SOCIAL PROBLEMS:
A CRITICAL THINKING APPROACH
SECOND EDITION

SOCIAL PROBLEMS: A CRITICAL THINKING APPROACH

SECOND EDITION

PAUL J. BAKER
Illinois State University

LOUISE E. ANDERSON
Kankakee Community College

DEAN S. DORN
California State University at Sacramento

Wadsworth Publishing Company, Belmont, California • A Division of Wadsworth, Inc.

Sociology Editor: *Serina Beauparlant*
Senior Editorial Assistant: *Marla Nowick*
Designer: *Wendy Calmenson*
Print Buyer: *Karen Hunt*
Permissions Editor: *Robert Kauser*
Production: *Sara Hunsaker/Ex Libris*
Copy Editor: *Barbara Salazar*
Cover Designer: *Vargas/Williams/Design*
Cover Photo: *© 1992 Geoffrey Gove/*
          The Image Bank
Compositor: *Bi-Comp, Inc.*
Printer: *R. R. Donnelley & Sons*

1 2 3 4 5 6 7 8 9 10—97 96 95 94 93

**Library of Congress
Cataloging-in-Publication Data**

Baker, Paul J.
    Social problems: a critical thinking
approach/Paul J. Baker.
    Louis E. Anderson, Dean S. Dorn.—2nd ed.
        p.   cm.
    Includes bibliographical references and
index.
    ISBN 0-534-19014-6 (acid-free paper)
    1. Sociology. 2. Social problems. 3.
Criticism (Philosophy) 4. Journalism—Social
aspects. I. Anderson, Louis E. II. Dorn,
Dean S. III. Title.
    HM51.B176 1993
    361.1—dc20   92-8896
                                      CIP
    ISBN 0-534-19014-6

CONTENTS

CHAPTER 3   Guidelines for Critical Reasoning   53

CHAPTER 4   Applying Guidelines: A Case Study in Critical Reasoning   75

PART II   CASE STUDIES FROM JOURNALISM AND SOCIOLOGY   91

The Second Edition of this book offers both continuity and change. A third author, Dean Dorn, has joined the team and we continue to explore new ways to enhance thoughtful engagement in the college classroom. A central postulate of sociology instruction guides our work: *The fact that students can read is no indication that they can think.* We do not despair of these circumstances and see little point in blaming students for their limited capacities as critical thinkers. Rather, we see the need for constructive teaching-learning strategies that help students bring reading and thinking together as an integral process. This book is designed to help students become thoughtful citizens who are capable of making sound judgments about a variety of contemporary social problems. We have written this book for the college classroom; but our larger goal is to nurture well-informed citizens through life-long learning skills. In his provocative book, *Coming to Public Judgment,* Daniel Yankelovich challenges educators to "develop the kind of intelligence needed to make public judgments" (1991, p. 242). We

have written a text-reader that responds to Yankelovich's challenge. We hope our readers will find new avenues of mindful engagement that are so essential in making democracy work in a complex world.

The Unique Contributions of a Critical Thinking Approach

The critical thinking approach of this book contrasts sharply with virtually all other social problems texts, which are typically designed as works of exposition. According to *Webster's Unabridged Dictionary, exposition* is "the art of presenting a subject matter in detail apart from criticism, argument or development" (1971, p. 802). The expository approach presents social problems as an elaborate set of conclusions dutifully packaged with graphs, statistical tables, inserts, cartoons, interesting photographs, and scientific theories. Even those works of exposition that are well written and thoughtful presentations of social problems inevitably encourage students to assume the passive role of memorizing the author's account.

We offer an alternative approach: a work of criticism. In contrast to exposition, *Webster's Unadbridged Dictionary* defines *criticism* as "the art of evaluating or analyzing with knowledge and propriety works of art or literature . . . or other literary matters (as moral values or the soundness of scientific hypothesis and procedures)" (1971, p. 538). Criticism involves actively evaluating and analyzing the ideas presented by an author. Students are not asked to memorize anything in this book of readings. They are taught instead to evaluate the logical and empirical adequacy of articles written by journalists and social scientists.

The first four chapters provide students with the analytical tools essential to the critical reading of the selections in the next eighteen chapters. Nothing in this book is written for the purpose of passive learning; the accent is on active learning. Part I equips students with critical thinking capabilities. Part II provides them with the opportunity to apply their critical reasoning skills to sixty-three selections from journalism and sociology.

Four Features Intended to Enhance Critical Thinking

1. *Social Problems as Constructed Realities.* Students are taught to examine social problems as constructed realities promoted by numerous professional and special-interest groups. No group or profession (sociology included) can claim to be sufficiently wise to present definitive knowledge about any single social problem. This critical perspective, grounded in the sociology of knowledge, liberates students from the pretentious and unrealistic task of trying to find the correct answer to a particular social problem.

2. *Mutual Appreciation for Both Journalism and Sociology.* Students learn to appreciate the fact that journalists and sociologists are in the same business. Both produce factual information and plausible explanations to account for various social problems. Both journalism and sociology have organizations and professional cultures that provide guidelines for creating and distributing social knowledge. The two knowledge-producing professions share many similarities and also have striking differences, for example, divergent methods of data analysis and interpretation. We attempt to demystify these two professions in order to help students feel more confident in their critical appraisal of statements made by journalists and sociologists. Furthermore, this book helps cultivate the rhetorical mode of comparison; students gain greater understanding of both fields by making conscious comparisons between them.

3. *Essential Skills of Criticism.* We present five core topics of critical reasoning that are pertinent to any statement about a social problem. Students learn to determine the adequacy of:

a. definition
b. evidence
c. cause-effect relationships
d. value assertions and assumptions
e. logical consistency in the line of reasoning about solutions

These topics of critical reasoning are intended to be applied to all selected readings in the book.

Special note to instructor: We have designed three student worksheets to help students practice these five critical thinking skills. It is available in the Instructor's Manual and can be reproduced for classroom use.

4. *The Integrity of Case Materials.* The editors of sociology readers sometimes make extensive revisions of the original documents by deleting major portions of the original work. We have avoided this practice and have presented original documents

in their entirety. With rare exception, we have not edited our selections; we want students to study each document as it was originally intended by the author. Only when students recognize and appreciate the full development of the author's line of reasoning can they determine the logical and empirical adequacy of a selection.

These four aspects of critical reasoning are intended to help students become more sophisticated readers of print journalism and more knowledgeable consumers of social science literature. The application of reasoning skills to situations outside the classroom is encouraged. We want our book to stimulate further interest in the life-long tasks of thoughtful deliberation about social issues.

This Book Is Designed to Be Flexible: Five Ways It Can Be Used

The Second Edition has expanded the case materials from eight to eighteen themes. Selections from journalism and sociology have grown from 32 to 63. Pagination and the table of contents create an artificial order for these themes and essays. But the readings do not need to be read in the same sequence found in the table of contents. We suggest five strategies for organizing the case materials.

1. *Follow the Table of Contents Selectively.* Critical thinking cannot be rushed. The critical analysis of essays will require more time than conventional reading habits of memorizing definitions and descriptive information. Teachers and students are cautioned to avoid the curse of coverage. This may involve selecting some essays for careful study and ignoring others. Since the readings offer a rich array of topics and essays, the teachers and students should have little difficulty in locating a critical mass of worthwhile case materials.

2. *Begin by Studying Short Popular Es-*

says. In contrast to the First Edition, we provide numerous short essays on various social problems that were originally written as commentaries for the opinion page of newspapers and popular magazines. These short essays allow students ample opportunity to develop the thinking skills introduced in Chapters 3 and 4. Students may want to practice their capabilities for critical thinking with these essays. Three chapters include several essays for this purpose: Chapter 5, Inequality and Gender; Chapter 10, Drugs; Chapter 13, The Homeless.

3. *Lead with Journalism; Follow with Sociology.* The teacher could assign all journalism articles during the first phase of the course, to be followed by the sociology selections. Since the journalism pieces are a bit easier to criticize, this method might give students added self confidence. As their reasoning skills improve, the more difficult sociological literature could be introduced.

4. *Divide Selections into Micro and Macro Perspectives.* In this approach, the course might open with social psychological themes of interpersonal relations and the analysis of small natural groups; the second phase of the course would turn to societal themes of long-range social trends and the institutional structures of nations. This course might conclude with an examination of essays that attempt to bridge the micro and macro worlds with a more comprehensive understanding of a particular social problem.

Special note to instructor: The instructor's manual will provide suggestions for this approach, including a guide to the readings as micro, macro, or both.

5. *Supplement Selections with Sources from the Library and the Street Corner.* Instructors can supplement this book with newspapers, magazines, and one or more paperbacks from sociology and journalism. This book invites students to see the study

of social problems as the beginning of a long journey to enlightened citizenship. It is not sufficient to understand the ongoing debates of a complex democracy. For this reason, teachers may want to extend the limits of the book by assigning essays from a wide range of sources found in airport lobbies, most grocery stores, libraries, and well-stocked bookstores.

Acknowledgements

The Second Edition of this book represents continued interest and commitment to the educational goals of critical thinking by a host of people who have supported this project at one time or another. The preface to the First Edition acknowledged numerous persons from the Teaching Projects of the American Sociological Association, Illinois State University, Kankakee Community College, University of Illinois (Urbana), The Fund for the Improvement of Post-Secondary Education, and Wadsworth Publishing Company. We are now pleased to add a new generation of supporters who assisted us during the past three years.

In 1989 we conducted a survey of all those teachers who had adopted the First Edition. Many teachers of social problems responded with detailed suggestions on ways to improve the Second Edition. We learned much from this survey and are grateful for their thoughtful reflections. Professor Harvey Choldin of the University of Illinois (Urbana) gave his social problems class a special final assignment: Write a book review of *Social Problems: A Critical Thinking Approach* offering suggestions on how the book could be improved in the Second Edition. These reviews provided many important insights.

In addition, the following instructors prepared their own insightful and invaluable reviews of the Second Edition manuscript: Lucille Baker, Tompkins Cortland Community College; Richard E. Bradford, Western New Mexico University; Cynthia A. Kempinen, Pennsylvania State University; Kenneth M. Moore, Oklahoma State University; Lawrence H. Joyce, SUNY-Cobleskill; Elizabeth Morrissey, Frostburg State University; William Watson, University of District of Columbia; and Anita Wilson, Bismark State Community College.

Considerable editorial assistance was provided by Stephen Baker and Seth Baker. They worked for room and board in the Baker household; but their efforts were invaluable to an overcommitted father. Thanks also to Sue Locke for typing several drafts of the first four chapters. The Second Edition would still be little more than new ideas and good intentions without the persistent sense of urgency and wonderful sense of humor of Serina Beauparlant and her able assistant, Marla Nowick. Thank you for keeping us on task.

Once again, Paul and Louis are grateful to their wives, Sharon and Dee, for continued good-natured support of this writing project. Finally, we express thanks to all our students who patiently continue to learn from us, while we continue to learn from them.

A FRAMEWORK
FOR CRITICAL ANALYSIS

Imagine that you are about to begin a long automobile journey of twelve to eighteen weeks. The journey covers some familiar territory, but much of the traveling will be through unknown regions of the country. One indispensable item for this venture is a road map. A map is a marvelous aid for providing a sense of direction. One piece of paper small enough to be held in your lap can provide a coherent view of highway networks extending thousands of miles.

For the next twelve to eighteen weeks the reader of this page will undertake a different kind of journey—a trip through the familiar and unfamiliar territory of social problems. In Part I, we want to prepare you for this journey by developing a road map for studying the huge and complicated world of social controversy. Part I helps the reader gain a distinctive perspective on reading assignments taken from a wide assortment of newspapers, popular magazines, and scholarly journals. It provides a thinker's map to guide your study of the verbal terrain of authors who write about the private troubles and public issues of the late twentieth century.

We approach the study of social problems from a distinctive perspective, noting first the diversity of perspectives that can in fact be applied to this study. Many interest groups (for example, American Medical Association, American Bar Association, Sierra Club, Roman Catholic Church, Daughters of the American Revolution) make special claims with regard to the most appropriate way to define and solve certain social problems. These conflicting claims cannot be resolved by social scientists, who have difficulty agreeing among themselves. It is important to know that no professor, no textbook, and no professional group is sufficiently informed to achieve a full understanding of social problems.

This book rests on the conviction that the study of social problems should not be approached by memorization of "correct" answers. Rather, a student must start by learning how to think critically and how to ask questions. The capacity to probe beyond ready-made answers requires a strategy of inquiry; the first three chapters develop such a strategy.

Four core ideas constitute the strategy of critical inquiry espoused in this book. The first idea is that social problems are social constructs. They are created by aroused citizens who see a need to improve some aspect of society. Various groups and individuals create an endless stream of statements about social conditions that they define as urgent problems. Through books, scientific articles, editorials, speeches, government reports, letters to the editor, and sermons, they strive to create a definition of a problem that is more persuasive than competing definitions. But the debates never move toward an ultimate objective truth that enjoys universal consensus. Rather, the diverse statements about social problems serve the interests of those who promote them. As historical and social constructions, social problems are always in a state of change.

The second core idea is that social issues are the concerns of groups. A group may be as a small as a married couple or as large as the world population. A social problem may be approached from the perspective of a small number of people whom it affects (a micro perspective) or it may be viewed more broadly, as a national or global problem (a macro perspective).

Third, social phenomena are explored with varying degrees of concreteness and abstraction. Sometimes the focus is on a particular incident (an accident at a nuclear power plant, for example), and at other times the focus is on a general trend or abstract principle (such as the human capacity to construct and administer nuclear power systems that are cost-effective and safe). The social world is interpreted sometimes through vivid description, at other times through general principles. In Chapter 2 we show the importance of micro/macro and concrete/abstract distinctions for both journalism and sociology.

Chapter 3 introduces the fourth key strategy of inquiry: a short list of critical thinking topics essential to any thoughtful assessment of a social problem. The topics cover critical questions of logic and evidence and can be applied to a wide assortment of statements written by journalists and social scientists.

The strategy of critical inquiry developed in this book, then, rests on four themes. Essays and articles about social problems are:

1. Socially constructed realities within a societal context.

2. Constructed along a continuum at either the micro or macro level.

3. Constructed along a continuum as either concrete descriptions or abstract generalizations.

4. Subject to logical and empirical scrutiny.

Because the essays of journalists and sociologists are human constructions of social reality, they should not be accepted uncritically as absolute truth.

Students should not accept uncritically the positions of the men and women who wrote the reading selections in Part II. The readings in this book are like other artifacts of human construction—they need to be seen in context and subjected to critical appraisal. Part I provides a set of critical thinking tools that will equip the reader for this task.

CHAPTER 1

SOCIAL PROBLEMS: CONSTRUCTED REALITIES OF CIVIC KNOWLEDGE

INTRODUCTION

We make you a promise: This book will bring rigor and excitement to the demanding task of studying complex social issues. It provides the tools that make a difference in the way thoughtful people confront many critical issues in the late twentieth century. This new way of reasoning will give you the lifelong ability to see to the heart of information and ideas found in the countless newspapers, magazines, and books dedicated to an informed and open society.

The central purpose of this book is to help students prepare for the arduous task of informed citizenship by teaching them to become critical readers. Journalism and social science are indispensable instruments of enlightened dialogue in a democratic society. Students can exercise their full freedom of expression and thought only by becoming critical consumers of journalism and social science; that is, critical readers of the many written accounts—editorials, news stories, magazine essays, scholarly articles, public opinion polls—that describe and explain the social problems of our day. The thinking skills described in this book will strengthen students' capacity to be both informed and free.

FACING THE PERPLEXITIES OF PLURALITY

The complete study of social problems is such a bewildering task that it is beyond the capacities of even the most brilliant scholars. No one can be fully informed about such problems, for three reasons. First, the list of social problems is almost endless. For many decades, sociology textbooks, public opinion surveys, mass media commentaries, and government reports have generated a continuous stream of information on phenomena defined as social problems: war, overpopulation, underpopulation, poverty, racial conflict, street crime, mental illness, international terrorism, government regulation, drug dependency, aging, unemployment, urban decay, television violence, pornography, overcrowded prisons, child abuse, abortion, government corruption, white-collar crime, alienated youth, campus unrest, sex discrimination, women's liberation, prostitution, deteriorating environment, poor schools, high taxes, homelessness, the decline of the family, increasing rates of herpes and AIDS. Everything from pot to potholes has been defined as a social problem. Some problems (prostitution, poverty, crime) persist over many centuries; others (international terrorism, campus unrest, urban riots) burst upon the scene with startling ferocity. At any given moment, however, the range of phenomena considered to be social problems is so broad and diverse as to be beyond the manageable comprehension of anyone.

A second difficulty is that one person can never fully comprehend or reconcile the many professional perspectives from which a given social problem is viewed. Prostitu-

tion, for example, has been studied by journalists, sociologists, psychologists, criminologists, and lawyers. Each field of study brings a distinct stock of expert knowledge to the problem, and even within a single field, such as sociology, scholars adopt a variety of perspectives. Some sociologists emphasize the disorganized social environment of prostitutes, others stress personal pathologies, and still others stress the progression of situations through which one gradually drifts to an underworld lifestyle (Heyl 1979:34). Experts in many fields selectively examine different aspects of every social problem. The way accountants, for example, look at white-collar crime differs from the ways lawyers, sociologists, and psychologists view it. These various perspectives never add up to one totally integrated picture. The different professional frames can never be merged into a single frame.

A third factor is the effect of highly diverse value assumptions and belief systems on analysis of a given problem. Because people have highly divergent value commitments, they have radically different ideas about what in fact constitutes a problem. A situation that one person sees as a problem may be seen as a solution by someone else. Antiabortionists, for example, believe that abortion is a major problem, while pro-choice advocates see abortion as an appropriate solution for women who define their pregnancy as a problem. In 1967 President Lyndon Johnson established affirmative action guidelines to help eradicate racial discrimination in the United States. His solution in turn became a problem for executives in universities and corporations, who argued that excessive regulation denied them the freedom to hire the most qualified people. Some people enjoy pornography and believe the more titillation, the better. Others dislike pornography but are willing to tolerate it as part of an open society, fearing government censorship more than pornography. Still others would like to see more censorship and less pornography. Whether a given situation constitutes a social problem depends on one's values.

The perplexities of plurality—too many topics to cover, too many theoretical perspectives to analyze, and too many conflicting value positions to be reconciled—make a comprehensive and definitive treatment of social problems impossible. What, then, can be said about an intelligible understanding of social problems? Since the broad topic of social problems is not a coherent field of study, how can one proceed with any kind of analysis? The solution is to develop a short list of key ideas, all very general, that can be applied to various social problems. In this book we develop a basic framework in the first four chapters, then apply it to various discussions of social problems by journalists and sociologists in Chapters 5 through 22. This framework can also be applied to any number of additional topics. We provide a general way of thinking that has broad application.

The perplexities of plurality require us to avoid the overwhelming task of memorizing bushels of minutiae. Plurality requires a simple and straightforward approach. This book abandons a glossary list of concepts, brief summaries of important studies, and odd pieces of statistical information in favor of a short list of core ideas that can be applied to the wide array of contemporary social problems.

THE POINT OF DEPARTURE: THE SOCIETAL CONTEXT

Social problems must always be seen in a societal context. They exist because members of society at a given point in time have become conscious of a condition that is undesirable and subject to improvement. According to Herbert Blumer, "A social problem does not exist unless it is recognized by that society to exist" (1971:301–2). Many undesirable conditions are not social problems in the minds of the vast majority of people at the time; child abuse before 1877, for example, and many sexist practices before the 1960s. When people start to talk about undesirable conditions because they believe something can be done about them, then these conditions become a social problem.

No established or official procedure for recognizing social problems exists. No one is elected, appointed, or trained to identify society's problems; rather, social problems gain recognition through numerous interest groups, social movements, enterprising journalists, political campaigns, and accidents of history. Sometimes a book is widely read as a statement about some social ill that needs to be cured. Poverty has been rediscovered several times through such highly publicized books as *How the Other Half Lives* (Riis 1890/1957) and *The Other America* (Harrington 1962). A social problem sometimes gains recognition through a single dramatic episode. The nuclear accidents at Three Mile Island and Chernobyl, for example, highlighted the complex problems of safety in a nuclear age. No simple pattern explains how social problems come to be recognized, but in some way a sizable number of people must become convinced of the need for action.

People become interested in social problems for a wide variety of reasons. They may have been victimized by an avoidable tragedy and want to do something about it. Thousands of people, for example, have lost loved ones in auto accidents caused by intoxicated drivers. In recent years, MADD (Mothers Against Drunk Drivers) has conducted a spirited campaign to enact stricter laws against drunk driving. Some people recognize social problems because of their religious affiliation. Quakers and Mennonites are committed to peace, the Roman Catholic clergy and some Protestants are against abortion, and the Jewish community has many organizations dedicated to combating anti-Semitism. Journalists sometimes take a special interest in a particular social problem, such as corruption in government, street crime, or the evils of bureaucracy. The list of persons interested in social problems goes on. In a democratic society with a free press, no one has a monopoly on identifying social problems or suggesting solutions. Many people and organizations play a role in calling attention to a condition that needs to be changed. Concerned people and the noise they make in support of their cause provide the societal context for the study of social problems.

Once identified, social problems are not fixed entities that can be studied in the same way one might study the cell structure of a leaf or the chemical composition of a rock. A social problem cannot be analyzed apart from its context. Such problems are fluid and multifaceted, and they require close and constant attention to many subjective feelings and objective circumstances. To see the many sides of a social problem, one must keep abreast of changing trends and conflicting perceptions. The pulse of the public constantly registers shifting opinions, journalists search for new ways to

write stories, politicians make new campaign promises, and social scientists examine new findings that require reinterpretation of favorite theories. Social problems are always surrounded by forces of change as advocates seek reform, opponents support the status quo, and politicians try to stay on the winning side.

Social scientists who study social problems are sensitive to this larger societal context that allows for many patterns of change. Some social problems show persistent and gradual change over time. Whatever the topic, a social problem must be studied in the societal context in which the public and its leaders debate the nature of undesired conditions and the need for action.

Social problems are often closely aligned with social movements. Whether the cause is women's rights, a cleaner environment, or stopping abortion, groups dramatize the urgency of change. Periods of wide public attention are accompanied by a sense of turmoil created by conflict among competing interest groups and their divergent demands for action. The mass media often exaggerate these tense situations and present them as scenes of chaos. Social problems sometimes appear in the form of riots, protest demonstrations, or strident speechmaking; a sense of alarm fills the air. A broader view of the societal and cultural context of social problems, however, indicates that the momentary appearance of chaos does not tell the whole story. The continuity of order accompanies the disorderly disruptions that surround controversial issues. In the United States, for example, much stability is found in core values that allow considerable change within the broader context of continuity. As early as the 1820s, Alexis de Tocqueville detected the tendency of public opinion to remain stable for long periods of time. Many sociologists throughout the twentieth century have observed core values in the United States that provide stability during heated moments of debate and deliberation about the pressing issues of the day.

The Framework of Dominant Values

We have mentioned the significance of value conflicts in the emergence of social problems. In the United States, a clash of values is only half of the picture. Equally important is the framework of dominant values within which social problems are debated. Controversy does not exist in a social and cultural environment in which anything goes.

We make no effort here to provide an exhaustive list of core values held by most Americans. Instead we describe three value orientations that often influence the way the public, politicians, journalists, and social scientists in the United States view social problems: ① a strong commitment to individualism and a corresponding aversion to collectivism, ② strong faith in equality and achievement as the basic guidelines for the successful attainment of the American dream, and ③ adherence to principles of tolerance and openness to the practical requirements of change as a gradual process. These core values do not fit into a unified value system but are loosely joined in a wide variety of patterns that coalesce in a distinctive way around a particular social problem at any given time. The values that influence the definition of race relations in the 1990s, for example, differ considerably from those of the 1890s.

Individualism.   One of the values that does most to shape opinion and policy in regard to many social problems is a firm commitment to individual responsibility. "We are a nation that sings praises to the spirit of rugged individualism. Seven out of ten believe that anyone who works hard can get ahead in this country" (Bloomgarden 1983:47).

People who succeed often attribute their good fortune to their individual effort. Likewise, people who suffer from poverty, limited education, or unemployment are often scorned for weakness of character or limited ambition. Since Americans often define social problems in terms of individual accountability, they harbor a deep suspicion of collective solutions. Labor unions and government policies are often attacked by those who desire minimum restraints on the individual. No idea is more certain of defeat in the United States than a proposal that becomes labeled as "socialistic."

Equality and achievement.   One of the tenets of individualism is the belief that "all men are created equal." This statement does not mean that all men and women are equally endowed with the same talents but that all people have the same chance for success. This proposition leads to a second major value—the belief that achievement is a good thing and is possible for anyone who really tries. Paradoxically, equality and achievement are often in conflict. The United States is highly stratified, with a few people enjoying great success, most being average, and many struggling near the bottom. This picture hardly portrays a society that enjoys the virtues of equality; rather, it represents a willingness to celebrate the claims of achievement. We preach equality and then promote no end of schemes (more education, the lottery, how-to-get-rich books) whose outcomes make people as unequal as possible. A society that celebrates achievement seems to require more losers than winners. Yet this imbalance undermines the claim of equality. Some critics are disturbed by this paradox and argue that the social system is rigged in favor of the privileged minority.

Tolerance and gradual change.   The third cultural theme that influences perspectives on social problems in the United States is a willingness to remain open to and tolerant of many opinions while we search for the moderate middle ground where solutions to problems can be discovered. Although Americans take great pride in a legal system that allows for a wide range of opinion on almost every topic imaginable, most citizens have a strong aversion to extremist positions. John Kenneth Galbraith once said that Americans like to debate between the thirty-five-yard lines. Extremist views such as those of the Ku Klux Klan often receive headline attention, but few people identify with extremists. The situation of Jane Fonda provides an interesting example of Americans' open spirit. During the Vietnam War, Fonda strongly denounced her government's foreign policy and went to Hanoi to discuss peace with the North Vietnamese. At the time of Fonda's visit, most Americans were opposed to her mission but were still willing to let her and other critics stage their widely publicized protests against the war. People who disagreed with her politics nevertheless continued to enjoy her movies, and in the 1980s they stayed in shape with her exercise plan. In the 1990s she enjoys a new celebrity role as the wife of one of America's foremost entrepreneurs, Ted Turner.

The tolerance for diverse opinions while shunning extremism is closely related to the belief that gradual change is always preferred to radical change. The image of the United States as a society that makes orderly progress by means of the sober work of practical-minded people enjoys almost universal consensus. Pragmatists search for moderate solutions in the middle ground, and politicians who see politics as "the art of the possible" win praise.

One might easily make the case that America is a society of bigotry and racial hatred, since its history is blighted by slavery, the genocide of American Indians, Jim Crow laws, race riots, and the internment of Japanese-Americans during World War II. Although these harsh realities must never

be denied, there is another side to the American way of life. Over the past hundred years, blacks have gained their civil rights as citizens, and many are currently moving into the mainstream of American society (Hamilton 1982; Farley 1984). Many Europeans who migrated to American shores between 1870 and 1910 belonged to antagonistic ethnic groups that seemed determined to keep their homeland identities, but the forces of gradual change are clearly apparent in the 1990s. The American melting pot, stirred by intermarriage and geographical mobility, is creating new citizens who will never think of themselves as Poles, Italians, Irish, Russians, or Ukrainians; the third and fourth generations are finally becoming fully assimilated Americans (Glazer 1984). This search for a middle ground does not imply the absence of serious problems for disadvantaged minorities. Rather, it illustrates deep distrust of radical solutions.

We see the same tendency toward gradual change in the environmental issue. In 1962 Rachel Carson wrote *Silent Spring*. In the next several years, attention increasingly focused on the alarming problems of polluted rivers, smog, acid rain, and toxic wastes. But Americans are not demanding radical change. The public and policy makers alike "no longer see protecting the environment as a 'crisis' issue; it is now widely perceived as a *management* issue" (Bloomgarden 1983:48; italics in original). A broad consensus unifies American society. "The public's commitment to the environment indicates a deep-seated conviction that we can progress toward a strong economy and a sound environment" (Bloomgarden 1983:51). The struggle for a cleaner environment goes on in the 1990s, but it is unlikely to be won by the demands of zealots.

The values of individualism, aversion to collectivism, equality, achievement, tolerance, pragmatism, and an optimism about gradual progress are integral to deliberations on a wide range of social problems. Ordinary citizens, political leaders, journalists, and social scientists often formulate definitions of a problem and possible solutions by giving implicit or explicit consideration to these cultural themes. Whether these values hover in the background or are placed up front for specific attention, they are the accepted framework for the vast majority of people who consider or influence public issues.

Narrowing the Framework to Print Journalism and Sociology

People are able to engage in meaningful dialogue about social problems because they share core values that guide consideration of key issues. Understanding the societal and cultural context is a prerequisite to understanding the nature of social problems in the modern world. But this contextual framework is too broad and unmanageable as a framework for rigorous analysis of specific problems. We deliberately narrow this framework by giving special attention to two occupational perspectives—print journalism and sociology—from which every major social problem in the twentieth century has been approached. Figure 1.1 shows how journalism and sociology relate to the broad framework.

The largest frame in Figure 1.1, the world of infinite human phenomena, includes every conceivable human event that anyone could ever imagine, from bumping a stranger in a ticket line to pushing a button for nuclear war. People are constantly bombarded by actions initiated by others (such as taking a phone call or hearing a baby wake from her nap), and they return the favor (by laughing at the friend's telephone story or picking up the awakened baby) in perpetual moments of reciprocity.

Although this stream of events flows on with very little self-conscious reflection, on rare occasions some particular activity will arouse a keen sense of self-consciousness. Individuals reflect on their activities in an attempt to find meaning in something out of the ordinary. In recent years, for example, many young people have become rather casual about their premarital sexual activities. Some have reflected on the morality of these newly discovered pleasures, but many others have been forced to reexamine the meaning of such behavior by accounts of herpes and AIDS. Judeo-Christian values have been momentarily linked to medical science. A new social awareness has arisen in the common culture of everyday life as the ancient sin of extramarital intercourse has become a medical risk. Life for some people has become more complicated as they contemplate this new social problem.

Innumerable human phenomena are interpreted through common symbolic systems—language, money, uniforms, gestures—that allow the actions to have special meaning as self-conscious happenings. Some occasions are festive, such as a birthday party, while others may be sad, such as a funeral. A few of these everyday occurrences are selectively transformed into private or public problems. When the public defines an occurrence as problematic, journalists report it as a news event. In the early 1980s, medical specialists were examining patients who exhibited an acquired immune deficiency syndrome (AIDS). This obscure disease soon came to the attention of the press.

Millions of people, famous and obscure, go to the doctor every day for every conceivable ailment. The proportion of cases that capture public attention is probably 0.01 percent or less. But when Rock Hudson planned to travel to Paris for treatment of AIDS, his trip became a major news event. He made front-page headlines; his disease became one of the major topics of media coverage in the summer of 1985. Numerous occurrences in the life of Hudson and his

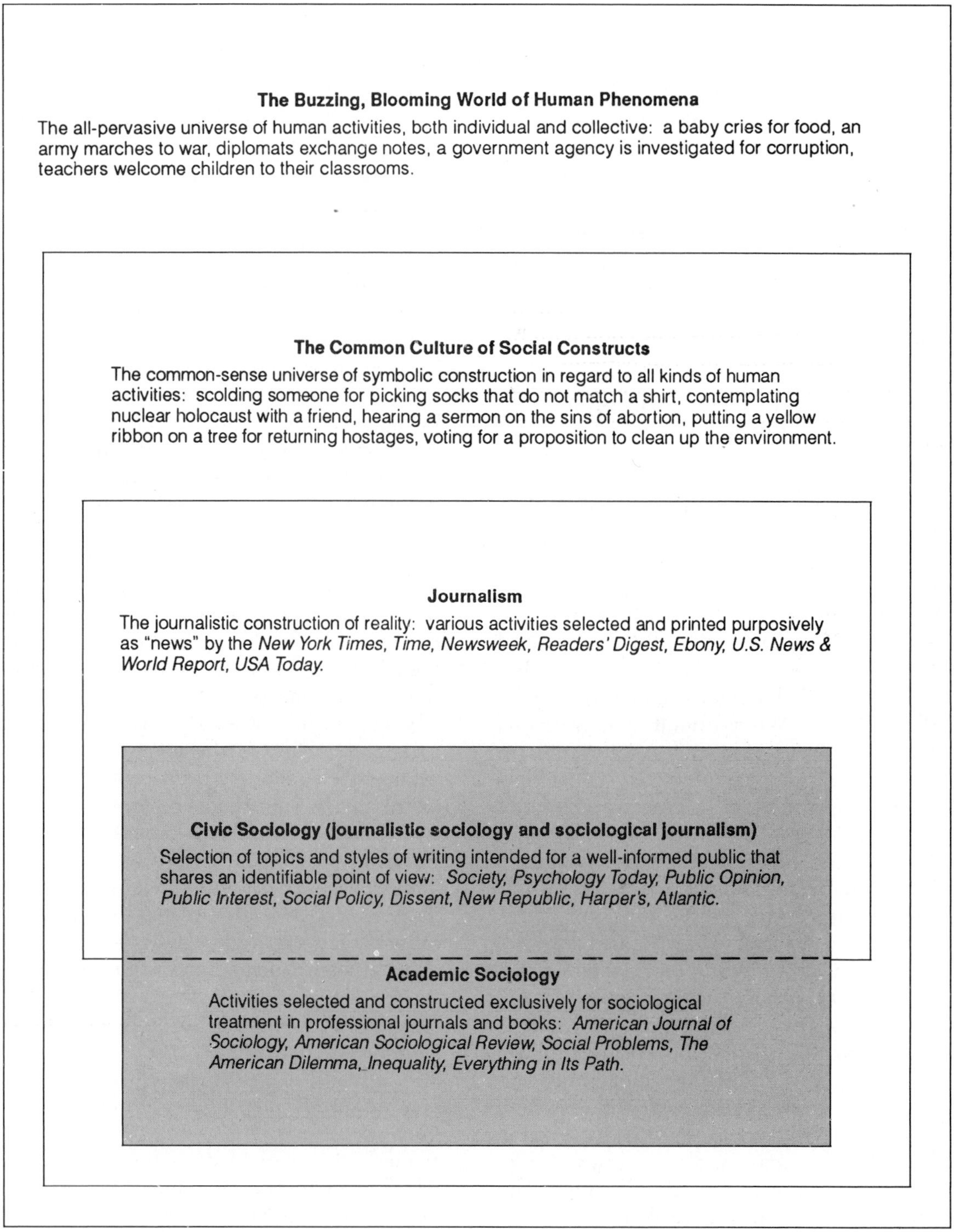

The Buzzing, Blooming World of Human Phenomena

The all-pervasive universe of human activities, both individual and collective: a baby cries for food, an army marches to war, diplomats exchange notes, a government agency is investigated for corruption, teachers welcome children to their classrooms.

The Common Culture of Social Constructs

The common-sense universe of symbolic construction in regard to all kinds of human activities: scolding someone for picking socks that do not match a shirt, contemplating nuclear holocaust with a friend, hearing a sermon on the sins of abortion, putting a yellow ribbon on a tree for returning hostages, voting for a proposition to clean up the environment.

Journalism

The journalistic construction of reality: various activities selected and printed purposively as "news" by the *New York Times, Time, Newsweek, Readers' Digest, Ebony, U.S. News & World Report, USA Today.*

Civic Sociology (journalistic sociology and sociological journalism)

Selection of topics and styles of writing intended for a well-informed public that shares an identifiable point of view: *Society, Psychology Today, Public Opinion, Public Interest, Social Policy, Dissent, New Republic, Harper's, Atlantic.*

Academic Sociology

Activities selected and constructed exclusively for sociological treatment in professional journals and books: *American Journal of Sociology, American Sociological Review, Social Problems, The American Dilemma, Inequality, Everything in Its Path.*

FIGURE 1.1

Societal Context of Civic Knowledge: Journalism and Sociology doctors also became media events; that is, journalists "mediated" between Hudson and the public with "news" about his condition. This private episode in the life of one famous movie star helped create a new social problem as millions of people reappraised the sexual habits and moral guidelines of a nation threatened by an epidemic of significant scope. By the 1990s the AIDS crisis has reached catastrophic proportions as whole societies in Africa and several major cities in the United States cope with the costly burden of treating the patients.

Defining the societal and cultural context of a modern nation necessarily depends on a huge mass media system. The world out there where movie stars are afflicted with AIDS and politicians debate the merits of new medical practices is mediated for us by journalists who choose to expose us to certain occurrences they believe are worth knowing about. The public as well as social scientists are heavily dependent on journalists who select an infinitesimally small fraction of human activities to be transformed into the news of the day. Journalists for weekly magazines (*U.S. News & World Report, Time, Newsweek*) select an even smaller number of the newsworthy events of the past seven days for summary and analysis. Each day and each week, journalists selectively construct a special reality that is consumed as the news.

The "Civic Sociology" box in Figure 1.1, overlapping the "Journalism" and "Academic Sociology" boxes, is of special interest to us. Many of the selections in Chapters 5 through 22 are instances of sociological

journalism or journalistic sociology. The nature of these authors and their magazines are explored in Chapter 2. At this point it is sufficient to note that journalism and sociology are not always distinct fields of inquiry. As Figure 1.1 indicates, a common area of inquiry exists in which journalists investigate social problems and write about them in a way that is reminiscent of the work of sociologists, who in turn write on topics for a general audience in a way that is not unlike the work of some journalists.

The smallest box in Figure 1.1 identifies knowledge disseminated by sociologists writing for other sociologists. At meetings of professional groups, such as the American Sociological Association and the Society for the Study of Social Problems, sociologists present papers on their latest theories, report new research findings, and reexamine classic works of the past. Various social problems are reviewed at these meetings, and many of the papers presented are then revised for publication in academic journals such as the *American Sociological Review*, the *American Journal of Sociology, Social Forces*, and *Social Problems*. Sociologists write for their colleagues in a highly technical fashion. As professional scholars who have been trained in graduate school, they assume that their readers already know technical concepts and sophisticated statistical procedures. These authors have no intention of reaching the general public; on the contrary, the emphasis is on expert knowledge written for fellow experts who look at social problems through a sociological prism.

MULTIPLE PERSPECTIVES ON SOCIAL PROBLEMS

Common-sense notions of the larger society, journalistic accounts, and social research often have a common agenda where

perplexing social problems are concerned, but their perspectives may lead them to different conclusions. The differences are clearly seen in the contrasting approaches to two violent episodes: a rape-murder in Philadelphia and the killing of four students by the National Guard in Ohio.

An Episode of Murder and Rape

On Palm Sunday in 1966, three men broke into the West Philadelphia home of three women—an eighty-year-old widow, her forty-four-year-old daughter, and a fourteen-year-old granddaughter. The intruders viciously beat and raped the women and looted the house. "The grandmother was found unconscious by the police and lying in a pool of blood"; she later died of her wounds. The mother and daughter were hysterical (Schwartz 1968:509).

Newspapers covered the story extensively, and editors called for new measures that would protect women in their homes and on the streets. The public outrage unleashed by this heinous crime had a powerful impact on public officials in Philadelphia and throughout Pennsylvania. Judges clamped down on all defendants accused of crimes that involved bodily injury. Within three weeks of the event, state legislators considered bills that would double the existing penalties against rape. By votes of 48 to 0 and 202 to 0, the Senate and House amended the Pennsylvania Penal Code to provide harsher penalties for rape and attempted rape. Five weeks after banner headlines first reported the crime, the governor signed the new law. Persons convicted of rape with bodily injury now faced a sentence of fifteen years to life.

Newspapers reported citizens' satisfaction with the swift action of politicians. One legislator who sponsored the new crime laws summarized the views of many Pennsylvanians when he declared:

The passage of this bill is a major breakthrough in the fight on crime throughout the State and especially in Philadelphia, and will bring about a definite deterrent on future rapists. When the word is circulated among these vicious criminals that they will be swiftly and severely punished; when they get the message that our organized society will not tolerate the violation of our women, these men will think twice before committing these uncivilized acts. (Schwartz 1968:510)

To editors, newspaper readers, judges, legislators, and other concerned citizens, the situation seemed obvious: A terrible crime had been committed and appropriate action was necessary. If existing sanctions did not deter rapists, then it was reasonable to believe that stricter punishment would. Everyone seemed convinced that the problem had been defined correctly and an appropriate solution found.

Sociologists, by training less likely to accept such quick solutions as a lengthened prison sentence, had not been prominent in the public demand for a tougher law. The sociologist Barry Schwartz investigated the actual impact of the new law to determine whether the new penalties had the desired deterrent effect on the rate of rape and attempted rape in Philadelphia. "If the new law had a desirable effect, a perceptible drop in the monthly rape rates could be expected after May 12, 1966 or even in April, the period of greatest public outrage in which much well-publicized planning for the new penalties took place" (Schwartz 1968:510). Probing the matter more systematically than journalists and ordinary citizens did, Schwartz unearthed facts that raised serious doubts about the deterrent effect of increased penalties on convicted rapists. Schwartz had as much compassion for rape victims as judges, legislators, and newspaper editors did, but he did not share their confidence in the effectiveness of a quick solution.

When Schwartz checked the police and court records in Philadelphia, he discovered that the number of rapes committed was the same in 1965 and 1966. He probed further to determine any pattern of change over the previous eight years. His findings were unequivocal: "The proportion of forcible rapes by adult offenders has not declined" (Schwartz 1968:512). Contrary to the hopes of public officials, Schwartz concluded that "Pennsylvania's new deterrent strategy against rape was a failure as far as Philadelphia is concerned" (p. 514).

In this case study we see the different perspectives of political leaders, journalists, and sociologists. The common-sense solution offered by legislators is based on the premise that penalties deter crimes; from this premise it follows that the more severe the penalty, the greater the deterrence. Journalists assumed their appropriate roles in this case by reporting news of both the crime and the deliberations of legislators and the governor. Furthermore, they supported the legislative effort on their editorial pages. Sociologists entered the picture to reassess the taken-for-granted premise that more severe penalties make for fewer crimes. By making systematic statistical comparisons of the rape rates before and after the amendment to the penal code was signed into law, sociologists were able to determine the effectiveness of the increased penalties for rape. Their findings were reported in a sociological journal and gained little or no attention from the citizens of Philadelphia, who still believe that stricter law enforcement will solve the problem of street crime.

The Killings at Kent State

Reaction to the student unrest that swept campuses in the United States from 1964 to 1970 offers a more complex picture of the multiple perspectives that journalists and sociologists bring to a controversial topic. No incident better illuminates these contrasting perspectives than the killing of four

Kent State University students by the Ohio National Guard on May 4, 1970.

The Kent State episode began with President Nixon's decision to send troops into Cambodia. Within twenty-four hours, students at most campuses in the United States were holding mass demonstrations to protest Nixon's war policy. On Friday evening, May 1, a crowd of 500 students at Kent State hurled rocks and bottles at police; students also damaged stores in downtown Kent. The next evening, the ROTC building was burned, and Governor James A. Rhodes sent the National Guard to restore order. Sunday was a day of confusion, but no major violence took place. On Monday, May 4, tension between a crowd of 300 students and a company of National Guardsmen led to a sudden and unexpected occurrence: Soldiers marched up Blanket Hill overlooking a parking lot, suddenly turned, faced the students, and began firing. When the shooting stopped thirteen seconds later, four students lay dead or dying and nine others were wounded.

The brief moments before and after this shooting became the subject of intense scrutiny by many interested people—hundreds of newspaper reporters; the President's Commission on Campus Unrest, chaired by Governor William Scranton of Pennsylvania; a special grand jury of Portage County, Ohio; the FBI; James Michener, commissioned by *Reader's Digest* to investigate and report on the incident; attorneys for the dead and wounded students; the Board of Church and Society of the United Methodist Church; and a sociologist, Jerry Lewis, who happened to be nearby at the fatal moments.

The first accounts of the Kent State tragedy, written immediately after the event for the daily newspapers, dramatized the shootings as a confrontation precipitated by unruly students. The newspapers mentioned sniper fire, and the impression was often given that the four students killed were campus radicals. Many accounts were sympathetic to the National Guard, often portraying the students as misfits who were disloyal to their nation. Letters to the editor by Ohio residents were overwhelmingly antagonistic toward the students. Some citizens even believed "they should have shot more of them" (quoted in Rudwick & Meier 1972:84).

In subsequent weeks, journalists substantially revised these early accounts, and other investigations recreated the events and drew new conclusions. Twenty days after the killings, for example, a special report by the *Akron Beacon Journal* tried to correct many of the original hysterical impressions initially accepted as truth by many television viewers and newspaper readers. The *Beacon* concluded soberly:

The four victims did nothing that justified their deaths. They threw no rocks nor were they politically radical. No sniper fired at the National Guard. The Guardsmen fired without order to do so. It was not necessary to kill or wound any students. There is no evidence to support suggestions by university and city officials that four members of the Students for a Democratic Society (SDS) planned and directed the trouble. (Stone 1971:105)

These conclusions were based on more than four hundred interviews with people who were at Kent State on the fateful day. The *Beacon*'s reappraisal was only one of many efforts to recapture and interpret the course of events surrounding the tragedy.

Figure 1.2 illustrates some of the many versions of the truth written in the weeks, months, and years after the event. Early accounts were softened by additional evidence. The President's Commission on Campus Unrest prepared a detailed report of the Kent State affair but avoided any statements that would implicate the guardsmen in criminal offenses. An independent

journalist, I. F. Stone, took sharp exception to the commission's report and portrayed the situation as a case of murder by guardsmen who unfortunately went unpunished. James Michener (1971) saw the situation differently; he described and interpreted it as a sad tragedy created by outside radicals who came to Kent State as violent agitators. Two journalists who spent three months at Kent State wrote an angry refutation of Michener's version. They claimed that Michener's theory of outside agitation was "a study in distortion" (Eszterhas & Roberts 1971:35–40). For several years after the tragedy, as Peter Davies studied thousands of pages of testimony and hundreds of photographs, he became convinced that an order was initiated at the White House and "loosely conveyed" to the guardsmen. "Taking orders from above, at least ten guardsmen conspired to open fire at the students on a prearranged signal" (Bills 1982:153).

The sociological perspective, also shown in Figure 1.2, was developed by a sociology professor who was one of the faculty members serving as campus marshals in an effort to keep peace between students and guardsmen. Professor Jerry Lewis spent the next several months investigating and writing about the event as a sociologist (Lewis 1971, 1972; Lewis & Adamek 1973, 1975). Lewis began his work with many of the same descriptive questions—Who? What? When? Where?—raised by journalists and law enforcement officials. But as a sociologist he approached the question Why? in a distinctly different way, by viewing the Kent State confrontation as an episode in collective behavior.

Why did the situation explode? Lewis answered this question by carefully examining students' shifting moods. According to Lewis, students drastically redefined the situation after the guardsmen arrived on campus. Governor Rhodes expected the

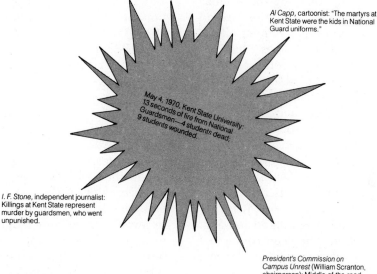

Peter Davies, independent investigator: A "loosely conveyed order initiated at the White House" was eventually passed down to the guardsmen, who conspired to kill the students. The behavior of the students was a circumstance of accidents.

Immediate news coverage: Stories report riot conditions, radical students, sniper fire, and National Guardsmen who fired after being under attack. Images suggest a major confrontation from a mass of students and a small band of guardsmen.

James Michener, writer for *Reader's Digest:* Campus radicals and outside agitators conspired to create a riot at Kent State. The behavior of the National Guardsmen was the culmination of a series of accidental circumstances.

Al Capp, cartoonist: "The martyrs at Kent State were the kids in National Guard uniforms."

May 4, 1970, Kent State University: 13 seconds of fire from National Guardsmen—4 students dead; 9 students wounded.

I. F. Stone, independent journalist: Killings at Kent State represent murder by guardsmen, who went unpunished.

Professor Jerry Lewis, campus peacemaker, witness, and sociologist: Killings are an aspect of collective behavior. Guardsmen's presence on campus radicalized students and created disorder. Guardsmen then used force in an attempt to restore order.

Twenty days later, special report by *Akron Beacon Journal:* Sober fact-finding assessment that viewed the episode as a tragedy. "The four victims did nothing to justify their deaths. . . . It was not necessary to kill or wound any students."

President's Commission on Campus Unrest (William Scranton, chairperson): Middle-of-the-road assessment. Actions of some students were "violent," "dangerous," "reckless," "irresponsible." But the "indiscriminate" firing by guardsmen was "unnecessary," "unwarranted," and "inexcusable." No judgment on the criminality of the guardsmen was made.

FIGURE 1.2

Kent State Killings: One Explosive Moment and Many Divergent Accounts

guardsmen to pacify Kent State students, but their presence had the opposite effect. Students were radicalized by the use of force. The guardsmen unwittingly created new problems of disorder that then led to an extreme reaction on Blanket Hill.

The agony of Kent State was not officially closed until January 4, 1979, when civil litigation resulted in a court settlement of $675,000 for six wounded victims and the parents of the four dead students (Kelner & Munves 1980). Many people have since reflected on the lessons to be learned from this tragedy. We have used the incident to illustrate a fundamental proposition about journalism and social science: The same incident is often reconstructed in highly divergent ways. No single vision ever unifies the views of the many reporters and sociologists who write about the social problems of their day. While accepting this plurality, we also see the need to find coherence in this many-sided vision of the social world.

SOCIAL PROBLEMS AND THE CIVIC KNOWLEDGE CONTINUUM

The episodes in Philadelphia and at Kent State illustrate the range of ideas and the various avenues for publishing those ideas in a modern society such as the United States. Each day writers on human affairs generate millions of sentences that are transformed into newspaper columns, magazine stories, best-selling books, articles in academic journals, and scholarly books intended for fellow experts and research libraries. Journalists and social scientists present their observations and arguments in diverse arenas. But they have one thing in common: an eagerness to place their ideas in broader circulation for critical scrutiny. Writers enjoy seeing their work in print. This private satisfaction is related to a significant civic function. They contribute to a huge mass of information and ideas we have designated as civic knowledge.

Civic knowledge is the accumulated body of thought that is shared by citizens who take an active interest in their community, their nation, and increasingly the world. Civic knowledge is part of the civic culture associated with communities of all sorts: small towns, big cities, states, nations, and ultimately the global community. Some aspects of civic knowledge are highly local (neighborhood housing conditions, the closing of a factory) and others are national or global (changing economic conditions, rising tension between nations). Elise Boulding (1988) presents a vision of an evolving global civic culture that transcends the traditional governmental systems of nation-states. Some of the social problems we shall explore are global issues, but most of our attention is directed at the national level, with particular scrutiny of policy disputes confronting citizens and civic leaders in the United States.

Civic knowledge is not a static body of information to be memorized. It is a fluid and loosely organized system of information, beliefs, values, arguments, and claims of causal relationships (Gamson & Modigliani 1989; Hilgartner and Bosk 1988). As an evolving system of thought, it is constantly undergoing revision. The processes of change evolve each day as new laws are passed, new court decisions are handed down, new political leaders are elected, and new statistics are published about rising crime rates, a widening income gap between the rich and the poor, or declining test scores of indifferent adolescents. Journalists and social scientists play active roles in revising civic knowledge. Changing conditions and new events create a constant need to reinterpret various aspects of the specialized and everyday knowledge that experts and ordinary citizens use to reach judgments about all kinds of social circumstances. What does it mean that increasing numbers of people are homeless? Why do American students do so poorly on achievement tests in comparison with children in Europe and Japan? Why have the fertility rates of all modern industrial societies reached new lows? Why does the United States have the highest rate of teenage pregnancy among all industrial societies? Can the free-enterprise system address adequately the problems of urban blight? Should corporations be required to provide special leave for parents whose children are sick? These questions and dozens more are on the minds of journalists and sociologists, who search for new ways to understand the elusive dynamics of our highly complex modern society. As they report new evidence of emerging problems or discuss new explanations for old problems, their published accounts become part of the civic knowledge available for others to debate.

Writers in many professional fields contribute to the civic knowledge of a modern society. A partial list includes jurists, social workers, educators, physicians, police officers, government officials, professors in all the social sciences, analysts of finance and business, military experts, feminists, and religious leaders. Writers in these fields have a vital interest in civic matters. Their diverse contributions help to shape a highly complex cultural enterprise. No one can grasp civic knowledge in its entirety. Here we examine one small part of the total picture: the written work of sociologists (and other social scientists who are sociologically inclined) and journalists. Writers in both fields publish their ideas in newspapers, magazines, and books. We recognize journalists and sociologists as important knowledge producers who create observations and insights that help other citizens gain a

better understanding of the social world in which they live. It is the responsibility of those who consume these written products to criticize what they are reading. This book is designed as a manual for people beginning such lifelong pursuits.

The writings of journalists and sociologists can be constructed as a continuum between polar extremes (see Figure 1.3). At one end of the continuum, journalists are busy writing accounts of recent events for daily newspapers and weekly magazines. At the other end of the continuum, academic sociologists write highly technical research reports on some specialized aspect of a particular social issue. There is also an important body of literature between the extremes of popular journalism and academic sociology. We designate this intermediate literature as either journalistic sociology or sociological journalism. We will clarify these terms shortly. First let us investigate popular journalism and academic sociology.

Civic Sociology

	Popular Journalism	Sociological Journalism	Journalistic Sociology	Academic Sociology
Types of Literature and Examples	Daily newspaper Weekly magazine	Monthly magazines Books	Periodic journals Books	Periodic journals Books
Degree of Immediacy and Timeliness	High	Moderate	Moderate	Low
Gatekeeping for Authors	Primarily journalists; Occasionally social scientists (open gate)	Primarily journalists; Sometimes social scientists (open gate)	Exclusively social scientists (closed gate)	Exclusively sociologists (closed gate)
Audience	"Person on the street"	"Well-informed citizen"	"Well-informed citizen"	"Expert"

FIGURE 1.3
Civic Knowledge: The Journalism–Sociology Continuum

Popular Journalism

Every city of even modest size has at least one newspaper. The chief local journalists are the editor and reporters who cover the local daily events in their region. Editors also write daily editorials on every topic imaginable and the citizens offer their opinions in letters to the editor. Additional news from the nation and the world is provided by the wire services and syndicated columnists who interpret current events two or three times each week. In metropolitan papers, guest commentators address a wide range of public issues of particular importance to them. In any given year several sociologists and other social scientists write such opinion pieces.

The vast majority of newspapers are identified with a particular community (*The Chicago Tribune*, say, or the *Sacramento Bee*). But for many decades the *Wall Street Journal* and the *Christian Science Monitor* have served a broader readership throughout the nation, and more recently *USA Today* has gained a large national readership. Advances in electronic communication allow the *New York Times* to be published simultaneously in several locations throughout the nation. This prestigious Eastern paper is now read in all regions of the country. Though these four papers enjoy wide circulation from coast to coast, none can be considered to be *the* national newspaper of the United States. No newspaper enjoys such recognition.

Each week a number of popular magazines are delivered to homes and newsstands. The leading weekly magazines are *Time, Newsweek*, and *U.S. News & World Report*. Each magazine has a cover story that focuses on a celebrity newsmaker (such as a new appointee to the Supreme Court), a major news event (such as war in the Middle East), or a social problem that has been receiving increased public attention (such

as the difficulties faced by working mothers). Much space is devoted to a weekly summary of the key events covered in daily newspapers (such as the travels of presidents, debates in Congress, and treaty negotiations on other continents). Other sections of the magazine cover recent developments in fashion, movies, music, health, sports, religion, education, and the economy. These trendy accounts help readers feel up to date about the world around them. The colorful photographs and snappy writing style make for easy reading; the broad coverage of topics and insider gossip about celebrities create a sense of worldly sophistication.

Daily newspapers and weekly news magazines have much in common as popular and immediate journalism. They are written for the "person on the street" who wants to get a quick view of local and world events in an easily readable style. Since the publisher intends to reach a mass audience, the sentences are short and the vocabulary is simple. Newspapers must be readable by the ordinary citizen; but the stories and commentary must also be timely. A fundamental claim of the newspaper and weekly magazine is the timely coverage of the most recent events available to the journalist. Nothing is more stale and uninteresting to readers than an old story. Nothing is more enjoyable for reporters and editors than to scoop the competing paper or magazine with a late-breaking story their competitor has missed. The writing is done by three types of journalists: reporters, who write stories; editors, who offer opinions; and commentators, who interpret events. Professional experts on social problems are also invited to write letters to the editor or commentaries for the editorial page. Among the experts who frequently write guest columns are sociologists and other social scientists. In this role, they practice the KISS principle: Keep It Short and Simple. Jargon is eliminated and elaborate explanations are reduced to manageable terms for ordinary readers.

Academic Sociology

In many respects the world of academic sociology is in sharp contrast to that of popular journalism. Sociologists study social problems with the primary intent of sharing their work with other sociologists, not with the general public. Since sociologists are self-consciously scholarly in their endeavors, they pay special attention to their methods of investigation, their theories of explanation, and their claims of originality. When sociologists publish their results, they are fully aware that other sociologists may dispute the soundness of their findings or the logic of their explanations. The public has little interest in sociological disputes about methods, theories, or claims of originality. Neither do academicians in other fields (psychologists, for instance, have their own disputes to enjoy). Thus most sociologists spend most of their careers talking and writing among themselves, hoping that colleagues will recognize their work as truly significant.

The writings of sociologists are typically published as either articles in scholarly journals, chapters in books, or full-length books. Scholarly articles in sociology journals (such as *American Sociological Review* and *Social Problems*) are screened closely by other sociologists. The author submits an essay to the editor of a sociology journal; the editor sends the essay to two or three critics, who then recommend its acceptance or rejection. Editors of leading sociology journals reject far more essays than they publish. Chapters in books are usually not screened in the same fashion. The editor of the book selects experts in various fields who have already established their reputations as scholars and asks them to write chapters on certain themes according

to criteria that the editor has determined at the outset. Each year sociologists write hundreds of full-length books about all kinds of social problems. A few of these books become classics in the field (Frederick Thrasher's *The Gang*, Edwin Sutherland's *White Collar Crime*), but most books remain obscure. Sociologists review their books in a special journal titled *Contemporary Sociology*. A shorter list of books is also reviewed in such journals as *American Journal of Sociology* and *Social Forces*.

Specialized scholarship is of great importance to academic sociology. The field comprises many specialties. Some sociologists concentrate on particular topics of study (Chicano street gangs, say, or elderly people in nursing homes); other sociologists specialize in the use of particular research methods (such as ethnographic field methods or statistical analysis of census data). And finally, some sociologists narrow their interest to one particular theory of human society and social relationships (such as functional theory, conflict theory, or phenomenology). Most people outside academic sociology find these specialized works of little value, but these differences often inspire strong loyalties and intense debates inside the field.

Specialization also extends to the journals that publish sociological scholarship. Throughout the world, a short list of perhaps twenty to thirty journals is of general interest to most sociologists; many other journals deal with specialized areas of study. *Sociological Abstracts*, a comprehensive publication that summarizes sociology journal articles, has identified 191 sociology journals published in various nations. An international abstracting service covering crime and juvenile delinquency, *Criminology and Penology Abstracts*, has identified 186 journals that are currently read by criminologists. The *Women Studies Abstracts* summarizes articles in 32 journals, and articles on poverty, summarized in *Human Resources Abstracts*, can be found in 130 journals. Obviously the academic social sciences as a total field of human thought with many fields of study and specialized interests is both large and complex. An international index to the literature of the social and behavioral sciences, *Social Sciences Citation Index*, reviews scholarly works in 1,951 journals. If each journal published 50 articles each year, approximately 100,000 works of scholarship would be made available, exclusive of the hundreds of books that are published. With so many sources to review, it is impossible for academic experts to know all that can be known about social problems in the late twentieth century. The magnitude of such an enterprise should keep all the professors humble.

Popular journalists are always thinking about tomorrow's headlines or next week's cover story. They work on the cutting edge of timeliness (Gans 1979). Sociologists never deal with such short time frames. A major sociological study may take three to five years. Sociologists also enjoy the freedom to study social problems of the past. With a keen eye for historical materials, they sometimes examine a social problem for several decades or even centuries (Erikson 1966). Sociologists are not totally indifferent to the times in which they live; many hope that their work will be relevant to contemporary debates about current issues. But timeliness is a much broader concept for sociologists than it is for journalists hurrying to make their deadlines.

Popular journalism and academic sociology are at the extreme ends of the broad continuum of civic knowledge. But a great deal of serious writing by journalists and sociologists can be found between these polar extremes. Let us now examine the middle way: civic sociology.

Civic Sociology: Sociological Journalism and Journalistic Sociology

Civic sociology comprises the writings of journalists, social scientists, and other reflective people who stand back from the immediate events of the day and offer thoughtful interpretations of significant trends and developments that are currently attracting public attention. The chief contributors to civic sociology are journalists and social scientists, but the intended audience is a broad group of readers who want to be well informed. Civic sociology has been a crucial part of American public affairs throughout the twentieth century. The authors of this enlightenment tradition see their work as thoughtful "public conversation," open to the voices of others who see the need to connect ideas to action (Bellah et al. 1985; Baker & Rau 1990; Janowitz 1972).

Figure 1.3 shows two kinds of civic sociology: sociological journalism and journalistic sociology. The first kind is written by journalists who examine issues more thoroughly than the editors and reporters who are working on daily and weekly deadlines. These journalists take the time to become knowledgeable about a particular social problem. Sometimes this in-depth study involves an extensive review of current writings by experts and other journalists. Sociological journalism can also require the expenditure of considerable time and energy to investigate a problem firsthand through interviews, observations of social conditions, or direct witness of congressional hearings and court proceedings. Journalists who have contributed to the civic culture of this century include Jacob Riis (*How the Other Half Lives*), Walter Lippmann (*Public Opinion*), and Studs Terkel (*Working*).

Not all journalists work under the tight

time constraints and the KISS formula of popular journalism. Some journalists are expected to pay more attention to the details of carefully collected evidence, and they give more thought to the way they conceptualize issues. They spend more time doing research on their topic, have more freedom to develop their ideas, and are given more space to spell out the issues. More fully developed ideas about social problems appear in magazines that have a smaller readership than such giant publications as *Time* and *Newsweek*. There are many such magazines, some relatively new and others established cultural institutions of many decades. Our short list of important magazines that publish civic sociology includes *Harper's, The Washington Monthly, The New Republic, The Nation, The Atlantic, Ms., The Progressive, Across the Board,* and *Commentary.*

The editorial staffs of all these magazines are dominated by journalists who are searching for and screening manuscripts they consider of general interest to their readers. They are not self-consciously committed to sociology or any other social science. When social scientists publish articles in these magazines, they are expected to write for an audience that appreciates well-written English, not academic jargon. At this point the writings of the social scientists are being reviewed by journalists whose priorities are ideas clearly expressed for nonspecialists. The rules of the game are written by journalists, who also serve as referees. Their goal is to generate public interest in issues they deem significant in the broader debates on social policy.

Journalists who seek to reach the public with ideas about social problems are not limited to writing essays for magazines. They may also write books intended for the general public. Numerous social problems have been debated as a result of such works:

Harry M. Caudill's *Night Comes to the Cumberlands,* Tom Wicker's *No Time to Die,* Alvin Toffler's *Future Shock,* Ken Auletta's *The Underclass.* These books have become part of the civic culture of American public policy.

The second kind of civic sociology, journalistic sociology, consists of works of scholarship by sociologists and other social scientists intended for academic colleagues as well as the general public. Many sociologists have looked beyond the immediate circle of fellow experts and written essays and books for interested citizens who are eager for a better understanding of the social problems of their time. Among the more distinguished contributors of this tradition are E. A. Ross (*Sin and Society*), Robert and Helen Lynd (*Middletown*), C. W. Mills (*The Power Elite*), David Riesman (*The Lonely Crowd*), Robert Bellah and his colleagues (*Habits of the Heart*), Charles Perrow (*Normal Accidents*), Gunnar Myrdal (*The American Dilemma*), and Lenore Weitzman (*The Divorce Revolution*).

Sociologists do not have the sense of immediacy that popular journalists face, but if they want to contribute to the public debates about current social issues, they must produce essays and books that are timely. If divorced women need more equitable laws to protect their children's financial security, there is little to be gained and much to lose by delaying the publication of new insights or research findings. Scholarship on such topics of public concern must be timely in a broad sense; it need not be rushed out this week.

Sociologists also publish essays in various magazines and journals that are edited primarily by sociologists or other social scientists. These journals are not popular with most people on the street, but they are read by a broad range of citizens who have an interest in public affairs. Some of the magazines and journals that publish the works of sociologists are *The Futurist, Public Interest, American Demographics, Wilson Quarterly, Society, Psychology Today, Dissent,* and *Social Policy.*

Figure 1.3 suggests that civic sociology is the domain of journalists and social scientists. For the purposes of this book, this position seems reasonable; but the full list of contributors to civic sociology is longer. Many others contribute to this literature as activists, political leaders, or interested observers of human affairs. For example, a longshoreman in San Francisco, Eric Hoffer, wrote a provocative book, *The True Believer,* which was widely acclaimed as an insightful study of social movements in the twentieth century. Sometimes novelists turn from their fictional work to write penetrating essays, as James Baldwin did when he wrote *The Fire Next Time,* on race relations. Jimmy Carter and Robert McNamara have written extensively on the global problems facing the international community since their political careers ended (Kidder 1987). Since social problems touch everyone, it is not surprising to learn that thoughtful people of public affairs have on occasion written important books and essays about the collective need for better answers to pressing issues.

Another group of writers worthy of mention are the social activists who call attention to troubling social conditions and then offer bold proposals for their solution. These visionary people may be trained in any number of fields, but their training is less important than their convictions and affiliation with like-minded activists who see an urgent need for change. Writing books and essays that call for reform is an important twentieth-century tradition in American civic culture. In recent decades several activists have written important books in the field of civic sociology. Betty Friedan's *Feminine Mystique* ignited the feminist movement in the 1960s. After she wrote her book, Friedan founded the National Organization for Women (NOW) and worked with other feminists on a broad agenda for social reform. In the 1960s Michael Harrington created national awareness of the pervasive problems of poverty in his widely acclaimed book *The Other America.* Harrington, a Socialist, was of a more radical political bent than most of his readers, but he helped to set a new national agenda for government initiatives. Other activist writers worthy of mention include Frances Moore Lappe (*Diet for a Small Planet*), who helped to create a new awareness of global hunger, and Lisebeth Schorr (*Within Our Reach*), who has written a compelling account of successful strategies to break the cycle of poverty in which millions of American families have been trapped. Activist writers play a crucial role in helping to generate the public agenda on social problems. Often their books are controversial, but journalists and sociologists acknowledge their capacity to draw attention to social problems that demand public debate and governmental consideration.

JOURNALISM AND SOCIOLOGY: A COMPARATIVE APPRECIATION

In 1905 an American sociologist, E. A. Ross, began a series of articles on corporate crime in the *Atlantic Monthly.* Two years later his articles were published as a book, *Sin and Society.* These essays combine Ross's remarkable skills as a sociologist, journalist, and social critic. In a foreword to the book, President Theodore Roosevelt praised Ross for his ability to articulate complex issues in regard to the control of unlawful activities of the new corporate giants in the United States. "You insist," wrote Roosevelt, "as all healthy-minded patriots should insist, that public opinion, if only sufficiently enlightened and aroused, is equal to the necessary regenerative tasks and can yet dominate the future" (Ross 1907:xxxix). These words have a quaint ring today, but Roosevelt's message is similar to ours: Public opinion can be enlightened only when journalists and social scientists provide carefully crafted statements about social problems. The writings of sociological journalists and journalistic sociologists have the potential to help citizens go about the work of creating a saner future.

Sociologists and journalists often share concerns and audiences. Some sociologists may enjoy attacking journalists and vice versa, but their quarrel is minor in comparison with their common goal: increasing understanding of the social problems confronting modern societies in the last years of the twentieth century. Jeremy Tunstall suggests that

there is more in common between sociologists and journalists than either side might care to admit. Both occupations are interested in the seamy side of life; both occupational ideologies stress that reality is shielded by facades, things that are not what they seem, and that many social appearances have been deliberately contrived. Both sociologists and journalists often anticipate deceit, self-seeking and corruption in public life. (Tunstall 1971:277)

Journalism and sociology also have similar strategies of observation. Sociologists rely on participant observation, survey methods, and government statistics. Journalists use the same means of gathering information in modified form. As participants in various social groups, reporters study and record real-life situations. A dramatic exam-

ple of participant observation is the journalist Tom Wicker's account (1975) of his four harrowing days as a mediator in the Attica prison riot. The sociologists Gresham Sykes (1958) and James Jacobs (1978) conducted similar participant observation studies within the walls of maximum-security penitentiaries, but their books are less dramatic and more theoretical than Wicker's. Survey methods are used by a thriving polling industry, which regularly sells its findings to newspapers and magazines (see Wheeler 1976). The opinion polls of George Gallup, Louis Harris, and Daniel Yankelovich offer editors a continuous news source on topics ranging from foreign policy to pot smoking. During presidential elections, computer analysts and pollsters apply sophisticated survey techniques that were initially developed by Samuel Stouffer and Paul Lazarsfeld, two distinguished empirical sociologists of this century. Finally, journalists share sociologists' interest in government statistics. Like sociologists, they turn to the Uniform Crime Reports of the FBI to gain an understanding of changing crime patterns. Occasionally journalists such as Ben Wattenberg (1976) assess massive files of government data to convey a broader picture of the changing social structure of the United States.

The factors shared by journalism and sociology—common interests, writers, audiences, and methods of observation—should not obscure fundamental differences. Ruth Jacobs contrasts her entry into the field of sociology with her many years as a reporter: "Unlike journalism, sociology is not confined to reporting and interpretation. Public interest and novelty justify journalism, but sound theory justifies sociology" (Jacobs 1970:350). Journalists often approach the topic of race, for example, by reporting and interpreting landmark Supreme Court decisions in cases involving school desegregation, busing, and affirmative action; sociologists, by contrast, write about race relations in broader terms of conflict and assimilation over many decades in group settings that range from classrooms and neighborhoods to the armed forces.

Some academic sociologists hold the notion that their discipline ranks above the daily news grind of journalists. In some circles, well-written and popular sociological writing is put down as "mere journalism." But the fact that writers approach social reality in different ways does not necessarily mean that one method is superior to the other. We share the views of Max Weber, who had extensive knowledge of the press:

Not everybody realizes that a really good journalistic accomplishment requires at least as much "genius" as any scholarly accomplishment, especially because of the necessity of producing at once and "on order," and because of the necessity of being effective, to be sure, under quite different conditions of production. It is almost never acknowledged that the responsibility of the journalist is far greater, and that the sense of responsibility of every honorable journalist is, on the average, not a bit lower than that of the scholar, but rather, higher. This is because, in the very nature of the case, irresponsible journalistic accomplishments and their often terrible effects are remembered. (Weber 1946:80)

The work of both journalists and sociologists is serious and exciting. We hope you have gained an appreciation for both perspectives.

CONCLUSION

Journalism and sociology are deeply entangled in the social controversies of the twentieth century. Professionals in both fields frequently proclaim their objectivity and detachment from the passions of partisan affairs and often claim neutral ground in the swirling debates of the moment. But such claims should not lead to an uncritical appraisal of their accounts of social problems, which pursue many hidden agendas. Neither field enjoys the privilege of standing on Mount Olympus with a set of self-sufficient answers to the many perplexing questions of our day.

The challenging task for thoughtful students is to understand the social and cultural context in which professional knowledge producers such as journalists and sociologists create a wide array of written information: books, research articles, front-page headlines, editorials. The key term is *context*. Sociology and journalism both function as knowledge-producing enter-

prises within the larger context of the changing common-sense constructions of human affairs. But this relationship is not one of simple harmony; for many reasons, sociologists and journalists often find themselves in conflict with various segments of the public. Occasions of tension are especially frequent in the investigation of controversial social problems.

This book is committed to helping students better understand both journalism and sociology, because both professions are of vital importance in a free and open society that cherishes the values of enlightenment. Readers must be thoughtful critics of these two fields. We do not assume the superiority of either journalism or sociology. Comparative notions of relative superiority and inferiority confuse the more fundamental issue of recognizing the context and purpose of each field. Students should learn to enjoy reading sociology in college. Whether the reading of social science literature becomes a lifelong habit or one's reading focuses primarily on local newspapers and weekly magazines, deliberation of social problems requires a critical understanding of how sociology and journalism construct plausible statements about the social world. Attention also must be given to the basic reasoning skills that can be used to assess any statement about any social problem. These concerns are addressed in the next three chapters.

References

Baker, Paul, and William Rau. 1990. The cultural contradictions of teaching sociology. In Herbert Gans, ed., *Sociology in America,* pp. 169–187. Newbury Park, Calif.: Sage.

Baldwin, James. 1963. *The fire next time.* New York: Dial.

Bellah, Robert, Richard Madsen, William Sullivan, Ann Swindler, and Steven Tipton. 1985. *Habits of the heart.* New York: Harper & Row.

Bills, Scott L. 1982. Kent State/May 4: *Echoes through a decade.* Kent, Ohio: Kent State University Press.

Bloomgarden, Kathy. 1983. Managing the environment: The public's view. *Public Opinion* 6:47–51.

Blumer, Herbert. 1971. Social problems as collective behavior. *Social Problems* 18:298–306.

Boulding, Elise. 1988. *Building a global civic culture: Education for an interdependent world.* Syracuse, N.Y.: Syracuse University Press.

Carson, Rachel. 1962. *Silent spring.* Boston: Houghton Mifflin.

Caudill, Harry M. 1962. *Night comes to the Cumberlands.* Boston: Little, Brown.

Erikson, Kai. 1966. *Wayward puritans.* New York: Wiley.

Eszterhas, J., and M. Roberts. 1971. A study in distortion. *The Progressive* 35:35–40.

Farley, Reynolds. 1984. *Blacks and whites: Narrowing the gap?* Cambridge, Mass.: Harvard University Press.

Friedan, Betty. 1963. *The feminine mystique.* New York: Norton.

Gamson, William, and Andrea Modigliani. 1989. Media discourse and public opinion on nuclear power: A constructionist approach. *American Journal of Sociology* 95:1–37.

Gans, Herbert. 1979. *Deciding what's news.* New York: Vintage.

Glazer, Nathan. 1984. The structure of ethnicity. *Public Opinion* 7:2–5.

Hamilton, Charles V. 1982. Integrating the American dream. *Public Opinion* 5:45–47.

Harrington, Michael. 1962. *The other America.* New York: Macmillan.

Heyl, Barbara Sherman. 1979. *The madam as entrepreneur: Career management in house prostitution.* New Brunswick, N.J.: Transaction.

Hilgartner, Stephen, and Charles Bosk. 1988. The rise and fall of social problems: A public arenas model. *American Journal of Sociology* 94:53–78.

Hoffer, Eric. 1951. *The true believer: Thoughts on the nature of mass movements.* New York: New American Library.

Jacobs, James. 1978. *Statesville.* Chicago: University of Chicago Press.

Jacobs, Ruth. 1970. The journalistic and the sociological enterprises as ideal types. *American Sociologist* 5:347–50.

Janowitz, Morris. 1972. Professionalization of Sociology. *American Journal of Sociology* 78:105–35.

Kelner, Joseph, and James Munves. 1980. *The Kent State coverup.* New York: Harper & Row.

Kidder, Rushworth M., ed. 1987. *An agenda for the 21st century.* Cambridge, Mass.: MIT Press.

Lappé, Frances Moore. 1982. *Diet for a small planet.* New York: Ballantine.

Lewis, Jerry M. 1971. Review essay: The telling of Kent State. *Social Problems* 19:2, 267–79.

Lewis, Jerry M. 1972. A study of the Kent State incident using Smelser's theory of collective behavior. *Sociological Inquiry* 42:2, 87–96.

Lewis, Jerry M., and Raymond J. Adamek. 1973. Social control violence and radicalization: The Kent State case. *Social Forces* 51:3, 342–47.

Lewis, Jerry M., and Raymond J. Adamek, 1975. Social control violence and radicalization: Behavior data. *Social Problems* 22:5, 663–74.

Lippmann, Walter. 1961. *Public opinion*. New York: Macmillan.

Lynd, Robert, and Helen Lynd. 1929. *Middletown*. New York: Harcourt, Brace & World.

Michener, James. 1971a. Kent State—Campus under fire. *Reader's Digest*. March, 98:57–63, 240–60.

Michener, James. 1971b. Kent State—What happened and why. *Reader's Digest*. April, 98:217–70.

Mills, C. W. 1956. *The power elite*. New York: Oxford University Press.

Myrdal, Gunnar. 1944. *The American dilemma: The Negro problem and modern democracy*. New York: Harper.

Perrow, Charles. 1984. *Normal accidents*. New York: Basic Books.

Riesman, David. 1960. *The lonely crowd*. New Haven: Yale University Press.

Riis, Jacob. 1890/1957. *How the other half lives*. New York: Hill & Wang.

Ross, E. A. 1907. *Sin and society*. Boston: Houghton Mifflin.

Rudwick, Elliot, and August Meier. 1972. The Kent State affair: Social control of a putative value-oriented movement. *Sociological Inquiry* 42:2, 81–86.

Schorr, Lisebeth. 1988. *Within our reach*. New York: Doubleday.

Schwartz, Barry. 1968. The effect in Philadelphia of Pennsylvania's increased penalties for rape and attempted rape. *Journal of Criminal Law, Criminology, and Police Science* 59:509–15.

Stone, I. F. 1971. *The killings at Kent State: How murder went unpunished*. New York: New York Review.

Sutherland, Edwin. 1983. White collar crime. New Haven, Conn.: Yale University Press.

Sykes, Gresham. 1958. *Society of captives*. Princeton, N.J.: Princeton University Press.

Terkel, Studs. 1972. *Working*. New York: Avon.

Thrasher, Frederick. 1963. *The gang: A study of 1,313 gangs in Chicago*. Abridged. Chicago: University of Chicago Press.

Toffler, Alvin. 1970. *Future shock*. New York: Random House.

Tunstall, Jeremy. 1971. *Journalists at work*. London: Constable.

Wattenberg, Ben. 1976. *The real America: A surprising examination of the state of the union*. New York: Putnam.

Weber, Max. 1946. Politics as vocation. In C. W. Mills and H. Gerth, eds., *From Max Weber*. New York: Oxford University Press.

Weitzman, Lenore. 1985. *The divorce revolution*. New York: Free Press.

Wheeler, Michael. 1976. *Lies, damn lies, and statistics*. New York: Liveright.

Wicker, Tom. 1975. *A time to die*. New York: Ballantine.

CHAPTER 2

SOCIAL PROBLEMS: DISCOURSE ABOUT PRIVATE TROUBLES AND PUBLIC ISSUES

INTRODUCTION

We have seen that both journalism and sociology are dedicated to the study of social problems. We identified much variety in these two professions, but we also recognized many occasions when their work overlaps as they seek to reach citizens who want to be well informed about social issues. For the past hundred years each generation of inquiring citizens has turned to journalism and sociology in its quest for better understanding of social problems of all kinds. Journalists and sociologists share the roles of observers and interpreters of social change and social controversy. These common roles are deeply embedded in the nation's civic culture. Both professions are part of a larger complex system of democratic institutions that work best in a climate of open inquiry and spirited public debate.

We have argued that journalism and sociology are important institutions in a modern society. This chapter examines some of the rudimentary features of discourse in both

29

professions. We will explore some of the special ways in which journalists and sociologists go about constructing statements about the social world. A number of questions come to mind. How is social knowledge constructed by journalists and sociologists? Does each profession have a unique approach to the study of social issues? Or are there important similarities? To what extent is each field grounded in more basic features of social knowledge that are shared by other members of society? What are the basic building blocks of human thought that allow ordinary citizens and experts to reflect upon their common concerns? These questions focus our attention on the basic elements of social thought that allow journalists and sociologists to construct plausible accounts of social problems. We begin this inquiry by examining the common-sense discourse of people in all walks of life.

ELEMENTARY FEATURES OF SOCIAL KNOWLEDGE

Most people become aware of social problems through various networks of communication. Words and images are communicated to the general public through television, newspapers, magazines, and books. Journalists and social scientists spend much of their time transforming various kinds of evidence (everyday impressions, government statistics, court transcripts, interviews) into elaborate statements about social problems. In this sense, social problems are constructed realities; that is, the problems become a reality because journalists and social scientists have decided that certain kinds of events and statistical trends should be defined as social problems. In the past decade, for example, journalists have written hundreds of stories about the problem of homelessness in the United States. One can sit at the kitchen table in a small town or in an affluent suburb and read about this problem. City dwellers may see homeless people every day on their way to work, but it is not necessary to meet homeless people to know about their plight. Writers and television crews have done the work for the ordinary citizen; they have gone to the rescue missions, talked to street people, consulted experts, and interviewed community leaders.

These writers then transform their impressions into a plausible account about homelessness. The account may appear as a series in a metropolitan paper (Mathews 1985), a detailed research monograph (Wiseman 1979), or a government report (Cuomo 1983). By reading various accounts or watching television reports, people can become aware of the problems of homelessness without ever meeting a homeless person. Through the efforts of others, homelessness becomes a constructed reality of importance to the public.

The process of constructing a problem is always guided by two elementary aspects of societal knowledge. First, social reality is perceived along a continuum from small groups (friends and family) to large societal systems (nation-states and multinational corporations). College professors, newspaper columnists, and friends at the local bar all grasp the difference in magnitude between the intimate quarrels of lovers and the diplomatic struggles of superpowers. Second, social reality is constructed along a continuum from concrete to abstract. Everyone, whether a peasant or a scholar, has a wide range of experiences out of which impressions of the world are shaped—the laughter of friends, the anguish of pain, the disappointment of defeat, the sadness of death, the first news of war. These raw experiences are interpreted through a common culture and take on special meaning as abstract moral principles or sweeping empirical generalizations.

Social problems can thus be perceived along two polar dimensions: microscopic/macroscopic and concrete/abstract. Figure 2.1 combines these two dimensions to form a metaphoric space of four divergent orientations. The scope of awareness spans all social groups, from the smallest to the largest; the degree of generality ranges from descriptions of raw experience to universal claims of wisdom and truth. The elementary features of social knowledge found in common-sense culture, journalism, and sociology all have similar dual orientations. A similarity of tendencies, however, does not imply like knowledge systems. The micro-concrete category for journalism, for ex-

ample, is somewhat different from the micro-concrete category for sociology. Descriptive sociological studies are rarely so concrete as the detailed stories found in newspapers.

Despite the differences among common sense, journalism, and sociology, journalists and sociologists continually rely on common-sense knowledge in their endeavor to understand social problems. The dual orientations (micro/macro and concrete/abstract) are embedded in the common culture and provide the symbolic foundation for journalism and sociology. These dual tendencies in the common-sense world are so important that they demand brief elaboration.

Micro/Macro

Personal relationships sustain human existence. People are bound together in relatively small groups of two, twenty, or even two hundred. They pair up to date, marry, enjoy a coffee break, share a dorm room, do a lab experiment, or gossip. Miniature worlds of two often expand to three, four, five, or fifteen when people double-date, have children, play poker, or attend a family reunion. People enter close networks in schools, churches, neighborhoods, fraternities, sororities, civic groups, and a host of other small-scale groups. These diverse social settings facilitate personal familiarity with routine expectations and special events. Word spreads fast when the first black family moves to an all-white neighborhood; the marital problems of neighbors often are exposed beyond their four walls; when the garbage is not collected, a municipal labor dispute is brought to the public's attention.

People are not frozen at one level of social consciousness but are able to acknowledge social groups that transcend their family, friends, and local community. Modern

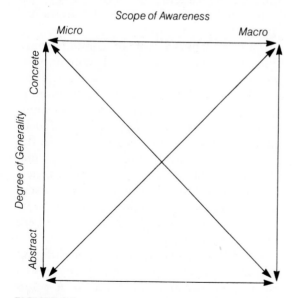

FIGURE 2.1

Field of Perception for Assessment of Social Problems: Common Sense, Journalism, Sociology

human discourse constructs images of labor unions; the medical profession; city, state, and federal bureaucracies; giant corporations; regions of the country; nation-states; continents; and the world order. The language related to these large social entities is often imprecise and the generalizations are frequently sweeping: "Affirmative action weakens the willpower of minorities to work for high achievement." "The welfare system undermines the family." "Because the Midwest is dominated by smokestack industries, it will continue to suffer economic decline." "World population is out of control and disaster is inevitable." Everyday labels such as "city hall," "the media," "public opinion," "the military establishment," "conglomerates," "the Mafia," and "Catholic hierarchy" identify social structures as constraining and directing forces and provide glimpses of a remote social terrain. The social vision of ordinary citizens is not limited to parochial affairs. As people construct images of total societies, they perceive giant forces of power, economic development, national security, social welfare, war, and peace.

Concrete/Abstract

A second aspect of common sense is the degree of generality with which people express ideas. At one extreme, people recount in vivid detail such experiences as seeing a fire, watching teenagers steal a bicycle, or witnessing the aftermath of a race riot. These concrete experiences are recalled as unique events, each taking place at a specific time and place. At the other extreme, people generalize rather abstractly about events they have witnessed or heard of. Generalities come quickly to the lips: "Buildings are burned to collect insurance"; "Our permissive society lets young people get away with murder"; "Riots happen because of low moral standards in the

ghetto." In August 1990, millions of Americans watched the sudden invasion of Kuwait by Iraqi soldiers. In the ensuing months the massive military buildup in Saudi Arabia was daily news. The sequence of concrete events in the Middle East was soon transformed into new images of American soldiers in a Muslim world where pin-ups, beer, and women drivers are forbidden. Many American citizens were puzzled about longstanding disputes between Arab states that were created by the British in the 1920s. Ordinary American citizens have no sense of the detailed history of such British creations as Iraq, Jordan, and Kuwait. They search for a coherent picture of Middle Eastern affairs and wonder if easy generalizations of right and wrong created by the sudden turn of events in which old enemies become new allies. Was the Iraq of 1990 similar to Nazi Germany of 1940? Was Saddam Hussein as evil as Hitler? There are no easy answers and many people are left with the Psalmist's ancient question "Why do nations conspire, and people plot in vain?" (Ps. 2:1).

The two dimensions of common-sense thinking (micro/macro and concrete/abstract), though independent of each other, are also related. Figure 2.2 depicts the relationship between these two dimensions. People have concrete impressions of both small and large social entities (such as the local precinct and the big-city political machine); they also understand abstract generalizations at both the micro and the macro levels (such as "Delinquency is caused by broken homes" and "High crime rates are related to poverty").

On different occasions and for different reasons, people apply varying degrees of abstract or global understanding. A priest administering the last rites to an injured soldier in Panama, for example, does not use the occasion to explain the direction of American foreign policy since the Truman

Scope of Awareness

		Micro: Small-scale social structures and social settings	Macro: Large-scale social structures and social settings
Degree of Generality	*Concrete:* Awareness of specific events at a particular time and place; unique occurrences understood in their uniqueness	*Micro-concrete* 1. Learning about a neighbor child who was abused 2. Knowing a friend who had an abortion	*Macro-concrete* 1. Seeing TV coverage of new laws to protect children (e.g., Child Abuse and Prevention Treatment Act, 1973) 2. Reading or hearing about the Supreme Court decision on abortion, *Roe v. Wade* (1973)
	Abstract: General principles and ideas that are believed to be true and that explain numerous (if not all) specific instances	*Micro-abstract* 1. Discussing the theories about the causes of child abuse (e.g., "abusers were abused when they were children") 2. The moral dilemmas and ultimate questions about abortion or keeping the baby	*Macro-abstract* 1. Following debates about the rights of families versus the responsibilities of the state to intervene in family life 2. Thinking about current policy debates between pro-life and pro-choice political factions in the abortion controversy

FIGURE 2.2

Ways of Knowing: The Common Culture and Common-Sense Consciousness

Doctrine. On the other hand, citizens attempting to understand the United States' expenditure of billions of dollars and thousands of lives in Korea, Vietnam, Lebanon, Panama, and Iraq would consider general policy issues such as the collapsing colonial empires of France and England, the rise and fall of the Communist bloc, and the political instability of developing nations. Mourning for a friend slain on a foreign battlefield is not dependent on general policy questions. Common sense allows people to think of personal tragedies in personal terms and of global strategies in global terms.

FEATURES OF SOCIAL KNOWLEDGE IN JOURNALISM

The professional norms of journalism provide reporters, editors, pundits, and freelance writers with a loose set of guidelines for selecting, describing, and interpreting worrisome events that will be defined by journalists and acknowledged by readers as social problems. All journalists have three crucial tasks: to select a topic to investigate, to describe people and events that have been investigated, and to interpret the events within a larger framework of human understanding and civic importance. Sometimes these guidelines are rather routine and mechanical. For example, each day reporters check in at the police station to cover the daily arrest reports. At other times the guidelines are more open ended and creative (for example, Bob Woodward and Carl Bernstein's famous investigation of the Watergate scandal that led to Richard Nixon's resignation [1974]). At the local as well as the national and international levels, journalists are often the first to observe the events, tell the story, and reflect on its meaning. Journalists like to claim that they write the first draft of history as the great events of our time are occurring.

Journalists have assignments at such places as burning buildings, political rallies, and the Supreme Court. Each day agencies of all kinds, from the courthouse to the White House, release information that reporters transform into stories and editors use as bases for their opinions. The raw data compiled by agencies are often cooked by public relations officers, who shape this in-formation with the intent of projecting positive images of their organization. Journalists then face the task of recognizing the biases and deciding whether additional sources are necessary to get a more balanced perspective.

Some reporters and freelance writers investigate highly complex situations such as the operations of street gangs in metropolitan areas, embezzlement in the savings and loan industry, and the plight of the small town when the surrounding rural area faces economic decline. A journalist's assignment may take a few hours or several years. It may be as simple as picking up a press release or as complex as determining some of the causes of a major social catastrophe such as the AIDS epidemic or racial disturbances in several American cities. Journalists play a central role in the production of information and ideas about all the social problems that concern the citizenry. The topics are virtually endless, from the welfare of inner-city children to international treaties on pollution control. Journalists select a topic that they or their editors consider important to cover, find pertinent information about it, and provide an analysis that allows readers to gain some understanding of what it all means.

FOUR TYPES OF SOCIAL KNOWLEDGE IN NEWSPAPERS AND MAGAZINES

We have been considering journalism as a process of creating and interpreting news. It can also be understood as a kaleidoscopic world of highly diverse statements about the social world. Numerous forms of social knowledge crowd into each daily newspaper and popular magazine. Using the dual dimensions of social affairs, we can identify four types of social knowledge: micro-concrete, micro-abstract, macro-concrete, and macro-abstract. News items in these four categories tend to resemble common-sense discourse, although the terminology has been changed to correspond to journalistic language.

The micro/macro dimension. The micro/macro dimension distinguishes between private affairs and public issues. The micro world of private affairs is a constant source of public curiosity. People never tire of learning about weddings, divorces, births, deaths, job promotions, and the social lives of celebrities. Space is devoted to such items as Leona Hemsley's first day in jail and her subsequent appeals for freedom, Amy Carter's first day at Thaddeus Stevens School and her later enrollment at Brown University, and Roger Keith Coleman's conviction of rape and murder and his subsequent plea to avoid the electric chair. Whether they concern the murder of a Mafia boss or the temper tantrum of a tennis player, these momentary episodes in the private lives of well-known people become instant news in a media-saturated world. Even widely publicized private affairs do not automatically become public issues.

The macro world of public issues concerns changes in the larger social structures of corporations, governments, and civic affairs. Reported events in the public-issues arena are often assessed in terms of their potential impact on millions of people. Journalists cover such topics as election returns, Supreme Court decisions, legislative action, impeachment proceedings, and meetings between world leaders. Politicians make news when they commit government resources to Medicaid, veterans' benefits, unemployment benefits, and food stamps. These same politicians also make news when they attack the welfare system and excessive government spending.

The concrete/abstract dimension. Journalistic knowledge expressed in concrete terms is referred to as a *story*; an abstract assessment of a social issue is labeled *analysis*. Stories emphasize specific events that occur only once. The gangland slaying of the Mafia boss Paul Castellano on December 16, 1985, for example, was dramatically reported in the press. Analysis emphasizes the general and recurrent features of social life. Within a week of Castellano's death, several published articles analyzed organized crime in the United States. Stories

probe questions of who, what, where, and when; analysis deals with questions that lie behind the stories—the why and the how.

Combining the two dimensions. The combined dichotomies of private affairs/public issues and stories/analysis create four types of journalistic knowledge, as shown in Figure 2.3: (1) stories of private affairs (Roger Keith Coleman, pleads his case but is executed, May 20, 1992), (2) stories of public issues (the Supreme Court rules on the death penalty as a constitutionally valid form of punishment, July 2, 1976), (3) analysis of private affairs (a psychiatrist reveals his theory of violent murder), and (4) analysis of public issues (an editorial examines the deterrence theory of capital punishment). These four categories of journalistic knowledge are ideal types. Not all news items fit one of the four categories perfectly. It is not always easy to distinguish between private affairs and public issues. Family news obviously falls under private affairs. But what about a story concerning a company that lays off eighty workers? Is the resulting unemployment a small-scale private affair that concerns eighty families, or is it a large-scale public issue that concerns the economy? This example does not belong exclusively in either category as a distinct case of micro-level or macro-level behavior but can best be understood as intermediate between the two extremes. Many intermediate points lie along the continuum from micro level to macro level. Similarly, varying degrees of concrete description and abstract generalization are present in stories and news analysis.

The course of events can shift a news item from one type of journalistic knowledge to another. In 1990 a private scandal was reported in the newspapers about the financial escapades and luxurious lifestyle of Charles Keating. His personal story of wrongdoing was soon linked to the larger

Scope of Awareness

		Micro (private affairs)	Macro (public issues)
		Small social groups, social structures, and social settings	Large social groups, social structures, and social settings
Degree of Generality	*Concrete (stories)* — Descriptive stories of particular people and events at specific times, places. Emphasis on questions of who, what, when, where	*Micro-concrete* Stories of private affairs; local news of families, social clubs, churches, human interest stories—e.g., "police car stolen"	*Macro-concrete* Stories of public issues; news of importance in economic and political arenas—e.g., Supreme Court decisions, passage of crucial legislation, bills vetoed by the president
	Abstract (analysis) — Analytical statements exploring general topics that affect many people in different places and times. Emphasis on questions of why, how	*Micro-abstract* Analysis of private affairs; discussion of problems of interpersonal relations—e.g., affairs of home, office, and community; popularized writings from psychology and sociology	*Macro-abstract* Analysis of public issues, editorials, syndicated columns; the commentaries that interpret public issues—e.g., Walter Lippmann, James Reston, David Broder, George Will

FIGURE 2.3

Ways of Knowing: Journalism

issue of the savings and loan crisis. As the story of Charles Keating unfolded, it soon encompassed the careers of five United States senators—"The Keating Five"—who had taken campaign contributions from the financier and consulted with him about an undesirable bank audit by federal regulators. Now the drama moved to the ethical conduct of senators and the politics of campaign contributions and "constituent services" to the wealthy. A new public issue had now emerged: Does representative government favor the wealthy at the expense of ordinary citizens? The behavior of one highly ambitious man, Charles Keating, generated stories of an extravagant lifestyle

as well as the analysis of government policies to regulate the savings and loan industry as well as political contributions to powerful incumbent congressmen.

The fact that journalists often write for a mass audience under severe time pressure does not diminish the significance of journalism as a crucial source of knowledge about social issues. Though many news items may be of fleeting interest and others undeniably trivial, it is still important to recognize that many journalists write thoughtful stories and commentaries about pressing social problems. Many examples of such work are found in the selections in Chapters 5 through 22 of this book. The articles and editorials we have selected represent a tiny fraction of the voluminous literature available in hundreds of newspapers and thousands of magazines. The strong interest of print journalists in social problems can be documented by the hundreds of articles published in newspapers and magazines that are listed in various indexing systems (such as *Reader's Guide, Facts on File, and Editorials on File*) that guide readers to articles on crime, poverty, drug abuse, mental illness, racial discrimination, bureaucracy, and many other topics that concern sociologists as well as journalists.

We have been emphasizing the work of popular journalists, but the same four types of social knowledge are found in more sophisticated journalism as well. Let us investigate both types of journalism.

Micro-Concrete: Narrative of a Personal Tragedy

Edmund Perry, a young black man, was sometimes described as "the hope of Harlem." Eddie had recently graduated from Phillips Exeter Academy and was planning to attend Stanford University in the fall. On June 12, 1985, he was killed by a white plain-clothes police officer. His death was widely reported in the press, and many critics, black and white, were outraged by the actions of an apparently overzealous police officer. Thirteen days later a grand jury declared the killing "justifiable homicide" and "within departmental guidelines." The grand jury found that Eddie and his brother were trying to mug the police officer, who then fired in self-defense. The story ended just as quickly as it had begun.

A freelance reporter, Robert Anson, had been following the news accounts, and he was puzzled: How could this tragedy happen to such a promising young man? He began an intensive investigation of the case by visiting Exeter and reading background in-

formation on the black community, and eventually he interviewed 115 people. Anson's careful probing of Edmund Perry's life in the contrasting worlds of Harlem and Exeter revealed a deeply troubled young man who was struggling with his success. Anson's book, *Best Intentions* (1987), offers a complex account of a young person unable to resolve the conflicting pressure of his two worlds.

Micro-Analysis: Interpreting the Black Experience

Robert Anson provides a vivid narrative of one black teenager's life in the conflicting worlds of racial tension, poverty, illicit drugs, and the alluring promises of upward mobility. What does this mean to live in a society where so many black youths face the despair of violence and death? During the past three decades this question has been asked many times by journalists who want to write more than another account of yet another death. The "why" question searches for the meaning of a broad range of experiences shared by many black males. One black journalist, Bob Teague, has reflected on the meaning of being a black man in America. He wrote his *Letters to a Black Boy* (1968) the same year Edmund Perry was born. On the first page of this provocative work Teague writes, "All black men are insane. And that includes your daddy." He goes on: "Almost any living thing would quickly go mad under the unrelenting exposure to the climate created and reserved for black men in a white racist society."

Teague's book is an introspective account of thousands of life experiences he has faced and learned about from other black people. His advice to his son is an interpretive essay on the interpersonal world of black-white relations in the United States. His concerns are similar to those discussed in the writings of such black psychiatrists as Alvin Poussaint (1970) and William Grier and Price Cobbs (1968), who explore the depths of anger and rage so frequently experienced by black Americans. This reflective literature adds new understanding to the disturbing story of the education and killing of Edmund Perry.

Macro-Concrete: Story of a Billion-Dollar Empire

At the macro level, many sociological journalists also present descriptive accounts of important events and trends as well as interpretive essays that offer explanations of these events. A good macro description of a major social problem is found in Guy Gugliotta and Jeff Leen's comprehensive history of the rapid emergence of the Colombian cocaine empire in the 1980s (1989). Their *Kings of Cocaine* is a raw story of shootouts, assassinations, drug seizures, raids, kidnappings, fast profits, high living, and pathetic addiction. The people who built this billion-dollar empire are presented as shrewed and violent entrepreneurs, bloody henchmen, corrupt judges, and dictators on the make. On the other side of the drug war, the battle is fought by captured traffickers who turn against their partners in crime in exchange for leniency, dedicated Drug Enforcement agents, determined prosecutors, and overwhelmed police officers who can never fully grasp the magnitude of the Colombian connection.

Gugliotta and Leen have written a comprehensive story of the leading drug lords and their staunchest opponents in the press, the Colombian government, and the U.S. Drug Enforcement Agency. It is a dramatic narrative of ruthless actions and big dollars for the profiteers while law enforcement agents struggle against the odds to stem the tide of Colombia's largest export business.

Macro-Analysis: Interpreting a War on Drugs

Kings of Cocaine is a descriptive account of one of the most explosive social problems of our time. But another journalist, Tina Rosenberg, moves beyond the narrative of drug lords' exploits to offer a broader understanding of what the drug war is all about. She has reviewed this book in *The New Republic* in a lengthy essay, "The Kingdom of Cocaine" (1989). Her review picks up where Gugliotta and Leen leave off. The book's "real lesson, the idea most important for thinking about cocaine today," is the persistence of this illicit enterprise that employs approximately half a million Colombians. Rosenberg writes, "Colombian crackdowns come and go, huge seizures come and go, arrests come and go, martyrs come and go . . . and cocaine remains" (p. 26).

Recognizing the repetitive character of the violent episodes, Rosenberg probes deeper with a sociological question: How does one explain the persistent social and cultural patterns of cocaine production and distribution? She then examines the social structure of Colombia as a nation where lucrative employment and needed hard currency for the national treasury provide strong incentives to keep the illicit system going. The police, the press, and the politicians have all been attacked brutally by death squads. The instruments of corruption are as highly developed in Colombia as the tools of violence. Millions of dollars are paid to bribe police officers, prosecutors, judges, military officers, and politicians. The return favor is immunity from prosecution and even from investigation. In short, cocaine "has destroyed, through corruption or violence, the institutions that might once have been able to fight it" (p. 26).

Tina Rosenberg respects Gugliotta and Leen as reporters who have "written as complete a story of the Medellín traffickers as we are likely to get" (p. 26). But their story of assassinations, arrests, and drug seizures does not reflect an understanding of the societal arrangements that continue to support the big business of cocaine. This is not a fight with a band of criminals who are outlaws. It is a struggle "against a large part of Colombia society" (p. 32). From this more detached perspective, the heroic efforts of some courageous people offer little assurance of victory. The problem is too deeply embedded in the entire society.

We have observed more than once that print journalism is a highly diverse field. Journalists write their stories and analyze the meanings of events and trends at many levels of sophistication. They sometimes fight a deadline for a story that will be forgotten in two weeks. On other occasions, journalists take several months or years to investigate a social problem and write a series of articles or a book that has significant impact on public debate. Sometimes journalists focus on the small world of one person; at other times they examine complex government policies that have an impact on millions of citizens. Journalism is an open field that places few constraints on the breadth of topics to be investigated or the depth of analysis to be rendered. Readers must be aware of this diversity as they read critically the multitude of essays and books on every social problem that gains public attention.

THE SOCIOLOGICAL PERSPECTIVE

Sociology provides a special perspective on human relationships. Some aspects of human behavior become "figures" that stand out clearly, while others are given minimal attention and become "ground," the background against which the figures are highlighted. Specifically, the sociological perspective focuses on patterned relations among people engaged in human activity. The uniqueness of the individual fades into the background as attention focuses on the relationships among people. People are related through economic, political, and religious activities, through schools and families, and by social contacts. The sociologist is interested in all kinds of human interaction.

Sociologists study relational patterns between groups of people. They may, for instance, compare relations among American mothers, fathers, and children with patterns found in an Israeli kibbutz or among the Hopi of New Mexico. Sociologists are interested in family patterns across social class lines and how these patterns relate to economic and political behavior. Organizations such as schools, churches, corporations, and college sororities are studied, as well as behavior within a political party or by groups of political opponents. In short, sociologists search for patterns of interactions wherever they are found. The interaction may be a fluid process such as friendship, or it may be crystallized, as in the legal structure of a society.

But what happens to the individual in a study of patterned and recurrent relationships? Characteristics with general social meaning that locate the individual in his or her relation to others are brought into the foreground, while the features that make an individual unique fade into the background. A person's gender, for example, locates that individual in the social world. Males and females are expected to behave in certain ways regardless of their unique personalities. Mothers are expected to share certain behavioral patterns and fathers certain others. College professors, newspaper editors, plumbers, and morticians engage in their occupations in individual ways, yet each occupation has acquired a set of general expectations related to the behavior of its members.

Male, female, mother, father, college professor, and *plumber* are terms that denote specific relationships with other people. To the sociologist, these titles denote status, a social position in relation to others. Each status is associated with a cluster of roles, a set of expectations for the behavior of the person occupying a particular social position. The word *mother,* for example, represents both a status (a woman's position in relation to her children) and a role (a general set of expectations in regard to her behavior). Sociologists highlight the relational aspects of an individual, such as rural or urban residence, religious affiliation, club memberships, education, age, and race. These characteristics have social meanings and affect behavior, beliefs, and attitudes. Though sociologists do not ignore idiosyncratic features or deny their importance, the individual's unique attributes are not their focus.

The sociologist looks to social structure or organization to explain social issues (Merton 1968:104). The pattern studied can be characteristic of a group as a whole, such as the value system of a society, or arrangements of parts of a group, such as the percentage of people unemployed. Social patterns can be either ongoing interactions (such as husband-wife-child relationships in families of low socioeconomic standing) or formal patterns of human relations (such as the hierarchy of authority and decision making in a bureaucracy).

Sociologists do not believe that social issues originate in the innate qualities of individuals. Much crime is seen as part of the organization of urban industrial society and is explained as one of the consequences of patterned inequality. In the same way, poverty is seen as deriving from inequality of opportunity rather than from any innate defects of poor people. Many contemporary social problems, such as race relations, central-city slums, and environmental pollution, have their roots in changing social structures. Changes in sex roles are perceived as attempts to change a social structure that has restrained women for thousands of years. The reality of social issues is constructed with primary concern for the social structures in which human behavior occurs.

DUAL DIMENSIONS OF SOCIOLOGICAL KNOWLEDGE: CONCRETE/ABSTRACT AND MICRO/MACRO

We have argued that discourse in everyday affairs and in journalism has polar tendencies that range from concrete description to abstract generalizations and from small interpersonal situations to global issues. The same polar tendencies are found in sociology. Sociology is both theoretical (abstract) and empirical (concrete); it develops abstract explanatory generalizations based on factual evidence. Both theory and empirical evidence should be present in any sociological work, but the balance between them varies. Some sociologists, such as Talcott Parsons, Jurgen Habermas, and Jeffrey Alexander, stress theoretical analysis. Data that test the validity of their ideas have not been systematically collected. Parsons, for example, has constructed an elaborate theory of social classes but has not developed specific research on people who are part of the upper, middle, and lower classes. Other sociologists, such as Cecil North, Paul Hatt, Peter Rossi, Paul Siegel, and Robert Hodge, have collected detailed information on the prestige ratings of various occupations in the United States. Their works are recognized as sophisticated empirical research but remain essentially descriptive and devoid of central theoretical concerns.

Most sociologists avoid the extremes of "armchair theorizing" and "dustbowl empiricizing" by adopting theories of the middle range. "Middle-range theory involves abstractions, of course, but they are close enough to observed data to be incorporated in propositions that permit empirical testing," writes Robert K. Merton (1968:39). An excellent example of middle-range theory is the work of Richard Cloward and Lloyd Ohlin (1960), who formulated a theory about delinquent subcultures after reviewing numerous descriptive accounts of gangs. They contend that these subcultures represent an attempt by lower-class boys to cope with the inconsistency between the acceptance of conventional goals and the experience of limited opportunities for success. According to Cloward and Ohlin, the frustration created by this inconsistency leads to gang activities. Several sociologists have attempted to test the adequacy of this theory empirically. Merton's formulation of the middle range, however, remains an ideal not always attainable. Studies continue to be written with various degrees of abstraction three decades after Merton offered his classic reconciliatory formula. While some sociological works are located in the middle, many other studies continue to be primarily theoretical or empirical.

THEORY IN SOCIOLOGY

Sociology has produced many social theories, and sociologists are often in disagreement about the proper way to describe and classify them. We will not review the wide range of theories or the heated debates on their relative importance. Rather, we will concentrate our attention on three sociological perspectives that have evolved during the past hundred years or more: conflict theory, structural-functionalism, and symbolic interactionism. These three frameworks have been consciously nurtured by four or five generations of sociologists who have tenaciously pursued a particular vision of society and its problems. We accept Randall Collins's assertion that these three perspectives "have a claim to be considered the core traditions of sociology" (1985:ix).

Conflict theory. Observers of society have no difficulty recognizing the human propensity for conflict. The Old Testament is a gold mine of ancient stories about social disharmony: Cain and Abel's nasty family feud, the Philistines' big giant and the Israelites' little David, the mighty struggle with the Pharaoh of Egypt for the liberation of a chosen people. Conflict has existed for a long time, but the first sociological formulation of such antagonistic forces did not emerge until the middle of the nineteenth century. At that time a student of philosophy who had turned to journalism made a profound discovery: The economic wealth generated by industrial production creates a deep division between workers, who own only their own labor, and capitalists, who own the factories, the land, and the system for distributing goods. Karl Marx (1818–1883) developed a theory of society that emphasized the unavoidable conflict between the two great social classes of modern industrial societies: the workers and the capitalists. Society is best understood as an arena of conflict between these two major social forces.

Marx predicted that the workers of the world would eventually overthrow the capitalist system. This prediction has not been borne out in the most advanced industrial societies of Western Europe, North America, or Asia. Some predominantly agricultural societies, most notably Russia, had a communist revolution, but this case of radical change did not appear inevitable in all societies. Furthermore, the revolution has ended in massive hardship for most of the Russian people. Does this mean that Marx's conflict theory was wrong? The answer is yes and no. Marx's predictions have not come true, but his idea that society is filled with tension as social classes struggle for resources, prestige, and power provides one of the most important insights of modern social science. Marx's work stimulated many scholars to examine society in terms of fundamental conflicts among all kinds of groups. Marx emphasized economic issues and social classes, but other sociologists recognize a long list of potential sources of antagonism between a dominant group and a subordinate group. In the largest social system of all, the international community of nations, conflict is apparent in hot and cold wars between governments of sovereign countries. In the United States, such conflicting groups include blacks and whites, men and women, northern industrial states and western agrarian states, European immigrants who claimed the land and the Native Americans who were driven off of it, Protestants and Catholics, bankers and farmers, labor unions and corporations, homosexuals and religious fundamentalists,

suburbs and central cities, young workers who pay high rates of social security taxes and retirees who, having paid those taxes during their working years, now enjoy the benefits. This is not an exhaustive list of conflicting groups, but it illustrates the fundamental point of conflict theory: a modern society is made up of many competing interests that inevitably generate tensions and unresolved perceptions of deprivation or inequality among some members of society.

Structural-functionalism. A noted French sociologist, Emile Durkheim (1857–1917), developed a sophisticated theory of social structure and social function. Durkheim's importance rests on the fact that other sociologists (especially Robert Merton) were able to use his insights as a foundation for their own functionalist theories. Durkheim's theory begins with a major premise: virtually all aspects of human life are socially structured. That is, human beings live with an elaborate set of social constraints derived from culture (customs, laws, rituals) and social groups (tribes, families, communities, churches, governments). People do not stand outside these forces and decide whether or not to conform to the dictates of society. On the contrary, the full range of human experiences is embedded in the social structure, and people conform with little sense of choice. We are socially coerced, and we rarely realize it. Even well-publicized acts of nonconformity (wearing punk clothes or disrupting a lecture by someone whose views one finds offensive) are quickly assimilated into the social order as ritualized behavior that is socially structured.

The functionalists insist that people live, work, play, and dream inside social structures that have powerful positive and negative consequences. *Social structure* refers to the many social arrangements that hold us together in meaningful relationships (marriage, school, bowling teams), and *function* means those consequences that result from these arrangements (regulating sexual behavior, learning essential knowledge and skills, enjoying the conviviality of friendly competition). Social structures have social consequences. This truism seems all too obvious, but it is bafflingly difficult to understand. Not all consequences are apparent; many of the more important ones seem hidden. The police and courts, for example, have the obvious purpose of catching criminals and keeping order; yet functionalists insist that there is more to it than a good-guys-versus-bad-guys social arrangement. Society needs crime and criminals just as much as it needs policemen and judges. Lawbreakers are necessary for law abiders, because lawbreakers show conformists the moral boundaries of appropriate behavior. Paradoxically, the unanticipated consequence of crime is the maintenance of a morally healthy society.

Just as social structures can vary in size from small groups to worldwide social institutions, consequences can vary in magnitude from local and limited to global and massive. The widely developed system of pensions, for example, is intended to help each person have a good life after retirement. But this system, which is designed to serve the needs of private families, has also generated trillions of dollars that now flow through the stock markets of Tokyo, London, and New York in a world economy dominated by institutional brokers. The irony is that the workers of the world have now invested in capitalism in a very big way. The vast majority of workers do not want to see a revolution; their retirement benefits are at stake.

Symbolic interactionism. The third major perspective in contemporary sociology begins with the realization that human activity takes place in social situations. People are incessantly active, and their activities frequently take place in the presence of others. The interactionist perspective is interested in the patterns of behavior found in these micro settings. Social reality can be studied by careful observation of the thousands of social situations at the person-to-person level. Sociologists have studied hundreds of social settings in hundreds of thousands of social situations—hospitals, classrooms, factory floors, bars, restaurants, laundromats, rescue missions, street corners, and newsrooms—in the past seventy-five years. No situation is too small or too trivial. All the world's a stage, and sociologists are interested in every actor and every scene of the drama.

George Herbert Mead and his student Herbert Blumer played crucial roles in developing the interactionist perspective. They insisted that the interactional setting be studied as a rich environment of words, cues, gestures, nonverbal messages, and images. Interaction is never examined in purely physical or mechanical terms; rather, emphasis is on the meanings people assign to their own and each other's behavior. Human interaction involves the sharing of symbols. The girl may blush when the boy across the room winks. The mere twitch of the eyelid becomes significant when both parties give the gesture the same meaning. People live in a culture that overflows with significant symbols. These symbols have special meanings on the many occasions when people gather to pray, tell jokes, play cards, call their broker, cash a check, or vote for the next sheriff. Human interaction is necessarily symbolic; therefore, sociologists of this theoretical persuasion often define their perspective as symbolic interactionism.

It is not difficult to see how these three sociological traditions can be applied to the study of social problems. Each theory provides a distinctive framework for studying some important aspects of a social problem. Symbolic interaction is often identified with micro studies of society's outcasts. Much research has focused on deviant lifestyles and deviant occupational careers. Symbolic interactionists pursue a basic question: How do people construct social meaning and purposive action in the marginal zones of social life? How do these disreputable people (hustlers, prostitutes, thieves, winos, drug addicts, gang members) interact with official and unofficial agents of social control (policemen, psychiatrists, social workers, street preachers)? People who live on the edge of middle-class propriety are often considered to be in need of special help. They constitute a social problem. Symbolic interactionists withhold moral condemnation and sympathetically probe the network of relationships and situations that sustain these marginal people's faith so that their precarious lives have purpose and meaning.

Conflict theory is most often identified with macro sociology. The study of social problems from this perspective involves thorough examination of those groups that systematically gain advantages over other groups. Social problems are understood as fully entrenched structural arrangements that perpetuate distinct disadvantages for such groups as blacks, women, and the long-term unemployed. In the field of race relations, for example, much has been written on the difficult problems facing blacks in inner cities where unemployment rates are extremely high. A Marxian conflict theorist sees this problem as a case of advanced capitalism and a split labor market. For various historical reasons, blacks enjoyed high levels of employment in the earlier decades of the twentieth century, but in recent decades they have found it more difficult to compete for jobs as capitalists have increasingly automated or moved factories to foreign sites where there is abundant cheap labor and little resistance from labor unions (Bonacich 1976). A major social problem in America is the notable disparity in power and resources between multinational corporations and unemployed residents of the central cities.

Structural functionalism is often viewed as a macro perspective that examines how one part of society affects another. But functional theory has also been applied to many micro-level issues. In the area of crime, for example, Travis Hirschi (1983) argues that, at the micro level, the structure of families in which both biological parents are present functions more successfully to control the behavior of children. At the macro level, Robert Nisbet observed in 1983 that about 25,000 murders occurred each year in the United States, and the situation has worsened since then. Nisbet considers our high level of violence to be directly related to disintegrating institutions. A societal-level change has occurred in the United States. Disintegration of the community that morally condemns the loss of life has led to a rampant increase in murders. Clearly, this structural change and its undesirable consequences can be defined as a social problem.

SOCIOLOGICAL METHODS

Sociologists do not restrict their work to the development and refinement of theories; they have also devoted much attention to the concrete aspects of social problems. They have pursued numerous strategies that can lead to better descriptive accounts of social conditions. These strategies are designated as sociological methods.

Once sociologists have selected a research area (such as crime) and limited their topic to manageable proportions (such as the study of delinquent gangs, white-collar crime, or prison conditions), they must choose their methods of observation. Because the most appropriate method varies with the research topic, sociologists must weigh the advantages and disadvantages of each approach for their particular research. Three common methods are survey research, participant observation, and analysis of census data and other government statistics.

Survey research. Sociologists who engage in survey research—the most common research method in sociology—use either mailed questionnaires or carefully structured interviews. This technique involves at least seven distinct stages. The researcher must:

1. Articulate the problem in order to identify key variables.
2. Construct a questionnaire or interview schedule that incorporates the research concepts.
3. Determine the population sample.
4. Mail the questionnaires or conduct the interviews.
5. Code the questionnaires or interview schedules.
6. Tabulate the results on a computer.
7. Interpret the computed results and write a final report.

Many refinements and subtle skills are associated with each of the seven stages. For example, sociologists strive to construct questions that minimize the possibility of a bias effect on respondents; they avoid questions that incorporate opinions. Such phrases as "the right-wing tendencies of the Republican party" and "the socialistic tendencies of the Democratic party" are avoided in favor of more neutral terms.

Survey analysts have explored numerous social problems, and some of their studies are recognized as classics of empirical scholarship: *The People's Choice* (Lazarsfeld et al. 1948), *The American Soldier* (Stouffer et al. 1949), *Christian Beliefs and Anti-Semitism* (Glock & Stark 1966), *Communism, Conformity, and Civil Liberties* (Stouffer 1955), *Protest and Prejudice* (Marx 1969), *Social Class and Mental Illness* (Hollingshead & Redlich 1958), *Equality of Educational Opportunity* (Coleman et al. 1966), and *To Dwell among Friends* (Fischer 1982). Sociologists claim to know much about the attitudes, beliefs, and opinions of Americans, and a great deal of this knowledge rests on the findings of research surveys.

Participant observation. Participant observation provides the sociologist with the opportunity to observe a group situation and participate in it simultaneously. The sociologist who uses this research technique spends time with members of the group being studied and observes daily routines and unusual events as a participant in the action and at the same time as someone removed from it. Although it is a difficult research role to master and the number of capable field investigators is relatively small, sociologists have observed many diverse groups and social situations. Their resulting books and articles provide an awareness of such intimate social worlds as mental hospitals (Goffman 1961), inner-city slums (Suttles 1968; Liebow 1967), working-class taverns (Le Masters 1975), universities (Becker et al. 1969), assembly lines (Roy 1959), small towns (Vidich & Bensman 1960), urban ethnic communities (Gans 1962), prisons (Jacobs 1978), and television news bureaus (Altheide 1974).

Census data and other vital statistics. Since 1790 the United States government has surveyed the total population once each decade. In addition, the Bureau of the Census and other government agencies such as the Department of Labor have conducted hundreds of surveys during the past forty years. The data generated by these surveys are compiled in numerous documents. The highlights of this descriptive information are found in such publications as almanacs and the *U.S. Fact Book*, and the raw data collected by the Bureau of the Census are available to research scholars on computer tapes. Sociologists use this survey material to analyze such large-scale issues as human migration in metropolitan areas, the growing proportion of women in the labor force, and the social and economic advancement of blacks. The data collected by the government help sociologists understand such broad societal changes as the dispersal of the black population, once concentrated in the rural South, to cities throughout the United States. City planners, educators, and civic leaders often call on sociologists to interpret the changing social conditions revealed by census data.

Other sources of sociological data. The empirical methods used by sociologists are not limited to survey research, participant observation, and analysis of census data. Many relevant data are found in archives; sociologists sometimes use archives to test a theory against events in a distant historical period. Kai Erikson (1966), for example, studied the witch trials in Massachusetts in order to test Emile Durkheim's theory of deviance. Edwin Sutherland (1983) studied corporation reports and court records in his classic study *White Collar Crime*. Sutherland (1937) also pioneered in the study of a criminal subculture when he hired an anonymous criminal to write an autobiography, *The Professional Thief*. Investigations are occasionally conducted in quasi-experimental fashion. Richward Schwartz and Jerome Skolnick (1964) created a fictional employment agency with four hypothetical clients seeking jobs. They found that companies are reluctant to hire anyone who has been charged with a crime, even when the person has been acquitted. Our legal system asserts that every defendant is innocent until proven guilty, but this study shows that in the real world, the innocent are often treated as if they were guilty.

FOUR TYPES OF SOCIAL KNOWLEDGE IN SOCIOLOGY

Though no clear division exists between theoretical analysis and empirical analysis, each tends to construct a somewhat different reality. Sociologists' skills are analogous to those of modern camera crews. They zoom in on small details in face-to-face encounters and with equal mastery adjust their lenses to capture the broad panoramas of large groups. Social interactions of interest to sociologists range from those between two people to those between whole societies. At the micro end of this range are studies of interactions between friends, among family members, and among cliques in organizations. A sociologist may study the informal relations between prisoners and their guards or among members of an inner-city gang. At the micro end are studies of societies or major social structures within them, such as the stratification system of social classes or political institutions. Other macro studies may focus on the assimilation of ethnic groups into the mainstream of American society or the social transformation of medicine into a major corporate industry regulated and supported by various government agencies.

The range in size of social units studied by sociologists is extensive; no precise line divides micro and macro studies. Sociological research is also concerned with social organizations of intermediate size. Sociologists study communities ranging from small villages to large cities, churches with memberships numbering from fewer than 100 to more than 3,000, and bureaucracies of any size. Mid-sized organizations studied by sociologists include schools, school districts, universities, prisons, prison systems, institutions of higher education, hospitals, libraries, professions, insane asylums, political parties, volunteer groups, and factories. Size is sometimes the key variable used to explain dissimilar internal arrangements of organizations (Kasarda 1974). Sociologists also study small groups that exist within larger organizations, such as factories (Roy 1959), bureaucracies (Blau 1955), and armies (Shils & Janowitz 1948). While the distinction between microanalysis and macroanalysis helps us recognize extremes in sociological studies, size is more than a matter of small versus large.

The distinction between micro and macro studies can be related to the distinction between abstract and concrete. Sociological studies demonstrate various combinations of abstraction and scale. Sociologists conduct studies that are macro-theoretical (Peter Evans's [1988] work on the world economy), micro-theoretical (Albert Cohen's [1955] theory of delinquent boys), macro-empirical (Reynolds Farley's [1984] study of the social and economic gains of blacks), and micro-empirical (Frederick Thrasher's classic study of 1,313 Chicago gangs). Micro/macro and concrete/abstract are dimensions of the multiple realities within sociology. They are extreme tendencies rather than definitive categories that

encompass all sociological studies. Figure 2.4 outlines some of the general features of academic sociology.

Another dimension of sociological studies, the number of units in the sample, contributes to their diversity. A sociologist may study one marriage, ten marriages, five thousand marriages, or all the marriages in the United States. The results often depend on the number studied. Likewise, a sociologist may study class structure in the United States, in all industrialized nations, or in all known societies for which scholars have data. The number of units analyzed can be few or many whether the study is micro or macro, theoretical or empirical.

An analysis of a single unit is known as a case study. Alvin Gouldner's (1954) study of a gypsum plant and Elliot Liebow's (1969) focus on one street corner are both case studies. Among the more famous case studies in American sociology are investigations of a single community: *Middletown* (Lynd & Lynd 1929), *The Social Life of a Modern Community* (Warner & Lunt 1941), *Elmtown's Youth* (Hollingshead 1975), *Who Governs?* (New Haven) (Dahl 1961), and *Community Power Structure* (Atlanta) (Hunter 1953). Case studies enrich our understanding of various aspects of social life but raise doubts about whether their findings can be generalized. A case study's scope is narrow; demographers (population analysts) take a broad view, often using census data to enumerate each case of a particular attribute in the entire population. Demographers draw on millions of individual cases to discuss such social issues as migration from rural to urban areas and the growing number of women in the labor market.

The size of the sample is the sum of the units studied. Unit size and sample size are independent of each other. An international survey concerning premarital sexual affairs may include several thousand cases, but the unit of analysis—paired relationships—is

Scope of Awareness

	Micro: Small-scale social structures and social settings	Macro: Large-scale social structures and social settings
Concrete: (empirical emphasis) Descriptive studies that focus on specific time periods, places, and groups. While unique features of groups are not emphasized, they are acknowledged as important	*Micro-concrete* Empirical accounts of the interpersonal relationships of home, neighborhood, work, school, church, prison	*Macro-concrete* Empirical accounts of large-scale social structures such as political, economic, and military institutions; attention often given to significant changes and social trends
Abstract: (theoretical emphasis) Theoretical statements that emphasize universal claims; explanations of social processes and social structures extending to all times, all places, and all groups	*Micro-abstract* Theoretical statements of interpersonal relationships and personal adjustments such as marriage, sex roles, age cycle, socialization	*Macro-abstract* Theroetical statements about societal structures such as contending interest groups, power conflicts, social classes, ideological systems

Degree of Generality (left axis label)

FIGURE 2.4
Ways of Knowing: Sociology

exceedingly small. Max Weber's (1963) monumental case studies of world religions and economic structure are macroscopic in scale (unit size) but narrow in scope (sample size) because the number of major religions is small.

Daniel Yankelovich and Kenneth Keniston share an interest in the changing attitudes and beliefs of young people. Although these issues are predominantly micro in scale, Yankelovich (1974) interviewed thousands of young people, and Keniston (1968) studied twelve young people in depth. In the 1970s, several sociologists became interested in communes. Benjamin Zablocki (1971) conducted a case study of a single commune, the Brüderhof; Rosabeth Moss Kanter (1972) studied several dozen contemporary communes as well as thirty communes established in the United States between 1780 and 1860. The scale of analysis for both studies is micro, but the scope of one study is narrow and that of the other broad.

THE SOCIAL PROBLEM AS MICROCOSM IN THE MACROCOSM

Up to this point, we have presented the micro-macro distinction as polar opposites, a friendly gathering at the local bar versus an august assemblage of world leaders. Thoughtful people who analyze social problems go beyond this simple distinction to note the importance of the interrelationship of micro and macro systems. It is not merely a matter of small versus big; we need to understand the larger societal network of institutional arrangements in which the small group is embedded.

The words that head this section paraphrase a subhead in Arthur Vidich and Joseph Bensman's classic *Small Town in Mass Society*: "Springdale as a Microcosm in the Macrocosm" (1960:321). Many local residents of Springdale believed that their rural community was a self-contained universe of friendly people who enjoyed living some distance from any large city. But the image of a self-sufficient community is illusory. Vidich and Bensmen "found external sources and origins for everything that the community cherished as being most genuinely representative of its own spirit" (p. 318). Springdale exists in a mass society in which crucial aspects of community life (the curriculum of the schools, the merchandise in stores, health regulations in the restaurant, evening entertainment on radio and television) are all determined by powerful decision makers in large corporations and government bureaucracies. Springdale cannot be understood as an isolated small town. Rather, the small world of neighbors, shopkeepers, and farmers must be seen in terms of its many connections to the external forces of a complex mass society.

Vidich and Bensman's perspective on micro-macro relationships has been developed by a group of sociologists who investigated a plant closing in a small town in Indiana. Monticello is a community of 5,000 people with an RCA plant that once employed up to 1,200 workers. In 1982 the plant closed, and four sociologists later examined the international context of the event as well as its local costs (Perrucci et al. 1988). These sociologists were interested in the circumstances that led to such a drastic decision as well as the social and psychological consequences for the displaced workers and other people in Monticello. They devote a chapter to the international, national, and regional contexts of economic changes and political responses. The town of Monticello, the state of Indiana, the Midwest region, and the United States are all part of a global political economy in which markets and capital are constantly shifting. Because capitalism is increasingly international in scope and international competition is increasingly severe, workers in a local factory (however loyal and skilled they may be) cannot feel immune to the broader forces of economic change.

Many social problems can be understood in terms of the microcosm of private troubles and the macrocosm of public policy. Many ordinary people suffer all kinds of hardship. Sociologists can look at the hardships one at a time, as personal burdens that people must bear; but it is often more useful to look at the many levels of power that shape public debate on appropriate strategies to ameliorate the private troubles. Among the social scientists who have attempted to see both the small worlds of suffering and the larger worlds of political and economic action (or inaction) is Daniel Patrick Moynihan (1987), who has written extensively on the fate of American families and the responsibility of the federal government. Ronald Bayer's *Private Acts, Social Consequences: AIDS and the Politics of Public Health* (1989) examines a whole range of social institutions that have responded with varying degrees of effectiveness to the AIDS epidemic. William Julius Wilson (1987) has spent several years investigating the rapid deterioration of inner-city communities as broad economic changes have led to the massive exodus of manufacturing industries. In each of these cases, social problems are investigated at two levels simultaneously: the local interpersonal setting of hardship and the societal context of public policy.

CONCLUSION

Ordinary people engaged in everyday discourse, journalists, and academic social scientists all tend to look at social problems as either private troubles or public issues. Further, discourse in all three areas tends to be either concretely descriptive or somewhat abstract, with claims of broader application to many similar circumstances. These polar tendencies allow students of social problems to see that there are four pure types of social knowledge: micro-concrete, micro-abstract, macro-concrete, and macro-abstract. All of us who aim to be well informed about social problems must recognize these tendencies. It can be the first crucial step toward a critical awareness of how a writer has constructed a statement about a social problem.

The task of sorting out different kinds of social knowledge as either micro or macro is the beginning of a series of mental initiatives. The next big challenge is to see crucial connections and context as micro worlds of private troubles are incorporated in macro settings of public policy debates. It is one thing to empathize with American soldiers who cross the world to challenge a dictator; it is quite another thing to understand the international relationships that place American soldiers in jeopardy more often than those of any other nation. Are other countries less worried about evil? Does the nature of "international order" require some big nations to be more assertive? Will historians of the next century look back on the latter half of the twentieth century as the era of pax Americana? Is this the great moment in American history—a period when the nation promotes world order while millions of its people suffer the hardships of poverty? Is there any way to understand a connection between the global expansion of American foreign policy and the steady decline of its local communities? There are micro issues and macro issues. And there is the constant challenge to connect the two.

References

Altheide, David. 1974. *Creating reality.* Beverly Hills, Calif.: Sage.

Anson, Robert Sam. 1987. *Best intentions: The education and killing of Edmund Perry.* New York: Vintage.

Bayer, Ronald. 1989. *Private acts, social consequences: AIDS and the politics of public health.* New York: Free Press.

Becker, Howard S., et al. 1969. *Making the grade.* New York: Wiley.

Blau, Peter. 1955. *Dynamics of bureaucracy.* Chicago: University of Chicago Press.

Bonacich, Edna. 1976. Advanced capitalism and black/white relations in the United States: A split labor market interpretation. *American Sociological Review* 41:34–51.

Cohen, Albert. 1955. *Delinquent boys.* New York: Free Press.

Coleman, James S., et al. 1966. *Equality of educational opportunity.* Washington, D.C.: U.S. Government Printing Office.

Collins, Randall. 1985. *Three sociological traditions.* New York: Oxford University Press.

Cuomo, Mario M. 1983. *1933/1983—Never again: A report to the National Governors' Association Task Force on the Homeless.* Portland, Me.

Dahl, Robert. 1961. *Who governs?* New Haven, Conn.: Yale University Press.

Erikson, Kai T. 1966. *Wayward puritans.* New York: Wiley.

Evans, Peter. 1988. Development and the world economy. In Neil Smelser, ed., *Handbook of sociology,* Beverly Hills, Calif.: Sage.

Farley, Reynolds. 1984. *Blacks and whites: Narrowing the gap?* Cambridge, Mass.: Harvard University Press.

Fischer, Claude, 1982. *To dwell among friends.* Chicago: University of Chicago Press.

Gans, Herbert. 1962. *The urban villagers.* New York: Free Press.

Glock, Charles Y., and Rodney Stark. 1966. *Christian beliefs and anti-Semitism.* New York: Harper & Row.

Goffman, Erving. 1961. *Asylums.* Garden City, N.Y.: Doubleday.

Goshko, John. 1976. FBI begins Hays enquiry. *Washington Post,* May 25, p. 1.

Gouldner, Alvin. 1954. *Industrial bureaucracy.* Glencoe, Ill.: Free Press.

Grier, William H., and Price M. Cobbs. 1968. *Black rage.* New York: Basic Books.

Gugliotta, Guy, and Jeff Leen. 1989. *Kings of cocaine.* New York: Simon and Schuster.

Hirschi, Travis. 1983. Families and crime. *The Wilson Quarterly* 7:132–39.

Hollingshead, August. 1975. *Elmtown's youth.* New York: Wiley.

Hollingshead, August, and F. Redlich. 1958. *Social class and mental illness.* New York: Wiley.

Hunter, Floyd. 1953. *Community power structure.* Chapel Hill, N.C.: University of North Carolina Press.

Jacobs, James. 1978. *Statesville.* Chicago: University of Chicago Press.

Kanter, Rosabeth Moss. 1972. *Commitment and community.* Cambridge, Mass.: Harvard University Press.

Kasarda, John. 1974. The structural implications of social system size: A three-level analysis. *American Sociological Review* 39:19–28.

Keniston, Kenneth. 1968. *Young radicals.* New York: Harcourt, Brace & World.

Lazarsfeld, Paul F., B. Bereleson, and H. Goudet. 1948. *The people's choice.* New York: Columbia University Press.

Le Masters, E. E. 1975. *Blue collar aristocrats.* Madison: University of Wisconsin Press.

Liebow, Elliot. 1967. *Talley's corner.* Boston: Little, Brown.

Lynd, Robert, and Helen Lynd. 1929. *Middletown.* New York: Harcourt, Brace & World.

Marx, Gary. 1969. *Protest and prejudice.* New York: Harper & Row.

Mathews, Jay. 1985. Down and out by choice. *Washington Post,* August 25, pp. A1, A22.

Merton, Robert K. 1968. *Social theory and social structure.* 3d ed. New York: Free Press.

Moynihan, Daniel Patrick. 1987. *Family and nation.* New York: Harcourt Brace Jovanovich.

Nisbet, Robert. 1983. Crime and punishment. *Across the Board* 20:4–8.

Perrucci, Carolyn, Robert Perrucci, Dena Targ, and Harry Targ. 1988. *Plant closing: International context and social costs.* New York: Aldine–De Gruyter.

Poussaint, Alvin F. 1970. A Negro psychiatrist explains the Negro psyche. In Robert V. Guthrie, ed., *Being black: Pychological–sociological dilemmas*, pp. 15–25. San Francisco: Canfield.

Rosenberg, Tina. 1989. The kingdom of cocaine. *New Republic* 26–34.

Roy, Donald. 1959. "Banana time" job satisfaction and informal interaction. *Human Organization* 18:158–68.

Rubington, Earl, and Martin S. Weinberg, eds. 1981a. *The study of social problems: Five perspectives.* New York: Oxford University Press.

Rubington, Earl, Martin S. Weinberg, and Sue Keifer Hammersmith, eds. 1981b. *The solution of social problems: Five perspectives.* New York: Oxford University Press.

Schwartz, Richard, and Jerome Skolnick. 1964. Two studies of legal stigma. In Howard S. Becker, ed., *The other side.* New York: Free Press.

Shils, Edward, and Morris Janowitz. 1948. Cohesion and disintegration in the Wehrmacht in World War II. *Public Opinion Quarterly* 12:280–94.

Stouffer, Samuel. 1955. *Communism, conformity, and civil liberties.* New York: Wiley.

Stouffer, Samuel, et al. 1949. *The American soldier.* Princeton, N.J.: Princeton University Press.

Sutherland, Edwin. 1937. *The professional thief.* Chicago: University of Chicago Press.

Sutherland, Edwin. 1983. *White collar crime.* New Haven, Conn.: Yale University Press.

Suttles, Gerald. 1968. *The social order of the slum.* Chicago: University of Chicago Press.

Teague, Bob. 1968. *Letters to a black boy.* New York: Walker.

Thrasher, Frederick. 1927. *The gang: A study of 1,313 gangs in Chicago.* Chicago: University of Chicago Press.

Vidich, Arthur, and Joseph Bensman. 1960. *Small town in mass society.* Garden City, N.Y.: Doubleday.

Warner, W. Lloyd, and Paul Lunt. 1941. *The social life of a modern community.* New Haven, Conn.: Yale University Press.

Weber, Max. 1963. *The sociology of religion.* Boston: Beacon.

Wilson, William Julius. 1987. *The truly disadvantaged: The inner city, the underclass, and public policy.* Chicago: University of Chicago Press.

Wiseman, Jacqueline. 1979. *Stations of the lost.* Chicago: University of Chicago Press.

Woodward, Bob, and Carl Bernstein. 1974. *All the president's men.* New York: Simon & Schuster.

Yankelovich, Daniel. 1974. *The new morality.* New York: McGraw-Hill.

Zablocki, Benjamin. 1971. *The joyful community.* Baltimore: Penguin.

CHAPTER 3

GUIDELINES FOR CRITICAL REASONING

INTRODUCTION

Nothing is mysterious or snobbish about critical reasoning. People practice it when they read movie reviews, discuss the betting odds on NFL favorites, or select a used car. But not all moviegoers, NFL gamblers, or car drivers are critical thinkers. Critical reasoning is a special way of looking at the world. It begins with a willingness to be attentive to information and opinion and requires a readiness to raise questions and probe beyond the appearance of things. To be critical demands both a discerning attitude and sound thinking skills. In the modern world, which offers so many interests, people choose to be critical in some areas and totally naive in others. The same person who can make discriminating judgments about a new pair of running shoes may be gleefully ignorant about an economic debate between two presidential candidates. People make choices in deciding to apply critical reasoning to those things that matter to them. We hope that students will decide to be critical thinkers about social problems, for we are convinced that social issues are so important to everyone that they demand thoughtful consideration.

No mechanical formula will turn readers into critical thinkers. Although we want to help students to think more logically, we do not present our case with syllogisms or truth tables. Instruction in critical reasoning is found in books on informal logic; we recommend these works as valuable guides to improved thinking.[1] Our approach, though based on ideas found in these books, is more simple and straightforward. We have selected a few basic topics that we believe are the first steps toward a better understanding of statements written about social problems. These topics of criticism are designed to help you gain an awareness of issues that you might otherwise overlook. Once you are aware of these topics, your native intelligence and good sense should enable you to sort out the strengths and weaknesses of a particular essay.

We have suggested that critical reasoning need not be a highly technical exercise with elaborate rules of formal argument. We also emphasize at the outset that the term *critical* does not necessarily imply a negative point of view. We all know people who take pleasure in putting down others' ideas. For our purposes, such faultfinding is unreasonable. *Webster's New Dictionary of Synonyms* describes the ideal thinking process that we hold up as our standard: "an effort to see a thing clearly, truly, and impartially so that not only the good in it may be distinguished from the bad and the perfect from the imperfect, but also that it as a whole may be fairly judged or valued" (1984:199). One can be critical yet appreciative. Critical reasoning sometimes leads to a highly favorable assessment of a statement. The issue is not one of condemning or praising but of evaluating fairly. We appeal to rational reflection, not mindless acrimony.

---

[1] For more information on informal logic and critical reasoning, see Scriven 1976; Barry 1983; Toulmin et al. 1979.

A DEFINITION OF CRITICAL REASONING

We now offer a more specific definition of critical reasoning: *Critical reasoning is the assessment of the logical and empirical adequacy of a nonfictional statement.* A critical thinker determines the adequacy of either someone else's or his or her own statements. This definition is the cornerstone of this book; all subsequent readings are examined in light of their logical and empirical adequacy.

Given the importance assigned to the definition of critical reasoning, it deserves further explanation. The definition refers to *nonfictional statements* because the rules of reasoning are different in the world of fiction. For example, novelists can make up evidence to suit their artistic purposes; they can invent characters, towns, or whole societies (past, present, or future). Journalists and sociologists do not enjoy such poetic freedom. The people and places in their stories must correspond to the real world. This important distinction does not make fictional writing less valuable for students of social problems. On the contrary, novels are important sources of knowledge about the character and nature of human societies and social life. No sociologist or journalist had greater insight into or perception of race relations in twentieth-century America than such black novelists as James Johnson, Richard Wright, Ralph Ellison, and James Baldwin. Fictional literature contains genuine value for students of social problems; however, the criteria for assessing the works of novelists are somewhat different from those applied to writings by journalists and sociologists.

A statement is considered *adequate* if it is sufficient for the purpose at hand. The first task of criticism is to determine the nature of a piece and the intent of its author. No absolute measuring scale determines adequacy or inadequacy. Rather, one must explore the extent of adequacy given the intentions of the author and the expectations of the author's audience. A statement can be satisfactory for one audience (ordinary citizens who read daily newspapers) and unsatisfactory for another (academic social scientists who read professional journals). Since notions of adequacy are related to authors' intentions and audiences, it is inappropriate to make comparative judgments between articles written by journalists and those written by sociologists. The critical study of journalism and sociology is not carried out with the intent of declaring one superior or inferior to the other.

Empirical adequacy refers to the extent to which a statement is supported by factual information. Are the writer's claims based on observations that can be verified by others? Or is the writer making claims that neither he nor anyone else could ever substantiate? Both journalists and sociologists insist on the importance of reliable facts. Both groups also hold to professional standards of objectivity in reporting the facts. Readers of journalism and sociology likewise expect objective and accurate information in the pieces they read. Given these common professional standards and audience expectations, it is only reasonable to examine the empirical adequacy of essays on social problems.

Whether the medium is *Reader's Digest, Mother Jones,* or the *Annals of the Political and Social Sciences,* the sequence in which most authors present their ideas varies remarkably little. An author begins by calling attention to a problem and then presents supporting evidence about the seriousness of the problem and some of its causes. The article ends with recommendations for a solution. Logicians divide this general pattern of reasoning into two broad categories: premises (ideas in the first part of the essay) and conclusions (ideas that pertain to solutions). In both journalism and social science, authors are expected to state their case in a logically consistent fashion. Readers who use critical reasoning ask a fundamental question: Do the conclusions follow logically from the premises? Careful consideration of this question determines the extent of *logical adequacy.*

We have presented a definition of critical reasoning for this book. We now elaborate on our definition by discussing five topics of criticism pertinent to any statement about a social problem. As critical thinkers, readers need to determine the adequacy of:

1. Definition of the problem.
2. Supporting evidence.
3. Statements about cause-effect relationships.
4. Value assertions or assumptions.
5. Logical consistency in the line of reasoning about solutions.

These are challenging topics; mastery cannot be conferred by one book or one social problems course. We provide only an elementary introduction to these topics of reasoning, but we offer a beginning. Persons who incorporate these concerns into their reading habits will be wiser for the effort.

DETERMINING THE ADEQUACY OF STATEMENTS THAT DEFINE THE PROBLEM

Identifying the Thesis

We have suggested that many essays on social problems written by both journalists and social scientists follow a conventional sequence: They open with a statement of the problem, provide supporting arguments, and conclude with recommendations for solution. If this format is used, the first task of the critical reader is to study carefully the opening paragraphs and inquire about the author's thesis. Is it clearly stated? Can the reader find the main point that gives the entire essay its central focus? If the point of departure is not clear, there is little likelihood that either the journey or the final destination will make much sense.

Identifying the writer's basic thesis is not always easy. The author may not adopt the conventional format of an opening proposition followed by other premises and a conclusion. The thesis may in fact be scattered throughout the essay and never stated explicitly. If the writer is vague about the thesis, the reader must exert additional mental energy in order to make the writer's implicit position explicit. The writer has created extra work for the reader; the reader may return the favor by judging the essay to be less than adequate in its articulation of the problem.

Clarifying the Meanings of Key Terms

Writers develop their line of reasoning through the use of key terms. It is important for readers to identify these terms and examine the way they are being defined. Writers define terms in various ways. Some are logically sound and others are sloppy or fallacious. For example, a writer will sometimes give a term more than one meaning without warning the reader, perhaps unconsciously. Shifting the meaning of a key word undermines any possibility of the reader's understanding just what the problem is. The tendency for words to be shifty is especially perplexing in the field of social problems, because key words are often loaded with multiple meanings created by conflicting groups in society. Is *abortion* "murder," a "victimless crime," or "the natural right of a woman to her own body"? Is *homosexuality* a "sin," "a psychiatric illness," "deviant behavior," or "an alternative lifestyle"? *Bureaucracy* is one of those spongy words that refers to just about every malady of the organizational world one can imagine—worker laziness and incompetence, inefficient management, rigid and tall ladders of power, indifferent treatment of the public, excessive regulation through unnecessary paperwork, indulgent privileges of government elites, inflexible adherence to petty rules, government waste. It seems as if everyone at one time or another has had a grievance against government officials. Some people vent their hostility when they define *bureaucracy*.

Readers must determine how an author has arrived at a definition. Writers use three common practices:

1. Common usage as found in a standard dictionary.
2. Expert usage derived from a specialist's dictionary.
3. Stipulated usage created for the purposes of the essay at hand.

All three approaches to definition are acceptable. Readers must not go merrily along with whatever the author states, however; they need to examine the author's strategy of usage and determine its acceptability. For example, in this chapter we have stipulated a definition of critical reasoning that cannot be found in any standard dictionary or technical reference book. Elements of the definition correspond closely to standard usage, and many ideas are adapted from a classic essay by an expert in critical thinking (Ennis 1962). Our definition is not necessarily better or worse than others found in *Webster's* or in logic textbooks; it is merely the one we have stipulated for the purposes of this book.

The first step in clarifying definitions is to consult a standard dictionary. If the author's use of key terms does not match that of the dictionary, then careful thought must be given to understanding the author's point of view. Is she creating her own stipulated terms? Are these stipulated terms broadly consistent with standard usage? Is she taking her key words from a specialized vocabulary? How do specialized terms compare with standard terms? The answers to these questions must all lead to one crucial point: The reader must understand what key words mean. Readers can consider definitions of terms adequate if they convey the distinctive characteristics of the object or thing being defined and are consistent with other aspects of the essay.

DETERMINING THE ADEQUACY OF STATEMENTS ABOUT EVIDENCE

Identifying the Evidence

A heated debate about a social problem rarely proceeds very far before someone demands evidence to support a crucial claim. The same need for evidence exists for critical readers. They want to know what kind of evidence the writer has to support his or her thesis. Two types of evidence are found in social-problem essays: (1) primary data collected by the author and (2) secondary data borrowed from another source. Determining which kind of data the author is using is an important preliminary step to any appraisal of evidence.

Primary sources.   If the writer reports that he has collected his own evidence, the reader must examine the methods and findings used. In Chapter 2 we mentioned various observational strategies found in journalism and sociology, including field observations, sample surveys, intensive interviews, and archival investigations. Each strategy describes the social world in its own way. No method is totally accurate, but we do not demand perfection. The question we ask is a practical one: To what extent is the evidence sufficient for the case being made? In answering this question, we must first ascertain the methods of data collection and the nature of the findings. If an observer who does not know the Chinese language spends three weeks in the Republic of China on a government-sponsored tour, the likelihood of obtaining meaningful empirical evidence is limited. Yet in the 1970s, when China admitted Western reporters and social scientists, many accounts of Chinese society were based on just this type of limited observation. Readers would justifiably have more confidence in evidence gathered by an investigator who is fluent in the language, free to travel without restriction, and able to spend several months or years in the country. Such conditions are rarely possible in China.

Secondary sources.   Many writers describe social problems without firsthand knowledge of the social conditions that are so disturbing to them, relying instead on data collected by others. Perhaps the most common source of data for journalists and sociologists is the government. Data about every conceivable social problem—crime, divorce, suicide, unemployment, pollution, auto accidents—are compiled by local, state, and federal agencies. Other secondary sources of information include news accounts by the daily press; public opinions collected by pollsters (for example, Gallup); and special studies commissioned or conducted by foundations (such as the Carnegie Foundation), private agencies (such as the Educational Testing Service), and pressure groups (such as Amnesty International). The list of sources is almost endless. Since journalists and sociologists frequently rely on secondhand accounts of the social world, careful consideration must be given to the sources of information writers use to describe social problems.

No hard and fast rules of evidence can be used to determine the adequacy of secondary sources, but some important issues must be kept firmly in mind. First, readers should look for a specific reference to the original source. Citations allow the reader to make an independent inquiry of the same evidence or an investigation into similar sources that might corroborate the writer's evidence. The more vague an author is about sources, the lower the credibility of the evidence. Once the reader has identified the sources of evidence, questions of adequacy must be examined. Robert and Dale Newman suggest fourteen "principles of use to the consumers of evidence." Here are six guidelines they recommend (Newman & Newman 1969:87):

1. *Accessibility.* The more accessible the situation being reported on, to both the reporters and their audience, the more credible the report.

2. *Authenticity.* The greater the presumption of authenticity, the higher the credibility of a document.

3. *Internal consistency.* The higher the internal consistency of work, the more credible the author's testimony.
4. *Carefulness of generalization.* The more careful the generalizations of a writer, the higher the credibility of his testimony.
5. *Expertise.* The greater the relevant expertise of an author, the higher his credibility.
6. *Objectivity.* The greater the objectivity of an author, the more credible his testimony.

In each instance, the principle can be turned into a question; for example, How objective is the author? The answer to such questions is frequently not an either/or declaration but rather a matter of determining the extent of credibility. A better question might be: To what extent is the author objective?

Hasty and Sweeping Generalizations

The Newmans' principle of careful generalizations is especially important in the study of social problems, because writers sometimes make either hasty or sweeping generalizations. There are two kinds of hasty generalizations. The first kind is a general conclusion drawn from too few specific cases; for example, a report on crime may cite a few dramatic instances and then draw the inference that a "crime wave" is under way. A famous reporter, Lincoln Steffens (1931), described just such an incident during his newspaper career in New York City. The second kind of hasty generalization is a conclusion drawn from atypical instances. In the 1960s, student unrest on a limited number of campuses by a small group of atypical students was exaggerated by many commentators into reports of a whole generation of young people in rebellion. A few extreme examples of violent confrontation came to typify many (if not all) college campuses, yet a careful appraisal of evidence would not warrant such hasty generalizations.

A writer makes sweeping generalizations when he or she makes a bold assertion as though it were self-evident yet offers no supporting evidence or appropriate qualification. Some writers make grandiose statements about social problems—crowded cities, welfare cheaters, sexist institutions, worker alienation—on the premise that all reasonable people share their general impressions of the world. In almost all instances, a careful examination of evidence suggests that the situation is more diverse and complicated than the sweeping generalizations make it seem. For example, despite the sweeping claims of some journalists, most city streets in the United States in the 1980s are not overcrowded; in slum areas, in fact, they are more likely to be starkly barren, with abandoned buildings and vacant lots.

Statistical Rhetoric and the Vitality of Mythical Numbers

Statistics are commonly used to make a persuasive case about the seriousness of a social problem. There is something convincing about hard numbers. They appear objective and authoritative. How could anyone dispute such official-looking data? In other words, statistics have rhetorical value. Clearly, statistics are an important source of evidence, but they should never be accepted uncritically. If readers are to be sensitive to various sources of bias, they must have some understanding of the relationship between the sample and the population it is alleged to represent. In the 1950s, Alfred Kinsey conducted a study of the sexual activities of American women. His sample contained a disproportionate number of students and female prisoners, hardly a cross section of American women, yet his statistics were often cited as being representative of all women.

Another source of bias involves the agency that collects the statistics. The Uniform Crime Reports, for example, summarize data made available by police departments. Police records are based on complaints by victims and arrests by police. Statistics on some kinds of crime—auto theft and murder, for example—more accurately reflect actual illegal activities than reports of other types—rape, aggravated assault, possession of illicit drugs. When sociologists compare crime rates from police records with victim surveys and self-reported confessions, they find that official statistics greatly underestimate the total amount of criminal behavior that actually occurs in society.

Also helpful to consider are the motives of those who promote statistical information. Government agencies sometimes benefit from presenting shocking statistics to legislators reviewing budget requests for the coming year. Similarly, if a problem such as drug addiction is accelerating at an "alarming rate," then law enforcement agencies and rehabilitation clinics will need more money to curb "the growing menace." Careful students of drug statistics have noted repeated occasions when the incidence of drug addiction has been exaggerated by self-serving officials who want to project visions of a big social problem. One official count claimed 200,000 addicts in New York City; a more rigorous and thoughtful estimate was 70,000 (Singer 1971; Reuter 1984). Readers must realize that any estimates of illegal drug sales or addiction are constructed on highly tenuous assumptions. Drug statistics, like all other statistical reports, must be read with caution.

DETERMINING THE ADEQUACY OF STATEMENTS ABOUT CAUSE-EFFECT RELATIONSHIPS

Thinking about social problems requires consideration of cause-effect relationships. According to the conventional wisdom, knowing the causes of a problem, whether it be poverty, juvenile delinquency, crime, drug addiction, racial prejudice, or child abuse, is the first step toward finding a remedy. If the causes of a problem can be recognized, then perhaps a cure can be found. Conventional wisdom is well established, yet no area of critical reasoning is more challenging and difficult for journalists and social scientists alike. Despite the high demand for understanding of the causes of such perennial topics as crime, poverty, personal pathology, and war, the supply of fully developed cause-effect explanations is very limited.

Identifying Causes and Effects

The search for key elements of cause-effect relationships begins with questions of why and how. According to the writer, why does the problem exist? How did the problem become so serious? What kinds of conditions are associated with what kinds of consequences? Does the writer blame some particular person, policy, group, or social condition? In social science literature, reference may be made to determinants, predictors, and statistical correlations between independent and dependent variables to explain causal relationships.

The logic of causation in social problems literature is rather straightforward: Initial conditions or events lead to undesirable outcomes. This logic requires the identification of causes and effects in terms of a flow of action that has a recognizable time sequence. Sometimes the temporal sequence is stated as descriptive narrative, with specific events occurring in chronological order. For example, many commissioned studies of urban race riots reconstruct the crucial sequence of events that led up to the fateful social explosion. Other social analysts deal with the temporal order in analytical terms. Though no specific events are described, the types of variables studied necessarily require a recognition of time. For example, a study of academic achievement among young adults assumes that such factors as parents' education, parents' income, and the students' IQ scores precede high school accomplishments. These background factors are used to explain why some students drop out of high school and others go on to graduate.

Identifying cause-effect relationships is not always easy. Steps involved include asking basic questions of why and how, searching for key concepts, noting how the key concepts are related to each other, and recognizing the flow of action that requires a time sequence. After identifying statements of causation, the critical reader must next assess their adequacy.

Necessary, Sufficient, and Contributory Conditions

The logical principles of necessary and sufficient conditions are helpful to an elementary understanding of causation. Vincent Barry provides the following definitions of terms:

A necessary cause is a condition that must be present if the effect is to occur.

A sufficient cause is a condition that by itself will bring about the effect.

A necessary and sufficient cause is a condition that must be present for the effect to occur and one that will bring about the effect alone and of itself. (Barry 1983:169–70)

We illustrate these principles with a discussion of causes of IQ scores. If *A* is a *sufficient* condition for *B*, then whenever *A* occurs, *B* must follow. This does not rule out other reasons sufficient for producing *B*. For example, a poor vocabulary is a sufficient condition to cause a low IQ score, but other causes (such as limited mental capacity as a biological fact of life) also account for low IQ scores. When *A* is a *necessary* condition for *B*, then if *A* does not occur, *B* cannot occur. This does not mean that *B* always occurs when *A* occurs. An adequate vocabulary, though necessary to achieve a high score, is no guarantee of a high IQ score. Formally speaking, an adequate vocabulary is a necessary though not sufficient condition to cause a high IQ score. Factors such as race, sex, and family income are neither necessary nor sufficient to explain high or low IQ scores.

In the study of social problems, relatively few cases exist in which an author can insist on a theory of causation that meets the logical requirements of necessary and sufficient conditions.[2] It is far more common for thoughtful journalists and sociologists to identify several conditions that *contribute* to a given effect. "A contributory cause is a factor that helps create the total set of conditions, necessary or sufficient, for an effect" (Barry 1983:170). A given effect can have many contributory causes.

---

[2] For one of the few instances, see Lindesmith's (1947) theory of opiate addiction.

Contributory causes are sometimes stated as probabilities; the language of probability allows varying degrees of influence to be assigned to any given cause. For example, since children from broken homes do not always become juvenile delinquents and not all juvenile delinquents come from broken homes, one can say that a broken home is neither a necessary nor a sufficient condition for juvenile delinquency. But broken homes do have an effect on delinquency as a contributory cause. Children from broken homes have a higher probability of becoming delinquents than those from intact homes.

Simple and Complex Statements of Causation

Readers must be wary of any commentary on a social problem that reduces the explanation to a single cause. The oversimplification of assuming a single cause for a crucial event (such as Watergate) or undesirable condition (such as high crime rates) can only be considered mischievous or naive. A seemingly simple question involving cause and effect often becomes complex. In many cases, several causal factors are related to many effects.

Lamar Empey (1982) illustrates the character of multicausal complexity in his discussion of delinquent behavior. He begins by observing that scholarly research supports five cause-effect statements about delinquent behavior:

1. The weaker the attachment between parents and child, the greater the delinquent behavior.
2. The weaker the attachment to the school, the greater the delinquent behavior.
3. The lower the academic achievement, the greater the delinquent behavior.

4. The weaker the commitment to conventional means for success, the greater the delinquent behavior.
5. The greater the identification with peers in the face of serious conflict with authority, the greater the delinquent behavior.

Each of these statements can be depicted as an independent causal factor, as Empey illustrates in Figure 3.1 (Empey 1982:292).

Researchers consider the model in Figure 3.1 to be an oversimplification. They realize that various causes can also be interdependent; for example, the weaker the attachment between parents and child, the weaker the attachment to school. Empey suggests that the causal relationships of independent and interdependent factors can be reconstructed as in Figure 3.2 (Empey 1982:294).

While Figure 3.2 demonstrates considerably greater complexity than Figure 3.1, it is still not sufficiently complex to allow for any detailed appraisal of delinquency. Researchers have observed that delinquency itself can become a factor in further weakening ties with parents, attachment to school, and so forth. In other words, delinquent behavior has reciprocal effects on the independent factors. Delinquency leads to more tenuous relationships at home and school, which in turn intensify the likelihood that

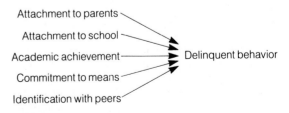

FIGURE 3.1

Independent Predictors of Delinquent Behavior

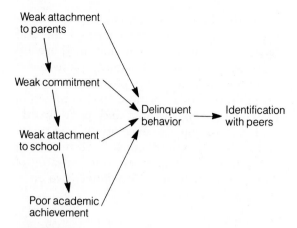

FIGURE 3.2

An Alternative Model for Examining Independent and Interdependent Predictors

the delinquent behavior will continue. Empey illustrates this highly complex model in Figure 3.3 (Empey 1982:295).

Empey's analysis demonstrates that a short list of five contributory causes of delinquency can lead to a complex maze of reciprocal relationships. The five simple arrows of Figure 3.1 have grown to eighteen in Figure 3.3. This added complexity does not ensure perfect predictions; one can speak only in probabilities. Many sociologists employ partial correlation models that

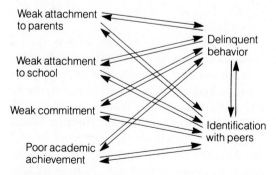

FIGURE 3.3

Independent, Interdependent, and Reciprocal Predictors of Delinquent Behavior

attach a relative numerical weight to each of the arrows.

Common Fallacies of Causation

There are two common fallacies of causation in the study of social problems. The first confuses a simple sequence of events with cause and effect. The fact that night follows day is no indication that the sun causes the moon. Such reasoning, however, is very common in social policy debates. Government action at one point in time is often blamed for a subsequent social problem. For example, after courts ordered the integration of public schools in some cities through special busing plans, some social analysts, observing white families leaving the central cities for the suburbs, concluded that busing caused "white flight." Critics of the white-flight thesis noted that whites had been leaving central cities for many years for a variety of reasons; attributing the white exodus from central cities to busing is therefore unreasonable (see Coleman 1976 vs. Farley 1976).

Another instance of confusion of sequence with causation is seen in debates about poverty policies, which often begin with the assertion that New Deal legislation in the 1930s somehow caused the current "welfare mess." Many people believe that a national policy of public assistance has unwittingly created a dependent and docile class of welfare recipients. Conditions facing welfare clients in the 1980s are seen as having been caused by government policies of the 1930s.

The second fallacy of causation confuses coincidence and cause. Two factors that coexist are often labeled as cause and effect. For example, although household crowding in cities is believed to cause neighborhood blight, some urban sociologists believe this conclusion may be the result of faulty reasoning. "Crowding should be viewed as an effect rather than a cause. . . . It is an effect of poverty and fertility and is more like an urban pathology itself than a cause of other pathologies" (Choldin 1979:189).

In the field of social problems, confusing coincidence with causation is sometimes called the "evil causes evil" fallacy. In this case, two undesirable conditions are joined together through the assumption that one causes the other. For example, journalists and sociologists have frequently identified poverty as an evil that causes any number of other evils. At one time or another, poverty has been blamed for poor health, mental depression and apathy, failure in school, and family instability. But in each of these instances, the reverse is equally plausible—poor health may cause poverty. It is also possible that little or no causal connection exists between poverty and poor health. Bad neighborhoods cause crime, and crime causes bad neighborhoods. Such reasoning does little to advance an understanding of cause and effect; it merely labels two coinciting conditions.

DETERMINING THE ADEQUACY OF STATEMENTS ABOUT VALUES

Finding the Values of Bold Partisans and Timid Neutralists

In 1906 President Theodore Roosevelt borrowed a scene from Bunyan's *Pilgrim's Progress* to criticize journalists who seemed preoccupied with the "muck" in American society, condemning them as muckrakers. Roosevelt's anger was aroused by the moral convictions of journalists determined to expose corruption and social injustice. This episode illustrates the important influence of values in studies dealing with social problems. Though the great muckraking era ended in 1912, some journalists and sociologists still feel the urge to write about social problems in the muckraking tradition. Writers investigating a social problem boldly criticize at the same time. This crusading spirit is evident in the titles of the following books, written by journalists and sociologists: Mary A. Mendelson, *Tender Loving Greed: How the Incredibly Lucrative Nursing Home "Industry" Is Exploiting America's Old People and Defrauding Us All* (1974); Michael Brown, *Laying Waste: The Poisoning of America by Toxic Chemicals*

(1980); Charles Perrow and Mauro Guillen, *The AIDS Disaster: The Failure of Organizations in New York and the Nation* (1990); William J. Wilson, *The Truly Disadvantaged* (1987); Mary Ann Mason, *The Equality Trap* (1986); Richard Sennett and Jonathan Cobb, *The Hidden Injuries of Class* (1973); Ray Rist, *The Urban School: A Factory for Failure* (1973). These titles telegraph the value judgments of the authors; before the book is opened, bad things have already been named. For these writers, moral criticism is closely related to social investigation.

Some journalists and sociologists do not investigate social problems in a muckraking style yet are committed to the expression of strong moral convictions in their writings. In their preface to *The War over the Family* (1984), Brigitte and Peter Berger assert, "This book is unabashedly partisan" (p. vii). The Bergers are not muckrakers, but they are strong supporters of the "bourgeois family." Whether investigating social wrongs or defending established institutions, writers in the social problems field often declare their values unequivocally.

A partisan approach, however, is not the only method used in the study of social problems. Some journalists and sociologists take the opposite approach and attempt to conceal their value judgments altogether. In the name of objectivity, they take a position of value neutrality. They believe that adherence to rules of neutrality will minimize bias and that minimal bias, in turn, will allow greater opportunity for discovery of the truth, which provides the only hope of solving social problems in a rational manner. In short, they believe that the knowledge can advance only when students of social problems put their values aside and assume a value-neutral position.

Professional disagreement over partisanship versus value neutrality cannot be resolved here. We call attention to the issue because we believe that the reader begins to assess values by searching for the partisan who may be either shouting or lurking in the essay. Readers intent on critically appraising the nature of values in social problems literature must first ask: To what extent are value convictions stated in an open and straightforward fashion? To what extent are value positions concealed and understood only through careful analysis of implicit meanings?

Identifying Three Kinds of Statements: Empirical, Conceptual, Evaluative

Identifying value statements is important. The task can best be performed by readers who also recognize statements that are not evaluative. We suggest a comparative strategy: Look for evaluative statements by noting which statements are empirical and conceptual. These three modes of expression, which abound in social problems literature, are defined as follows:

1. Empirical statement—a statement of fact based on observations that can be con-

firmed or disconfirmed by the observations of others.

2. Conceptual statement—a general idea that indicates hypothetical relationships between things or categories.

3. Evaluative statement—a judgment of worth indicating what is desirable or undesirable.

Empirical and conceptual statements are often associated with the discussions of evidence and cause-effect relationships. The three types of statements are summarized and illustrated in Table 3.1.

Here let us examine the question of value statements more closely. Such statements assume some general principle or criterion that serves as a basis for judging worthiness. If a person argues that the death penalty is wrong, then it is assumed that some general principle about the sanctity of life or the nature of punishment informs the person's value judgment. This general principle may in turn rest on specific criteria established by religious beliefs, secular ethical teachings, or humanistic reflections.

We agree with the distinction made by the philosopher John Wilson (1956) that "value statements are not attitude statements" (p. 66). In the case of attitudes, one need not justify one's sentiments; in the case of value statements, one should be willing to develop a rationale and criteria for one's position. Someone might say, "I'm repulsed by the idea of the death penalty." If, when challenged to defend this position, the person responds, "I have no reason, it's just my feelings," he or she has an attitude about the death penalty that is not grounded in any general principle.

It is important to identify the criteria being used to assert value judgments. What standards determine a particular decision about what is good or bad? Value criteria may be derived from many sources—religious beliefs, a political philosophy, science, the ideologies of capitalism and com-

TABLE 3.1 Three Kinds of Statements about Social Problems

	Empirical Statement	Conceptual Statement	Evaluative Statement
Definition of terms	A statement of fact based on observations that can be confirmed or disconfirmed by the observations of others	A general idea that indicates hypothetical relationships between things or categories	A value judgment indicating what is desirable or undesirable
Related terms sometimes used interchangeably	Evidence, facts, factual information, descriptive statement, statistics	Theoretical statement, abstraction, causal model, paradigm	Normative statement, moral statement, opinion, values, ideology
Illustrative statements: *Juvenile delinquency*	The first juvenile court was established in Chicago in 1899.	The weaker the attachment between parents and child, the greater the likelihood of delinquent behavior.	The innocence of youth is best served by a juvenile court that keeps youngsters away from hardened criminals.
Drug use	The use of marijuana is much more common among young adults (ages 18 to 35) than older adults (age 65 and older).	Young persons with personal problems are more likely to become involved in illicit drug use.	Marijuana is so detrimental to a person's physical and emotional health that it should never be legalized.
Poverty	In 1990, 31.5 million persons, or 12.8% of the U.S. population, were below the official poverty line.	Limited education contributes to poverty, but poverty, in turn, contributes to limited education. Therefore, limited education is both a cause and an effect of poverty.	Most welfare payments go to support people who are lazy or have loose morals.
Race relations	During the past several years, unemployment rates for blacks and whites indicate a consistent ratio of 2 to 1. In other words, blacks are disproportionately unemployed.	Insecure and frustrated persons in a majority group are more likely to form negative images of persons in minority groups.	Many white Americans are hypocrites who believe in equality but refuse to vote for qualified black candidates.

munism—that are equally justifiable. While empirical statements can be verified as true or false, unfortunately no similar process can verify value statements. The philosophers W. V. Quine and J. S. Ullian summarize this problem of logic:

Disagreements about principles can stubbornly resist rational resolution. The person who thinks that animal life is more highly valued than human amusement is unlikely to be swayed by the arguments of the modern huntsman, and conversely. (Quine & Ullian 1970:92)

Quine and Ullian's example of hunting may seem trivial, but the same rational problem applies to nations hunting nuclear weapon installations in space.

Though reasoning skills cannot resolve fundamental disagreements about principles, critical thinkers can seek clarification of the principles drawn on and a better understanding of the implications of these principles for a given situation. For example, the Roman Catholic church has argued for centuries that under certain circumstances a just war is possible. But can the criteria of a just war be met under new circumstances of modern technology? Are the components of a just war feasible given the first-strike capabilities of nuclear weapons? No rules of logic are applicable to such questions; nevertheless, a critical thinker studying social problems will ask: Are the criteria sufficiently clear to explain how a given value judgment is made?

The process of clarifying value statements requires the identification of value objects and evaluative terms. *Value objects* can be physical objects (nuclear plants, littered streets), events (the assassination of John Kennedy), people (the Boston Strangler), actions (smoking pot), institutions (the family, higher education), communities (Chicago), or groups (the Mafia, General Motors Corporation). Value objects can be either particular persons, places, and dates

or general categories. They can be highly specific (the nuclear accident at Three Mile Island) or vague (capitalism, modernization). In short, almost anything you can observe or imagine can be a value object.

Evaluative terms make judgments about value objects and prescribe specific action. Many words with positive or negative connotations—such as *authentic, bad, decent, cynical, nice, sincere, strong, rancorous, wholesome*—are used as evaluative terms that express a preferential meaning for a specific object and precede a call for action. For example, "The Three Mile Island accident demonstrates the dangerous and foolish risk of nuclear power plants; all nuclear power stations should be phased out" or "The heinous crime of a rapist-murderer justifies capital punishment."

Ways of Approaching Values in the Study of Social Problems

Journalists and sociologists disagree about how they should treat values in the study of social problems. While many different opinions and perspectives are applied to the problem of values, we limit our comments to common strategies found in various books, magazines, and professional journals.

Criticizing the prevailing value system. Some journalists and sociologists assume the role of critics of the status quo and articulate their values in a direct challenge to current beliefs and practices. Journalists in this tradition often write for radical newspapers and magazines such as *In These Times* and *Mother Jones*. Many modern sociologists, identifying themselves as Marxists, openly criticize capitalist institutions and the free-enterprise system. For example, in *Schooling in Capitalist America* (1976) Samuel Bowles and Herbert Gintis ridicule many popular beliefs regarding education and the opportunity to get ahead as pernicious myths that primarily serve the interests of the dominant class. They espouse the creation of a "working-class consciousness" as a prelude to a revolutionary movement.

Discerning readers have no difficulty identifying the values of an avowed social critic. The more difficult problem is being sufficiently knowledgeable of the writer's stock of wisdom about the "Truth." If a reader knows nothing about Marx, following a Marxist critique of America may be difficult. In similar fashion, ignorance of Catholicism may lead to problems in understanding a Jesuit's ethical position on abortion. Many of Milton Friedman's conservative arguments about economics and government policy rest on a historical appreciation of nineteenth-century liberalism. In order to understand the bearing of values on controversies related to social problems, a person must be knowledgeable about various ideological perspectives.

Analyzing value dilemmas.   Other sociologists and journalists approach values as a point of departure for analysis of social problems. One of the most distinguished and influential books in the field of social problems is Gunnar Myrdal's *An American Dilemma* (1944). Myrdal was a Swedish economist selected by the Carnegie Foundation in the late 1930s to study race relations in the United States. Having had no previous interest in the study of race relations, he began his work with no preconceived ideas. Myrdal approached the topic of race relations by examining the conflict between two value systems: the American creed of equal rights versus the customs of segregation and the denial of rights. His book repeatedly called attention to the gap between American ideals of "the land of the free" and the realities of discrimination.

Myrdal developed a sophisticated theory of value analysis that provides useful guidelines for students of social problems. Essentially, the social investigator examines "sets of coexisting value premises" to determine how members of a society deal with contradictory value commitments—for example, the contradictory values of prison policies that assert the importance of both rehabilitation and deterrence. Many people praise the values of individual autonomy and the freedom to "do your own thing," while others deplore the weak social ties suggested by unstable family life, extensive recreational use of illicit drugs, and neglect of elderly parents. A final example of a value dilemma is provided in a study by two experts on public opinion polls. When questioned on the growth of government regulation over the past several years, a majority of those polled consistently opposed greater regulation. At the same time, "a majority has also voiced approval of existing regulation and indicated that it did not want to roll back the tide" (Lipset & Schneider 1979:6).

Value conflicts represent contradictory forces in society, and social problems are often integral to these conflicts. Social scientists and journalists study social problems by identifying these contradictions. Myrdal's theory recognizes the improbability of a simple reconciliation. "We cannot assume a convergence of interest. We stand continuously before research tasks where a clash of interests and valuations is part of the problem" (Myrdal 1953:242). Students of social problems cannot escape contradictory values but must face them squarely with the tools of rationality.

Testing Ideal Values with Inconvenient Facts

Many of the great muckrakers in American journalism and sociology have studied social problems by first endorsing the ideals of society—democracy, fair play, decent care for children, honesty in government—and then investigating situations that contradict these ideals. No work better illustrates the clash of official ideals and investigative facts than Lincoln Steffens' *The Shame of the Cities* (1904). At the turn of this century, Steffens exposed the corruption of city leaders who espoused democratic virtues in the chambers of government while engaging in corruption behind the scenes. Steffens' moral crusade is illustrated by his description of Chicago: "First in violence, deepest in dirt; loud, lawless, unlovely, ill-smelling, irreverent, new; an over-grown gawk of a village, the 'tough' among cities, a spectacle for the nation" (p. 163). Steffens was a reformer who believed that the first step toward better municipal government was exposure of bad government. Once people recognized the existence of corruption, they would demand new leaders and new laws.

The contrast between the ideal and the real, the "ought" and the "is," facilitates a straightforward assessment of a social problem. The greater the gap, the bigger the scandal and the more urgent the need for reform. Though the ideal and the real never meet, a comparison of the two often leads to new efforts to understand changing social conditions. In the 1990s, many questions are being asked about the fact that while virtually everyone goes to school, many children do not learn what they should. Hope for improvement in schools rests upon a better understanding of why educational ideals are so difficult to achieve. Even though this approach to studying social problems is not always highly sophisticated, it is still a highly effective way to examine crucial issues in a democratic society. Individuals and societies sometimes benefit by measuring actual achievements against the yardstick of ideal expectations.

Analyzing Values As Causes and Effects

Journalists and sociologists see values as part of a larger network of cause-effect relationships. Values are vital to all human endeavors; their vitality stems from the fact that consequences follow from them. Values can also be seen as the effects of particular circumstances. Writers observe the emergence of evil social forces such as Nazism in Germany, lynchings in the United States, racism in the West, and authoritarian personalities and try to explain the phenomena. People's perplexity over the sudden ascendancy of undesirable value systems creates a profound need for satisfactory explanation. Condemned to search for meaning, we seek assistance from many sources, including journalism and the social sciences. The quest for an explanation of the cause of "evil values" helps us reconstruct an ethically plausible world in refutation of the hypothesis of moral chaos. For example, after a major war, writers assume the tedious task of reconstructing the social and historical forces that led up to it, thereby explaining the colossal human carnage. Such inquiry is more than an effort to satisfy idle curiosity.

Values can also have consequences that are problematic for various groups in society. Some social problems are defined as the unintended (and undesirable) consequences of social policies intended to be benevolent. For example, the juvenile court system was established in Chicago in 1899 for the purpose of saving children from the vile adult prison system. Yet a distinguished Chicago attorney insists that "the child welfare and juvenile justice systems do much more harm than good" (Murphy 1974:vii; see also Platt 1969). Indictment of a morally approved institution is not uncommon in social criticism.

Critics refute any simplistic line of reasoning that argues that policies based on values of goodness will necessarily lead to beneficial results. Such reasoning is often used to explain how the goodwill of founders led them to establish schools, hospitals, parks, and children's camps. But the relationship between values and consequences is more than a matter of goodness begetting more goodness. Indeed, sociologists take special interest in studying the paradox that the good intentions of reformers can lead to policies that are more harmful than the conditions the reformers are trying to improve. For example, Christopher Jencks and James Crouse (1982) point out that aptitude tests such as the ACT and the SAT were originally designed to promote fairness in college admission policies. The consequences, however, despite good intentions, have not been greater fairness at the admissions gate but, unwittingly, the denigration of scholastic achievement in high school. A second example illustrates this paradox of unanticipated negative consequences of intended reform. The good people who led the temperance movement (for example, the WCTU) helped establish Prohibition, which in turn led to a lucrative underground liquor business controlled by mobsters. The massive patronage of illegal merchants created a cynical disregard for the law on the part of many formerly law-abiding citizens. The creation of underground business and cynicism toward the law may have been more detrimental to society than the original problem of alcohol consumption. We are not suggesting that noble values necessarily lead to ignoble results but rather that values often have unpredictable consequences. Sometimes there is virtue in being skeptical of good intentions.

ASSESSING LOGICAL CONSISTENCY IN AN ARGUMENT

Seeing Connections and Combinations among Elements of an Argument

We have considered four key elements in the construction of statements about social problems: definition, evidence, cause-effect relationships, and values. Readers must now consider how these elements are connected. They are like pieces of a jigsaw puzzle; readers search for the parts (the elements) and then make connections between them in order to see the larger picture. This puzzle-solving process requires a great amount of concentration and patience. Questions that provide clues to the logical coherence of an author's line of reasoning include: Do the pieces fit together? Are any pieces missing?

The ideas that make up an argument are not always presented as isolated and discrete elements. For example, the three kinds of statements—empirical, conceptual, evaluative—in Table 3.1 are not always easily identifiable in the same way as canned goods on a grocery shelf. The elements of reasoning are not necessarily obvious on first inspection. Journalists and social scientists often write sentences and paragraphs that combine description with conceptual analysis, evaluation with supporting evidence, conceptual schemes with normative proclamations, and so forth. The reader must be able to recognize not only isolated statements of description, causal analysis, and evaluation but also various combinations of these three modes of thought.

Recognizing distinctions as well as combinations can be illustrated by the use of facts and values. In some cases, factual and evaluative statements can easily be distinguished. "John Kennedy was president of the United States" is obviously a different type of statement from "John Kennedy was a good president." Many evaluative terms, however, assign value and describe at the same time; in such instances, distinguishing fact from value is more difficult. For example, if a person said "General George Patton was an impetuous leader on the battlefield," some might argue that the term *impetuous* gives a factual description of Patton. Others might perceive the same word as more evaluative and minimally factual. While a clear distinction between facts and values is not always possible, the reader can get a better idea of the intentions of the author by studying the context in which a particular statement is made.

The fusion of description, causal analysis, and evaluation is illustrated by a passage in Kai Erikson's *Everything in Its Path*. Erikson studied Buffalo Creek, West Virginia, a community that had been destroyed by a flood after the collapse of a makeshift dam built by the coal company. In his conclusion, he placed the tragic incident within a larger context of cultural change.

The people of Appalachia have been the victims of one long, sustained disaster brought about by the pillaging of the timber reserves, the opening of the coal fields, the emergence of the Depression, and the introduction of welfare as a way of life; and the effect of these and other developments in the life of the region has been to create shift in the gravitational field and to destroy that old balance. If we had a chart to indicate the flow of change across that cultural field, it would be covered with arrows showing drifts away from individual freedom to enforced conformity, from self-assertion to passivity, from ability to disability, from tidiness to an almost sullen kind of slovenliness, and from independence to an ever-growing dependency. All of the vectors of change indicated on our chart would have to be counted as movements toward less satisfactory potentialities in the field, even if we used no other base line than the standards of the people concerned. (Erikson 1976:250–51)

In this passage, the reader notes historical description of change combined with clear causal and evaluative implications. Erikson evaluates the changes as negative and blames them on outside agencies.

The overall line of reasoning in an essay is best understood by beginning at the end. In the last several paragraphs of an essay or the last chapter of a book, the author often raises the basic question: What can be done to solve the problem? The answer can be seen as the logical conclusion to the essay. Not all essays on social problems have solution statements, however. In some cases, authors simply point out the difficulty of finding an adequate solution, while in others they ignore the question altogether. Just as readers are urged to study the opening paragraphs to determine an author's definition of a social problem, so must they study the concluding paragraphs to find an author's solution. Two questions need to be asked: (1) According to the author, what should be done? (2) Do the recommendations for action follow logically from earlier premises? In other words, readers must assess the full line of reasoning developed by the author. Conclusions about how to solve the problem must be compatible with previous assertions about the nature of the problem.

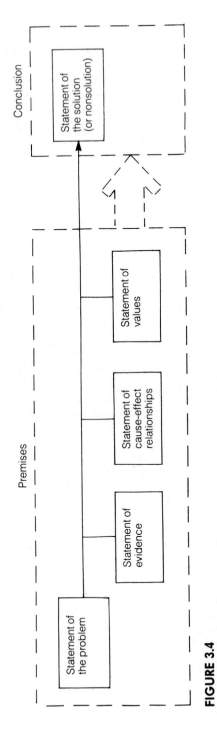

FIGURE 3.4

A Critical Reasoning Scheme Designed for Analysis of Statements about Social Problems

CONCLUSION

Figure 3.4 provides an overview of the critical reasoning process developed in this chapter. The reader's task is to identify various elements of an author's argument, to assess the empirical and logical adequacy of those elements, to see the connections among them, and finally to assess the logical consistency of the author's line of reasoning. Critical readers rarely master all aspects of this reasoning process, but even elementary efforts at critical reasoning yield powerful results. Awareness of an author's way of reasoning is the first full step toward the mature exercise of freedom.

The basic analytical issues for determining the adequacy of a statement about a social problem and key questions for each issue are outlined below:

I. Analysis of elements (problem, evidence, cause-effect relationships, values, solutions):
  A. Readers must have the capacity to *identify* various elements. Key questions:
    1. How implicit or explicit are the elements?
    2. Are the elements clearly identifiable?
    3. How vague and ambiguous are the elements?
  B. Readers must have the capacity to *determine the logical and empirical adequacy* of the elements. Key questions:
    1. How credible are the elements in the statements?
    2. Are the elements sufficiently developed to articulate the line of reasoning?
II. Analysis of total statement:
  A. Readers must have the capacity to *recognize relationships* between the elements. Key question:
    1. Are the elements meaningfully connected?
  B. Readers must have the capacity to *determine the logical consistency* between and among the elements. Key questions:
    1. How coherent is the line of reasoning?
    2. Does the conclusion logically follow from the premises?

These questions are examined in the next chapter.

References

Barry, Vincent. 1983. *Good reason for writing.* Belmont, Calif.: Wadsworth.

Berg, Ivar. 1971. *Education and jobs: The great training robbery.* Boston: Beacon.

Berger, Brigitte, and Peter Berger. 1984. *The war over the family.* New York: Anchor/Doubleday.

Bowles, Samuel, and Herbert Gintis. 1976. *Schooling in capitalist America.* New York: Basic Books.

Brown, Michael. 1980. *Laying waste: The poisoning of America by toxic chemicals.* New York: Pantheon.

Choldin, Harvey. 1979. Crowding and slums: A statistical exploration. In Michael Lewis, ed., *Research in social problems and public policy* 1:179–94.

Coleman, James S. 1976. Liberty and equality in school desegregation. *Social Policy* 6:9–13.

Ehrenreich, Barbara. 1983. *The hearts of men.* New York: Anchor/Doubleday.

Empey, Lamar. 1982. *American delinquency: Its meaning and condition.* Homewood, Ill.: Dorsey.

Ennis, Robert. 1962. The concept of critical thinking. *Harvard Educational Review* 32:81–111.

Erikson, Kai. 1976. *Everything in its path*. New York: Simon & Schuster.

Farley, Reynolds. 1976. Is Coleman right? *Social Policy* 6:14–23.

Jencks, Christopher, and James Crouse. 1982. Should we relabel the SAT . . . or replace it? *Phi Delta Kappan* 63:659–63.

Lindesmith, Alfred R. 1947. *Opiate addiction*. Bloomington, Ind.: Principia.

Lipset, Seymour Martin, and William Schneider. 1979. The public view of regulation. *Public Opinion* 6:6–13.

Mason, Mary Ann. 1986. *The equality trap: Why working women shouldn't be treated like men*. New York: Simon & Schuster.

Mendelson, Mary A. 1974. *Tender loving greed*. New York: Vintage.

Murphy, Patrick. 1974. *Our kindly parent—the state*. New York: Viking.

Myrdal, Gunnar. 1944. *The American dilemma: The Negro problem and modern democracy*. New York: Harper.

Myrdal, Gunnar. 1953. The relation between social theory and social policy. *British Journal of Sociology* 4:210–42.

Newman, Robert, and Dale Newman. 1969. *Evidence*. Boston: Houghton Mifflin.

Perrow, Charles and Mauro Guillen. 1990. *The AIDS disaster: The failure of organizations in New York and the nation*. New Haven, Conn.: Yale University Press.

Platt, Anthony. 1969. *The child savers*. Chicago: University of Chicago Press.

Quine, W. V., and J. S. Ullian. 1970. *The web of belief*. New York: Random House.

Reuter, Peter. 1984. The (continued) vitality of mythical numbers. *Public Interest* 75:135–47.

Rist, Ray. 1973. *The urban school: A factory for failure*. Cambridge, Mass.: M.I.T. Press.

Scriven, Michael. 1976. *Reasoning*. New York: McGraw-Hill.

Sennett, Richard, and Jonathan Cobb. 1973. *The hidden injuries of class*. New York: Vintage.

Singer, Max. 1971. The vitality of mythical numbers. *Public Interest* 23:3–9.

Steffens, Lincoln. 1904. *The shame of the cities*. New York: Hill & Wang.

Steffens, Lincoln. 1931. *The autobiography of Lincoln Steffens*. New York: Harcourt Brace.

Toulmin, Stephen, Richard Rieke, and Allan Janik. 1979. *An introduction to reasoning*. New York: Macmillan.

Webster's new dictionary of synonyms. 1984. Springfield, Mass.: G. & C. Merriam.

Wilson, John. 1956. *Language and the pursuit of truth*. London: Cambridge University Press.

Wilson, William Julius. 1987. *The truly disadvantaged*. Chicago: University of Chicago Press.

CHAPTER 4

APPLYING GUIDELINES:
A CASE STUDY
IN CRITICAL REASONING

INTRODUCTION

Chapter 3 presented a set of critical tools to be used by thoughtful readers of journalism and social science and summarized some basic principles of criticism in a somewhat formal and abstract fashion. But abstract principles are of little use unless they can be applied to concrete situations. In this chapter we outline the practical procedures for criticizing an essay on an important social problem.

A HEURISTIC GUIDELINE FOR CRITICISM

The guidelines for criticism presented in this chapter are heuristic; that is, they provide directions for analyzing a statement about a social problem but make no claim to be the only way to criticize the writings of journalists and social scientists. The guidelines provide practical assistance by helping the reader sort out various issues in an organized fashion. Scholars in rhetoric and logic have written about many important topics that we do not mention. Although we have limited our analysis to four steps, these elementary procedures are not necessarily the best method to use on all occasions.

The four steps of critical reasoning shown in Figure 3.4 involve two basic kinds of thinking: (1) using the power of reasoning to identify and criticize various aspects of an essay and (2) recognizing that an essay has parts as well as a whole. These two mental tasks are displayed in Figure 4.1 in a way that identifies each of the four steps. Each step mentioned in Figure 4.1 requires the careful pursuit of several additional questions. Though we do not intend to present an exhaustive set of questions related to each of the four steps, the following outline provides a comprehensive point of departure.

Step 1: Identify Topics

A. Identification of various topics found in the essay.
   1. Identifying the definition of the problem.

Tasks of Reasoning

	Identifying Topics	*Criticizing Topics*
Seeing the Parts	A. Step 1 1. Finding the definition of the problem 2. Finding the evidence 3. Finding cause-effect relationships 4. Finding values 5. Finding solutions	B. Step 2 1. Determining the adequacy of definitions 2. Determining the adequacy of evidence 3. Determining the adequacy of cause-effect relationships 4. Determining adequacy of values 5. Determining the adequacy of solutions
Seeing the relationships and the Whole	C. Step 3 1. Finding the author's line of reasoning 2. Summarizing the author's ideas as a total argument with premises and conclusion	D. Step 4 1. Determining the adequacy of the author's line of reasoning 2. Overall assessment of the argument as empirically sound and logically consistent

(Tasks of Perceiving)

FIGURE 4.1
Four Steps of Criticism

a. What is the nature of the social problem?

b. Can the reader find a thesis statement or key sentences that represent the author's main concern?

c. If a thesis statement cannot be found, can the thesis be summarized in the reader's own words?

d. What are the key terms or definitions in the essay?

2. Identifying evidence.

a. What types of evidence are presented?

b. Does any discussion of methodology accompany primary evidence?

c. Are specific sources cited for secondary evidence?

3. Identifying cause-effect relationships.

a. What is the author's basic idea about cause-effect relationships?

b. Can specific words or phrases be found that state causes and corresponding effects?

c. Can blame statements be found or constructed? Are there villains (causes) and victims (effects)?

d. To what extent is the author's model of causality simple or complex? Is there a simple cause-effect relationship or are several causes related to several effects?

4. Identifying value assertions and assumptions.

a. What is the author's basic value position?

b. Are the author's values stated implicitly or explicitly?

c. Is it possible to find value objects and corresponding words or phrases that are evaluative terms?

5. Identifying solutions or nonsolutions.

a. What is the author's conclusion about the social problem? Is there any statement about a solution or a nonsolution?

Step 1 requires a great deal of work. At least fifteen questions merit careful thought. Not all of these questions are equally appropriate for all essays about social problems, and some of the questions can be answered with a simple recognition that they are not applicable. For example, an analysis of newspaper editorials never involves consideration of primary evidence. The most important result of the first step is identifying key topics. The answers to the questions asked in Step 1 establish the foundation for the next three steps.

Step 2: Determine Logical and Empirical Adequacy

B. Determination of the logical and empirical adequacy of the topics.

1. Assessing the definition of the problem.

a. Is the author's major thesis clearly stated?

b. Are key terms and definitions clearly stated?

c. Are terms and definitions used in a consistent fashion?

2. Assessing evidence.

a. Are sources of factual information clearly identified?

b. Is evidence sufficiently objective for the purposes at hand?

c. Is evidence sufficiently accurate and up to date for the purposes at hand?

d. Are sweeping or hasty generalizations offered without appropriate qualifications?

3. Assessing cause-effect relationships.

a. Are causal statements plausible and empirically sound?

b. Whether causality is simple or complex, is it adequate for the purposes at hand?

4. Assessing value assertions or assumptions.
   a. Are value objects and evaluative terms clearly stated, or are they ambiguous?
   b. Are the criteria of value judgments sufficiently explicit?
   c. Are the criteria of value judgments and the value judgments themselves adequately articulated and defended?
   d. Are factual statements distinguished from evaluative statements?
5. Assessing the solution statement.
   a. Is a statement of solution (or nonsolution) stated with sufficient clarity?
   b. Does the solution statement appear to be plausible? Where does the author's position fall along a continuum of plausibility: wildly utopian (extreme optimism), pragmatically in the middle range (emphasis on practicality), or morbidly despairing (extreme pessimism)?

Step 2 involves determining adequacy for the purposes at hand. Has the author made a good case for her definition of the problem, her evidence, her analysis of relationships, and her value judgments, or has she been too vague in her statement of the problem? Is her evidence limited, without sufficient documentation? Are her value assertions little more than sweeping indictments of "bad guys" and all the evil in the world? These questions require the reader to make judgments on matters that frequently cannot be divided into simple categories of adequate or inadequate. There are varying degrees of adequacy and inadequacy. Readers can sometimes make black-and-white distinctions, but more often they need to recognize various shades of gray.

Step 3: Recognize Relationships among Topics

C. Identification of the author's line of reasoning.
   1. Identifying the author's line of reasoning as an argument. What are the relationships between and among the elements of the premise (i.e., definition, evidence, causality, values) and the conclusion?
      a. How is the conclusion related to the premise?
      b. Can all five elements of the agreement (definition, evidence, causality, values, and solution) be outlined to show the line of reasoning?
   2. Summarize the author's line of reasoning.

Step 3 involves seeing the essay as a total statement and requires recognizing relationships that form a line of reasoning with a beginning, a middle, and an end. The key phrase for Step 3 is "line of reasoning." What is the connecting thread that holds various elements of the argument together? The line of reasoning is analogous to the plot in a novel or play; it is the organizing framework that allows the author to integrate various parts into a coherent whole.

Just as paintings, monuments, and cathedrals can be viewed as total objects of art, so statements about social problems can be seen as total works of nonfiction. Whether the statement is an editorial in a local newspaper, an essay in *Harper's Magazine*, or a two-volume work on race relations (Myrdal's *American Dilemma*), its author has a line of reasoning that organizes various elements, such as evidence and causality, into a larger pattern of relationships. The discerning reader must always be searching for the organizing focus that gives meaning to the statement as a whole.

Step 4: Determine the Logical Consistency of the Line of Reasoning

D. Determination of logical consistency in the author's line of reasoning.
  1. Assessing the logical consistency of the author's line of reasoning.
      a. Are the four elements of the premise (definition, evidence, causality, values) stated in a logically consistent fashion?
      b. How coherent is the total line of reasoning from premises to conclusion? Does the conclusion about solving the social problem follow logically from the premises?
  2. Overall assessment.

The fourth step is the grand finale in this exercise of criticism. The first three steps having pointed the way, the final question can be asked: Does the author offer a logically consistent line of reasoning? This question rests on a critical examination of the logical relationship between the premises and the conclusion.

This final moment in critical reasoning rests on the reader's appraisal of the previous three steps. If statements of causality were considered inadequate in Step 2, then little likelihood exists that logical consistency will be found in Step 4. A chain is only as strong as its weakest link. If some parts of the argument are faulty, then the total statement will be weakened accord-

ingly. If one part of the essay includes numerous hasty and sweeping generalizations, then the total argument cannot be logically sound. Sound reasoning of the whole requires full support from all the parts.

The four steps may seem elaborate and complicated. We have raised many questions, but we are not persuaded that all of them are so important as to require meticulous attention every time someone reads the daily newspaper or a *Time* essay. The most important aspect of these guidelines is the logic of critical inquiry suggested by the four steps outlined in Figure 4.1. Readers proceed by finding key parts of an author's argument, determining their logical and empirical adequacy, and then examining the essay as a whole. Once readers grasp the author's basic argument, they must judge its logical consistency. No foolproof procedures or fail-safe mechanical formulas for critical reasoning can be given, but these four steps and the questions accompanying them will point discerning readers in the right direction as they probe a long list of interesting social problems.

We have outlined a practical guide to critical reasoning. It is now time to test these procedures with a specific case study. In the last analysis, the only way to become a critical thinker is to practice on actual statements by journalists and social scientists. We begin by analyzing Christopher Jencks's essay on the financial plight of divorced women with children.

INSTRUCTIONS FOR CRITICAL ANALYSIS OF JENCKS'S ESSAY

Perhaps the most important aspect of critical analysis is the need to read something more than once. An essay should be read at least twice. The first reading should be a quick overview of the author's position. The second reading should involve a slower concentration on key points mentioned in the four steps. Readers of this text can look forward to reading all the selections twice, the first time quickly and the second time with more focused concentration on key points of identification and criticism.

On the second reading of Jencks's essay, jotting down a few notes will be helpful.

These notes can be used to make points of comparison with our critical appraisal of Jencks in the concluding section of this chapter. We have numbered each paragraph to assist the reader in this analysis.

DIVORCED MOTHERS, UNITE!

CHRISTOPHER JENCKS

1. Now that the equal rights amendment has been defeated, America needs to come to grips with the economic implications of male supremacy. So long as men and women marry and pool their economic resources, as tradition dictates they should, the fact that men receive 70 percent of the nation's income has no effect on women's material well-being—though it does have psychological effects. But women are less and less likely to be married. As a result, the disparity between men's and women's living standards is growing wider every year.

2. Economic inequality between the sexes is especially serious when couples with children stop living together. Despite *Kramer vs. Kramer,* the mother still ends up with the children in more than nine cases out of 10. Some mothers get a little child support from the father, and most work. But despite the women's movement, the average woman who worked full-time through-

From *Psychology Today,* November 1982. Copyright © 1982 Sussex Publishers, Inc. Reprinted with permission of *Psychology Today.*

Christopher Jencks, professor of sociology and urban affairs at Northwestern University, is the author of Who Gets Ahead? (Basic Books, 1979). *Known for his fresh ideas on social reform, he has also proposed giving parents vouchers for their children's education and replacing the Scholastic Aptitude Test with achievement tests.*

out 1979 still earned only 57 percent of what her male counterpart earned—just as she did in 1959. Hence the typical mother ends up with less money to support herself and her children than her husband has to support himself alone.

3. Indeed, after following a national sample of married women from 1971 to 1978, economists Greg Duncan and James Morgan at the University of Michigan found that women who got divorced and did not remarry typically experienced a 50 percent decline in family income. The skid would undoubtedly have been even worse had not a large fraction of these women gone to work. Divorced mothers do not have to pay for the absent father's food, clothing, and other expenses, but the father's departure does not reduce the family's housing bill, and working tends to raise child-care expenses.

4. If a mother remarries, Duncan and Morgan found, her living standard usually rises even more dramatically than it drops when she separates, exceeding what it was before her first husband left. (It may be that women who can't "marry up" don't remarry at all.) But the transition from one husband to another typically takes about five years, and a growing minority of women with children never remarry. Even for those who do, the years without a male breadwinner are typically a period of acute economic hardship. The fact that they were only poor temporarily does not mean that they suffered any less, and the fact that marrying a man—any

man—seems to be the only way out of poverty is morally deplorable and leads to a lot of bad marriages.

5. The great irony of this state of affairs emerged when Duncan and Morgan followed husbands from 1971 to 1978. Whereas divorce had typically lowered the living standard of both mothers and children, it had typically raised that of fathers.

6. The spread of mother-child families has transformed the character of American poverty. A generation ago the poor were mostly old people who could not work, black people who could get only menial jobs, and rural whites eking out a living from marginal farms and small businesses. The political and demographic upheavals of the 1960s and 1970s changed all that.

7. Congressmen worried about reelection have raised Social Security benefits for the aged even faster than the cost of living, so that people over 65 are now less likely to be poor than people under 15. The civil-rights movement opened up better jobs for blacks, reducing the wage differential between black and white men and almost eliminating it between black and white women. The uneducated rural poor mostly died off, and their better-educated children moved to urban areas, making rural poverty considerably less common than it used to be.

8. But these gains were largely offset by the steady increase in families without a male breadwinner. Such families have always been poor, but unlike other sorts of poor families, very little has been done to help them. Almost half of all mother-child families live below the federal poverty line, and the percentage has hardly changed over the last generation. Such families have also become much more numerous. Only 8 percent of all children lived in mother-child families in 1960, but 12 percent did in 1970, and by 1980, 19 percent did. Recent experience suggests that at least a quarter of all white children and two-thirds of all black children born in the 1970s can expect to spend part of their childhood in such a family. As a result, poverty is increasingly a problem of women and children.

9. Despite a lot of loose talk about the development of a "permanent underclass" in America, immune to the benefits of economic progress, the evidence suggests that, in fact, the new complexion of poverty makes it less and less likely to be permanent.

10. For blacks, poorly educated whites, and people in rural areas, poverty often was a fixed condition; old people, too, seldom escaped poverty once they fell into it. For the mother-child families who increasingly dominate today's "underclass," poverty is quite often temporary, beginning, as the Duncan and Morgan studies show, the day the man who supports them moves out and ending when another man moves in.

11. Such hardship is not inevitable. Just as the elderly improved their economic situation by pressuring Congress to raise Social Security benefits, and blacks improved their situation by pressuring whites to give them better jobs, divorced, separated, and single mothers could improve their lot by pressuring Congress and state legislatures to overhaul both child-support laws and the welfare system, which have long been national scandals.

12. Because of the way existing laws about child support work, absent fathers hardly support their children at all. According to a 1979 Census Bureau survey, for example, only half of all divorced mothers received any money whatever from their children's father during 1978. Even those who got something seldom got much. Payments averaged just over $1,000 per child for the entire year. The situation was even worse among mothers who were separated but not divorced, only a third of whom had gotten any money during the previous year. Among mothers who had never been legally married, only 6 percent of them got any financial support from their children's father.

13. Absent fathers are not, it is true, usually rolling in cash, and almost all divorced fathers feel that their divorce settlements have left them strapped. Yet such fathers almost always have more money and fewer expenses than divorced mothers. For the typical divorced couple with children, neither of whom has remarried, the economic situation in 1978 was roughly as follows: The husband's income was about $14,000, while the wife's income, exclusive of child support, was about $8,000. The mother had custody of the couple's two children, whose presence almost doubled her household expenses. For all family members to have ended up with the same stan-

dard of living, the mother and children would have needed about $14,000 of the family's $22,000 total income. To achieve this, divorce courts would have had to require the father to pay the mother $6,000, leaving the father $8,000 to support himself.

14. What actually happened was quite different. Since half of all fathers paid nothing and the other half paid $1,000 per child, the average payment for two children was $1,000, not $6,000. As a result, the typical father had more money to support himself than his former wife had to support both herself and the children.

15. The first step toward reforming this system would be for legislatures—or, better yet, Congress—to establish explicit rules about how much absent parents should contribute to their children's support. The absent parent's financial obligation should depend solely on objective economic considerations, like the father's income, the mother's income, and the number of children involved.

16. Under our present system, if the parents cannot agree about what constitutes reasonable child support, they must take the question to court, where the outcome depends on each lawyer's skill in blackening the other side's reputation, and on who the judge happens to be. Such a procedure encourages acrimony, often leaving one or both parents feeling that they have been victims of gross injustice. Small wonder that the father often does not pay. We need a system in which battles of this type are fought at a societal rather than an individual level.

17. If legislatures rather than judges determined the absent parent's obligations, we would have a National Organization of Single Parents lobbying for higher payments, and a League of Divorced Fathers arguing for lower ones. When the legislature resolved these conflicting claims, its judgment would bind everyone—at least until the following year, when agitation for change would begin again. Fathers might complain even louder about their onerous obligations, just as they now complain about their tax obligations, but they would at least know that everyone in their economic situation was paying the same amount, and they would be less likely to feel that their former wives were victimizing them.

18. The second critical reform is to collect the

money that fathers owe. At present, this is the mother's responsibility. If the father doesn't pay, the mother must find money somewhere to hire a lawyer to begin harassing the father. Even if the mother does this, her chances of success are by no means good, since the courts have no effective machinery for enforcing a judgment that someone owes someone else money. In the end, the average father will pay only two-thirds of what the court orders him to pay.

19. The best way out of this unfair situation is to turn over the collection and distribution of child support to the tax authorities, who are already in the business of extracting money from people who would rather not pay. Failure to pay should be subject to the same penalties as failure to pay one's income tax, including criminal penalties for willful evasion. Ideally, since many fathers no longer live in the same states as their children, and since many states have no income tax and hence no system for ascertaining their residents' incomes, the whole business should be handled by the Internal Revenue Service. Failing that, the federal government should at least take responsibility for tracing delinquents and collecting what they owe.

20. There will, of course, always be some fathers who die, some who disappear without a trace, and some who have no money. In these cases the state should act as a surrogate father, providing the mother with a minimum benefit to supplement her other income. But if mothers have an economic incentive to help the government trace absent fathers, such cases should not be all that numerous.

21. Any serious political effort to improve the economic situation of families without male breadwinners will also have to replace Aid to Families with Dependent Children with a system that is more compatible with basic American values about work. As now constituted, AFDC encourages idleness. It provides benefits to women who do not work, and it sharply reduces these benefits when a woman takes a job. Indeed, the Reagan Administration's recent "reforms" of AFDC mean that recipients will typically lose almost a dollar in benefits every time they earn a dollar. In most states this means that a woman with several children will have no economic incentive to work unless she can find a job

that pays substantially above the normal wage for working women. Of course, many women would rather work than take welfare, and significant numbers work even though they would be better off economically on AFDC. But precisely because two-thirds of all women who head families with children also work, a program like AFDC, which encourages other women in the same situation not to work, strikes both legislators and the public as unnecessary and subversive of the work ethic. Because legislators dislike AFDC, they keep benefits punitively low.

22. Rather than continuing their losing campaign to improve AFDC benefits, reformers who want to help families without a male breadwinner should look for an alternative that might command broader popular support. Mothers who can't work—a sizable fraction of AFDC recipients—should be supported through programs designed exclusively for the disabled. Mothers who can work should be guaranteed jobs.

23. To be sure, most AFDC mothers are short on technical skills, and some are also short on the personality traits that employers value. Even when they find jobs, some of these women have trouble keeping them. The only way I can see to insure that all these women have a chance to work steadily is to subsidize their employers for part—or, in some cases, all—of the cost of hiring

them. Such subsidies could end up costing taxpayers more than AFDC costs now. But because such a program would appear to support the work ethic instead of subverting it, both taxpayers and legislators would almost certainly be willing to spend the extra amount.

24. A system built on the assumption that women earn half of what men earn and always end up with the children when a couple separates is hardly a feminist's dream. Nor is it mine. But sexual equality in earnings is still a long way off. And despite increased judicial reliance on nominally joint custody agreements, children who live with only one parent are more likely to live with their mother today than they were 20 years ago. In 1960, 14 percent of all children under 18 who lived with only one parent were living with their fathers; by 1980, the figure was down to 9 percent. (Most of these fathers were probably widowers.)

25. A system of increased child-support payments from absent fathers and guaranteed jobs for mothers is probably our best bet for keeping mother-child families out of poverty. At least it would be consistent with most people's notions about work and parental responsibility, which our present system is not, and it would narrow the economic gap between men and women at all economic levels.

Identifying Critical Reasoning Topics in Jencks's Essay: Step 1

Defining the problem and any special terms. We begin by looking for key topics in Jencks's essay. The first question, which concerns a definition of the social problem, is answered in a thesis statement at the beginning of the second paragraph: "Economic inequality between the sexes is especially serious when couples with children stop living together." The fundamental problem is defined as economic inequality between the sexes. Despite the women's movement, many women face financial difficulties; this situation is especially severe for single women with children.

Jencks does not use technical definitions, but several key words and phrases are crucial to his argument. They include *poverty, mother-child families, temporary versus permanent underclass, the work ethic, Aid to Families with Dependent Children (AFDC),* and *solving problems at an individual versus a societal level.* How Jencks uses these key terms will become apparent in our examination of his line of reasoning (steps 3 and 4).

Identifying evidence. The chief source of evidence in this essay is a national sample of men and women who were followed from 1971 to 1978. The evidence is secondary, since it was originally collected by Duncan and Morgan. Jencks also uses statistical data from the census bureau.

Identifying cause-effect relationships. Jencks makes several statements concerning cause-effect relationships. His most important analysis deals with the cause of poverty for many divorced mothers. These women are poor because their husbands do not provide the necessary child support. Most husbands neglect their former wives and children, while they enjoy increased wealth after divorce. Causation is straightforward: The poverty of divorced mothers is caused by the failure of former husbands to provide necessary child support. Furthermore, the courts fail to enforce the financial provisions of a divorce settlement, leaving the woman stranded with the children and with little hope of economic security until she remarries. The cause-effect relationship is rather simple: Mothers who divorce become poor; mothers who remarry (and most do) regain their prosperity. Fathers who divorce become more prosperous; if they remarry, they remain prosperous. The American dream often becomes a nightmare when mothers must raise their children alone.

Another discussion of causation concerns AFDC and the motivation of a mother to take a job outside the home. According to Jencks, "AFDC encourages idleness. It provides benefits to women who do not work, and it sharply reduces these benefits when a woman takes a job" (paragraph 21). This current causal arrangement has a direct bearing on Jencks's argument for reform of the AFDC system.

Identifying value assertions and assumptions. A surface reading of the essay clearly indicates Jencks's basic values with regard to economic inequality between the sexes. He dislikes various features of the current system that create inequality and wants to see greater equality. Several value objects and evaluative terms provide clues

to Jencks's position. Three paired instances of value objects and evaluative terms illustrate Jencks's value judgments.

Value Object	(verb)	Evaluative Term
situation: "Marrying a man" as "the only way out of poverty"	(is)	"morally deplorable" (paragraph 4)
situation: "no effective machinery for enforcing" child support	(is)	"unfair" (paragraphs 18 and 19)
social system: "a system built on the assumption that women earn half of what men earn and always end up with the children when a couple separates"	(is)	"hardly a feminist dream" (paragraph 24)

These examples, along with many other statements, indicate Jencks's moral commitment to greater equality between the sexes.

Identifying solutions to the social problem. Jencks is very clear about his recommendations to reform the current system of sexual inequality. In the last paragraph of the essay, he writes, "A system of increased child-support payments from absent fathers and guaranteed jobs for mothers is probably our best bet for keeping mother-child families out of poverty."

Criticizing Critical Reasoning Topics in Jencks's Essay: Step 2

Determining the adequacy of the definition of the problem. Jencks's thesis statement and many other comments leave little doubt about the nature of the problem. He also uses terms with clarity. While no official statistical definition of *poverty* is given, he leaves little doubt about the meaning of the economic disparity between men and women. The only point of confusion occurs in Jencks's discussion of AFDC recipients. Up to this point in the article, the whole issue has focused on divorced mothers and their need for greater support from their former husbands. But Jencks suddenly shifts focus to a larger group of single mothers that includes divorcees and women who have never married. How many divorced mothers also need a subsidized job and how many divorced mothers could make it financially with the recommended reforms in the divorce laws is not clear. Jencks never clarifies the distinction between the two groups of deprived single mothers.

It is interesting to note that Jencks's criticism of fathers does not apply to men who impregnate women they do not marry. No mention is made of the financial responsibilities of these fathers. Instead, the government, corporations, and hard-pressed mothers are held to account for the bills of these elusive fathers.

Determining the adequacy of the evidence. Jencks makes broad empirical assertions about the economic disparity between men and women. Is it possible to obtain independent verification of his claims? We have faced this question by turning to a readily available source, *The Statistical Abstract of the United States: 1984.* Several tables in the *Abstract* provide information on income and type of household (Table 758, p. 461; Table 760, p. 462; Table 767, p. 466). In every case, the same basic pattern is reported. In 1982, married couples with children had an income of approximately $25,000 ($6,300 per household member), while mother-child families had approximately $10,500 ($3,375 per household member). Jencks's assertions are confirmed; the disparity is indeed great.

A second critical point needs to be made about the evidence. Jencks relies on the empirical work of Duncan and Morgan (see Duncan 1984). Close reading of this evidence indicates a highly valuable source of information. Unlike most social surveys, which study a single sample at one point in time, the Duncan and Morgan data are from a longitudinal study. They provide an invaluable opportunity to see how the same people actually change over time. Presented with the longer view of a group of men and women over a seven-year period, one can determine the extent of hardship faced by divorced mothers and divorced fathers.

Determining the adequacy of the cause-effect relationships. Causal statements about the relationship between divorce and financial strain on mother-child families rest on longitudinal data, which provide strong support for simple cause-effect statements about divorce and the hardships of divorced mothers. Jencks is on less solid ground in his discussion of the relationship between AFDC and idleness. In this instance, no specific evidence is presented to support this case. He offers sweeping generalizations that appear plausible by the canons of common sense, but he fails to support his claims with documented data.

Determining the adequacy of the value assertions and assumptions. Jencks's commitment to greater economic equality between the sexes leads to two additional value assertions. The first concerns the injustice facing divorced mothers when their former husbands walk away from their responsibilities. Since local and state courts allow husbands to be irresponsible, enacting federal legislation that requires the executive branch of government to coerce collection of child-support payments is crucial. This solution expresses a second major value assumption, namely, that the federal government should become an active agent in helping single mothers who face private troubles. Jencks's belief in a strong central government is also expressed in his proposal to subsidize employers who agree to hire low-skilled single mothers.

Criteria for these values are never spelled out. For example, Jencks does not cite moral literature from the Judeo-Christian heritage that places firm responsibility on fathers to support their children, nor does he call attention to the *Playboy* philosophy, which recommends hedonistic irresponsibility for fun-loving men who enjoy the company of Bunnies rather than dull wives (Ehrenreich 1983). Such value criteria support the importance of private virtues. Jencks has little to offer in this area.

Jencks focuses on the macro arena by recommending policies for government. Little attention is given to the micro level, where private citizens face moral responsibilities. For example, Jencks accepts the status quo of high divorce rates as an inevitable fact of modern life. Some people would argue that he should recognize the virtues of the nuclear family and place greater emphasis on helping husbands and wives keep their families together in the first place. Why he accepts high divorce rates as OK and then argues for an enlarged welfare system as an improvement in society is never articulated in the essay.

Determining the adequacy of the solutions. Jencks is more than clear about his solution to the problems facing mother-child families, but some people would suggest that his reforms are unrealistic. Despite growing interest in the feminization of poverty in America and in the need for fathers to be supportive, many people would not want to see the IRS acting as Big Brother. Also, Jencks's suggestion of subsidizing employers who hire single mothers goes counter to current trends to hold the line on welfare programs. While the liberal reforms he puts forth are plausible, they are certainly controversial.

Identifying Jencks's Line of Reasoning: Step 3

Seeing connections among the five elements of the argument. Each of the topics in the premise is connected to the others in this essay. Definition of the problem (financial inequality of single mothers) is supported by evidence (the Duncan and Morgan survey). The causes of poverty are supported by longitudinal data gathered from men and women over a seven-year period. The value of the unfairness of sexual inequality is closely tied to the definition of the problem. These basic themes in the premise provide the rationale for proposed reforms; the conclusion follows from the premise.

A summary of the line of reasoning. Figure 4.2 summarizes Jencks's argument. This outline suggests that Jencks actually analyzed two problems stemming from different causes and requiring different remedies: the plight of divorced mothers and the unemployability of AFDC mothers. But the egalitarian values of Jencks lead him to the same ideal outcome—adequate income for all mother-child families. We are not suggesting that the outline in Figure 4.2 is the only way to break down Jencks's essay. It merely provides a framework for identifying parts and their relationships.

Criticizing Jencks's Line of Reasoning: Step 4

Logical consistency of premise and conclusion. Jencks does a fine job of articulating key ideas in his premise that lead to his conclusion. His line of reasoning is especially clear for the recommended reform of current divorce laws. Because concern for divorced mothers dominates the essay, some confusion arises when the AFDC problem is introduced. The solution of needed changes in AFDC policies is not tightly connected to the earlier issues concerning divorced women. This confusion, however, is

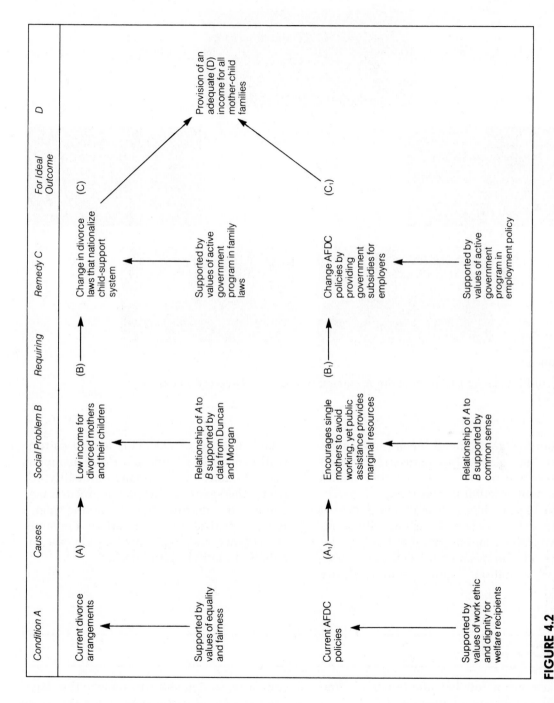

FIGURE 4.2

An Outline of the Line of Reasoning in Jencks's "Divorced Mothers, Unite!"

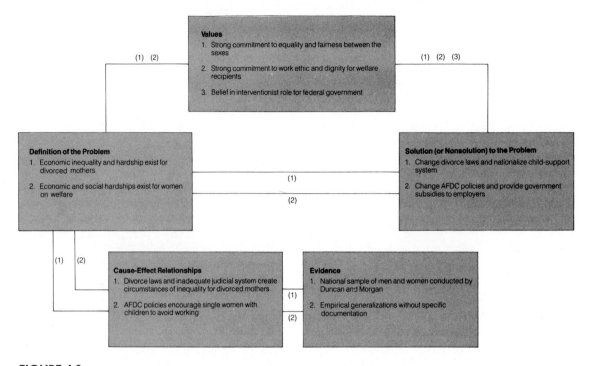

FIGURE 4.3

Relationships among Elements of the Argument in Jencks's "Divorced Mothers, Unite!"

a minor flaw that reflects incomplete analysis of the relationship between divorced mothers and AFDC mothers rather than a major contradiction in reasoning.

The logical pieces of the Jencks puzzle fit together in a coherent fashion. Relationships between and among the five key elements of the argument (definition, evidence, causation, values, solutions) are established by Jencks. This logical pattern is illustrated in Figure 4.3. From his opening statement on "economic inequality between the sexes" to his closing recommendation to "narrow the economic gap," Jencks consistently uses various elements of evidence and logic to make his case on behalf of mother-child families.

CONCLUSION

We have given detailed attention to the empirical and logical adequacy of Jencks's essay. This exercise in critical reasoning is intended to help students develop and use similar reasoning skills to analyze the sixty-three selections in this book. Each essay can be read with the same scrutiny we have given "Divorced Women, Unite!"

Critical thinking is no different from any other learned skill. At first, it seems strange and awkward. With a little practice, the sense of self-confidence grows. In time, conscientious and persistent effort brings proficiency. We are hopeful that such cumulative learning will be the experience of readers of this book. Jencks's essay is a learning example, the first step in the journey toward critical reasoning. Each subsequent essay in the book provides a new opportunity to sharpen critical thinking skills. By the time the last essay is read, habits of critical reasoning will have been formed that can serve thoughtful citizens on a wide variety of occasions. Such is our ultimate dream.

References

Duncan, Greg J. 1984. *Years of poverty, years of plenty*. Ann Arbor, Mich.: Survey Research Center–Institute for Social Research.

Ehrenreich, Barbara. 1983. *The hearts of men: American dreams and the flight from commitment*. New York: Doubleday.

U.S. Bureau of the Census. 1984. *The statistical abstract of the United States: 1984*. Washington, D.C.: Government Printing Office.

PART II

CASE STUDIES
FROM JOURNALISM
AND SOCIOLOGY

This section can be be described as a source-book of case materials that illustrate contemporary analysis of social problems by some of the leading journalists and sociologists who help to shape American civic culture. It is a collection of essays that covers a wide range of situations commonly recognized as social problems. The essays are complete and intact statements, just as they first appeared in newspapers, popular and specialized magazines, scholarly journals, technical reports, and books. With one exception—"Opportunities Denied, Opportunities Diminished: Discrimination in Hiring," by The Urban Institute—none of the essays has been edited or abridged. There is an important reason for publishing the essays in their entirety: It is the only way to be fair-minded about an author's work. An abridgement of an essay would destroy its original character and integrity. How could you read these selections critically if you did not know the author's full argument as he or she presented it? We want readers to learn to appreciate the art of essay writing about social problems. And we want the writers to make their cases as they intended.

Since contemporary statements about social problems are richly diverse in both content and form, we have deliberately provided a sampling of essays that express this diversity. In terms of *form*, essays range from very short commentaries found in daily newspapers to full-length articles published in magazines and scholarly journals. We have also included chapters from books, a technical report, and lengthy book reviews. In terms of *content*, we have selected essays that cover a wide spectrum of ideological views—liberal, middle of the road, and conservative. We do not seek or prescribe a politically correct view of any social problem. Our sample of essays on any given topic will not please all readers. A sample large enough to include something to please everyone would require several volumes. We do not intend to offend our readers with our particular selections. Since we cannot please everyone, we earnestly suggest that readers actively pursue additional essays found in abundance at any academic or public library.

Readers of these essays must guide their critical judgment by one of the principle rules of criticism: Determine the intention of the author and the audience for whom he or she is writing. Comparisons between journalism and sociology should not involve judgments of superiority or inferiority. It is as inappropriate to consider journalists inferior to sociologists because they express themselves less technically and are less rigorous in their methodology as it is to scorn sociologists because they write in jargon and devote considerable attention to academic disputes that are of no concern to anyone outside the field. Each essay in the next eighteen chapters should be read with clear awareness of the author's intention and the kind of readers for whom it was written.

INEQUALITY
AND GENDER

INTRODUCTION

All societies have distinct role expectations for men and for women. In the United States these expectations have been undergoing change for many decades. Today Americans live in a world of diverse family patterns and conflicting images of ideal lifestyles for men and women. The conventional norms of the first half century defined a successful woman as a wife and mother who stayed home to carry out a full array of household duties. The husband and father was expected to stay away from the home most of the day, earning enough money to pay the bills. Many adults still live by these expectations, but the traditional pattern is no longer held up as an ideal to be emulated by everyone. Times have changed; there is no return to yesteryear.

Although the women's movement and political controversies about such issues as the Equal Rights Amendment and sexual harassment suggest that changing sex roles is a recent issue, this is far from the case. Broad trends can be identified over the past hundred years. Women have increased their participation in the labor force from 18 percent in 1900 to over 50 percent today, and they give birth to fewer children than women did in the past. In 1910 the birth rate was 30 per 1,000 population; by the 1990s it had declined to 16 per 1,000. These two trends—increasing participation in the labor force and decreasing family size—suggest that major long-term changes have restructured the role expectations of men and women. These changes are complex. The fact that more women are joining the labor force as full-time workers does not mean that a single sex-role pattern is emerging. On the contrary, we are living in a period of diverse family patterns. According to Kathleen Gerson, "the domestic woman who builds her life around children and homemaking persists, but she now coexists with a growing number of working mothers and permanently childless women."[1]

Women today face hard choices as they make decisions about work, career, and motherhood. Despite women's liberation, women still earn less than men in the workplace and are still expected to do most of the work in the home. Women work substantially more hours each week in the home and at the workplace than men do. Women are working harder than ever, yet many do not enjoy the benefits of full equality. How is it that personal effort is not enough to make women truly free, financially secure, and equal to men? The six selections in this chapter respond to this question in various ways.

Two of the essays, by Joan Beck and Arlie Hochschild, address the problems facing married women who hold jobs. While women have been liberated to pursue careers outside the home, their husbands have not felt compelled to compensate for these additional hours of work by assuming half of the household duties. These women still carry the burden of most of the "women's work" around the house. Beck, a journalist, has addressed the problem by summarizing major themes that Hochschild, a sociologist, developed in a book on the quandary of women who come home from the workplace to their second shift, in the house. An excerpt from her book appeared in a daily newspaper, the *Sacramento Bee*. These two essays illustrate the common concern of journalists and sociologists for a more equitable division of labor in the home.

The other four selections in this chapter shift the focus to gender inequality in the workplace. Felice Schwartz has written a highly controversial essay on mothers in management careers for one of the leading business journals in the United States, the *Harvard Business Review*. Unlike earlier feminist writers who emphasized discrimination in the workplace, Schwartz calls attention to what she claims are the additional costs of hiring and promoting women executives. "The cost of employing women in management is greater than the cost of employing men." This simple claim generates highly diverse implications for corporate policies and career choices. Marilyn Gardner is sympathetic to Schwartz's position in her essay "The Truth about Working Women." For Barbara Ehrenreich and Deirdre English, Schwartz's claims are anything but the truth. Readers of these three selections must make their own thoughtful assessment. How strong are Schwartz's argument and evidence? Is Gardner helping to clarify Schwartz's position, or merely confusing the more significant issues that Ehrenreich and English expose? These questions are far from settled; but they help identify crucial issues that men and women in the late twentieth century must address.

---

[1] Kathleen Gerson, *Hard Choices: How Women Decide about Work, Career, and Motherhood* (Berkeley and Los Angeles: University of California Press, 1985), p. 9.

1. MEN DRAGGING FEET ON HELPING WORKING WIVES IN THE HOME

JOAN BECK

There she is, Ms. America. Dressed for success. Briefcase in one hand, preschooler clutching the other. On the fast track at work. Supermom at home. The woman who has it all, 1990s model.

What she also has is most of the housework and child care—and a husband who is far more skilled at evading his fair share than she is at cajoling or bargaining or gently persuading him to do it.

But that's old stuff. Dozens of books, hundreds of articles, millions of women have all made that point and nothing much changes. Women still work a full shift for pay and then go home to work a second shift without pay or help—and often without thanks.

Even couples who say they believe in sharing child care and housework rarely do, says Arlie Hochschild, University of California/Berkeley professor. Her new book, "The Second Shift," is the latest hot addition to the poor-tired-supermom genre and is as much an apologia for men as an indictment of them.

Men simply haven't been able to change as fast as women have in recent years, Hochschild generalizes. "Female culture" has shifted more rapidly than "male culture." And the point of clash is not so much in the workplace as in the home. "Men's underlying feelings about taking responsibility at home have changed much less than women's feelings have changed about forging some kind of identity at work," she says.

Women now work about 15 hours longer each week than men do, Hochschild figures, averaging data in several major studies. That adds up to an extra month of 24-hour days a year.

Only about 20 percent of the men in the dozens of two-income couples Hochschild surveyed share family chores equally. Most of what

men do is selective—taking a child to the zoo rather than being responsible for daily baths, grilling a steak on occasion rather than getting dinner regularly.

Women's move into the work force gives them more status, more independence, she notes. But because women's work at home has always been undervalued, husbands of working wives who are pressured to help more with the housekeeping or child care feel they become devalued if they give in.

Men who are not doing well in their own careers, men who still cling to male-dominated family patterns, men who fear losing status find it particularly difficult to share housework, Hochschild explains. They dare not give in to what they choose to consider a wife's bossiness; helping around the house can seriously threaten their masculine identity.

Often, a woman in such a marriage senses her husband's fragility, backs off from asking his help with chores and caters to him at home in traditional ways so he need not risk further loss of self-esteem by doing devalued "women's work."

Having a wife at home to tend a man's house and care for him is a privilege, Hochschild points out. If he takes on an equal share of the tasks at home, he essentially loses that privilege. But that is hard to put into words, so a man may simply say, "I wasn't brought up to do housework."

Why don't wives lean harder on husbands to do a fairer share at home? Hochschild suggests several reasons. A man's job is still seen as more important to society and to a family than a woman's, so he deserves the breaks, the restorative leisure, the right to be catered to. A women who loves a man and understands the competitive pressures he faces wants to give him the emotional support he needs.

Women also get worn down by male tactics. Men may play incompetent, burning food, shopping carelessly, acting helpless, requiring endless instructions, so they won't be asked to help again. They may make excuses: The beds don't need to be made, the house doesn't look messy. They may not do a job until repeatedly asked, then complain about being nagged. Women also tend to feel more guilty about short-changing children and tolerating a messy house and undone laundry than men do.

Because women usually can earn less than men, they have greater need for the protections of marriage and are usually willing to put more effort into keeping a relationship going—even if it means 15 hours of extra work every week, says Hochschild.

But even a husband who helps very little at home can be deeply affected by the smoldering resentment his wife feels and his need to steel himself against that resentment. She may then withdraw emotionally. Their sex life may suffer. They may drift apart. Divorce is more likely to happen over this issue than about money or sex, Hochschild says.

The solutions Hochschild proposes have all been pushed before. She wants tax breaks for employers who offer family leaves, job-sharing, part-time work and flexible hours. She advocates tax credits to developers to build affordable housing near jobs and shopping. She urges more and better day care. She points to the need to upgrade homemaking and child care so men will be more comfortable sharing.

And she wants to update the rules and expectations of marriage so that the work-sharing couples—the happiest among the dozens she studied—can become the role models of the future.

That's the least we can do for beleaguered men, who are now stuck in the transition stage of the most significant social revolution of this century.

---

2.   THE TRUTH ABOUT WORKING WOMEN

MARILYN GARDNER

During the past quarter century, Felice Schwartz has probably spent more time studying women's career issues than anyone else in the United States. In 1962 she founded Catalyst, a nonprofit women's business-research group in New York. Since then, Ms. Schwartz and her colleagues have published an impressive array of studies on such issues as parental leave, child care, relocation, dual-career couples, and flexible benefits.

But suddenly Schwartz the long-time ally of professional women is being treated like a traitor. Earlier this year she had the courage—some would say the temerity—to go public in the Harvard Business Review with a sobering, hitherto unpublicized fact of corporate life in the '80s:

From *The Christian Science Monitor*, March 21, 1989. Reproduced with permission.

"The cost of employing women in management is greater than the cost of employing men."

Women's careers, she explains, noting the obvious, are often interrupted by childbearing and childrearing. One corporate study reported a rate of turnover for women 2½ times greater than that for men. Another found that half of the women who took maternity leave returned to work late or not at all. As a consequence, she writes, "The money corporations invest in recruitment, training, and development is less likely to produce top executives among women than among men."

Feminists are worried that Schwartz's findings will give employers new reasons to discriminate against women. They also fear that children will continue to be seen as a "women's issue," rather than as a family issue.

As one litigation lawyer in Boston, the mother of two young children, says in criticizing the report, "It's hard enough for women without having these employers with their smug smiles saying, 'See, I knew there was a reason I didn't want to deal with women.'"

Yet what has been largely ignored in the furor is Schwartz's attempt to offer solutions that will reduce turnover and thus lower the cost of employing women.

She calls for more flexible leave policies for both men and women. She also makes a case for part-time work as "the single greatest inducement to getting women back on the job expeditiously." Specifically, she believes job-sharing—two part-time employees taking responsibility for one job—is the most promising form of part-time employment and "will be the most widespread form of flexible scheduling in the future."

During the late '70s, when my daughter was still in elementary school, I spent two years in a job-sharing post in the promotion department of this newspaper. My partner and I shared an office, a desk, and one full-time copywriting position. She worked three days a week. I worked two. When one of us went on vacation, the other stepped in full-time.

Although we sacrificed some benefits, the flexibility—and the sense of well-being it gave us and our families—more than compensated. Equally important, the arrangement proved valuable to the department.

These creative solutions are still the exception. But as Schwartz points out, they will need to become much more the rule as employers, faced with a shrinking labor pool, seek ways to retain bright, well-educated workers, male and female.

Until now, a conspiracy of silence on family issues has prevailed in corporate America. As Rep. Pat Schroeder (D) of Colorado explained in an interview with The Monitor, "It's OK to talk to an employer about parking, about hours, about the lunch room, about physical fitness, but you just don't bring up the family."

By breaking the taboo, by daring to bring up the family and its effects on corporate costs, Schwartz has set off a heated debate that could eventually strengthen the workplace. Her timing, in fact, may be fortuitous. A parental leave bill is scheduled to reach the House floor in May.

When it does, perhaps the debate can take a positive approach. Instead of arguing about how much it will cost companies to give new parents 10 weeks of unpaid leave, lawmakers and employers could consider this: How much will it cost *not* to provide parental leave? How much turnover might be avoided if companies sought to help parents meet their needs during the critical years of infancy and early childhood?

Schwartz and her now-famous article will not be the last word. There must be more studies, and new ways of measuring women's value to employers. But as a successful pragmatist she deserves a fair hearing, and her suggested solutions merit more than cursory dismissal by the ideologues.

If Schwartz can be seen as an agent of change rather than the enemy, she may, in the metaphor of her organization, prove to be a catalyst for further reforms in the workplace.

3.   BLOWING THE WHISTLE ON THE "MOMMY TRACK"

BARBARA EHRENREICH and DEIRDRE ENGLISH

When a feminist has something bad to say about women, the media listen. Three years ago it was Sylvia Hewlett, announcing in her book *A Lesser Life* that feminism had sold women out by neglecting to win child-care and maternity leaves. This year it's Felice Schwartz, the New York–based consultant who argues that women—or at least the mothers among us—have become a corporate liability. They cost too much to employ, she argues, and the solution is to put them on a special lower-paid, low-pressure career track— the now-notorious "mommy track."

The "mommy track" story rated prominent coverage in the *New York Times* and *USA Today*, a cover story in *Business Week*, and airtime on dozens of talk shows. Schwartz, after all, seemed perfectly legitimate. She is the president of Catalyst, an organization that has been advising corporations on women's careers since 1962. She had published her controversial claims in no less a spot than the *Harvard Business Review* ("Management Women and the New Facts of Life," January–February 1989). And her intentions, as she put it in a later op-ed piece, seemed thoroughly benign: "to urge employers to create policies that help mothers balance career and family responsibilities."

Moreover, Schwartz's argument seemed to confirm what everybody already knew. Women haven't been climbing up the corporate ladder as fast as might once have been expected, and women with children are still, on average, groping around the bottom rungs. Only about 40 percent of top female executives have children, compared to 95 percent of their male peers. There have been dozens of articles about female dropouts: women who slink off the fast track, at age 30-something, to bear a strategically timed baby or two. In fact, the "mommy track"—mean-

ing a lower-pressure, flexible, or part-time approach to work—was neither a term Schwartz used nor her invention. It was already, in an anecdotal sort of way, a well-worn issue.

Most of the controversy focused on Schwartz's wildly anachronistic "solution." Corporate employers, she advised, should distinguish between two categories of women: "career-primary" women, who won't interrupt their careers for children and hence belong on the fast track with the men, and "career-and-family" women, who should be shunted directly to the mommy track. Schwartz had no answers for the obvious questions: How is the employer supposed to sort the potential "breeders" from the strivers? Would such distinction even be legal? What about *fathers*? But in a sense, the damage had already been done. A respected feminist, writing in a respected journal, had made a case that most women can't pull their weight in the corporate world, and should be paid accordingly.

Few people, though, actually read Schwartz's article. The first surprise is that it contains *no* evidence to support her principle claim, that "the cost of employing women in management is greater than the cost of employing men." Schwartz offers no data, no documentation at all—except for two unpublished studies by two *anonymous* corporations. Do these studies really support her claim? Were they methodologically sound? Do they even exist? There is no way to know.

Few media reports of the "mommy track" article bothered to mention the peculiar nature of Schwartz's "evidence." We, however, were moved to call the *Harvard Business Review* and inquire whether the article was representative of its normal editorial standard. Timothy Blodgett, the executive editor, defended the article as "an expression of opinion and judgment." When we suggested that such potentially damaging "opinions" might need a bit of bolstering, he responded by defending Schwartz: "She speaks with a tone of authority. That comes through."

From *Ms. Magazine*, July/August 1989, pp. 56–58. Reprinted with permission.

(The conversation went downhill from there, with Blodgett stating sarcastically, "I'm sure your article in *Ms.* will be *very* objective." Couldn't fall much lower than the *Harvard Business Review,* we assured him.)

Are managerial women more costly to employ than men? As far as we could determine—with the help of the Business and Professional Women's Foundation and Women's Equity Action League—there is no *published* data on this point. A 1987 government study did show female managerial employees spending less time with each employer than males (5 years compared to 6.8 years), but there is no way of knowing what causes this turnover or what costs it incurs. And despite pregnancy, and despite women's generally greater responsibility for child-raising, they use up on the average only 5.1 sick days per year, compared to 4.9 for men.

The second surprise, given Schwartz's feminist credentials, is that the article is riddled with ancient sexist assumptions—for example, about the possibility of a more androgynous approach to child-raising *and* work. She starts with the unobjectionable statement that "maternity is biological rather than cultural." The same thing, after all, could be said of paternity. But a moment later, we find her defining maternity as ". . . a continuum that begins with an awareness of the ticking of the biological clock, proceeds to the anticipation of motherhood, includes pregnancy, childbirth, physical recuperation, psychological adjustment, and continues on to nursing, bonding, and child-rearing."

Now, pregnancy, childbirth, and nursing do qualify as biological processes. But slipping child-rearing into the list, as if changing diapers and picking up socks were hormonally programmed activities, is an old masculinist trick. Child-raising is a *social* undertaking, which may involve nannies, aunts, grandparents, day-care workers, or, of course, *fathers.*

Equally strange for a "feminist" article is Schwartz's implicit assumption that employment, in the case of married women, is strictly optional, or at least that *mothers* don't need to be top-flight earners. The "career-and-family woman," she tells us, is "willing" and "satisfied" to forgo promotions and "stay at the middle level." What about the single mother, or the wife

of a low-paid male? But Schwartz's out-of-date—and class-bound—assumption that every woman is supported by a male breadwinner fits in with her apparent nostalgia for the era of the feminine mystique. "Ironically," she writes, "although the feminist movement was an expression of women's quest for freedom from their home-based lives, *most women were remarkably free already* [emphasis added]."

But perhaps the oddest thing about the "mommy track" article—even as an "expression of opinion and judgment"—is that it is full of what we might charitably call ambivalence or, more bluntly, self-contradictions. Take the matter of the "glass ceiling," which symbolized all the barriers, both subtle and overt, that corporate women keep banging their heads against. At the outset, Schwartz dismisses the glass ceiling as a "misleading metaphor." Sexism, in short, is not the problem.

Nevertheless, within a few pages, she is describing the glass ceiling (not by that phrase, of course) like a veteran. "Male corporate culture," she tells us, sees both the career-primary and the career-and-family woman as "unacceptable." The woman with family responsibilities is likely to be seen as lacking commitment to the organization, while the woman who *is* fully committed to the organization is likely to be seen as "abrasive and unfeminine." She goes on to cite the corporate male's "confusion, competitiveness," and his "stereotypical language and sexist . . . behavior," concluding that "with notable exceptions, men are still more comfortable with other men."

And we're supposed to blame *women* for their lack of progress in the corporate world?

Even on her premier point, that women are more costly to employ, Schwartz loops around and rebuts herself. Near the end of her article, she urges corporations to conduct their own studies of the costs of employing women—the two anonymous studies were apparently not definitive after all—and asserts confidently ("of course I believe") that the benefits will end up outweighing the costs. In a more recent *New York Times* article, she puts it even more baldly: "The costs of employing women pale beside the payoffs."

Could it be that both Felice Schwartz and the

editors of the *Harvard Business Review* are ignorant of that most basic financial management concept, the cost-benefit analysis? If the "payoffs" outweigh the costs of employing women—runny noses and maternity leaves included—then the net cost may indeed be *lower* than the cost of employing men.

In sum, the notorious "mommy track" article is a tortured muddle of feminist perceptions and sexist assumptions, good intentions and dangerous suggestions—unsupported by any acceptable evidence at all. It should never have been taken seriously, not by the media and not by the nation's most prestigious academic business publication. The fact that it was suggests that something serious *is* afoot: a backlash against America's high-status, better paid women, and potentially against all women workers.

We should have seen it coming. For the past 15 years upwardly mobile, managerial women have done everything possible to fit into an often hostile corporate world. They dressed up as nonthreatening corporate clones. They put in 70-hour workweeks; and of course, they postponed childbearing. Thanks in part to their commitment to the work world, the birthrate dropped by 16 percent since 1970. But now many of these women are ready to start families. This should hardly be surprising; after all, 90 percent of American women do become mothers.

But while corporate women were busily making adjustments and concessions, the larger corporate world was not. The "fast track," with its macho camaraderie and toxic work load, remains the only track to success. As a result, success is indeed usually incompatible with motherhood—as well as with any engaged and active form of fatherhood. The corporate culture strongly discourages *men* from taking parental leave even if offered. And how many families can afford to have both earners on the mommy track?

Today there's an additional factor on the scene—the corporate women who *have* made it. Many of them are reliable advocates for the supports that working parents need. But you don't have to hang out with the skirted-suit crowd for long to discover that others of them are impatient with, and sometimes even actively resentful of, younger women who are trying to combine career and family. Recall that 60 percent of top female executives are themselves childless. Others are of the "if I did it, so can you" school of thought. Felice Schwartz may herself belong in this unsisterly category. In a telling anecdote in her original article, she describes her own problems with an executive employee seeking maternity leave, and the "somewhat awkward conversations" that ensued.

Sooner or later, corporations will have to yield to the pressure for paid parental leave, flextime, and child care, if only because they've become dependent on female talent. The danger is that employers—no doubt quoting Felice Schwartz for legitimation—will insist that the price for such options be reduced pay and withheld promotions, i.e., consignment to the mommy track. Such a policy would place a penalty on parenthood, and the ultimate victims—especially if the policy trickles down to the already low-paid female majority—will of course be children.

Bumping women—or just fertile women, or married women, or whomever—off the fast track may sound smart to cost-conscious CEOs, but eventually it is the corporate culture itself that needs to slow down to a human pace. No one, male or female, works at peak productivity for 70 hours a week, year after year, without sabbaticals or leaves. Think of it this way. If the price of success were exposure to a toxic chemical, would we argue that only women should be protected? Work loads that are incompatible with family life are themselves a kind of toxin—to men as well as women, and ultimately to businesses as well as families.

4. THE AWFUL QUANDARY OF WORKING MOTHERS

ARLIE HOCHSCHILD and ANN MACHUNG

REFLECTIONS FOR LABOR DAY

She is not the same woman in each magazine advertisement, but she is the same idea. She has that working-mother look as she strides forward, briefcase in one hand, smiling child in the other. Literally and figuratively, she is moving ahead. Her hair, if long, tosses behind her; if it is short, it sweeps back at the sides, suggesting mobility and progress. There is nothing shy or passive about her. She is confident, active, "liberated." She wears a dark tailored suit, but with a silk bow or colorful frill that says, "I'm really feminine underneath."

She has made it in a man's world without sacrificing her femininity. And she has done this on her own. By some personal miracle, this image suggests, she has managed to combine what 150 years of industrialization have split wide apart—child and job, frill and suit, female culture and male.

When I showed a photograph of a supermom like this to the working mothers I talked to in the course of researching my book on their lot, many responded with an outright laugh. One daycare worker and mother of two, ages 3 and 5, threw back her head: "Ha! They've got to be kidding about her. Look at me, hair a mess, nails jagged, 20 pounds overweight. Mornings, I'm getting my kids dressed, the dog fed, the lunches made, the shopping list done. That lady's got a maid."

Even working mothers who did have maids couldn't imagine combining work and family in such a carefree way. "Do you know what a baby *does* to your life, the 2 o'clock feedings, the 4 o'clock feedings?" Another mother of two said:

"They don't show it, but she's whistling"—she imitated a whistling woman, eyes to the sky—"so she can't hear the din." They envied the apparent ease of the woman with the flying hair, but she didn't remind them of anyone they knew.

The women I interviewed—lawyers, corporate executives, word processors, garment pattern cutters, daycare workers—and most of their husbands, too, felt differently about some issues: how right it is for a mother of young children to work a full-time job, or how much a husband should be responsible for the home. But they all agreed that it was hard to work two full-time jobs and raise young children.

How well do couples do it? The more women work outside the home, the more central this question. The number of women in paid work has risen steadily since before the turn of the century, but since 1950 the rise has been staggering. In 1950, 30 percent of American women were in the labor force; in 1986, it was 55 percent. In 1950, 28 percent of married women with children between 6 and 17 worked outside the home; in 1986, it had risen to 68 percent. In 1950, 23 percent of married women with children under 6 worked. By 1986, it had grown to 54 percent. We don't know how many women with children under the age of 1 worked outside the home in 1950; it was so rare that the Bureau of Labor kept no statistics on it. Today half of such women do. Two-thirds of all mothers are now in the labor force; in fact, more mothers have paid jobs (or are actively looking for one) than nonmothers. Because of this change in women, two-job families now make up 58 percent of all married couples with children.

Since an increasing number of working women have small children, we might expect an increase in part-time work. But actually, 67 percent of the mothers who work have full-time jobs—that is, 35 hours or more weekly. That proportion is what it was in 1959.

If more mothers of young children are stepping into full-time jobs outside the home, and if most couples can't afford household help, how much more are fathers doing at home? As I began exploring this question I found many studies on the hours working men and women devote to housework and childcare.

For example, one national random sample of 1,243 working parents in 45 American cities, conducted in 1965–66 by Alexander Szalai and his co-workers, found that working women averaged three hours a day of housework while men averaged 17 minutes; women spent 50 minutes a day of time exclusively with their children; men spent 12 minutes. On the other side of the coin, working fathers watched television an hour longer than their working wives, and slept a half hour longer each night. A comparison of this American sample with 11 other industrial countries in Eastern and Western Europe revealed the same difference between working women and working men in those countries as well.

In a 1983 study of white middle-class families in greater Boston, Grace Baruch and R. C. Barnett found that working men married to working women spent only three-quarters of an hour longer each week with their kindergarten-aged children than did men married to housewives.

Szalai's landmark study documented the now familiar but still alarming story of the working woman's "double day," but it left me wondering how men and women actually felt about all this. He and his co-workers studied how people used time, but not, say, how a father felt about his 12 minutes with his child, or how his wife felt about it. Szalai's study revealed the visible surface of what I discovered to be a set of deeply emotional issues: What should a man and woman contribute to the family? How appreciated does each feel? How does each respond to subtle changes in the balance of marital power? How does each develop an unconscious "gender strategy" for coping with the work at home, with marriage, and, indeed, with life itself? These were the underlying issues.

But I began with the measurable issue of time. Adding together the time it takes to do a paid job and to do housework and childcare, I averaged estimates from the major studies on time use done in the 1960s and 1970s, and discovered that women worked roughly 15 hours longer each week than men. Over a year, they work an *extra month of 24-hour days a year*. Over a dozen years, it was an extra year of 24-hour days. Most women without children spend much more time than men on housework; with children, they devote more time to both housework and child care. Just as there is a wage gap between men and women in the workplace, there is a "leisure gap" between them at home. Most women work one shift at the office or factory and a "second shift" at home.

Each marriage bears the footprints of economic and cultural trends which originate far outside marriage. A rise in inflation which erodes the earning power of the male wage, an expanding service sector which opens up jobs for women, new cultural images—like the woman with the flying hair—that make the working mother seem exciting, all these changes do not simply go on around marriage. They occur within marriage, and transform it. Problems between husbands and wives, problems which seem "individual" and "marital," are often individual experiences of powerful economic and cultural shock waves that are not caused by one person or two. Quarrels that erupt result mainly from a friction between fast-changing women and slower-changing men, rates of change which themselves result from the different rates at which the industrial economy has drawn men and women into itself.

There is a "his" and "hers" to the economic development of the United States. In the latter part of the 19th century, it was mainly men who were drawn off the farm into paid, industrial work and who changed their way of life and their identity. At that point in history, men became more different from their fathers than women became from their mothers. Today the economic arrow points at women; it is women who are being drawn into wage work and women who are undergoing changes in their way of life and identity. Women are departing more from their mothers' and grandmothers' way of life, men are doing so less.

Both the earlier entrance of men into the industrial economy and the later entrance of women have influenced the relations *between* men and women, especially their relations within marriage. The former increase in the number of men in industrial work tended to increase the power of men, and the present growth in the number of women in such work has somewhat increased the power of women. On the whole, the entrance of men into industrial work did not destabilize the family whereas *in the absence of other changes,* the rise in female employment has gone with the rise in divorce.

Beneath the image of the woman with the flying hair, there has been a real change in women without much change in anything else.

The exodus of women into the economy has not been accompanied by a cultural understanding of marriage and work that would make this transition smooth. The workforce has changed. Women have changed. But most workplaces have remained inflexible in the face of the family demands of their workers. And at home, most men have yet to really adapt to the changes in women. This strain between the change in women and the absence of change in much else leads me to speak of a "stalled revolution."

Brought to America by the tradition of the European Enlightenment, the belief in human progress easily fit the open American frontier, the expanding national and international economy, and the movements for racial and gender equality. Like most Americans over at least two centuries, most of the men and women I interviewed for this study said they believed "things were getting better." They said they believed men "are doing more at home than before." In small measure, this is true.

But the young do not promise to usher in a new era. Corporations have done little to accommodate the needs of working parents, and the government has done little to prod them. The nuclear family is still the overwhelming choice as a setting in which to rear children. Yet we have not invented the outside supports the nuclear family will need to do this job well. Our revolution is in danger of staying stalled.

Certainly this is what has occurred in the Soviet Union, the other major industrial society to draw a majority of its childbearing women into the labor force. Since industrialization, Soviet women have worked outside the home and done the lion's share of the second shift, too. "You work?" the Soviet joke goes. "You're liberated."

A stalled revolution has been mistaken for the whole revolution. And some commentators in the USSR argue that there, too, the extra burden on working mothers is behind the rising rate of divorce.

As more women enter the labor force, will the divorce rate rise in China? In Japan? In India? In Australia? Cultures differ, but this fundamental problem is the same.

Can we do better than this? The answer depends on how we make history happen. Just as individuals have gender strategies, so do governments, corporations, schools, factories and men's clubs. How a nation organizes its work force and daycare centers, how its schools train the young, reflects the work and family roles it envisions for each sex.

The Reagan government said it was "pro-family," and confused being "pro-family" with being against women's work outside the home. In an age in which over 70 percent of wives and mothers work outside the home, and in which the rate is still climbing, the Reagan administration's Panel on the Family only offered as its pro-family policy a package of measures against crime, drugs and welfare. In the name of "protecting" the family, the Republicans proposed to legalize school prayer and eliminate family planning services. They did nothing to help parents integrate work and family life. And we have to ask whether when marriages end due to the strains of this life, it is pro-family or anti-family to make life in two-job families so very hard? As working women become an interest group, a voting bloc, and a swing vote in elections, the issue of policies to ease life in two-job families is likely to become a serious issue of public policy in years ahead—if they can envision a solution.

We really need, as Frank Furstenberg has suggested, a Marshall Plan for the Family. It would look to other progressive industrial nations for a model of what could be done. In Sweden, for example, upon the birth of a child, every working couple is entitled to 12 months of paid parental leave, nine months at 90 percent of the person's salary plus an additional three months at about $300 a month. The mother and father are free to divide this year off between them as they wish. Any working parent of a child under 8 has the opportunity to work no more than six hours a day, at six hours' pay. Parental insurance offers parents money for work time lost to visit a child's school or care for a sick child. That's a "pro-family" policy.

An honestly pro-family policy in the United States would give tax breaks to companies that encourage "family leave" for new fathers, job sharing, part-time work and flex time. Through comparable worth, it would pull up wages in "women's" jobs. It would go beyond half-time work (which makes it sound like a person is only doing "half" of something else that is "whole") by instituting lower-hour, more flexible "family phases" for all regular jobs filled by parents of young children.

The government would give tax credits to developers who build affordable housing near places of work and shopping centers, with nearby meal-preparation facilities, as Delores Hayden describes in her book *Redesigning the American Dream*. It would create warm and creative daycare centers. If the best daycare comes from elderly neighbors, students, grandparents, they could be paid to care for children. Traveling vans for daycare enrichment could roam the neighborhoods as the ice-cream man did in my childhood.

In these ways, the American government could create a "safer environment" for the two-job family. It could draw men into children's lives, reduce the number of children in "self-care," and make marriages happier. These reforms could even improve the lives of children whose parents divorce, because research has shown that the more involved fathers are with their children *before* divorce, the more involved they are with them *afterwards*. If the government encouraged corporations to consider the long-range interests of workers and their families, they would save on long-range costs due to higher incidence of absenteeism, turnover, juvenile delinquency, mental illness, and welfare support for single mothers.

These are the real pro-family reforms. If they seem "utopian" today, we should remember that in the past, the eight-hour day, the abolition of child labor, and the vote for women once seemed utopian too. Among top-rated employers listed in *The Hundred Best Companies to Work For in America*, many offer country-club membership, first-class air travel, and million-dollar fitness centers. Only a handful offer job sharing, flex time, or part-time work. Not one provides on-site daycare and only three offer childcare deductions—Control Data, Polaroid, and Honeywell are exceptions. In his book *Megatrends*, John Naisbitt reports that 83 percent of corporate executives believed that more men feel the need to share the responsibilities of parenting; yet only 9 percent of corporations offer paternity leave.

Public strategies are linked to private ones. Economic and cultural trends bear on marital tensions in ways it would be useful for families to understand, and we need to apply an interpretation of marriage that highlights the links between the two. When I talked with Nancy Holt about working two jobs and raising a child at this period in history, I talked about "the uneven rate of change," about the greater difference between her life and her mother's than that between Evan's and his father's. We discussed the differences between her gender ideology and Evan's. We explored the cautionary tales that might be holding each version of manhood and womanhood in place. I pointed out her strategies—a sharing showdown, cutting back at work—and I named Evan's—resistance. We discussed how Nancy's resentment at Evan's refusal to share the second shift might have emerged in how she handled Joey. We explored how the give and take of credit for each partner's contributions to the second shift created imbalances in their marital economy of gratitude. The questions I asked the Holts are only a start in exploring how family life is situated in a wider circle of influence; such questions begin what for each couple would have to be a long, careful look in the cultural mirror.

The happiest two-job marriages I saw were between men and women who did not load the former role of the housewife-mother onto the woman, and did not devalue it as one would a bygone "peasant" way of life. They shared that role between them. What couples called "good communication" often meant that they were good at saying thanks for one tiny form or another of taking care of the family. Making it to the school play, helping a child read, cooking dinner in good spirit, remembering the grocery list, taking responsibility for the "upstairs." These were the silver and gold of the marital exchange. Up until now, the woman married to the "new man" has been one of the lucky few. But as the government and society shape a new gender strategy, as the young learn from example, many more women and men will be able to enjoy the leisurely bodily rhythms and freer laughter that arise when family life is family life and not a second shift.

5. MOTHERS IN CAREERS

FELICE N. SCHWARTZ

BUSINESS MAKES ADJUSTMENTS

The cost of employing women in management is greater than the cost of employing men. This is a jarring statement, partly because it is true, but mostly because it is something people are reluctant to talk about. A new study by one multinational corporation shows that the rate of turnover in management positions is 2½ times higher among top-performing women than it is among men. A large producer of consumer goods reports that one half of the women who take maternity leave return to their jobs late or not at all. And we know that women also have a greater tendency to plateau or to interrupt their careers in ways that limit their growth and development. But we have become so sensitive to charges of sexism and so afraid of confrontation, even litigation, that we rarely say what we know to be true. Unfortunately, our bottled-up awareness leaks out in misleading metaphors ("glass ceiling" is one notable example), veiled hostility, lowered expectations, distrust, and reluctant adherence to Equal Employment Opportunity requirements.

From "Management Women and the New Facts of Life," by Felice N. Schwartz, *Harvard Business Review,* January–February 1989, pp. 65–76. Reprinted with permission. Copyright © 1989 by the President and Fellows of Harvard College; all rights reserved.

Ms. Schwartz is president of Catalyst, an organization that advises businesses on women's career development.

Career interruptions, plateauing, and turnover are expensive. The money corporations invest in recruitment, training, and development is less likely to produce top executives among women than among men, and the invaluable company experience that developing executives acquire at every level as they move up through management ranks is more often lost.

The studies just mentioned are only the first of many, I'm quite sure. Demographic realities are going to force corporations all across the country to analyze the cost of employing women in managerial positions, and what they will discover is that women cost more.

But here is another startling truth: The greater cost of employing women is not a function of inescapable gender differences. Women *are* different from men, but what increases their cost to the corporation is principally the clash of their perceptions, attitudes, and behavior with those of men, which is to say, with the policies and practices of male-led corporations.

It is terribly important that employers draw the right conclusions from the studies now being done. The studies will be useless—or worse, harmful—if all they teach us is that women are expensive to employ. What we need to learn is how to reduce that expense, how to stop throwing away the investments we make in talented women, how to become more responsive to the needs of the women that corporations *must* employ if they are to have the best and the brightest of all those now entering the work force.

The gender differences relevant to business fall into two categories: those related to maternity and those related to the differing traditions and expectations of the sexes. Maternity is biological rather than cultural. We can't alter it, but we can dramatically reduce its impact on the workplace and in many cases eliminate its negative effect on employee development. We can accomplish this by addressing the second set of differences, those between male and female socialization. Today, these differences exaggerate the real costs of maternity and can turn a relatively slight disruption in work schedule into a serious business problem and a career derailment for individual women. If we are to overcome the cost differential between male and female employees, we need to address the issues that arise when female socialization meets the male corporate culture and masculine rules of career development—issues of behavior and style, of expectation, of stereotypes and preconceptions, of sexual tension and harassment, of female mentoring, lateral mobility, relocation, compensation, and early identification of top performers.

The one immutable, enduring difference between men and women is maternity. Maternity is not simply childbirth but a continuum that begins with an awareness of the ticking of the biological clock, proceeds to the anticipation of motherhood, includes pregnancy, childbirth, physical recuperation, psychological adjustment, and continues on to nursing, bonding, and child rearing. Not all women choose to become mothers, of course, and among those who do, the process varies from case to case depending on the health of the mother and baby, the values of the parents, and the availability, cost, and quality of child care.

In past centuries, the biological fact of maternity shaped the traditional roles of the sexes. Women performed the home-centered functions that related to the bearing and nurturing of children. Men did the work that required great physical strength. Over time, however, family size contracted, the community assumed greater responsibility for the care and education of children, packaged foods and household technology reduced the work load in the home, and technology eliminated much of the need for muscle power at the workplace. Today, in the developed world, the only role still uniquely gender related

is childbearing. Yet men and women are still socialized to perform their traditional roles.

Men and women may or may not have some innate psychological disposition toward these traditional roles—men to be aggressive, competitive, self-reliant, risk taking; women to be supportive, nurturing, intuitive, sensitive, communicative—but certainly both men and women are capable of the full range of behavior. Indeed, the male and female roles have already begun to expand and merge. In the decades ahead, as the socialization of boys and girls and the experience and expectations of young men and women grow steadily more androgynous, the differences in workplace behavior will continue to fade. At the moment, however, we are still plagued by disparities in perception and behavior that make the integration of men and women in the workplace unnecessarily difficult and expensive.

Let me illustrate with a few broadbrush generalizations. Of course, these are only stereotypes, but I think they help to exemplify the kinds of preconception that can muddy the corporate waters.

Men continue to perceive women as the rearers of their children, so they find it understandable, indeed appropriate, that women should renounce their careers to raise families. Edmund Pratt, CEO of Pfizer, once asked me in all sincerity, "Why would any woman choose to be a chief financial officer rather than a full-time mother?" By condoning and taking pleasure in women's traditional behavior, men reinforce it. Not only do they see parenting as fundamentally female, they see a career as fundamentally male—either an unbroken series of promotions and advancements toward CEOdom or stagnation and disappointment. This attitude serves to legitimize a woman's choice to extend maternity leave and even, for those who can afford it, to leave employment altogether for several years. By the same token, men who might want to take a leave after the birth of a child know that management will see such behavior as a lack of career commitment, even when company policy permits parental leave for men.

Women also bring counterproductive expectations and perceptions to the workplace. Ironically, although the feminist movement was an expression of women's quest for freedom from their home-based lives, most women were remarkably free already. They had many responsibilities, but they were autonomous and could be entrepreneurial in how and when they carried them out. And once their children grew up and left home, they were essentially free to do what they wanted with their lives. Women's traditional role also included freedom from responsibility for the financial support of their families. Many of us were socialized from girlhood to expect our husbands to take care of us, while our brothers were socialized from an equally early age to complete their educations, pursue careers, climb the ladder of success, and provide dependable financial support for their families. To the extent that this tradition of freedom lingers subliminally, women tend to bring to their employment a sense that they can choose to change jobs or careers at will, take time off, or reduce their hours.

Finally, women's traditional role encouraged particular attention to the quality and substance of what they did, specifically to the physical, psychological, and intellectual development of their children. This traditional focus may explain women's continuing tendency to search for more than monetary reward—intrinsic significance, social importance, meaning—in what they do. This too makes them more likely than men to leave the corporation in search of other values.

The misleading metaphor of the glass ceiling suggests an invisible barrier constructed by corporate leaders to impede the upward mobility of women beyond the middle levels. A more appropriate metaphor, I believe, is the kind of cross-sectional diagram used in geology. The barriers to women's leadership occur when potentially counterproductive layers of influence on women—maternity, tradition, socialization—meet management strata pervaded by the largely unconscious preconceptions, stereotypes, and expectations of men. Such interfaces do not exist for men and tend to be impermeable for women.

One result of these gender differences has been to convince some executives that women are simply not suited to top management. Other executives feel helpless. If they see even a few of their valued female employees fail to return to

work from maternity leave on schedule or see one of their most promising women plateau in her career after the birth of a child, they begin to fear there is nothing they can do to infuse women with new energy and enthusiasm and persuade them to stay. At the same time, they know there is nothing they can do to stem the tide of women into management ranks.

Another result is to place every working woman on a continuum that runs from total dedication to career at one end to a balance between career and family at the other. What women discover is that the male corporate culture sees both extremes as unacceptable. Women who want the flexibility to balance their families and their careers are not adequately committed to the organization. Women who perform as aggressively and competitively as men are abrasive and unfeminine. But the fact is, business needs all the talented women it can get. Moreover, as I will explain, the women I call career-primary and those I call career-and-family each have particular value to the corporation.

MOVING TO A SELLER'S MARKET

Women in the corporation are about to move from a buyer's to a seller's market. The sudden, startling recognition that 80% of new entrants in the work force over the next decade will be women, minorities, and immigrants has stimulated a mushrooming incentive to "value diversity."

Women are no longer simply an enticing pool of occasional creative talent, a thorn in the side of the EEO officer, or a source of frustration to corporate leaders truly puzzled by the slowness of their upward trickle into executive positions. A real demographic change is taking place. The era of sudden population growth of the 1950s and 1960s is over. The birth rate has dropped about 40%, from a high of 25.3 live births per 1,000 population in 1957, at the peak of the baby boom, to a stable low of a little more than 15 per 1,000 over the last 16 years, and there is no indication of a return to a higher rate. The tidal wave of baby boomers that swelled the recruitment pool to overflowing seems to have been a one-time phenomenon. For 20 years, employers had the pick of a very large crop and were able to choose males almost exclusively for the executive track. But if future population remains fairly stable while the economy continues to expand, and if the new information society simultaneously creates a greater need for creative, educated managers, then the gap between supply and demand will grow dramatically and, with it, the competition for managerial talent.

The decrease in numbers has even greater implications if we look at the traditional source of corporate recruitment for leadership positions—white males from the top 10% of the country's best universities. Over the past decade, the increase in the number of women graduating from leading universities has been much greater than the increase in the total number of graduates, and these women are well represented in the top 10% of their classes.

The trend extends into business and professional programs as well. In the old days, virtually all MBAs were male. I remember addressing a meeting at the Harvard Business School as recently as the mid-1970s and looking out at a sea of exclusively male faces. Today, about 25% of that audience would be women. The pool of male MBAs from which corporations have traditionally drawn their leaders has shrunk significantly.

Of course, this reduction does not have to mean a shortage of talent. The top 10% is at least as smart as it always was—smarter, probably, since it's now drawn from a broader segment of the population. But it now consists increasingly of women. Companies that are determined to recruit the same number of men as before will have to dig much deeper into the male pool, while their competitors will have the opportunity to pick the best people from both the male and female graduates.

TWO TYPES OF CAREER WOMEN

Under these circumstances, there is no question that the management ranks of business will include increasing numbers of women. There remains, however, the question of how these women will succeed—how long they will stay,

how high they will climb, how completely they will fulfill their promise and potential, and what kind of return the corporation will realize on its investment in their training and development.

There is ample business reason for finding ways to make sure that as many of these women as possible will succeed. The first step in this process is to recognize that women are not all alike. Like men, they are individuals with differing talents, priorities, and motivations. For the sake of simplicity, let me focus on the two women I referred to earlier, on what I call the career-primary woman and the career-and-family woman.

Like many men, some women put their careers first. They are ready to make the same trade-offs traditionally made by the men who seek leadership positions. They make a career decision to put in extra hours, to make sacrifices in their personal lives, to make the most of every opportunity for professional development. For women, of course, this decision also requires that they remain single or at least childless or, if they do have children, that they be satisfied to have others raise them. Some 90% of executive men but only 35% of executive women have children by the age of 40. The *automatic* association of all women with babies is clearly unjustified.

The secret to dealing with such women is to recognize them early, accept them, and clear artificial barriers from their path to the top. After all, the best of these women are among the best managerial talent you will ever see. And career-primary women have another important value to the company that men and other women lack. They can act as role models and mentors to younger women who put their careers first. Since upwardly mobile career-primary women still have few role models to motivate and inspire them, a company with women in its top echelon has a significant advantage in the competition for executive talent.

Men at the top of the organization—most of them over 55, with wives who tend to be traditional—often find career women "masculine" and difficult to accept as colleagues. Such men miss the point, which is not that these women are just like men but that they are just like the *best* men in the organization. And there is such a shortage of the best people that gender cannot be allowed to matter. It is clearly counterproductive to disparage in a woman with executive talent the very qualities that are most critical to the business and that might carry a man to the CEO's office.

Clearing a path to the top for career-primary women has four requirements:

1. Identify them early.
2. Give them the same opportunity you give to talented men to grow and develop and contribute to company profitability. Give them client and customer responsibility. Expect them to travel and relocate, to make the same commitment to the company as men aspiring to leadership positions.
3. Accept them as valued members of your management team. Include them in every kind of communication. Listen to them.
4. Recognize that the business environment is more difficult and stressful for them than for their male peers. They are always a minority, often the only woman. The male perception of talented, ambitious women is at best ambivalent, a mixture of admiration, resentment, confusion, competitiveness, attraction, skepticism, anxiety, pride, and animosity. Women can never feel secure about how they should dress and act, whether they should speak out or grin and bear it when they encounter discrimination, stereotyping, sexual harassment, and paternalism. Social interaction and travel with male colleagues and with male clients can be charged. As they move up, the normal increase in pressure and responsibility is compounded for women because they are women.

Stereotypical language and sexist day-to-day behavior do take their toll on women's career development. Few male executives realize how common it is to call women by their first names while men in the same group are greeted with surnames, how frequently female executives are assumed by men to be secretaries, how often women are excluded from all-male social events where business is being transacted. With notable exceptions, men are still generally more comfortable with other men, and as a result women miss many of the career and business opportunities that arise over lunch, on the golf course, or in the locker room.

The majority of women, however, are what I call career-and-family women, women who want to pursue serious careers while participating actively in the rearing of children. These women are a precious resource that has yet to be mined. Many of them are talented and creative. Most of them are willing to trade some career growth and compensation for freedom from the constant pressure to work long hours and weekends.

Most companies today are ambivalent at best about the career-and-family women in their management ranks. They would prefer that all employees were willing to give their all to the company. They believe it is in their best interests for all managers to compete for the top positions so the company will have the largest possible pool from which to draw its leaders.

"If you have both talent and motivation," many employers seem to say, "we want to move you up. If you haven't got that motivation, if you want less pressure and greater flexibility, then you can leave and make room for a new generation." These companies lose on two counts. First, they fail to amortize the investment they made in the early training and experience of management women who find themselves committed to family as well as to career. Second, they fail to recognize what these women could do for their middle management.

The ranks of middle managers are filled with people on their way up and people who have stalled. Many of them have simply reached their limits, achieved career growth commensurate with or exceeding their capabilities, and they cause problems because their performance is mediocre but they still want to move ahead. The career-and-family woman is willing to trade off the pressure and demands that go with promotion for the freedom to spend more time with her children. She's very smart, she's talented, she's committed to her career, and she's satisfied to stay at the middle level, at least during the early child-rearing years. Compare her with some of the people you have there now.

Consider a typical example, a woman who decides in college on a business career and enters management at age 22. For nine years, the company invests in her career as she gains experience and skills and steadily improves her performance. But at 31, just as the investment begins to pay off in earnest, she decides to have a baby. Can the company afford to let her go home, take another job, or go into business for herself? The common perception now is yes, the corporation can afford to lose her unless, after six or eight weeks or even three months of disability and maternity leave, she returns to work on a full-time schedule with the same vigor, commitment, and ambition that she showed before.

But what if she doesn't? What if she wants or needs to go on leave for six months or a year or, heaven forbid, five years? In this worst-case scenario, she works full-time from age 22 to 31 and from 36 to 65—a total of 38 years as opposed to the typical male's 43 years. That's not a huge difference. Moreover, my typical example is willing to work part-time while her children are young, if only her employer will give her the opportunity. There are two rewards for companies responsive to this need: higher retention of their best people and greatly improved performance and satisfaction in their middle management.

The high-performing career-and-family woman can be a major player in your company. She can give you a significant business advantage as the competition for able people escalates. Sometimes too, if you can hold on to her, she will switch gears in mid-life and reenter the competition for the top. The price you must pay to retain these women is threefold: you must plan for and manage maternity, you must provide the flexibility that will allow them to be maximally productive, and you must take an active role in helping to make family supports and high-quality, affordable child care available to all women.

The key to managing maternity is to recognize the value of high-performing women and the urgent need to retain them and keep them productive. The first step must be a genuine partnership between the woman and her boss. I know this partnership can seem difficult to forge. One of my own senior executives came to me recently to discuss plans for her maternity leave and subsequent return to work. She knew she wanted to come back. I wanted to make certain that she would. Still, we had a somewhat awkward con-

versation, because I knew that no woman can predict with certainty when she will be able to return to work or under what conditions. Physical problems can lengthen her leave. So can a demanding infant, a difficult family or personal adjustment, or problems with child care.

I still don't know when this valuable executive will be back on the job full-time, and her absence creates some genuine problems for our organization. But I do know that I can't simply replace her years of experience with a new recruit. Since our conversation, I also know that she wants to come back, and that she *will* come back—part-time at first—unless I make it impossible for her by, for example, setting an arbitrary date for her full-time return or resignation. In turn, she knows that the organization wants and needs her and, more to the point, that it will be responsive to her needs in terms of working hours and child care arrangements.

In having this kind of conversation it's important to ask concrete questions that will help to move the discussion from uncertainty and anxiety to some level of predictability. Questions can touch on everything from family income and energy level to child care arrangements and career commitment. Of course you want your star manager to return to work as soon as possible, but you want her to return permanently and productively. Her downtime on the job is a drain on her energies and a waste of your money.

THE NEED FOR BUSINESS FLEXIBILITY

For all the women who want to combine career and family—the women who want to participate actively in the rearing of their children and who also want to pursue their careers seriously—the key to retention is to provide the flexibility and family supports they need in order to function effectively.

Time spent in the office increases productivity if it is time well spent, but the fact that most women continue to take the primary responsibility for child care is a cause of distraction, diversion, anxiety, and absenteeism—to say nothing of the persistent guilt experienced by all working mothers. A great many women, perhaps most of all women who have always performed at the highest levels, are also frustrated by a sense that while their children are babies they cannot function at their best either at home or at work.

In its simplest form, flexibility is the freedom to take time off—a couple of hours, a day, a week—or to do some work at home and some at the office, an arrangement that communication technology makes increasingly feasible. At the complex end of the spectrum are alternative work schedules that permit the woman to work less than full-time and her employer to reap the benefits of her experience and, with careful planning, the top level of her ability.

Part-time employment is the single greatest inducement to getting women back on the job expeditiously and the provision women themselves most desire. A part-time return to work enables them to maintain responsibility for critical aspects of their jobs, keeps them in touch with the changes constantly occurring at the workplace and in the job itself, reduces stress and fatigue, often eliminates the need for paid maternity leave by permitting a return to the office as soon as disability leave is over, and, not least, can greatly enhance company loyalty. The part-time solution works particularly well when a work load can be reduced for one individual in a department or when a full-time job can be broken down by skill levels and apportioned to two individuals at different levels of skill and pay.

I believe, however, that shared employment is the most promising and will be the most widespread form of flexible scheduling in the future. It is feasible at every level of the corporation except at the pinnacle, for both the short and the long term. It involves two people taking responsibility for one job.

Two red lights flash on as soon as most executives hear the words "job sharing": continuity and client-customer contact. The answer to the continuity question is to place responsibility entirely on the two individuals sharing the job to discuss everything that transpires—thoroughly, daily, and on their own time. The answer to the problem of client-customer contact is yes, job sharing requires reeducation and a period of adjustment. But as both client and supervisor will quickly come to appreciate, two contacts means that the customer has continuous access to the

company's representative, without interruptions for vacation, travel, or sick leave. The two people holding the job can simply cover for each other, and the uninterrupted, full-time coverage they provide together can be a stipulation of their arrangement.

Flexibility is costly in numerous ways. It requires more supervisory time to coordinate and manage, more office space, and somewhat greater benefits costs (though these can be contained with flexible benefits plans, prorated benefits, and, in two-paycheck families, elimination of duplicate benefits). But the advantages of reduced turnover and the greater productivity that results from higher energy levels and greater focus can outweigh the costs.

A few hints:

- Provide flexibility selectively. I'm not suggesting private arrangements subject to the suspicion of favoritism but rather a policy that makes flexible work schedules available only to high performers.
- Make it clear that in most instances (but not all) the rates of advancement and pay will be appropriately lower for those who take time off or who work part-time than for those who work full-time. Most career-and-family women are entirely willing to make that trade-off.
- Discuss costs as well as benefits. Be willing to risk accusations of bias. Insist, for example, that half time is half of whatever time it takes to do the job, not merely half of 35 or 40 hours.

The woman who is eager to get home to her child has a powerful incentive to use her time effectively at the office and to carry with her reading and other work that can be done at home. The talented professional who wants to have it all can be a high performer by carefully ordering her priorities and focusing on objectives rather than on the legendary 15-hour day. By the time professional women have their first babies—at an average age of 31—they have already had nine years to work long hours at a desk, to travel, and to relocate. In the case of high performers, the need for flexibility coincides with what has gradually become the goal-oriented nature of responsibility.

Family supports—in addition to maternity leave and flexibility—include the provision of parental leave for men, support for two-career and single-parent families during relocation, and flexible benefits. But the primary ingredient is child care. The capacity of working mothers to function effectively and without interruption depends on the availability of good, affordable child care. Now that women make up almost half the work force and the growing percentage of managers, the decision to become involved in the personal lives of employees is no longer a philosophical question but a practical one. To make matters worse, the quality of child care has almost no relation to technology, inventiveness, or profitability but is more or less a pure function of the quality of child care personnel and the ratio of adults to children. These costs are irreducible. Only by joining hands with government and the public sector can corporations hope to create the vast quantity and variety of child care that their employees need.

Until quite recently, the response of corporations to women has been largely symbolic and cosmetic, motivated in large part by the will to avoid litigation and legal penalties. In some cases, companies were also moved by a genuine sense of fairness and a vague discomfort and frustration at the absence of women above the middle of the corporate pyramid. The actions they took were mostly quick, easy, and highly visible—child care information services, a three-month parental leave available to men as well as women, a woman appointed to the board of directors.

When I first began to discuss these issues 26 years ago, I was sometimes able to get an appointment with the assistant to the assistant in personnel, but it was only a courtesy. Over the past decade, I have met with the CEOs of many large corporations, and I've watched them become involved with ideas they had never previously thought much about. Until recently, however, the shelf life of that enhanced awareness was always short. Given pressing, short-term concerns, women were not a front-burner issue. In the past few months, I have seen yet another change. Some CEOs and top management groups now take the initiative. They call and ask us to show them how to shift gears from a respon-sive to a proactive approach to recruiting, developing, and retaining women.

I think this change is more probably a response to business needs—to concern for the quality of future profits and managerial talent—than to uneasiness about legal requirements, sympathy with the demands of women and minorities, or the desire to do what is right and fair. The nature of such business motivation varies. Some companies want to move women to higher positions as role models for those below them and as beacons for talented young recruits. Some want to achieve a favorable image with employees, customers, clients, and stockholders. These are all legitimate motives. But I think the companies that stand to gain most are motivated as well by a desire to capture competitive advantage in an era when talent and competence will be in increasingly short supply. These companies are now ready to stop being defensive about their experience with women and to ask incisive questions without preconceptions.

Even so, incredibly, I don't know of more than one or two companies that have looked into their own records to study the absolutely critical issue of maternity leave—how many women took it, when and whether they returned, and how this behavior correlated with their rank, tenure, age, and performance. The unique drawback to the employment of women is the physical reality of maternity and the particular socializing influence maternity has had. Yet to make women equal to men in the workplace we have chosen on the whole not to discuss this single most significant difference between them. Unless we do, we cannot evaluate the cost of recruiting, developing, and moving women up.

Now that interest is replacing indifference, there are four steps every company can take to examine its own experience with women:

1. Gather quantitative data on the company's experience with management-level women regarding turnover rates, occurrence of and return from maternity leave, and organizational level attained in relation to tenure and performance.

2. Correlate this data with factors such as age, marital status, and presence and age of chil-

dren, and attempt to identify and analyze why women respond the way they do.

3. Gather qualitative data on the experience of women in your company and on how women are perceived by both sexes.

4. Conduct a cost-benefit analysis of the return on your investment in high-performing women. Factor in the cost to the company of women's negative reactions to negative experience, as well as the probable cost of corrective measures and policies. If women's value to your company is greater than the cost to recruit, train, and develop them—and of course I believe it will be—then you will want to do everything you can to retain them.

We have come a tremendous distance since the days when the prevailing male wisdom saw women as lacking the kind of intelligence that would allow them to succeed in business. For decades, even women themselves have harbored an unspoken belief that they couldn't make it because they couldn't be just like men, and nothing else would do. But now that women have shown themselves the equal of men in every area of organizational activity, now that they have demonstrated that they can be stars in every field of endeavor, now we can all venture to examine the fact that women and men are different.

On balance, employing women is more costly than employing men. Women can acknowledge this fact today because they know that their value to employers exceeds the additional cost and because they know that changing attitudes can reduce the additional cost dramatically. Women in management are no longer an idiosyncrasy of the arts and education. They have always matched men in natural ability. Within a very few years, they will equal men in numbers as well in every area of economic activity.

The demographic motivation to recruit and develop women is compelling. But an older question remains: Is society better for the change? Women's exit from the home and entry into the work force has certainly created problems—an urgent need for good, affordable child care; troubling questions about the kind of parenting children need; the costs and difficulties of diversity in the workplace; the stress and fatigue of combining work and family responsibilities. Wouldn't we all be happier if we could turn back the clock to an age when men were in the workplace and women in the home, when male and female roles were clearly differentiated complementary?

Nostalgia, anxiety, and discouragement will urge many to say yes, but my answer is emphatically no. Two fundamental benefits that were unattainable in the past are now within our reach. For the individual, freedom of choice—in this case the freedom to choose career, family, or a combination of the two. For the corporation, access to the most gifted individuals in the country. These benefits are neither self-indulgent nor insubstantial. Freedom of choice and self-realization are too deeply American to be cast aside for some wistful vision of the past. And access to our most talented human resources is not a luxury in this age of explosive international competition but rather the barest minimum that prudence and national self-preservation require.

6. WOMEN AND WAGES

JUNE O'NEILL

A decade ago, a popular button worn by women's-rights activists bore the slogan "59 cents" (out of every dollar). The reference was to the most frequently cited measure of the wage gap, the ratio of women's to men's annual full-time earnings, a ratio that had remained fixed at around the 60-percent level for many years. Indeed, some observers claim to have traced the 60-percent ratio back to biblical times, citing the Lord's conversation with Moses in Chapter 27 of Leviticus in which he decreed—for purposes of tithing—that an adult woman should be valued at 30 shekels of silver compared to a man's 50 shekels.

In point of fact, the female-to-male wage ratio in the United States was only 46 percent in 1890. It had increased to 58 percent by 1939, but it did not go much above this level for the next four decades. The persistence of the 60-percent pay ratio at the end of the 1970s was particularly frustrating and puzzling because women's role in the economy had apparently undergone dramatic change in the post–World War II period. Women's participation in the workplace had soared, and the feminist movement had grown in size and influence. Moreover, equal-pay-and-employment legislation had been enacted in the 1960s, followed by more strenuous implementation of affirmative action in the 1970s. Yet the observed gender wage gap did not respond. At the close of the 1970s, advocacy groups were impatient with existing antidiscrimination measures. It was at this time that new and more radical measures were sought to increase women's earnings, for example, comparable-worth regulation of pay rates (which would have dramati-

cally limited the influence of the market and increased the role of the government in determining wages).

Starting in the early 1980s, however, women's earnings began to rise more rapidly than men's, and the gender gap narrowed. Between 1981 and 1989, the female-to-male earnings ratio increased from 59 to 68 percent, again measured in terms of annual full-time earnings. Earnings of females and males can be measured in other terms; the ratio is considerably higher than 68 percent when women and men of similar productivity are compared.

Why did the wage gap narrow in the 1980s and not before? A closer examination of the data shows that the recent gains were not really a sudden departure from the past. Basic changes in women's work-related skills had been occurring prior to the 1980s, but they were obscured by changes in the composition of the work force. As women with little work experience and lower levels of schooling shifted from home activities to market work, they joined employed women with considerable work experience and relatively high educational levels, a process that diluted the overall skill level of the expanding group of employed women. During the 1980s, however, the work experience, schooling, and training of employed women increased relative to men's; moreover, changes in market demand for different types of skills were generally more favorable to women than to men. But perhaps the most important factor in the 1980s and continuing today is that increasingly the female work force is composed of women who, from an early age, expect to be working from the time of leaving school until retirement, and who, like men, are making the kinds of schooling and occupational choices that enhance earnings later on.

This is not to say that discrimination played no role in inhibiting women's progress. Unquestionably, women were once restricted in their work choices. For example, before World War II

From *The American Enterprise*, November/December 1990, pp. 25–33. Copyright © 1991 by *The American Enterprise*. Distributed by The New York Times Special Features. Reprinted with permission.

June O'Neill is director of the Center for Study of Business and Government at Baruch College of the City University of New York.

many firms and public school systems maintained "marriage bars," policies that prohibited the hiring of married women or the retention of women after they married. Such restrictions and other less overt ones have been eliminated or considerably eased over the years. Although federal antidiscrimination legislation may have helped effect the change, that link is by no means clear. As Princeton economist Claudia D. Goldin has shown, economic contingencies, not legislation, led to the removal of marriage bars by the early 1950s. And the fact that the wage gap narrowed most rapidly during the years of the Reagan administration, when affirmative action was hardly a priority, should dispel any theories about a direct link between affirmative action and women's wages. However, the women's movement and the civil rights movement may have been important catalysts in the process of changing attitudes about women's rights to equal treatment in the workplace.

PATTERNS OF CHANGE ACROSS GENERATIONS

In seeking explanations for the differential in earnings between women and men, one can rule out many factors, such as family background and quality of schooling, that typically account for much of the gap in earnings between other (for example, racial and ethnic) groups. Women and men grow up in the same families, live in the same neighborhoods, and attend the same schools. Nonetheless, the skills that women and men acquire have differed significantly because of deeply rooted differences in the roles in the family assumed by men and women. Men have been expected to be the breadwinners, while women have been responsible for the care of home and children. In the past, these home responsibilities precluded market work after marriage, but over the years women have greatly expanded the extent of their paid work outside the home.

The way in which women's work participation has evolved from one generation to the next is depicted in Figure 1, which shows participation at different ages for eight cohorts of American women born ten years apart. It is clear that virtually all cohorts attained higher levels of market participation than the preceding cohort, despite fluctuations in the economy and changes in the age of marriage and in birthrates. Economic and demographic changes, however, have clearly left their stamp on the pattern and degree of change in each cohort's labor-market experience.

The difficulty in the past of combining marriage and children with market work is evident in the pattern of the earliest cohort shown (born 1886–1895), which reached its highest level of labor-force participation (37 percent) at ages 20–24 before many had married. The proportion working among married women in this cohort never went much beyond 10 percent at any stage in their life cycle. However, the depression of the 1930s is likely to have curtailed work opportunities among those who might have worked when their children were grown. And the marriage bars may have been a factor as well.

Starting weakly with the cohort born 1896–1905 and continuing more strongly in each subsequent cohort, a clear pattern develops of rising labor-force participation after age 25 and as the cohort ages. A low point in work participation is seen at the ages when women usually marry and when their children are still young, but when their children are grown, married women enter the labor market, and participation rates rise. The rising wages and expanding job opportunities during World War II and the postwar years undoubtedly provided strong incentives for married women to make these transitions to market work.

The cohorts born 1916–1925 and 1926–1935 include the high-fertility women who were the mothers of the baby-boom generation. During their childbearing years, their participation in market work was not substantially higher than that of earlier cohorts, but it rose to successively higher levels as they reached their late thirties and forties. Despite high (but declining) fertility, the cohort born 1936–1945 was more likely than earlier generations to remain in the labor force or to enter it during their childbearing ages, and they have moved into the labor force in record numbers as they reached their thirties and forties.

The two most-recent cohorts have broken still

more sharply with the past. Their labor-force participation was initially high at entry-level ages, and it has not taken the characteristic dip as they reached their late twenties, a reflection of delayed marriage, low fertility, and an increasing tendency for mothers of young children to work. In 1960, only 19 percent of married women with children under age six were in the labor force; by 1987, the proportion was 57 percent. Among wives whose children are in the 6–17-year age range, the proportion in the labor force is now 71 percent.

The life-cycle participation profiles in Figure 1 shows that the proportion of all women working increased from generation to generation; but to better understand the change in the wage gap, we need more information about the change in the skills and experience levels of the growing subset of women who work. Were the working women accumulating more years of work experience over their lifetimes, comparing one generation with the next? This cannot be read directly from Figure 1, but it can be inferred. The results

may seem counterintuitive. When the cohort profile rises steeply from age 30 to age 50, as it does for each of the four cohorts born 1906–1915 through 1936–1945, it is evident that a substantial proportion of those in the work force at ages 40 and 50 could not have worked for many years since the proportion working was so much lower at age 30. By contrast, the profile of the cohort born 1886–1895 is relatively flat; the proportion of women working is roughly the same at age 50 as at age 30. It is quite possible, therefore, that women from this early cohort who were at work at age 50 had accumulated as many or more years of work experience as their counterparts from later cohorts, although only a minority of women in the early cohort—largely single women—would have been in this situation.

One inference that might be drawn from a comparison of these cohort profiles is that, quite paradoxically, increases in the proportion of women working were not likely to be associated with significant increases in the lifetime work experience (years worked) of employed women

FIGURE 1

Labor force participation rates at different ages by birth cohort

Sources: U.S. Department of Labor, Bureau of Labor Statistics, *Handbook of Labor Statistics* and various releases for data referring to labor force rates in 1950 and later.

over much of the post–World War II period. This inference has been confirmed by recent studies that have estimated the number of years of work experience accumulated by working women, measured at different points in time over the century. These studies find little gain in cumulated years of work experience when 45-year-old working women in 1980 are compared with 45-year-old working women in 1950.

In sum, an important component of market skills is acquired through years of work experience, and work experience did not rise among the growing group of working women over much of the post–World War II period. It was also the case that the married women who entered the labor force at later stages in their lives had relatively lower schooling levels compared to men as well as to women who were already working. While the working women of 1950 had completed more years of schooling than men, by 1980 the advantage had shifted to men. Therefore, in terms of both schooling and work experience, the market skills of working women did not increase relative to those of men over the period 1950–1980, and as a consequence there was no reason for the gender gap in wages to narrow.

Black women are an important exception to the overall pattern; they acquired substantial work experience relative to white women as well as to men early in the post–World War II period. By 1967, black women workers age 40–44 had accumulated three more years (22 percent) of work experience than white women workers of the same age. Their education level also rose relatively rapidly during these years, although it remained behind that of white women. As a consequence of this increase in work-related skills, black women's earnings rose rapidly relative to the earnings of virtually any other group. . . . [T]he ratio of black women's earnings to black men's earnings increased steadily from 51 percent in 1939 to 70 percent in 1970, reaching 85 percent by 1989. Relative to white women's earnings, the earnings of black women rose from only 38 percent in 1939 to 82 percent in 1970 and have been 90 percent or more since the mid-1970s. (Although federal affirmative-action policies may have contributed to the surge in black women's earnings during the mid-1970s, it is not

likely to explain the substantial relative gains in black women's earnings in earlier periods and certainly not from 1939 to 1960.)

Black women make up only 11 percent of all women, hence, the trends observed for all women (all races) are essentially dominated by the trends of white women. It is among recent cohorts of white women that patterns of work participation have shown a marked change. White women have caught up with black women and have recently maintained high levels of participation through their twenties, thirties, and for the 1946–1955 cohort, into their forties.

Data tabulated from the Labor Department's National Longitudinal Surveys of Labor Market Experience confirm that the working women who reached ages 25–39 in the 1980s (all races combined) have accumulated significantly more work experience since leaving school than their counterparts born 10 to 15 years before them. Partly reflecting these rising experience levels, the ratio of women's earnings to men's began to rise during the 1970s among age groups in their twenties and thirties, and the trend accelerated during the 1980s. This is evident in Table 1, which shows the earnings ratios tabulated by age over the period 1960–1988. For the period 1980–1988, two kinds of earnings ratios are shown, one based on the annual income of full-time, year-round workers, and the other based on hourly earnings. Because women who work "full time" (35 hours a week or more) on average work 8–10 percent fewer hours a week than men who work full time, the hourly earnings ratios are higher than the annual earnings ratios.

The increase in the work experience gained by younger cohorts is likely to have an even greater impact on their future earnings because their work experience has been more correctly anticipated. Many work-related investment choices are made at younger ages: years of schooling, subjects or professional training in school, geographic location. In the past, women were much less likely than men to invest in lengthy vocationally oriented training because they did not expect that they would be working enough years to justify it. In fact, until the late 1970s, only a minority of young women anticipated that they would be working during their married years. The National Longitudinal Sur-

TABLE 1   Female-to-male Earnings Ratios by Age

Ages	Annual Income of Full-time Year-round Workers				Hourly Earnings of Current Workers*	
	1960	1970	1980	1988	1980	1988
20–24	80.6	74.0	77.7	88.5		
25–35	65.1	64.9	68.6	76.1	73.0	80.3
35–44	57.6	53.9	56.2	64.8	61.1	66.9
45–54	58.0	56.3	54.3	61.7	56.1	62.8
55–64	64.5	60.3	56.7	58.0	57.1	60.8

Note: Hourly earnings were calculated from the microdata files of the current population survey. Annual income data (left) are based on recall. Respondents are asked about income over the last year. Hourly earnings data (right) come from a monthly survey of current earnings.
Source: Annual income data are from U.S. Bureau of the Census, Current Population Reports, Series P-60.

vey found that only 28 percent of white women ages 14–24 in 1968 reported that they planned to be working at age 35. When this group actually reached age 35 in the 1980s, more than 70 percent of them were in the labor force. Their underestimation of their future labor-force participation must surely have influenced their early career preparations (or lack of preparation). More recent survey data show a dramatic change in expectations: the vast majority of young women (72 percent of white women ages 14–21 in 1979) now report an intention to work at age 35.

Changing work expectations are also reflected in rising female enrollments in higher education. In 1960, women received 35 percent of all bachelor's degrees in the United States; in the 1980s, women have been receiving somewhat more than half of these degrees. Women have rapidly increased their professional training as well. In 1968, women received only 8 percent of the medical degrees; the proportion rose to 31 percent in 1986. Among M.B.A.s, the female share rose from 3 percent to 31 percent over the same period. Similarly, women received 4 percent of the law degrees in 1968 and 39 percent in 1986.

This recent trend in women's increased investment in schooling is likely to reinforce the rise in work experience and contribute to relative increases in the earnings of women workers.

WHY THE GENDER WAGE GAP DECLINED IN THE 1980S

Closer analysis reveals several factors that have contributed to narrowing the wage gap during the 1980s. The analysis is based on data from the U.S. Census Bureau's *Current Population Survey,* and it is confined to white men and women in the 20–44 age group. The female-to-male hourly earnings ratio for this group increased from 65.6 percent in 1977 to 71.4 percent in 1987.

The data indicate that over the decade women's skills increased relative to men's in terms of schooling, work experience, and occupations. Although women still complete slightly fewer years of schooling than men, this differential narrowed; at the postsecondary-school level, women gained one-third of a year and men one-fifth of a year, narrowing the differential to only

0.14 of a year. This small gain was important because the monetary return to an additional year of postsecondary schooling was increasing.

Consistent with their overall increased schooling level, women entered occupations that require greater skill, as measured by the number of years of specific vocational preparation required to qualify for the occupation. Although women still hold occupations with lower training requirements in greater numbers than men, the difference has narrowed by about 29 percent over the decade.

An important obstacle to the analysis of gender differentials in earnings is the scarcity of information on lifetime employment patterns. The standard annual surveys of earnings conducted by the Census Bureau do not include questions about work history. While age or, more precisely, the number of years since leaving school is a reasonable proxy for the work experience of men, it is not for women, who typically are out of the labor force for a period of time in their twenties or early thirties. To provide some clues about work experience, other measures related to experience can be examined.

It is possible, for example, to identify intermittent workers who have either joined or left the labor force during the year and who are likely to have less experience than those who have been in the labor force all year. Taking these variables into account, labor-force turnover among women declined over the decade. Twelve percent of women who worked during 1977 were labor-force "leavers"; that is, they had left the labor force by March of the following year (compared to 3 percent of men). At the end of the decade, 7.5 percent of women were labor-force leavers. The proportion of women who joined the labor force during the year also declined, although it remained higher than that for men. The decline in turnover implies that women were staying in the work force longer and increasing their experience.

Combining data for 1977–1987, it is possible to estimate the extent to which changes in the work patterns of women and men can account for the change in the gender gap. I have conducted such an analysis for workers with children and for workers without children. Since caring for children is the most important reason why women work less than men, women who do not have children typically accumulate more work experience than women with children and are, therefore, more nearly comparable to men in numbers and patterns of years actually worked.

This analysis shows that the wage gap narrowed by slightly less than one percent per year from 1977 to 1987 for both workers with children and those without children. Changes in the proportion joining and leaving the labor force explain 13 percent of the decline in the wage gap among women with children; they explain little of the decline among workers without children since turnover is less a factor for childless women. When changes in schooling, in the industrial mix, and in occupational skills levels are added to the list of variables, 24 percent of the gain in women's relative wages is explained for workers with children and 33 percent for those with no children.

WHAT WE STILL DON'T KNOW ABOUT THE GENDER WAGE GAP

Since less than half of the convergence in the wage gap can be accounted for by the changes in the characteristics noted, the remainder must be attributable to the effects of factors that could not be measured (such as actual work experience) or to changes over the decade in the market rewards for different skills. Evidence from other sources shows that women in the 20–44 age group did increase their work experience, and this factor undoubtedly contributes to the otherwise unexplained part of the narrowing in the wage gap.

Changes in the economy also played a role through effects on the market rewards to occupational skills. The relative wage of male workers in blue-collar occupations fell by about 6 percent from 1977 to 1987. About 45 percent of men are employed in blue-collar jobs, compared to only about 10 percent of women. The decline in earnings in blue-collar work relative to white-collar work can account for about 20 percent of the otherwise unexplained part of the narrowing in the wage gap.

The evidence reviewed indicates that, unlike the pattern of preceding decades, there was a significant narrowing in skill differentials between working men and women during the 1980s and that this convergence in skills contributed to the convergence in wages. In addition, changes in relative wages in the economy—in particular, the relative decline in the earnings of blue-collar workers—worked to the relative disadvantage of men and also contributed to the narrowing of the wage gap.

Some women are still likely to be constrained by household responsibilities in their choice of jobs, so job characteristics such as shorter hours, more flexible schedules, and a location close to home are likely to be obtained at the price of lower pay rates. But clearly, the extreme specialization of tasks in the home that characterized the early part of the century have diminished. Women are much more likely to work in the market than in the past. The average working woman in her early fifties today has worked in 63 percent of the years since leaving school, and many of these work years have involved part-time or part-year work. Employed women in their early thirties, however, have worked in 75 percent of the years since leaving school.

Table 1 shows one reason why the female-to-male wage ratio declines with age: women's work experience falls relative to men's as age increases. In 1988, the pay ratio was 76.1 percent at ages 25–34, and it declined to 65 percent at ages 35–44 and to 58 percent at ages 55–64. In part, the pattern reflects cohort differences rather than age alone. The older women of today are the mothers of the baby-boom generation, the vast majority of whom as young women in the 1950s expected to raise a family, care for a home, and in exchange be supported by their husbands. During the 1960s, rising wage levels and an expanding service sector made work increasingly more attractive, and rising divorce rates made marriage less secure. A large proportion of this cohort entered the labor force in their thirties and forties. Their earnings were bound to be lower than men's of the same age since they had been out of the labor force during the ages when careers are established. Today's younger cohorts of women are working longer, and they are better prepared because they have anticipated their career needs. As a result, their earnings are not likely to fall behind men's as they age to the same extent as in prior generations.

DOES DISCRIMINATION ACCOUNT FOR THE PAY GAP?

Despite the advances of the past decade, women still earn less than men. George Washington University economist Barbara Bergmann and others attribute the pay gap to "widespread, severe, ongoing discrimination by employers and fellow workers." It is difficult to marshal evidence on the extent to which the gender gap in pay is explained by discrimination. Discrimination cannot be directly measured. Instead, researchers estimate the extent to which differences in labor-market productivity appear to explain the gap and then attribute the unexplained remainder to discrimination. Such a conclusion is premature, however, when productivity differences are not accurately measured, and this is often the case. Typically, data are unavailable on lifetime patterns of work experience, work expectations, and the intensity and nature of work investments. As these are the key areas in which men and women differ, there is considerable room for interpretation and disagreement.

Table 2 illustrates the difficulty. It shows female-to-male hourly earnings ratios in 1987 for

TABLE 2 Female-to-male Hourly Earnings Ratios (1987, white workers, ages 20–44)

	With Children	Without Children
Standardized for age and region only	62.7	86.3
Standardized for age, region, schooling, industry, occupational-skill level, and labor force turnover	72.0	90.7

Source: Microdata files of the *Current Population Survey*, March 1988

white workers in the 20–44 age range. The data are again from the *Current Population Survey,* which does not contain information on years of work experience. Based on other evidence, it is known that women without children are less likely to be intermittent workers than women with children. The pay ratio is 86 percent when women and men without children are compared, but it is only 63 percent when women and men with children are compared. An adjustment is made for other factors related to productivity: years of schooling, major industrial classification, the skill level of the job (measured as years of training required to perform the job), and labor-force turnover. After controlling for these factors, the wage ratio rises to 72 percent among workers with children and to 91 percent among workers without children.

Men and women without children are much more likely to be comparable in terms of years of work experience than men and women with children, but not entirely so. Many of the women who have not had a child expect to have one someday, and consequently they may not have invested in work skills to the same extent as men or committed career women. Similarly, many men without children may be planning to have a family, and their work efforts may be greater as a result.

Other kinds of data that provide additional information on work preparation and motivation indicate similarly small differentials once these factors are taken into account. For example, an analysis of female-to-male pay differentials in the federal government found that among college graduates under the age of 35 about 70 percent of the gap could essentially be explained by degree level, years of government experience, and particularly important, field of college major, leaving an unexplained gap of 5 percent. Men in the federal government were much more likely to have engineering degrees than women, which was a big factor in the type of occupation they were prepared to fill.

These results are not conclusive, but they do suggest that differences in earnings attributable solely to gender are likely to be much smaller than is commonly believed, probably less than 10 percent.

POLICY IMPLICATIONS

In the past, women who chose (or would have chosen) to have careers were likely to find their paths filled with obstacles that society had erected to preserve women's role in the home. These discriminatory barriers, however, were probably not the major cause of pay differences between men and women, because women's decisions about work were rooted in real economic forces affecting the family. Over the years, attitudes toward women's market work have changed considerably as the economic reward for market work increased and as women became an increasingly important presence in the labor market. Market pressures have generated self-correcting mechanisms: as the costs of denying employment to women have mounted, prejudices have diminished.

Overt discrimination against women in pay and in promotion is now against the law. Women who believe they have been treated unfairly do, therefore, have legal recourse. Nonetheless, new policies have been advocated that would enlarge the role of government in affecting women's working conditions and pay. Prominent among current proposals are those that would mandate employer benefits related to time off for childbearing and special child-care needs and for determining comparable-worth pay. Provisions for maternal leave are now formally and informally present in the workplace. When arranged voluntarily on an individual basis, they suit the particular situation of the firm and the woman. When mandated by government, they become an additional cost of employing women of childbearing age. Provisions such as these are reminiscent of past protective legislation that imposed maximum-hours restrictions on women's employment and thereby limited women's employment opportunities.

Comparable worth is a mechanism for raising women's pay directly by requiring a firm to equalize pay between occupations dominated by women and occupations dominated by men when these occupations are determined by job evaluations to be of "comparable worth." Since there is no uniform way to rank occupations by worth, a comparable-worth policy would ultimately lead to politically administered wages that would depart from the market system of wage determination.

There is, however, a more efficient and fair way to remove pay differentials among occupations if these differentials are due to discrimination. If males get higher pay in male-dominated occupations, then presumably women are being kept out, otherwise they would be seeking to enter these jobs (as would men who work in mixed or predominantly female jobs). The appropriate response to discriminatory barriers would be to eliminate them. They are a violation of Title VII of the Civil Rights Act and illegal under the law. However, if women do not choose to seek the higher-paying male-dominated jobs—for example, because these jobs have countervailing costs in the form of a long training period or unpleasant working conditions—then the pay differential is not discriminatory. In fact, the differential is what the market requires to attract workers to the different jobs.

During the past decade, women's earnings have risen more rapidly than men's, and the pay gap has narrowed substantially. These gains have come about because more recent cohorts of women have been accumulating more work experience and, in anticipation, have better prepared themselves for a career. This is evident in the large increase in women's enrollment in higher education and in their more numerous entry into higher-paying occupations such as law and medicine that were once almost exclusively male.

Women and men still do not have the same earnings. Some of the remaining differential may be due to labor-market discrimination, but I believe that the differential is largely due to continuing gender differences in the priority placed on market work versus family responsibilities. Until family responsibilities are more equally shared, women are not likely to have the same pattern of market work and earnings as men. Technology has cooperated by reducing the burden of housework. But child care remains a responsibility that is more difficult to shift to the market.

It is impossible to predict how the arrangements of future generations will evolve; however, the relative rise in women's earnings is likely to be a spur to more sharing of home responsibilities and more ingenuity in the way such arrangements are handled.

WOMEN IN THE
THIRD WORLD

INTRODUCTION

In Chapter 5 we examined the problems many American women face as they juggle the competing demands of home and workplace. These problems are not unique to our society. In many respects, women in other societies around the world face even greater obstacles to the fulfillment of their aspirations. The two essays of this chapter examine some of the difficulties Third World women face in their homes, their communities, and their places of employment.

"Third World" is a key term in these essays. Just what does it mean? A brief explanation is in order. During the Cold War (from 1945 to 1990) two massive international coalitions were formed as deadly adversaries. Many nations joined the United States in such alliances as the North Atlantic Treaty Organization (NATO) to oppose an antagonistic bloc of nations aligned with the Soviet Union in the Warsaw Pact. Those nations aligned with the United States were known as the "First World"; those in the Soviet camp were identified as the "Second World." Many nations that did not belong to either of these two power blocs became known as the "Third World." None of these terms has ever been precisely defined, but the First World typically included the United States, Canada, Great Britain, Western Europe, Japan, Australia, and New Zealand. The Second World incorporated the Soviet Union, Eastern Europe, Cuba, and the People's Republic of China. The Third World included the nations aligned with neither bloc. In Belgrade, Yugoslavia, many of these nations formalized their neutrality in the Cold War by creating the Nonaligned Nations in 1961. Leaders of many of these nations expressed strong opinions about the need to remain independent of foreign domination.

The Cold War is over. With the disintegration of the USSR and its satellites, the Second World has come to an end. With their old enemy in disarray, the nations of the First World are increasingly going their own ways, though NATO remains. "First World" has little meaning now that the Second World has broken apart, yet undoubtedly we will still be speaking of the Third World for some time to come. The term has come to be synonymous with "developing" (that is, underdeveloped) nations, principally those of Africa, Asia, and Latin America, where the vast majority of people live in poverty.

The authors of the two essays in this chapter address problems faced by poor women of the Third World. They mention dire social conditions in twenty-eight nations. The gap between the wealthy industrial nations of the Northern Hemisphere and the poor, nonindustrial nations of the Southern Hemisphere is enormous. According to the 1992 _World Almanac_, the per capita gross national product (GNP) is $21,974 in the United States, $21,820 in Japan, and $13,020 in France. The per capita GNP reported for some of the nations mentioned in the next two essays, in contrast, is $790 in the Dominican Republic, $1,648 in Panama, $530 in Zambia, $180 in Bangladesh, $625 in the Philippines, and $430 in Indonesia. During the past several decades the gap between rich and poor nations continued to grow. In developing nations women often carry a disproportionate burden in these conditions of extreme poverty.

Both essays describe the division of labor in developing nations and its implications for women. "Division of labor" is an important idea in the social sciences; "between men and women" is understood. The authors in the following essays call attention to the systematic bias in work assignments, arguing that the division of labor is far from equal. Women typically work harder at highly valued tasks for a small fraction of the rewards reserved for men.

Barbara Ehrenreich and Annette Fuentes emphasize a shift in the meaning of "division of labor": labor is now divided between nations as well as between men and women. Many employers are multinational firms with headquarters in the United States or Japan. The young Third World women they employ are at their mercy. The authors describe these young women as victims of exploitation. Key questions as you read this essay focus on values, evidence, and solutions. How do the authors' values influence their line of reasoning? The managers are given little opportunity to argue their point of view. Can you imagine how they would counter Ehrenreich and Fuentes's argument?

Whereas Ehrenreich and Fuentes see the issues of gender and the division of labor in the light of a global economy, Nafis Sadik examines them in the light of the internal structure of each Third World nation. His discussion focuses on the crucial roles women play in the non-money economy as well as the money economy. What does Sadik mean when he says that women "are the agents of change to bring about better lives for billions of people in the Third World"? How can these invisible people bring about massive change? Few questions are more important at the end of the twentieth century.

7. LIFE ON THE GLOBAL ASSEMBLY LINE

BARBARA EHRENREICH and ANNETTE FUENTES

In Ciudad Juárez, Mexico, Anna M. rises at 5 A.M. to feed her son before starting on the two-hour bus trip to the maquiladora (factory). He will spend the day along with four other children in a neighbor's one-room home. Anna's husband, frustrated by being unable to find work for himself, left for the United States six months ago. She wonders, as she carefully applies her new lip gloss, whether she ought to consider herself still married. It might be good to take a night course, become a secretary. But she seldom gets home before eight at night, and the factory, where she stitches brassieres that will be sold in the United States through J. C. Penney, pays only $48 a week.

In Penang, Malaysia, Julie K. is up before the three other young women with whom she shares a room, and starts heating the leftover rice from last night's supper. She looks good in the company's green-trimmed uniform, and she's proud to work in a modern, American-owned factory. Only not quite so proud as when she started working three years ago—she thinks as she squints out the door at a passing group of women. Her job involves peering all day through a microscope, bonding hair-thin gold

wires to a silicon chip destined to end up inside a pocket calculator, and at 21, she is afraid she can no longer see very clearly.

Every morning, between four and seven, thousands of women like Anna and Julie head out for the day shift. In Ciudad Juárez, they crowd into *ruteras* (run-down vans) for the trip from the slum neighborhoods to the industrial parks on the outskirts of the city. In Penang they squeeze, 60 or more at a time, into buses for the trip from the village to the low, modern factory buildings of the Bayan Lepas free trade zone. In Taiwan, they walk from the dormitories—where the night shift is already asleep in the still-warm beds—through the checkpoints in the high fence surrounding the factory zone.

This is the world's new industrial proletariat: young, female, Third World. Viewed from the "first world," they are still faceless, genderless "cheap labor," signaling their existence only through a label or tiny imprint—"made in Hong Kong," or Taiwan, Korea, the Dominican Republic, Mexico, the Philippines, but they may be one of the most strategic blocs of womanpower in the world of the 1980s. Conservatively, there are 2 million Third World female industrial workers employed now, millions more looking for work, and their numbers are rising every year. Anyone whose image of Third World women features picturesque peasants with babies slung on their backs should be prepared to update it. Just in the last decade, Third World women have become a critical element in the global economy and a key "resource" for expanding multinational corporations.

From *Ms. Magazine*, January 1981. Reprinted with permission of Barbara Ehrenreich and *Ms. Magazine.*

Barbara Ehrenreich is a feminist journalist and activist and a co-author of "For Her Own Good" (Anchor, 1979). Annette Fuentes has worked on the staff of "Seven Days" magazine. This article was made possible through a support grant from the Windom Fund.

It doesn't take more than second grade arithmetic to understand what's happening. In the United States, an assembly line worker is likely to earn, depending on her length of employment, between $3.10 and $5 an hour. In many Third World countries, a woman doing the same work will earn $3 to $5 a *day*. According to the magazine *Business Asia*, in 1976 the average hourly wage for unskilled work (male or female) was 55 cents in Hong Kong, 52 cents in South Korea, 32 cents in the Philippines, and 17 cents in Indonesia. The logic of the situation is compelling: why pay someone in Massachusetts $5 an hour to do what someone in Manila will do for $2.50 a day? Or, as a corollary, why pay a male worker anywhere to do what a female worker will do for 40 to 60 percent less?

And so, almost everything that can be packed up is being moved out to the Third World; not heavy industry, but just about anything light enough to travel—garment manufacture, textiles, toys, footwear, pharmaceuticals, wigs, appliance parts, tape decks, computer components, plastic goods. In some industries, like garment and textile, American jobs are lost in the process, and the biggest losers are women, often black and Hispanic. But what's going on is much more than a matter of runaway shops. Economists are talking about a "new international division of labor," in which the process of production is broken down and the fragments are dispersed to different parts of the world. In general, the low-skilled jobs are farmed out to the Third World, where labor costs are minuscule, while control over the overall process and technology remains safely at company headquarters in "first world" countries like the United States and Japan.

The American electronics industry provides a classic example: circuits are printed on silicon wafers and tested in California; then the wafers are shipped to Asia for the labor-intensive process by which they are cut into tiny chips and bonded to circuit boards; final assembly into products such as calculators or military equipment usually takes place in the United States. Garment manufacture too is often broken into geographically separated steps, with the most repetitive, labor-intensive jobs going to the poor countries of the southern hemisphere. Most Third World countries welcome whatever jobs come their way in the new division of labor, and the major international development agencies—like the World Bank and the United States Agency for International Development (AID)—encourage them to take what they can get.

So much any economist could tell you. What is less often noted is the *gender* breakdown of the emerging international division of labor. Eighty to 90 percent of the low-skilled assembly jobs that go to the Third World are performed by women—in a remarkable switch from earlier patterns of foreign-dominated industrialization. Until now, "development" under the aegis of foreign corporations has usually meant more jobs for men and—compared to traditional agricultural society—a diminished economic status for women. But multinational corporations and Third World governments alike consider assembly-line work—whether the product is Barbie dolls or missile parts—to be "women's work."

One reason is that women can, in many countries, still be legally paid less than men. But the sheer tedium of the jobs adds to the multinationals' preference for women workers—a preference made clear, for example, by this ad from a Mexican newspaper: *We need female workers; older than 17, younger than 30; single and without children: minimum education primary school, maximum education one year of preparatory school [high school]: available for all shifts.*

It's an article of faith with management that only women can do, or will do, the monotonous, painstaking work that American business is exporting to the Third World. Bill Mitchell, whose job is to attract United States businesses to the Bermudez Industrial Park in Ciudad Juárez, told us with a certain macho pride: "A man just won't stay in this tedious kind of work. He'd walk out in a couple of hours." The personnel manager of a light assembly plant in Taiwan told anthropologist Linda Gail Arrigo: "Young male workers are too restless and impatient to do monotonous work with no career value. If displeased, they sabotage the machines and even threaten the foreman. But girls? At most, they cry a little."

In fact, the American businessmen we talked to claimed that Third World women genuinely enjoy doing the very things that would drive a man to assault and sabotage. "You should watch these kids going into work," Bill Mitchell told us. "You don't have any sullenness here. They smile." A top-level management consultant who specializes in advising American companies on where to relocate their factories gave us this global generalization: "The [factory] girls genuinely enjoy themselves. They're away from their families. They have spending money. They can buy motorbikes, whatever. Of course it's a regulated experience too—with dormitories to live in—so it's a healthful experience."

What is the real experience of the women in the emerging Third World industrial work force? The conventional Western stereotypes leap to mind: You can't really compare, the standards are so different. . . . Everything's easier in warm countries. . . . They really don't have any alternatives. . . . Commenting on the low wages his company pays its women workers in Singapore, a Hewlett-Packard vice-president said, "They live much differently here than we do. . . ." But the differences are ultimately very simple. To start with, they have less money.

The great majority of the women in the new Third World work force live at or near the subsistence level for one person, whether they work for a multinational corporation or a locally owned factory. In the Philippines, for example, starting wages in U.S.-owned electronics plants are between $34 to $46 a month, compared to a cost of living of $37 a month; in Indonesia the starting wages are actually about $7 a month less than the cost of living. "Living," in these cases, should be interpreted minimally: a diet of rice, dried fish, and water—a Coke might cost a half-day's wages—lodging in a room occupied by four or more other people. Rachael Grossman, a researcher with the Southeast Asia Resource Center, found women employees of U.S. multinational firms in Malaysia and the Philippines living four to eight in a room in boardinghouses, or squeezing into tiny extensions built onto squatter huts near the factory. Where companies do provide dormitories for their employees, they are not of the "healthful," collegiate variety implied by our corporate informant. Staff from the American Friends Service Committee report that dormitory space is "likely to be crowded, with bed rotation paralleling shift rota-tion—while one shift works, another sleeps, as many as twenty to a room." In one case in Thailand, they found the dormitory "filthy," with workers forced to find their own place to sleep among "splintered floorboards, rusting sheets of metal, and scraps of dirty cloth."

Wages do increase with seniority, but the money does not go to pay for studio apartments or, very likely, motorbikes. A 1970 study of young women factory workers in Hong Kong found that 88 percent of them were turning more than half their earnings over to their parents. In areas that are still largely agricultural (such as parts of the Philippines and Malaysia), or places where male unemployment runs high (such as northern Mexico), a woman factory worker may be the sole source of cash income for an entire extended family.

But wages on a par with what an 11-year-old American could earn on a paper route, and living conditions resembling what Engels found in 19th-century Manchester are only part of the story. The rest begins at the factory gate. The work that multinational corporations export to the Third World is not only the most tedious, but often the most hazardous part of the production process. The countries they go to are, for the most part, those that will guarantee no interference from health and safety inspectors, trade unions, or even free-lance reformers. As a result, most Third World factory women work under conditions that already have broken or will break their health—or their nerves—within a few years, and often before they've worked long enough to earn any more than a subsistence wage.

Consider first the electronics industry, which is generally thought to be the safest and cleanest of the exported industries. The factory buildings are low and modern, like those one might find in a suburban American industrial park. Inside, rows of young women, neatly dressed in the company uniform or T-shirt, work quietly at their stations. There is air conditioning (not for the women's comfort, but to protect the delicate semiconductor parts they work with), and high-volume piped-in Bee Gees hits (not so much for entertainment as to prevent talking).

For many Third World women, electronics is a prestige occupation, at least compared to other kinds of factory work. They are unlikely to know that in the United States the National Institute on Occupational Safety and Health (NIOSH) has placed electronics on its select list of "high health-risk industries using the greatest number of toxic substances." If electronics assembly work is risky here, it is doubly so in countries where there is no equivalent of NIOSH to even issue warnings. In many plants toxic chemicals and solvents sit in open containers, filling the work area with fumes that can literally knock you out. "We have been told of cases where ten to twelve women passed out at once," an AFSC field worker in northern Mexico told us, "and the newspapers report this as 'mass hysteria.'"

In one stage of the electronics assembly process, the workers have to dip the circuits into open vats of acid. According to Irene Johnson and Carol Bragg, who toured the National Semiconductor plant in Penang, Malaysia, the women who do the dipping "wear rubber gloves and boots, but these sometimes leak, and burns are common." Occasionally, whole fingers are lost. More commonly, what electronics workers lose is the 20/20 vision they are required to have when they are hired. Most electronics workers spend seven to nine hours a day peering through microscopes, straining to meet their quotas.

One study in South Korea found that most electronics assembly workers develop severe eye problems after only one year of employment: 88 percent had chronic conjunctivitis; 44 percent became nearsighted; and 19 percent developed astigmatism. A manager for Hewlett-Packard's Malaysia plant, in an interview with Rachael Grossman, denied that there were any eye problems: "These girls are used to working with 'scopes.' We've found no eye problems. But it sure makes me dizzy to look through those things."

Electronics, recall, is the "cleanest" of the exported industries. Conditions in the garment and textile industry rival those of any 19th-century (or 20th) sweatshop. The firms, generally local subcontractors to large American chains such as J. C. Penney and Sears, as well as smaller manufacturers, are usually even more indifferent to the health of their employees than the multinationals. Some of the worst conditions have been documented in South Korea, where

the garment and textile industries have helped spark that country's "economic miracle." Workers are packed into poorly lit rooms, where summer temperatures rise above 100 degrees. Textile dust, which can cause permanent lung damage, fills the air. When there are rush orders, management may require forced overtime of as much as 48 hours at a stretch, and if that seems to go beyond the limits of human endurance, pep pills and amphetamine injections are thoughtfully provided. In her diary (originally published in a magazine now banned by the South Korean government) Min Chong Suk, 30 a sewing-machine operator, wrote of working from 7 A.M. to 11.30 P.M. in a garment factory: "When [the apprentices] shake the waste threads from the clothes, the whole room fills with dust, and it is hard to breathe. Since we've been working in such dusty air, there have been increasing numbers of people getting tuberculosis, bronchitis, and eye diseases. Since we are women, it makes us so sad when we have pale, unhealthy, wrinkled faces like dried-up spinach. . . . It seems to me that no one knows our blood dissolves into the threads and seams, with sighs and sorrow."

In all the exported industries, the most invidious, inescapable health hazard is stress. On their home ground United States corporations are not likely to sacrifice productivity for human comfort. On someone else's home ground, however, anything goes. Lunch breaks may be barely long enough for a woman to stand in line at the canteen or hawkers' stalls. Visits to the bathroom are treated as privilege; in some cases, workers must raise their hands for permission to use the toilet, and waits up to a half hour are common. Rotating shifts—the day shift one week, the night shift the next—wreak havoc with sleep patterns. Because inaccuracies or failure to meet production quotas can mean substantial pay losses, the pressures are quickly internalized; stomach ailments and nervous problems are not unusual in the multinationals' Third World female work force. In some situations, good work is as likely to be punished as slow or shoddy work. Correspondent Michael Flannery, writing for the AFL-CIO's *American Federationist*, tells the story of 23-year-old Basilia Altagracia, a seamstress who stitched collars onto ladies' blouses in the La Romana (Dominican Republic) free trade zone (a heavily guarded industrial zone owned by Gulf & Western Industries, Inc.):

"A nimble veteran seamstress, Miss Altagracia eventually began to earn as much as $5.75 a day. . . . 'I was exceeding my piecework quota by a lot.' . . . But then, Altagracia said, her plant supervisor, a Cuban émigré, called her into his office. 'He said I was doing a fine job, but that I and some other of the women were making too much money, and he was being forced to lower what we earned for each piece we sewed.' On the best days, she now can clear barely $3, she said. 'I was earning less, so I started working six and seven days a week. But I was tired and I could not work as fast as before.' " Within a few months, she was too ill to work at all.

As if poor health and the stress of factory life weren't enough to drive women into early retirement, management actually encourages a high turnover in many industries. "As you know, when seniority rises, wages rise," the management consultant to U.S. multinationals told us. He explained that it's cheaper to train a fresh supply of teenagers than to pay experienced women higher wages. "Older" women, aged 23 or 24, are likely to be laid off and not rehired.

We estimate, based on fragmentary data from several sources, that the multinational corporations may already have used up (cast off) as many as 6 million Third World workers—women who are too ill, too old (30 is over the hill in most industries), or too exhausted to be useful any more. Few "retire" with any transferable skills or savings. The lucky ones find husbands.

The unlucky ones find themselves at the margins of society—as bar girls, "hostesses," or prostitutes.

At 21, Julie's greatest fear is that she will never be able to find a husband. She knows that just being a "factory girl" is enough to give anyone a bad reputation. When she first started working at the electronics company, her father refused to speak to her for three months. Now, everytime she leaves Penang to go back to visit her home village she has to put up with a lecture on morality from her older brother—not to mention a barrage of lewd remarks from men outside her family. If they knew that she had actually gone out on a few dates, that she had been to a discotheque, that she had once kissed a young man who said he was a student . . . Julie's stomach tightens as she imagines her family's reaction. She tries to concentrate on the kind of man she would like to marry: an engineer or technician of some sort, someone who had been to California, where the company headquarters are located and where even the grandmothers wear tight pants and lipstick— someone who had a good attitude about women. But if she ends up having to wear glasses, like her cousin who worked three years at the "scopes," she might as well forget about finding anyone to marry her.

One of the most serious occupational hazards that Julie and millions of women like her may face is the lifelong stigma of having been a "factory girl." Most of the cultures favored by multinational corporations in their search for cheap labor are patriarchal in the grand old style: any young woman who is not under the wing of a father, husband, or older brother must be "loose." High levels of unemployment among men, as in Mexico, contribute to male resentment of working women. (Ironically, in some places the multinationals have increased male unemployment—for example, by paving over fishing and farming villages to make way for industrial parks.) Add to all this the fact that certain companies—American electronics firms are in the lead—actively promote Western-style sexual objectification as a means of insuring employee loyalty: there are company-sponsored cosmetics classes, "guess whose legs these are" contests, and swimsuit-style beauty contests where the prize might be a free night for *two* in a fancy hotel. Corporate-promoted Westernization only heightens the hostility many men feel toward any independent working women—having a job is bad enough, wearing jeans and mascara to work is going too far.

Anthropologist Patricia Fernandez, who has worked in a *maquiladora* herself, believes that the stigmatization of working women serves, indirectly, to keep them in line. "You have to think of the kind of socialization that girls experience in a very Catholic—or, for that matter, Muslim— society. The fear of having a 'reputation' is enough to make a lot of women bend over backward to be 'respectable' and ladylike, which is just what management wants." She points out that in northern Mexico, the tabloids delight in playing up stories of alleged vice in the *maquiladoras*—indiscriminate sex on the job, epidemics of venereal disease, fetuses found in factory rest rooms. "I worry about this because there are those who treat you differently as soon as they know you have a job at a *maquiladora*," one woman told Fernandez. "Maybe they think that if you have to work, there is a chance you're a whore."

And there is always a chance you'll wind up as one. Probably only a small minority of Third World factory workers turn to prostitution when their working days come to an end. But it is, as for women everywhere, the employment of last resort, the only thing to do when the factories don't need you and traditional society won't—or, for economic reasons, can't—take you back. In the Philippines, the brothel business is expanding as fast as the factory system. If they can't use you one way, they can use you another.

There has been no international protest about the exploitation of Third World women by multinational corporations—no thundering denunciations from the floor of the United Nations' general assembly, no angry resolutions from the Conference of the Non-Aligned Countries. Sociologist Robert Snow, who has been tracing the multinationals on their way south and eastward for years, explained why: "The Third World governments *want* the multinationals to move in. There's cutthroat competition to attract the corporations."

The governments themselves gain little revenue from this kind of investment, though—especially since most offer tax holidays and freedom from export duties in order to attract the multinationals in the first place. Nor do the people as a whole benefit, according to a highly placed Third World woman within the UN. "The multinationals like to say they're contributing to development," she told us, "but they come into our countries for one thing—cheap labor. If the labor stops being so cheap, they can move on. So how can you call that development? It depends on the people being poor and staying poor." But there are important groups that do stand to gain when the multinationals set up shop in their countries: local entrepreneurs who subcontract to the multinationals; Harvard- or Berkeley-edu-

cated "technocrats" who become local management; and government officials who specialize in cutting red tape for an "agent's fee" or an outright bribe.

In the competition for multinational investment, local governments advertise their women shamelessly, and an investment brochure issued by the Malaysian government informs multinational executives that: "The manual dexterity of the Oriental female is famous the world over. Her hands are small, and she works fast with extreme care. . . . Who, therefore, could be better qualified by nature and inheritance, to contribute to the efficiency of a bench-assembly production line than the Oriental girl?"

The Royal Thai Embassy sends American businesses a brochure guaranteeing that in Thailand, "the relationship between the employer and employee is like that of a guardian and ward. It is easy to win and maintain the loyalty of workers as long as they are treated with kindness and courtesy." The facing page offers a highly selective photo-study of Thai womanhood: giggling shyly, bowing submissively, and working cheerfully on an assembly line.

Many "host" governments are willing to back up their advertising with whatever amount of brutality it takes to keep "their girls" just as docile as they look in the brochures. Even the most polite and orderly attempts to organize are likely to bring down overkill doses of police repression:

- In Guatemala in 1975 women workers in a North American–owned factory producing jeans and jackets drew up a list of complaints that included insults by management, piecework wages that turned out to be less than the legal minimum, no overtime pay, and "threats of death." In response, the American boss made a quick call to the local authorities to report that he was being harassed by "Communists." When the women reported for work the next day they found the factory surrounded by two fully armed contingents and military police. The "Communist" ringleaders were picked out and fired.

- In the Dominican Republic, in 1978, workers who attempted to organize at the La Romana industrial zone were first fired, then obligingly arrested by the local police. Officials from the AFL-CIO have described the zone as a "modern slave-labor camp," where workers who do not meet their production quotas during their regular shift must stay and put in unpaid overtime until they do meet them, and many women workers are routinely strip-searched at the end of the day. During the 1978 organizing attempt, the government sent in national police in full combat gear and armed with automatic weapons. Gulf & Western supplements the local law with its own company-sponsored motorcycle club, which specializes in terrorizing suspected union sympathizers.

- In Inchon, South Korea, women at the Dong-II Textile Company (which produces fabrics and yarn for export to the United States) had succeeded in gaining leadership in their union in 1972. But in 1978 the government-controlled, male-dominated Federation of Korean Trade Unions sent special "action squads" to destroy the women's union. Armed with steel bars and buckets of human excrement, the goons broke into the union office, smashed the office equipment, and smeared the excrement over the women's bodies and in their hair, ears, eyes, and mouths.

Crudely put (and incidents like this do not inspire verbal delicacy), the relationship between many Third World governments and the multinational corporations is not very different from the relationship between a pimp and his customers. The governments advertise their women, sell them, and keep them in line for the multinational "johns." But there are other parties to the growing international traffic in women—such as the United Nations' Industrial Development Organization (UNIDO), the World Bank, and the United States government itself.

UNIDO, for example, has been a major promoter of "free trade zones." These are enclaves within nations that offer multinational corporations a range of creature comforts, including: freedom from paying taxes and export duties; low-cost water, power, and buildings; exemption from whatever labor laws may apply in the country as a whole; and, in some cases, such security features as barbed-wire, guarded checkpoints, and government-paid police.

Then there is the World Bank, which over the past decade has lent several billion dollars to finance the roads, airports, power plants, and even the first-class hotels that multinational corporations need in order to set up business in Third World countries. The Sri Lankan garment industry, which like other Third World garment industries survives by subcontracting to major Western firms, was set up on the advice of the World Bank and with a $20 million World Bank loan. This particular experiment in "development" offers young women jobs at a global low of $5 for a six-day week. Gloria Scott, the head of the World Bank's Women and Development Program, sounded distinctly uncomfortable when we asked her about the bank's role in promoting the exploitation of Third World women. "Our job is to help eliminate poverty. It is not our responsibility if the multinationals come in and offer such low wages. It's the responsibility of the governments." However, the Bank's 1979 World Development Report speaks strongly of the need for "wage restraint" in poor countries.

But the most powerful promoter of exploitative conditions for Third World women workers is the United States government itself. For example, the notoriously repressive Korean textile industry was developed with the help of $400 million in aid from the U.S. State Department. Malaysia became a low-wage haven for the electronics industry, thanks to technical assistance financed by AID and to U.S. money (funneled through the Asian Development Bank) to set up free trade zones. Taiwan's status as a "showcase for the free world" and a comfortable berth for multinationals is the result of three decades of financial transfusions from the United States. On a less savory note, the U.S. funds an outfit called the Asian-American Free Labor Institute, whose ostensible purpose is to encourage "free" (*i.e.*, non-Communist) trade unions in Asia, but whose actual mission is to discourage any truly militant union activity. AAFLI works closely with the Federation of Korean Trade Unions, which was responsible for the excrement-smearing incident described above.

But the most obvious form of United States involvement, according to Lenny Siegel, the director of the Pacific Studies Center, is through "our consistent record of military aid to Third

World governments that are capitalist, politically repressive, and are not striving for economic independence." Ironically, says Siegel, there are "cases where the United States made a big investment—through groups like AAFLI or other kinds of political pressure—to make sure that any unions that formed would be pretty tame. Then we put in even more money to support some dictator who doesn't allow unions at all." And if that doesn't seem like a sufficient case of duplicate spending, the U.S. government also insures (through the Overseas Private Investment Corporation) outward-bound multinationals against any lingering possibility of insurrection or expropriation.

What does our government have to say for itself? It's hard to get a straight answer—the few parts of the bureaucracy that deal with women and development seem to have little connection with those that are concerned with larger foreign policy issues. A spokesman for the Department of State told us that if multinationals offer poor working conditions (which he questioned), this was not their fault: "There are just different standards in different countries." Offering further evidence of a sheltered life, he told us that "corporations today are generally more socially responsible than even ten years ago. . . . We can expect them to treat their employees in the best way they can." But he conceded in response to a barrage of unpleasant examples, "Of course, you're going to have problems wherever you have human beings doing things." Our next stop was the Women's Division within AID. Staffer Emmy Simmons was aware of the criticisms of the quality of employment multinationals offer, but cautioned that "we can get hung up in the idea that it's exploitation without really looking at the alternatives for women." AID's concern, she said, was with the fact that population is outgrowing the agricultural capacity of many Third World countries, dislocating millions of people. From her point of view, multinationals at least provide some sort of alternative: "These people have to go somewhere."

Anna, for one, has nowhere to go but the maquiladora. Her family left the farm when she was only six, and the land has long since been bought up by a large commercial agribusiness company. After her father left to find work north of the border, money was scarce in the household for years. So when the factory where she now works opened in the early 1970s, Anna felt it was "the best thing that had ever happened" to her. As a wage-earner, her status rose compared to her brothers with their on-again, off-again jobs. Partly out of her new sense of confidence, she agreed to meet with a few other women one day after work to talk about wages and health conditions. That was the way she became what management called a "labor agitator" when, six months later, 90 percent of the day shift walked out in the company's first south-of-the-border strike.

Women like Anna—or Julie K. in Malaysia—need their jobs desperately. They know the risks of organizing. Beyond that, there's the larger risk that—if they do succeed in organizing—the company can always move on in search of a still-docile, job-hungry work force. Yet thousands of women in the Third World's industrial work force have chosen to fight for better wages and working conditions. Few of these struggles reach the North American media. We know of them from reports, often fragmentary, from church and support groups:

- Nuevo Laredo, Mexico, 1973: 2,000 workers at Transitron Electronics walked out in solidarity with a small number of workers who had been unjustly fired. Two days later, 8,000 striking workers met and elected a more militant union leadership.

- Mexicali, Mexico, 1974: 3,000 workers, locked out by Mextel (a Mattel subsidiary), set up a 24-hour guard to prevent the company from moving in search of cheaper labor. After two months of confrontations, the company moved away.

- Bangkok, Thailand, 1976: 70 young women locked their Japanese bosses out and took control of the factory. They continued to make and sell jeans and floppy hats for export, paying themselves 150 percent more than their bosses had.

- South Korea, 1977: 3,000 women at the American-owned Signetics plant went on a hunger strike for a 46.8 percent wage hike above the 39 cents an hour they were receiving. Since an actual walkout would have been illegal, they remained in the plant and held a sit-in in the cafeteria. They won a 23 percent increase.

- South Korea, 1978: 1,000 workers at the Mattel toy company in Seoul, which makes Barbie dolls and Marie Osmond dolls, staged a work slowdown to protest their 25-cents-an-hour wages and 12-hour shifts.
- South Korea, 1979: 200 young women employees of the YH textile-and-wig factory staged a peaceful vigil and fast to protest the company's threatened closing of the plant. On August 11, the fifth day of the vigil, more than 1,000 riot police, armed with clubs and steel shields, broke into the building where the women were staying and forcibly dragged the women out. Twenty-one-year-old Kim Kyong-suk was killed during the melee. It was her death that touched off widespread rioting throughout Korea that many thought led to the overthrow of President Park Chung Hee.
- Ciudad Juárez, Mexico; September, 1980: 1,000 women workers occupied an American Hospital Supply Corporation factory. They demanded better working conditions, paid vacations, and recognition of the union of their choice. The women, who are mostly in their teens and early twenties, began the occupation when 180 thugs, which the company claims were paid by a rival union, entered the factory and beat up the women's leaders. The occupation is over, but the struggle goes on.

Regarding the 1979 vigil in South Korea, Robert Snow points out: "Very few people realize that an action which began with 200 very young women factory workers led to the downfall of a government. In the 1980s, Third World factory women like this are going to be a political force to reckon with." So far, feminism, first-world style, has barely begun to acknowledge the Third World's new industrial womanpower. Jeb Mays and Kathleen Connell, cofounders of the San Francisco-based Women's Network on Global Corporations, are two women who would like to change that. "There's still this idea of the Third World woman as 'the other'—someone exotic and totally unlike us," Mays and Connell told us. "But now we're talking about women who wear the same styles in clothes, listen to the same music, and may even work for the same corporation. That's an irony the multinationals have created. In a way, they're drawing us together as women."

Saralee Hamilton, an AFSC staff organizer of a 1978 conference on "Women and Global Corporations" (held in Des Moines, Iowa) says: "The multinational corporations have deliberately targeted women for exploitation. If feminism is going to mean anything to women all over the world, it's going to have to find new ways to resist corporate power internationally." She envisions a global network of grass-roots women capable of sharing experiences, transmitting information, and—eventually—providing direct support for each other's struggles. It's a long way off; few women anywhere have the money for intercontinental plane flights or even long-distance calls, but at least we are beginning to see the way. "We all have the same hard life," wrote Korean garment worker Min Chong Suk. "We are bound together with one string."

8.   INVESTING IN WOMEN: THE FOCUS OF THE NINETIES

NAFIS SADIK

Women are at the heart of development. They are the agents of change to bring about better lives for billions of people in the Third World. They are central to the goal of sustainable development—economic and social progress that does not risk the integrity of the environment.

But they cannot fully realize their potential unless their basic living conditions are improved. They must have better health care, more rational workloads at home, more and better jobs outside the home and higher social status.

And above all, they must be given greater control of their own destinies by gaining a voice in how many children they will bear and by breaking their dependence on children as a major source of security and status.

Using the latest United Nations figures and results from the new demographic and health surveys now being released, as well as recent data from three major world conferences, the 1989 State of World Population Report looks at the totality of factors that help determine the number of their children, as well as the reverse—how smaller families affect their lives for the better.

To get down to the basics, in much of the Third World, women control most of the non-money economy, including subsistence farming and domestic labour, as well as major areas of the money economy (trading the "informal sector" and wage employment). In the developing world, women generally have the double burden of both inside and outside the home to support their families.

Much of this work is unrecognized and those who do it can expect no support. Their health suffers, their work suffers, their children suffer. Development itself is held back as a result.

The costs of ignoring the needs of women are uncontrolled population growth, high infant and child mortality, a weakened economy, ineffective agriculture, a deteriorating environment, a generally divided society and a poorer quality of life for all. Poor living conditions, it is generally agreed, are both a cause and effect of rapid population growth and need to be tackled together.

Many women, especially in developing countries, have few choices in life outside marriage and children. They tend to have large families because that is expected of them. Investing in women means widening their choice of strategies and reducing their dependence on children for status and support.

Family planning is one of the most important investments, because it represents the freedom from which other freedoms flow.

Investment in women must be aimed at removing the barriers preventing them from reaching their full potential. That means granting them equal access to land, to credit and to rewarding employment, as well as establishing their personal and political rights.

Households headed by women are the poorest in the world. Women are not permitted to own land in Colombia, Nepal, Kenya, Ethiopia, Panama, Chile, Iraq and Egypt. New land-reform laws exclude divorced women from land ownership in Zambia, Tanzania, Ethiopia and Nepal. In India 35 percent of the rural landless population are comprised of woman-headed households, compared with 20 percent in the country as a whole.

A change in any one aspect of women's lives—for good or ill—affects every other aspect. Increasing the availability of family planning will have its full effect on fertility when both women and men are prepared to use it. Improv-

From *Populi*, United Nations Population Fund, vol. 16, no. 2, 1989, pp. 5–19. Reprinted with permission.

Dr. Nafis Sadik is executive director, UNFPA.

ing girls' education will make its full impact when it is accompanied by better employment opportunities; better jobs are irrelevant if women are too burdened by child-bearing and domestic work to take advantage of them.

Making the necessary changes means recognizing women not only as wives and mothers, but as vital and valuable members of society. It means rethinking development plans from the start so that women's rights and needs are taken into account at every stage—so that women's status and security is derived from their entire contribution to society, rather than mainly from child-bearing.

Few would argue against providing women with better welfare services; but making investment in women a development priority will require a major change in attitudes not only by developing countries but by financial and lending institutions. Unfortunately, increasing economic pressures in the last few years have caused more than 35 of the world's poorest countries to cut health spending by 50 percent and education by 25 percent.

This burden has fallen hardest on the poor, and hardest of all on poor women.

The challenge for those who believe that women's contributions are central to development, and that investment in women should take priority, even in societies under severe economic stress, is daunting; they must make an irresistible case for the change.

Change of some kind cannot be avoided. In the face of population growth, the urban explosion, the deepening environmental crisis, escalating international debt and growing poverty in many of the poorest of the developing countries, many authorities agree that some kind of fundamental rethinking is long overdue. The concept of "sustainable development," in which human and natural resources are brought into a dynamic equilibrium, is one response.

Women, as we have seen, have a central part in any system of sustainable development.

Taking the long view, investing in women has a finite if unquantifiable economic value. The return will be an approach to development which will make the most effective use of the world's limited resources: slower, more balanced growth in the labour force and security for

the family and, most important the possibility of better health, education, nutrition and personal development not only for women but for all people.

Investing in women is not a panacea. It will not put an end to poverty, erase the gross inequalities between people and countries, slow the rate of population growth, rescue the environment, or guarantee peace. But it will make a critical contribution towards all those ends. It will have an immediate effect on some of the most vulnerable of the world's population. And it will help create the basis for future generations to make better use of both resources and opportunities.

World population is currently 5.2 billion. It is projected to increase by over 90 million each year until the end of the century. All but 6 million of each year's increase will live in developing countries. According to the United Nations, the population at the end of this century will be about 6.25 billion and about 8.5 billion by 2025. It may stop growing at 10 billion, about double its present size, perhaps a century from now.

To secure the projected drop in fertility, the number of women using family planning will have to rise to 730 million (58 percent) in 2000 and finally to 1.218 billion (71 percent or the present level in industrial countries) by 2025. In sub-Saharan Africa this would mean a tenfold increase in family-planning users by 2025.

The status of women will be crucial in determining future population growth rates. The extent to which women are free to make decisions affecting their lives may be the key to the future not only of the poor countries but of the richer ones too.

When children cease to be a major source of women's security, women have smaller families. To these women, family planning services are essential.

The most effective route to smaller families is to provide women with the means of social and economic independence: full rights in the family and society, access to income and career development, education and health care, and a real say in the decisions that affect their lives, of which one of the most important is family size.

But many young women are still trapped within a web of traditional values which assign a very high status to childbearing and almost none to anything else she can do. Increasing a woman's capacity to decide her own future, enhancing her overall status—her access to education, to land, to agricultural extension services, to credit, to employment—as an individual in her own right has a powerful effect, not least on her fertility.

But a major obstacle must be overcome. Discrimination against girls is ingrained in many developing nation societies. To start with, sons are generally preferred to daughters. Parents expect little from a girl once she marries and leaves home. Before marriage she starts working at an earlier age than her brothers, and toils harder and longer. Research in Bangladesh found that boys under five were given more food than girls and that girls were more likely to be malnourished in times of famine. A study in India found that boys were fed richer foods than girls.

Discrimination against girls continues as they grow older. In the developing world as a whole 65 percent of girls were in primary school in 1985 compared with 78 percent of boys. In secondary school, 37 percent of girls and 48 percent of boys were enrolled. The inequities persist. There is no maternity leave for a tea-picker on a plantation in Malawi or for a woman working on a building site in India. But if a pregnant woman is overworked and underfed she is more likely to have a small and weak baby. Low-birth-weight babies are more vulnerable to infection: they are 13 times more likely to die of infectious disease than normal babies.

Between 20 and 45 percent of women of child-bearing age in the developing world do not eat the recommended minimum of 2,250 calories a day under normal circumstances, let alone the extra 285 a day they need when they are pregnant. Heavy manual work combined with poor nutrition for mothers results in low-birth-weight babies and an inferior supply of breast milk. Compounding the problems for women is the prevalence of teenage marriages and teenage pregnancies.

It has been estimated that 40 percent of all 14-year-old girls alive today will have been pregnant at least once by the time they are 20. In Bangladesh four out of five teenage girls are mothers and in Africa as a whole, three out of four teenagers. Africa has the highest rate of births to very young mothers: 40 percent of births to teenagers occur among women aged 17 or under, compared with 39 percent in Latin America, 31 percent in Asia and 22 percent in Europe.

One reason for these high rates is that family planning programmes tend to be aimed at married women; worldwide, three quarters of girls under 15, and half of those 16 or over, have no access to family planning information.

Childbirth anywhere in the world has its risks, particularly without proper antenatal care and attention during and after delivery. For most women in developing countries the risks are multiplied. One out of every 21 African women will die as a result of pregnancy or childbirth. The figure is 1 in 38 South Asian women, and 1 in 90 women in Latin America. One in five women die before menopause in Afghanistan, Benin, Cameroon, Malawi, Mali, Mozambique, Nepal, Nigeria and North Yemen.

Yet every one of those deaths—over 500,000 a year, or one every minute of every day—could be prevented. A woman in Africa is 200 times more likely to die as a result of bearing her children than a European woman. More women die of maternal causes in India in one month than in North America, Europe, Japan and Australia put together in one year. The last recorded maternal death in Iceland was in 1976.

Abortion can also be a deadly experience for women in the developing world. Between 20 and 33 percent of all pregnancies are deliberately terminated, which means that approximately 150,000 abortions are performed every day. That adds up to between 50 and 60 million a year, of which only 33 million are performed legally.

In Ethiopia, for instance, 54 percent of obstetric deaths are the result of botched abortions. That so many women are willing to go through it speaks for their desire to control their fertility. That their numbers are actually increasing—from an estimated 30 million a year in 1981 to 60 million in 1988—is evidence of the failure of family planning services to keep pace with demand.

A further burden is having babies in quick succession. For a mother whose body has not yet recovered from a previous birth, these babies are the least likely to survive.

Every death brings the next birth a little nearer. United Nations figures from 25 developing countries reveal that couples experiencing the death of one child are likely to have larger families than those whose children all survived. The more recent the death, the greater the likelihood of an additional child.

The mothers' experience of loss means that they will be the least likely to use family planning, which could save not only their children's lives but their own. Nearly half of maternal deaths could be avoided simply by preventing unwanted pregnancy.

The Safe Motherhood Conference pointed out that most developing countries allocate less than 20 percent of their health budgets to maternal and child health programmes, and the majority of that goes to child health. With no action on maternal mortality, there could be 600,000 deaths in the year 2000. With action to halve the rate of maternal mortality, and fertility 25 percent lower than United Nations projections, the number could be reduced to 225,000.

The recent international focus on safe motherhood has drawn attention to practical, affordable solutions to the problem of maternal and infant mortality.

The World Bank has proposed a three-pronged health care approach: stepping up health services in the community, improving the referral system, and providing transport between the different levels in the system.

The Bank estimates that if more prosperous countries were to allocate an extra $2 per person per year to upgrading their health services along the lines they suggest, there would be a 50 percent drop in maternal mortality rates. For poorer countries, an outlay of just $1 per person per year would reduce maternal mortality by 25 percent.

Health, like charity, begins at home. But there are times when women need help from the health services. Unfortunately there is evidence that those who need help the most may be the least likely to receive it.

The nearest hospital, for instance may be far away and the roads bad. This also touches upon a basic problem. Unfortunately hospitals in most countries tend to act like enormous high-tech sponges sucking in health finance. Though three quarters of health problems could be solved by primary health care, 75 percent of the health budget in developing countries may be spent on doctors and hospitals.

Three quarters of the health problems in the developing world could be solved by a simple combination of prevention and cure: enough of the right food, clean water to drink, safe sanitation, access to family planning, immunization, and basic drugs.

This is primary health care in a nutshell: an initiative that tries to shift the focus of attention away from doctors and nurses and towards parents and village health workers, away from hospitals and operating theatres and towards communities and homes. By its nature it focuses attention on women.

Despite the fact that women are responsible for children from embryo to adulthood, they are so often the sole breadwinners of the household. Because they are the providers as well as the recipients of health care, womens own health requires safeguarding above all.

The distinction the modern world likes to make between economic activity and household work makes no sense when applied to women's lives in much of the developing world. Their productive work has to be fitted in around the crushing needs of feeding and clothing families.

An independent, adequate income would make women less reliant on husbands and children and reduce the need for sons as props for old age. Women would value daughters as much as sons and share the benefits of extra income equally. The result would be a new generation of healthy, confident, secure and forward-looking young women ready to take their place in society.

Nevertheless, the evidence linking women's employment with lower fertility and mortality is contradictory. One study of 60 developing countries found that women working outside tended to have fewer children than those working at home or in the fields and plantations, even when other factors, such as education, urban living and industrialization of the economy, were taken into account. But surveys of Turkey, Thailand and other countries have given opposite results.

Research conducted in 38 countries found

that only at higher socio-economic levels does employment become a viable alternative to bearing children, thus showing a positive effect on fertility rates. This becomes a strong effect only when combined with other measures of women's improved status, plus a vigorous family-planning programme. In Bangladesh, for instance, research on 425 women found their status was completely unaffected by their employment because of the menial nature of the work and their paltry wages.

Reliance on women for cheap, unskilled or partly skilled labour represents a massive waste of human and economic resources. Better education and employment at a higher level would reduce the social and economic cost of large families and enable women to make their full contribution to development.

Women's employment figures—the number of actual jobs held outside the home—are often a cruel misrepresentation of the actual amount of work that women do. A look at regional participation rates shows why. In Africa, for instance only 22.9 percent of women were considered to be in the labour force in 1985, defined as either "performing some work for wage or salary, in cash or in-kind," or "self-employed" performing "some work for profit or family gain, in cash or in-kind."

But women are responsible for between 60 and 80 percent of the food grown in Africa. Somehow their hours of planting, weeding, picking, threshing and winnowing have become invisible when national statistics are being compiled.

The same is true of their care of livestock, their vegetable growing, their trading, as well as the myriad activities normally classified as "housework"—fetching water and firewood, pounding grain, preserving fish and meat, cooking, cleaning, sewing, weaving, washing and mending clothes, teaching children and nursing them when they are ill, and caring for old or disabled family members.

In Pakistan, where one survey of village women found them putting in 63 hours of work a week, only 13.9 percent of women aged between 25 and 54 are considered to be "economically active." In Rwanda, where women were found to work three times as much as men, only 55 percent of women are considered to be "economi-

cally" active, exactly the same percentage as men.

Throughout the Third World, most of women's work is in what might be called the "non-money economy." There is no wage for the four to six hours a day a Mexican woman spends grinding grain if she lives too far from the mill; or the 1.3 hours the average Indian woman spends cooking even when there is a mill nearby; or the three hours spent preparing food in Indonesia, the 2.6 hours in Nepal and the 3.5 hours in Bangladesh.

In order to survive, a growing number of the most impoverished in developing countries are forced into a ferocious assault on their environment. In the process they use up resources which could sustain them and their families in the future. In the rural areas of developing countries, women are responsible for water, fuelwood, and much of the agriculture. Their cumulative activities have profound effects on the world's water supply, tree cover and farmland.

Today typical forests are being felled at a rate of 11 hectares a year; topsoil is being washed away by wind and rain at the rate of 26 billion tons a year; new stretches of desert are appearing at a rate of 6 million hectares a year; and build-up of salt and stagnant water threatens half of the world's irrigated cropland.

The effects are felt most acutely at the lowest level—by individual people, often the poorest and least powerful of people, most often by the women.

It is they who have to walk farther and farther each year to fetch firewood from the dwindling woodlands; they who must search for hours for a stretch of unpolluted water; and they who must cope with the effects of environmental degradation and pollution on their own and their family's health.

Reducing women's workload and making their labour more profitable might also help reduce family size, which would reduce the load still further. Benefits for mothers would spill over into benefits for daughters.

There are many other examples demonstrating the multiplier effects of taking women seriously as breadwinners and improving their access to productive resources.

Every large-scale survey in developing countries has discovered that the education of women is one of the most universal and reliable predictors both of their own fertility and of their children's health. This effect holds good regardless of school curricula and different cultures, and even though other factors, such as income and employment opportunities, come into play.

Today 65 percent of girls and 78 percent of boys in the developing world are in primary school—20 and 11 percent more than a decade ago. Secondary school enrolment rates are lower—with only 37 percent of girls and 48 percent of boys in school—but this is still 29 and 16 percent more than 10 years ago. But if current trends continue, literacy will continue to win the race against population growth.

In almost every country studied in recent years, educated women have been found to have fewer children than their less educated or uneducated sisters. In Brazil, for instance, uneducated women have an average of 6.5 children each, those with secondary education only 2.5. In Liberia women who have been to secondary school are 10 times more likely to be using family planning than women who have never been to school at all.

A study of four Latin American countries revealed that education was responsible for between 40 and 60 percent of the decline in fertility in the last decade. The authors suggested that this effect might soon be seen around the world.

The families of educated mothers are likely to be healthier as well as smaller. Mothers' education may be even more important to their children's health than flush toilets or piped water, or even food intake. Studies put the difference in child mortality (deaths of children between the ages of one and five) as high as 9 percent for every year the mother was at school. In Peru, for instance, educated women had healthier children regardless of whether there was a clinic or hospital nearby. Educated women tend to be older when they get married, are more likely to be employed and live in the city than uneducated women.

Recent research has turned up the fact that educated women are more likely to have antenatal care and ensure that their births are attended by a trained person. Their children are more likely to have health cards and to be immu-

nized. They even have fewer episodes of diarrhoea than the children of less educated women.

Educated women are more likely to stand up for themselves. In Kerala, India, for instance, educated women, however poor, seem to believe they have a right to good health care. Conversely, lower-class Nepalese women expected and received worse treatment from health staff; illiterate women in Ibadan, Nigeria, fared similarly. If women's confidence is higher in clinic and hospital waiting rooms, it is likely to be higher at home too. Research from Nigeria, Bangladesh and Mexico confirms that educated women tend to communicate more with their husbands, to be more involved in family decisions and to be more respected—more able, in other words, to plan what happens in their lives.

The world spends around $3 billion a year on family planning services for developing countries. Half of this is accounted for by only two countries, China and India, which spend $1 billion and $0.5 billion respectively. In addition, $0.5 billion is contributed by international donors, $0.5 billion by other national governments in the developing world and $0.5 billion by the users themselves.

The contribution of international donors increased from $168 million to $512 million between 1971 and 1985, by just $2 million a year in real terms, nowhere near sufficient to keep pace with growing numbers and growing needs. In the worst of the recession from 1979 to 1982, there was an actual decline in the real value of family planning assistance of around $13.5 million a year.

For many countries, cuts in assistance mean cuts in services. But governments are also cutting back their own budgets for social services because of the escalating economic crisis. Recent figures reveal that 37 of the poorest countries have cut health spending by 50 percent and education by 25 percent in the last four years.

It is against this backdrop that a woman's need for family planning must be seen. It costs $10 to $20 a year to provide her with the means to control her own fertility, to safeguard her own health and that of her children, to give her the chance to plan her life. An additional $2 billion a year from now until the year 2000 would ensure that 500 million women were given that chance by the year 2000.

For 3 million of those women it could literally be the chance of a lifetime Without family planning, that number of women's lives will be needlessly lost.

It would save the lives of more than 5 million babies and young children. It would also mean that the average number of children born to each woman in the world would drop from 3.4 in 1980–1985 to 3.1 by the year 2000. And this would keep the world's population well on course to stabilization.

Compared with today's total annual expenditure of $3 billion on family planning, an additional $2 billion seems huge, especially when necessary back-up health services are added on. But that extra $2 billion represents just 2 percent of all development assistance.

It is calculated that there would be 35 percent fewer births in Latin America, 33 percent fewer in Asia and 27 percent fewer in Africa if women were able to have the number of children they wanted, and correspondingly fewer women dying in childbirth.

RECOMMENDATIONS

These recommendations are addressed mainly to governments. However, international organizations and nongovernmental organizations also have a wide responsibility in this area.

Sustainable development can only be achieved with the full and equal participation of women, when population, environmental and development linkages are adequately translated into policies and programs, and when social sectors are given equal priority with economic growth.

1.   Equality of Status

Despite the Decade for Women and the recommendations of the International Conferences of 1975 and 1985, many declarations and much rhetoric, women in many parts of the world and in many communities have still not reached equality in status with men. In many ways this is a reflection of lack of understanding of the issues and the pervasiveness of deep-seated attitudes and belief systems.

There is an urgent need to change the attitudes of decision makers and leaders in favour of equality of status for women and to ensure commitment to this cause at the highest levels of society.

A legal and attitudinal framework which provides a basis for equality of status is essential. All countries should:

- ratify and implement the International Convention on the Elimination of All Forms of Discrimination against Women;
- review the legal system to remove barriers to women's full participation in society and the family on an equal basis with men, and to eliminate the legal basis for discrimination;
- educate both men and women at all levels, starting in the school system, to accept the principle that women and men are equal in value and have equal rights in society and the family;
- promote women's access to decision-making and leadership positions in government and the private sector, and ensure women's involvement in the design and implementation of programmes affecting women.

2.   Documenting and Publicizing Women's Vital Contribution To Development

There is still a shortage of vital quantitative and qualitative information on women. National data collection systems do not yet accurately document women's contribution to development. All countries should:

- ensure that national statistics on employment, mortality and morbidity are disaggregated by sex;
- investigate and quantify women's unpaid work and their work in the informal sector;
- assign an economic value to women's unpaid work;
- ensure timely and regular availability of socio-economic indicators on women;
- provide the widest possible audience with accurate and full information on women's productive and reproductive responsibilities.

3. Increasing the Productivity of Women and Lessening the Double Burden of Women

While women contribute two thirds of the hours worked in the world, they only earn about one tenth of the world's income and own only about 1 percent of the world's property. Women's working conditions are more difficult than those of men, particularly because women's access to production resources is restricted. All countries should:

- repeal all laws and practices preventing or restricting women from owning and administering productive resources;
- recognize that women's access to technology and training has to be guaranteed in all aspects of the economy, not only in those occupations and tasks traditionally perceived as a woman's domain;
- ensure that women have access to credit without collateral and improve access to markets in the agricultural and informal sector;
- establish and enforce laws of equal pay for work of equal value;
- measures to relieve women's workload, including improved domestic technology and better family planning services, should be a priority;
- all women should have access to safe water and fuel supply in or within reasonable distance of their homes;
- child-care should be a standard feature of workplaces on the same basis as other facilities;
- child-care and maternity leave should be on the same footing as health insurance and sick leave.

4. Providing Family Planning

Giving women the ability to choose when and whether to have children has powerful positive effects on their health, on the health of their children, and on their ability to involve themselves in the world outside the confines of the household. Providing family planning services may be one of the best ways of investing in women. It also has a profound effect on population growth. Countries should:

- provide high quality services and a wide variety of family planning methods so that women can choose the one that best suits their needs;
- provide appropriate and special family planning information and services for men, teenagers, unmarried and newly married women, people who tend to be excluded from services which are usually combined with maternal and child health care;
- provide full information about possible side effects of family planning so that women can make an informed choice;
- ensure that women are consulted and involved at every level in the organization of family planning services so that services are provided by appropriate staff in appropriate places at appropriate times;
- ensure that prevention and treatment of infertility is an effective part of MCH/FP services;
- include IEC and counselling about AIDS as an integral part of family planning services and promote the use of condoms in AIDS prevention;
- integrate family planning into mother and child health care services and other sectoral activities;
- improve the quality of contraceptive care and ensure that services are user-friendly and client-oriented.

5. Improving the Health of Women

The most dangerous time for both a mother and her baby is usually the weeks surrounding birth. High infant death rates have serious effects on a woman's sense of security, and dangerous labour, if it does not result in a mother's death, can cause much long-term suffering and disability. Countries should:

- train traditional birth attendants in hygiene, in promoting the benefits of birth spacing and in ensuring that "at risk" births take place in a clinic setting;
- concentrate interventions particularly on women who have lost two babies;

- provide supplementary food for malnourished mothers, especially young teenage mothers, to help reduce the incidence of low-birth-weight babies to fewer than 10 percent of live births by the year 2000;
- monitor nutrition of pre-school children, with separate norms for boys and girls, and ensure that at least 90 percent of children have a weight for age corresponding to international reference norms;
- educate parents about the need to care equally for their daughters as for their sons;
- train women to assume supervisory and decision-making roles in the health sector.

6.   Expanding Education

Educating girls gives them some of the basic skills and confidence to begin taking control of their lives, and opens up opportunities for them in the world outside the home. Education is perhaps the strongest variable affecting the status of women. Countries should:

- expand girls' enrolment in school and their retention in the school system by active recruitment, counselling of drop-outs and reducing school fees if necessary;
- halt the practice of expelling pregnant teenagers from school and encourage them to continue their education before and after the birth;
- include sex education, family planning and family responsibility in school curricula for children before they reach the age of first sexual experience;
- encourage both girls and boys to study the whole range of subjects;
- establish a framework of appropriate policies and programmes to bring about appropriate attitudinal and behavioural changes among both women and men.

7.   Goals for the Year 2000

Specific goals are needed to ensure progress in implementing these recommendations. UNFPA has proposed that governments should:

- increase international assistance for family planning programmes from $0.5 billion to $2.5 billion per year until the year 2000;
- make family planning a development priority, ranked alongside major economic investments, and with an allocation of not less than 1 percent of GNP in the countries concerned;
- extend family planning services to 500 million women by the year 2000;
- ensure that no person lives more than one hour's walk away from a health facility providing basic health care and family planning, and that no one lives more than two hours' travelling time from basic emergency facilities;
- ensure that all women pay at least one visit to a health care facility during pregnancy;

   reduce maternal mortality by at least 50 percent by the year 2000, especially in those countries where such mortality is very high (higher than 100 maternal deaths per 100,000 births);
- reduce infant mortality to 50 per 1,000 live births by the year 2000, especially in those countries where infant mortality is high;
- expand girls' enrolment in primary school to at least 75 percent by the year 2000. In countries where girls' enrolment is particularly low, ensure that the ratio of girls to boys in primary school is at least 4:5 by the year 2000;
- expand girls' enrolment in secondary school to at least 60 percent by the year 2000. In countries where girls' enrolment is particularly low, ensure that the ratio of girls to boys in secondary school is at least 3:5 by the year 2000;
- combat women's illiteracy so that at least 70 percent are able to read and write by the year 2000.

These goals cover not only population but also some of the specific concerns of many other agencies and organizations working in the field of development. A co-operative and co-ordinated effort and committed leadership is essential to ensure their achievement.

CHAPTER 7

SOCIAL CLASSES AND WELFARE POLICY

INTRODUCTION

The Industrial Revolution generated enormous wealth for some nations. The economic opportunities it generated, however, have been accompanied by occasional downward spirals of depression and persistent poverty for some people who live outside the circle of affluence. A paradox can be seen in this era of economic growth. As societies such as France, Germany, England, and the United States grew wealthy, some journalists and social scientists became increasingly alarmed about the problems of poverty. Perhaps the most famous alarmist of all, Karl Marx, was both a journalist and a social scientist at various times in his life. Marx edited a Cologne newspaper in 1842 and later wrote articles for the *New York Daily Tribune*. He also wrote numerous important essays and books on the need to transform the wealth generated by industrialization into a more equitable society for all. One of Marx's most important disciples, Vladimir Lenin, founded a communist nation and launched an international movement to eliminate the extremes of wealth and poverty universally found in capitalist nations.

Marx died more than 100 years ago and Lenin's vision of an egalitarian communist order officially died in 1991, when the Soviet Union came to an end. The communist movement may be passing into the dustbin of history, but journalists and social scientists in the capitalist nations are still locked in debate over the issue of poverty in the midst of affluence. Views seem to differ sharply on every aspect of the issue: defining the problem of poverty, establishing its cause, finding appropriate evidence, clarifying ideological and value positions, and determining an adequate social policy. This chapter examines some of these issues by focusing on the persistent problems of poverty and the unfinished task of developing a social welfare system that seems to make sense for the people who receive assistance as well as for those who provide it.

Robert Reich takes the issues of poverty and affluence in new directions. He observes an important recent trend: the poorest segment of American society is getting poorer and the richest segment is getting richer. Why? His answer avoids simplistic attacks against heartless and witless politicians. Instead, Reich takes a global view of the division of labor in a rapidly developing world economy. His analysis of the causes of the growing disparity between the rich and the poor is fundamental to an appreciation of the prospects he sees for closing the gap.

E. J. Dionne takes a searching look at contemporary confusion about the nature and meaning of equality as a social ideal. Politicians, journalists, and social scientists seem to have lost sight of what public *goals* should be for the less fortunate members of society and the *means* to achieve those goals. In this climate of confusion, it is important to examine some of American's fundamental values in respect to individual rights and responsibilities as well as the government's responsibility to provide for the general welfare—the welfare of all its citizens. Dionne's essay raises more questions than it answers, but we believe that generating meaningful questions about social inequality is the first step toward formulating new answers to the poverty problem and an appropriate social welfare system.

The third essay, by Nicholas Lemann, calls attention to the historical evolution of American industrial cities and the waves of ethnic groups that settled there to begin their rise from wretched slums and public disrepute. Taking a long view of poverty and affluence in the industrial city, Lemann sees good reasons to be hopeful. How does Lemann use history as his guide to strategies to overcome current problems of poverty?

Conservative critics of the American welfare system have argued that government assistance to the poor has played a major role in perpetuating poverty. The welfare system creates dependency and undermines traditional values of hard work, sacrifice, and discipline. Charles Murray has used this argument to attack the American welfare system on many occasions. Here he extends his critique of government policies by examining the British underclass. As a seasoned debater on questions of poverty and public policies, Murray is aware of the importance of stipulating definitions, marshaling evidence, articulating values, making causal inferences, and drawing logically consistent conclusions. This complex essay provides many opportunities for critical assessment of Murray's reasoning skills. Readers must decide whether Murray has made a convincing case for the causes and consequences of the British underclass. What are the implications for poverty in the United States?

9.   WHY THE RICH ARE GETTING RICHER AND THE POOR POORER

ROBERT B. REICH

Between 1978 and 1987, the poorest fifth of American families become 8 percent poorer, and the richest fifth became 13 percent richer. That means the poorest fifth now have less than 5 percent of the nation's income, while the richest fifth have more than 40 percent.

This widening gap can't be blamed on the growth in single-parent lower-income families, which in fact slowed markedly after the late 1970s. Nor is it due mainly to the stingy social policies of the Reagan years. Granted, food stamp benefits have dropped 13 percent since 1981 (in real terms), and many states have failed to raise benefits for the poor and unemployed to keep up with inflation. But this doesn't come close to accounting for the growing persistence of economic inequality in the United States. Rather, this disturbing trend is connected to a profound change in the American economy as it merges with the global economy. And because the merging is far from complete, this trend will not stop all by itself anytime soon. It is significant that the growth of inequality can be seen most strikingly among Americans who have jobs. Through most of the postwar era, the wages of Americans at different income levels rose at about the same pace. Although different workers occupied different steps on the escalator, everyone moved up together. In those days poverty was the condition of *jobless* Americans, and the major economic challenge was to create enough jobs for everyone. Once people were safely in the work force, their problems were assumed to be over. Thus "full employment" became a liberal rallying cry.

But in recent years Americans with jobs have been traveling on two escalators—one going up, the other going down. In 1987 the average

hourly earnings of nonsupervisory workers (adjusted for inflation) were lower than in any year since 1966. Middle-level managers fared much better, although their median real earnings were only slightly above the levels of the 1970s. Executives, however, did spectacularly well. In 1988 alone, CEOs of the 100 largest publicly held industrial corporations received raises averaging almost 12 percent.

Between 1978 and 1987, as the real earnings of unskilled workers were declining, the real incomes of investment bankers and other securities industry workers rose 21 percent. It is not unusual for a run-of-the-mill investment banker to bring home comfortably over a million dollars. Meanwhile, the number of impoverished *working* Americans climbed by nearly two million, or 23 percent, during those same years. Nearly 60 percent of the 20 million people who now fall below the Census Bureau's poverty line are from families with at least one member in full-time or part-time work.

The American economy now exhibits a wider gap between rich and poor than it has at any other time since World War II. The most basic reason, put simply, is that America itself is ceasing to exist as an economic system separate from the rest of the world. One can no more meaningfully speak of an "American economy" than of a "Delaware economy." We are becoming but a region—albeit still a relatively wealthy region—of a global economy. This is a new kind of economy whose technologies, savings, and investments move effortlessly across borders, making it harder for individual nations to control their economic destinies.

We have yet to come to terms with the rise of the global corporation, whose managers, shareholders, and employees span the world. Our debates over the future of American jobs still focus on topics such as the competitiveness of the American automobile industry or the future of

Adapted from *The New Republic,* May 1, 1989. Reprinted with permission.

American manufacturing. But these issues are increasingly irrelevant.

New technologies of worldwide communication and transportation have redrawn the economic playing field. American industries no longer compete against Japanese or European industries. Rather, a company with headquarters in the United States, production facilities in Taiwan, and a marketing force spread across many nations competes with another, similarly wide-ranging company. So when General Motors, say, is doing well, that probably is good news for a lot of executives in Detroit, and for GM shareholders across the globe, but it isn't necessarily good news for a lot of assembly-line workers in Detroit, because there may, in fact, be very few GM assembly-line workers in Detroit, or anywhere else in America. The welfare of assembly-line workers in Detroit may depend, instead, on the health of corporations based in Japan or Canada.

More to the point, even if those Canadian and Japanese corporations are doing well, those Detroit workers may be in trouble. For they are increasingly part of an international labor market, encompassing Asia, Africa, Western Europe, and, perhaps before long, Eastern Europe. With relative ease corporations can relocate their production centers to take advantage of low wages. So American workers find themselves settling for low wages in order to hold on to their jobs. More and more, your "competitiveness" as a worker depends not on the fortunes of any American corporation, or of any American industry, but on what function you serve within the global economy.

In order to see in greater detail what is happening to American jobs, it helps to view the work that most Americans do in terms of new categories that reflect how U.S. workers fit into the global economy. Essentially, three broad categories are emerging. I call them: (1) symbolic-analytic services; (2) routine production services; and (3) routine personal services.

1. Symbolic-analytic services are based on the manipulation of information: data, words, and oral and visual symbols. Symbolic analysis comprises some (but by no means all) of the work undertaken by people who call themselves lawyers, investment bankers, commercial bankers, management consultants, research scientists, academics, public-relations executives, real estate developers, and even a few creative accountants. Also, many advertising and marketing specialists, art directors, design engineers, architects, writers and editors, musicians, and television and film producers.

Some of the manipulations of information performed by these symbolic analysts offer ways of more efficiently deploying resources or shifting financial assets, or of otherwise saving time and energy. Other manipulations grab money from people who are too slow or naive to protect themselves. Still others serve to entertain the public.

Most symbolic analysts work alone or in small teams. If they work with others, they often have partners rather than bosses or supervisors. Their work environments tend to be quiet and tastefully decorated, often within tall steel-and-glass buildings. When they are not analyzing, designing, or strategizing, they are in meetings or on the telephone—giving advice or making deals. Many of them spend an inordinate amount of time in jet planes and hotels. They are generally articulate and well groomed. The vast majority are white males.

Symbolic analysis now accounts for more than 40 percent of America's gross national product, and almost 20 percent of our jobs.

The services performed by America's symbolic analysts are in high demand around the world. The Japanese are buying up the insights and inventions of America's scientists and engineers (who are only too happy to sell them at a fat profit). The Europeans, meanwhile, are hiring our management consultants, business strategists, and investment bankers. Developing nations are hiring our civil and design engineers; and almost everyone is buying the output of our pop musicians, television stars, and film producers.

The same thing is happening with the global corporation. The central offices of these sprawling entities, headquartered in America, are filled with symbolic analysts who manipulate information and then export their insights around the world via the corporation's far-flung operations. IBM, for instance, doesn't export machines from the United States; it manufactures its machines in factories all over the globe. IBM world headquarters, in Armonk, New York, exports just strategic planning and related management services.

Thus has the standard of living of America's symbolic analysts risen. They increasingly find themselves part of a global labor market, not a national one. And because the United States has a highly developed economy, and an excellent university system, they find that the services they have to offer are in high demand around the whole world. This ensures that their salaries are quite high.

Those salaries are likely to go even higher in the years ahead, as the world market for symbolic analysis continues to grow. Foreigners are trying to learn these skills and techniques, to be sure, but they still have a long way to go. No other country does a better job of preparing its most fortunate citizens for symbolic analysis than does the United States. None has surpassed America in providing experience and training, often with entire regions specializing in one or another kind of symbolic analysis (New York and Chicago for finance, Los Angeles for music and film, the San Francisco Bay area and greater Boston for science and engineering). In this we can take pride. But for the second major category of American workers—the providers of routine production services—the future doesn't bode well.

2. Routine production services involve tasks that are repeated over and over, as one step in a sequence of steps for producing a finished product. Although we tend to associate these jobs with manufacturing, they are becoming common in banking, insurance, wholesaling, retailing, health care—all industries employing millions of people who spend their days processing data, often putting information into computers or taking it out.

Most people involved in routine production services work with many other people who do similar work, within large, centralized facilities. They are overseen by supervisors, who in turn are monitored by more senior supervisors. They are usually paid an hourly wage. Their jobs are often monotonous. Most of the workers do not have a college education. Those who deal with metal are mostly white males; those who deal

with fabrics or information tend to be female and/or minorities.

Decades ago, those kinds of workers were relatively well paid. But in recent years America's providers of routine production services have found themselves in direct competition with millions of foreign workers, most of whom work for a fraction of the pay American workers get. Through the miracle of satellite transmission, even routine data processing can now be undertaken in relatively poor nations, thousands of miles away from the skyscrapers where the data are finally used. This fact has given management ever greater power in bargaining talks. If routine production workers living in America don't agree to reduce their wages, then the work often goes abroad.

And it has. In 1950, routine production services constituted about 30 percent of our gross national product and well over half of American jobs. Today such services represent about 20 percent of the GNP and one-fourth of jobs. And the scattering of foreign-owned factories placed here to circumvent American protectionism isn't going to reverse the trend. So the standard of living of America's routine production workers will likely keep declining. The dynamics behind the wage concessions, plant closings, and union-busting that have become commonplace won't be stopped without a major turnaround in labor organizing or political action.

3. Routine personal services also entail simple, repetitive work, but, unlike routine production services, they are provided in person. Included in this employment category are restaurant and hotel workers, barbers and beauticians, retail sales personnel, cab drivers, household cleaners, day-care workers, hospital attendants and orderlies, truck drivers, and—among the fastest-growing of all careers—custodians and security guards.

Like production workers, providers of personal services are usually paid by the hour. They are also carefully supervised and rarely have more than a high school education. But unlike people in the other two categories of work, they are in direct contact with the ultimate beneficiaries of what they do. And the companies they work for are often small. In fact, some routine personal-service workers become entrepreneurs. (Most new businesses and new jobs in America come from this sector—which now constitutes about 20 percent of GNP and 30 percent of jobs.) Women and minorities make up the bulk of routine personal-service workers.

Apart from the small number who strike out on their own, these workers are paid poorly. They are sheltered from the direct effects of global competition, but not the indirect effects. They often compete with undocumented workers willing to work for low wages, or with former or would-be production workers who can't find well-paying production jobs, or with labor-saving machinery (automated tellers, self-service gas pumps) dreamed up by symbolic analysts in America and manufactured in Asia. And because they tend to be unskilled and dispersed among small businesses, personal-service workers rarely have a union or a powerful lobby group to stand up for their interests. When the economy turns sour, they are among the first to feel the effects.

These workers will continue to have jobs in the years ahead and may experience some small increase in real wages. They will have demographics on their side, as the American work force shrinks. But for all the foregoing reasons, the gap between their earnings and those of the symbolic analysts will continue to grow if present economic trends and labor conditions continue.

These three functional categories—symbolic analysis, routine production services, and routine personal services—cover at least three out of four American jobs. The rest of the nation's work force consists mainly of government employees (including public school teachers), employees in regulated industries (like utility workers), and government-financed workers (engineers working on defense weapons systems), many of whom are sheltered from global competition. One further clarification: Some traditional job categories overlap several of these categories. People called "secretaries," for example, include those who actually spend their time doing symbolic analysis work closely allied to what their bosses do; those who do routine data entry or retrieval of a sort that will eventually be automated or done overseas; and those who provide routine personal services.

The important point is that workers in these three functional categories are coming to have different competitive positions in the world economy. Symbolic analysts hold a commanding position in an increasingly global labor market. Routine production workers hold a relatively weak position in an increasingly global labor market. Routine personal service workers still find themselves in a national labor market, but for various reasons they suffer the indirect effects of competition from workers abroad.

How should we respond to these trends? One response is to accept them as inevitable consequences of change, but to try to offset their polarizing effects through a truly progressive income tax, coupled with more generous income assistance—including health insurance—for poor working Americans. (For a start, we might reverse the extraordinarily regressive Social Security amendments of 1983, through which poor working Americans are now financing the federal budget deficit, often paying more in payroll taxes than in income taxes.)

A more ambitious response would be to guard against class rigidities by ensuring that any talented American kid can become a symbolic analyst—regardless of family income or race. But America's gifted but poor children can't aspire to such jobs until the government spends substantially more than it does now to ensure excellent public schools in every city and region and ample financial help when they are ready to attend college.

Of course, it isn't clear that even under those circumstances there would be radical growth in the number of Americans who become research scientists, design engineers, musicians, management consultants, or (even if the world needed them) investment bankers and lawyers. So other responses are also needed. Perhaps the most ambitious would be to increase the numbers of Americans who could apply symbolic analysis to production and to personal services.

There is ample evidence, for example, that access to computerized information can enrich production jobs by enabling workers to alter the flow of materials and components in ways that increase efficiency. Production workers who have broader responsibilities and more control over how production is organized cease to be "routine" workers—becoming, in effect, symbolic analysts at a level very close to the production process. The same transformation can occur in personal-service jobs. Consider, for example, the checkout clerk whose computer enables her to control inventory and decide when to reorder items from the factory.

The number of such technologically empowered jobs, of course, is limited by the ability of workers to learn on the job. That means a far greater number of Americans will need a good grounding in mathematics, basic science, reading, and communication skills. So once again, comfortably integrating the American work force into the new world economy turns out to rest heavily on education. (Better health care, especially prenatal and pediatric care, would also figure in here.)

Education and health care for poor children are apt to be costly. Since poorer working Americans, already under a heavy tax load, can't afford it, the cost would have to be borne by wealthier Americans—who also would have to bear the cost of any income redistribution plans designed to neutralize the polarizing domestic effects of a globalized economy. Thus a central question is the willingness of the more fortunate American citizens—especially symbolic analysts, who constitute much of the most fortunate fifth, with 40 percent of the nation's income—to bear the burden. But here lies a catch-22. For as our economic fates diverge, the top fifth may be losing its sense of connectedness with the bottom fifth

(or even the bottom half) that would elicit such generosity.

The conservative tide that has swept the land during the past decade surely has many causes, but the fundamental changes in our economy should not be discounted as a major factor. It is now possible for the most fortunate fifth to sell their expertise directly in the global market, and thus maintain and enhance their standard of living, even as that of other Americans declines. There is less and less basis for a strong sense of interclass interdependence in America. Meanwhile, the fortunate fifth have also been able to insulate themselves from the less fortunate, by living in suburban enclaves far removed from the effects of poverty. Neither patriotism nor altruism may be sufficient to overcome these realities. Yet without the active support of at least some of the fortunate fifth, it will be more difficult to muster the political will necessary for change.

George Bush speaks eloquently of "a thousand points of light" and of the importance of generosity. But so far his administration has set a poor example. A minuscule sum has been budgeted for education, training, and health care for the poor. The president says we can't afford any more. Meanwhile, he pushes a reduction in the capital gains tax rate—another boon to the fortunate fifth.

On withdrawing from the presidential race of 1988. Paul Simon of Illinois said, "Americans instinctively know that we are one nation, one family, and when anyone in that family hurts, all of us hurt." Sadly, that is coming to be less and less the case.

10. THE IDEA OF EQUALITY IS PROVING UNEQUAL TO THE DEMANDS OF TODAY

E. J. DIONNE, JR.

Egalitarianism: It died during Ronald Reagan's 1980s but the full impact of its demise, according to numerous social policy analysts, is just beginning to be felt in American society.

The half-century-old concept that government has a responsibility to narrow the gap between rich and poor—a responsibility that Republicans and Democrats had largely accepted since the time of Franklin D. Roosevelt's New Deal—no longer guides the design of American economic policies.

Instead, inequality is now being widely defended as a source of productivity, economic growth and individual striving for excellence. Polls show that this view resonates with the American public. According to one survey, only 29 percent of Americans see redistribution of income as a government responsibility.

The country's politics reflect this outlook. When Democratic Sen. Daniel Patrick Moynihan of New York recently proposed reducing the Social Security tax burden on working- and middle-class Americans, even Moynihan did not suggest taxing the rich at a higher rate instead. Nevertheless, few Democrats embraced Moynihan's egalitarian idea of cutting taxes on working people; his proposal appears stillborn.

International conditions also have affected attitudes toward egalitarianism. The collapse of communism has put socialists and other supporters of strong government controls on the defensive.

Seymour Martin Lipset, a political sociologist at Stanford University, says that the intellectual trend toward greater acceptance of inequality

has taken hold throughout the industrial world, to the point where even socialist parties are acknowledging that "for an economic system to work, you have to have unequal rewards."

Supporters of greater economic equality are fighting back, arguing that the intellectual trend in favor of inequality has reached its high tide and that disparities between the wealthy and the rest of society have grown so wide that an egalitarian backlash is inevitable.

But advocates of more equal distribution of incomes and wealth concede that the intellectual climate today is hostile. "Intellectual criticism of the egalitarian position has become bolder and more vigorous," says Marshall Cohen, a philosopher at the University of Southern California and the editor of Philosophy and Public Affairs. "A generation ago, the liberal welfare consensus was the general position."

The shift in the intellectual argument is reshaping American society and public policy. The concept of a progressive income tax, for example, has been substantially eroded. In the 1950s, when Dwight D. Eisenhower was president, the richest people were taxed at a nominal top rate of 91 percent. Today, in accord with the conservative theory that lower taxes on the well-to-do promote job-creating investment and hard work, the top rate has been cut to 28 percent.

At the same time, there has been a significant drop in the buying power of welfare benefits. According to Christopher Jencks, a sociologist at Northwestern University, the purchasing power of the typical welfare recipient fell by 16 percent from 1976 to 1988.

The working poor also lost ground. Between 1981 and 1989, the minimum wage lost 44 percent of its value. Even with the increase that went into effect on April 1, the purchasing power of the minimum wage was 24 percent below its 1981 level.

According to Jeff Faux, president of the Economic Policy Institute, a liberal research center in Washington, the 1980s saw the first substantial change in the distribution of wealth and income in the United States since World War II.

The institute's analysts, whose findings broadly parallel those of other economists, concluded that the share of the nation's wealth owned by the top 10 percent of its households rose from 67.5 percent to 73.1 percent between 1979 and 1988. The share of after-tax family income earned by the top 10 percent rose from 29.5 percent in 1980 to an estimated 34.9 percent in 1990. In the same periods, the income share of the bottom 10 percent dropped from 1.7 percent to 1.4 percent. (This poorest group consists of net debtors, so they have "negative wealth.")

The broad middle class—the 60 percent of Americans between the richest and poorest— saw its share of family income decline from 50.2 percent in 1980 to an estimated 46.5 percent in 1990.

The decline in intellectual support for economic equality has affected thinking on social policy. Policy-makers seem more inclined than ever to attribute disparities in people's fortunes to the failures of individuals rather than to flaws in the economic system.

Kate O'Beirne, deputy director for domestic policy studies at the conservative Heritage Foundation, notes that poverty research is concentrating more and more on the problems faced by single-mother families and on the importance of "family stability and the work ethic" in lifting people out of poverty. She says the trend toward an emphasis on self-help and individual responsibility is visible across the political spectrum.

The quest for a more equal distribution of income and wealth has always been problematic in the United States, given the heavy emphasis in the nation's creed on self-improvement and achievement.

Isabel Sawhill, a senior fellow at the Urban Institute and a supporter of greater equality, says she learned the power of the achievement ethic when, as a college professor, she made a hypothetical offer to students to trade their grade on an exam for the average grade of the class—provided that they agreed in advance to accept the average class grade for their entire year's work.

"I never had a majority of students accept the offer," she says. "They always said, 'We don't want to change the rules of the game this time, because next time we might do better.'"

Democratic Rep. Barney Frank of Massachusetts, an outspoken liberal, notes that this self-reliance ethic took deep hold in the United States because the country lacked the feudal and aristocratic traditions of Europe that gave huge advantages to those born into the right families. In the United States, inequalities of wealth and income have been seen as more legitimate, he says, partly because of the presumption that the better-off have earned their advantages.

It is clear that Americans are more wary of economic leveling than the citizens of other industrial countries.

According to poll results published in the American Enterprise magazine, only 29 percent of Americans agreed that "it is the responsibility of the government to reduce the differences in income between people with high incomes and those with low incomes." In Austria and Italy, more than 80 percent agreed with the same proposition; in West Germany and Britain, more than 60 percent agreed.

But the impulse toward equality has been more popular in the United States in the past, notably during the Great Depression. "The promise of America was not that everyone would become rich, but that just about everyone could have a decent standard of living," says Robert Shapiro, an economist who is vice president of the centrist Progressive Policy Institute. "Egalitarianism became popular during the New Deal because, suddenly, that middle-class standard was threatened and people wanted the government to do something to restore the American dream."

New Deal economists legitimized the striving for greater equality by explaining the cause of the Great Depression as a failure to spread purchasing power—money—broadly enough. Using the government to give money to the unemployed and the poor was thus defended not simply as morally correct but also as economic good sense.

"There was a kind of reigning ideology that redistribution was good for growth," says Northwestern's Jencks, a coauthor of "Inequality," a study of the causes of income disparities published in the early 1970s. "And with a relatively high rate of growth [after World War II], the idea was that redistribution wouldn't hurt anybody and wouldn't cost very much." But after the struggles of the 1960s and early 1970s, the egalitarian idea became much more controversial.

Faux of the Economic Policy Institute says advocates of equality erred in the 1960s when they turned their attention almost exclusively to the problems of poverty. "In the 1930s, 1940s, and 1950s, the problem of inequality was seen as the gap between people who worked for a living and people who clipped coupons," he says, referring to those who lived mainly on the proceeds of investments. "What happened in the 1960s is that inequality became exclusively a problem of poor people."

Todd Gitlin, a sociologist at the University of California at Berkeley, says the postwar prosperity led ever larger numbers of Americans to doubt that greater income equality would do anything to help them. "Middle-class people took equality as a threat to level them down," he says. "What is striking is the decline of the impulse to level up."

In the 1960s the push for civil rights further redefined the issue of equality, making it largely a racial concern.

Randall Kennedy, a professor at Harvard Law School, says the successes of the civil rights movement encouraged advocates of the less affluent to cast as many problems as they could in racial terms.

"Things that were mainly class problems were redefined as racial problems, because in the American legal structure there is no problem with class discrimination," he says, "whereas there is a constitutional problem with racial discrimination."

Kennedy says that in the heyday of the civil rights movement, this strategy produced many successes for egalitarians. But over time, the close link between race and the idea of equality led many whites to see egalitarianism as a threat to their incomes and opportunities.

Jencks says the move away from equality also grew out of popular frustration over the failures—both real and imagined—of Lyndon B. Johnson's Great Society. "There's an impulse to say that if you couldn't fix it by what we did in the '60s, then the hell with it," Jencks says. "It was the domestic equivalent of the Vietnam War."

The economic problems of the 1970s—notably high inflation and sluggish growth—further undermined the egalitarian idea. Irving Kristol, one of the nation's most influential conservative thinkers, says the country came to accept the conservative view that "if you have an overemphasis on economic equality, you frustrate economic growth." Kristol says that through the pro-incentive policies of supply-side economics, the message of the New Deal was turned on its head: Redistribution was no longer the friend of a productive economy, but its enemy.

Liberals still disagree, and many predict a revival of egalitarianism. For example, Jo-Ann Mort, communications director for the Amalgamated Clothing and Textile Workers Union, says, "America is falling behind economically because of inequalities in education levels and job training and because it is creating so many low-wage, dead-end jobs." She says, "For both political and moral reasons, the country is again going to discover the merits of equality."

Michael Novak, a resident scholar at the conservative America Enterprise Institute, argues to the contrary that the collapse of the Communist economies of Eastern Europe has strengthened the argument that too much state intervention in the distribution of wealth and the management of industry endangers liberty and economic productivity.

George Weigel, a conservative who runs the Ethics and Public Policy Center in Washington, says events in Eastern Europe will inevitably play back into the American debate, promoting the idea that "if the goal is economic growth, the system of choice is the market system." He adds: "Coming to that point of view means a willingness to concede differences in the distribution of wealth." For the moment, at least, that seems a fair description of the American mood.

11.   MAKING IT: THE UNDERCLASS CYCLE

NICHOLAS LEMANN

The Irish, crowding into the cities, posed problems in housing, police, and schools; they meant higher taxes and heavier burdens in the support of poorhouses and private charitable institutions. Moreover, the Irish did not seem to practice thrift, self-denial and other virtues desirable in the "worthy, laboring poor." They seemed drunken, dissolute, permanently sunk in poverty.

> —William V. Shannon, *The American Irish*

Hardly less aggressive than the Italian, the Russian and Polish Jew . . . is filling the tenements of the old Seventh Ward to the river front, and disputing with the Italian every foot of available space in the back alleys of Mulberry Street. The two races, differing hopelessly in much, have this in common: They carry their slums with them wherever they go, if allowed to do it. . . . The Italian and the poor Jew rise only by compulsion.

> —Jacob Riis, *How the Other Half Lives*

The present always imputes a degree of innocence to the past. One of many possible examples is our attitude toward the underclass, which is, essentially, that no similar social problem has ever existed in urban America—and that therefore the problem can't be solved. An ethnic group living in isolated slums in the very heart of our prosperous cities; fatal disease spreading as a result of irresponsibly licentious behavior; rampant welfare dependence; out-of-control violent crime; abuse of lethal intoxicants; rampaging youth gangs; rich, swaggering criminals who sit atop the society of the slum; a breakdown of family values; a barely disguised feeling among the

prosperous classes that perhaps the poor are inherently not up to being fully functioning Americans—the whole picture has been around, intermittently, in this country since about 1850.

Historically, alarm about urban ethnic poverty arises with the arrival in our cities of a large group of immigrants who are visibly very different from middle-class America. The first such group was the peasant Irish, who began coming here in the 1840s. Within a decade, there were large Irish slums; the Irish dominated the resources of the jails, public hospitals and social-welfare agencies; and the fear of where all this would lead was an important factor in national politics. In the late 1880s, after immigrants from eastern and southern Europe had established their own urban slums, another substantial wave of concern about the underclass began, and one of its many consequences was a major political realignment that led to the heyday of Progressivism.

Worries about the turn-of-the century underclass led to strict limits on immigration, and this created labor shortages in the cities. The abundance of unskilled jobs began attracting large numbers of southern blacks to the cities starting around the time of World War I. This black migration intensified with World War II and the boom years that followed it, which vastly increased the demand for labor and coincided with the mechanization of agriculture in the South. The number of black migrants from South to North in the '40s, '50s, and '60s was greater than the number of Irish, Jews, or Italians or Poles who came to the cities during their peak years of migration. It should not be surprising that, like the earlier migrations, the black migration, which lasted until about 1970, should have brought the issue of slum life back to the fore, and contributed to another political realignment—the shift of the presidential electorate to the Republican Party in the late '60s.

From *The Washington Post*, May 21, 1989. Reprinted by permission of Nicholas Lemann.

SLUMS IN THE 1890s

It is impossible to read Jacob Riis's *How the Other Half Lives*, published in 1890, without noticing the parallels between Riis's concerns and those of middle-class reformers in the big cities today. Rotgut liquor seemed every bit as dangerous then as crack does today; in fact, his chapter called "A Raid on the Stale-beer Dives" is an eerily precise parallel to those television shows in which a camera crew accompanies the police to a crack house. The saloon-keeper was the equivalent of the drug-dealer, the only visibly affluent male in the slum (except for the numbers king, whose function in recent years has been taken over by local government lotteries). Teenage gangs were even worse than they are now, in the sense that one of their usual activities, according to Riis, was assaulting police officers.

Riis even shared some of the suspicions of present-day conservatives that social problems may add to, rather than diminish, the conditions they seek to alleviate. "Ill-applied charity," Riis felt, was creating a class of people who didn't bother to look for work. Cholera, bred by willfully unclean living, played the role AIDS does now. Teen-age girls were having babies and letting them run wild. Illiteracy was rampant. Murder was an "everyday crop."

In Riis's work, as in that of the other great liberal reformers of the day, there lurks just beneath the surface the idea that ethnicity is destiny. Obviously the same idea, again barely submerged, is around today, though it is reassuring to see how silly Riis's stereotypes seem after less than a century. "Penury and poverty are wedded everywhere to dirt and disease, and Jewtown is no exception," he wrote. "It could not well be otherwise in such crowds, considering especially their low intellectual status."

Riis saw the relatively small black population of New York as occupying a much higher plane: "Cleanliness is the characteristic of the negro in his new surroundings, as it was his virtue in the old. In this respect he is immensely superior to the lowest of the whites, the Italians and the Polish Jews. . . ." As late as World War I, blacks living in the North outscored Jews on the Army intelligence test.

I don't mean to argue that all the problems of the ghettos are simply going to go away over time—only that the current atmosphere of fatalism is unwarranted. What will happen is similar to what has happened in the past: The ghettos will become depopulated as everybody who can get a job moves out. This has been going on for two decades in the big-city black ghettos, virtually all of which were badly overcrowded in the mid-'60s and have an emptied-out look today. In the 1970s, the District of Columbia lost 16 percent of its population while its black-white ratio stayed almost exactly the same; there was a lot of black flight going on, too. If you define the underclass as people living in majority-poor inner-city neighborhoods (and social scientists are moving toward this kind of geographical definition), then instead of being the "growing problem" that everyone says it is, the underclass is a shrinking problem.

Of course, the more the employed migrate out of inner cities, the worse ghettos will become as neighborhoods: There will be still less of a social check on crime, less institutional structure, fewer intact families. (The main difference between today's ghettos and those that Riis wrote about is that there are so many fewer poor husband-wife families today—a difference that does make today's underclass more intractable but still not totally so.) Eventually, the out-migration will stop—though it hasn't stopped yet—and a dispirited core of people will be left behind to live in what will be, functionally, the urban equivalents of Indian reservations.

SOCIAL PROGRAMS

We should not sit around and watch this happen. External events have a tremendous effect on the ability of poor people to get out of the ghettos. The Irish middle class began to emerge when Irish political machines took over city halls and got access to the many thousands of decent-paying municipal patronage jobs. The immigrants Riis wrote about had the good fortune to arrive in the United States early in a long period of industrialization, in which unskilled jobs were plentiful and the economy was expanding.

The black migration out of the ghettos was spurred by the domestic initiatives of Lyndon Johnson, such as the Civil Rights Act, the Fair Housing Act, affirmative action and the large increase in black employment in government that began with the declaration of the War on Poverty. The proportion of the poor who escape poverty, and the speed with which they escape, are variable and depend greatly on economic trends and on what the government does.

Today, most discussion of the underclass is strongly influenced by the idea that government social programs can't possibly help. We believe we've tried everything; we believe none of it worked; we believe that if the programs that began in the late '60s had any effect at all, it was to make things worse. Most of this is wildly oversimplified, exaggerated, or untrue. The government's anti-poverty efforts were of limited size and duration—the heyday of poverty programs, as opposed to welfare programs, lasted only five years, from 1964 to 1968—and were built around a new, unproven idea: community action.

Moreover, progress was made: The percentage of Americans who are poor decreased substantially during the '60s, then leveled off in the '70s and rose in the '80s, when the government was cutting back its efforts. It's hard to find individual members of the underclass who are downwardly mobile—mostly they come from families that have always been poor.

Now we know a lot more about what kinds of poverty programs work. In general, what works is intensive efforts—not short-term, one-shot aid injections—to help poor children arrive at adulthood well-educated and trained for employment. These efforts ought to begin with prenatal care and continue through Head Start, special-education programs during the school years and job training of sufficient duration and intensity to teach real skills and good work habits. Ridding ghetto neighborhoods of crime would help, too. So would making long-term welfare recipients get jobs. All this is both expensive and intrusive, so it lacks a certain mom-and-apple-pie appeal. But it would do a lot of good.

Since the ghettos have deteriorated so much as places, it's tempting to say that the answer is to improve them as places. But this works only up to a point. Public safety, education and the housing stock in ghettos can and should be improved, but the idea of creating an independent economic base and a class of successful role models there is a persistent fantasy. This idea has a respectable ancestry in Booker T. Washington's vision of a black America made up of yeoman farmers and skilled artisans. But remember that Washington formulated his views during the height of Jim Crow and foresaw a totally segregated black America.

The vision of a self-sufficient ghetto doesn't work in a world in which, happily, successful blacks have the option of entering the mainstream economy and making much more money. There is no reason to hope, or to expect, that when people in the ghettos become successful enough to be role models, they won't leave. The idea that people who have already left will move back is even more unlikely absent a total overhaul of inner urban areas in which the ghettos themselves are displaced.

Economic development efforts in poor neighborhoods have been one of the conspicuous failures of the past generation, because it's murderously difficult to build businesses in neighborhoods that are rapidly losing population. The most publicized success stories involving ghetto development, such as Bedford-Stuyvesant in Brooklyn and South Shore in Chicago, really involve the residential stabilization of working-class neighborhoods, not the establishment of a neighborhood economic base.

Two sentiments about the underclass seem to prevail these days: First, the situation is completely hopeless; and second, the underclass can only be healed from within black America, through black leadership. The best answer to the first point is to look at the history of previous immigrant ghettos, which should lead to the conclusion that the situation is exactly as hopeless today as it has always been—which is to say, not hopeless at all. The second point is really an attitude, not a program. Does anyone really believe that if Benjamin Hooks of the NAACP—an organization of, by and for middle-class blacks—made daily speeches about drugs, crime and teen-age pregnancy, it would turn the ghetto around?

Jesse Jackson, to his credit, has been making such speeches for years. He is a hero in the ghettos, but he hasn't made the problems go away. The underclass is cut off from the rest of America, and what it needs is the direct intervention of the whole society, not just black society. A generation from now, the wild pessimism now prevailing about the underclass will seem dated; and so will our disinclination to see that the problem exerts a call to which the whole country must respond for both moral and practical reasons.

12.   THE BRITISH UNDERCLASS

CHARLES MURRAY

Is the underclass an American phenomenon? It often seems so. Reports about Western Europe's social democracies typically portray societies in which the low-income class is hardworking and responsible. Only the United States of America, these reports suggest, is stricken with a large urban population that seems mired at the bottom of society, disorganized and demoralized.

On the left, the blame for this situation is often ascribed to the United States's failure to adopt a generous welfare state, Sweden being the standard to which the United States should aspire. But it is also widely accepted by left and right alike that the underclass in the United States is unique in that it is predominantly black. It is also widely thought, though more controversially, that the historical experiences of American blacks help to explain today's underclass. Several theorists have focused on the legacy of slavery; Nicholas Lemann has emphasized the black sharecropper experience; William Julius Wilson calls attention to the elimination of manufacturing jobs that black city dwellers once held. Even people who assign more blame to bad contemporary policy than to history (I am one of them) take for granted that it is hard to find Caucasian counterparts to the poorest black neighborhoods in any large American city.

The question of a developing underclass in other Western countries is thus of special interest. If the United States is indeed alone, explanations based on the black experience and a stingy welfare state become more persuasive. If other countries have experienced similar trends, we have a basis for disentangling the factors in modernization, or in policy, or both, that stimulate the growth of what we have come to call an underclass. And so last year I accepted with considerable curiosity an invitation by the London *Sunday Times* to explore the possibility of an English underclass.

OLD CONCEPT, NEW LABEL

Because definition is always a problem when discussing the underclass, let me begin by providing mine. By "underclass" I refer not to poor people, but to a subset of poor people who chronically live off mainstream society (directly through welfare or indirectly through crime) without participating in it. They characteristically take jobs sporadically if at all, do not share the social burdens of the neighborhoods in which they live, shirk the responsibilities of fatherhood and are indifferent (or often simply incompetent) mothers.

The British were among the first to describe an urban underclass, never more evocatively than through Henry Mayhew's 1850 articles in the *Morning Chronicle*, which first drew the Victorians' attention to poverty. To Mayhew, what

From *The Public Interest*, no. 99 (Spring 1990), pp. 4–28. Copyright © 1990 National Affairs, Inc. Reprinted with permission.

we would call a member of the underclass was "distinguished from the civilized man by his repugnance to regular and continuous labor—by his want of providence in laying up a store for the future—by his inability to perceive consequences ever so slightly removed from immediate apprehension—by his passion for stupefying herbs and roots and, when possible, for intoxicating fermented liquors. . . ." Other popular labels for this kind of poor person were "dishonest," "undeserving," "unrespectable," "depraved," "debased," "disreputable," or "feckless."

As Britain entered the 1960s, this distinction between honest and dishonest poor people had been softened. The second kind of poor person was no longer "undeserving"; rather, he was the product of a "culture of poverty." But intellectuals as well as the man in the street continued to accept that poor people were not all alike. Most were doing their best under difficult circumstances; a small number were pretty much as Mayhew had described them. Then came the intellectual reformation that swept both the United States and Britain in the mid-1960s, bringing with it a new way of looking at the poor. Henceforth, the poor were to be homogenized. The only difference between poor people and everyone else, we were told, was that the poor had less money. More importantly, the poor were all alike. There was no such thing as the ne'er-do-well poor person—he was the figment of the prejudices of a parochial middle class. Poor people, *all* poor people, were equally victims, and would be equally successful if only society gave them a fair shake.

The difference between the United States and Britain was that the United States reached the future first. During the last half of the 1960s and throughout the 1970s, something strange and disturbing was happening among poor people in the United States. Poor communities, whose inhabitants had mostly been hard workers and good neighbors, began deteriorating. Drugs, crime, illegitimacy, homelessness, dropping out of school and the job market, casual violence—all the measures that were available to social scientists showed large increases, focused in poor communities. As the 1980s began, the growing population of "the other kind of poor people"

could no longer be ignored, and a label for it came into use: the underclass.

By and large, British intellectuals still disdain the term. In 1987, the social historian John Macnicol summed up the prevailing view in the *Journal of Social Policy,* writing dismissively that underclass was nothing more than a refuted concept periodically resurrected by conservatives "who wish to constrain the redistributive potential of state welfare." But there are beginning to be breaks in the ranks. Frank Field, the prominent Labour MP, has just published a book with "underclass" in its subtitle. The newspapers, watching the United States and seeing shadows of its problems in Britain, have begun to use the term.

And well they should. I must introduce caveats to that statement. My trip to Britain was a reconnaissance, not a full-scale study. I cannot estimate the size of the British underclass with any confidence. It is possible that the British underclass will for a long time prove less dysfunctional than the American variety. Despite the caveats, however, the warning signs of an underclass in Britain are reasonably clear. Britain does have an underclass as I have defined it—people living off mainstream society without participating in it—still largely out of sight and still smaller than the one in the United States. But it is growing rapidly. Within the next decade it could easily become as large (proportionately) as America's.

In making this case, I will concentrate on three phenomena that have turned out to be early-warning signals in the United States: illegitimacy, violent crime, and dropout from the labor force. I begin with illegitimacy, which in my view is the best predictor of an underclass in the making.

ILLEGITIMACY

To focus on illegitimacy still raises hackles in Britain, just as it did in America during the 1970s. Why should it be a "problem" that a woman has a child without a husband? Why can't a single woman raise a healthy, happy child, provided that she receives enough support from the state? Why is raising a child without having married any more of a problem than raising a child after a divorce? The very world "illegitimate" is intellectually illegitimate. Using it in a gathering of British academics is a faux pas, causing pained silence.

I nonetheless focus on illegitimacy rather than on the more general phenomenon of one-parent families because, in a world where all social trends are ambiguous, illegitimacy is less ambiguous than other forms of single parenthood. It is a matter of degree. Of course some unmarried mothers are excellent mothers and some unmarried fathers are excellent fathers. Of course some divorced parents disappear from their children's lives altogether and some divorces have more destructive effects on the children than a failure to marry would have had. Being without two parents is generally worse for the child than having two parents, no matter how it happens. But illegitimacy bespeaks an attitude on the part of one or both of the parents. If one stipulates that bearing (and keeping) a child is one of the most profoundly important human acts, then siring a child without intending to support it, or bearing and keeping a child without knowing one can take care of it, constitutes an

excellent proxy measure of the sort of irresponsibility that is the hallmark of the underclass.

Illegitimacy has been skyrocketing since 1979. I use "skyrocketing" advisedly. [Figure 1] is the graph for the years since World War II ended.

The postwar era divides into three parts. From the end of World War II until 1960, Britain enjoyed a very low and even slightly declining illegitimacy ratio. From 1960 through 1978, the ratio increased, but remained modest by international standards—as late as 1979, Britain's illegitimacy ratio of 10.6 percent was among the lowest rates in the industrialized West. Then, suddenly, during a period when fertility was steady, the illegitimacy ratio began to rise very rapidly—to 14.1 percent by 1982, 18.9 percent by 1985, and finally to 25.6 percent by 1988, thereby catching up with the United States in this unhappy statistic. (The most recent U.S. figures are for 1987, when the ratio stood at 24.5 percent and had been rising by about a percentage point per year.)

The sharp rise is only half of the story. The other and equally important half is that illegitimate births are not scattered evenly among the British population. There is much publicity

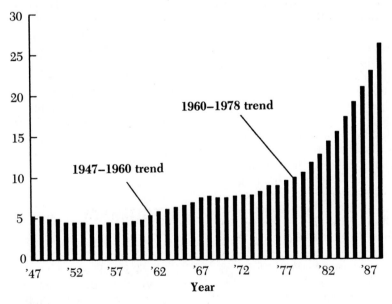

FIGURE 1
Percentage of British births born to single women.

about the member of the Royal Family who has a child without a husband or the socially prominent young career woman who deliberately decides to have a baby on her own, but these are comparatively rare events. The increase in illegitimate births is strikingly concentrated among the lowest social class.

This is especially easy to document in Britain, where one may fit together the Government Statistical Service's birth data on municipal districts with the detailed socioeconomic data from the general census. When one does so for the 169 metropolitan districts and boroughs in England and Wales for which data are available from both sources, the relationship between illegitimacy and social class (using the five-class classification used for many years by the Government Statistical Service) is so obvious that statistical tests become superfluous. Municipal districts with high concentrations of household heads in Class I (professional persons) have illegitimacy ratios in the low teens. Wokingham was lowest as of 1987, with only nine of every hundred children born illegitimate. Municipalities like Nottingham and Southwark, with populations most heavily weighted with Class V household heads (unskilled laborers), have illegitimacy ratios of more than 40 percent.

The statistical tests confirm the relationship. With just two measures—the percentage of people in Class V and the percentage of people who are "economically inactive"—the illegitimacy ratio in a community can usually be predicted within just three percentage points of the true number. Statistically, these two measures of economic status explain 51 percent of the variance—an extremely powerful relationship for just two independent variables. In short, the notion that giving birth to illegitimate babies is a general phenomenon, experienced by young career women and girls from middle-class homes as much as by others, is flatly at odds with the facts. There has been a proportional increase in illegitimate births among all communities, but the prevalence of illegitimate births is drastically higher among the lower-class communities than in the upper class.

The data I have just described are based on municipal districts. The picture worsens when we move down to the neighborhood level,

though precise numbers are hard to come by. If one assumes that the relationship of socioeconomic status to illegitimacy that holds between municipalities also holds between socioeconomic classes within municipalities, then a municipality with an overall ratio of 35 percent should be expected to have poor neighborhoods where most babies are illegitimate (just as black inner-city neighborhoods in the United States have much higher ratios than black middle-class neighborhoods).

When I raised these points with British demographers and sociologists, the reaction more often than not was, in effect, "So what?" I found that discussing the issue with British experts was like being in a time warp, hearing in 1989 the same rationalizations about illegitimacy that American experts used in the 1970s and early 1980s.

"Children from single-parent households do just as well as children from two-parent households." For example, there is the case of the National Child Development Study (NCDS), a longitudinal British sample that researchers have been following since 1968. The differences between children from one-parent families and two-parent families are due to social and financial circumstances, not to the parental situation, proclaims a set of studies, prepared under the auspices of the National Children's Bureau.

Assessing these conclusions is made difficult by technical problems with the studies' definitions of "single parent" and "two parent" families; for example, a child could be defined as coming from a one-parent family if he had ever been without two parents, even briefly. But the generic problem with such analyses, and these in particular, is that all forms of single parenthood tend to be lumped together, as if it makes no difference whether the mother is a widow, a middle-aged woman divorced after years of marriage, or a girl of twenty who has never married. All are "single parents," and all single-parent situations are supposed to be equal. But in fact, one particular form of single parenthood—illegitimacy—constitutes a special problem for society. Single-parent situations are radically unequal.

The change in the received wisdom on this topic in the U.S. has been remarkable. One example will serve to illustrate. In 1983 a statistic cited everywhere by those who wanted to debunk the reactionaries was that 50 percent of all U.S. welfare mothers were off the welfare rolls within two years. The idea of "welfare dependency" was a myth. Then in 1986 David Ellwood, the scholar whose work had popularized the 50-percent statistic, took a finer-grained look at the same data (the Panel Study of Income Dynamics at the University of Michigan), separating welfare mothers into different categories. The most important characteristic in predicting whether a woman left welfare quickly was her marital status at the time she had the baby. For never-married women, the average number of years on welfare was not the highly touted two years, but 9.3. British social-welfare scholars respond that in their country single mothers exit rapidly, basing their confidence about the 1980s on survey data about single women who had babies from the mid-1930s to the mid-1970s. The magic number once again is said to be two years.

"It's mainly a black problem." I heard this everywhere, from political clubs in Westminster to the demographics section of a government research office. The statement is correct in this one, very limited sense: blacks born in the West Indies have much higher illegitimacy ratios—about 48 percent of live births in the latest numbers—than all whites. But blacks constitute such a tiny proportion of the British population that their contribution to the overall illegitimacy ratio is minuscule. If there had been no blacks whatsoever in Britain, the overall British illegitimacy ratio of 25.6 percent in 1988 would have dropped by about one percentage point. Blacks are not causing Britain's illegitimacy problem.

"It's not as bad as it looks." In the United States, the line used to be that blacks have extended families, with uncles and grandfathers compensating for the lack of fathers. In Britain, the counterpart to this cheery optimism is that an increasing number of illegitimate births are jointly registered and that an increasing number of such children are born to people who live together at the time of birth. Both joint registration and living together are quickly called evidence of "a stable relationship."

The statements about joint registration and living together are factually correct. Of the 158,500 illegitimate births in England and Wales

in 1987, 69 percent were jointly registered. Of those who jointly registered the birth, 70 percent gave the same address, suggesting some kind of ongoing relationship. Both of these figures have increased—in 1961, for example, only 38 percent of illegitimate births were jointly registered, suggesting that the nature of illegitimacy in the United Kingdom has changed dramatically.

British commentators on social policy make much of the cohabitation figures without any apparent basis. Once again, the comparison with the United States is striking: American social scientists never demonstrated empirically, or even tried very hard to demonstrate, that the extended black family was able to compensate for the lack of a married father and mother. In any case, appeals to the extended family became more difficult as the years went on—without marriage, grandfathers and uncles too have become scarce. Ought Britons to assume that jointly registering a birth, or living together at the time of the birth, makes for a stable relationship that is just as good (or nearly as good) as a marriage? I pose it as a question because I don't have a solid empirical answer. But neither did any of the people who kept repeating the joint-registration and living-together numbers so optimistically.

It may at least be said that the anecdotal evidence on this issue is cause for concern. While in Britain, I visited poor neighborhoods in Birkenhead (across the Mersey from Liverpool) and Easterhouse, a huge council estate (the British label for a public housing project) outside Glasgow, and talked not only with single mothers but also with the remaining two-parent families who are trying to raise their own children in a predominantly single-parent environment. Their stores were remarkably similar to those that a family in a poor neighborhood of Detroit might tell.

The cohabiting couples that they described were not surrogate marriages, but more commonly relationships in which the father may have been living in the house when the child was born, but did not assume a father's responsibility to support or bring up the child. The relationships, moreover, tended to be transient and chaotic, with instances in which children with the same father but different mothers lived within a few doors of each other.

Some of the problems of trying to raise children in such an environment may seem trivial but are painfully poignant. Take, for example, the story of a Birkenhead father who told me about going to his little girl's Christmas play at school. He was the only father there—hardly any of the other children had fathers—and his daughter, embarrassed because she was different, asked him not to come to the school any more. But the problems with the breakdown of the married two-parent family go beyond poignancy.

The central problem is that kids tend to run wild in communities without fathers. The fewer the fathers, the greater the tendency. "Running wild" can mean that young children have no set bedtime. It can mean that they are left alone in the house at night while mummy goes out. It can mean that eighteen-month-old toddlers are allowed to play in the street. It can mean children who treat other children too aggressively. The same Birkenhead father and his wife raised their first daughter as they were raised, to be polite and considerate—and she suffered for it. Put simply, her schoolmates weren't being raised to be polite and considerate—they weren't being "raised" at all in some respects. With their second child, the Birkenhead parents eased up on their requirements for civil behavior, realizing that their children had to be able to defend themselves against threats that the parents hadn't faced when they were children. Their third child is still an infant, and the mother has made a conscious decision. "I won't knock the aggression out of her," she said to me. Then she paused, and added angrily, "It's *wrong* to have to decide that."

It is of course true that many families with children have those kinds of problems, not just poor single parents. But this is why the concentration of the underclass into particular neighborhoods is so devastating. A middle-class neighborhood almost certainly has many divorced parents, but the dominant family type is the two-parent family, which remains the visible model for youngsters growing up. Even if one particular youth lacks a father, he lives in a neighborhood in which fathers abound. When the one-parent family becomes the norm and father figures are scarce, the difficulties associated with the single-parent family seem to multiply. One must use "seem" because of the continuing scarcity of systematic investigations. But this is why the British example is so provocative, even on this anecdotal level. One becomes less inclined to assume that the breakdown of the American black family is a black problem fostered by black history.

CRIME

Crime is the next place to look for an underclass, for several reasons. First and most obviously, the habitual criminal is the classic member of an underclass, living off mainstream society by preying on it. Habitual criminals, however, are only part of the problem. Once again, the key issue is how a community functions, and crime can devastate a community in two especially important ways: first, to the extent that members of a community are victimized by crime, the community tends to become fragmented; second, to the extent that many people in a community engage in crime as a matter of course, the community's socializing norms change, as different kinds of men are idolized by boys and the standards of morality in general collapse.

Consider first the official crime figures, reported annually for England by the Home Office. As in the case of illegitimacy, I took for granted upon arrival that England had much lower crime rates than the United States. It therefore came as a shock to discover that England and Wales (which I will subsequently refer to as England) have a combined property-crime rate apparently as high, and probably higher, than that of the United States. (I did not compare rates with Scotland and Northern Ireland, which are reported separately.) I say "apparently," because Britain and the United States define property crime somewhat differently. But burglaries, which are similarly defined in both countries, provide an example. In 1988 England had 1,623 reported burglaries per 100,000 inhabitants, compared with 1,309 in the United States. Adjusting for the trans-Atlantic differences in definitions, England also appears to have higher rates of motor-vehicle theft than the United States. The rates for other kinds of theft seem to be roughly the same.

I wasn't the only one who was surprised at these comparisons. If you want to attract startled and incredulous attention in the U.K., mention casually that England has a higher property-crime rate than that notorious crime center of the Western world, the United States; no one will believe you.

The understandable reason why no one believes you is that *violent* crime in England remains much less frequent than in the United States, and it is violent crime, not property crime, that engenders most of the anxiety and anger about crime. Thus, in all of 1988, England recorded just 624 homicides. The United States averaged that many every eleven days—20,675 for the year.

That's the good news for Britain. The bad news is that the violent-crime rate in England has been rising very rapidly [Figure 2].

The size of the increase isn't as bad as it first looks, because England began with such a small initial rate. The rise is steep nonetheless, and it became much steeper in about 1968. Compare the gradual increase from 1950–1968 with what

happened subsequently. By 1988, England had 314 "offences of violence against the person" reported per 100,000 people. The really bad news is that England has been experiencing this increase despite demographic trends that should have led to a decrease. This point is important enough to explain at more length.

The most frequent offenders, the ones who puff up the violent-crime statistics, are males in the last half of their teens. As males get older, they tend to become more civilized. In England, the number of males in this troublesome age group increased throughout the 1970s, and this fact was widely used to explain the crime increase. But the number of English males aged fifteen to nineteen hit its peak in 1982 and has subsequently decreased both as a percentage of the population and in raw numbers (by a little more than 11 percent in both cases). Despite the reduction in the number of males in the highest-offending age group after 1982, the violent-crime rate in England from 1982 to 1988 rose by 43 percent.

"The increase is a statistical artifact," I was

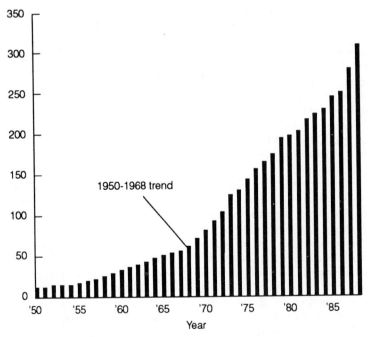

FIGURE 2

Violent crimes per 100,000 inhabitants, England and Wales

frequently told—another echo of the American dialogue in the 1960s and 1970s. One version of this argument is that crime just seems to be higher because more crimes are being reported to the police than before (because of greater access to telephones, for example, or because of the greater prevalence of insurance). This seems unlikely to do much better as an explanation than it did in the United States, where changes in reporting work both ways. Rape and sexual assault are more likely to be reported now, because of changes in public attitudes and judicial procedures regarding those crimes. But an anonymous purse-snatch is less likely to be reported, because the victim doesn't think it will do any good, and the drop-off in reporting for this reason is worst in the neighborhoods where crime is perceived to be out of control.

The most obviously spurious version of the "crime isn't really getting worse" argument uses rates of increase rather than the magnitude of increases to make the case. The best example in Britain is the argument that public concern about muggings in the early 1970s was simply an effort to scapegoat young blacks, and resulted in a "moral panic." Sociologist Stuart Hall and his colleagues made this case at some length in 1978 in a book entitled *Policing the Crisis,* in which, among other things, they argued with a straight face that because the rate of increase in violent crimes was decreasing, the public's concern was unwarranted. Applying their logic to recent trends, for example, the increase in violent crime in the 1950s was worse than the increase in the 1980s, because violent crime rose by 88 percent from 1950–1958, whereas it rose by only 60 percent from 1980–1988. The problem with this line of reasoning is apparent when one takes another look at the graph of violent crime shown above [Figure 2]. From 1950–1958, the violent-crime rate increased by thirteen crimes per 100,000 inhabitants. From 1980–1988, it increased by 118 crimes per 100,000 inhabitants.

The denial by intellectuals that crime really has been getting worse spills over into denial that poor communities are more violent places than affluent communities. To the people who live in poor communities, this doesn't make much sense. One man in a poor, high-crime community told me about his experience in an open

university where he had once taken a sociology course about poverty. The professor kept talking about this "nice little world that the poor live in," the man remembered. The professor scoffed at the reactionary myth that poor communities are violent places. To the man who lived in such a community, the professor was talking "bloody drivel." A few weeks later, a class exercise called for the students to canvass a poor neighborhood. The professor went along, but apparently he too suspected that some of his pronouncements were bloody drivel—he cautiously stayed in his car and declined to knock on doors himself. And that raises the most interesting question regarding the view that crime has not risen, or that crime is not especially a problem in lower-class communities: Do any of the British intellectuals who hold this view actually believe it, to the extent that they take no more precautions walking in a slum neighborhood than they do in a middle-class suburb?

In the United States, the arguments that crime isn't really getting worse have virtually disappeared, and an examination of the English crime statistics leads me to expect that the same thing will happen in Britain. The changes are too big to be explained away. If Britain follows the American model, after all the statistical artifacts are taken into account and debated it will be decided that England is indeed becoming more dangerous; that this unhappy process is not occurring everywhere, but disproportionately in particular types of neighborhoods; and that those neighborhoods turn out to be the ones in which an underclass is taking over. Reality will once again force theory to its knees.

VOLUNTARY UNEMPLOYMENT

If illegitimate births are the leading indicator of an underclass and violent crime a proxy measure of its development, the definitive proof that an underclass has arrived is that large numbers of young, healthy, low-income males choose not to take jobs. This decrease in labor-force participation is the most elusive of the trends in the growth of the British underclass.

The main barrier to understanding what's going on is the high unemployment of the 1980s.

The official statistics distinguish between "unemployment" and "economically inactive," but Britain's unemployment figures (like those in the U.S.) include an unknown but probably considerable number of people who manage to qualify for the benefit even if in reality very few job opportunities would tempt them to work. On the other side of the ledger, over a prolonged period of high unemployment the "economically inactive" category includes men who would like to work but have given up. To make matters still more complicated, there is the "black economy" to consider, whereby people who are listed as "economically inactive" are really working for cash, but not reporting their income to the authorities. So we are looking through a glass darkly, and I have more questions than answers.

The simple relationship of economic inactivity to social class is strong, just as it was for illegitimacy. According to the 1981 census data, the municipal districts with high proportions of Class V household heads also tend to have the highest levels of "economically inactive" persons of working age. This is another way of saying that you will find many more working-aged people who are neither working nor looking for work in the slums than in the suburbs. Some of them are undoubtedly discouraged workers, but two questions—applying specifically to lower-class young men—need to be asked and answered with much more data than are currently available.

First, after taking into account Britain's unemployment problems when the 1981 census was taken, were the levels of economic inactivity among young males consistent with the behavior of their older brothers and fathers during earlier periods? Or were young males dropping out more quickly and more often than in the past?

Second, Britain has for the last few years been conducting a natural experiment, with an economic boom in the South and continued high unemployment in the North. If lack of jobs is the problem, then presumably economic inactivity among lower-class healthy young males in the South has plummeted to insignificant levels. Has it?

The story that I heard from a variety of people in Birkenhead and Easterhouse was that the youths who came of age in the late 1970s risk becoming a lost generation. My sources did indeed ascribe the problem to the surge in unemployment at the end of the 1970s. "They came out of school at the wrong time," as one older resident of Easterhouse put it, and have never in their lives held a real job. They are now in their late twenties. As economic times improve, they are competing for entry-level jobs against people ten years younger, whom employers prefer to hire. But it's not just that, he added. "They've lost the picture of what they're going to be doing," he said. When he was growing up, he could see himself in his father's job. Not these young men.

This generation gap was portrayed to me as being only a few years wide. A man from Birkenhead in his early thirties—who had worked steadily after leaving school until he lost his job as an assembly-line worker in 1979—recalled how humiliated and desperate to work he had remained, even as his unemployment stretched from months into years. He—and the others in their thirties, forties, or fifties—were the ones showing up at six in the morning when jobs were advertised. They were the ones who sought jobs even if they paid less than the benefit rate. "The only income I wanted was enough to be free of the bloody benefit system," he said. "It was like a rope around my neck." The phrase for being on benefit that some of them used, being "on the suck," says a great deal about how little they like their situation. In passing, it should be noted that this way of looking at things is no small asset to Britain. In many inner cities of the U.S., the slang for robbing someone is "getting paid." Compare that inversion of values with the values implied by "on the suck." Britain in 1989 still has resources that seem to have been depleted in urban America.

But the same men who talk this way often have little in common with their sons and younger brothers. Talking to boys in their late teens and early twenties about jobs, I heard nothing about the importance of work as a source of self-respect and no talk of just wanting enough income to be free of the benefit system. To make a decent living, a youth of twenty-one explained to me, you need £200 a week—after taxes. He would accept less if it was all he could get. But he conveyed clearly that he would feel exploited. As for the government's employment, the Youth Training Scheme, that's "slave labor." Why, another young man asked me indignantly, should he and his friends be deprived of their right to full unemployment benefits just because they're not yet eighteen? It sounded strange to my ears—a "right" to unemployment benefits for a school-age minor who's never held a job. But there is no question in their minds that that's exactly what the unemployment benefit is: a right, in every sense of the word. The boys did not mention what they considered to be their part of the bargain. "I was brought up thinking work is something you are morally obliged to do," as one older man put it. With the younger generation, he said, "that culture isn't going to be there at all." The older men had anecdotes to back up these observations. During the extensive housing refurbishment now going on at Easterhouse, for example, the contractors are obliged to hire local youths for unskilled labor as part of a work-experience scheme. Thirty Easterhouse young men applied for a recent set of openings. Thirteen were accepted. Ten actually came to work the first day. By the end of the first week, only one was still showing up.

My hypothesis—the evidence is too fragmentary to call it more than that—is that Britain is experiencing a generation gap by class. Welleducated young people from affluent homes are working in larger proportions and for longer hours than ever. The attitudes and behavior of the middle-aged working class haven't changed much. The change is concentrated among lowerclass young men in their teens and twenties. It is not a huge change. I am not suggesting that a third or a quarter or even a fifth of lower-class young people are lounging about, indifferent to work. But an underclass doesn't have to be huge to become a problem.

That problem is remarkably difficult to fix. It seems simple—just make decent-paying jobs available. That's what we used to think in the United States, and we tried nearly everything to prove it—training programs, guaranteed jobs, special "socialization" programs that taught not only job skills but also "work readiness skills" like getting to work on time, "buddy" systems whereby an experienced older man tried to ease a trainee into the world of work. Controlled ex-

periments show that these strategies have consistently had little effect at best, no effect most commonly, and occasionally negative effects. Nor did the expanding economy of the 1980s do much good—the percentage of American black male youths out of the labor force was the same in 1989 as it had been in 1979, and it is still far above the rate for white male youths. The lesson that Britain is just beginning to learn is that it is irretrievably disastrous for young men to grow up without being socialized into the world of work. By remaining out of the work force during the crucial formative years, young men aren't just losing a few years of job experience. They are missing out on the time in which they need to be acquiring the skills and the networks of friends and experiences that enable them to establish a place for themselves—not just a place for themselves in the workplace, but a vantage point from which they can make sense of themselves and their lives. Furthermore, when large numbers of young men don't work, the communities around them break down, just as they break down when large numbers of young unmarried women have babies. The two phenomena are intimately related, as George Gilder has argued most eloquently.

LOSING GROUND IN BRITAIN

How big is the British underclass? It all depends on how one defines its membership; the size of the underclass can be made to look huge or insignificant, depending on what one wants the answer to be. It seems safe to conclude, however, that the underclass now poses a much smaller problem for Britain than for the U.S. If the crime and illegitimacy trends in Britain leveled off where they are now and the South's tight labor market spread to the North, Britain would continue to have an underclass but not one that would force major reform. Britain could continue to treat social policy as it has since the Beveridge Report, looking for ways to fine-tune social-welfare and criminal-justice systems that most Britons think work pretty well.

The question facing Britain is the same one facing the United States: How contagious is this disease? Is it going to spread indefinitely, or will it be self-containing? Imagine, for example, what Britain will be like ten years from now if the trends continue unabated. The results seem preposterous. If violent crime follows the steepening trendline it has displayed since 1969, by 1999 the British violent-crime rate will be double the rate that already is a source of such concern. In the case of illegitimacy, it is impossible to assume that the exponential curve in the treadline since 1970 will continue to steepen—if it were to do so, all British births would be illegitimate by the end of the century. But even if we assume more conservatively that the trend of the last ten years will continue linearly, more than 40 percent of births will be to single women by 1999. Because these results are so obviously preposterous, the question arises: Why might these projections be too high? Why may we reasonably expect that recent trends are caused by abnormal forces that are about to fade?

Here we reach questions about causation that are most controversial. In his recently published book, Labour MP Frank Field blames Mrs. Thatcher for the emergence of a British underclass. Field claims that the increased inequalities produced by rewarding the rich and punishing the poor have generated an underclass; change the policies, Field contends, and the underclass will diminish.

My interpretation and the interpretations of the left do not so much compete as pass in the night. As far as I can tell, inequality in general and Mrs. Thatcher's policies in particular hardly enter in. The slope in the graph in violent crime steepened most conspicuously in the late 1960s, long before Mrs. Thatcher came to power. The acceleration in the illegitimacy ratio was beginning in 1979, and was nearly as steep as it would ever get by Mrs. Thatcher's first full year in office. It is hard to credit that Mrs. Thatcher's influence on fertility behavior among single young women occurred within days of her election.

In any case, let me propose a more radical reason why the Thatcher government's policies have little to do with the development of an underclass: the relevant policies haven't changed that much under Mrs. Thatcher. Despite the many dramatic changes in Britain in other spheres, the culprits behind the trends that I have described have been largely unaffected.

The hypothesis I bring to interpreting events in Britain is directly analogous to the one I used in analyzing the American situation several years ago in *Losing Ground*. In talking about the underclass, we are really talking about phenomena that relate directly or indirectly to the behavior of people in their late teens and early twenties. Young people—not just poor young people, but all young people—try to make sense of the world around them. They behave in ways that reflect what they observe. In the 1960s and 1970s, social policy in Britain fundamentally changed what makes sense. The changes did not affect the mature as much as the young. They affected the affluent hardly at all. But the rules of the game did change fundamentally for low-income young people, changing behavior in their wake.

"Making sense of the world around them" has to be understood in terms of the judgment and the time frame of young people. People in their late teens and early twenties can be terribly foolish and short-sighted. Late adolescence is a critical time of life for shaping the future, and unfortunately also a time during which all of us—not just blacks and the poor—are prone to do things that can be self-destructive. Unlike middle-class youths, inner-city youngsters are likely to lack not just money, but also the education, the socialization to longer-term thinking, and the adult oversight that together would manage to rein them in.

In the U.S. context, the rules of the game changed during a reform period that stretched from the mid-1960s to the mid-1970s, and they changed in every sphere—education, criminal justice, and welfare; through legislation, court decisions, and administrative reforms; at the federal level and at the state level. What makes the British case intriguing is that the changes in intellectual fashion followed the same time schedule as in the United States, but the policy changes did not. Policy toward crime changed course during the late 1960s, whereas the most significant changes in policy toward single women with children occurred in the last half of the 1970s.

I begin with crime, assuming this commonsense view of the situation: if a criminal's chances of being punished go down, crime goes up. In every respect—the chances of getting caught, the chances of being found guilty, and the chances of going to prison—crime has become safer in Britain throughout the postwar period, and most dramatically safer since 1960.

The landmark legislation was the Criminal Justice Act of 1967, implemented in 1968, which for the first time introduced parole to Britain, mandated suspension of all sentences of less than six months, and in a variety of other ways legislated the same philosophy of criminal justice—less use of prisons, less talk of just deserts, more therapy, the advent of "minimal intervention"—that had been affecting United States criminal-justice policy in less cohesive and integrated ways throughout the 1960s.

Without trying to establish causal links between legislation and behavior here, I will simply review some of the salient trends that a thoughtful criminal, or prospective criminal, might reasonably have noticed. "Clear-up rates" are one example. ("Clearing up" a crime in Britain means that the police think they know who did it, regardless of what happens in the courts.) With a few crimes such as homicide, the clear-up rate has remained high and unchanged. But for a crime such as robbery, the clear-up rate, which had risen during the 1950s, fell from 61 percent in 1960 to 42 percent in 1970, dropped again to 29 percent by 1980, and dropped still further to 21 percent in 1987—an extremely large change. Reductions for other crimes have been smaller but significant.

If clear-up rates had been the only thing to change, the overall effect on the "safeness" of crime would have been modest. But while clear-up rates were falling, so was the likelihood of conviction after apprehension. When the Criminal Justice Act was passed, half of all cleared-up offenses resulted in a conviction. A decade later, in 1977, the proportion had fallen to 43 percent; a decade after that, to 30 percent.

Perhaps most importantly, the penalties imposed upon conviction changed. This last topic is a source of great misunderstanding, for prison is the most obvious form of punishment and prisons are commonly thought to be incapable of reducing crime. Partly, the misunderstanding arises from a confusion between the incapacity of prisons to rehabilitate offenders (which is reasonably well-documented) and their capacity to

deter potential offenders (which is not well-documented). Strict and consistent use of prisons, as once characterized Britain, can at the same time be miserably inefficient at rehabilitating criminals and spectacularly effective in deterring people from becoming criminals in the first place.

Another misunderstanding arises from the tendency to think in terms of the raw number of people in prison. As the number of people in prison rises but crime also continues to rise, the conclusion is loudly proclaimed that incarceration doesn't work. But if one is thinking in terms of risks, the obvious measure is not the number of people in prison, but rather the chances of going to prison if one commits a crime. That figure has plummeted, not only since the reform of 1967 but since the end of World War II. Prison sentences as a proportion of reported crimes fell by almost half from 1950 to 1967, then fell by another 30 percent in the single year after the reform was implemented, and have remained comparatively steady (though still falling slowly) since then.

But comparatively few offenders were sent to prison even in the tough old days. Thus a full analysis of the trends in punishment would consider fines as well as prison sentences, the use of cautions and suspended sentences, the effects of the parole system on actual time served, the delay between arrest and disposition, and a host of other factors that affect how a person arrested for a given crime in 1960 was treated differently from someone arrested for the same offense today. It seems evident from a variety of descriptions in the press and essays on the criminal-justice system that the use of penalties has fallen in every dimension—not just in severity, but in swiftness and certainty as well.

Even using simple measures, recent trends in penalties are at odds with the Thatcher government's reputation for being punitive and anticrime. The actual end products of the criminal-justice system haven't corresponded to the rhetoric. From 1982 to 1987, even as crime continued to rise, the number of convictions and prison sentences dropped—not just as a proportion of crimes, but in raw numbers. In 1982, 3.1 million indictable offenses were known to the police, and 475,000 people were found guilty of them; of these, 50,300 received unsuspended prison sentences. In 1987, 3.7 million indictable offenses were known to the police (up 19 percent), 386,000 people were found guilty of them (down 19 percent); of these, 41,700 received unsuspended prison sentences (down 17 percent). Can these figures be the product of a get-tough policy?

Because crime statistics are so subject to qualifications and punishment itself is debated so passionately, let me make clear what I am and am not saying. I'm not claiming that the official statistics are perfect, or that British law enforcement has gotten lax, or that one must ignore the complicated social forces associated with increases in crime. I do claim that committing a crime is much safer than it used to be, and that this trend still continues. That being the case, why shouldn't crime continue to increase? In fact, why shouldn't the slope of the increase in the graph of violent crime continue just as steeply for the next ten years? It might flatten out, but it is difficult to think of a good reason why.

Similarly, why shouldn't illegitimacy continue to increase? There is an obvious explanation for why single young women get pregnant: sex is fun and babies are endearing. Nothing could be more natural than for young men and women to want to have sex, and nothing could be more natural than for a young woman to want a baby. A better question than asking why single young women get pregnant is to ask why they don't. The obvious answer is that in the past it was very punishing for a single woman to have a baby. (If that seems too negative, then one may say that a young single woman who had a baby had to forgo many social and economic rewards. It amounts to the same thing.)

One type of punishment was social stigma (or one type of reward for virtue was social acceptance), and without doubt the sexual revolution of the 1960s markedly reduced the stigma. Leaving aside why this happened, it is reasonable to expect that illegitimacy would have risen in the 1960s even if social policy had remained unchanged. But in addition to stigma, until recently severe economic punishment awaited single mothers. For a poor single woman, supporting a baby alone was next to impossible. Having to do so was something to be actively avoided.

At this juncture, we come to the benefit system, another source of great controversy and confusion in Britain as in America. There is no evidence anywhere, including Britain, that large numbers of young women get pregnant so that they can get on welfare—or, in the British phrase, on benefit. (Sometimes they have a second child specifically so that they can remain on benefit, but that constitutes a comparatively minor part of the problem.) Rather, the problem in providing money to single women who have babies is that the income enables many young women to do something that they would naturally like to do. Such benefits don't have much effect on affluent women—the benefit rate is so far below what they consider their needs that they are not in any way "enabled" to have babies by the level of support being provided. For poor women, however, the benefit level can be quite salient in deciding whether having a baby is feasible. And the simple economic feasibility of raising a baby without the support of a father changed fundamentally during the 1970s.

In 1955, for example, an unmarried, unemployed mother with a single child under five had to get along on less than £22 a week; miserably little (all figures will be in 1987 purchasing power). It was almost impossible to survive on such a budget. Unless the mother had some other source of support, the only realistic option was putting the child up for adoption or into the care of the local authority. Having an illegitimate baby was brutally punishing if you were poor. (It was also punishing if you were rich, but for different reasons.) During the 1960s, the benefit grew, reaching about £36 by 1970—still an extremely slender stipend, though conceivably enough to get by on.

During the 1970s, the size of the benefit for single women began to rise more rapidly, increasing more than a third in purchasing power from 1970 to 1976 and reaching a high of £52 in 1980. Meanwhile, in 1977, the Homeless Persons Act was passed. Before, a single mother had to wait in queue for housing. The act stipulated that pregnant women and single mothers were to get some sort of housing immediately—and to go to the top of the queue for council housing—if they couldn't live with their parents and were otherwise homeless. Not surprisingly, large numbers of young women with babies suddenly found that they were unable to live with their parents.

The effect of all these changes was not continuous. The right analog for understanding the process is not a young woman with a calculator, following the latest quotations on benefits and deciding whether to change her fertility behavior. Rather, the analogy is the way a pot comes to boil. Thus, for example, I doubt that the Homeless Persons Act induced many young women to have babies so that they could get their own flats. Rather, the benefit increases and the Homeless Persons Act were steps in a quiet, cumulative process whereby having a baby as a single mother went from "extremely punishing" to "not so bad." By 1977 a poor young woman looking at the world around her could see that single mothers in their neighborhoods were getting along, whereas a similar young woman in the early 1960s would have looked around and concluded that being a single mother was to be avoided at all costs. The combination of cash and housing did not offer enough to appeal to the middle class, but it provided low-income young women with a standard of living no worse and often better than they endured with their parents. Meanwhile, sex was as much fun as ever and babies were as endearing as ever. By the end of 1978, the illegitimacy ratio had begun the rapid rise that has continued throughout the eighties. A series of changes in the benefit rates and collateral housing benefits lifted a large portion of low-income young women above the threshold where having and keeping a baby became economically feasible.

Following this logic, it doesn't make any difference if the benefit level stops getting higher, or even if it diminishes somewhat. As long as the benefit level is well above the threshold, the dynamics of social incentives will continue to work in favor of illegitimacy, as the advantages of legal marriage become less clear and its disadvantages more obvious. For men, the pressures to marry will continue to diminish. Given all this, I cannot see why the illegitimacy ratio would level off.

I have touched on only a few of the changes in British social policy that relate to the development of an underclass. State education was a lively topic of conversation among people with whom I talked everywhere; the stories sounded depressingly like the problems with urban public education in the United States. Drug abuse in Britain is reported to be increasing significantly. These developments all interact. When one leaves school without any job skills, barely literate, the job alternatives to crime or the dole are not attractive. Young men who are subsisting on crime or the dole are not likely to be trustworthy providers, which makes having a baby without a husband seem more plausible. If a young man's girlfriend doesn't need him to help support the baby, it makes less sense for him to plug away at a menial job and more sense to have some fun— which in turn makes hustling and crime more attractive, marriage less attractive. Without a job or family to give life meaning, drugs become that much more valuable as a means of distraction. The cost of drugs makes crime the only feasible way to make enough money to pay for them. The interconnections go on endlessly, and they help to explain why community norms lose their force, why the role of older adults in the community diminishes, why communal bonds loosen.

A DEARTH OF SOLUTIONS

The British in both parties still talk as if modest, incremental changes in one corner of the system can have an effect. The Conservatives continue to profess high hopes for youth employment programs, get-tough-on-crime reforms, and for the prospect of falling unemployment in the North. Labour seems genuinely to believe that Thatcherism is to blame and that a Labour government will bring back the good old days. And it would be foolhardy to assume too quickly that all of these voices are wrong. Britain is not the United States, and the most certain prediction is that British experience will be different from ours. At the close of this brief tour of several huge topics, let me be the first to acknowledge that I have skipped over complications and nuances and surely missed special British conditions of which I am ignorant.

Still, so much has been the same so far. In both countries, the same humane impulses and the same intellectual fashions drove reforms in social policy. The attempts to explain away the consequences have been similar, with British intellectuals in the 1980s—just like American intellectuals in the 1970s—saying that the problems aren't really as bad as they seem. And to the extent that the United States has had more experience than Britain with a growing underclass, the sad lesson we have to offer is our powerlessness to do much about an underclass once it exists. No matter how much money we spend on our cleverest social interventions, we don't know how to make teenagers who have grown up in an underclass culture into steady workers, we don't know how to make up for the lack of good parents, and, most critically, we don't know how to make up for the lack of communities that reward responsibility and stigmatize irresponsibility. Let me emphasize the words: *We do not know how.* It's not money we lack, but the capability to social-engineer our way out of this situation. Unfortunately, the impression persists that our social engineering simply hasn't been clever enough, and that we must strive to become more clever.

Another possibility was voiced first by another American visitor to Britain, Benjamin Franklin. "There is no country in the world where so many provisions are established for [the poor]," he wrote in 1766 about Britain to a British audience. "[S]o many hospitals to receive them when they are sick and lame, founded and maintained by voluntary charities; so many almshouses for the aged of both sexes, together with a solemn law made by the rich to subject their estates to a heavy tax for the support of the poor. . . . In short, you offered a premium for the encouragement of idleness, and you should not now wonder that it has had its effects in the increase of poverty."

We cannot say things so baldly in the last years of the twentieth century, but Franklin's analysis is not far from the mark. Some years ago I wrote for an American audience that the real contest about social policy is not between people who want to cut budgets and people who want to help. Watching Britain replay our history, I can do no better than repeat the same conclusion: when meaningful reforms finally do occur, they will happen not because stingy people have won, but because generous people have stopped kidding themselves.

RACE AND
SOCIAL INEQUALITY

INTRODUCTION

Problems of racial change have dominated public debate throughout the twentieth century. As the 1900s opened, African-Americans faced the oppressive force of Jim Crow laws in the South, which forbade everything, from voting to enjoying public parks and attending good schools and colleges. Most blacks eked out a living as tenant farmers or sharecroppers on land owned by whites. This unequal economic arrangement contributed further to the diminished social and political status of African-Americans. Many blacks escaped the poverty and oppressive customs of the South by moving to the booming industrial cities of the Midwest and East. As World War I created opportunities for work in such cities as Chicago, Detroit, Philadelphia, Newark, and Cleveland, blacks migrated in large numbers and soon gained vital turf in every major city in the United States.

Change did not come easily, however. At

the turn of the century, lynchings were still a frightening reality in the South, and in northern cities many whites violently resisted blacks' efforts to find new homes and jobs. Race riots occurred in East St. Louis (1917) and Chicago (1919). Some blacks continued to press northward, and others struggled to find a better life in the South.

Journalism and sociology played vital roles in the study of many aspects of race-related problems. W. E. B. Du Bois, Robert Park, and other pioneers in the field were intimately familiar with the rural roots of blacks who moved north to find new opportunities. It is worth noting that Park began his career as a journalist and later turned to sociology as a professor at the University of Chicago. Du Bois began his career as a bright young Ph.D. from Harvard who published many important studies of black life in rural and urban settings and later gained national attention as editor of *Crisis*, the journal of the National Association for the Advancement of Colored People (NAACP).

A major concern of W. E. B. Du Bois was the slow pace at which blacks were advancing in the United States. The Fourteenth Amendment to the U.S. Constitution guarantees full citizenship to blacks, yet the barriers to economic and social advancement were staggering. In the middle decades of the twentieth century, much attention focused on the civil rights movement, which promised to end segregation in all its forms. Thereafter, blacks supposedly would be as free to move ahead as any other group in the United States.

In 1964 a hopeful chapter in American history opened with the passage of the first major civil rights legislation since the 1860s. It was a time for optimisim. Yet the American dream still eludes large numbers of African-Americans. Bill McAllister presents sobering evidence of the difficul-

ties faced by a particularly imperiled group in the black community: young men. Karl Zinsmeister presents mixed results on the opportunities for advancement since the passage of the Civil Rights Act. His review of the evidence is not free of some strong biases as to who is responsible for some of the obstacles to black advancement.

Many of the concerns raised by McAllister and Zinsmeister are rooted in the changing character of the black family. Sociologists have studied the black family throughout the twentieth century. As early as the 1960s Daniel Patrick Moynihan expressed alarm about the growing proportion of black families without fathers in the home. Moynihan argued that the disintegration of the black family creates severe disadvantages for black youth. Jewell Handy Gresham challenges the Moynihan thesis as a longstanding white approach to the continuing disparities between the races. White's propensity to blame blacks for their poverty is unacceptable to Gresham. Her case deserves close attention.

The last essay in this chapter, by Loïc J. D. Wacquant and William Julius Wilson, offers a more complex argument than any of the others. These authors avoid the simplistic reasoning that places most of the blame for current conditions of poverty on a single factor. The disadvantages inner-city blacks face in the 1990s are unique to the history of race relations in the United States. Wilson has spent many years in efforts to disentangle the web of interrelated forces that so limit opportunities for so many Americans at the end of the twentieth century. The chain of causation in his argument and the supporting evidence require close scrutiny. His conclusions about the emergence and persistence of an urban underclass are in sharp contrast to those of Charles Murray.

13. THE PLIGHT OF YOUNG BLACK MEN IN AMERICA

BILL McALLISTER

Of Washington's record 372 murders in 1988, 351 of the victims were black and 235 of them, or 63 percent of the city's homicides, were males age 15 to 34.

This pattern has been typical for years in the nation's largest cities. In New York in 1987, the latest period for which figures are available, 534 of the city's 1,672 murder victims were young black males, according to the Crime Analysis Program Northeastern University in Boston. In Detroit, the figure was 352 of 686. In Baltimore, it was 116 of 226, and in Los Angeles, 233 of 811.

Soaring murder rates are the most dramatic effect of what many black sociologists describe as a much larger societal problem—the plight of young black men in America. By virtually every official index—mortality, health, income, education and marital status—black men have emerged as one of the most troubled segments of American society. Their worsening problems foreshadow grave difficulties for the black American family in the years ahead.

"We are in the process of watching our own demise," says Ed Pitt, former director of health and environmental services for the National Urban League, echoing a widespread, fatalistic attitude.

"Not since slavery has so much calamity and ongoing catastrophe been visited on black males," says Health and Human Services Secretary Louis W. Sullivan, the administration's highest-ranking black official. Although Sullivan is less alarmist than some blacks, he says the federal government must take stronger action to reverse the trends.

"To call these men an 'endangered species' would be nothing but hyperbole," Sullivan has said. "But I do not think it is an exaggeration to suggest that the young black American male is a species in danger. And in trouble."

Of all the problems confronting young black men, homicide is perhaps the most visible. New Orleans juvenile service officer Stanley Schofield tells of a teenage boy there who dresses in women's clothes for safety. Schofield says the youth has a quick answer for his appearance: "It's dangerous out there."

Homicide has become a leading cause of death among urban black men, who face a 1-in-10 chance of being killed during their lifetimes compared to a 1-in-80 chance for white men, according to congressional testimony. For black males age 15 to 24, homicide is the leading cause of death; one of every three black men age 20 to 24 who dies is a homicide victim, according to the Institute for Advanced Study of Black Family Life and Culture in Oakland.

The soaring murder rate has helped push overall death rates for black men to alarming levels at a time when mortality rates for whites are decreasing, according to Pitt. "That is historic. That is critical," he says. "It cries out for every urgent reaction we can come up with, because without young men to start and maintain our families, we can have no future on this continent."

The crisis that Sullivan, Pitt and many others perceive affects only a minority of the nation's 5.1 million black males age 15 to 34, but the adverse trends that have caused this alarm do touch many of them. Among the problems:

- Persistently high unemployment. Despite recent overall gains in employment among blacks, statistics developed by the Urban League show no narrowing of the historically large gap between employment rates of blacks and whites. By including individuals who have become so discouraged about finding a job that they are excluded from federal labor statistics, the league estimated that black

Americans are unemployed at a rate 2.2 times greater than that of whites.

- Continued high poverty rates. In 1987, one in three blacks was living below the poverty level, a number that has increased slightly since, according to the Center on Budget and Policy Priorities, a Washington research group. The number of black children under 18 living in poverty reached 45.6 percent in 1987, a rate higher than in the late 1960s or the 1970s, the center said.

- A decline in real income. Northeastern University's Center for Labor Market Studies found that young black men "clearly have fared worst in the new American economy of the 1980s." Average real income for black men age 20 to 29 fell by 27.7 percent between 1973 and 1987, a drop much deeper than the 17.8 percent decline the university said was recorded by all men the same age.

- A sudden decline in the percentage of black men seeking higher education. Enrollment of black men in the nation's colleges dropped by 34,000 between 1976 and 1986, the largest decline for any racial or ethnic group, according to the American Council on Education. The percentage of black men age 18 to 24 in college dropped from 35.4 percent in 1976 to 27.8 percent in 1987 despite an increase in the number of black graduates from high schools with college preparatory courses.

- A dramatic increase in black women heading households. The Rockefeller Foundation has reported that from 1890 until 1950, a higher percentage of black than white women were married. But since 1960, the number of black households headed by women has grown steadily. By 1988, almost six of 10 black families with children under age 18 were headed by a single parent and virtually all of those were headed by women, according to a recent Census Bureau report. (About two in 10 comparable white families were headed by women.)

"It's suicidal for black males to grow up in a house without black men," says Jawanza Kunjufu, a Chicago education consultant, echoing the fears of many blacks.

These problems have not surfaced without warning. Twenty-four years ago, Daniel Patrick Moynihan, then a labor Department official but now a Democratic senator from New York, issued the first government report warning that unstable families were causing many problems faced by black Americans. But today, many prominent blacks say that the problem has become so pervasive that the federal government has walked away, unable—or unwilling—to address it.

Gary L. Bauer, who handled family issues in the Reagan White House, says that he was well aware of the issue and raised it several times during Domestic Policy Council meetings. Bauer, now head of the private Family Resource Council in Washington, says of the council's response, "It may have been too much to bite off."

HHS Secretary Sullivan says that attitude has changed with George Bush in the White House. Bush is committed to using the federal government's resources to attack the problems because too many black Americans face a future that is both "a national disgrace and a national tragedy," Sullivan says.

Long active in minority health issues as a medical school administrator in Atlanta, Sullivan says he wants to become the Bush administration's point man for black Americans much as former surgeon general C. Everett Koop had become the Reagan administration's point man on the hazards of smoking. "I see my role as sounding the call to arms about the problem so we can get the nation to solve these problems," Sullivan says.

He insists that despite constraints on federal spending, "We have abundant resources." He says he will urge that federal funds be redirected to the effort. "I look on this as a very serious problem both for black Americans and the nation as a whole."

There is sharp division among black officials over what problems should be attacked and how. To some, the major problem confronting blacks is drugs. Others say it is jobs. Still others say it is education.

Democratic Rep. Major R. Owens of New York, for example, argues that education is the key issue that the federal government should address. Even so, Owens, like many black leaders, is skeptical of the government's attitude. "My feeling is that the federal government just doesn't care," he says. "The Bush administration is content with a public relations position . . . a lot of hype."

In the streets, the plight of young black men is linked by many blacks to charges that whites are secretly behind the surge of black violence. Wade W. Nobles, director of the Institute for Advanced Study of Black Family Life and Culture, is one of the black intellectuals who cites the numbers of whites controlling drug trafficking in South America as evidence that there may be an "orchestrated" genocide of black men.

Nobles and other prominent blacks say racism lies under many of the problems confronting black men. "The real nitty-gritty is that they [white Americans] are afraid of black men," Nobles says.

While few dispute that integration has improved the overall lot of the nation's 30 million blacks, some blacks say blacks have been indifferent to many problems affecting their race. "We really have allowed ourselves to be lulled to sleep at the tail end of the civil rights movement," says Joyce M. Ladner, a sociologist at Howard University in Washington.

Nobles and other black researchers argue that the problems confronting black men are so profound that the future of black Americans may be in question.

Sullivan and his aides say the federal government's current attitude is sincere, citing several steps taken by the Bush administration as proof of its commitment. Among those are changes in welfare to make it less likely that unemployed males are driven from the homes of their children, proposals to expand Medicaid coverage for poor pregnant women and their infants, and $20 million for prenatal-care demonstration projects.

The disparity between the health of black and white Americans is troublesome to many. Homicide is only one of the factors that have helped push black life expectancy downward from 69.7 years to 69.4 years in the latest study by the National Center for Health Statistics. Life expectancy for whites increased slightly from 75.3 to 75.4 years.

According to health statistics for 1988, black men also suffered higher death rates from heart disease (68 percent higher than the total population), strokes (90 percent higher), cancer (71 percent higher), liver ailments (126 percent higher) and diabetes (86 percent higher).

In Washington, cancer rates among black men are the highest in the nation, according to a study by the District of Columbia Commission of Public Health that suggested heavy alcohol use is an important factor. The same study showed that, in every disease category surveyed, blacks in Washington are more likely to die than are whites, a difference that officials blame on unequal access to health care and poor health habits.

Blacks, mostly males, account for one in four AIDS cases nationwide, according to Nobles, who says the number is likely to rise because it appears to be the product of needle-sharing, a widespread practice among poor blacks who use illegal drugs.

While blacks account for 12 percent of the U.S. population, they account for 46 percent of the nation's prisoners. Nearly nine of 10 black inmates are men and 54 percent of them are under 29 years of age, according to Nobles.

At the same time, many blacks, usually the more affluent, continue to move out of the central cities, where many of the problems are concentrated, leading sociologists to express fears of a growing black underclass.

Black males "are at risk of becoming a permanent drain on society and an uncontrollable danger to themselves and their communities," Nobles recently told a congressional committee.

Unless the lot of black men improves rapidly, Nobles said, the United States could see "the emergence of a permanent black underclass in the 21st century."

The lack of a federal response to many of the problems confronting black men has led to a proliferation of community programs designed to rebuild the black family around what many say is their African heritage, a culture based on a strong male figure.

In St. Louis, for example, Alderman Kujaliwa Kennedy runs a program called Simba Wachanga (Young Lions) that stress re-creation of African rites of passage, including dances, which members perform at public ceremonies. Chicago community leaders run a program called "Building Black Men."

Naim Akbar, a clinical psychologist at Florida State University, cites slavery and the civil rights movement as proof that black men can overcome severe obstacles.

It's important for us to understand that we have been through hell already," he said at an Urban League conference on black adolescents. "If we could do it before, we can do it again.

They've been killing black males ever since we got here."

"We need to systematically restructure the education possibilities so young people will see themselves as something other than slam-dunking perverts or pinball bums," Nobles told the Urban League meeting. "Look, if you don't do something quickly to save black boys, there ain't going to be another generation."

14.   BLACK DEMOGRAPHICS

KARL ZINSMEISTER

The Reverend Joseph Lowery, former aide to Martin Luther King, has said that "When America catches a cold, the black community gets pneumonia." Because of their particular susceptibility, black Americans and their problems have been one of this nation's most abiding concerns in the two decades since the urban riots of the late 1960s. And properly so.

But in our worry over black America's problems, we sometimes overlook its successes. And there have been many. The most visible have been in the political arena. From 1968 to 1987 the number of black elected officials nationwide rocketed up six times over, to a total of nearly 7,000. The number of black mayors increased from 48 to 303, and many of our most important cities, including Atlanta, Baltimore, Birmingham, Chicago, Detroit, Los Angeles, New Orleans, Philadelphia, and Washington, D.C. now have black chief executives.

Education levels—which are a touchstone to many other forms of success—have risen dramatically for blacks. The median number of school years completed by blacks rose from nine in

1968 to twelve in 1985. The fraction of all blacks twenty-five and older who finished high school doubled in the last twenty years—from 30 percent to 60 percent. Blacks with four years of college under their belt jumped from 4 percent to 11 percent. At present over 1.1 million blacks are enrolled in college. While still behind white levels, black educational attainment has increased much more rapidly than that for whites in the last twenty years.

In tandem with this big educational push, the number of blacks in high-status jobs has risen sharply. There are about 1.5 million black managers, business executives, and professionals today. One of the most encouraging changes since 1968 is the new prominence of black television anchors, black astronauts, black professors and authors, black leveraged buyout specialists, and black national security advisers.

Blacks have also made a big move into the suburbs, which Ben Wattenberg has described as "the locale of the American success story." Today one-quarter of all blacks live in the suburbs. Half of all black Americans now own their own homes.

The accomplishments are not universal. Blacks have not excelled in small business, for example, and in this country small businesses have typically been one of the classic social elevators. Nonetheless, the achievements of the

From *Public Opinion*, January/February 1988, pp. 41–44. Reprinted with permission of The American Enterprise Institute for Public Policy Research, Washington, D.C.

black middle class in recent years have been impressive.

Of course, the final indicator of "making it" is financial status. Here, too, the successes have been notable. Black families with two working parents now have about 85 percent of the income of similar white families. That is up from 73 percent in 1968. Astonishingly, under 7 percent of all black married couples are poor, after totaling up their cash income and government non-cash aid.

Among the most recent entrants to the labor force, the black-white income gap is even smaller—young, educated, married blacks have basically reached parity with their white counterparts. For people who have followed the traditional American path to success—finish high school, go to college, get married—the economic playing field is now level for both races.

Black per capita income today is about $7,500 for every man, woman, and child. This is a 50 percent increase, in constant dollars, over the 1968 level. (In this same period white per capita income rose 40 percent.) American blacks as a group now command a whopping $215 billion in purchasing power.

FINANCIAL STATUS

If you look closely at all black households, you can divide them into three rough groups: about one-third are comfortably middle class, with an annual income above $25,000, the median income in this country for households of all races. This category includes most of the college graduates and the black professionals, executives, and managers. Nearly 1.5 million of these black families have a yearly cash flow of $40,000 or more.

Another third of all black households are what might be called lower to medium middle class, with yearly incomes ranging from $25,000 down to $10,000. These families are working, most of them own their own homes, many of them live in the suburbs.

The final third of all black households have an annual income below $10,000. Nearly all of these households receive some sort of cash or non-cash government benefit, and even after these payments, about half of them are still be-

low the poverty level. These are the families with problems, and they receive a great deal of national attention.

Another way to estimate the size of the black underclass is to total some subpopulations. There are roughly 5 million blacks, primarily single mothers and their children, living on Aid to Families with Dependent Children payments. Assume each of the 1.5 million families also supports one other unreported adult. (As one welfare mother told the *New York Times*, "Most people on public assistance, the boyfriend gets his cut, no ifs and ands.") To this add the one million blacks, mostly men, who are in jail or on parole or probation. Add another one million career criminals on the rough assumption that there is at least one career criminal operating freely on the streets for every one under supervision. This is not an exhaustive list, and some of these categories may overlap. The total would appear to be about 8 million blacks, 30 percent of all, who might be thought of as the core of an underclass.

So long as it is understood that this lower third constitutes a minority of American blacks, it is entirely appropriate that public concern and policy focus on them. Their problems are severe, a threat not only to their own future welfare but also to the orderly functioning of American society as a whole.

The deepest of these problems, accounting for much of the turmoil that follows, is family deterioration. Divorce and separation rates are high for blacks. Marriage rates are relatively low. A tragically small number of all black children begin their lives in families with two parents present. Sixty percent of all black births now occur out of wedlock, compared with 34 percent in 1968 and around 20 percent in the 1950s. The majority of black unwed mothers and children end up—like white unwed mothers and children—on welfare, and their average period of dependency is over nine years.

Illegitimate births should not always be looked at in terms of the mother, however. Today an astounding 70 percent of all black fathers between the ages of eighteen and twenty-six—both married and unmarried—live apart from at least one of their children. Among those who are unmarried nearly all are absentee parents. What's more, 45 percent of all unwed black fathers age

twenty-four to twenty-seven have at least two illegitimate children, and 12 percent have at least
three, most often with different mothers.

The upshot of all this is that the two-parent
family is becoming the exception in the black
community. Just 36 percent of all black households are married couples today (versus 55 percent in 1968). Only 37 percent of all black children live with both parents (compared to 60
percent in 1968).

This was not always so. In Harlem in 1925,
despite serious economic and social pressures on
black families, 85 percent of them were "intact,"
economist Glenn Loury reports. By the time of
the Moynihan report in 1965, one-quarter of all
black families with children were single-parent
families. In 1985 it was over half.

Former Equal Employment Opportunity
Commission Chairwoman Eleanor Holmes Norton has described this splintering of the black
family as "a threat to the future of black people
without equal." Among its other untoward effects widespread matriarchy is now the leading
cause of poverty in the black community. Two
simple figures indicate the economic risks: black
married-couple families with children have a
poverty rate of about 9 percent after government
transfers. Among single-parent black families 35
percent are poor.

Officially, median family income for blacks
fell 5 percent from 1970 to 1980. A special study
by the U.S. Bureau of the Census, however,
shows that this was accounted for almost entirely
by deterioration of families. Had family structure
been the same in 1980 as it was ten years earlier,
black median family income would have increased over 11 percent in the decade. It was the
shift of many black families from the more-viable
form (two parents) to the less-viable form (one
parent) that caused a fall instead of a rise in overall black income.

LIFE FOR YOUNG BLACKS

Untenable finances are only the beginning of the
problem. The offspring of these decaying underclass families are connected with an enormous
portion of this country's social misery. Half of the
convicted felons in this country are young black

males. Most of their victims are other blacks—
homicide is now the leading cause of death
among black youth, and 95 percent of the assail-
ants are black. Last year New York City Police
Commissioner Benjamin Ward, who is black,
pointed out that most crime in New York is initiated by young black men. "Our little secret is out
of the box," he declared.

A major 1986 study by the National Bureau of
Economic Research reported that 27 percent of
the black inner-city males age sixteen to twenty-
four they surveyed admitted to being involved in
crimes in the past twelve months. Thirty-two
percent believed they could earn more from
street crime than from work. It is estimated that
between 20 and 75 percent of all income in
Harlem today is illegally gotten.

Feeding on all this is the drug trade. In the
NBER study 21 percent of inner-city youth admitted to using drugs stronger than marijuana.
Sixteen percent said they drank alcohol "every
day or almost every day." One of the grim consequences of drug abuse in the black community is
a very high level of AIDS infection. Over 50 percent of all women with AIDS are black, as are 62
percent of all infected babies.

Stating that elevated levels of intravenous
drug use as well as sexual promiscuity and homosexual activity accounted for the disproportionate share of AIDS cases among blacks, the
Reverend Joseph Lowery urged in May 1987
that blacks "adopt a liberating lifestyle that will
make them free of drugs and free of sexual irresponsibility and promiscuity." His statement
that "We've got to come back to basic, family-
oriented relationships, so we can overcome the
assault by AIDS" was endorsed by black public
health officials.

The cumulative effect of rising moral anarchy
is to make life barely tolerable for a significant
number of inner-city blacks. Charles Murray has
argued that in certain neighborhoods in this
country, because of environmental conditions,
"no one is out of poverty . . . no matter how
much money is coming in." A telling indication
of how far we have fallen in this regard came in
May 1987 when Washington, D.C. mayor Marion
Barry, as a gesture toward public education,
taught an eighth grade science class at a city
school. The mayor holds two degrees in chemis-

try, and on this occasion he was leading the school's gifted and talented class in a discussion on the food chain.

As talk turned to predation, then cannibalism, the mayor posed a question: "We don't eat other people, we just kill other human beings. We shoot them, cut them. How many of you," Barry asked his pupils, "know somebody who's been killed?"

There were nineteen students in the class, all black. Fourteen hands shot up. The teacher went around the room: How were they killed? "Shot." "Hit by truck." "Stabbing." "Shot." "Shot." "Drugs." "Shot." Remember, these were twelve-year-old children. And given that they were the gifted and talented class, you may assume they were from backgrounds more privileged than the average black urban child. Such is the extent to which we have allowed murder, overdose, and mayhem to become a routine part of the life of young blacks in inner cities.

And this is hardly unrepresentative material. In Detroit 102 black youngsters age sixteen or under were shot during the first four months of 1987 in gang and drug wars, nearly all of them by other children. A survey at one Detroit junior high school found that a third of the students knew someone their age who was selling drugs.

These examples hint at another fundamental problem for the black underclass: despite great hopes and high determination, other social institutions have had little success in compensating for the collapse of the lower-class black family. Not the churches, certainly not the welfare system, and unfortunately not the schools have been able to staunch the bleeding at the bottom of black society.

At least 50 percent of all black children fall within the jurisdiction of this nation's twelve largest inner-city public school systems. Those, of course, are the very schools that have declined the most in the last two decades. University of Chicago sociologist William Julius Wilson has reported that in 1984 only 47 percent of the students who entered Chicago public high schools four years earlier graduated on time. Of this minority less than a third were capable of reading at or above the national twelfth-grade level. Such is the extent to which black youth have been let down by our schools.

This latter pattern points toward the most serious of the problems facing the black underclass. And that is the sharp separation of the prosperous, well-adjusted top two-thirds of black Americans from the poor and broadly dysfunctional bottom third. One of the clearest afflictions of the black underclass is its isolation from the rest of American society: isolation not only from white America but from the example and promise of blacks who have made a success of themselves.

Yale psychology Professor Edmund Gordon, who is himself black, points out that in city schools, for instance, black teachers are often socially, psychologically, and politically distant from their black students. In a 1987 interview with the *Yale Almuni Magazine,* he characterized the split as "Negroes teaching black kids," a phrase intended to capture the "class difference between that black staff, which clearly perceived itself as middle class, and the mass of students, who are clearly lower class." The Kerner Commission report confirms that this division existed even in the late 1960s, stating: "The typical rioter was a [black] teenager or young adult . . . extremely hostile to both whites and middle-class Negroes."

Before the civil rights movement, Gordon points out, it was difficult for blacks to disassociate themselves from the ghetto. But once the movement was under way, "those of us who were upwardly mobile had a chance to escape the ghetto and . . . you found many black people who had made it up the ladder not only removing themselves from the black community physically but also removing themselves from it psychologically."

RELINKING SEPARATE INTERESTS

There is evidence that a disturbing anti-success ethic may now be taking root among some lower-echelon urban blacks. A year-long investigation by the *Washington Post* at a D.C. high school deemed "typical" reported in September 1987 that "Doing Well Is Not 'Cool' at Inner-City School." A study earlier in the same year by University of California and University of the District of Columbia professors found that many black students in urban areas do poorly in school and avoid success because their peers see use of standard English, studying, and pursuing academic interests as "acting white." One of the taunts applied to ambitious black students at such schools is "Oreo double stuff"—referring to the cookie that is black on the outside but has lots of white on the inside.

When interviewing black skilled blue-collar workers one also finds evidence of a pronounced bifurcation. While not as far removed culturally from the black underclass as, say, a black professor or Army colonel, black trades workers such as tile setters, electricians, and plasterers, as well as small businessmen such as store owners and goods carters often have economic and social profiles more like prosperous immigrants than poor blacks—working tremendous hours, saving large sums of capital, finding it difficult to recruit laborers from the communities that surround their inner-city work sites. In their powerful work efforts and their confidence, such individuals express little in common with persons living in a dispirited mailbox economy of government checks. One of the problems is that while blacks who are working are making more, many blacks are not working. As a result, today only 56 percent of black men are employed, compared to 70 percent in 1968. This despite the fact that 71 percent of the individuals surveyed by the NBER said they could get a minimum wage job "very easily or somewhat easily."

Today, economic inequality is much sharper among blacks than among other social groups. The top fifth of black families ranked by income currently make 13.8 times as much as the bottom fifth. Among whites the split is 8.6 times.

According to the Census Bureau, Prince George's County in southern Maryland had the most affluent and educated black population in the country in the early 1980s. But the same county also saw the number of blacks living in poverty within its border more than double in the previous decade.

In recent years a variety of black leaders including Marian Wright Edelman, Eleanor Holmes Norton, Joseph Lowery, and columnist William Raspberry have called for middle-class blacks to take a more active role in helping the black underclass. What is needed, they say, is a relinking of separated black interests.

This, however, will not be easy. For one thing current public policies on issues of race—affirmative action and quotas, electoral activism, and minority set-asides—provide aid almost exclusively to middle- and upper-class blacks. As such, William Julius Wilson and others have suggested, they may actually exacerbate the schism between the successful and the mired down.

Even more difficult, an alliance of the two parts of black America will require giving up the traditional belief that the main problem facing black America is white America. In an editorial on the Kerner Commission report published twenty years ago the *New York Times* commended the panel members for laying responsibility for the black community's traumas "where it belongs—on white racism."

With that as diagnosis the prescriptions were the predictable ones of an earlier era: "a swift reconstruction of the patterns that are comfortable for the white majority and the allocation of funds for jobs, education, and housing far beyond any [previously] contemplated." In particular 2 million government-sponsored jobs, 6 million units of public housing, more spending on schools and expanded welfare were called for. Today, it is harder to believe that those kinds of things will cure what ails black America. And it is less clear that the crucial change needed is for whites to "assume responsibility" for black progress.

In an era of abundant prosperity for many American blacks, where every measure of white racism shows it to be in sharp decline, where the crying imperative is no longer equal political rights but economic empowerment among a marginal black underclass, there is only so much white America can do. In its next phase black ambition must focus urgently upon economic activism, and black Americans must ask themselves what they can do for themselves and for their brothers. Repairing the tattered fabric of black family life, in particular, will require self-healing. The obstacle is no longer a simple "Them."

These are the best of times, and these are the worst of times for American blacks. Those who are struggling need badly those who have made it. An accounting between the two black nations would seem overdue.

15. THE POLITICS OF FAMILY IN AMERICA

JEWELL HANDY GRESHAM

The past is not dead. It's not even past.
—William Faulkner

In April 1844, Secretary of State John Calhoun, the pre-eminent Southern philosopher of States' rights, directed a letter to the British ambassador in Washington attesting that where blacks and whites existed in the same society, slavery was the natural result. Wherever the states changed that providential relationship, the blacks invariably degenerated "into vice and pauperism accompanied by the bodily and mental afflictions incident thereto—deafness, blindness, insanity, and idiocy." In the slave states, in contrast, the blacks improved greatly "in number, comfort, intelligence, and morals."

To prove his point, Calhoun supplied statistics from the 1840 census. The data showed a shocking rate of black insanity in New England: one out of every fourteen in Maine, every twenty-eight in New Hampshire, every forty-three in Massachusetts, etc. The overall figure for the North was almost ten times the rate in the South, where only one "lunatic" for every 1,309 blacks was shown in Virginia, one in 2,447 in South Carolina, etc.

At the time Calhoun wrote that letter, one of the country's leading newspapers had just broken the scandal of the plot by President Tyler's Administration to annex Texas as slave territory—a potential constitutional crisis certain to inflame the bitter North-South conflict. In that context, Calhoun's statistics were intended less for the British than for Congress, to which he forwarded copies.

There was only one flaw in his argument: The figures were false. Dr. Edward Jarvis of Massachusetts General Hospital, a leading specialist in the incidence of insanity, immediately challenged them. Joined by the prestigious American Statistical Association, Jarvis conducted an exhaustive study of every town and country in the free states in which black insanity had been reported by the Census Bureau. In case after case, the number of "insane" blacks proved larger than the state's total black population!

The A.S.A.'s comprehensive study—forwarded to former President John Quincy Adams in the House of Representatives—concluded that "it would have been far better to have no census at all, than such a one as has been published" and urged Congress either to correct the data or "discard or disown" it "as the good of the country . . . and as justice and humanity shall demand." But when Adams, as recorded in his diary, confronted Calhoun at the State Department, the latter "answered like a true slavemonger. . . . He writhed like a trodden rattlesnake on the exposure of his false report to the House . . . and finally said that where there were so many errors they balanced one another, and led to the same conclusion as if they were all correct." The A.S.A. report—blocked by the Speaker and the proslavery majority in the House—never reached the floor.

While these developments unfolded, Southern slaves were of course in no position to challenge the claims in which their welfare was critical. Nor did the free blacks of New York City under the leadership of the distinguished black physician/abolitionist James McCune Smith stand a chance of having their memorial to Congress protesting the "calumnies against free people of color" recognized. For those who held political power, it was imperative that blacks simply not exist except as objects, and the truth or falsity of what was said was beside the point. What mattered, then as now, was not the *facts* but only that the semblance of "substance" be provided for a time sufficient to confuse the issue and carry the day.

From *The Nation*, July 24/31, 1989, pp. 116–122. Copyright © 1989, The Nation Company, Inc. Reprinted with permission.

"THE NEED TO SEGREGATE OR QUARANTINE A RACE"

After the Civil War, the Calhoun view of the inherent degeneracy of blacks, which held that they could not survive outside slavery, was tenaciously clung to by the outnumbered whites of Mississippi. In 1865 the *Meridian Clarion* asserted with unconcealed satisfaction that the black race was doomed: "A hundred years is a long time to one man; but to a nation or a race, it is but a limited period. Well, in that time the negro will be dead."

In due course, Mississippi produced figures to prove it: The 1866 state census showed a more than 12 percent decline in the black population. Unfortunately for the prophets, however, this data was as accurate as Calhoun's: The 1870 Federal census showed an *increase* of more than 7,000, which turned out to be an undercount of between 50,000 and 75,000, corrected in the 1880 Federal figures.

Nonetheless, in the 1880s, the Reverend C. K. Marshall, the most prominent preacher in the state, predicted that "by January, 1920 . . . except for a few old people [who] will linger as the Cherokees do on their reservation . . . the colored population of the south will scarcely be counted."

With the passage of more years without apparent visible diminution in black ranks, however, white theories of a built-in biological solution to the black "problem" obviously had to be augmented. In *The Plantation Negro as Freeman* (1889), the historian Philip A. Bruce used the black family as a device for attacking all blacks. Bruce, the scion of a former Virginia slaveowner, simply advanced Calhoun's thesis: With the end of slavery, the loss of white "supervision" led to a severe and menacing deterioration in blacks' social and moral condition. The black family as such did not exist, he announced; black children, accordingly, were born into a state of moral degeneracy.

Bruce viciously castigated black women. Alluding to the alleged propensity of black men to rape white women, he asserted that they found "something strangely alluring and seductive . . . in the appearance of a white woman" because of the "wantonness of the women of his own race." The "fact" that black women failed to complain of being raped by men of their race counted as "strong proof of the sexual laxness of plantation women as a class."

Herbert Gutman called Bruce's work perhaps the most important connecting link between the "popular" views of African-American degeneracy in the 1880s and the supportive pseudoscientific works of the ensuing decades before World War I. These latter writings rested heavily on the pseudoscientific data of Social Darwinism—the doctrine of survival of the fittest. The historian George Frederickson explains the relevance of such theories in his book *The Black Image in the White Mind:*

If the blacks were a degenerating race with no future, the problem ceased to be one of how to prepare them for citizenship or even how to make them more productive and useful members of the community. The new prognosis pointed rather to the need to segregate or quarantine a race liable to be a source of contamination and social danger to the white community, as it sank ever deeper into the slough of disease, vice, and criminality.

THE DEVICE UPDATED

It was against these brutally repressive rationalizations still undergirding the Southern apartheid system after World War II that the civil rights revolution of the 1950s and 1960s erupted. And it was at the climactic stages of that struggle that Labor Department official Daniel Patrick Moynihan conceived, in December 1964, his supposedly secret "internal memorandum" on the black family.

Whether Moynihan knew his history or not, his report served the time-tested purpose: Whenever the system is in crisis (or shows signs of becoming transformed); whenever blacks get restless (or show strength); whenever whites in significant numbers show signs of coming together with blacks to confront their mutual problems (or enemies), the trick is to shift the focus from the real struggle for political and economic empowerment to black "crime," degeneracy, pathology and—in Moynihan's innovative twist—the "deterioration" of the black family (previously defined as nonexistent!).

Moynihan's report was subtitled "The Case for National Action." But just how much serious "action" it intended was made plain in the author's next "internal memo"—this time to Richard Nixon—counseling "benign neglect."

In the light of subsequent events it is interesting to discover in *Pat*, the Senator's biography, that it was presidential assistant Bill Moyers who, in May 1965, first brought the black family report, until then ignored, to Lyndon Johnson's attention and arranged for the President to deliver a major policy speech based on it.

Curiously, the Moyers-arranged speech bypassed all agencies of the government set up to aid the passage of the President's civil rights agenda. It was delivered at the graduation exercises of Howard University before an overwhelmingly black audience of thousands of students, parents, friends and dignitaries. Apparently few observers among the editors, journalists and scholars present found what Johnson did reprehensible. Howard was one of the colleges that had sent a sizable contingent of students into the revolutionary *nonviolent* Southern struggle which at that moment was galvanizing, inspiring and, in a thousand unforeseeable ways, transforming the nation. Before the young people whom he should have congratulated for the extraordinary example of sacrifice and heroism they were setting, the President emphasized the "historical" degenerate state of the families from which they came!

True, words of noble intent were there (as they were in Moynihan's original), and they heartened many. But so were the declarations of black degeneracy that reinforced the racism of many more and signaled the open-door policy for what was to come. Through the summer, however, the "secret" Moynihan report continued to be leaked to selected journalists. Then came the event that cemented its impact. Ten days after the August passage of the Voting Rights Act of 1965, Watts exploded—and in a mad scramble for instant wisdom, journalists turned to the black family report and drew on its conclusions as explanations for the violent civil disorders.

What did it explain? What were the causes of Watts and the succeeding ghetto rebellions? Not, as the Kerner commission concluded in 1967, the division of America into two societies, separate and unequal. Not historical white racism, Depression-level unemployment and the intolerable conditions of the ghetto that cut short the dreams and lives of millions of black men, women and children. Not at all. "Ours is a society," offered Moynihan, "which presumes male leadership in private and public affairs. . . . A subculture such as that of the Negro American, in which this is not the pattern, is placed at a distinct disadvantage." To overcome that disadvantage, he said, the malaise of the black family, characterized by the unnatural dominance of a "black matriarchy," had to be cured.

In contrast, Moynihan wrote: *"The white family has achieved a high degree of stability and is maintaining that stability."* (Emphasis added.) Against the backdrop of the next twenty-five years, this declaration would be hilarious were it not for the fact that, for untold millions of *white* working women—divorced, single and joint providers—the idealized patriarchal structure held up as an icon had always been a myth! Indeed, even as Moynihan wrote the words, the modern women's movement for equal rights and a sense of selfhood, submerged under the centuries-old domination of that very model, was being forged in the crucible of the civil rights struggle.

Those who found the Moynihan report useful were presumably unaware that the archetypal sexism on which it rests is inextricable from its racism. At any rate, the report signaled, at the very height of the civil rights movement, that Northern whites would pick up where the South was forced to leave off in blocking the long black struggle for parity with whites in American life.

LINE OF DESCENT

On January 25, 1986, Bill Moyers, Moynihan's original booster, invoked the full power of a prime-time, two-hour CBS Special Report to beam the old theme into millions of homes. The title: *The Vanishing Black Family—Crisis in Black America* (shades of the old Mississippi *Meridian Clarion*!). The East Texan, in sympathetic "liberal" guise, took cameras into a Newark, New Jersey, housing project for an "intimate" portrait of black teen-age welfare mothers, sexually irresponsible if not criminal youth, a smiling black male "superstud," and pervasive pathology all around. Moyers's report was directed not at the cause of the plight of the people whose confidences he elicited. Viewers were shown, rather, a pathology in black America so overwhelming and irredeemable as to leave the panel of blacks brought in at the end to "discuss" the subject helpless to dissipate the impact of the carefully selected imagery.

The result, whatever sympathy toward individual victims white viewers might have felt, and whatever responsibilities some might acknowledge that America has for its racist "past," could only be: First, to utterly terrify most as to the very nature of their fellow black citizens by reinforcing, with "liberal" authority, the most archetypal of racist myths, fears and stereotypes—a picture of "jungle" immorality and degeneracy, inarticulateness and sloth so rife that the onlookers could actually forget the terrible national corruption, wholesale public and private immorality, and other massive problems about them, in horrified fascination with the doings of these Others. And second, to make the situation seem so hopeless that "realistically" there is nothing to be done about it anyway. Racism is no longer the problem, self-destructiveness is. And if that is so, why continue to throw good taxpayer dollars after bad? In the words of the older black woman selected by Moyers to deliver the clincher at the end: "If Martin Luther King were alive, he would not be talking about the things I think he was talking about—labor and all that. He would be talking about the black family."

It is hard to believe that it was simply bad taste that led CBS to choose the very week of the first national celebration of King's birthday to televise his fellow Southerner's broadside. African-Americans had hardly had a moment to savor the honor to the martyred black minister before their psyches were so powerfully assaulted.

The extent of the commonplace manner in which deep-seated black response is blocked out from the larger society may be seen in several postscripts to the broadcast beginning when the National Black Leadership Roundtable, comprising the chief executive officers of more than 300 national black organizations, directed a detailed letter to CBS to protest the "untimely and in-deed . . . suspect" airing of an "unbalanced, unfair and frequently salacious" documentary.

The N.B.L.R. challenged the implication "that the *only* legitimate and sanctioned family form is nuclear and patriarchal," and observed:

One was left with the impression that black families generally do not have fathers in the home, but there was no serious examination of the reasons for the absence of the father within some black families. The unconscionable high levels of unemployment, underemployment, imprisonment, drug addiction and mortality among black men—effects of an economy which does not fully respond to the employment needs of all Americans—all play a role. . . . Single-parent families then, are not, as implied . . . the result of "immorality" or promiscuity, but rather are adaptive responses to economic and social forces.

Two months later CBS vice president of public affairs broadcasts Eric Ober, speaking for Moyers, replied. He refused to meet with Walter Fauntroy, N.B.L.R. president, or "any member of your group." And to the N.B.L.R. query as to what "experts" had been consulted within the black community, he replied that the "experts we consulted were primarily officials of the *Department of the Census*." (Emphasis added.) Little did he know the history.

The reinforcing white response was predictable. In early 1987, the Columbia University Graduate School of Journalism gave its highest award in broadcast journalism—the Alfred I. Du Pont-Columbia University Gold Baton for the "program judged to have made the greatest contribution to the public's understanding of an important issue"—to CBS News for the Moyers Special Report on "the disintegration of black family life."

Moyers's contribution lies not only in his restoration to primacy of old images through the power of television but in his encouragement of the willingness, indeed the eagerness, of large numbers of white Americans to have all that he portrayed be true at any cost so that the victims might deserve their fate. Such is the depth of the entrenched white desire to avoid facing the society's culpability for creating and maintaining the two ever more unequal "societies" the Kerner report asked us to face up to a generation before.

RESTRAINING THE "DARKER IMPULSES"

In such a climate, it is not surprising that politicians like "centrist" Democrat Charles Robb, L.B.J.'s son-in-law and former Virginia Governor, now Senator, promptly picked up Moyers's cue. Once upon a time, black people were the victims of white racism, Robb conceded in his keynote speech to a conference on the Johnson presidency. But that time has passed. "It's time to shift the primary focus from racism, the traditional enemy from without, to self-defeating patterns of behavior, the new enemy within."

Approval by establishment opinion makers was swift to follow. A *New York Times* editorial endorsed Robb's brand of "hard truth," and journalists flung the name of the messenger into the public arena as a worthy candidate for President.

In such a climate, the level of public tolerance of the intolerable increased. Even years before, there had been little reaction when, at a speech in New Orleans to the International Association of Chiefs of Police, President Reagan had drawn "applause and some whoops of approval" for remarks that included the following:

It has occurred to me that the root causes of our . . . growth of government and the decay of the economy . . . can be traced to many of the same sources of the crime problem. . . . Many of the social thinkers of the 1950s and '60s who discussed crime only in the context of disadvantaged childhoods and poverty-stricken neighborhoods were the same people who thought that massive government spending could wipe away our social ills. The underlying premise in both cases was a belief that there was nothing permanent or absolute about any man's nature—that he was a product of his material environment, and that by changing that environment . . . we could . . . usher in a great new era. The solution to the crime problem will not be found in the social worker's files, the psychiatrist's notes or the bureaucrat's budget. . . . Only our deep moral values and strong institutions can hold back that jungle and restrain the darker impulses of human nature.

Most black people knew immediately of which "jungle" and whose "darker impulses" Reagan was speaking, and that his words represented a not-so-subtle invitation to white-against-black terror.

Reagan's position was a *theological* one in the American Calvinist tradition, a division of the world into good and evil, with a scapegoat selected to serve as "sacrificial animal upon whose back the burden of unwanted evils is ritualistically loaded," in Kenneth Burke's definition. Through such projections, the culture thus expiates its sins and receives absolution.

The Reagan rhetoric directed to the assembled police officers was a direct corollary of his theological labeling of the Soviet Union as an "evil empire" (a remark now implicitly withdrawn in the case of the Russians, but not that of African-Americans!). It indicates how high is the level of responsibility for nationwide police practices of treating black Americans as if they are foreign enemies and, with sickening regularity, eliminating many. And it also indicates the treatment of a variety of foreign "enemies"— now mostly desperately struggling Third World countries—on the basis of a "moral" stance rooted in the myths of a fatalistically corrupt domestic system.

It is on this level that the politics of family— which is to say the politics of power and domination—threatens not only domestic but world social, political and economic order.

It is likewise on this level that the political manipulation of the intermingled race/sex/religion syndrome of the society is irrevocably wedded to violence; in its ultimate form, militaristic. For the identities of those who create the monsters in the mind (Toni Morrison calls the creations "grinning apes in the head") require ever vigilant attention to finding and confronting replicas in the external world.

It is this system of macho ethics that was successfully drawn upon in George Bush's march to the White House. True to tradition, the ultimate scapegoat tapped was a black male, the rapist Willie Horton (whether real or fancied does not traditionally matter), projected before millions via television and print.

Those who make use of such a repugnant and dangerous tactic—among them South Carolina's Lee Atwater, now chair of the Republican National Committee, and Texan James Baker 3d— know these traditions well. And they know further that it is not possible for the image of a black man accused of rape to be flashed before black

Americans by white men independent of the psychic association for blacks with lynchings. After the election, The *New York Times* not only contributed the verdict to history that the Bush campaign was "tough and effective," this preeminent sheet augmented that judgment with strident editorial criticism of black students at Howard for their successful protest action when Lee Atwater was suddenly named to the University's Board of Trustees.

While white perception of black criminality is readily evoked, white awareness of black anger or anguish has been not only historically avoided but, on the deepest psychic levels, guarded against. Existentially, the concept of black people as vulnerable human beings who sustain pain and love and hatreds and fears and joy and sorrows and degradations and triumphs is not yet permitted in the national consciousness. Hence the constant need of the dominant society, in age after age, to reinforce linguistic and ritualistic symbols that deny black humanity.

Historically, white terror is the sustaining principle of the system. Whether overtly applied or covertly threatened, not only has this basic device of subjugation never been nationally rejected, it has, on the contrary, always been sanctioned.

THE FAMILY AS UNIFYING PRINCIPLE

A few weeks after his election, George Bush addressed the Republican Governors Association in Alabama where, some months before, several black legislators had been arrested for trying to remove the Confederate Flag from above the State Capitol, presided over by Republican Governor Guy Hunt. The theme of the conference—"Century of the States"—resurrected overtones of Calhoun's old brand of States' rights. To this audience, a smiling Bush announced that building more prisons was a major domestic priority of his Administration (on education, he emphasized that the initiative would be left up to the states).

Only a few weeks later a smiling Bush assured a black gathering celebrating the birthday of Martin Luther King Jr. that he is committed to the fulfillment of King's dream of America, just as they are. That King's dream does not include the construction of prisons is immaterial. In the prevailing political realm, language does not matter: Symbols are all.

However, the renewed focus on the black family has introduced a sleeper. For the very technology of communication which carries the message of black pathology to white people conveys to blacks the unmistakable message that once again the dominant culture needs the assurance that black pathology prevails. Clearly, we must bestir ourselves to face the threat. Ironically, we have been handed a mighty weapon. To millions of ordinary human beings the family is not a symbol to be manipulated by opportunistic politicians but the essential nurturing unit from which they draw their being. For African-Americans (and for hundreds of millions of others), it is the institution around which our historical memories cling. Through the extended family of mothers, fathers, sisters and brothers, uncles and aunts, cousins and unsung numbers of others who simply "mothered" parentless children, black people "got over."

It is unbelievable that on the eve of the twenty-first century those who are still fashioning the political formula for WHO and WHAT make a family remain overwhelmingly male!

But it is women who give birth, and children who represent the one essential entity which must exist if the family does. It is simply inconceivable that women, that society, can any longer allow men to retain almost exclusive domain over the vital process of defining the human family.

The concept of "family" can and should be a unifying, rather than divisive, principle. Given the weight of U.S. history that we uniquely bear, black women should step forth collectively not only as blacks but as women, in the name of our lost children throughout history—including most urgently the present generation. One of the first steps is to confront, in all their ramifications, the racist/sexist myths historically concocted by opportunistic, ruthless or naïve white males in the interests of white-over-black and male-over-female dominance.

Never again should the future of black children—or children anywhere in the world—be left in such hands!

16.   POVERTY, JOBLESSNESS, AND THE SOCIAL TRANSFORMATION OF THE INNER CITY

LOÏC J. D. WACQUANT and WILLIAM JULIUS WILSON

The conspicuous problems of inner-city poverty and welfare cannot be understood, and therefore successfully tackled, in and of themselves: they do not emerge, develop and eventually dissolve in a social vacuum. Rather, they are the outcome of the historical interplay of forces and struggles that cut across the field of politics and public policy, the economic field, and the field of class and race relations.

Nonetheless, the public debate on welfare tends to pay scant attention to the basic societal processes that produce and sustain poverty in the first place. As a result, the malady is often ill-identified and the cure prescribed ends up falsely putting the blame on the victims (the poor) or on the programs of assistance designed to help them (welfare). The underlying causes for the emergence and ongoing crystallization of a black underclass, for instance, have typically been obscured by an excessive concern for the alleged individual deficiencies—behavioral, moral or cultural—of those who compose it, or worse yet, unfounded claims that such an underclass is one of the "counterintuitive" effects of welfare programs.

In this chapter, the *linkages between welfare and societal organization* are explored by unraveling recent social changes in the inner-city neighborhoods of the country's largest urban centers. In order to relate public aid to transformations in the social structure and political economy of these areas, we first survey the demographic and racial correlates of the rise of welfare among inner-city residents. We then document the adverse impact of deindustrialization and of

From *Welfare Policy for the 1990s*, ed. Phoebe H. Cottingham and David T. Ellwood (Cambridge, Mass.: Harvard University Press). Copyright © 1989 by the Rockefeller Foundation. Reprinted by permission of the publisher.

the shifts in the labor market on the economic opportunities of the urban poor. Drawing on a detailed examination of Chicago, we show how the class and institutional transformations undergone by central city ghettos in recent decades have further exacerbated the effects of the broader economic changes. In conclusion, we sketch out the implications of this analysis for the current public policy debate, arguing that its terms be broadened to include social structural factors and that the integration of economic and social policies be considered seriously.

WELFARE, JOBLESSNESS AND THE GROWING CONCENTRATION OF POVERTY, 1970–1980

The structure of poverty has undergone significant changes in recent years (see Wilson et al., 1988). Poverty has become at once more urban, more concentrated, and more deeply rooted in big cities, particularly in older industrial centers with vast, highly segregated black and Hispanic populations. Accordingly, the number of recipients of public assistance in these metropolises has soared. Today, welfare seems a fact of life in many poor neighborhoods of urban America. But increased welfare dependency is only a surface manifestation of deeper social changes.

The nature and magnitude of these changes can perhaps best be captured by tracing the demographic evolution of the ten largest central cities from 1970 to 1980. These metropolises alone comprised over half of the poor living in the 50 largest cities of the country in 1980, and over one third of all central-city poor over this decade.

One remarkable change is that although the total population of these ten cities dropped by 7 percent (from 21.8 to 20.2 million), owing to the exodus of more than 4 million whites, there was *a marked increase, both relative and absolute, in their poverty population.* The number of poor residents grew by 19 percent, from 3.1 to 3.8 million, while the overall poverty rate jumped from 14.6 to 18.7 percent. This increase was due entirely to the growth of poverty among minorities. Poor blacks and Hispanics reached 29 percent by 1980, compared to 11 percent of whites, while the national official poverty rate stagnated in the 11–13 percent range throughout this period (U.S. Bureau of Census, 1986a). Now, it is important to disaggregate these data and to look at individual cities, for this reveals recurrent contrasts between the old, waning, industrial centers of the Midwest and Northeast and the newer, booming metropolises of the South and West.

While Los Angeles, Dallas, and Houston recorded slight to moderate population gains from 1970 to 1980, due to increases in minority residents that more than offset a small outmigration of whites, Rustbelt cities all suffered demographic decline: Indianapolis lost 6 percent of its population, New York City and Chicago 9 percent, Philadelphia and Baltimore dropped 14 percent, and Detroit and Cleveland between one fourth and one fifth. In these cities whites moved out en masse, as can be seen in column 2 of Table 1, with Chicago and Cleveland losing one third of their white residents and Detroit a full one half. Only Philadelphia and Cleveland saw their black population slip, by 2 percent and 13 percent respectively, and Baltimore was the only large city where the Latino population did not rise. Everywhere else, black and Hispanic residents multiplied. These large cities are thus undergoing a process of *rapid racial polarization:* whereas whites made up 71 percent of their aggregate population in 1970, by 1980 this figure had dropped to 58 percent.

In spite of this depopulation, the number of poor rose rapidly everywhere, with the exception of Cleveland; by 30 percent in Los Angeles, 24 percent in Chicago, 20 percent in New York City, 16 percent in Philadelphia, Detroit, and Houston, 11 percent in Dallas and Indianapolis, and 7 percent in Baltimore. The only cities that did not experience an increase in the rate of poverty were Dallas (where it remained constant at 14 percent) and Houston (where it dipped

slightly to 13 percent). In all Rustbelt cities except Indianapolis poverty rates rose substantially (by a uniform 5 percentage points), to hover around 20–23 percent in 1980.

Growth of poverty is not the whole story, however. For there was an even *sharper increase in the population, both poor and nonpoor, living in poverty areas and especially in extreme poverty areas* in these ten cities. The number of residents living in poverty tracts rose by 34 percent overall and those in extreme poverty tracts more than doubled (from .9 to 2.1 million). Poverty areas naturally include both poor and nonpoor individuals; it is therefore worth noting that the increase in the poor population of these areas was even more pronounced, due exclusively to changes among blacks and Hispanics. This growth was particularly acute in five of the seven Rustbelt cities, as indicated in columns 4 and 5 of Table 1. In New York City, for example, the poor population residing in extreme poverty areas grew by a whopping 269 percent; in Chicago and Detroit by 162 percent and 117 percent; in Indianapolis by 150 percent, and in Philadelphia by 128 percent. By contrast, the number of poor living in the poorest neighborhoods of Los Angeles and Houston increased by only 17 percent, and decreased in Dallas by some 13 percent.

The differential rise of poverty across areas produced an *increasing concentration of the (minority) poor in the poorest sections of these cities.* In this decade, the number of poor residents found in extreme poverty tracts grew by 138 percent (from 428,000 to just over one million) as indicated in Table 2. This growing concentration of the poor in extreme poverty areas is almost entirely a minority phenomenon. As columns 6 and 7 of Table 1 show, the proportion of poor blacks living in extremely poor neighborhoods increased substantially in all seven Rustbelt cities: it doubled in Chicago (from 24 to 47 percent) and tripled in New York City (from 15 to 45 percent); it climbed from 35 to 43 percent in Cleveland, from 38 to 42 percent in Baltimore, from 25 to 39 percent in Philadelphia, from 13 to 22 percent in Detroit, and from 8 to 16 percent in Indianapolis. In the same period the concentration of poor blacks remained unchanged in Los Angeles and Houston and even decreased

TABLE 1 Changes in Population, Poverty, Poverty Concentration, and Welfare Receipt in the Ten Largest Cities, 1970–1980 (in Percentages)

City	Total Population	White Population	Poor Population	Population in Poverty Areas[a]	Population in Extreme Poverty Areas[b]	% of Blacks Living in Extreme Poverty Areas[b] 1970	% of Blacks Living in Extreme Poverty Areas[b] 1980	% of Families Receiving Public Assistance 1970	% of Families Receiving Public Assistance 1980	# of Families on Welfare	# of Families on Welfare in Poverty Areas[a]
New York City	−9	−29	+20	+53	+269	15	45	9.7	16.2	+44	+62
Chicago	−9	−32	+24	+62	+162	24	47	7.5	17.0	+95	+120
Philadelphia	−14	−23	+16	+56	+128	25	39	8.6	19.0	+93	+132
Detroit	−21	−51	+16	+50	+117	13	22	8.3	23.4	+119	+176
Baltimore	−14	−29	+7	+30	+33	38	42	9.7	21.0	+90	+106
Cleveland	−24	−33	−3	+31	+23	35	43	8.5	18.0	+53	+104
Indianapolis	−6	−11	+11	+38	+150	8	16	2.9	7.8	+161	+188
Los Angeles	+5	−16	+31	+75	+17	20	19	9.9	12.1	+23	+60
Houston	+29	+8	+16	−14	+18	17	16	3.9	5.2	+74	+52
Dallas	+7	−12	+11	+4	−13	33	28	4.5	6.0	+39	+43
Total	−7	−25	+19	+48	+138	22	38	8.9	15.0	+62	+88

a. Poverty areas are census tracts in which 20 percent or more of the population is poor.
b. Extreme poverty areas are census tracts in which 40 percent or more of the population is poor.

TABLE 2 Growing Concentration of Poverty by Race in the Ten Largest Central Cities, 1970–1980 (as Measured by the Number and Percentage of Residents Living in Tracts with Poverty Rates of 40% and More)

	1970		1980	
	n	*%*	*n*	*%*
Total population	918	4.2	2,048	10.2
Whites	233	1.5	336	2.9
Black	676	11.5	1,378	21.8
Hispanics	173	7.5	516	16.5
Poor population	428	13.5	1,016	26.9
Whites	110	6.7	144	10.9
Blacks	322	21.9	688	37.6
Hispanics	76	14.5	272	29.8

Source: U.S. Bureau of the Census (1973, 1985).
Note: Number *n* in thousands.

slightly in Dallas. Poor Hispanics were also disproportionately concentrated in extreme poverty areas, but this was more true of Puerto Ricans in Rustbelt cities than of Latinos of Mexican origin clustered in the Sunbelt. In Los Angeles, Dallas, and Houston, the three cities with the largest proportions of Mexicans, the number of Hispanics dwelling in extreme poverty tracts ranged from 5 percent to 7 percent; the figure for both Chicago and Detroit was 13 percent. By contrast, in the three cities with large numbers of Puerto Ricans, the proportion of Hispanic residents in depressed areas was typically high: 57 percent in Philadelphia, 45 percent in New York City, and 30 percent in Baltimore.

A clear majority of the roughly 1.5 million poor whites in the ten largest central cities in the United States lived in nonpoor areas throughout the decade of the 1970s (65 percent in 1970, 57 percent in 1980) and only a very small fraction of them lived in extremely poor areas. In sharp contrast, only 1 poor black in 6 and 1 poor Hispanic in 5 resided in a nonpoor neighborhood by 1980. Indeed, most poor blacks in these metropolises lived in tracts with poverty rates exceeding 30 percent—almost two thirds did so in 1980, up from one half only ten years before. Moreover, if one makes a distinction between Hispanic whites and non-Hispanic whites, as allowed by

the 1980 census reports, it turns out that a full two-thirds of all poor non-Hispanic whites lived in nonpoor areas in 1980, with a mere 6 percent residing in extreme poverty areas. Poor blacks are thus six times more likely to live in severely depressed neighborhoods than are poor non-Hispanic whites. This fact is crucial for understanding the formation of a black ghetto underclass.

Changes in the incidence and concentration of poverty were *closely related to changes in joblessness.* Thus while the unemployment rate for blacks increased nationwide from 6.3 percent in 1970 to 12.3 percent in 1980, in the poverty areas of Rustbelt central cities the situation was somewhat worse to start with, and it deteriorated at a more rapid pace. In Detroit, for instance, the unemployment rate for blacks living in poor tracts was already 10 percent in 1970 and shot up to 31 percent in 1980. In Philadelphia, the corresponding figures were 9 percent and 20.5 percent; in Chicago, 8.5 percent and 20.8 percent; in Cleveland, 10 and 18 percent; in Indianapolis, 12 and 22 percent; in Baltimore, 7 and 19 percent; in New York City, 6 and 15 percent. Once again, Sunbelt cities looked quite different: in Houston, black unemployment increased, but rates were significantly lower than either the national average or Rustbelt cities figures (from 3.7 percent to 8 percent); in Dallas, unemployment among black males residing in poverty areas actually dropped from 4.6 percent to 2.1 percent. In Los Angeles, levels were high but the increase was comparatively slight (from 12 to 15 percent).

Because official unemployment rates do not take into account those who have given up on the job search, employment rates are a better measure of the state of the labor market; they tell more accurately the worsening economic situation of inner-city blacks. For whereas national employment rates among white males sixteen years and older stayed around 70 percent throughout this decade, that of their black counterparts dropped from 63 percent to 56 percent. In the poverty areas of the Rustbelt cities, moreover, employment rates dropped to considerably lower levels. In Philadelphia, less than half (46 percent) of all black males living in poor tracts were employed in 1980, down from 61 percent only ten years before. In the poverty areas of Detroit, a staggering 60 percent of all black

males did not hold a job by 1980 (up from 39 percent in 1970). In the poor neighborhoods of Chicago, the black male employment rate fell from 62 percent to a mere 48 percent. And barely half of all black males living in New York's and Baltimore's poverty areas had gainful employment in 1980, a 20-point drop in a decade. Nothing of the sort happened in our Southern central cities: a full two-thirds of the black residents of the poverty areas of Dallas and Houston were employed in 1980 (down from three-fourths in 1970).

Given these general trends in poverty and unemployment, it should come as no surprise that, contrary to the national trend (the proportion of families receiving welfare payments stagnated at roughly 5 percent in urban America), public assistance receipt expanded noticeably in central-city areas over this decade (see Table 3). While the total number of families in these ten cities decreased by 4 percent, the number of families on public assistance grew by 62 percent, from

TABLE 3 Families Receiving Public Assistance, by Race, in the Ten Largest Central Cities, 1970–1980

	All Tracts		Tracts with 20% or More Poor		Percent of Families on Aid Living in Poverty Areas	
	1970	1980	1970	1980	1970	1980
Total						
n	466	754	275	518	59.1	68.7
%	84.0	15.0	21.8	29.7	—	—
Whites						
n	214	235	84	94	39.3	39.9
%	5.3	7.8	18.2	19.5	—	—
Blacks						
n	251	411	191	337	75.8	82.4
%	18.5	27.2	24.5	34.8	—	—
Hispanics						
n	96	172	96	130	69.5	76.0
%	17.8	23.6	26.7	31.3	—	—

Source: U.S. Bureau of the Census (1973, 1985).
Note: Number *n* in thousands.

466,000 (8.4 percent of all families) in 1970 to 754,000 (15 percent) in 1980, due almost entirely to increases among blacks and Hispanics. Moreover, 84 percent of this growth in the number of assisted families occurred in poverty areas. As of 1980, one of every three black or Latino families dwelling in a poverty area of these cities was on welfare (compared to a national figure of 23 percent for all black Americans).

The proportion of families on welfare who lived in poverty areas went up noticeably for both blacks and Hispanics in the 1970s, whereas it remained constant among whites. The net result was that, in 1980, white families composed only 18 percent of those receiving public assistance in poor neighborhoods, down from 31 percent in the previous decade. Among welfare recipients, then, we find once again a sharp contrast between a white population residing primarily in nonpoor areas (60 percent) and a black and Hispanic component heavily concentrated in poor tracts (82 percent and 76 percent respectively). The percentage of all families which both resided in poverty areas and received income from means-tested programs exhibits the same pattern: stable among whites where it represented a tiny minority (from 2 to 3 percent); on the rise among Hispanics (from 12 to 18 percent) and among blacks, among whom one of every four families was on welfare in a poverty area by 1980 (up from 14 percent ten years earlier).

City differences in rates of public assistance closely parallel those for poverty and unemployment, in spite of marked differences in rules of welfare eligibility and levels of support across states (see columns 8 and 9 of Table 1). Indeed, the three cities (Dallas, Houston, and Indianapolis) with the lowest levels of poverty, poverty concentration, and joblessness in 1970 also had the lowest rates of public assistance (less than 4.5 percent of all families). All the other cities had rates around 8 to 10 percent at that time. Over the ensuing ten years, the incidence of welfare receipt increased by about 6 to 12 percentage points in Rustbelt cities (reaching 23 percent in Detroit, 21 percent in Baltimore, and about 18 percent in New York City, Chicago, and Cleveland), while they rose by less than 2 percentage points in Los Angeles, Houston, and Dallas.

In summary, in the ten-year period from 1970 to 1980, and despite depopulation caused by the massive suburban flight of whites, the ten largest central cities of the country suffered an absolute and relative increase in poverty, accompanied by an even speedier growth in the population living in poor and extremely poor areas. For the most part, these trends applied to blacks and Hispanics, who have become increasingly concentrated in the most depressed neighborhoods of these cities. These demographic trends closely followed gross trends in unemployment, especially among blacks; the growth of unemployment and poverty, in turn, fueled the rapid expansion of welfare. Public assistance rose among blacks and Hispanics in all cities, but did so at a faster pace in their poverty areas. And on all indicators, the older industrial centers of the Rustbelt (particularly Chicago, Detroit, New York City, Philadelphia, and Baltimore) fared considerably worse than the cities of the West and South.

Although more research is needed to compare a larger set of cities and more closely examine the effects of their racial and industrial composition on poverty and welfare, this preliminary review suggests that massive and growing concentration of extreme poverty is a problem that plagues not a few specific urban areas, but metropolises that typically combine a large black population confined in highly segregated ghettos with an aging industrial structure, and which therefore suffered important employment losses in recent years.

DEINDUSTRIALIZATION AND THE DECLINING EMPLOYMENT BASE OF RUSTBELT CENTRAL CITIES

The rise and fate of the underclass—and hence the efficacy and need for welfare—are inextricably connected to the structure and performance of the American economy. At the macro level, poverty rates closely follow fluctuations in economic activity. Econometric research has established, for instance, that when unemployment goes up by one percentage point, the national poverty rate rises by 1.1 percent (whereas a one point increase in inflation is accompanied by only a 0.15 percent increase in poverty) (see Blank and Blinder, 1986; and Blinder and Esaki, 1978). Also, as the level of wages rises (after adjusting for inflation), poverty rates descend. When real wages stagnate or go down, as they have in recent years, the proportion of Americans in poverty, particularly among minorities, goes up. This connection could have been better understood by paying due notice to the continued weakening of the American economy. In the seventies, recessions occurred every few years and each cycle of boom and bust created higher levels of unemployment, forcing down wages in a stepwise fashion. Joblessness and diminishing real wages combined to increase poverty and related problems such as family breakup, welfare receipt, and crime.

More than by conjunctional fluctuations, the minority residents of large industrial metropolises have been especially hurt by the accelerating *structural economic changes* of the past three decades. The shift to service-producing industries, together with the relocation of plants abroad or to cheaper labor sites nationally (in the suburbs and in the South, where unions are weak and employers find themselves in a buyer's market), has led to enormous declines in entry-level blue-collar jobs, particularly in the older central cities of the Middle-Atlantic and Midwestern regions. Because of the disproportionate concentration of blacks in these goods-producing industries, particularly heavy manufacturing, such massive jobs cutbacks have disproportionately affected central-city blacks, and the poor in particular (see Levy, 1987).

Indeed, from 1958 to 1982, according to data from the censuses of manufacturers, the number of factories located in the Rustbelt cities plummeted, falling by one half or more in New York, Chicago, Philadelphia, and Detroit, and by 40 percent in Cleveland and Baltimore. By contrast, in the central cities outside the Northeast and Midwest the number of manufacturing establishments typically rose—by 6 percent in Los Angeles, by more than half in Dallas, and by 115 percent in Houston. In the period from 1967 to 1982 alone, New York City lost 39 percent of its 11,300 factories and Chicago 38 percent of 8,455. Forty-three percent of Philadelphia's plants disappeared, and Detroit, which was hit hardest of

all, lost more than 1,400, or nearly half, of its plants.

The impact of deindustrialization and plant relocation on the employment opportunities of inner-city residents has been nothing short of dramatic. In the last thirty-five years, Rustbelt central cities lost close to half of their total manufacturing employment and upwards of six-tenths of their production workers in this sector alone. Nationwide, the number of employees holding production jobs in manufacturing, that is, blue-collar workers up to and including foremen, increased by 6 percent in the years from 1958 to 1982 (from 11.6 to 12.4 million, with a peak of 13.7 million in 1977). But, as Figure 1 testifies, such jobs declined by more than one-half in New York City (from 670,000 to 311,000) and Chicago (from 390,000 to a meager 172,000), by 61 percent in Philadelphia (from 208,000 to 81,000) and Detroit (from 145,000 to 59,000), and by 54 percent in Cleveland and Baltimore. And the sharpest cuts in production employment in all six of these cities occurred after 1967. In fact, looking again at the 1967–1982 period, it can be seen that New York, Baltimore, and Cleveland lost half of their manufacturing blue-collar workers; Chicago and Philadelphia a full 55 percent; while Detroit lost a staggering 61 percent. This is in sharp contrast to Los Angeles, Dallas, and Houston, where blue-collar employment in the manufacturing sector increased, by 3, 21, and 109 percent respectively.

The economic predicament of inner-city residents can be better ascertained by tabulating together changes in the principal economic sectors, namely, manufacturing, retail trade, wholesale trade, and services. Table 4 reports these data for each of the ten largest cities in the country. The first column tallies the losses in total manufacturing employment (including jobs other than production) experienced by Rustbelt cities and the gains in Sunbelt cities from 1967 to 1982. The middle columns show how retail and wholesale trade aggravated this divergence: employment in both of these sectors decreased in all Rustbelt cities but increased in Los Angeles, Dallas, and Houston. More interestingly, the fourth and fifth columns of Table 4 reveal that the growth of services, observed in all cities, fell far short of providing adequate replacement for

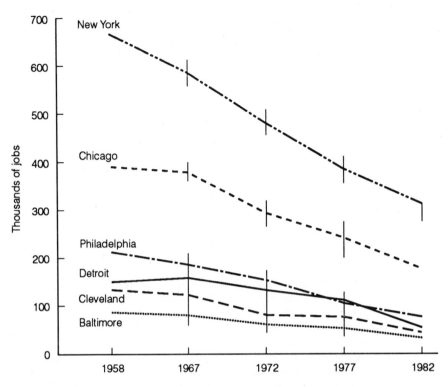

FIGURE 1

The decline of production jobs in the manufacturing sector of Rustbelt cities, 1958–82

TABLE 4 Employment Losses and Gains, by Economic Sector, in the Ten Largest Central Cities, 1963–1982 (in Thousands of Jobs)

City	Manufacturing	Retail Trade	Wholesale Trade	Selected Services	Balance
New York	−366	−85	−60	+118	−393
Chicago	−269	−64	−47	+57	−323
Philadelphia	−139	−22	−22	+12	−171
Detroit	−103	−34	−26	+9	−154
Baltimore	−48	−15	−9	−15	−87
Cleveland	−79	−17	−9	+7	−98
Indianapolis	−10	+4	+1	+9	+4
Los Angeles	+18	+45	+14	+135	+212
Dallas	+8	+38	+21	+55	+122
Houston	+76	+100	+62	+133	+371

Note: Trends in Indianapolis are not strictly comparable because of the incorporation of Marion county into the city after 1970.

the losses incurred in the other economic sectors in the Rustbelt. Indeed, in the urban centers of the industrial Midwest and Northeast, the gains in service employment came only to a fraction of the cutbacks in manufacturing production jobs alone. For instance, the 118,000 jobs gained in selected services in New York City from 1963 to 1982 represented less than 42 percent of those lost from 1967 to 1982 in blue-collar manufacturing employment alone; in Chicago, service employment increased by 46 percent, but this expansion amounted to but one fourth of the job decline in manufacturing production; in Philadelphia and Cleveland, the ratio was 1 for 9, in Detroit 1 for 10. The final result is that whereas overall employment increased noticeably in the cities of the Sunbelt, Rustbelt cities recorded a net loss of literally hundreds of thousands of jobs that far outstripped the decrease of their population.

In short, contrary to what is often believed, *the growth of service jobs in Rustbelt central cities has been moderate and has fallen far short of compensating for the staggering decline of manufacturing jobs.* And when one takes into account nonproduction manufacturing employment (retail and wholesale trade positions), the employment opportunities available to the growing population of the urban poor are even more limited.

It must be emphasized further that this metamorphosis of the employment base of the inner city entails much more than a simple, if drastic, reduction of the volume of job openings: it also means a switch to quite different kinds of job prospects. It is well known that service jobs which are not part of the knowledge-intensive service sectors (that is, those that are normally more accessible to the inner-city poor) are considerably less secure, provide far fewer benefits, and offer much lower pay than does traditional unionized, blue-collar work. A recent study by the Congressional Office of Technology Assessment found that of the 11.5 million workers who lost jobs because of plant shutdowns or relocations between 1979 and 1984, only 60 percent found new jobs, and of these, about half had taken pay cuts, often severe. Another study by Bluestone and Harrison has probed the proliferation of low-wage employment and linked it directly to the loss of jobs in the manufacturing

sector, the continued expansion of services, and the attendant reorganization of work toward more part-time schedules. This research also established that deindustrialization has triggered "an enormous downward wage mobility" that has disproportionately affected younger workers in the predominantly industrial states of the Midwest (Bluestone and Harrison, 1987). In the cities of the Rustbelt, then, the dwindling supply of employment has "magnified the competition for jobs among the urban black underclass, further diminishing chances for economic advancement" (Lichter, 1988). Most jobs that are now within reach of the urban poor (in terms of education, geographic location, skills, and so forth) also provide substantially lower monetary and welfare returns than was the case in previous decades. This, in turn, is part of a national trend toward increased income inequality among economic sectors and families, indeed, a general movement of class divergence that affects the entire American social structure.

For all these reasons, any public policy designed to alleviate poverty and reduce welfare dependency in America's large cities ought to take into account the consequences of these basic economic mutations. It bears stressing, at this juncture, that the relation between shifts in the economy and the rise of welfare receipt is never one-to-one and direct. It is mediated, among other factors, by local social structures and their institutional functioning. In this regard, recent transformations in the economy have not merely depleted the employment pool of poor central-city residents, generated extremely high levels of joblessness in Rustbelt cities, and contributed to the growing concentration of the poor; these broad economic shifts have also triggered wide-ranging, ramifying changes in the social life of the ghetto that go hand in hand with, and indeed further accelerate, the growth of public assistance.

CHICAGO'S INNER CITY: FROM INSTITUTIONAL GHETTO TO PHYSICAL GHETTO

The extent to which conditions in the inner city have deteriorated and the ways in which such deterioration fuels the expansion of welfare can

TABLE 5 Selected Social and Demographic Characteristics of Chicago's Ten Poorest Inner-City Neighborhoods, 1970–1980

	% of Families Below Poverty Level		% of Families Headed by a Female		% of Adults (Aged 16 or Over) Not in Labor Force		% of Population on AFDC-GA		% Change, 1970–1980		
	1970	1980	1970	1980	1970	1980	1970	1980	Population	Net Migration	Number of AFDC-GA Recipients
South Side											
Near South Side	37.2	42.7	41.0	76.0	55.2	62.4	22.4	72.8	−17.4	−28.0	+168.6
Douglas	31.1	42.6	43.0	70.0	48.9	57.0	24.3	36.6	−13.5	−33.0	+ 30.6
Oakland	44.4	60.9	48.0	79.0	64.3	76.0	38.4	60.5	− 8.4	−25.6	+ 44.1
Grand Boulevard	37.4	51.4	40.0	76.0	58.2	74.5	30.4	45.6	−32.9	−37.6	+ 0.7
Washington Park	28.2	43.2	35.0	70.0	52.0	67.1	23.2	48.2	−30.6	−35.7	+ 50.5
Englewood	24.3	35.8	30.0	57.0	47.7	61.9	21.8	41.4	−34.2	−46.2	+ 25.0
West Side											
Near West Side	34.7	48.9	37.0	66.0	44.6	64.8	26.9	44.4	−27.2	−37.9	+ 20.1
East Garfield Park	32.4	40.3	34.0	61.0	51.9	67.2	32.5	42.7	−39.5	−53.8	− 20.6
West Garfield Park	24.5	37.2	29.0	58.0	47.7	58.4	24.6	40.4	−30.1	−46.7	+ 14.8
North Lawndale	30.0	39.9	33.0	61.0	56.0	62.2	32.2	40.6	−35.1	−50.1	− 18.0
Chicago	12.2	16.8	29.7	27.0	41.5	44.8	8.5	16.9	−10.8	−17.3	+ 78.1

Sources: Chicago Fact Book Consortium (1984), City of Chicago (1973), and Chicago Area Geographic Information Study (no date).

best be ascertained by probing the transformations of the social and economic fabric of these decaying urban areas. Because of the long-standing importance of smokestack industries in its economy, together with its extreme levels of racial segregation and trends in the concentration of poverty that parallel those of other Rustbelt metropolises, the city of Chicago offers a particularly favorable terrain for unraveling these changes.

Table 5 offers a synoptic overview of the spectacular rise of social dislocations in Chicago's inner city. In a period of only ten years, conditions worsened dramatically in the black communities of the South and West Sides, increasing the

schism between poor black neighborhoods and the rest of the city (not to mention its suburbs). In 1970, the citywide percentage of families living under the poverty line in Chicago was around 12 percent; in the ghetto, these rates were already in the twenties and thirties for most neighborhoods. A decade later, the city's poverty rate had risen by less than 5 percent, but shot up an average of 12 percentage points in its poorest sections. In eight of the ten community areas that make up the historic core of the Black Belt, upwards of four families in ten were mired in poverty. Accompanying this rise of poverty was a proliferation of single-parent families: on the South Side, more than 70 percent of all house-

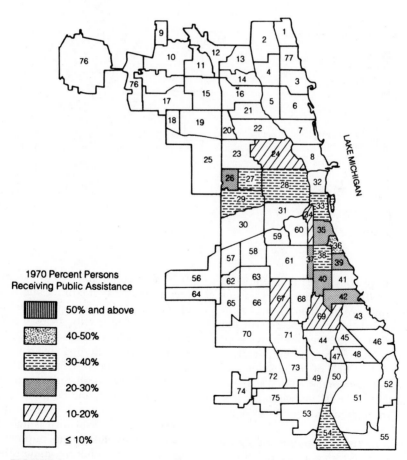

FIGURE 2

Public assistance in Chicago by community area, 1970–1980

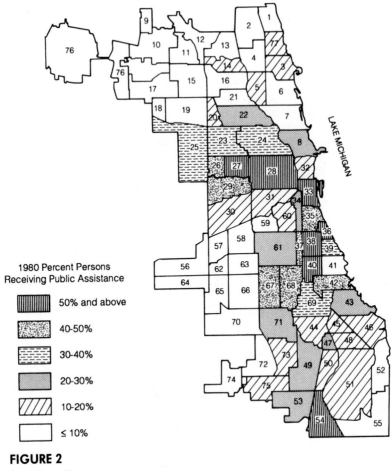

1980 Percent Persons
Receiving Public Assistance

▓	50% and above
▒	40-50%
≡	30-40%
▓	20-30%
╱	10-20%
□	≤ 10%

FIGURE 2
(*continued*)

holds were headed by women in 1980, compared to a level of about 40 percent ten years earlier and to a citywide figure of less than 27 percent in 1980. Even more spectacular was the growth and spread of public aid receipt. Despite heavy population losses due to voluminous outmigration (from one third to one half of the residents of these areas deserted them in those ten years), the number of recipients of AFDC and general assistance increased throughout the ghetto to reach unprecedented levels.

As can be seen in Figure 2, public assistance receipt in Chicago both rose and expanded rapidly over this decade, radiating outward from the poorest ghetto neighborhoods of the city. In 1970, four community areas had rates of welfare receipt of about one third, and in the poorest of all, Oakland, 41.5 percent of the total population was on welfare; only 14 of the 77 community areas had rates exceeding one in five. Ten years later, 28 did, including seven which topped the 50 percent mark. In Grand Boulevard, Oakland, and the Near South Side, respectively 61 percent, 71 percent, and 84 percent of the population were on one public assistance program or another in 1980. Not surprisingly, the neighborhoods hit hardest by unemployment and poverty, that is, the ghetto communities of the South Side and West Side, were those where welfare receipt rates grew most rapidly.

The juxtaposition of Figure 3, which captures changes in unemployment by community area, with Figure 2 evidences a clear geographical pattern in the growth and extension of public assistance that correlates tightly with the increase and spread of joblessness. In fact, each map is nearly a reproduction of the other. Together, they show how economic hardship and social dislocations have cumulated in the same areas of concentrated poverty.

It is well established in the sociological literature that economic hardships adversely impact the formation and stability of families. Research has consistently demonstrated, for example, a direct relation between the timing of marriage and

economic conditions: the more encouraging the latter, the earlier young people tend to marry. Once married, the higher the income of the couple, the lower their chance of divorce, and so on. In this connection, the weak employment status of a large and growing number of black males has been hypothesized as the main reason for the fact that blacks marry considerably later than whites and have much lower rates of remarriage, each of these phenomena being closely associated with the high incidence of out-of-wedlock births and female-headed households that has gripped the ghetto in recent years. Indeed, black women generally, but especially young black females residing in large cities, are facing a

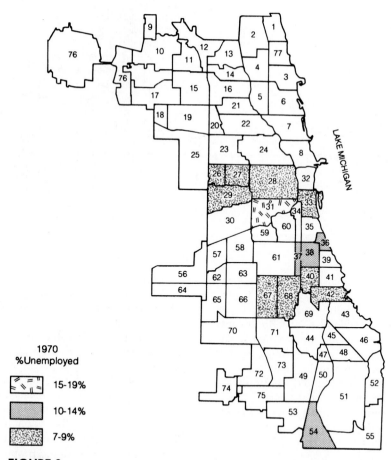

FIGURE 3

Unemployment in Chicago by community area, 1970–1980

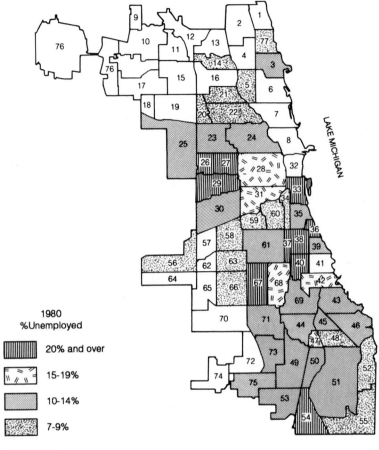

FIGURE 3
(*continued*)

shrinking pool of "marriageable" (that is, economically secure) men. And this problem is particularly acute in the ghetto areas of the inner city. For example, in Oakland, Grand Boulevard, and Washington Park, three areas which compose the heart of Chicago's black ghetto, the aggregate ratio of employed males over adult females has decreased sharply and continuously since 1950 (see Figure 4). At that time, there were between six and seven employed males for every ten adult women in these neighborhoods, a ratio close to the citywide figure of 73 percent. Thirty years later, this proportion had dropped to 56 percent in Chicago, but plummeted to 24 percent in Grand Boulevard, 29 percent in Washing-

ton Park, and a mere 19 percent in Oakland. No other group in urban America has experienced such a rapid and near-total depletion of the pool of marriageable men.

This argument involves no presumption that the marriage rate will rise automatically once a sufficient number of employed males are present in a neighborhood, for clearly a host of other factors are involved in the process of family formation, such as the cultural meaning of marriage, the balance of power between genders, the cultural acceptability of cross-racial or live-in unions, the age considered proper for mating, together with the differential age composition of gender groups, and so on. But, other things being

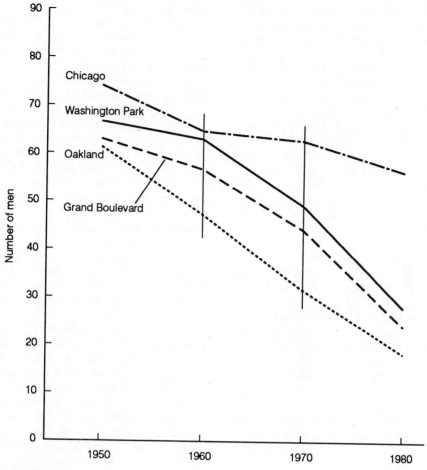

FIGURE 4

Employed men per 100 women in Chicago and three inner-city communities in Chicago

equal, a minimal pool of securely employed males is a necessary, if not a sufficient, condition for the smooth functioning of a stable marriage market; it is hard to deny that a large demographic deficit of such partners, as evidenced by Figure 4, places severe structural constraints on marriage processes, irrespective of the cultural idiom of the population in question. As Blau (1987) aptly puts it, "whether our choices are fully determined by our constitution, background, and experiences or whether we are entirely free to marry anyone who is willing to marry us, we cannot marry Eskimos if there are none around." When aggregate ratios of women (of all ages) per employed men drop to such lows as one for seven, it seems warranted to conclude that joblessness hinders family formation in the inner city.

The sharp drop in the pool of "marriageable" men is a reflection of a cumulation of economic and social dislocations that have fundamentally altered the social fabric of inner-city communities. Today's ghetto neighborhoods are not only very different from other urban neighborhoods: they are also quite different from what they were twenty or thirty years ago. The evolution of the class structure of the ghetto testifies to an increasing segregation of the most deprived segments of the black community. This is most clearly seen in the skyrocketing rates of labor market exclusion. The number of working adults in the inner-city neighborhoods of the South Side dropped by 50 percent in the decade from 1970 to 1980 alone. Whereas a majority of adults residing in Oakland, Grand Boulevard, and Washington Park were gainfully employed in 1950, by 1970, 57 percent of them did not hold a job, and in 1980 that figure had risen to a staggering 73 percent. By comparison, the employment rate for the city as a whole remained above 55 percent throughout this thirty-year period. As might be expected, the most severe losses occurred among blue-collar workers. In 1950, more than 35,800 residents of these three communities were laborers and operatives, and a full 6,600 were foremen and craftsmen. By 1980, these occupations added up to fewer than 6,200, a drop of more than 85 percent. The number of managers, professional, and technical staff living in these areas also dropped, from 5,270 in 1950 to 2,225 in 1980; the number of clerical and sales employees, from 10,300 to 5,200. These middle-class occupations represented at most 10 percent of the adult population of these ghetto neighborhoods at any time; by contrast, their proportion more than doubled among black adults in the entire city over that period to exceed 17 percent by 1980.

The fate of the black community of North Lawndale on the city's West Side vividly exemplifies the cumulative process of social and economic dislocation that has swept through Chicago's inner city. After a quarter-century of uninterrupted deterioration. North Lawndale resembles a war zone. Nearly half of its housing stock has disappeared since 1960; what remains is, in most cases, run-down and dilapidated. A recent survey of the area found that only 8 percent of its buildings were in good to excellent condition, with 10 percent on the verge of collapse and another 40 percent in need of major rehabilitation. The physical decay of the neighborhood is matched only by its social deterioration. Levels of crime in North Lawndale have reached astronomical proportions: in 1985, its murder rate was twice that of the city and six times the national figure. Police contacts with juveniles, for instance, were 20 times more frequent there than in the white neighborhoods on the North side of town, with 5 percent of all youths referred to court in the year 1980 alone. While infant mortality has dropped both nationwide and in Chicago, it has continued to climb in North Lawndale. In 1985 it peaked at 28 deaths per 1,000 live births, almost three times the national figure. According to recent counts, a full 70 percent of all babies born in this community are born out of wedlock. And half of all births are currently to mothers twenty-one years or younger, with one in seven to girls aged less than seventeen. The proportion of households headed by women doubled in the last decade, reaching 61 percent or twice the city average in 1980. At the same time, the percentage of those receiving welfare assistance, including Food Stamps and no-grants medical assistance, rose from one third to one half of the entire population.

This staggering explosion of social woes is closely related to a string of plant and store shutdowns that have gradually turned North Lawndale from a lively industrial and commercial hub into one of the most destitute ghetto communities of the city. Chicago still had more than 8,000 factories in 1970; by 1982, this figure was down to 5,200, a net loss of more than 35 percent. Because North Lawndale, like many inner-city neighborhoods across the country, depended heavily on smokestack industries for low-skilled jobs and steady income, it has shouldered more than its share of the costs of this deindustrialization. In its good days, the economy of this West Side community was anchored by two huge factories, the famous Hawthorne plant of Western Electric with over 43,000 jobs, and a Harvester plant employing some 14,000 workers; the world headquarters of Sears, Roebuck and Company was also located in its midst, bringing another 10,000 jobs. Lorean Evans, a resident of North Lawndale and head of a local economic development group, recalls how the whole area was "just a conglomerate of stores then. We had an auto center and banks, a York's department store, a Woolworth's. We had all kinds of specialty shops" (*Chicago Tribune*, 1985). There were, among others, a Zenith and a Sunbeam factory, a

Copenhagen snuff plant, an Alden's catalogue store, a Dell Farm food market and a post office bulk station. But things changed quickly: Harvester closed its gates at the end of the sixties and is now a vacant lot. Zenith, Sunbeam, and Alden, too, shut down their facilities. Sears moved most of its offices to the downtown Loop in 1973, leaving behind only its catalogue distribution center, with a work force of 3,000, until last year, when it was moved out of the state of Illinois. The Hawthorne factory gradually phased out its operations and finally closed down in 1984. As the big plants went, so did the smaller stores, the banks, and countless other businesses dependent for their sales on the wages paid by large employers. To make matters worse, scores of stores were forced out of business or pushed out of the neighborhood by insurance companies in the wake of the 1968 riots that swept through Chicago's West Side after the assassination of Martin Luther King. Tens of others were burned or simply abandoned. It has been estimated that the community lost 75 percent of its business establishments from 1960 to 1970 alone. Today North Lawndale has 48 state lottery agents, 50 currency exchanges, and 99 licensed bars and liquor stores, but only one bank and one supermarket for a population of some 50,000.

During the decades since the fifties, the easing of racial strictures on housing and the rapid improvement of economic opportunities for educated blacks in the corporate and public sectors, spurred by the civil rights movement and affirmative action legislation, led many black middle-class and stable working-class families to leave the ghetto (Wilson, 1980 and 1987). From 1970 to 1980, the number of poor families in North Lawndale decreased by one tenth, but the number of nonpoor families dropped by more than a third. The heavy bleeding of industrial jobs—the number of North Lawndale residents employed in manufacturing and construction declined by two thirds, from 15,200 in 1960 to less than 5,200 twenty years later—combined with the accelerating exodus of working families to produce a quadrupling of the official unemployment rate and an even sharper drop in employment rates. In 1980, a large majority of all adults (62 percent) living in North Lawndale did not hold a job, compared to only four in ten in 1950, when the

neighborhood enjoyed the same employment ratio as the rest of the city. These job losses resulted in a sharp drop in the median family income from 74 percent of the city average in 1960 to less than half in 1980. By then, 7 of the 27 census tracts that comprise North Lawndale had poverty rates in excess of 50 percent, while the overall poverty rate peaked at 43 percent, up from 30 percent only ten years before.

Needless to say, the heavy loss of entry-level jobs in industrial plants across the city and the accompanying outmigration of middle-class and stable working-class families were not the only factors involved in the growing social dislocations of Chicago's inner city. The "urban renewal" policy of the last thirty years contributed very directly to entrenching the underclass by concentrating massive public housing projects in the most segregated and poorest neighborhoods of the city (see Hirsch, 1983). Moreover, inner-city schools have declined along with the other institutions of the ghetto. Far from offering an avenue of upward mobility, or even of integration into the working class, let alone into the middle class, the public education system now serves to further solidify the social and economic isolation of the underclass. Of the 39,500 students who enrolled in the ninth grade of Chicago's public schools in 1980 and should have graduated in the spring of 1984, only 18,500 (or 47 percent) did so, and a mere 6,000 (15 percent) of them were capable of reading at or above the national twelfth-grade average. And educational failure was even more likely for those black and Hispanic students who attended nonselective segregated public high schools (as opposed to integrated or selective academic schools) and who represented two thirds of the original class of 1984. Of their cohort of 25,500 ninth-graders, a full 15,900 (63 percent) never finished their secondary schooling. Of the 9,600 who did graduate, 4,000 read at or below the junior level and a meager 1,900 or 7.6 percent read at or above the national average (Designs for Change, 1985). In the early 1980s, then, the probability that a youngster living in Chicago's inner city will successfully complete his or her high school education is of the order of 1 in 14, compared to a national chance of more than 1 in 3 (and 6 in 10 in selective academic high schools of the Chicago area).

Looking beyond high school, the fate of those privileged few who did graduate from inner-city high schools proves no brighter. Of the 16,000 graduates tracked by a recent study, only 31 percent held jobs and 32 percent were reported as unemployed. The paucity of school resources, the grossly skewed class and racial composition of its public, the severely limited chances of mobility it affords and the absence of a perceptible connection between educational and occupational success, all add up to make the school a mechanism of exclusion for the children of Chicago's ghetto residents. As a former superintendent puts it, inner-city public schools have become "reserves for the poor."

Changes in North Lawndale typify the social transformation of inner-city neighborhoods in Chicago. They reveal a shift from what we may, in ideal-typical terms, describe as an "institutional ghetto," largely duplicating the activities and organizational texture of the larger society, to a physical ghetto incapable of offering even the most basic resources, services, and opportunities. Our analysis of the increasing concentration of poverty, joblessness, and welfare receipt in other Rustbelt central cities, as well as of the bleeding of industrial jobs on which the urban poor have traditionally relied most, suggests that this bleak picture of Chicago's inner city is not unique. It indicates, rather, not only that life-conditions have dramatically worsened in the ghettos of the country's large metropolises, but also that these racial enclaves now harbor unprecedented concentrations of the most underprivileged segments of the urban poor.

EFFECTS OF THE SOCIAL AND INSTITUTIONAL TRANSFORMATION OF THE INNER CITY

Increased joblessness, poverty, and receipt of welfare do not simply result mechanically from having large numbers of poor together in the same areas. They signal, rather, a *transformation of the social and institutional structure of the inner city* which, given the profound economic changes discussed above, puts their residents in a radically more constraining situation than their

counterparts of earlier times or the poor of other neighborhoods.

First, in extreme poverty areas, the steady exodus of working- and middle-class families has removed an important "social buffer" that used to deflect the full impact of unemployment, thus leaving the ghetto poor more vulnerable to the kind of prolonged and increasing joblessness that has plagued inner-city communities in the 1970s and early 1980s as a result of uneven economic growth and periodic recessions (Wilson, 1987). The absence of stable working families makes it considerably more difficult to sustain basic institutions in the inner city, for it cuts deep into their membership and saps their base of support: banks, stores, professional services, and restaurants lose their best and most regular patrons; churches see their audience dwindle and their resources shrink; recreational facilities, block clubs, community groups, and other informal organizations also fail to retain their most likely users. The decline of these organizations, in turn, weakens means of formal and informal social control and contributes to increasing levels of crime and street violence, which helps accelerate the deterioration of the neighborhood.

Second, as we have seen, the concentration of poverty significantly impacts on the schools and educational processes. More specifically, with the lowering of the class composition of the student body and of the volume of "cultural capital" (Bourdieu, 1979) that children bring in from outside the school, chances of academic success are significantly reduced. The concentration of low-achieving students itself undermines teachers' morale and discipline. It also weakens the perception of a meaningful relation between education and work and thus decreases academic aspirations. The neighborhood in which the school is located is also less supportive of education and less demanding with regard to educational achievement. All of this makes it exceedingly difficult for the school to compete with other available sources of income and status, including nonconventional and illegal ones.

Third and most important, the class transformation of the inner city drastically cuts off employment channels. For one thing, there are fewer local businesses, service establishments, and stores around that can offer jobs—not only full-time positions on which a wage-earner might be able to raise a family, but also the kind of part-time jobs that are crucial to initiate youths into the world of work. Illegal activities such as drug dealing or fencing stolen goods are often the only readily available means by which teenagers from these communities can get the income they and their families need. As a result, many inner-city adolescents routinely become involved with crime rather than work at an early age. More crucially, though, inner-city residents become *isolated from the job networks* that permeate other neighborhoods. They lack the kind of informal contacts with employers or workers that are decisive in obtaining employment: with fewer kin, friends, or acquaintances holding jobs or in a position to influence hiring, they are less likely to learn about openings, to be recommended for, and to retain such jobs as might become available. A recent series of interviews with black residents of Chicago's inner city has shown that such contacts are indeed held to be decisive in the job hunt: when asked "what it takes to find a good job in Chicago today," a majority of respondents spontaneously mentioned "connections" as the most critical factor.

Fourth, as the structure of opportunity is distorted by the class transformation of the inner city, the social perception of this structure is also altered. When the objective probability of achieving a socially rewarding and stable life, symbolized by the presence of working- and middle-class families, decreases abruptly, conventional aspirations make much less sense and prove more difficult to sustain, and individuals are more likely to try to adjust to a condition that appears unchangeable and inevitable. This triggers a circular process that feeds back onto itself, whereby subjective expectations and hopes act to reinforce the objective mechanisms that limit prospects and avenues for mobility. In a neighborhood plagued by uninterrupted material and social decay and massive exclusion from the productive sphere of society, where stable employment opportunities are objectively minimal and where chances of economic self-sufficiency are simply not a reality for a large majority of the residents, it should not be surprising that many find it difficult to maintain a solid commitment to the labor force and belief in the economic prom-

ises of middle-class America. The experience of long and repeated spells of unemployment, or a succession of low-paying, dead-end jobs that cannot generate sufficient income to support a family are hardly conducive to a strong attachment to the labor market. As the German sociologist Claus Offe has remarked, "to the extent that the experience (or the anticipation) of unemployment, or involuntary retirement from worklife, increases, the more the effect of moral stigmatization and self-stigmatization generated by unemployment wears off because, beyond a certain threshold (and *especially if unemployment is concentrated* in certain regions and industries), it can no longer be accounted for plausibly in terms of individual failure or guilt" (Offe, 1985; emphasis added).

Thus it is the local social setting and its associated structure of opportunities which explain the behavior, aspirations, and hopes of inner-city residents. Far from arising from a self-reproducing culture of poverty, their disposition toward the future, which is characterized by what may appear (from the middle-class standpoint of someone whose life is objectively ordered and regular) as a certain lack of rational planning and personal ambition, is an expression of their objective future. And it is in this new structural context that the tangle of disruptions associated with poverty must be placed in order to be fully comprehended. The expansion of inner-city welfare, then, is not an autonomous force that generates other social problems, but a response to the complex interaction of economic and social forces that have severely reduced the opportunity prospects and resources of poor inner-city dwellers and led to their increasing social isolation. The implications of our analysis for social policy in general, and the current welfare reform discussion in particular, is the subject of our concluding section.

THE ECONOMY, THE UNDERCLASS, AND THE LIMITED VISION OF WELFARE REFORM

The *growth of welfare in large inner cities is but a surface manifestation of deeper social-struc-*

tural and economic changes, including deindustrialization, skyrocketing rates of joblessness, the increasing concentration of poverty, and racial polarization. Let us stress here that these sharp increases in public assistance and associated dislocations took place during the very period when both the eligibility requirements for public aid became tighter and the real dollar value of the basic welfare package (AFDC plus food stamps) went down (by 22 percent between 1972 and 1984; see Danziger and Gottschalk, 1985). Therefore they can hardly be attributed to the greater generosity of the welfare state. Disaggregating these data allowed us to show that the problems of rising poverty, joblessness and welfare dependency since 1970 have essentially struck the Rustbelt cities of New York City, Chicago, Philadelphia, Detroit, Cleveland, Indianapolis and Baltimore. Underlying these trends were sharp differences in the fate of the employment infrastructure of Sunbelt and Rustbelt metropolises. Whereas the pool of jobs increased steadily in all major economic sectors in the South and West from the late fifties to the early eighties, employment in manufacturing, retail trade, and wholesale trade declined dramatically in all of the Rustbelt centers. Indeed, the expansion of services in these central cities compensated for only a small portion of the losses caused by massive deindustrialization, so that by the end of this period they had incurred a net deficit of hundreds of thousands of the jobs generally most accessible to poor central-city residents.

These differences between older industrial centers situated in declining economic regions and the newer, growing, metropolises of the economically expanding Sunbelt demonstrate the importance of relating the evolution of public assistance to basic trends in the broader society and economy. In addition, as our account of the deterioration of Chicago's ghetto over recent decades testifies, the movement of these broader structures has had wide-ranging repercussions in the social fabric of inner-city communities, transformations which further exacerbated the impact of basic economic dislocations. The result is that the poor living in today's large urban ghettos are more concentrated and socially isolated than ever before. It is the complex articulation of all these factors—shifts in industrial base and the

accompanying recomposition of labor markets, together with demographic and racial changes, poverty concentration, and the local social structure—that constitutes the matrix of forces out of which welfare receipt evolves.

What implications does this analysis have for the current debate on welfare? In recent years, a liberal-conservative consensus on the question of welfare reform has emerged around the notions that (1) public assistance should be based on reciprocal responsibilities whereby society is obligated to provide assistance to welfare recipients, who in turn are obligated to society to behave in socially approved ways; and (2) able-bodied adult recipients should be required to prepare themselves for employment, to search for work, and to accept jobs when they are offered. Both of these themes were emphasized in the major welfare reform reports released in 1986 and 1987, and figure prominently in the House and Senate versions of the welfare reform legislation currently under discussion.

These two points of agreement are predicated on the implicit assumption that it is not the availability of (decent) jobs, but the willingness to work that is the obstacle to be vanquished on the road to self-sufficiency; that a "welfare ethos" has emerged which encourages recipients of public assistance to shirk their social obligations as citizens to work, to be educated, to form and maintain families, and to obey the law. In other words, *it is the moral fabric of individuals, not the social and economic structure of society, that is taken to be the root of the problem.* This assumption is in our opinion, both *unwarranted and untenable.* To date, no rigorous research can support such a view. Indeed, the basic timing and spatial patterning of mounting social dislocations and welfare receipt in recent years belie it. In many ways, this transformation of a societal problem into a question of individual attributes and incentives is little more than a modernized version of the sort of conventional attacks that have been launched against welfare programs since their inception by proponents of a market society.

Because those involved in the formulation of new welfare policy often share this individualistic and moralistic vision, they have paid too little attention to the broader economic and social-structural factors that are responsible for the crystallization of a large underclass and persistent welfare dependency. Except for the New York State Task Force (1986) report on welfare reform, submitted to Governor Cuomo, most calls for changes in the welfare system fail to consider the problems associated with the loss of jobs due to structural shifts in the economy and the periodic recessions that accompany them. These problems, ranging from family breakup and marriage delay to the deterioration of inner-city neighborhoods, are prime sources of continued welfare need.

If the structural forces that affect public assistance are not recognized, proposed programs for welfare reform will have minimal impact, should they be adopted. For example, an employment-oriented welfare program that is not part of a broad framework including some macro-management of the economy remains at the mercy of its vagaries. As Robert Reischauer has pointed out, "in recessionary periods, when jobs are scarce throughout the nation, a credible emphasis on work will be difficult to maintain. Unskilled welfare recipients will realize that they stand little chance of competing successfully against experienced unemployed workers for the few positions available. In regions of the country where the economy is chronically weak, this dilemma will be a persistent problem. Evidence from one such area, West Virginia, suggests that work-welfare programs can do little to increase the employment or earnings of welfare recipients if the local economy is not growing. A public sector job of last resort may be the only alternative in such cases" (Reischauer, 1987b).

Our analysis thus leads us to strongly favor the nonwelfare approach to welfare reform, that is, to move beyond workfare programs in favor of a comprehensive package of policies anchored in *economic measures designed to attack the structural roots of the problem, rather than treat its more apparent symptoms at the level of individuals.* A program that combines progressive welfare reform with a policy to create jobs and universal provision of child and health care would be far more effective in the long run in lifting people out of poverty and off the welfare rolls. But given the seriousness of the problems of poverty concentration and social dislocations in

the inner city, we also find it imperative to change the current tax laws in order to obtain the financial means necessary to launch comprehensive reforms in the areas of education, training and retraining, and child support assurance, and to expand the earned-income tax credit. Key to the success of such programs is their universal character, which will require putting an end to the categorization and balkanization of welfare in American political life. The debilitating bifurcation of welfare and social insurance policies is arguably the single greatest political impediment to a successful attack on poverty in this country.

The current poverty situation in the inner city calls for a comprehensive, social-democratic agenda of reform. We cannot discuss here such a program in detail. But the first and foremost item on this agenda would surely be full employment. There are several bills before Congress now that address issues of employment and that would do far more to enhance the lives of the poor than any of the current proposals of welfare reform. One of these bills, the Quality of Life Action Act (authored by Congressman Charles Hayes of Illinois and introduced on March 4, 1987), establishes a program for carrying out the Employment Act of 1946 and the Humphrey-Hawkins Full Employment and Balanced Growth Act of 1978, two laws which have never been implemented. Another bill, the Economic Bill of Rights (introduced on July 1, 1987, by Congressman Hayes along with Augustus F. Hawkins of California), outlines legislation patterned after President Franklin Roosevelt's original Bill of Economic Rights set forth in 1944. It affirms the commitment of the federal government to assure the eight basic rights originally introduced by President Roosevelt over forty years ago: (1) the right to useful paid employment; (2) the right to earn enough to provide an adequate living; (3) the right of every farmer to raise and sell agricultural products at a return which will provide a decent family living; (4) the right of every business, large and small, to trade in an atmosphere of freedom from unfair competition and domination by monopolies at home and abroad; (5) the right of every family to a decent home; (6) the right to adequate medical care and the opportunity to achieve and enjoy good health; (7) the right to adequate protection from the economic fears of old age, sickness, accident, and unemployment, and (8) the right to a good education. Items 1 and 2 and 5 through 8 would seem especially relevant to the present welfare debate. A less ambitious but no less important employment bill, the Guaranteed Job Opportunity Act, was recently introduced by Senator Paul Simon. This bill would establish a program of project-oriented jobs, modeled on the Works Progress Administration (WPA), that would guarantee job opportunities to every American citizen unable to find employment in the private sector.

Odd as it may seem, another chief concern of welfare reform should be the need to raise the minimum wage. It is not enough to require of a welfare recipient to be employed when such jobs as he or she may find do not pay enough to support a family. Today, upwards of 9 million Americans work and still officially live in poverty. The current minimum wage, after adjusting for inflation, is over 20 percent below its average of the 1970s and a third less than its peak of 1968. A full-time, year-round, minimum-wage worker earns about $6,968 in a year, coming 20 percent short of the poverty line for a family of three and 38 percent below for a family of four (compared to 120 percent in 1968). In 1985 about 7.5 million worked at the minimum wage, more than two thirds of them adults and three of every ten heads of households. Raising the minimum wage would appreciably improve the situation of the working poor.

The fact that the effects of welfare reform alone are likely to be extremely limited is another justification for going beyond it. There are, officially, over 32 million poor today in the United States (most of them children and women) and only one third of them receive public assistance: those not on the welfare rolls should not be forgotten. Universal programs provide the only means of including them among the beneficiaries of social spending. Furthermore, such social insurance programs have historically proved considerably more effective in fighting poverty than have means-tested programs (Burtless, 1986).

To conclude, welfare cannot be divorced from the diverse and profound changes that are reshaping the American social structure and the country's political economy. It is these underlying structural changes, and not the expansion of welfare programs or the mysterious ascendancy of a "culture of poverty," that are the moving force behind the growing social woes of large American cities and associated increases in public aid receipt. Policy responses must therefore aim not at ameliorating the assumed individual traits of the poor, but at checking the structural mechanisms that produce them. As we contemplate the political obstacles that stand in the way of devising and implementing a comprehensive program that would integrate economic, social, and tax policy to attack the roots of poverty not only in the inner city but in the larger society as well, we consider that the first essential step is to break out of the narrow vision of the current welfare debate and to change its terms in order to *bring the society and the economy back to center stage.*

References

Blank, R. M., and A. S. Blinder. 1986. Income distribution, and poverty. In S. H. Danziger and D. H. Weinberg, eds., *Fighting poverty: What works and what doesn't.* Cambridge, Mass.: Harvard University Press.

Blau, P. M. 1987. Contrasting theoretical perspectives. In J. C. Alexander, B. Giessen, R. Munch, and N. J. Smelser, eds., *The micro-macro link.* Berkeley: University of California Press.

Blinder, A. S., and H. Y. Esaki. 1978. Macroeconomic activity and income distribution in the postwar United States. *Review of Economics and Statistics* 60: 604–609.

Bluestone, B., and B. Harrison. 1987. *The great American job machine: The proliferation of low-wage employment in the U.S. economy.* Washington, D.C.: Joint Economic Committee.

Bourdieu, P. 1979. Les trois etats du capital culturel. *Actes di la recherche in sciences sociales* 30: 3–6.

Burtless, G. 1986. Public spending for the poor: Trends, prospects, and economic limits. In S. H. Danziger and D. H. Weinberg, eds., *Fighting poverty: What works and what doesn't.* Cambridge, Mass.: Harvard University Press.

Chicago Fact Book Consortium. 1984. *Local community fact book: Chicago metropolitan area.* Chicago: Chicago Review Press.

Chicago Tribune. 1985. *The American millstone: An examination of the nation's permanent underclass.* Chicago/New York: Contemporary Books.

City of Chicago. 1973. *Chicago statistical abstract, part I: 1970 Census, community area summary tables.* Chicago: Department of Development and Planning.

Danziger, S. H., and P. P. Gottschalk. 1985. The poverty of losing ground. *Challenge* May/June: 31–38.

Levy, F. 1987. *Dollars and dreams: The changing American income distribution.* New York: Russell Sage Foundation and Basic Books.

Lichter, D. T. 1988. Racial differences in underemployment in American cities. *American Journal of Sociology* 93/94: 771–793.

New York State Task Force. 1986. A new social contract rethinking the nature and purpose of public assistance. Report of the Task Force on Poverty and Welfare, submitted to Governor Mario Cuomo, Albany, N.Y.

Offe, C. 1985. *Disorganized capitalism: Contemporary transformations of work and politics.* Cambridge, Mass.: MIT Press.

Reischauer, R. D. 1987. Welform: Will consensus be enough? *The Brookings Review* 5: 3–8.

U.S. Bureau of the Census. 1973. *Low-income areas in large cities.* Census of the Population, 1970. Subject Reports, PC(2)-9b, 3 vols. Washington, D.C.: U.S. Government Printing Office.

U.S. Bureau of the Census. 1985. *Poverty areas in large cities.* Census of the Population, 1980, Subject Reports, PC80-2-8D. Washington, D.C.: U.S. Government Printing Office.

U.S. Bureau of the Census. 1986. *Money income and the poverty status of families and persons in the United States: 1985.* Current Population Reports, P-60, no. 154. Washington, D.C.: U.S. Government Printing Office.

Wilson, W. J. 1987. *The truly disadvantaged: The inner city and public policy.* Chicago: University of Chicago Press.

Wilson, W. J., R. Aponte, J. Kirschenman, and L. J. D. Wacquant. 1988. The ghetto underclass and the changing structure of urban poverty. In F. Harris and R. Wilkins, eds., *Quiet riots: Race and poverty in the United States.* New York: Pantheon Books.

CHAPTER 9

RACE AND EMPLOYMENT OPPORTUNITIES

INTRODUCTION

The social standing of most Americans in the late twentieth century is directly related to opportunities for good employment. Any comparison between African-Americans and whites in the area of employment indicates that blacks suffer persistent disadvantages. The two most striking comparative statistics that demonstrate this inequality over many decades are (1) the consistently higher rates of unemployment for blacks (typically twice the rate for whites regardless of educational background) and (2) the disproportionately fewer high-paying, high-prestige jobs available to blacks. While a few trends are encouraging and the statistics fluctuate from time to time, there is little likelihood of a color-blind work world in the foreseeable future. The grim fact is unavoidable: in the area of employment, the gap between blacks and whites is still enormous. The United States is a long way from approaching racial equality in the workplace.

Numerous sociologists have explored various factors in an effort tó explain the persistent disparity between the occupational attainments of whites and blacks. In Chapter 8 two major explanations were offered. Zinsmeister restated Moynihan's thesis about the disintegration of the black family, and Wacquant and Wilson called attention to the spatial dislocation between inner-city neighborhoods and suburban jobs. Another frequent explanation for the slow advancement of African-Americans is the limited educational opportunities found in inner-city schools and tracking systems that place many black students in low-achievement programs. Each of these explanations may have some merit, but many sociologists and social critics have argued that the most important factor is also the most obvious: white employers discriminate against black job applicants. This argument rests on overwhelming evidence that talented blacks have repeatedly been rebuffed when they have sought opportunities to move up the occupational ladder.

The 1964 Civil Rights Act made discrimination in hiring illegal, and President Lyndon Johnson's executive order of 1967 establishing affirmative action required employers to seek out qualified African-Americans. These policies were intended to end the shameful practices of the past. Many people believe these official actions succeeded, and some critics of affirmative action are convinced that the problem now is reverse discrimination: less qualified blacks are hired ahead of more qualified whites. What is the situation today? Are employers still discriminating against blacks? Or is the problem reverse discrimination? Perhaps it is neither. Have we achieved the ideal of color-blind hiring practices? These important questions have been addressed by a research team at the Urban Institute.

The public often thinks of conflict between the races in terms of dramatic episodes, such as the beating of a black civilian by white police officers. Such extreme situations are examined in an effort to understand broader and more pervasive attitudes and actions. One of the problems with the analysis of extreme episodes is the difficulty of making appropriate generalizations from an isolated case. Are all white policemen hostile to all black civilians? Or is the ugly incident an exception that represents "a few bad apples" in the police department? The Urban Institute's research team is aware of the challenging requirements of studying enough episodes of discrimination (or non-discrimination) under appropriately controlled circumstances to make sound empirical generalizations about the hiring of blacks and whites in the 1990s. These researchers have conducted a sophisticated study of discrimination in hiring in the United States. The reader must study more than the conclusions they reach; it is equally important to study the methodology by which the authors gathered their statistical evidence. Finally, the reader must study critically the authors' interpretation of their findings.

One of the most important aspects of any statistical study is the authors' interpretation of the "facts" they have gathered and reported. Numbers never speak for themselves. The authors must decide what the findings mean. The Urban Institute's researchers interpret their data as strong evidence of job discrimination. But the editors of *The New Republic* studied the same numbers and came to different conclusions. Can both interpretations of the facts be right? Readers must weigh the evidence and draw their own conclusions.

Assessments of the perplexing relations between blacks and whites in the United States have often been rather gloomy. We conclude Chapter 9 with a success story of dramatic improvement in attitudes and actions among blacks and whites. Charles

Moskos examines the recent history of integration in the armed forces. He is a military sociologist who has done many studies of social life in the army. His analysis of successful integration in the army poses an interesting paradox for those who want to see similar benefits in civilian settings. The extreme degree of control that military leaders exercise over every aspect of a soldier's life gave them the opportunity to enforce non-discrimination policies while holding everyone to a high standard of performance. Does successful integration in a free society require special controlled circumstances that limit the citizen's freedom? Moskos offers an important case study of successful integration in a racially divided society that cherishes freedom yet needs to solve serious problems of prejudice and discrimination.

17. OPPORTUNITIES DENIED, OPPORTUNITIES DIMINISHED: RACIAL DISCRIMINATION IN HIRING

MARGERY AUSTIN TURNER, MICHAEL FIX, and RAYMOND J. STRUYK, with VERONICA M. REED, AMINA H. N. ELMI, WENDY ZIMMERMANN, and JOHN G. EDWARDS

BACKGROUND AND INTRODUCTION

There is little evidence, based on direct observation, concerning the extent and character of hiring discrimination in the United States. Specifically, little is known about how often minorities are treated less favorably than equally qualified majority job applicants. Despite this fact, beliefs about employment discrimination's scope and impact are fervently held—as debate over HR 1, the Civil Rights Act of 1991, makes clear. The result is that "much of the debate over the future of civil rights in employment is characterized by high ratios of rhetoric to fact" (Donohue and Siegelman 1991).

This report presents the findings of the Employment Discrimination Study, a pilot study

measuring the extent of unfavorable treatment experienced by young black males applying for entry-level jobs in two metropolitan areas. Data were obtained from "hiring audits" conducted in Chicago and Washington, D.C., in the summer of 1990. Briefly, the findings indicate that, in the two metropolitan areas studied, young black job seekers were unable to advance as far in the hiring process as their white counterparts 20 percent of the time; black testers advanced farther than their white counterparts 7 percent of the time. In addition, blacks were denied a job that was offered to an equally qualified white tester 15 percent of the time; white testers were denied a job when their black counterparts received an offer in 5 percent of the audits.

HR 1, the Civil Rights Act of 1991, is the successor to legislation passed by the U.S. Congress in 1990 but vetoed by President George Bush. The 1990 and 1991 bills represent a congressionally led effort to restore and extend protections for employees and job applicants that were limited by a series of decisions handed down by the U.S. Supreme Court in its 1988 and 1989 terms. Those Court decisions are consistent with much of the administrative (versus congressional) poli-

From Urban Institute Report 91-9 (August 1991). Washington, D.C.: The Urban Institute Press. This essay is abridged. Some footnotes and tables are renumbered. Reprinted with permission of The Urban Institute Press.

cymaking that has taken place in the civil rights field over the past decade. That is, both judges and administration policymakers have taken as their point of departure the belief that American society has made great progress in combatting discrimination and that the nation is well on the way to becoming a color-blind society. These assumptions are supported by some scholars who claim that most overt discrimination has been eliminated (e.g., Strauss 1990) and by others who argue that the residual discrimination is not worthy of "elimination by state coercion" (e.g., Epstein 1990).

In fact, however, there is no empirical evidence that discrimination has been eliminated, and the belief that it has been substantially eradicated is not universally endorsed, even by moderate and conservative lawmakers. For example, Supreme Court Justice Harry Blackmun, dissenting in *Wards Cove Packing Co.* v. *Atonio* (1989)—perhaps the most far-reaching Court opinion on employment rights to emerge from the 1988 term[1]—stated: "[O]ne wonders whether the majority still believes that race discrimination—or, more accurately, race discrimination against nonwhites—is a problem in our society, or even remembers that it ever was."

The concerns of those who suspect that discrimination persists have been reinforced by public opinion data developed by the National Opinion Research Center (NORC) at the University of Chicago. Although opinion research has consistently revealed a steady decline in prejudice among Americans,[2] the report released by the NORC in January 1991 found that *a majority* of whites still believe that both blacks and Hispanics are not only more inclined than whites to prefer welfare, but are also lazier, more prone to

violence, less intelligent, and less patriotic. Although these responses do not represent evidence of discriminatory attitudes or behavior by employers, they do "easily disabuse the belief that Americans are approaching a color and creed blind society . . ." (Smith 1990). Further, these racial and ethnic images are "significant predictors of support for racial integration programs . . . and desired social distance."

Recent data on worker perceptions also raise concerns about the possible persistence of discrimination in employment. A 1990 random survey of 803 adults commissioned by the *National Law Journal* (Swoboda 1990) revealed the perception of pervasive discrimination. Fifty-one percent of those interviewed—48 percent of whites and 64 percent of blacks—said that all or most "employers practice some form of discrimination in their hiring and promotion practices, regardless of their official policies." In addition, 5 percent of white respondents and 25 percent of black respondents believed they had been discriminated against on the basis of race or ethnicity; 23 percent of whites and 36 percent of blacks believed they had been discriminated against for this or other reasons.[3]

Finally, a recent survey of employers in Chicago focused explicitly on employer perceptions of blacks and their attractiveness as job candidates (Kirschenman and Neckerman 1991). This study found that employers consistently relate race to inferior education, lack of job skills, and unreliable job performance. The authors concluded that "Chicago's employers did not hesitate to generalize about race or ethnic differences in the quality of the labor force. Most associated negative images with inner-city workers, and particularly with black men."

Employment Discrimination and Joblessness Among Black Males and Youth

Evidence of the economic gains of black males, like evidence of attitudinal change, reveals un-

---

[1]*Wards Cove Packing Co.* v. *Atonio,* 109 S.Ct. 2115 (1989), quoting 2133–36. Among other things, the decision makes it more difficult for plaintiffs in disparate impact cases to establish a prima facie case, reduces the burden on employers once that case has been established, and reduces employers' burden in justifying challenged business practices. See, generally, Belton (1990).

[2]For example, Schumann, Steeh, and Bobo (1985) concluded that discriminatory beliefs (e.g., "blacks are inferior to whites") have been steadily declining in the population at large over the past 40 years.

[3]Data from Swoboda (1990) and unpublished tabulations of the survey results provided to The Urban Institute.

even progress. The economic status of black men relative to white men has improved along a number of dimensions in the past 20 years: the wage gap has narrowed, the share of black men working as managers and professionals has increased, and the share of black men whose income exceeds the white median tripled between 1939 and 1979 (Heckman and Verkerke 1990). In the 1980s, some further narrowing of the earnings gap between blacks and whites occurred among those working, but this was accompanied by a sharp reduction in black male labor force participation rates, especially for those with low levels of education. Thus, the extent of blacks' overall progress in recent years is ambiguous (Jaynes 1990).

These negative employment trends are even more pronounced among black male youths, where the relative rate of joblessness (42 percent versus 19 percent for white male youths) is strikingly high.[4] These high rates of joblessness mean that too many young black men will never gain a foothold in the "formal economy"—a fact that imposes severe costs on them and the society as a whole.

Rees (1986) advanced three hypotheses to explain high rates of joblessness among young black males—hypotheses that may also explain differing levels of labor force participation for the black male population as a whole. They include:

- Entry-level jobs are moving away from the inner city, leaving blacks with reduced access to employment opportunities in comparison with their white counterparts;
- Employers discriminate against black youth in the hiring process, so that blacks are rejected from jobs that are available; and
- Young black men are poorly qualified for employment, owing either to the inferior quality of central city schools or because the social milieu of these youths gives low priority to the

attributes that lead to school or job performance.

All three of these possible explanations have proven difficult or impossible to test empirically with much rigor. Recent analyses of job suburbanization or deconcentration have generated the most robust findings, indicating that this "spatial mismatch" is having an increasingly large impact on black employment (Holzer 1989). Using data from the Philadelphia metropolitan area, Ihlanfeldt and Sioquist (1990) estimated that between 30 percent and 50 percent of the employment gap between black and white youth can be explained by job accessibility. Supporting data are also presented for Chicago and Los Angeles.[5]

Assuming that these estimates assign the correct order of magnitude to decentralization, the majority of the difference between joblessness or employment rates of blacks and whites still remains unexplained. Obviously, differences in schooling and training are important factors. So also are differing levels of participation in the underground or drug economy (Reuter et al. 1990), the devastating employment consequences of serving time in prison (Freeman 1990), the availability of entry-level jobs that require comparatively low skills and education (Bendick and Egan 1988), and the number, policies and effectiveness of job-training programs (Gregory 1988). Nevertheless, the question remains: to what degree does hiring discrimination explain residual differences?

Although there is an extensive literature on black and white wage differentials and the discriminatory practices they may reflect, there has been little empirical investigation of discrimination in hiring, as Donohue and Siegelman (1991) recently noted. As the evidence cited here indicates, more progress has been made in reducing wage differentials between white and black workers than in reducing the gap in labor force participation. As a result, discrimination at the

---

[4]Data presented in Rees (1986), April 1985. Joblessness includes those out-of-school young men who do not have jobs. It differs from unemployment in that it includes the jobless who are not looking for work as well as those who are searching for a position.

[5]Ihlanfeldt and Sioquist (1990) have also investigated the effects of decentralization on the earnings of central-city blacks. For a general review of this literature, see Jencks and Mayer (1990).

hiring stage may well represent the more pressing issue in employment today.

Analyses of the extent of hiring discrimination may not only explain differing labor force participation rates; they should also help frame remedies to this problem. For example, if it is the case that firms move away from the central city to escape minority workers, then racial and other minorities can expect to be discriminated against if they apply for positions in the suburbs. This scenario, in turn, suggests that attitudinal change and enforcement of antidiscrimination laws should precede, or at any rate accompany, efforts to increase minorities' access to suburban employment. If, on the other hand, minorities are no more likely to encounter discrimination in the suburbs than in the central city, then policymakers can focus on strategies for increasing access to the suburban workplace, while pursuing metropolitan-wide enforcement of employment discrimination protections.

Hiring Audit Methodology

This study employs the "hiring audit" methodology pioneered by Cross et al. (1990) in a parallel study of discrimination against Hispanic job seekers in Chicago and San Diego. The techniques for conducting hiring audits build directly on the substantial experience developed in the past 15 years in conducting systematic audit studies of discrimination in housing (Turner, Struyk, and Yinger 1990; Wienk et al. 1979).[6]

In a hiring audit, a minority group tester and majority group tester are carefully matched on all attributes that could affect the hiring decision. Specifically, they are paired in terms of age, physical size, education, experience, and other

"human capital" characteristics, as well as such intangibles as openness, apparent energy level, and articulateness. While many of these attributes can be assigned for the purposes of the audit (years of school completed and prior work experience, for example), matching others requires very careful assessment and pairing of individual candidates. Once auditors have been matched, an opening for an entry-level job is identified in the local newspaper and each auditor separately attempts to inquire about the position, complete an application, obtain an interview, and be offered the job. The incidence of differential treatment is determined by comparing the experiences and outcomes for the two auditors.

In this study, a total of 476 audits were conducted by 10 pairs of testers. Audits were conducted in Washington, D.C. and Chicago in summer 1990. Although we followed many of the sampling field procedures used by Cross and his colleagues (1990), we developed more comprehensive measures of differential treatment and employed a different statistical technique for reporting the extent of unfavorable treatment experienced by blacks.[7] Subordinate goals of our study were experimental: to further advance the "technology" of testing in the employment context and to improve tools for analyzing and interpreting the results.

HIRING AUDIT METHODOLOGY

This [section] summarizes the basic methodology of the Employment Discrimination Study. Specifically, we discuss the choice of metropolitan areas in which to conduct the study; the way in which job vacancies were sampled; the number of valid audits completed and their distribution in each city among occupations and types of business; and procedures for recruiting, matching, and training auditors at the two sites.

---

[6]Like its predecessor Hispanic-Anglo hiring audit study, this work is a pilot project to develop the first reliable information on hiring discrimination against black youths and to continue development of a methodology for documenting the incidence and forms of hiring discrimination. There have also been parallel studies conducted in Canada and the United Kingdom, which appear to follow a broadly similar methodology, although actors were used as testers. For a description of the findings, see Reitz (1988).

---

[7]This statistical technique was developed as part of the national Housing Discrimination Study audit project, whose field work was done in 1989. For a description of the basic technique, see Turner et al. (1990).

Selecting Metropolitan Areas

Given the experimental character of the project and the resources available, it was clear that statistically significant numbers of audits could be carried out to measure discrimination in two metropolitan areas. This means that our results are not representative of all urban areas or the nation as a whole. Three criteria guided the selection of the two sites:

1. The metropolitan areas had to be major conurbations, each important in its own right so as to make the results of general interest.
2. Each area had to have been included in the 1989 national Housing Discrimination Study, conducted for the U.S. Department of Housing and Urban Development (HUD) by The Urban Institute (Turner et al. 1990). Twenty-five areas were included in the HUD project, all with substantial minority populations.[8] The Employment Discrimination Study would thus contribute to a growing body of information on discrimination in selected metropolitan areas.
3. The two sites had to differ in terms of industrial structure, labor market tightness, demographic composition, and other factors.

Based on these criteria, the Washington, D.C., and Chicago metropolitan areas were selected. Washington, D.C., is the home of the Committee on Strategies to Reduce Chronic Poverty at the Greater Washington Research Center, one of six community planning and action projects funded by the Rockefeller Foundation to examine the conditions of, and seek remedies to, persistent poverty. Extensive analysis has recently been undertaken of the city's poverty population and of the local economy (Carr et al. 1988), raising questions among local leaders about the role of racial discrimination in explaining comparatively low rates of labor force participation among young black males. In part, the present study is an attempt to respond to those questions. Chicago was one of the two sites for The Urban Institute's Hispanic-Anglo hiring study (Cross et al. 1990), enabling us to make approximate comparisons between the level of discrimination against blacks and Hispanics. Both Chicago and Washington are major metropolitan areas, and both were included in the HUD housing audit study (Turner et al. 1990). They also differ sharply from each other in several important respects.

First, Chicago's employment is more heavily concentrated in production jobs and in the sales and service sectors compared to Washington's (see table 1). Forty-six percent of Washington's employment is among executives, professional specialty, and technician positions, compared with 30 percent for Chicago. Second, the Washington labor market was, until the summer of 1990, tight and growing, whereas Chicago's has been comparatively loose and stagnant. Over the 1986–88 period, employment in Washington expanded by 6.3 percent compared to 1.6 percent in Chicago. Over the same period, the unemployment rates in the two areas averaged 2.9 and 6.9 percent, respectively.[9] These differences are important because, as Freeman (1990) has demonstrated, black youth unemployment rates are sensitive to overall labor market conditions.

A third difference between Chicago and Washington pertains to the proportion of blacks in the population. In 1980 blacks constituted roughly comparable proportions of the two metropolitan areas' population (20 percent in Chicago, 28 percent in Washington). However, blacks constituted 70 percent of District of Columbia inhabitants compared with 40 percent of those living within the City of Chicago. A fourth difference is that residential racial segregation in the Chicago metropolitan area is greater than that in Washington. For example, on a measure of the extent to which blacks are isolated spatially from whites, Chicago scored 0.828 whereas Washington scored 0.672. (The average score for all metropolitan areas is 0.488.)[10] In fact, Massey and Denton (1989) included Chicago among 10

---

[8] All areas in the Housing Discrimination Study had central cities of over 100,000 population in 1980, and in those in which black-white audits were conducted, blacks constituted at least 12 percent of the 1980 population (the national average percentage of blacks in metropolitan areas).

---

[9] Data from U.S. Bureau of Labor Statistics (1987, 1988, 1989b).

[10] Figures from Massey and Denton (1989).

TABLE 1 Percentage Distribution of Employed Male Civilians in the Chicago and Washington, D.C., Metropolitan Areas, by Occupation, 1988

	Chicago	Washington, D.C.
Executive, administrative, and managerial	15.1	19.3
Professional specialty	12.7	20.9
Technicians	2.3	5.9
Sales	13.2	9.0
Administrative support, including sales	8.1	8.5
Service occupations	11.8	8.9
Precision production, craft and repair	15.8	14.7
Machine operators, assemblers, and inspectors	7.0	1.7
Transportation and materials moving	6.2	4.7
Handlers, equipment cleans, etc.	7.0	4.1
Total	100.0	100.0

Sources: U.S. Bureau of Statistics (1988, 1989b).

"hypersegregated" metropolitan areas in the U.S.

One of our initial hypotheses was that residents of the two areas might differ in attitudes toward hiring minorities. In Washington the massive presence of the federal government, which has actively promoted affirmative hiring and other equal opportunity programs for years, might have set a tone for the entire community.[11] Another hypothesis was that employment by black-owned firms would differ between the two areas. However, in 1987, employees of black-owned firms constituted only 1.5 percent of all workers in the Washington area and 0.3 percent in the Chicago area; presumably, therefore, the presence of these firms is not a factor.[12]

The diversity of the two metropolitan areas is a strength of the study. A finding that black youths are substantially discriminated against in both labor markets would *suggest* a pervasive pattern of discrimination in America's urban labor markets and argue for a strong program of auditing and enforcement of equal opportunity laws.

Sampling Job Vacancies

To ensure statistically significant results for both Washington, D.C., and Chicago, we estimated we would need to complete between 200 and 250 audits in each site. Samples of this size are adequate to detect differences of 15 percentage points between white-favored and black-favored outcomes.[13] The sampling process consisted of two separate steps. First, the sample frame was defined. Second, specific job vacancies were drawn from this frame for auditing.

[11]Government positions themselves are not included among those audited, however, because the federal hiring process was expected to differ so significantly from that of private employers.

[12]Chicago data are for the primary metropolitan statistical area (PMSA) (Cook, Du Page, and McHenry counties), and those for Washington, D.C., are for the standard metropolitan statistical area (SMSA). Data on black employees of black-owned firms are from the U.S. Bureau of the Census (1990), and those on total employment are from the U.S. Bureau of Labor Statistics (1989a).

[13]Although this report does not focus on the "net" estimates of discrimination (percentage of white-favored minus percentage of black-favored outcomes), it is nevertheless essential to plan for sample sizes large enough to ensure detectable differences between the share of white-favored and black-favored outcomes.

The sampling frame. The principal require-ment for drawing a random sample is that the universe must be defined so that each job va-cancy in the selected occupations has an equal chance of being drawn.[14] In the United States jobs are obtained through: (1) personal contacts; (2) direct application (i.e., a job seeker visits a business in search of work, but is not directed there by an ad or referral); and (3) intermediaries such as newspaper ads and employment services (Holzer 1987).

In the Hispanic-Anglo audit study, Cross and his colleagues (1990) explored the possibility of developing a sampling frame for the first two job sources and ultimately concluded that this was not feasible. Therefore, they turned to newspa-per help-wanted ads. They listed the principal advantages of using newspapers in a short-term hiring audit as:

- Newspaper ads are one of the main sources of employment information used by young adults. Surveys show that 30 percent to 60 per-cent of young adults use newspaper classified ads as a job-search method (Holzer 1988; U.S. Bureau of Labor Statistics 1989c).[15]

- Newspaper ads, particularly for sales, service, clerical, and blue collar jobs, are roughly rep-resentative of the distribution of all job vacan-cies in broad occupational categories (Abra-ham 1987).

- As a single source, newspaper classified ads provide centralized access to a large number of jobs (thousands of ads appear every weekend in big-city newspapers). These ads are rela-tively simple to sample.

- Newspaper ads serve as a productive, low-cost approach for a hiring audit because each ad represents an employer who is presumably ready to make a job hiring decision, in contrast to direct application where employers often let applications languish without any progress or resolution.

- Both minority and majority job seekers can use newspaper ads (i.e., information about the availability of these jobs is open to everyone).

- It is believed that employers who advertise in the newspaper tend to discriminate less than those who hire through personal contact and direct application. Thus, a newspaper classi-fied ad sampling frame provides a conservative, lower-bound estimate of disparate treatment.

We followed Cross et al. (1990) and used the classified ads in each area's major newspaper ex-clusively as the sampling frame. Not all adver-tised jobs or advertising employers were in-cluded, however. We chose to sample low-skill, entry-level jobs requiring limited experience, because these jobs are typically filled by high school graduates in the 18–24 age range. They include occupations in hotel, restaurant and other services, retail sales, office work, manage-ment (mainly trainee positions), technical areas, and general labor, including manufacturing. These low-skill, entry-level occupations repre-sent precisely the types of jobs where the bulk of young adults begin their working careers. The damage done by discrimination at this entry point is compounded by reducing future upward mobility and can discourage young men from even seeking regular employment.

Not all entry-level jobs are appropriate for an audit study. Numerous jobs were judged ineligi-ble by us because they required such credentials as a specialized driver's license or equipment such as a tool chest. Other jobs eliminated were part-time, temporary, and government posi-tions.[16] Also excluded were jobs filled through intermediaries such as an employment service.

Drawing the sample. Random samples of ad-vertisements for job vacancies were drawn weekly from Sunday issues of the *Washington Post* and the *Chicago Tribune* during a five-week period in early summer 1990. The ads drawn in the sampling procedure each Sunday by the site

---

[14]This section draws heavily on Cross et al. (1990:13–17).

[15]For data on sources of information found by all work-ers in finding jobs, see Corcoran, Datcher, and Duncan (1980).

[16]Government jobs obviously account for an important share of the Washington, D.C., job market. Neverthe-less, these jobs were excluded because the government hiring process was expected to differ so significantly from that of private employers.

TABLE 2 Disposition of Sampled Job Vacancies

	Chicago	Washington, D.C.
Initial sample[a]	414	375
Replacements[b]	76	111
Ineligibles and invalids[c]	272	228
Valid audits	218	258

a. Number of ads drawn by initial sampling of the Sunday newspaper.
b. Job vacancies sampled as replacements of initial sample vacancies found to be ineligible. The initial sample plus replacements equals the total number of audits initiated, 490 in Chicago and 486 in Washington.
c. Includes jobs already filled and cases in which both auditors were screened out on the telephone or in which neither auditor could make contact with the employer after repeated tries. Includes ineligible ads from both the initial and replacement samples.

supervisor were audited the following week. About 60 percent of the ads contained announcements for more than one job opening for the same type of position. In drawing the sample, each advertised position was given an equal chance of being selected, but multiple openings for the same position (e.g., three waiters at one restaurant) were treated as a single position.

Sample size and composition. Altogether, 218 valid audits were completed in Chicago and 258 in Washington (table 2). These successful audits resulted from 490 and 486 total audits initiated in the two sites, respectively. The initiated audits include both those drawn in the first sampling on Sunday and replacements to the first sample. About half of the audits initiated resulted in a valid audit. The remaining audits that were initiated proved to be either "ineligible" for inclusion in the sample or "invalid" because (1) the jobs had already been filled, (2) one or both auditors was screened out on the telephone, or (3) the auditors could not make contact with the employer after repeated tries.

Valid audits include all those in which both auditors appeared in person to submit an application and in which at least one auditor was able to at least submit an employment application. The distribution of valid audits by disposition is shown in table 3; almost 90 percent of the audits ran the full course to a possible job offer or denial of a job by the employer. The balance were either terminated somewhere in the process or

"truncated" because an employer audited in the final two weeks had not made a job-offer decision by the close of field operations. Terminations occurred when employers required applicants to take tests or attend training sessions or when auditors encountered someone they knew at the job site or reported that employers seemed suspicious of their identities or applications.

As shown in table 4, job vacancies audited in both sites were heavily concentrated in the service and retail trade sectors. Interestingly, the difference in the overall industrial composition of the two cities was not reflected in the distribution of entry-level job vacancies advertised. Among the more commonly audited positions in both sites were office support, restaurant help, and retail sales. Comparatively few production jobs were advertised.

Auditor Selection and Training

The hiring audits were conducted by 10 pairs of full-time paid auditors, 5 pairs in each of the two audit sites.[17] Careful recruitment, matching, and

---

[17]All the audit pairs were assigned the same number of advertisements from each week's sample. Their success in completing audits varied somewhat by site and by pair, but, on average, each pair in Chicago completed 44 audits over a six week period, and each pair in Washington, D.C., completed 52 audits over the same period.

TABLE 3 Types and Number of Valid Audits

	Chicago	Washington, D.C.	Number	Percent
Completed Valid audits; neither terminated nor truncated	191	227	418	88
Terminated Valid audits terminated because of expected events	9	10	19	4
Truncated Valid audits started in last two weeks of study in which employer did not make a job-offer decision for at least one tester	18	21	39	8
Totals	218	258	476	100

training of auditors was integral to the success of the study. The auditors, one black and one white, were carefully matched to control for all "job-relevant" characteristics. Specifically, these were experience, education, age, and physical strength and size. Audit partners were made identical in a defined set of job qualifications and trained so that other attributes—demeanor, openness, articulateness, and energy level—were as similar as possible. Race was the only important difference between the two members of each audit team.

Male college students between the ages of 19 and 24 were recruited from major universities in the Chicago and Washington, D.C., metropolitan areas. Job announcements seeking research assistants, and accompanied by letters explaining that the sex and age stipulations were bona fide occupational requirements, were mailed to university employment and placement offices, social science departments, minority affairs offices, and select professors. Respondents were screened over the telephone, and all who met the job requirements were invited to apply and received an initial interview. Twenty-three applicants in Washington and thirty-one applicants in Chicago were initially interviewed for the ten auditor positions in each site. After initial interviews, all qualified applicants were independently interviewed by two additional individuals, consensus was reached about whom to hire, and preliminary audit teams were formed.

Conventional appearance was the major selection criterion—average height, average weight, conventional dialect, and conventional dress and hair. This made audit partners potentially interchangeable, except where we were able to find similarly unique partners. Most audi-

TABLE 4 Distribution of Audited Positions by Sector and Occupation (percentage of valid audits)

	Chicago	Washington, D.C.
Sector		
Construction	0.9	2.7
Manufacturing	2.8	3.1
Retail trade	31.7	29.8
Service	64.7	65.5
Transportation	0.0	1.6
Occupation		
Services:		
Hotel	11.0	3.9
Other	15.1	3.5
Restaurant	21.6	19.8
Total	47.7	27.2
Sales	26.6	20.2
Office	14.2	26.4
General labor	6.9	18.6
Technical	1.8	0.4
Management	2.8	7.4

tors were between the ages of 19 and 21 and between 5′8″ and 5′10″ tall. However, there was a team comprising a 6′4″, bearded, 23-year-old white partner and a 6′2″, bearded, 24-year-old black partner in Washington. And, in Chicago, there was a team of 24-year-old graduate students who had both studied abroad.

All auditors participated in a five-day training session, the overriding goal of which was to make paired auditors as similar as possible. On the first day of training, auditors were videotaped during a mock interview and pairs were finalized by consensus of senior project staff based on similarities in appearance, mannerisms, personality, and interview style.[18] The first day of training also included an introduction to employment discrimination, equal employment opportunity, and a review of project design and methodology. The second day was spent creating the auditors' biographies. The biographies— a record of the auditors' fictitious personas— detailed their personal, school and past employment histories. Most of the auditors posed as recent high school graduates, with limited work experience including summer and after-school jobs as waiters or busboys, parking lot attendants, and file clerks. Some of the older pairs posed as having a maximum of two years' work experience since high school graduation and some community-college course work.

The auditors were required to memorize all information on their biographies. Two days were spent on instructions for conducting an audit, learning a standardized method for filling out job applications, filling out the survey instrument, and completing simulated audits. These simulated audits were critical because they allowed the auditors to experience every stage of the hiring process and to learn to properly complete applications and survey instruments. In these mock audits, the auditors were also able to observe and critique their partners in different interview situations, trainers were able to point out and help minimize differences in the way partners come across to employers, and auditors learned to match their responses in a wide range

of circumstances. On the final day of training, the audit pairs went on practice audits, giving them one real audit experience before actual auditing began.

UNFAVORABLE TREATMENT OF BLACK JOB SEEKERS

Young black men applying for entry-level jobs face a substantial chance of being treated less favorably than comparable white applicants. In 20 percent of the audits conducted in Washington, D.C., and Chicago, the white applicant advanced farther in the hiring process than his black counterpart, and in 15 percent the white applicant was offered a job whereas his equally qualified black partner was not. Blacks were favored over comparable white applicants in a much smaller share of cases; in 7 percent of the audits the black advanced farther in the hiring process, and in 5 percent only the black received a job offer.

Opportunities Denied—Outcomes of the Hiring Process

The ultimate indicator of success in the job application process is, of course, a job offer. But no job seeker, however well qualified, can expect to receive an offer for every application he submits. Since auditors are competing against real applicants for every position, it is unreasonable to expect one or both to receive an offer in every case. In fact, only 33 percent of the audits culminated in job offers.[19]

A more useful measure of success, therefore, is how far into the hiring process an auditor was able to advance. Given their comparable characteristics and qualifications, both members of the audit teams should have had equal success in advancing through the application and interview stages, whether or not one or both ultimately received a job offer. When black applicants are unable to advance as far as equally qualified

---

[18]Two of the preliminary pairings in Washington, D.C., were changed based on this process.

[19]The rate was lower in Chicago (24 percent), where the job market was soft, and higher in Washington, D.C. (40 percent).

whites, they are effectively denied equal opportunities to compete for employment.

As reported in table 5, white applicants advanced farther in the hiring process than their black counterparts in 20 percent of the audits, whereas black auditors advanced farther than their white partners in 7 percent of the audits.[20] In other words, when a young black man applies for an entry-level position for which an equally qualified white candidate is also competing, there is a one in five chance that the black will be unable to advance as far in the process as an equally qualified white. Correspondingly, when a young white man applies for an entry-level position for which an equally qualified black candidate is also competing, there is a 7 percent chance that the white will be less successful than the black. Thus, given equally qualified white and black candidates, one white and the other black, if differential treatment occurs, it is three times more likely to favor the white than to favor the black.

In the majority of the cases where one auditor advanced further than his partner, he received a job offer whereas his partner did not. In 15 percent of the audits, only the white partner received a job offer (see table 6). This accounts for 75 percent of the cases where the white auditor advanced father in the hiring process than his black counterpart.[21] The black auditor was the only member of the team to receive a job offer in 5 percent of the audits (71 percent of the cases in which the black auditor advanced further in the hiring process). Again, therefore, if an equally qualified white and black are in competition, differential treatment is three times more likely to favor the white than to favor the black.

At what stage in the hiring process is differential treatment most likely to occur? As illustrated by table 7, both black and white auditors were generally successful in submitting a job application; the incidence of unfavorable treatment at this initial stage was only 2 percent. Once be-

---

[20]The t-statistics in this and subsequent tables test whether the observed incidences of unfavorable treatment are significantly different from zero. See appendix A for complete details.

[21]In the remaining cases, the white auditor advanced farther but still received no job offer.

TABLE 5 Opportunity Denied: Who Advanced Farther in the Hiring Process? (percent of all completed audits)

	Percent	t-Statistic
White advanced farther	20**	11.7
Black advanced farther	7**	4.5
Number of audits	438	

Note: ** indicates that percentage differs from zero at a 1 percent significance level.

TABLE 6 Opportunity Denied: Who Got a Job Offer? (percentage of all completed audits)

	Percent	t-Statistic
Only white received offer	15**	7.0
Only black received offer	5**	4.1
Number of audits	438	

Note: ** indicates that percentage differs from zero at a 1 percent significance level.

TABLE 7 Opportunity Denied by Stage at which Unfavorable Treatment Occurred (percentage of audits with both partners remaining at that stage)

	Percent	t-Statistic
Application		
White favored	2*	2.42
Black favored	0	——a
Number of audits	476	
Interview		
White favored	9**	7.45
Black favored	3**	4.33
Number of audits	465	
Job offer		
White favored	8**	4.25
Black favored	4**	4.10
Number of audits	220	

Notes: ** indicates that percentage differs from zero at a 1 percent significance level. * indicates that percentage differs from zero at a 5 percent significance level. a. Dash (——), not applicable.

yond the application stage, however, differential treatment was equally likely to occur at the formal interview stage or the job-offer stage. In 9 percent of the audits where both partners submitted an application, only the white partner received a formal interview (compared to 3 percent in which only the black was interviewed). And in 8 percent of the audits where both partners received a formal interview, only the white partner received a job offer (compared to only 4 percent in which only the black was offered a job).

There appears to be some variation in the prevalence of discrimination between labor markets. As shown in table 8, the incidence of unfavorable treatment toward blacks is higher in Washington, D.C., than in Chicago. In Washington, blacks face a 23 percent chance of being denied opportunities to advance through the hiring process, compared to a 17 percent chance in Chicago. However, this difference is not statistically significant at the 5 percent level. The share of cases in which white auditors received a job

offer but their equally qualified black partners did not was 19 percent in Washington compared to only 10 percent in Chicago, and this difference is statistically significant at a 1 percent level. The share of black-favored outcomes does not differ between the two metropolitan areas.

Opportunities Denied—Steering in the Hiring Process

In addition to being denied opportunities to advance through the hiring process, blacks were "steered" to less-desirable jobs than their white counterparts in a small but significant share of all audits, whether or not a job was actually offered. In some cases, blacks benefited from job steering. Overall, though, whites were slightly more likely to be favored than their black counterparts.

To document possible steering, the auditors

TABLE 8 Opportunity Denied by Metropolitan Area
(percent of all completed audits)

	Chicago	Washington, D.C.
Who advanced farther?		
White favored		
Percent	17**	23**
t-statistic	5.9	16.4
Black favored		
Percent	8*	7**
t-statistic	2.2	9.3
Who got a job offer?		
White favored		
Percent	10**	19**
t-statistic	3.8	11.0
Black favored		
Percent	5	6**
t-statistic	1.6	17.6
Number of audits	197	241

Note: ** indicates that percentage differs from zero at a 1 percent significance level. * indicates that percentage differs from zero at a 5 percent significance level.

TABLE 9. Differences in Job Quality (percentage of all completed audits)

	Chicago	Washington, D.C.	Total
White favored			
Percent	4**	5**	5**
t-statistic	7.9	7.9	9.4
Black favored			
Percent	2*	3*	3*
t-statistic	1.3	1.8	2.3
Number of audits	214	258	472

Note: ** indicates that percentage differs from zero at a 1 percent significance level. * indicates that percentage differs from zero at a 5 percent significance level.

were asked to indicate whether the jobs for which they were considered corresponded to the advertised positions for which they applied. When auditors reported that they were considered for a different job than the advertised position, they were asked to indicate whether this job was better, worse, or about the same as the advertised position. Wages, hours, and status were used in determining whether one job was better than another.

As an illustration, one audit team responded to an advertisement for sales personnel at a car dealership. The white auditor was considered for and offered a position in new car sales, whereas the black auditor was told that the only positions available were in used car sales. In another case, a team applied for an advertised position for a receptionist. The black was offered a job as a factory worker whereas the white was considered for the receptionist position. As illustrated by table 9, blacks were steered to less-desirable jobs than their white counterparts in 5 percent of the audits. Blacks were considered for more desirable jobs than their white partners in 3 percent of the audits. The same pattern of job steering occurred in both Chicago and Washington, although the incidence was higher for Washington.

SUMMARY AND CONCLUSIONS

The Urban Institute's hiring audit study demonstrates that unequal treatment of black job seekers is entrenched and widespread.[22] The re-

---

[22]Use of the term "widespread" to describe the extent of discrimination found in this study derives from prior legal analysis and application of the term by the General Accounting Office (GAO) of the U.S. Specifically, the 1986 Immigration Reform and Control Act (IRCA) calls for the initiation of a process that could lead to the termination of the employer sanctions authorized by IRCA if the GAO were to find that sanctions had led to a "widespread pattern of discrimination" against eligible workers (Immigration and Naturalization Act, Section 274A(1)(1)(A)). After extensive analysis of IRCA's legislative history as well as U.S. civil rights legislation, the GAO determined that a "widespread pattern of discrimination" exists if there is a "serious pattern" and more than just a "few isolated cases of discrimination" (GAO, Immigration Reform; Employers Sanctions and the Question of Discrimination; GAO/GGD 90-62, March 1990). In the case of IRCA, the Comptroller General concluded that the introduction of discriminatory practices by 10 percent of all employers should be termed "widespread" for the purposes of the act. This level of discrimination is roughly half that found in this report.

search contradicts claims that hiring practices today either favor blacks systematically or are effectively color-blind. In the Washington, D.C., and Chicago metropolitan areas, blacks receive unfavorable differential treatment 20 percent of the time they compete against comparable whites for entry-level positions. In contrast, whites receive unfavorable differential treatment 7 percent of the time they compete against comparably qualified blacks.

Over the last 25 years, black men have gained substantial ground relative to white men with regard to wages, income, and access to managerial positions. However, almost no progress has been made in labor force participation and unemployment rates. Indeed, recent trends show a widening gap between blacks and whites on these indicators. Arguments about reasons for this trend are not supported by systematic evidence, since most research on discrimination in employment has focused on relative wage rates, and little is known about either the extent or character of discriminatory hiring practices.

The Urban Institute, sponsored by the Rockefeller Foundation, has conducted the first study to directly measure differential treatment of white and black job seekers applying for entry-level employment. The study employed the "audit" methodology, which has been used extensively for over a decade to test for discrimination in housing, and was pioneered in the employment context by a 1989 Urban Institute study of discrimination against Hispanic job seekers. In the current hiring audit, ten pairs of young men—each pair consisting of a black and a white—were carefully matched on all characteristics that could affect a hiring decision, and were trained to behave as similarly as possible in an interview setting. They applied in turn for entry-level jobs (requiring no special skills, experience, or training) advertised in the newspaper, and each applicant reported his treatment at every stage of the hiring process. Since both applicants were the same with respect to job qualifications, experience, and demeanor, systematic differences in treatment by employers can only be attributable to race. This methodology effectively catches employers in the act of discriminating.

A total of 476 hiring audits were conducted in the metropolitan areas of Washington, D.C., and Chicago during summer 1990. In one out of five audits, the white applicant was able to advance farther through the hiring process than his equally qualified black counterpart. In other words, the white was able to either submit an application, receive a formal interview, or be offered a job when the black was not. Overall, in one out of seven, or 15 percent, of the audits, the white was offered a job although his equally qualified black partner was not.[23]

In contrast, black auditors advanced farther than their white counterparts on only 7 percent of the audits, and the black auditors received job offers whereas their white partners did not in 5 percent of the audits. In sum, if equally qualified black and white candidates are competing for a job, differential treatment, when it occurs, is three times more likely to favor the white applicant than the black.

These results show that despite extensive legislative and regulatory protections and incentives to hire minorities, unfavorable treatment of young black men is widespread and pervasive across firms offering entry-level jobs in the Washington, D.C., and Chicago metropolitan areas. Moreover, the audit results indicate that reverse discrimination—favoring a black applicant over an equally qualified white—is far less common.

The hiring audit results should be viewed as realistic estimates of the incidence of discrimination in the two metropolitan areas we studied, for three reasons. First, the reported measures of differential treatment focus on outcomes of the hiring process, and do not include instances of discouraging treatment (negative comments, longer waits for scheduled appointments, cursory interviews), which were experienced by black applicants in as many as half the audits. Second, the job openings for which black and white auditors applied were selected from the classified advertisements of major metropolitan newspapers, and discrimination is presumably

---

[23]All statistical results presented in this summary are significant at the 99 percent confidence level.

lower for advertised positions than for positions filled by less-public mechanisms, such as word of mouth, postings at the job site, or use of recruiters or employment agencies. Finally, all of the auditors participating in this study were actually college students who were overqualified for the positions for which they applied; they were articulate and poised, spoke and dressed conventionally, and posed as having had prior job experience. One would expect both blacks and whites with these characteristics to appear as exceptionally attractive candidates to prospective employers. In particular, the qualifications of the black auditors were substantially higher than those of the average black applicant for entry-level jobs.

Results from The Urban Institute's earlier audit study of discrimination against Hispanic job seekers, conducted in Chicago and San Diego, indicate that Hispanics appear even more likely than blacks to be denied equal opportunity for advancement through the hiring process. Specifically, in 31 percent of the Hispanic-Anglo audits, the majority applicant advanced farther through the hiring process, compared to 20 percent of the black-white audits.

Overall levels of discrimination differed between the two metropolitan areas we studied. Despite the presence of the federal government with its long-standing equal opportunity policies, the incidence of unfavorable treatment was substantially higher in Washington than in Chicago. Specifically, whites advanced farther than their black counterparts 23 percent of the time in Washington, D.C., compared to 17 percent of the time in Chicago. And whites were offered jobs but their black partners were not in 19 percent of the Washington audits, compared to 10 percent of the Chicago audits. Outcomes favoring the black partner occurred at approximately the same rate in the two labor markets.

The likelihood of discrimination against blacks was not found to vary substantially between central city and suburban locations; blacks are no more likely to encounter unfavorable treatment by employers in suburban (and predominantly white) locations than in central city (and predominantly black) locations. This evidence contradicts the view that blacks encounter more discrimination when they seek employment in the suburbs, although it is important to keep in mind that only firms advertising available positions in the metropolitan newspaper were included in the audit study.

The type of job for which a minority applies proves to be the most important predictor of the likelihood of discrimination. In general, minorities are more likely to encounter discrimination in entry-level clerical jobs and in jobs involving client sales and service than in blue collar positions. Of the eight job categories with above-average levels of discrimination, six are in clerical or sales and service positions. In other words, discrimination against blacks appears to be highest in the types of jobs offering the highest wages and future income potential.

The fact that black job seekers in Washington, D.C., and Chicago were unable to advance as far in the hiring process as equally qualified whites in one out of five audits indicates that unfavorable treatment of black job seekers is widespread, and that discrimination contributes to black male unemployment and nonparticipation in the labor force. The results also contradict the view that reverse discrimination is commonplace. Evidence from hiring audits indicates that pressures to dismantle the machinery of civil rights enforcement are premature. Indeed, the prevalence of disparate treatment in the hiring process means that greater efforts are needed to detect discrimination and to provide victims with access to justice.

These results argue for a shift in the allocation of enforcement resources. In the years after the passage of the Civil Rights Act in 1964, enforcement resources—as measured by charges brought before the Equal Employment Opportunity Commission and employment discrimination cases—showed [a] marked shift from hiring incidences to terminations (Donohue and Siegelman 1991:46). Our finding of substantial discrimination in hiring indicates a need to reverse this trend.

References

Abraham, K. 1987. "Help-wanted advertising, job vacancies, and unemployment." *Brook-*

ings Papers on Economics Activity, no. 1: 207–48.

Belton, R. 1990. "The dismantling of the Griggs disparate impact theory and the future of Title VII: The need for a third reconstruction." *Yale Law and Policy Review* 8:223.

Bendick, Marc, Jr., and Egan, Mary Lou. 1988. *JOBS: Employment opportunities in the Washington metropolitan area for persons with limited employment qualification.* Washington, D.C.: Greater Washington Research Center.

Carr, Oliver T., Jr., et al. 1988. *Opportunity ladders: Can area employment possibilities improve the prospects for Washingtonians in long-term poverty?* Washington, D.C.: Greater Washington Research Center.

Corcoran, Mary, Datcher, Linda, and Duncan, Greg. 1980. "Most workers find jobs through word of mouth." *Monthly Labor Review* 103 (8): 33–35.

Cross, H., Kenney, G., Mell, J., and Zimmermann, W. 1990. *Employer Hiring Practices: Differential treatment of Hispanic and Anglo job seekers.* Washington, D.C.: Urban Institute Press.

Donohue, J. J., and Siegelman, P. 1991. "The changing nature of employment discrimination litigation." Draft. Chicago: Northwestern University School of Law.

Epstein, Richard A. 1990. "The paradox of civil rights." *Yale Law and Policy Review* 8 (2): 299–319.

Freeman, R. 1990. "Employment and earnings of disadvantaged young men in a labor shortage economy." Working Paper 3444. Cambridge, Mass: National Bureau of Economic Research.

Gregory, Vikki L. 1988. *ET: Employment and training activities serving predominantly low-income residents of Washington, D.C., with limited employment qualifications.* Washington, D.C.: Greater Washington Research Center.

Heckman, James J., and Verkerke, J. Hoult. 1990. "Racial disparity and employment dis-

crimination law: An economic perspective." *Yale Law and Policy Review* 8 (2): 276–99.

Holzer, H. 1989. "The spatial mismatch hypothesis: What has the evidence shown?" Michigan State University Working Paper. Lansing: Michigan State University.

———. 1988. "Search methods used by unemployed youth." *Journal of Labor Economics* 6 (1): 1–20.

———. 1987. "Job search by employed and unemployed youth." *Industrial and Labor Relations Review* 40 (4): 601–11.

Ihlanfeldt, K. R., and Sioquist, D. L. 1990. "Job accessibility and racial differences in youth employment rates." *American Economic Review* 80 (1): 267–76.

Jaynes, G. D. 1990. "The labor market status of black Americans: 1939–1985." *Journal of Economic Perspectives* 4 (4): 9–24.

Jencks, C., and Mayer, S. 1990. "Residential segregation, job proximity, and black job opportunities." In L. Lynn, Jr., and M. G. H. McGeary (eds.), *Inner-city poverty in the United States,* pp. 187–222. Washington, D.C.: National Academy Press.

Kirschenman, Joleen, and Neckerman, K. M. 1991. "We'd love to hire them but . . . : The meaning of race for employers." In Christopher Jencks and Paul E. Peterson (eds.), *The urban underclass.* Washington, D.C.: Brookings Institution.

Massey D. S., and Denton, N. A. 1989. "Hypersegregation in U.S. metropolitan areas: Blacks and Hispanic segregation along five dimensions." *Demography* 26 (3): 373–91.

Rees, A. 1986. "An essay on youth joblessness." *Journal of Economic Literature* 24:613–28.

Reitz, J. G. 1988. "Less racial discrimination in Canada, or simply less racial conflict? Implications of comparisons with Britain." *Canadian Public Policy* 14 (2): 424–41.

Reuter, Peter, MacCoun, Robert, Murphy, Patrick, Abrahamse, Allan, and Simon, Barbara. 1990. *Money from crime: A study of the economics of drug dealing in Washington, D.C.* Santa Monica, Calif.: Rand.

Schumann, H., Steeh, C., and Bobo, L. 1985. _Racial attitudes in America: Trends and interpretations._ Cambridge, Mass.: Harvard University Press.

Smith, T. W. 1990. _Ethnic images._ General Social Sciences Topical Report 19. Chicago: National Opinion Research Corp.

Strauss, D. A. 1990. "The law and economics of racial discrimination in employment." Paper presented at the Georgetown University Conference on the Law and Economics of Racial Discrimination in Employment, November 30, Washington, D.C.

Swoboda, F. 1990. "Workplace discrimination perceived as prevalent." _Washington Post,_ July 9, p. A12.

Turner, M. A., Struyk, R., and Yinger, J. 1991. _Housing discrimination study synthesis._ Washington, D.C.: Urban Institute.

U.S. Bureau of the Consensus. 1990. _1987 survey of minority-owned business enterprises: Black._ Publ. #MB87-1. Washington, D.C.: U.S. Government Printing Office.

U.S. Bureau of Labor Statistics. 1989a. _Employment, hours, and earnings: States and areas, 1972–87._ Bulletin 2320, vols. 1–2. Washington, D.C.: U.S. Government Printing Office.

———. 1989b. _Geographic profile of employment and unemployment._ Bulletin 2327. Washington, D.C.: U.S. Government Printing Office.

———. 1988. _Geographic profile of employment and unemployment._ Bulletin 2305. Washington, D.C.: U.S. Government Printing Office.

———. 1987. _Geographic profile of employment and unemployment._ Bulletin 2279. Washington, D.C.: U.S. Government Printing Office.

Wienk, R. E., Reid, C. E., Simonson, J. C., and Eggers, F. J. 1979. _Measuring discrimination in American housing markets: The housing market practices survey._ Washington, D.C.: U.S. Department of Housing and Urban Development.

18.   IN BLACK AND WHITE

THE NEW REPUBLIC

It's rare that the issue of racial discrimination in the workplace is the subject of more than conjecture and hysteria, which is why the recent report by the Urban Institute on racism in hiring for entry-level jobs comes as such a relief. It contains some of the most reliable data ever on who actually discriminates against whom, where, how—and even when—in the job market. Bravely, it treats affirmative action as discrimination—not merely as some completely cost-free panacea. And it deploys a social science methodology, which, though limited, provides perhaps the most reliable way of testing the extent to which Americans actually discriminate against each other.

It's a shame, then, that the report's conclusions were simply portrayed in the press as proof that old-fashioned white-on-black racial discrimination is still endemic. (This was not simple misrepresentation: the report's conclusion itself described such discrimination as "widespread and pervasive.") The report was further interpreted as bolstering the argument for the civil rights bill now before Congress and was deemed

From _The New Republic,_ June 10, 1991, pp. 7–8. Reprinted with permission.

to have knocked a hole in the fashionable idea that affirmative action is now a greater problem than old-fashioned bigotry. In fact, the evidence presented in the report makes for far more complicated reading than these easy conclusions suggest. Indeed, part of its persuasiveness lies in the very complexity of the portrait it paints.

The institute hired twenty male college students—ten white and ten black—and carefully matched them in black-white pairs so that each had virtually identical skills, résumés, appearances, and demeanors. They were then sent out in Washington, D.C., and Chicago to apply for a range of jobs advertised in newspapers. Their progress was monitored not simply to see whether one received a job offer and the other did not, but to examine each stage of the application process, to check for the subtlest of racial bias. In all, more than 400 separate job searches were subsequently thrown into a computer.

In 80 percent of the job searches, both the white and the black applicants were offered equivalent jobs. In 15 percent, the white received a job offer over the black; in 5 percent, the black got the job, and the white didn't. When the study looked further for evidence of discrimination at earlier stages of the application process—verbal discouragement over the phone, long waiting periods for interviews, and so on—it found another 7 percent of the job searches revealed some level of discrimination. That left 73 percent of the job searches with no evidence of discrimination at all.

What are we to make of this relatively low level of bias? Frankly, we think it's good news. We don't know, of course, exactly what a similar report would have found, say, in 1961, because such a report does not exist. But it doesn't take much agonizing to recognize that 73 percent fairness represents something close to a transformation in racial attitudes in a matter of decades. There are caveats, of course: 27 percent bias is still 27 percent too much. But the visceral, structural, overwhelming injustice of not so long ago has been dramatically reduced.

The report contained further twists of encouraging news. There was no evidence that racial discrimination against blacks occurs more often in suburban and predominantly white neighborhoods than in the inner city. In Washington,

D.C., all government jobs were excluded, suggesting that, given the high level of affirmative action in government employment, blacks probably fare better in D.C. than the study suggests. In Chicago, blacks were actually *more* likely than whites to receive favorable treatment in the early stages of job application.

There was only sporadic evidence, moreover, that the more sophisticated the job and the skills required, the more likely it was that blacks would be subject to discrimination. In some cases, in fact, the reverse seemed to be the case. The study found, for example, that if you were black, you would be least likely to suffer discrimination in applying for white-collar positions in hotels, banking, retail, and real estate in Chicago. You were most likely to suffer discrimination in applying for a blue-collar position in retail in Washington, D.C. (All in all, by the way, D.C. comes across as a far more discriminatory city than Chicago.) What could be happening, of course, is that white-collar employers are more likely to hire with affirmative action foremost in their minds. But the data, even here, are too mixed to draw any firm conclusions.

Where racial discrimination is at its most personal and direct—when an interviewer is of a different race than the interviewee—the report uncovered an interesting finding. It could not find any statistically significant relationship between the race of the interviewer and the race of the successful applicant. In the only slight caveat to this, the report found that a black interviewer was much more likely to discriminate racially in favor of a black interviewee than a white interviewer with a white interviewee, but the number of cases in which this happened was too small to be statistically reliable. In other words, our traditional view of the racist job interviewer is simply not substantiated in real life.

The Urban Institute report tells a largely convincing story that few people in today's civil rights controversies wish to hear. It offends the right by showing that old-fashioned discrimination is still clearly a greater problem than affirmative action in those less elevated professions where reverse discrimination has yet to take hold. (It tells us nothing, of course, about whether affirmative action is the key to eliminating old-fashioned discrimination; or, for that matter, about whether it actually makes matters worse.) But its key finding is one that will surely offend the established "civil rights" lobby more. It is that both forms of discrimination, though deplorable, are actually the exception in today's American work environment. They certainly cannot begin to account for the scope of the crisis in much of black America today. Focusing on them, as the Democrats' obsessive civil rights bill posturing does, is a fatal distraction from the vital matter at hand.

The vital matter, as we have noted many times before, is that far too few black Americans can enter the job market with competitive skills in the first place. It is that the collapse of the black family, the inner-city drug epidemic, the violent crime that now besieges a central part of black America, and the decline of public education have made the premise of the Urban Institute study a blithe and distant dream. This report is fascinating and welcome. But it should stand as a goad to mobilize against the real tragedy, rather than as an invitation to be obsessed by a false one.

19.   HOW DO THEY DO IT?

CHARLES MOSKOS

The first thing that strikes a visitor to an Army dining facility (as the mess hall as been renamed) is that the sergeants sit at their own tables. The bigger dining facilities even have partitions separating the sergeants from the lower enlisted ranks. The second notable thing is the easy mixing of the races. Black and white soldiers eat together in seemingly random fashion. The bantering that goes on across the tables seems to have no particular racial direction. What a contrast with the self-imposed segregation found in most college dining halls today.

The Army is not a racial utopia by any means. Beneath the cross-race bantering, an edge of tension often lurks. A black soldier puts it as follows: "It's invisible, but you feel the racism of a lot of the white guys. The whites are still top dog

and the brothers know it." A white soldier sees it another way: "Blacks get away with things a white can't. Whites get the shaft." Still, give or take a surly remark here, a bruised sensibility there, the races do get on remarkably well. Under the grueling conditions of Desert Storm not one racial incident occurred that was severe enough to come to the attention of the military police.

It hasn't always been this way. Throughout the Vietnam War race relations were terrible. By the early 1970s race riots were rampant, an outcome of both perceived and real discrimination against blacks in the military along with spillover from the racial and political turmoil in society at large. Racial conflict did not disappear with the all-volunteer Army, instituted in 1973. Fights between black and white soldiers were endemic in the 1970s, an era that is now called "the time of troubles." Army recruiters were drawing from the poorest and toughest elements of America. Drugs and hooliganism infected the barracks.

But starting in the early 1980s, recruitment policies changed and tensions between the races eased. The key factor in improved recruiting was

From *The New Republic*, August 5, 1991, pp. 16–20. Reprinted with permission.

Charles Moskos, a former draftee, is professor of sociology at Northwestern University and author of *A Call to Civic Service* (Free Press).

the Army's introduction of GI bill–type benefits, which help pay for college expenses after leaving the service. Today, as over the past decade, almost all recruits are high school graduates coming from the lower-middle and working classes. But the different economic background of soldiers explains only part of the overall improvement. After all, racial tensions have sharpened in society at large during the same period at all income levels. So what is it that works in the military? Six factors can be identified, each having some lessons for race relations in civilian society.

1. The Level Playing Field. In many ways the Army is what sociologist Marion J. Levy Jr. aptly calls "a radical meritocracy." Basic training is the leveling experience par excellence. The mandatory short haircuts, the common uniform, the rigors of eight weeks of infantry training, all help to reduce pre-existing civilian advantage. For many youths from impoverished backgrounds, successful completion of basic training is the first occasion in which they can outshine those coming from privileged backgrounds.

The Army also can provide an academic boost not often available in civilian employment. The Basic Skills Education Program (BSEP), started in 1976, is a bootstrap operation in remedial reading, writing, and mathematics. BSEP students are selected by company commanders to attend an on-post school for four hours daily in the morning. The remainder of their work day is devoted to normal company duties. BSEP enrollees have below-average test scores and are usually high school dropouts. The course varies from two to six weeks and is particularly beneficial for young soldiers who, though lacking in good schooling, have the leadership potential to become sergeants. Although the Army shies away from baldly stating it, BSEP students are mainly black. What is important is that doing well in the BSEP is definitely not seen as "acting white." It is considered a realistic investment in one's future career.

Blacks and whites diverge during selection for advanced training because black soldiers tend to score lower than whites on aptitude tests, though they score much higher than black youth in civilian society. Blacks are most likely to be found in general clerical work, supply, and food service, fields in which they make up about 60 percent of the work force. They are much less likely to be found in highly technical fields; only 9 percent of those in electronic warfare, for example, are black. Still, whatever a soldier's work assignment, rank and promotion in the enlisted ranks are roughly equivalent between the races, certainly more so than in civilian life.

In the combat arms, such as the infantry, black participation is about 25 percent in today's Army, somewhat lower than the overall black percentage in the Army, but about double that of their numbers in the American population. As it turns out, blacks made up 15 percent of the soldiers killed in the Gulf war.

2. No Discrimination. The Army's stated goal is absolute commitment to equal opportunity and non-discrimination regardless of race—with no qualifications. This principle is no longer debated at any level in the military. By contrast, equal opportunity for women is also a stated principle, but the role of women continues to be a roiling source of contention.

An important symbol of the Army's emphasis on non-discrimination is found in the officer evaluation report. Among the fourteen categories in the evaluation, one states: "supports equal opportunity." Normally these reports are completed by the immediate supervisor and reviewed by the next highest person in the chain of command. A similar evaluation system operates for sergeants. Anything less than a favorable rating in this category means the end of one's military career.

Few people are given a negative check on their equal opportunity box. But the box is more than pro forma: it serves as an organizational reminder of the importance of race relations. Whatever racist sentiments sergeants or officers may hold, one will practically never hear such sentiments openly expressed in mixed-race groups and even rarely in all-white groups. It is not so much that military leaders are innocent of racism, but anyone hoping to stay in the Army must avoid any innuendo of racism, lest it appear in an evaluation report.

3. Hierarchy. Ironically, perhaps, the tremendous emphasis on rank helps erode racial feelings by producing cross-race solidarity within ranks. It also breaks down cross-racial solidarity across ranks. A soldier being harassed by a sergeant of the same race soon abandons notions that common racial origin overrides all, especially when his misery is being shared by a person of another race. The social barriers in the Army lie not so much between whites and blacks as between lower-ranking soldiers and sergeants, and between enlisted persons and officers. That hierarchy, really inequality, can reduce racism is one of the paradoxes of military life.

4. Goals, Not Quotas.   Guidelines for promotion boards state: "The goal for this board is to achieve a percentage of minority and female selection not less than the selection rate for all officers being considered." This means that if the goal is not met, the board must defend its decisions. Thus the pressure to meet the goals is strong, and in most cases they are met. But if they are not met and further review indicates they cannot be without violations of standards, then the chips fall where they may.

The process goes like this. The board takes into consideration past assignments, physical standards, evaluation ratings, promotability to the next level after the one under consideration, education, and training credentials. The top candidates are quickly selected and the bottom ones just as quickly eliminated. In reality, goals become operative only in the gray middle. As one well-informed white officer put it, "Only fully qualified people are promoted, but not necessarily the best qualified. But don't forget, we are talking micromillimeter differences in these cases."

If this looks like a quota by another name, remember that the number of blacks who are promoted from captain to major, a virtual prerequisite for an officer seeking an Army career, is usually below the goal. The underpromotion of black captains causes the Army heartburn and creates frustration among junior black officers. The most plausible explanation for the shortfall is that about half of all black officers are products of historically black colleges, where a disproportionate number of the more recent graduates do not acquire the writing and communication skills

necessary for promotion to staff jobs. Promotions through colonel and the general ranks show little racial difference.

One last remark on the goals versus quotas distinction. The military has no hint of two promotion lists, whites being compared only with whites, blacks with blacks. On the sticky issue of racial representation in promotions, the Army has come up with a system that satisfies neither the pro- nor anti-quota viewpoints—but it works.

5. Social Engineering.   The military has at its command means of training and surveillance that are rarely found in civilian society. Of course, social control isn't the only mechanism for better race relations—look at prisons. But it clearly plays a part. During the time of racial troubles in the 1970s, the Army developed the most extensive training and staffing program of equal opportunity anywhere. The program was sponsored by the Army Research Institute for the Behavioral and Social Sciences (ARI).

ARI funded extensive analysis of race relations unequaled in civilian culture. The role of black social scientists was pivotal. John S. Butler of the University of Texas statistically isolated the effect of institutional racism in promotion rates and showed that "smarter" blacks were *less likely* to be promoted than blacks with lower test scores. James A. Thomas and Peter Nordlie (a white) conducted research that found that the Army's initial race relations courses were reproducing white backlash sentiments. Richard O. Hope, former director of race relations research for the Defense Department, conducted extensive evaluation studies that led to a mainstreaming of race relations programs into the command structure. The ability of these sociologists to monitor racial attitudes over a period of time and to use the data to inform policy was a luxury afforded only by the military's social control of its members.

The research led to race relations programs formulated by something called the Defense Equal Opportunity Management Institute (DEOMI), located at Patrick Air Force Base in Florida. Even during a time of budgetary cutbacks, DEOMI's future is secure. It trains equal opportunity instructors for all the services, and in recent years has received frequent requests from civilian organizations for advice on how to set up race relations programs. Most of the instruction deals with race relations history and military policy. But what is most vivid in the memory of DEOMI graduates is the "shock treatment"—sensitivity-type courses to bring them "to grips with their underlying racial attitudes and feelings," in the cliché of the trade.

At one level the sensitivity courses veer close to putting whites on the defensive, though whites are never described as ipso facto racists simply because they occupy a dominant position in American society. But the important element of DEOMI's sensitivity course involves role playing, whites seeing situations from the standpoint of a minority member—or minorities taking the viewpoint of majority members.

A favorite pedagogical device is to present a "problem." One night in the barracks, a white soldier shouts "nigger" at a black soldier. Several blacks jump the white soldier. A barracks melee breaks out, with the races going at each other. The next day everybody is tense waiting for new trouble. What is to be done? School solution: let everybody cool off, have NCOs (noncommissioned officers) talk to their soldiers in groups and individually, bring in officers if necessary, ascertain exactly what happened, take appropriate action. A racial epithet is cause for punishment in the Army. An enlisted man can be charged with incitement to riot for such an action. An NCO or officer could additionally be charged with conduct unbecoming an NCO or officer. Also, a superior can be accountable for *not* taking action when he or she observes racist behavior.

DEOMI graduates, mainly NCOs, are assigned throughout the Army. They monitor racial incidents, look for patterns of racism in assignments and promotions, conduct ethnic observances, and give equal opportunity training to locally based NCOs. Full-time equal opportunity (EO) NCOs are assigned to each brigade, and in turn train battalion and company NCOs who are assigned EO responsibilities as an additional duty. Over time, race relations has shifted from a responsibility of specialized staff toward being regarded as an integral part of a commander's responsibilities. EO NCOs, at the commander's request, also administer surveys on race relations and general unit morale. At one time, being a race relations NCO could marginalize one's Army career. Today it is considered a "good ticket to be punched," one that can be a help on the way up to first sergeant or sergeant major.

In the late '70s an extraordinary twelve or fourteen hours were devoted to race relations in basic training, with follow-up throughout the soldier's term in service. NCOs as well as recruits were required to take race relations training. Many white soldiers resented these courses, considering them exercises in white guilt. But studies showed the courses did make whites more attuned to black feelings once the accusatory tone of the earlier courses was replaced by a "how do we solve this problem?" approach.

More important, perhaps, the mandatory race relations courses sent a strong signal to black soldiers that the Army was serious about equal opportunity. In the more benign era of today, equal opportunity courses have been cut back to just one hour in basic training, but race relations remains an integral part of the senior NCO education. As a sign of the times, the emphasis has shifted toward sexual harassment issues.

6. Blacks in Leadership Roles. If there is a black center to the Army, it is among the 85,000 black NCOs. Blacks are one-and-a-half times more likely than whites to reenlist. Many see themselves as the main transmission belt of the values of discipline and self-improvement of the old black bourgeoisie. As a black sergeant told me, "We are the only good role models continuously in contact with young blacks. We have the responsibility of talking values to a captive audience."

Black NCOs can easily recognize a part of themselves in the character of Master Sergeant Vernon Walters in the movie *A Soldier's Story*, set in the days of the segregated Army. Sergeant Walters is obsessively concerned that blacks not play the fool in front of whites. What's different today, of course, is that black NCOs lead soldiers of all races. Black sergeants take umbrage at any whisper they are partial to blacks. Indeed, an analysis of evaluation reports by Charles Hines, a black major general who holds a Ph.D. in sociology, shows that black sergeants grade "average" black soldiers more severely than white sergeants do. If there is any racial favoritism in superior-subordinate relations, it is certainly not black favoring black. African-American sergeants have gone a long way to assuage white feelings of reverse discrimination. This cannot be over-emphasized as the military is the only place in America where whites are routinely bossed around by blacks.

Above the ranks of non-commissioned officers in the Army is the officer corps, where 7,000 blacks serve. Twenty-six blacks hold flag rank, 6 percent of all Army generals. And of course Colin L. Powell, chairman of the Joint Chiefs of Staff, is the first black to head the American military. In terms of black participation and achieve-ment, the Army still has a way to go, but few civilian institutions approach it.

The senior Army black leadership feels a spe-cial concern for the Army's junior black officers. In 1975 a group of black senior officers founded Rocks, an association named after Brigadier Gen-eral Roscoe O. Cartwright, who was killed in an airplane crash the year before. Cartwright, or "Rock" as he was better known, was an es-teemed role model and mentor for many of the black officers who entered the Army in the 1960s. Rocks is dedicated to mentoring junior black officers and does not view itself as a pres-sure group. Its philosophy, in the words of a black general, is: "We want to tell the younger black officers that there will be plenty of bumps on the road, but you have to get over them so you can remove them later for those behind you."

The point that distinguishes this from black role models in civilian life is that senior Army blacks tend to eschew any social agenda that premises black advancement on racial politics and supplication to benevolent whites. In their bootstrap conservatism and rejection of the ide-ology of victimhood, senior black sergeants and officers differ from an important segment of the black civilian leadership.

How to put these lessons into civilian prac-tice? This question is becoming more urgent with the rapid drawdown of the military now un-der way. The armed forces will shrink from 2.1 million to 1.6 million people by 1996, dispropor-tionately affecting the number of blacks in the Army. A smaller post–cold war military means not only fewer blacks in the military, but also fewer black veterans. Studies of veterans show that military service has a substantial positive ef-fect on earnings and employment for those who are black or Hispanic. Though I have never seen it mentioned by researchers of poverty, the end of conscription may be one of the causes of the growth of a black underclass. By my calculations some 30,000 fewer black males annually will be entering the military during the drawdown than would have entered at the rate of the peacetime draft.

But the drawdown also presents an opportu-nity. Though it may be difficult to replicate mili-tary conditions in the civilian sector, we might draw a moral of what can serve as the functional equivalent of the military. In 1989 Senator Sam Nunn and Representative Dave McCurdy intro-duced legislation crafted by the Democratic Leadership Council to create a voluntary pro-gram of national youth service. Young people who perform a stint of civilian service would re-ceive post-service educational benefits along the lines of the GI Bill for military veterans. This innovative legislation ran against the something-for-nothing philosophy of welfare liberals and the every-man-for-himself attitude of libertarian conservatives. A pilot program of national ser-vice was signed into legislation in November 1990, but its implementation has been held up by the Bush administration, which opposes the establishment of a civilian youth corps.

Any national service program would do well to emulate the military by placing the emphasis on the service performed, rather than on those who perform it. After all, we do not have a mili-tary to help young people mature or to give them jobs—though these are certainly important and desirable consequences. The Army is attractive to many blacks because there are enough blacks in it to promise a certain degree of social comfort and professional support. But even more impor-tant, there are enough non-black and non-poor people to prevent the Army from being thought of as a "black" institution or a haven for society's underclass.

The Army, in short, delivers the uplift but not the stigma of a government social program. Whatever successes the military has had for turning dead-end youth into responsible citizens have been largely due to the discipline of the armed forces being legitimated on other than overt welfare grounds, for example, national defense, patriotism, and citizenship obligation. Those very conditions peculiar to the armed forces that serve to re-socialize poor youth toward productive ends depend directly and ultimately upon the military not being defined as an employer of last resort or as a welfare agency. The same must be true for civilian youth programs.

So what can be transferred? Maybe a broad lesson: race relations can best be transformed by an unambiguous commitment to non-discrimination coupled with uncompromising standards of performance. Added to this, another fact: the military of the 1970s recognized that its race problem was so critical that it was on the verge of self-destruction. That realization set in motion the steps that have led to today's relatively positive state of affairs. As racial division seems to be growing in American society at large, we must come to that same realization.

CHAPTER 10

DRUGS:
LICIT AND ILLICIT

INTRODUCTION

Few issues in twentieth-century America have generated more controversy than determining which drugs should be legal and which illegal. The use of drugs, however potent or mild, is not inherently criminal. At various times during this century, many people have enjoyed such drugs as alcohol, heroin, LSD, and marijuana without any interference by the police. Yet on other occasions, the sale or possession of the same drugs, perceived as an alarming social problem, has created widespread hysteria. Experts in many professional fields have taken an interest in the perplexing questions related to the use and abuse of various drugs. The seven selections in this chapter examine some of these questions.

The first essay, by Mark Isikoff, examines a major drug that devastates millions of lives each year, yet remains the legal drug of choice for a sizable public: alcohol. Isikoff does not recommend prohibition, but he raises serious questions about official moral crusaders who denounce the evils of some drugs and seem to ignore the destructive qualities in others.

The crusade against drugs takes many forms. Susan LaCroix reports on one of the most controversial: criminal prosecution of women who give birth to addicted infants. This strategy attacks the problem of drug abuse as a crime. Does this solution give appropriate consideration to the point of view of physicians or social workers? Is the solution worse than the problem?

Rufus King is a major scholar and critic of the many wars on drugs that have been launched from Washington, D.C., and state capitals during most of this century. In his judgment, these campaigns come and go with the political seasons, but one thing remains constant: they never succeed. Why? During the past decade many critics have joined King in his criticism of the conventional law enforcement strategy for dealing with drugs that are defined as "illicit."

William Bennett presents a frightening picture of the mass addiction that could be expected if anyone could buy hard drugs in the open market at sharply reduced prices. Is it best to protect people against their own inclinations to seek temporary euphoria? Bennett and Wilson and DiIulio are sufficiently frightened by widespread drug use to see the need to pay the costs of surveillance over national borders and local communities. Bennett argues from a strong value position. Wilson and DiIulio are less moralistic and more sensitive to the high costs of current enforcement policy. In the last analysis they are willing to pay the high price of prohibition.

Richard Dennis approaches this issue by asking crucial questions about the cost of the law enforcement approach. Ethan A. Nadelmann also examines issues of cost; but he broadens the debate by looking at the international context in which the United States carries out its drug campaign. Given the global character of the problem, is there any reason to believe the war on drugs can ever be won?

20. THE NATION'S ALCOHOL PROBLEM IS FALLING THROUGH THE CRACK

MARK ISIKOFF

Last summer, amid a barrage of news accounts about crack-dealing gangs spreading through Iowa, Republican Gov. Terry E. Branstad appointed F. H. Mike Forrest, a blunt-talking former Army Reserve officer and retired lawyer, as the state's first "drug czar."

From *The Washington Post National Weekly Edition,* April 9–15, 1990, pp. 30–31. Copyright © 1990, The Washington Post. Reprinted with permission.

But soon after taking office, Forrest says, he discovered that the state's most serious drug problem had nothing to do with crack. And what's more, neither the news media nor anybody else wanted to hear about it.

"The worst problem we face in Iowa, by far, is alcohol abuse," says Forrest. "Yet in the public mind, I'm not certain people see that. . . . Every time I start talking about it, all the television people turn off those cameras. And all those good quotations I give them never get used."

Forrest is not alone in his frustration. While the Bush administration and state governments pour billions of new dollars into fighting illegal drugs, a growing number of public health officials fear that this effort has overshadowed the far more damaging and pervasive problems caused by alcohol abuse.

This is especially true in many midwestern and Rocky Mountain states where officials say the toll from alcohol—measured by highway fatalities, teenage drinking and thousands of babies born with fetal alcohol syndrome—dwarfs the problems created by cocaine and other illegal drugs.

And they charge the Bush administration with exacerbating the imbalance by omitting alcohol from its drug control strategy and directing that new treatment aid to the states be spent exclusively for illegal drug users rather than alcohol abusers.

"It doesn't make any sense," says Jan Smaby, Minnesota's new drug policy director. "Alcohol is the number one abused drug here by a landslide. . . . Particularly in a state like Minnesota, it's just ridiculous to say we're going to talk about illegal drugs—we're not going to talk about alcohol.

But the imbalance is not on the federal level alone. For much of the past year, Iowa's news media and political leaders have been preoccupied with reports of crack cocaine and other illegal drugs sweeping the state.

Police officials have reported crack seizures in remote rural communities, and in Des Moines, where drug arrests jumped 169 percent last year, police are worried about a potential outbreak of drive-by shootings and other violence among rival drug gangs this summer.

But at the same time, many officials say there is little hard evidence that cocaine has penetrated widely into the general population. Consistent with national trends, the last statewide survey of high school students here showed that weekly use of marijuana and other illegal drugs

What Is Abused Where?
Number of Patients Admitted for Treatment in Selected Areas

	Alcohol	Other Drug		Alcohol	Other Drug
Alaska	8,650	1,528	Nevada	9,320	1,613
California	108,000	64,408	New Hampshire	4,087	773
Colorado	50,667	4,032	North Carolina	19,164	4,144
D.C.	5,696	5,173	Oregon	32,578	6,594
Florida	60,551	18,142	Pennsylvania	35,203	32,571
Iowa	18,282	4,713	Puerto Rico	3,341	14,766
Kansas	10,476	3,289	South Carolina	27,512	6,361
Kentucky	14,284	4,730	Texas	10,650	12,290
Maine	16,395	2,760	Utah	11,450	2,240
Maryland	18,127	18,320	Virginia	48,608	12,534
Minnesota	44,155	7,628	West Virginia	10,996	2,024
Montana	8,845	2,135	Wisconsin	72,335	12,501
Nebraska	19,563	2,221	Total U.S.	1,217,285	518,851

Note: Figures are for fiscal 1988. Data for alcohol client admissions in California and Virginia are estimated. Figures for Colorado represent episodes, not admissions. Figures for D.C. are based on provisional year and expenditure reported. For Puerto Rico, alcohol figures include only state agency clientele and drug client admissions data are estimated.

Source: State Alcohol and Drug Abuse Profile, FY 1988. Data are included only for those programs that received funds administered by the state drug agency.

had dropped by more than half between 1978 and 1987, while regular alcohol use (also illegal for teenagers) was on the rise.

Meanwhile, Des Moines school officials say that although they see almost no signs of drug abuse in the public schools, they do see alarming increases in binge drinking, weekend beer parties and other alcohol-related problems. "They are literally drinking until they fall down or throw up," says Barb Madden-Bittle, nurse at 1,400-student Roosevelt High School. "I see a real increase in alcohol—it's really worrisome. . . . But the kids are telling us that it's really okay because it's not marijuana or crack."

"The way people view this problem—it's distorted, it's warped," says Harold Hughes, a former Iowa governor and recovered alcoholic who now runs a private substance-abuse treatment clinic. "People panic when they hear about drugs. . . . But it's alcohol that is killing, maiming and crippling people and filling our jails. . . . It's doing 10 times more damage than all the illegal drugs put together."

Confronted with an increasing number of such complaints, national drug policy director William J. Bennett tells audiences that his mandate from Congress is to be "The drug czar, not the health czar."

At a recent meeting in Omaha, members of the National Commission on Drug Free Schools told Bennett they wanted to begin their upcoming report to President Bush with a powerful warning about the dangers of alcohol abuse among the nation's youth. But Bennett, the commission's co-chairman, warned panel members that they were forgetting their "homework assignment" and risked losing their credibility if they concentrated on alcohol.

"The point is, right now, the American people are eager to get this drug thing behind us," Bennett says. "There are opportunities to talk about alcohol. . . . Why are people changing the subject? . . . There are still some neighborhoods in parts of America where crack is tearing the hell out of places."

In other forums, Bennett has drawn a sharp distinction between alcohol and illegal drug use, which he says "degrades the human character."

"We regard drug use as morally wrong," Bennett said in a recent speech to the conservative-oriented Heritage Foundation. Unlike "90 percent" of alcohol consumption, he said, when illegal drugs are used, "the primary object is to zonk out."

But many public health officials contend that the distinction is not quite so clear-cut and may give rise to cynicism about the anti-drug effort.

The Department of Health and Human Services recently estimated that 15.1 million Americans are suffering from alcoholism or alcohol dependence—more than five times the government's estimated number of regular cocaine or crack users (about 3 million) and more than 30 times the estimated number of heroin addicts (500,000).

A study by the Centers for Disease Control released last month found that alcohol contributed to the deaths of 105,095 people in 1987, including 57,230 deaths from cirrhosis of the liver and other diseases, 20,282 highway fatalities and 8,552 suicides.

Perhaps more significant, given public concern about the links between crack and crime, the CDC study found that 9,107 of the nation's homicides in 1987 were alcohol-related, or about 46 percent of the total. In cities such as the District of Columbia, police have estimated that as many as 60 percent of murders are "drug related," but say that most result from turf wars and other disputes related to distribution rather than crimes spurred by consumption.

These numbers are striking, some public health experts say, because of the dramatic shift in spending for substance abuse prompted by the federal government's drug war.

Under the Bush administration's latest budget proposal, all of the proposed $100 million increase for block-grant funding of state substance-abuse treatment programs must be spent exclusively for illegal drug users.

Yet two-thirds of the 1.7 million Americans seeking treatment from such programs last year reported alcohol as their primary problem, according to a recent national survey by the National Association of State Alcohol and Drug Abuse Directors.

In Iowa, four of five people seeking treatment were admitted for alcohol, while in Nebraska and Colorado, nine of 10 treatment admissions were for alcohol.

Many state officials acknowledge that these figures may be misleading because alcoholics are more likely to openly admit their problems. But at the same time, they say, it is increasingly common to find treatment patients who are "polydrug abusers," addicted to both alcohol and illegal substances.

"The overwhelming majority of people are seeking treatment for alcohol or alcohol in combination with other drugs," says Diane Canova, director of public policy for the alcohol and drug abuse directors group. "For us, to have [an anti-drug] policy that excludes alcohol doesn't mirror reality."

Even the mounting national concern over crack-addicted babies may be out of proportion, some health officials say. In Iowa, local hospitals report that they continue to see far more babies suffering from fetal alcohol syndrome—a set of birth defects that can include low birth weight, a diminished cranium, distorted facial features and slow cognitive and muscle development.

Some doctors and researchers now believe that at least some of the adverse symptoms detected in "crack babies" may actually be the consequence of alcohol use by the mother. Rizwan Shah, who treats many inner city patients [in Des Moines] as medical director of the Family Ecology Center at Iowa Methodist Hospital, says, "For every one cocaine baby, I see five or six with fetal alcohol syndrome."

But sometimes, she says, it is difficult to tell what may have caused the low birth weight or slow motor coordination of a newborn infant. "I have yet to see a cocaine-using mother who had not also used alcohol," she says.

Forrest says that when he read in a recent medical newsletter about the link between fetal alcohol syndrome and mental retardation, it reinforced his determination to "raise consciousness" about the state's alcohol problem. "That got my attention," he says. "There are probably academicians who would say, 'We've known that for years.' But as one member of the general public, I didn't. And I have to assume a lot of other people didn't either."

Nevertheless Forrest acknowledges that his efforts have been largely ignored. Over the past 18 months, the threat of illegal drugs has rocketed into the forefront of public discussion here.

Private polls taken in this year's Senate race show that drugs are "one of the top two" issues on voters' minds, about even with the economy and ahead of abortion and the environment, according to Phil Roeder, spokesman for Democratic Sen. Tom Harkin, who is using the slogan "Drug Free by '93" as part of his reelection campaign. Much of the reason, Roeder says, is that Iowans have watched national television news coverage of drug-related violence in cities such as Washington, D.C., and Los Angeles "and are saying, 'We're not going to let that happen here.'"

Not surprisingly, most of the concern over drugs is centered in Des Moines, the state's largest city with a population of 191,000. Last year, the police department called crack a "growing epidemic" and the City Council passed a resolution declaring fighting drugs the city's top priority.

About the same time, the police began a policy of inviting local television news crews to accompany the narcotics squad as it made drug arrests. "It makes dramatic film—people see officers running into a home with sledgehammers, guns drawn," says police spokesman Thomas Van Baale. "People see that and they get scared." Police say there was legitimate reason to worry. In the city's largest public housing project, the Homes of Oakridge, drug dealers had moved into many apartments and were dealing crack. Many were being supplied by gangs from Los Angeles and Chicago.

Mayor John Dorrian, who recently appointed a panel of business and community leaders to develop an anti-drug strategy, says the drug problem has "touched the lives of everybody" in the city, even his own family. His 26-year-old daughter entered a cocaine treatment program last year after losing her job as medical technician.

But police officials say that visible evidence of crack and other illegal drug use remains largely limited to a 20-block low-income neighborhood just north of the central business district. And although drug arrests more than doubled last year, at least in part because the city hired more narcotics officers, overall crime—including murders, robberies and burglaries—dropped by 10 percent.

"I don't think the drug problem has increased, but our awareness of what's going on has," says Pete Rounds, chief of the police department's narcotics division.

Mark Horstmeyer, public relations director for the Des Moines school system, says the system in recent years has beefed up its drug education programs, but quickly adds: "We don't have a drug problem in the schools. . . . I sometimes think the TV is playing it up a little because they think it's exciting."

Indeed, some students say crack smokers they see on the streets—known here as "geekers"—are mostly in their thirties and are objects of ridicule.

"We all make fun of geekers," says Azim Rashad, a 16-year-old junior at Roosevelt High. "The police are trying to say all of Des Moines is filled with dope. I think they're just trying to get some more money."

21. JAILING MOTHERS FOR DRUG ABUSE

SUSAN LaCROIX

Butte County, California, seems an unlikely place for babies to be born already exposed to cocaine and heroin. The quiet agricultural region three hours' drive northeast of San Francisco is noted for its almonds and olives, not the problems of the inner city, where the estimated rates of drug-exposed newborns have reached as high as 25 percent. But with the hospitals in this county of 175,000 people delivering a growing number of infants with symptoms of drug exposure, Michael Ramsey, the local District Attorney, decided something had to be done.

Last October, after consulting with area hospital administrators, mental health workers and law enforcement officials, Ramsey announced that county hospitals would start screening all newborns exhibiting symptoms of exposure to a controlled substance. Any positive test results might then be used as evidence to prosecute the mothers for illegal drug use—a misdemeanor that, unless the offender enters a drug treatment

From *The Nation*, May 1, 1989, pp. 585–588. Copyright © 1989. The Nation Company, Inc. Reproduced with permission.

Susan LaCroix is an associate at the Center for Investigative Reporting in San Francisco.

program, carries a mandatory sentence of ninety days in jail. The plan, believed to be the first of its kind in the nation, has drawn harsh criticism from attorneys, health care workers and civil rights activists across the country, who question the legality and ethics of inviting criminal-justice authorities into the delivery room. Judith Rosen, a founder of California Advocates for Pregnant Women, offers the following scenario.

A woman has just given birth and in walks someone from the Child Protective Services who wants the mother to be candid about her drug habits so that C.P.S. can help her and the infant. An Assistant District Attorney enters and begins, "You have the right to remain silent. . . ." The mother takes advantage of her constitutional rights and refuses to say anything. She then might be labeled "uncooperative" by social service agencies and would risk having her baby taken away.

Rosen knows this terrain well. In 1986, as a volunteer attorney for the American Civil Liberties Union in San Diego, she criticized the treatment of Pamela Rae Stewart. The 27-year-old mother had been arrested, jailed and prosecuted on a charge of criminally contributing to her baby's death by using illicit drugs and ignoring doctors' advice to stay off her feet and abstain from sexual intercourse during her pregnancy. Rosen argued that it was no crime to disobey a doctor's orders and asked, "Are we, as women, to have perfect babies and be subject to prosecution if we don't?"

The case against Stewart was dismissed in 1987, when San Diego municipal court Judge E. Mac Amos Jr. ruled in a pretrial motion that the District Attorney's office erred in invoking a 1925 child-support law to prosecute her. Although this California statute makes it a crime for a parent willfully to withhold medical care from a child, and specifically includes the fetus in its definition of the word "child," it generally applies to situations in which pregnant women seek support payments from estranged husbands.

Were it not for the Stewart dismissal, Butte County's District Attorney Ramsey might have attempted to apply the same statute to drug users in his jurisdiction. The mothers of the county's drug-exposed infants "certainly appear to be abusing children," Ramsey says. But the courts have not recognized drug abuse by pregnant women as child abuse. So, says the D.A., he devised a "creative way of using the law": prosecuting for illegal drug use rather than for child abuse or "fetal neglect." This way, Butte County would be able to circumvent some of the legal issues raised in the Stewart case, such as whether a woman's basic right to privacy can be sacrificed to the state's interest in the health of her fetus. Also at stake is whether she can be branded a criminal for not following a doctor's orders despite court rulings that patients have the right to refuse medical care.

Such issues lie at the heart of a growing conflict between maternal autonomy and the extent of fetal rights, a conflict involving pregnant women's control over their behavior as well as their medical treatment during pregnancy. The Butte County controversy addresses only one behavior issue—drug use—in what conceivably includes any activity or environmental hazard that may harm the fetus, such as smoking, alcohol consumption and hazards in the workplace. Feminists and civil rights advocates worry that the trend, if unchecked, could lead to the prosecution of pregnant women for even poor eating and exercise habits.

How far will the law go in enforcing a doctor's judgment that conflicts with the mother's wishes? In a survey published in the May 1987 *New England Journal of Medicine,* medical institutions in eighteen states and the District of Columbia reported thirty-six attempts over a five-year period to override through law a pregnant woman's refusal of therapy. In the interest of the fetus, hospitals have sought and obtained court orders for Caesarean sections, intrauterine transfusions and hospital detention of pregnant women against their will. Court orders for Caesareans were granted in all but one of fifteen instances. A Gallup poll commissioned by *Hippocrates* magazine and published last May showed that support for intervention extends beyond the medical community to the general public. Nearly half those surveyed agreed that a woman who smokes cigarettes or drinks alcohol while pregnant—or refuses to have a Caesarean birth as recommended by her doctor—should be held legally liable for any related harm done to the fetus. Such findings are particularly puzzling in light of the general legal trend toward honoring patients' control over medical decisions. Recent court rulings have sharply restricted forced medication of psychiatric patients and have allowed mentally competent adults to refuse drug treatment, surgery and blood transfusions.

While acknowledging that pregnancy complicates the issue, advocates of reproductive freedom argue that forcing women to assume medical risks and forfeit their legal autonomy in a manner not required of men and nonpregnant women treads on the generally accepted privileges of medical patients: The common-law rights to bodily integrity and the constitutional rights of liberty, privacy and religious freedom. The courts have generally interpreted these rights to allow patients to refuse medical treatment when they disagree with a doctor's advice or object on religious grounds, such as in cases where Jehovah's Witnesses refuse blood transfusions. Many rulings, however, have denied pregnant women these rights, even forcing them to undergo major surgery when their religion forbids it.

Ramsey says he simply wants to prevent Butte County's women from harming their unborn children, by controlling their abusive behavior.

He may be unable to change most of their behavior—smoking, drinking and other potentially harmful activities—but targeting illicit drug users is within his power. However, the plan Ramsey calls creative, critics call draconian. "A lot of people are very upset because they think it's punitive and not productive," says Lucy Quacinella, an attorney with Legal Services of Northern California in Butte County. Citing a severe lack of county drug programs and treatment services, she says, "The real issue is that women are not getting the treatment they need before the baby is born." Ramsey counters that the prospect of a jail sentence will work as an incentive for drug-addicted women to enroll in "diversion" programs that allow some such women to avoid incarceration. "People with substance abuse problems do not voluntarily get into these treatment programs," he says. He is confident that, faced with a choice between the drug diversion program or jail, women will choose treatment.

This argument is profoundly misleading, charges Judith Rosen, the advocate for pregnant women. "First of all, it's not up to the D.A. whether or not a woman gets into treatment" through diversion, she says. Only the courts determine eligibility, and the criteria for diversion are so narrow that it's very likely most of the women will be ineligible. Under the California penal code, a woman does not qualify if she has previously been convicted of illegal drug use or of any felony in the past five years, if she has previously been diverted to treatment or if she has ever had probation or parole revoked. Furthermore, a movement in California seeks to repeal the diversion law in hope of sending more drug users to jail. "We don't know that diversion will even be in effect a year from now." Rosen says.

Whether or not the law is repealed, Rosen predicts that most women prosecuted for illegal drug use will end up in jail, and that their babies will flood the state's already overburdened foster care programs. In jail, Rosen warns, "the mother won't get drug treatment, she won't get parenting classes and she won't get off the self-destructive cycle she's on." Meanwhile, the separation of mother and child could destroy what psychologists and social workers agree is a critical bonding period, causing emotional and psychological damage to the infant and feelings of overwhelming guilt and depression in the mother.

Perhaps the most widespread concern, voiced by obstetricians, lawyers and health care workers, is that the threat of drug testing and prosecution will frighten women away from seeking medical aid. The result may be a greater number of what San Francisco deputy city attorney Lori Giorgi calls "toilet-bowl babies"—babies born at home, in toilets and bathtubs and on kitchen floors, without medical attention. "We're seeing more and more of them because their mothers are too scared to go to the hospital," Giorgi says. "They're afraid their babies will be taken away."

Drug use among expectant mothers is a growing problem nationwide. While few studies have been completed on drug-exposed infants, a cross-section sampling of thirty-six U.S. hospitals compiled last summer by the National Association for Perinatal Addiction Research and Education in Chicago revealed that 11 percent of the women in those hospitals had used illegal drugs during pregnancy, including cocaine, marijuana, heroin, amphetamines and PCP. The effects of these drugs on fetuses and newborns include prematurity or stillbirth, prenatal strokes, tremors, deficient motor reflexes and learning disabilities.

As pressure grows to deal with the problem of drug babies, other states are considering punitive measures against substance-abusing pregnant women and new mothers. In Pennsylvania, for example, State Senator Jim Greenwood sponsored legislation last June to amend the civil child abuse law to include penalties for the presence of drugs or symptoms of fetal alcohol syndrome in newborns. Several other states, including Florida, Massachusetts and New Jersey, already have child abuse and neglect statutes designed to protect any infant harmed prenatally by its mother's drug abuse. Related punitive actions have also been taken by the courts. In Washington, D.C., a Superior Court judge last year sentenced a woman convicted of second-degree theft to 180 days in jail—an unusually harsh punishment for a first-time offender—because she was pregnant and tested positive for cocaine.

But such punitive action is not the answer—

in Washington, Butte County or elsewhere. "If these mothers were walking away from treatment, I might feel differently," says Ann O'Reilly, director of family and children's services for the San Francisco Department of Social Services. "But they're not walking away from treatment—they're walking away from waiting lists."

Although Federal spending on drug treatment and prevention has increased substantially in the past several years, public clinics are still financially strapped and not equipped to deal with the crisis. Butte County is one of many in the United States that offers little or no treatment or support services for pregnant drug users. Women in the county addicted to heroin, for example, must travel eighty-five miles for treatment, to a private outpatient clinic in Sacramento, which charges $200 a month for a methadone maintenance program. Without methadone, sudden withdrawal from heroin can be deadly to both mother and baby, but in Butte County the treatment price is

out of reach even for many middle-income women.

What is not out of reach is jail sentences for pregnant drug users—a quick fix that makes it appear that something fundamental is being done about this public-health crisis. Butte County has yet to prosecute a mother under the new plan, but the A.C.L.U. vows to oppose District Attorney Ramsey's actions—in court, if necessary. Meanwhile, other organizations, including the American College of Obstetricians and Gynecologists, are speaking out against the trend toward forced medical treatment of pregnant women. But the U.S. Supreme Court is soon to hear arguments in *Webster v. Reproductive Health Services*, and if that leads to a reversal of *Roe v. Wade*, pregnant women's autonomy will be drastically altered. An adverse ruling would not only affect abortion but would open the door for just the kind of intervention Ramsey and others seek in their misguided attempt to protect the unborn from drugs.

---

22. A WORTHLESS CRUSADE

RUFUS KING

Drug-law reformers missed a fine opportunity last fall when President Bush and drug czar Bennett launched their Great War on Drugs—and then beat a hasty retreat. That retreat would come rapidly is hardly a surprise. We have been unsuccessfully fighting the "war" that Bush chose to redeclare for seven decades. Now, however, Mr. Bennett has rekindled the controversy, calling his critics morally scandalous intellectuals who propose "pseudo-solutions" and speak

---

From *Newsweek*, January 1, 1989. Reproduced with permission from the author.

Rufus King, a Washington lawyer, served several congressional investigations and has written extensively on drug-law reform.

with "ignorant sneers." Such attacks are not usually made from strength.

Let me start with some numbers Mr. Bennett doesn't often use. The National Institute on Drug Abuse reports that the official 1988 toll of drug-caused deaths in 27 U.S. cities, the best available measure of the nation's "drug problem," was, for cocaine products, 3,308, for heroin and morphine, 2,480, and, of course, for marijuana zero. "Emergency-room mentions" in the same cities totaled only 62,141. For comparison, smoking killed 390,000 last year and alcohol killed at least 100,000. Alcohol is responsible for more fetal damage than crack and remains *the* major menace on our highways.

The last Reagan drug-war budget was $3.4 billion. President Bush's initial request was nearly $6 billion, which he raised to $7.9 billion in his Sept. 5 speech. His strategy called for roughly these proportions: 75 percent for "interdiction" and enforcement; 15 percent for education and prevention, and 10 percent for treatment.

Could anyone be serious about interdicting drug supplies when the plants that produce drugs grow almost anywhere? More than 50 years ago U.S. Narcotics Commissioner Harry Anslinger told Congress that the armed forces and the FBI together couldn't stop the smuggling of illegal drugs across our enormous land and sea borders, and that is still obviously true. And our efforts to stop the growing of drug crops in other countries are an embarrassing tale.

When President Nixon and Attorney General Mitchell came to Washington in 1969 on their law-and-order platform, they faced a problem: law enforcement on the nation's streets is not a federal responsibility. Despite all their purple rhetoric they couldn't *do* much. So they began pumping up the drug menace. But they found that even there the limelight had to be shared with Congress on the domestic front, so they launched interdiction abroad, which they could coordinate with their exclusive control over U.S. foreign policy. Remember Operation Intercept, which virtually closed the Mexican border for a disastrous three weeks? And the pressure the Nixon administration put on Turkey, a minor producer of opium, which nearly drove Turkey out of NATO?

Get-tough enforcement measures, such as "shock incarceration" for users and talk of the headman's ax for pushers, have all been tried before. The long sentences and mandatory minimums of the 1950s choked the courts, strained and disrupted prisons and drove black-market prices higher, with all the attendant corruption and disrespect for law. The latest assault on personal freedom is compulsory testing for nearly everyone, so we can all be kept "drug free."

Drug education and "prevention" are also old stuff, often nothing but sheltered employment for bureaucrats and freeloaders. Generations of education about the dangers of alcohol (in my grade school they used to show us how whisky could cook an egg) have had little effect. Cigarette use is declining not from preventive warnings on packages but through changes in cultural values in the population.

If treatment means honest counseling by a professional in a white coat for those who seek it, and medical relief when addicts require it, treatment programs can indeed help. But that isn't the focus. "Treatment" has often been a euphemism for imprisonment without the protections of the criminal-law system. Today it's "boot camps."

Like smokers and alcoholics, most users of illegal drugs poison themselves because they *want* to be intoxicated. No human force—apart from drug-free imprisonment—and there aren't many U.S. prisons where inmates can't get drugs—can do them much good until they want help. Many eventually "age out"—simply come to a point where they have had enough. But many more drug users, reportedly up to 40 percent in some places, who *are* ready to quit are turned away by long waiting lists and sent back to the street.

Members of Congress and state lawmakers are still trampling one another to outdo the president in lavish outlays and tough posturing. But three weeks after the president's TV performance (he even used a faked exhibit, remember?), the White House began its retreat. Mr. Bennett's deputies were quoted predicting there would be no "overnight success," that the administration's goals were "only guesses" and that the program was almost like "pin the tail on the donkey." And for pure cynical politics, this from a senior White House official: "We have an out (for failure): this was not under the control of the national government."

We reformers are on a roll. Some of the drug-policy rascals may soon be turned out, unless Mr. Bennett comes up with better arguments. It took the nation only 13 years to recognize that Prohibition had been a disastrous mistake. Isn't it about time, after all these decades of folly and failure, that we open our eyes to the realities of this mistake too? Let's hear it for legalization!

23.   SHOULD DRUGS BE LEGALIZED?

WILLIAM BENNETT

Since I took command of the war on drugs, I have learned from former Secretary of State George Shultz that our concept of fighting drugs is "flawed." The only thing to do, he says, is to "make it possible for addicts to buy drugs at some regulated place." Conservative commentator William F. Buckley, Jr., suggests I should be "fatalistic" about the flood of cocaine from South America and simply "let it in." Syndicated columnist Mike Royko contends it would be easier to sweep junkies out of the gutters "than to fight a hopeless war" against the narcotics that send them there. Labeling our efforts "bankrupt," federal judge Robert W. Sweet opts for legalization, saying, "If our society can learn to stop using butter, it should be able to cut down on cocaine."

Flawed, fatalistic, hopeless, bankrupt! I never realized surrender was so fashionable until I assumed this post.

Though most Americans are overwhelmingly determined to go toe-to-toe with the foreign drug lords and neighborhood pushers, a small minority believe that enforcing drug laws imposes greater costs on society than do drugs themselves. Like addicts seeking immediate euphoria, the legalizers want peace at any price even though it means the inevitable proliferation of a practice that degrades, impoverishes and kills.

I am acutely aware of the burdens drug enforcement places upon us. It consumes economic resources we would like to use elsewhere. It is sometimes frustrating, thankless and often dangerous. But the consequences of not enforcing drug laws would be far more costly. Those consequences involve the intrinsically destructive nature of drugs and the toll they exact from our society in hundreds of thousands of lost and broken lives . . . human potential never realized . . . time stolen from families and jobs . . . precious spiritual and economic resources squandered.

That is precisely why virtually every civilized society has found it necessary to exert some form of control over mind-altering substances and why this war is so important. Americans feel up to their hips in drugs now. They would be up to their necks under legalization.

Even limited experiments in drug legalization have shown that when drugs are more widely available, addiction skyrockets. In 1975 Italy liberalized its drug law and now has one of the highest heroin-related death rates in Western Europe. In Alaska, where marijuana was decriminalized in 1975, the easy atmosphere has increased usage of the drug, particularly among children. Nor does it stop there. Some Alaskan schoolchildren now tout "coca puffs," marijuana cigarettes laced with cocaine.

Many legalizers concede that drug legalization might increase use, but they shrug off the matter. "It may well be that there would be more addicts, and I would regret that result," says Nobel laureate economist Milton Friedman. The late Harvard Medical School psychiatry professor Norman Zinberg, a longtime proponent of "responsible" drug use, admitted that "use of now illicit drugs would certainly increase. Also, casualties probably would increase."

In fact, Dr. Herbert D. Kleber of Yale University, my deputy in charge of demand reduction, predicts legalization might cause "a five-to-six-fold increase" in cocaine use. But legalizers regard this as a necessary price for the "benefits" of legalization. What benefits?

1. Legalization will take the profit out of drugs. The result supposedly will be the end of criminal drug pushers and the big foreign drug wholesalers, who will turn to other enterprises because nobody will need to make furtive and dangerous trips to his local pusher.

But what, exactly, would the brave new world of legalized drugs look like? Buckley stresses

From *Reader's Digest*, March 1990, pp. 90–94. Reprinted with permission. © 1990 by The Reader's Digest Assn., Inc.

that "adults get to buy the stuff at carefully regulated stores." (Would you want one in your neighborhood?) Others, like Friedman, suggest we sell the drugs at "ordinary retail outlets."

Former City University of New York sociologist Georgette Bennett assures us that "brand-name competition will be prohibited" and that strict quality control and proper labeling will be overseen by the Food and Drug Administration. In a touching egalitarian note, she adds that "free drugs will be provided at government clinics" for addicts too poor to buy them.

Almost all the legalizers point out that the price of drugs will fall, even though the drugs will be heavily taxed. Buckley, for example, argues that somehow federal drugstores will keep the price "low enough to discourage a black market but high enough to accumulate a surplus to be used for drug education."

Supposedly, drug sales will generate huge amounts of revenue, which will then be used to tell the public not to use drugs and to treat those who don't listen.

In reality, this tax would only allow government to *share* the drug profits now garnered by criminals. Legalizers would have to tax drugs heavily in order to pay for drug education and treatment programs. Criminals could undercut the official price and still make huge profits. What alternative would the government have? Cut the price until it was within the lunch-money budget of the average sixth-grade student?

2. Legalization will eliminate the black market. Wrong. And not just because the regulated prices could be undercut. Many legalizers admit that drugs such as crack or PCP are simply too dangerous to allow the shelter of the law. Thus criminals will provide what the government will not. "As long as drugs that people very much want remain illegal, a black market will exist," says legalization advocate David Boaz of the libertarian Cato Institute.

Look at crack. In powdered form, cocaine was an expensive indulgence. But street chemists found that a better and far less expensive—and far more dangerous—high could be achieved by mixing cocaine with baking soda and heating it. Crack was born, and "cheap" coke invaded low-income communities with furious speed.

An ounce of powdered cocaine might sell on the street for $1200. That same ounce can produce 370 vials of crack at $10 each. Ten bucks seems like a cheap hit, but crack's intense ten- to 15-minute high is followed by an unbearable depression. The user wants more crack, thus starting a rapid and costly descent into addiction.

If government drugstores do not stock crack, addicts will find it in the clandestine market or simply bake it themselves from their legally purchased cocaine.

Currently crack is being laced with insecticides and animal tranquilizers to heighten its effect. Emergency rooms are now warned to expect victims of "sandwiches" and "moon rocks," life-threatening smokable mixtures of heroin and crack. Unless the government is prepared to sell these deadly variations of dangerous drugs, it will perpetuate a criminal black market by default.

And what about children and teen-agers? They would obviously be barred from drug purchases, just as they are prohibited from buying beer and liquor. But pushers will continue to cater to these young customers with the old, favorite come-ons—a couple of free fixes to get them hooked. And what good will anti-drug education be when these youngsters observe their older brothers and sisters, parents and friends lighting up and shooting up with government permission?

Legalization will give us the worst of both worlds: millions of *new* drug users *and* a thriving criminal black market.

3. Legalization will dramatically reduce crime. "It is the high price of drugs that leads addicts to robbery, murder and other crimes," says Ira Glasser, executive director of the American Civil Liberties Union. A study by the Cato Institute concludes: "Most, if not all, 'drug-related murders' are the result of drug prohibition."

But researchers tell us that many drug-related felonies are committed by people involved in crime *before* they started taking drugs. The drugs, so routinely available in criminal circles, make the criminals more violent and unpredictable.

Certainly there are some kill-for-a-fix crimes, but does any rational person believe that a cut-rate price for drugs at a government outlet will stop such psychopathic behavior? The fact is that under the influence of drugs, normal people do not act normally, and abnormal people behave in chilling and horrible ways. DEA agents told me about a teen-age addict in Manhattan who was smoking crack when he sexually abused and caused permanent internal injuries to his one-month-old daughter.

Children are among the most frequent victims of violent, drug-related crimes that have nothing to do with the cost of acquiring the drugs. In Philadelphia in 1987 more than half the child-abuse fatalities involved at least one parent who was a heavy drug user. Seventy-three percent of the child-abuse deaths in New York City in 1987 involved parental drug use.

In my travels to the ramparts of the drug war, I have seen nothing to support the legalizers' argument that lower drug prices would reduce crime. Virtually everywhere I have gone, police and DEA agents have told me that crime rates are highest where crack is cheapest.

4. Drug use should be legal since users only harm themselves. Those who believe this should stand beside the medical examiner as he counts the 36 bullet wounds in the shattered corpse of a three-year-old who happened to get in the way of his mother's drug-crazed boyfriend. They should visit the babies abandoned by cocaine-addicted mothers—infants who already carry the ravages of addiction in their own tiny bodies. They should console the devastated relatives of the nun who worked in a homeless shelter and was stabbed to death by a crack addict enraged that she would not stake him to a fix.

Do drug addicts only harm themselves? Here is a former cocaine addict describing the compulsion that quickly draws even the most "responsible" user into irresponsible behavior: "Everything is about getting high, and any means necessary to get there becomes rational. If it means stealing something from somebody close to you, lying to your family, borrowing money from people you know you can't pay back, writing checks you know you can't cover, you do all those things—things that are totally

against everything you have ever believed in."

Society pays for this behavior, and not just in bigger insurance premiums, losses from accidents and poor job performance. We pay in the loss of a priceless social currency as families are destroyed, trust between friends is betrayed and promising careers are never fulfilled. I cannot imagine sanctioning behavior that would increase that toll.

I find no merit in the legalizers' case. The simple fact is that drug use is wrong. And the moral argument, in the end, is the most compelling argument. A citizen in a drug-induced haze, whether on his back-yard deck or on a mattress in a ghetto crack house, is not what the founding fathers meant by the "pursuit of happiness." Despite the legalizers' argument that drug use is a matter of "personal freedom," our nation's notion of liberty is rooted in the ideal of a self-reliant citizenry. Helpless wrecks in treatment centers, men chained by their noses to cocaine—these people are slaves.

Imagine if, in the darkest days of 1940, Winston Churchill had rallied the West by saying, "This war looks hopeless, and besides, it will cost too much. Hitler can't be *that* bad. Let's surrender and see what happens." That is essentially what we hear from the legalizers.

This war can be won. I am heartened by indications that education and public revulsion are having an effect on drug use. The National Institute on Drug Abuse's latest survey of current users shows a 37-percent decrease in drug consumption since 1985. Cocaine is down 50 percent; marijuana use among young people is at its lowest rate since 1972. In my travels I've been encouraged by signs that Americans are fighting back.

I am under no illusion that such developments, however hopeful, mean the war is over. We need to involve more citizens in the fight, increase pressure on drug criminals and build on anti-drug programs that have proved to work. This will not be easy. But the moral and social costs of surrender are simply too great to contemplate.

24. THE ECONOMICS OF LEGALIZING DRUGS

RICHARD J. DENNIS

Last year federal agents in southern California broke the six-dollar lock on a warehouse and discovered twenty tons of cocaine. The raid was reported to be the largest seizure of illegal narcotics ever. Politicians and law-enforcement officials heralded it as proof not only of the severity of our drug problem but also of the success of our interdiction efforts, and the need for more of the same. However, in reality the California raid was evidence of nothing but the futility and irrationality of our current approach to illegal drugs. It is questionable whether the raid prevented a single person from buying cocaine. Addicts were not driven to seek treatment. No drug lord or street dealer was put out of business. The event had no perceptible impact on the public's attitude toward drug use. People who wanted cocaine still wanted it—and got it.

If the raid had any effect at all, it was perverse. The street price of cocaine in southern California probably rose temporarily, further enriching the criminal network now terrorizing the nation's inner cities. William Bennett, the director of national drug-control policy, and his fellow moral authoritarians were offered another opportunity to alarm an already overwrought public with a fresh gust of rhetoric. New support was given to a Bush Administration plan that is meant to reduce supply but in fact guarantees more money to foreign drug lords, who will soon become the richest private individuals in history.

Indeed, Americans have grown so hysterical about the drug problem that few public figures dare appear soft on drugs or say anything dispassionate about the situation. In a 1989 poll 54 percent of Americans cited drugs as the nation's greatest threat. Four percent named unemployment. It is time, long past time, to take a

clear-eyed look at illegal drugs and ask what government and law enforcement can really be expected to do.

Drug illegality has the same effect as a regressive tax: its chief aim is to save relatively wealthy potential users of drugs like marijuana and cocaine from self-destruction, at tremendous cost to the residents of inner cities. For this reason alone, people interested in policies that help America's poor should embrace drug legalization. It would dethrone drug dealers in the ghettos and release inner-city residents from their status as hostages.

Once the drug war is considered in rational terms, the solution becomes obvious: declare peace. Legalize the stuff. Tax it and regulate its distribution, as liquor is now taxed and regulated. Educate those who will listen. Help those who need help.

Arguments for the benefits of drug legalization have appeared frequently in the press, most of them making the point that crime and other social hazards might be reduced as a result. This article presents an economic analysis of the benefits of legalizing drugs.

SOME WRONG WAYS TO DISCUSS THE DRUG PROBLEM

In order to make any sort of sane argument about drugs, of course, we have to decide what the problem is. That isn't as simple as it might seem, Bennett's thirty-second sound bites notwithstanding. It's easier to say what the drug problem is not.

The drug problem is not a moral issue. There's a streak of puritanism in the national soul, true, but most Americans are not morally opposed to substances that alter one's mind and mood. That issue was resolved in 1933, with the repeal of Prohibition. There is no question that drugs used to excess are harmful; so is alcohol. Americans seem to have no moral difficulty with the notion that adults should be allowed to use alcohol as they see fit, as long as others are not harmed.

The drug problem is not the country's most important health issue. The use of heroin and cocaine can result in addiction and death; so can the use of alcohol and tobacco. In fact, some researchers estimate the yearly per capita mortality rate of tobacco among smokers at more than a hundred times that of cocaine among cocaine users. If the drug-policy director is worried about the effect on public health of substance abuse, he should spend most of his time talking about cigarettes and whiskey.

The drug problem is not entirely a societal issue—at least not in the sense that it is portrayed as one by politicians and the media. Drug dealing is a chance for people without legitimate opportunity. The problem of the underclass will never be solved by attacking it with force of arms.

So what is the problem? The heart of it is money. What most Americans want is less crime and less profit for inner-city thugs and Colombian drug lords. Less self-destruction by drug users would be nice, but what people increasingly demand is an end to the foreign and domestic terrorism—financed by vast amounts of our own money—associated with the illegal drug trade.

This, as it happens, is a problem that can be solved in quick and pragmatic fashion, by legalizing the sale of most drugs to adults. Virtually overnight crime and corruption would be reduced. The drug cartels would be shattered. Public resources could be diverted to meaningful education and treatment programs.

The alternative—driving up drug prices and increasing public costs with an accelerated drug war—inevitably will fail to solve anything. Instead of making holy war on the drug barons, the President's plan subsidizes them.

Laws protecting children should obviously be retained. Some might question the effectiveness of combining legal drug use by adults with harsh penalties for the sale of drugs to minors. But effective statutory-rape laws demonstrate that society can maintain a distinction between the behavior of adults and that of minors when it truly believes such a distinction is warranted.

Legalization would require us to make some critical distinctions among drugs and drug users, of course. The Administration's plan approaches the drug problem as a seamless whole. But in fact crack and heroin are harmful in ways that marijuana is not. This failure to distinguish among different drugs and their consequences serves only to discredit the anti-drug effort, especially among young people. It also disperses law-enforcement efforts, rendering them hopelessly ineffective. Instead of investing immense resources in a vain attempt to control the behavior of adults, we should put our money where the crisis is. Why spend anything to prosecute marijuana users in a college dormitory when the focus should be on the crack pusher in the Bronx schoolyard?

The appropriate standard in deciding if a drug should be made legal for adults ought to be whether it is more likely than alcohol to cause harm to an innocent party. If not, banning it cannot be justified while alcohol remains legal. For example, a sensible legalization plan would allow users of marijuana to buy it legally. Small dealers could sell it legally but would be regulated, as beer dealers are now in states where beer is sold in grocery stores. Their suppliers would be licensed and regulated. Selling marijuana to minors would be criminal.

Users of cocaine should be able to buy it through centers akin to state liquor stores. It is critical to remove the black-market profit from cocaine in order to destabilize organized crime and impoverish pushers. Selling cocaine to minors would be criminal, as it is now, but infractions could be better policed if effort were concentrated on them. Any black market that might remain would be in sales of crack or sales to minors, transactions that are now estimated to account for 20 percent of drug sales.

Cocaine runs the spectrum from coca leaf to powder to smokable crack; it's the way people take it that makes the difference. Crack's effects on individual behavior and its addictive potential place it in a category apart from other forms of cocaine. The actual degree of harm it does to those who use it is still to be discovered, but for the sake of argument let's assume that it presents a clear danger to people who come in contact with the users. A crack user, therefore, should be subject to a civil fine, and mandatory treatment after multiple violations. Small dealers should have their supplies seized and be subject to moderate punishment for repeat offenses. Major dealers, however, should be subject to the kinds of sentences that are now given. And any adult convicted of selling crack to children should face the harshest prison sentence our criminal-justice system can mete out.

The same rules should apply to any drug that presents a substantial threat to others.

A serious objection to legalizing cocaine while crack remains illegal is that cocaine could be bought, turned into crack, and sold. But those who now buy powder cocaine could take it home and make it into crack, and very few do so. Moreover, legal cocaine would most likely be consumed in different settings and under different circumstances than still-illegal crack would be. Researchers believe that more-benign settings reduce the probability of addiction. Legalization could make it less likely that cocaine users will become crack users. In addition, an effective dose of crack is already so cheap that price is not much of a deterrent to those who want to try it. No price reduction as a result of the legalization of cocaine, then, should lead to a significant increase in the number of crack users.

As for heroin, the advent of methadone clinics shows that society has realized that addicts require maintenance. But there is little practical difference between methadone and heroin, and methadone clinics don't get people off methadone. Heroin addicts should receive what they require, so that they don't have to steal to support their habit. This would make heroin unprofitable for its pushers. And providing addicts with access to uninfected needles would help stop the spread of AIDS and help lure them into treatment programs.

WHAT THE DRUG WAR COSTS AND WHAT WE COULD SAVE

The major argument against legalization, and one that deserves to be taken seriously, is a possible increase in drug use and addiction. But it can be shown that if reasonable costs are assigned to all aspects of the drug problem, the benefits of drug peace would be large enough to offset even a doubling in the number of addicts.

Any numerical cost-benefit analysis of drug legalization versus the current drug war rests on assumptions that are difficult to substantiate. The figures for the costs of drug use must be estimates, and so the following analysis is by necessity illustrative rather than definitive. But the numbers used in the analysis below are at least of the right magnitude; most are based on government data. These assumptions, moreover, give the benefit of the doubt to the drug warriors and shortchange proponents of drug legalization.

The statistical assumptions that form the basis of this cost-benefit analysis are as follows:

The social cost of all drug use at all levels can be estimated by assuming that America now has two million illicit-drug addicts. Slightly more than one million addicts use cocaine (including crack) about four times a week; 500,000 addicts use heroin at about the same rate. This means that there are about 1.5 million hardcore addicts. Some experts argue that the figures for addiction should be higher. An estimate of the social cost of drug use should also take into account casual use, even if the social cost of it is arguable; 10 million people, at most, use cocaine and other dangerous drugs monthly. To ensure a fair estimate of social cost, let's assume that America now has two million drug addicts.

Legalization would result in an immediate and permanent 25 percent increase in the number of addicts and the costs associated with them. This projection is derived by estimating the number of people who would try hard drugs if they were legalized and then estimating how many of them would end up addicted. In past years—during a time when marijuana was more or less decriminalized—approximately 60 million Americans tried marijuana and almost 30 million tried cocaine, America's most popular hard drug. (It is fair to assume that nearly all of those who tried cocaine also tried marijuana and that those who haven't tried marijuana in the past twenty-five years will not decide to try decriminalized cocaine.) This leaves 30 million people who have tried marijuana but not cocaine, and who might be at risk to try legal, inexpensive cocaine.

In a 1985 survey of people who voluntarily stopped using cocaine, 21 percent claimed they did so because they feared for their health, 12 percent because they were pressured by friends and family, and 12 percent because the drug was too expensive. The reasons of the other half of those surveyed were unspecified, but for the purpose of this exercise we will assume that they stopped for the same reasons in the same proportions as the other respondents. (Interestingly, the survey did not mention users who said they had stopped because cocaine is illegal or out of fear of law enforcement.) It seems reasonable to assume that many people would decide not to use legalized drugs for the same reasons that these experimenters quit. Therefore, of the 30 million people estimated to be at risk of trying legal cocaine, only about a quarter might actually try it—the quarter that is price-sensitive, because the price of cocaine, once the drug was legalized, would plummet. This leaves us with approximately 7.5 million new cocaine users. How many of them could we expect to become cocaine addicts? The estimate that there are now one million cocaine addicts suggests a one-in-thirty chance of addiction through experimentation. Thus from the 7.5 million new users we could expect about 250,000 new addicts, or an increase of 25 percent over the number of cocaine addicts that we now have. We can assume about the same increase in the number of users of other hard drugs.

Those who argue that wide availability must mean significantly higher usage overlook the fact that there is no economic incentive for dealers to push dirt-cheap drugs. Legalization might thus lead to less rather than more drug use, particularly by children and teenagers. Also, the public evinces little interest in trying legalized drugs. Last year, at the direction of this author, the polling firm Targeting Systems Inc., in Arlington, Virginia, asked a nationwide sample of 600 adults, "If cocaine were legalized, would you personally consider purchasing it or not?" Only one percent said they would.

The drug war will result in a 25 percent decrease in drug use. That's the midpoint in William Bennett's ten-year plan to cut drug use by 50 percent by the year 2000. Since this figure is based on Bennett's official prediction, we might expect it to be highly optimistic. But to demonstrate the enormous benefits of legalization, let's accept his rosy scenario.

The drug war will cost government at all levels $30 billion a year. Keeping drugs illegal costs state and local law-enforcement agencies approximately $10 billion a year—a conservative figure derived from the costs of arresting, prosecuting, and imprisoning several hundred thousand people a year for drug violations. Bennett recently implied before Congress that state governments will need to spend as much as $10 billion in new money when he was asked about what it will cost to keep in prison a higher proportion of the country's 20 million or more users of hard and soft drugs. The drug war will also cost the federal government about $10 billion a year, mostly in law enforcement—about what Congress has agreed to spend in the next fiscal year.

If marijuana and cocaine were legalized and crack and all drugs for children remained illegal, about 80 percent of current illegal drug use would become legal. This would permit savings of 80 percent—or $8 billion—of the current costs of state and local law enforcement. By rolling back the war on drugs, we could save up to all $20 billion of projected new federal and state expenditures.

The current dollar volume of the drug trade is approximately $100 billion a year. If Bennett's prediction is accurate and drug consumption is cut by half over the next ten years, Colombian drug lords will still receive, on average, $3.75 billion a year, assuming that they net five percent of gross receipts—a conservative estimate. The money reaped by drug lords can be used for weapons, planes, and bombs, which could necessitate U.S. expenditures of at least one dollar to combat every dollar of drug profits if a drug war turned into real fighting.

If legalized, taxed drugs were sold for a seventh or an eighth of their current price—a level low enough for illegal dealing to be financially unattractive—the taxes could bring in at least $10 billion at the current level of usage.

The most important—and most loosely defined—variable is the social cost of drug use. The term "social cost" is used indiscriminately. A narrow definition includes only health costs and taxes lost to the government through loss of income, and a broad definition counts other factors, such as the loss of the personal income itself and the value of stolen property associated with drug use. The Alcohol, Drug Abuse, and Mental Health Administration has estimated that drug and alcohol abuse cost the nation as much as $175 billion a year, of which alcohol abuse alone accounts for at least $115 billion. These figures probably include costs not really related to drug use, as a result of the Administration's zeal to dramatize the drug crisis. We will assume that $50 billion a year is a realistic estimate of the share for drug use.

Once these usually qualitative factors have been assigned numbers, it is possible to estimate how much the drug war costs in an average year and how much drug peace might save us. Again, this assumes that 25 percent fewer people in a mid-point year will use drugs owing to a successful drug war and 25 percent more people will use drugs with the establishment of drug peace.

If we choose drug peace as opposed to drug war, we'll save $10 billion a year in federal law enforcement, $10 billion a year in new state and local prosecution, about $8 billion a year in other law-enforcement costs (80 percent of the current $10 billion a year), about $6 billion a year in the value of stolen property associated with drug use (80 percent of the current $7.5 billion), and $3.75 billion a year by eliminating the need to match the Colombians' drug profits dollar for dollar. We'll also benefit from taxes of $12.5 billion. These social gains amount to $50.25 billion.

If use rises 25 percent, instead of declining by that amount, it will result in a social cost of $25 billion (50 percent of $50 billion). Therefore, the net social gain of drug peace is $25.25 billion. If legalization resulted in an immediate and permanent increase in use of more than 25 percent, the benefits of drug peace would narrow. But additional tax revenue would partly make up for

the shrinkage. For example, if the increase in use was 50 percent instead of 25 percent, that would add another $12.5 billion in social costs per year but would contribute another $2.5 billion in tax revenue.

At the rate at which those numbers converge, almost a 100 percent increase in the number of addicts would be required before the net benefits of drug peace equaled zero. This would seem to be a worst-case scenario. But to the drug warriors, any uncertainty is an opportunity to fan the flames of fear. Last year Bennett wrote, in *The Wall Street Journal*, "Of course, no one . . . can say with certainty what would happen in the U.S. if drugs were suddenly to become a readily purchased product. We do know, however, that whenever drugs have been cheaper and more easily obtained, drug use—and addiction—have skyrocketed." Bennett cited two examples to prove his thesis: a fortyfold increase in the number of heroin addicts in Great Britain since the drug began to be legally prescribed there, and a 350 percent increase in alcohol consumption in the United States after Prohibition.

In fact experts are far from certain about the outcome of the British experiment. The statistics on the increase in the number of drug abusers are unreliable. All that is known is that a significant rise in the number of addicts seeking treatment took place. Moreover, according to some estimates, Britain has approximately sixty-two addicts or regular users of heroin per 100,000 population (for a total of 30,000 to 35,000), while the United States has 209 heroin addicts or users per 100,000 population, for a total of 500,000. And very few British heroin addicts engage in serious crime, unlike heroin addicts in America. Bennett's criticism notwithstanding, the British apparently have broken the link between heroin addiction and violent crime.

As for Prohibition, its effects were hardly as dramatic as Bennett implied. During 1916–1919 per capita consumption of pure alcohol among the U.S. drinking-age population was 1.96 gallons a year; during Prohibition it dropped to 0.90 gallons; after Repeal, during 1936–1941, it went up about 70 percent, to 1.54 gallons.

And how does Bennett explain the experience of the Netherlands, where the decriminalization of drugs has resulted in decreased use? Does he think that what made all the difference in Holland is the fact that it has a smaller underclass than we do? In essence, the Dutch policy involves vigorous enforcement against dealers of hard drugs, official tolerance of soft drugs such as marijuana and hashish, and decriminalization of all users. The number of marijuana users began decreasing shortly after the Dutch government decriminalized marijuana, in 1976. In 1984 about four percent of Dutch young people age ten to eighteen reported having smoked marijuana—roughly a third the rate among minors in the United States. In Amsterdam the number of heroin addicts has declined from 9,000 in 1984 to fewer than 6,000 today. Over that same period the average age of addicts has risen from twenty-six to thirty-one, indicating that few new users have taken up the habit. And there is no evidence that crack has made inroads among Dutch addicts, in contrast to its prevalence in America.

Amsterdam is a capital city close in size (population 695,000), if not in culture and economic demographics, to Washington, D.C. (population 604,000). Amsterdam had forty-six homicides last year, of which perhaps 30 percent were related to the drug trade. Washington had 438 homicides, 60 to 80 percent of which were drug-related. The rate of homicides per 100,000 population was 6.6 in Amsterdam, less than a tenth the rate of 72.5 in Washington.

Holland's strategy is one of only two that have been shown to cause a real decline in drug use. The other is Singapore's, which consists of imposing the death penalty on people caught in possession of as little as fifteen grams of heroin. If this is Bennett's fallback position, perhaps he should say so explicitly.

SOME OBJECTIONS CONSIDERED

The fear that legalization would lead to increased drug use and addiction is not, of course, the only basis on which legalization is opposed. We should address other frequently heard objections here.

Crack is our No. 1 drug problem. Legalizing other drugs while crack remains illegal won't solve the problem. Although crack has captured the lion's share of public attention, marijuana has always commanded the bulk of law-enforcement interest. Despite de facto urban decriminalization, more than a third of all drug arrests occur in connection with marijuana—mostly for mere possession. Three fourths of all violations of drug laws relate to marijuana, and two thirds of all people charged with violation of federal marijuana laws are sentenced to prison (state figures are not available).

Crack appears to account for about 10 percent of the total dollar volume of the drug trade, according to National Institute on Drug Abuse estimates of the number of regular crack users. Legalizing other drugs would free up most of the law-enforcement resources currently focused on less dangerous substances and their users. It's true that as long as crack remains illegal, there will be a black market and associated crime. But we would still reap most of the benefits of legalization outlined above.

Legalization would result in a huge loss in productivity and in higher health-care costs. In truth, productivity lost to drugs is minor compared with productivity lost to alcohol and cigarettes, which remain legal. Hundreds of variables affect a person's job performance, ranging from the consumption of whiskey and cigarettes to obesity and family problems. On a purely statistical level it can be demonstrated that marital status affects productivity, yet we do not allow employers to dismiss workers on the basis of that factor.

If legal drug use resulted in higher social costs, the government could levy a tax on the sale of drugs in some rough proportion to the monetary value of those costs—as it does now for alcohol and cigarettes. This wouldn't provide the government with a financial stake in addiction. Rather, the government would be making sure that users of socially costly items paid those social costs. Funds from the tax on decriminalized drugs could be used for anti-drug advertising, which could be made more effective by a total ban on drug advertising. A government that licenses the sale of drugs must actively educate its citizens about their dangers, as Holland does in discouraging young people from using marijuana.

Drug legalization implies approval. One of the glories of American life is that many things that are not condoned by society at large, such as atheism, offensive speech, and heavy-metal music, are legal. The well-publicized death of Len Bias and other harrowing stories have carried the message far and wide that drugs are dangerous. In arguing that legalization would persuade people that drug use is safe, drug warriors underestimate our intelligence.

Any restriction on total legalization would lead to continuing, substantial corruption. Under the plan proposed here, restrictions would continue on the sale of crack and on the sale of all drugs to children. Even if black-market corruption continued in those areas, we would experience an immediate 80 percent reduction in corruption overall.

Legalization is too unpredictable and sweeping an action to be undertaken all at once. It would be better to establish several test areas first, and evaluate the results. The results of such a trial would probably not further the case of either side. If use went up in the test area, it could be argued that this was caused by an influx of people from areas where drugs were still illegal; if use went down, it could be argued that the area chosen was unrepresentative.

Even if current drugs are legalized, much more destructive drugs will be developed in the future. The most destructive current drug is crack, which would remain illegal. Many analysts believe that the development of crack was a marketing strategy, since powder cocaine was too expensive for many users. If cocaine had been legal, crack might never have been marketed. In any case, if a drug presents a clear danger to bystanders, it should not be legal.

No matter how the government distributes drugs, users will continue to seek greater quantities and higher potency on the black market. If the government restricts the amount of a drug that can be distributed legally, legalization will fail. It must make drugs available at all levels of quantity and potency. The government should regulate the distributors but not the product itself. The model should be the distribution of alcohol through state-regulated liquor stores.

Legalizing drugs would ensure that America's inner cities remain places of hopelessness and despair. If drugs disappeared tomorrow from America's ghettos, the ghettos would remain places of hopelessness and despair. But legalization would put most drug dealers out of business and remove the main source of financing for violent gangs. At the least, legalization would spare the inner cities from drug-driven terrorism.

Marijuana in itself may be relatively harmless, but it is a "gateway drug." Legalization would lead its users to more harmful and addictive drugs. While government studies show some correlation between marijuana use and cocaine addiction, they also show that tobacco and alcohol use correlate with drug addiction. Moreover, keeping marijuana illegal forces buyers into an illegal market, where they are likely to be offered other drugs. Finally, 60 million Americans have tried marijuana, and there are one million cocaine addicts. If marijuana is a gateway drug, the gate is narrow.

Legalizing drugs would aggravate the growing problem of "crack babies." The sale of crack would remain illegal. Even so, it is difficult to believe that anyone ignorant or desperate enough to use crack while pregnant would be deterred by a law. Laws against drug use are more likely to deter users from seeking treatment. Crack babies probably would have a better chance in a less censorious environment, in which their mothers had less to fear from seeking treatment.

Drug use in the United States can be seen as a symptom of recent cultural changes that have led to an erosion of traditional values and an inability to replace them. There are those who are willing to pay the price to try to save people from themselves. But there are surely just as many who would pay to preserve a person's right to be wrong. To the pragmatist, the choice is clear: legalization is the best bet.

25.   CRACKDOWN

JAMES Q. WILSON and JOHN J. DiIULIO JR.

According to the projections, crime was supposed to be under control by now. The postwar baby-boom generation, which moved into its crime-prone years during the early 1960s, has grown up, yielding its place to the (proportionately) less numerous baby-bust generation. With relatively fewer 18-year-olds around, we should all be walking safer streets.

And in fact for most people crime *has* gone down. The Census Bureau's victimization surveys tell us that between 1980 and 1987 the burglary rate declined by 27 percent, the robbery rate by 21 percent. Despite what we hear, 3,000 fewer murders were committed in 1987 than in 1980. Even in some big cities that are in the news for the frequency with which their residents kill each other, the homicide rate has decreased. Take Los Angeles: despite freeway shootings and gang warfare, there were 261 fewer murders in 1987 than in 1980, a drop of more than 20 percent.

But in specific enclaves the horror stories are all too true. In south central Los Angeles, in much of Newark, in and around the housing projects of Chicago, in the South Bronx and Bedford-Stuyvesant sections of New York, and in parts of Washington, D.C., conditions are not much better than they are in Beirut on a bad day. Drugs, especially crack, are sold openly on street corners; rival gangs shoot at each other from moving automobiles; automatic weapons are carried by teenagers onto school playgrounds; innocent people hide behind double-locked doors and shuttered windows. In Los Angeles there is at least one gang murder every day, Sundays included. A ten-foot-high concrete wall is being built around the junior high school one of us attended, in order, the principal explained, to keep

stray bullets from hitting children on the playground.

The problem is drugs and the brutal struggles among competing gangs for control of the lucrative drug markets. The drug of choice is crack (except in Washington, where it is PCP). The crack craze has led to conditions far worse than were found in these same neighborhoods a decade or so ago, when heroin was the preferred drug. The reasons for the change are not reassuring.

Crack is a stimulant; heroin is a sedative. Crack produces exceptional euphoria; heroin produces, after a quick "rush," oblivion. Crack (and PCP) addicts are often stimulated to acts of violence and daring that make them dangerous to themselves as well as to others; heroin addicts are rarely violent when high—the drug even depresses the sexual drive.

Crack is marketed by competitive distribution systems, some of whose members are fighting—literally—to establish monopoly control. Heroin (at least on the East Coast) was marketed in a criminal environment dominated by established monopolies that were well equipped, in muscle and in political connections, to protect their market shares with a minimum of random violence.

Crack users have no attractive chemical alternative. The drug is far more rewarding than any substitute. Heroin users who had progressed to the point where they wanted nothing but relief from the pains of withdrawal and the diseases caused by intravenous injection could take oral methadone. The heroin substitute, though addictive, required no injections, prevented withdrawal pains, and (in the correct dosages) produced little or no "high."

In short, certain neighborhoods of our larger cities are being ravaged by a drug that consumers find more alluring than heroin, that stimulates rather than sedates its users, that suppliers must use violence to sell, and that therapists are at a loss to manage by chemical means.

From *The New Republic*, July 10, 1989, pp. 21–25. Reprinted with permission.

Attempting to suppress the use of drugs is very costly. Some people therefore conclude that we must eliminate all the costs of law enforcement by repealing the laws that are being enforced. The result would be less crime, fewer and weaker gangs, and an opportunity to address the public health problems in a straightforward manner.

But legalizing drugs would also entail costs. Those costs are hard to measure, in part because they are to a large degree moral and in part because we have so little experience with legalized drugs.

There is an obvious moral reason for attempting to discourage drug use: the heavy consumption of certain drugs ravages human character. These drugs—principally heroin, cocaine, and crack—are for many people powerfully reinforcing. The pleasure or oblivion they produce leads many users to devote their lives to seeking pleasure or oblivion, and to do so regardless of the cost in ordinary human virtues, such as temperance, duty, and sympathy. The dignity, autonomy, and productivity of users is at best impaired, at worst destroyed.

Some people think society has no obligation to form and sustain the character of individuals. Libertarians would leave all adults free to choose their own habits and seek their own destiny so long as their behavior did not cause any direct harm to others. But most people, however willing they may be to tolerate human eccentricities and support civil liberties, act as if they believe that government, as the agent for society, is responsible for helping to instill certain qualities in the citizenry. This was the original reason for mandatory schooling. We not only want to train children to be useful, we want to train them to be decent. It is also the reason that virtually every nation that has been confronted by a sharp increase in addiction to any psychoactive substance, including alcohol, has enacted laws designed to regulate or suppress its use.

Great Britain once allowed physicians to prescribe opiates for addicts. The system worked reasonably well so long as the addicts were middle-class people who had become hooked as a consequence of receiving pain-killers in hospitals. But when thrill-seeking youth discovered heroin, the number of addicts increased *40-fold*,

and so Britain ended the prescription system. It was replaced at first with a system of controlled dispensation from government clinics, and then with a system of substituting methadone for heroin coupled with the stringent enforcement of the laws against the latter.

Even if we were to decide that the government had no responsibility for character formation and should regulate only behavior that hurts other people, we would still have to figure out what to do about drug-dependent people—because such a dependency does hurt other people. A heroin addict dreamily enjoying his euphoria, a crack smoker looking for the next high, a cocaine snorter eager for relief from his depression—these users are not likely to be healthy people, productive workers, good parents, reliable neighbors, attentive students, or safe drivers. Moreover, some people are harmed by drugs that they have not chosen to use. The babies of drug-dependent women suffer because of their mothers' habits. We all pay for drug abuse in lower productivity, more accidents, higher insurance premiums, bigger welfare costs, and less effective classrooms.

The question is whether the costs of drug use are likely to be higher when the drug is illegal or when it is legal. In both cases society must pay the bill. When the drug is illegal, the cost consists of the law enforcement costs (crime, corruption, extensive and intrusive policing), the welfare costs (poorer health, lost wages, higher unemployment benefits, more aid to families with dependent children, and various treatment and prevention programs), and the moral costs (debased and degraded people). If the drug were legal, the bill would consist primarily of the welfare costs and the moral costs. And there would still be law enforcement costs: the costs of enforcing tax collection if the drugs were sold, or of preventing diversion if the drugs were distributed through the health care system, and the costs in either case of keeping the drugs out of the hands, lungs, and veins of minors. Legalization without some form of regulation is inconceivable; the more stringent the regulation, the higher the law enforcement bill.

Which scenario will be costlier? The answer chiefly depends on how many people will use the drug. We have a rough idea of how many people regularly use heroin and cocaine despite its illegality. How many will regularly use it under the legal scenario?

No one really knows, but it will almost surely be many more than now. The free market price of cocaine is probably no more than five percent of its present black market price. Even allowing for heavy taxes, Stanford's John Kaplan has estimated that the free market price would be no more than 20 percent of what it now costs. The consumption of a widely desired, pleasure-inducing substance without question will increase dramatically if the price is cut by 80 percent to 95 percent.

Moreover, the true price of the drug is the mandatory cost plus the difficulty and inconvenience of the search for it and the risk associated with consuming a product of unknown quality. Though drugs are sold openly on the streets of some communities, for most people—especially for novice, middle-class users—they are hard to come by and often found only in threatening surroundings. Legalization will make the drug more attractive, even if the price actually rises, by reducing the costs of searching for it, negotiating a transaction, and running the risk of ingesting a dangerous substance. The combined effect of lowered market prices and lowered transaction costs will be very great.

Just how great cannot be known without trying it. And one cannot try it experimentally, for there is no way to run a meaningful experiment. The increase in use that would occur if people in one neighborhood or patients at one clinic were allowed to buy the drug at its market cost can give us no reliable information on how many people would use the drug if it were generally available. And the experiment would have irreversible effects. Moreover, as the British experience showed, there is no such thing as "controlled distribution." Inevitably there will be massive leaks of government-supplied drugs into the black market.

We already have the "benefits" of one quasi-experiment. So long as cocaine was available only in its relatively expensive powdered form, its use was pretty much concentrated among more affluent people. But with the invention of crack, which can be sold in single low-priced doses rather than by the high-priced gram, cocaine use increased sharply.

We believe that the moral and welfare costs of heavy drug use are so large that society should continue to enforce the laws against its use for the sake of keeping the number of users as small as possible. But we recognize that by adopting this position, we are placing a heavy burden on those poor communities where drug use is endemic. We are allowing these neighborhoods to be more violent than they would be if the drug were legal. Since we do not live in such communities, we must ask ourselves whether our preferences can be justified to people who do.

The answer to that question is given by the testimony of those who live in the midst of the problem. They want drugs kept illegal. They say so and their representatives in Congress say so. We hope that our libertarian critics will not accuse the people of Watts, Anacostia, and the South Bronx of suffering from false consciousness on this matter. These people know what drug use is and they don't like it.

But if drugs are to be kept illegal, we have a special responsibility to prevent the streets of inner-city neighborhoods from being controlled by those who seek to profit from the trade. We have not done a very good job of this.

In some places there may not be enough police. In others the cops are just badly used, as when the focus is on making a case against "Mr. Big," the local drug kingpin. There are two things wrong with this. First, nothing is easier than replacing Mr. Big; indeed, often the police get evidence on him from tips supplied by his would-be replacement. Meanwhile the distribution of drugs goes on unabated. Second, arresting Mr. Big does nothing to improve the lives of the decent people in the neighborhood who want the drug dealers off the street.

Many cities, notably New York, have recognized this and are concentrating on street-level dealers. The NYPD has wrested control from the drug dealers in parts of the Lower East Side, all of Washington Square Park, much of West 107th Street, and other places. But they have done so at a cost, what Aric Press of *Newsweek* calls the criminal justice equivalent of bulimia. The police go on an arrest binge, and then, "overwhelmed and overfed, the rest of the system—prosecuters, defenders, judges, and jailers—has spent its days in an endless purge, desperately trying to find ways to move its population before it gets hit with another wave tomorrow." The purgatives included granting early release to some inmates and trying to shift other city prisoners to state penitentiaries; pressuring the governor to authorize the appointment of more judges while encouraging faster plea bargaining to clear the crowded dockets; and building "temporary" holding facilities for new arrestees.

The District of Columbia has begun to enter the bulimia phase. The number of people going through the criminal justice system on drug charges has exploded. Between 1983 and 1987 drug arrests increased by 45 percent, drug prosecutions by over 500 percent, drug convictions by over 700 percent. Clearly judges and prosecutors were starting to get tough. But until very recently, the toughness stopped at the jailhouse door. As recently as 1986, only seven percent of the adults arrested on drug charges—and only 20 percent of those convicted on such charges—were sent to the city's principal correctional facility at Lorton. Then, suddenly, the system lurched into overdrive. Between 1986 and 1987 the number of drug incarcerations more than doubled, so that by the end of the year an adult arrested on a drug charge had a one-in-five chance of going to jail, and one convicted on such a charge had a one-in-two chance of winding up at Lorton.

This means that, until very recently, the price of drug dealing in Washington has been quite low. Those who say that "law enforcement has failed" should remember that until the last two years it was barely tried. Police Chief-designate Isaac Fulwood says that the same dealer may be arrested eight or nine times in the space of a few weeks. The city has been operating a revolving-door criminal justice system.

One reason for the speed with which the door revolves is that in Washington, as in most parts of the country, the prisons are jammed full. Another factor is that professional drug dealers know they can get a favorable plea bargain if they threaten to make the system give them a full trial, replete with every conceivable motion. The mere threat

of such a demand is ordinarily enough to ensure that an attractive bargain is offered.

How can an overtaxed system help protect people in the drug-ridden neighborhoods? Building more conventional prisons is part of the answer, but that takes a lot of time, and no one wants them in their back yard. The goal is to take drug dealers off the streets for a longer period than the time it takes to be booked and released. One step is to ensure that no good arrest is washed out for want of prosecution because of a shortage of judges, prosecutors, and public defenders. These are not cheap, but candidates for these posts are more readily available than vacant lots on which to build jails.

Nevertheless, prisons are still needed and can be had, provided we are willing to think of alternatives to conventional holding tanks. One is to reserve regular prison space for major traffickers and to use parts of present (or all of former) military camps as boot camps for lower-level dealers. At these minimum-security camps, inmates would receive physical training, military discipline, and drug-abuse treatment, all under the direction of military personnel and with the aim of preparing them for a life that would combine, to the extent possible, the requirement of regular drug tests and the opportunity for gainful employment.

Meanwhile, the chances of released inmates rejoining old gangs can perhaps be reduced by enforcing a law, such as the one recently passed in California, that makes mere membership in certain gangs illegal and attaches civil or criminal penalties to parents who knowingly allow their children to join them.

Critics of punishment object that (1) incarceration is not a deterrent, either because young drug dealers are not "rational" or because drug trafficking is so lucrative as to make short stays behind a fence worth it; and that (2) the only true solution to the drug problem is to reduce the demand for drugs by education and treatment. We are tempted to respond to these views by pointing out that, insofar as we can tell, each is wrong in whole or in substantial part. Instead, let's assume that these views are entirely correct. They are also irrelevant.

At this stage, we are not trying to deter drug

sales or reduce drug use. All we wish to do is to reassert lawful public control over public spaces. Everything else we may wish to achieve—reducing the demand for drugs, curing the users of drugs, deterring the sale of drugs—can only be done after the public and the police, not the dealers and the gangs, are in charge of the neighborhoods. In the short run, this can be done by repeatedly arresting every suspected dealer and user and sending them through the revolving door. If we cannot increase the severity of the penalties they face, we can at least increase the frequency with which they bear them. In police terms, we want to roust the bad guys.

After the bad guys find they are making repeated trips to the same prison camps, the decent people of the neighborhood must form organizations willing and able to work with the police to keep the bad guys from regaining control of the streets. The Kenilworth-Parkside area of Washington shows what can be done. A few years ago this neighborhood, the site of a public housing project, was an open-air drug market that spawned all manner of crime. In 1982 a tenants' committee led by Kimi Gray formed a corporation and assumed control of the housing project. Though the residents were primarily unwed mothers living on welfare, over the next five years their association collected the rents, ran the buildings, enforced school attendance on the children, and got rid of the addicts. In 1988 the association signed a contract to purchase the project from the government.

A key to the Kenilworth-Parkside group's accomplishment lies in its cooperation with the police. Gray and her colleagues set up neighborhood watch groups, held police-community meetings, and helped the police find and arrest drug dealers and street criminals.

Much is made these days of "community-oriented" policing. Both of us have written favorably about it and the problem-solving, police-neighborhood collaboration that lies at its heart. But the success stories are always in communities in which the people are willing to step forward and the police are willing to meet them halfway. Where open-air drug markets operate every night, where Uzi-toting thugs shoot rival and bystanders alike, it is a brave or foolhardy resident who will even testify against a criminal,

much less lead an anti-crime crusade. But once the police have shown that they can control the streets, even if the dealers they have chased off spend only brief (albeit frequent) periods in prison camp, there is an opportunity to build new partnerships.

The drugs-crime problem ultimately will be solved only when the demand for drugs is dramatically reduced. Though it is necessary to make major investments in overseas crop eradication, the interdiction of international drug shipments, and the control of our borders, there is scarcely an experienced law enforcement officer in the country who does not believe that controlling the sources of supply is much more than a holding operation.

How do we reduce demand? We do not know. Realizing that is the beginning of wisdom. The greatest mischief is to assume that the demand for drugs will decline only when there is less racism and poverty, better schools and more jobs, more religion, and better-quality television.

Recall how the heroin epidemic finally ended. At one time the number of new addicts seemed to be rising exponentially despite the ending of the Turkish supply of illicit opium and the breaking up of the French processing laboratories. Now we have a fairly stable number of confirmed addicts whose ranks seem not to be increasing and may be decreasing. This was accomplished by three things: death, testing, and methadone.

Youngsters who were ready to ignore the lectures of their teachers or the blandishments of public-service television commercials were not so ready to ignore the testimony of their everyday experiences. Heroin addicts were dying from drug overdoses, dirty needles, and personal neglect. Doing heroin no longer seemed as glamorous as it did when one first heard about it from jazz musicians and big-time crooks.

The military began a rigorous program of testing, which continues to this day. There were sanctions attached to being found out—often a delay in being returned home, possibly military punishment, and probably a dishonorable discharge. Drug use in the military dropped dramatically, and has stayed low.

Heroin addicts who were burned out by their long and increasingly unsatisfying bout with the drug often turned to methadone as a way of easing the pain and stabilizing their lives. If they stayed with it, they had a good chance of benefiting from the counseling and training programs made available to them.

These three prevention measures are not likely to be as effective with cocaine and crack addicts. Some users are dying from these drugs, but smoking crack still seems to many users to be far more exciting and much less dangerous than injecting heroin. In time, enough people will ruin their lives so that even the fantastic high that crack produces will begin to seem unattractive to potential users. But that time is not here yet.

Testing works, but only if it is done rigorously and with real consequences, ranging from immediate counseling to discharge or punishment. As yet few civilian institutions seem prepared (or able) to do what the armed forces did. It is hard enough for private employers to test, and they are not subject to the search-and-seizure provisions of the Fourth Amendment. Opposition from employee groups and civil libertarians shows little sign of abating. Some government agencies are testing, but they are doing so gingerly, usually by limiting tests to workers such as prison guards and customs agents, who are in obviously sensitive positions. It is hard to imagine many schools adopting a testing program, though some are trying.

And there is no cocaine equivalent for methadone, though science may yet find one.

That doesn't leave much: some school-based drug-education programs that look promising but have not (as yet) proved their efficacy, and many treatment programs that can have some success—provided the patient is willing to stay in them.

"Willing": that is the key. Heavy drug use is an addiction about which we have, in other contexts, already learned a great deal. Fifty years ago we knew as little about dealing with alcoholism as we now know about cocaine abuse. Today we know enough about alcoholism to realize the key steps to coping with it.

First and foremost: addicts will not get better until they first confront the fact that they are addicts. Alcoholics Anonymous knows this full well, making it the cornerstone of its Twelve Steps. The families of alcoholics are taught they did not cause and can neither control nor cure the addictive behavior—the disease—of the alcoholic. The deaths of others and an inescapable testing program can help provoke among drug users what the destruction of the lives of alcoholics sometimes stimulates—a recognition that they are powerless in the face of the drug and they need the help of others like themselves.

Among the heroin treatment programs that have worked, even without methadone, are those that have involved some aspect of confrontation. Therapeutic communities provide this, but they tend to reach relatively few people. The civil commitment program (technically, Civil Addict Program) in California reached more. It worked this way: an addict (usually arrested by the police) was incarcerated for a brief period, followed by release into the community under instructions to report regularly for a urine test. A parolee with a dirty urine test was reincarcerated on the original charge.

Douglas Anglin and William McGlothlin at UCLA were able to compare the drug use of two similar groups—one that had been sent through the Civil Addict Program and another that had been sent to it but was quickly released from its testing requirements through some legal error made in the commitment proceedings. Those who went through the full program reduced their narcotic use and criminality over a five-year follow-up period at a rate three times greater than the control group.

This raises the possibility that frequent drug testing, backed up by the revocation of parole or of probation for those who fail, may help produce (out of either fear or growing self-awareness) that willingness to confront the fact of addiction that is the prerequisite of successful treatment. Though experts disagree about the role of coercion in treatment programs, an impressive number of studies suggest that cocaine-using arrestees will rarely volunteer for treatment unless they are subject to considerable legal pressure.

Harry Wexler and Douglas Lipton, two experienced drug researchers, have summarized what they have learned about intervening with drug offenders this way: "The criminal justice system must frequently and systematically supervise cocaine-heroin users so that they have less time for crime and drug use." This means urine testing as a condition of probation or parole.

The advocates of treatment and prevention sometimes argue as if these programs can be made to work under wholly voluntary arrangements, provided enough treatment slots are available. Indeed, the helping atmosphere makes treatment seem preferable to the callous toughness of law enforcement strategies. This is sometimes true, but for the majority of addicts it is a serious error, akin to thinking that alcoholics will follow their doctors' advice, if there are enough doctors around. Alcoholics need some measure of coercion; AA supplies it, through the peer pressure generated at regular meetings of other alcoholics. Cocaine users will require even more pressure because coke is far more pleasure-giving than alcohol.

Much of what we have said here will seem pointless to those who still believe that every social problem must be viewed as an indictment of society and its failure to eliminate the "root causes" of its ills. But when it comes to addictive

behaviors, the symptoms are the causes. We do not know why some people try cocaine and then drop it, others try it and abuse it, and still others do not try it at all. We do not know the answers to those questions with respect to alcohol abuse either, and we have been studying that "symptom" pretty seriously for the last half century. What we do know is that addiction is a self-sustaining reaction that spreads as the addictive drug becomes more easily available.

We must begin with the facts, not with theories. The facts are these: some parts of our cities are being destroyed by gangs competing for the right to destroy lives by selling drugs. Those gangs have to be defeated, even if it means hiring more judges and building more correctional facilities. After that we can help communities reorganize themselves so that the good people control the streets and the teachers, doctors, and scientists have a chance to find out what will prevent another addictive epidemic from breaking out when some chemist discovers a drug that is even cheaper and more euphoria-inducing than crack. And that last event, we can be certain, will happen.

26.   THE CASE FOR LEGALIZATION

ETHAN A. NADELMANN

What can be done about the "drug problem"? Despite frequent proclamations of war and dramatic increases in government funding and resources in recent years, there are many indications that the problem is not going away and may even be growing worse. During the past year alone, more than thirty million Americans violated the drug laws on literally billions of occasions. Drug-treatment programs in many cities are turning people away for lack of space and

From *The Public Interest*, Summer 1988, pp. 3–31. Reprinted with permission.

funding. In Washington, D.C., drug-related killings, largely of one drug dealer by another, are held responsible for a doubling in the homicide rate over the past year. In New York and elsewhere, courts and prisons are clogged with a virtually limitless supply of drug-law violators. In large cities and small towns alike, corruption of policemen and other criminal-justice officials by drug traffickers is rampant.

President Reagan and the First Lady are not alone in supporting increasingly repressive and expensive anti-drug measures, and in believing that the war against drugs can be won. Indeed, no "war" proclaimed by an American leader during the past forty years has garnered such sweeping bipartisan support; on this issue, liberals and conservatives are often indistinguishable. The fiercest disputes are not over objectives or even broad strategies, but over turf and tactics. Democratic politicians push for the appointment of a "drug czar" to oversee all drug policy, and blame the Administration for not applying sufficient pressure and sanctions against the foreign drug-producing countries. Republicans try to gain the upper hand by daring Democrats to support more widespread drug testing, increasingly powerful law-enforcement measures, and the death penalty for various drug-related offenses. But on the more fundamental issues of what this war is about, and what strategies are most likely to prove successful in the long run, no real debate—much less vocal dissent—can be heard.

If there were a serious public debate on this issue, far more attention would be given to one policy option that has just begun to be seriously considered, but which may well prove more successful than anything currently being implemented or proposed: legalization. Politicians and public officials remain hesitant even to mention the word, except to dismiss it contemptuously as a capitulation to the drug traffickers. Most Americans perceive drug legalization as an invitation to drug-infested anarchy, Even the civil-liberties groups shy away from this issue, limiting their input primarily to the drug-testing debate. The minority communities in the ghetto, for whom repealing the drug laws would promise the greatest benefits, fail to recognize the costs of our drug-prohibition policies. And the typical middle-class American, who hopes only that his children will not succumb to drug abuse, tends to favor any measures that he believes will make illegal drugs less accessible to them. Yet when one seriously compares the advantages and disadvantages of the legalization strategy with those of current and planned policies, abundant evidence suggests that legalization may well be the optimal strategy for tackling the drug problem.

Interestingly, public support for repealing the drug-prohibition laws has traditionally come primarily from the conservative end of the political spectrum: Milton Friedman, Ernest van den Haag, William F. Buckley, and the editors of the *Economist* have all supported it. Less vocal support comes from many liberals, politicians not among them, who are disturbed by the infringements on individual liberty posed by the drug laws. There is also a significant silent constituency in favor of repeal, found especially among criminal-justice officials, intelligence analysts, military interdictors, and criminal-justice scholars who have spent a considerable amount of time thinking about the problem. More often than not, however, job-security considerations, combined with an awareness that they can do little to change official policies, ensure that their views remain discreet and off the record.

During the spring of 1988, however, legalization suddenly began to be seriously considered as a policy option; the pros and cons of legalization were discussed on the front pages of leading newspapers and news magazines, and were debated on national television programs. Although the argument for legalization was not new, two factors seem to have been primarily responsible for the blitz of media coverage: an intellectual rationale for legalization—the first provided in decades—appeared in my article in the Spring issue of *Foreign Policy* magazine; more importantly, political legitimacy was subsequently bestowed upon the legalization option when Baltimore Mayor Kurt Schmoke, speaking to the National Conference of Mayors, noted the potential benefits of drug legalization and asked that the merits of legalization be debated in congressional hearings.

The idea of legalizing drugs was quickly denounced by most politicians across the political spectrum; nevertheless, the case for legalization appealed to many Americans. The prominent media coverage lent an aura of respectability to arguments that just a month earlier had seemed to be beyond the political pale. Despite the tendency of many journalists to caricature the legalization argument, at long last the issue had been joined. Various politicians, law-enforcement officials, health experts, and scholars came out in favor of drug legalization—or at least wanted to debate the matter seriously, On Capitol Hill, three or four congressmen seconded the call for a debate. According to some congressional staffers, two dozen additional legislators would have wanted to debate the issue, had the question arisen after rather than before the upcoming elections. Unable to oppose a mere hearing on the issue, Congressman Charles Rangel, chairman of the House Select Committee on Narcotics, declared his willingness to convene his committee in Baltimore to consider the legalization option.

There is, of course, no single legalization strategy. At one extreme is the libertarian vision of virtually no government restraints on the production and sale of drugs or any psychoactive substances, except perhaps around the fringes, such as prohibiting sales to children. At the other extreme is total government control over the production and sale of these goods. In between lies a strategy that may prove more successful than anything yet tried in stemming the problems of drug abuse and drug-related violence, corruption, sickness, and suffering. It is one in which government makes most of the substances that are now banned legally available to competent adults, exercises strong regulatory powers over all large-scale production and sale of drugs, makes drug-treatment programs available to all who need them, and offers honest drug-education programs to children. This strategy, it is worth noting, would also result in a net benefit to public treasuries of at least ten billion dollars a year, and perhaps much more.

There are three reasons why it is important to think about legalization scenarios, even though most Americans remain hostile to the idea. First, current drug-control policies have failed, are failing, and will continue to fail, in good part because they are fundamentally flawed. Second, many drug-control efforts are not only failing, but also proving highly costly and counter-productive; indeed, many of the drug-related evils that Americans identify as part and parcel of the "drug problem" are in fact caused by our drug-prohibition policies. Third, there is good reason to believe that repealing many of the drug laws would not lead, as many people fear, to a dramatic rise in drug abuse. In this essay I expand on each of these reasons for considering the legalization option. Government efforts to deal with the drug problem will succeed only if the rhetoric and crusading mentality that now dominate drug policy are replaced by reasoned and logical analysis.

WHY CURRENT DRUG POLICIES FAIL

Most proposals for dealing with the drug problem today reflect a desire to point the finger at those most removed from one's home and area of expertise. New York Mayor Ed Koch, Florida Congressman Larry Smith, and Harlem Congressman Charles Rangel, who recognize government's inability to deal with the drug problem in the cities, are among the most vocal supporters of punishing foreign drug-producing countries and stepping up interdiction efforts. Foreign leaders and U.S. State Department and drug-enforcement officials stationed abroad, on the other hand, who understand all too well why it is impossible to crack down successfully on illicit drug production outside the United States, are the most vigorous advocates of domestic enforcement and demand-reduction efforts within the United States. In between, those agencies charged with drug interdiction, from the Coast Guard and U.S. Customs Services to the U.S. military, know that they will never succeed in capturing more than a small percentage of the illicit drugs being smuggled into the United States. Not surprisingly, they point their fingers in both directions. The solution, they promise, lies in greater source-control efforts abroad and greater demand-reduction efforts at home.

Trying to pass the buck is always understandable. But in each of these cases, the officials are half right and half wrong—half right in recognizing that they can do little to affect their end of the drug problem, given the suppositions and constraints of current drug-control strategies; half wrong (if we assume that their finger-pointing is sincere) in expecting that the solution lies elsewhere. It would be wrong, however, to assume that the public posturing of many officials reflects their real views. Many of them privately acknowledge the futility of all current drug-control strategies, and wonder whether radically different options, such as legalization, might not prove more successful in dealing with the drug problem. The political climate pervading this issue is such, however, that merely to ask that alternatives to current policies be considered is to incur a great political risk.

By most accounts, the dramatic increase in

drug-enforcement efforts over the past few years has had little effect on the illicit drug market in the United States. The mere existence of drug-prohibition laws, combined with a minimal level of law-enforcement resources, is sufficient to maintain the price of illicit drugs at a level significantly higher than it would be if there were no such laws. Drug laws and enforcement also reduce the availability of illicit drugs, most notably in parts of the United States where demand is relatively limited to begin with. Theoretically, increases in drug-enforcement efforts should result in reduced availability, higher prices, and lower purity of illegal drugs. That is, in fact, what has happened to the domestic marijuana market (in at least the first two respects). But in general the illegal drug market has not responded as intended to the substantial increases in federal, state, and local drug-enforcement efforts.

Cocaine has sold for about a hundred dollars a gram at the retail level since the beginning of the 1980s. The average purity of that gram, however, has increased from 12 to 60 percent. Moreover, a growing number of users are turning to "crack," a potent derivative of cocaine that can be smoked; it is widely sold in ghetto neighborhoods now for five to ten dollars per vial. Needless to say, both crack and the 60 percent pure cocaine pose much greater threats to users than did the relatively benign powder available eight years ago. Similarly, the retail price of heroin has remained relatively constant even as the average purity has risen from 3.9 percent in 1983 to 6.1 percent in 1986. Throughout the southwestern part of the United States, a particularly potent form of heroin known as "black tar" has become increasingly prevalent. And in many cities, a powerful synthetic opiate, Dilaudid, is beginning to compete with heroin as the preferred opiate. The growing number of heroin-related hospital emergencies and deaths is directly related to these developments.

All of these trends suggest that drug-enforcement efforts are not succeeding and may even be backfiring. There are numerous indications, for instance, that a growing number of marijuana dealers in both the producer countries and the United States are switching to cocaine dealing, motivated both by the promise of greater profits and by government drug-enforcement efforts

that place a premium on minimizing the bulk of the illicit product (in order to avoid detection). It is possible, of course, that some of these trends would be even more severe in the absence of drug laws and enforcement. At the same time, it is worth observing that the increases in the potency of illegal drugs have coincided with decreases in the potency of legal substances. Motivated in good part by health concerns, cigarette smokers are turning increasingly to lower-tar and -nicotine tobacco products, alcohol drinkers from hard liquor to wine and beer, and even coffee drinkers from regular to decaffeinated coffee. This trend may well have less to do with the nature of the substances than with their legal status. It is quite possible, for instance, that the subculture of illicit-drug use creates a bias or incentive in favor of riskier behavior and more powerful psychoactive effects. If this is the case, legalization might well succeed in reversing today's trend toward more potent drugs and more dangerous methods of consumption.

The most "successful" drug-enforcement operations are those that succeed in identifying and destroying an entire drug-trafficking organization. Such operations can send dozens of people to jail and earn the government millions of dollars in asset forfeitures. Yet these operations have virtually no effect on the availability or price of illegal drugs throughout much of the United States. During the past few years, some urban police departments have devoted significant manpower and financial resources to intensive crackdowns on street-level drug dealing in particular neighborhoods. Code-named Operation Pressure Point, Operation Clean Sweep, and so on, these massive police efforts have led to hundreds, even thousands, of arrests of low-level dealers and drug users, and have helped improve the quality of life in the targeted neighborhoods. In most cases, however, drug dealers have adapted relatively easily by moving their operations to nearby neighborhoods. In the final analysis, the principal accomplishment of most domestic drug-enforcement efforts is not to reduce the supply or availability of illegal drugs, or even to raise their price; it is to punish the drug dealers who are apprehended, and cause minor disruptions in established drug markets.

THE FAILURE OF INTERNATIONAL DRUG CONTROL

Many drug-enforcement officials and urban leaders recognize the futility of domestic drug-enforcement efforts and place their hopes in international control efforts. Yet these too are doomed to fail—for numerous reasons. First, marijuana and opium can be grown almost anywhere, and the coca plant, from which cocaine is derived, is increasingly being cultivated successfully in areas that were once considered inhospitable environments. Wherever drug-eradication efforts succeed, other regions and countries are quick to fill the void; for example, Colombian marijuana growers rapidly expanded production following successful eradication efforts in Mexico during the mid-1970s. Today, Mexican growers are rapidly taking advantage of recent Colombian government successes in eradicating marijuana in the Guajira peninsula. Meanwhile, Jamaicans and Central Americans from Panama to Belize, as well as a growing assortment of Asians and Africans, do what they can to sell their own marijuana in American markets. And within the United States, domestic marijuana production is believed to be a multi-billion-dollar industry, supplying between 15 and 50 percent of the American market.

This push-down/pop-up factor also characterizes the international heroin market. At various points during the past two decades, Turkey, Mexico, Southeast Asia (Burma, Thailand, and Laos), and Southwest Asia (Pakistan, Afghanistan, and Iran) have each served as the principal source of heroin imported into the United States. During the early 1970s, Mexican producers rapidly filled the void created by the Turkish government's successful opium-control measures. Although a successful eradication program during the latter part of the 1970s reduced Mexico's share of the U.S. market from a peak of 87 percent in 1975, it has since retained at least a one-third share in each year. Southwest Asian producers, who had played no role in supplying the American market as late as 1976, were able to supply over half the American market four years later. Today, increasing evidence indicates that drug traffickers are bringing unprecedented quantities of Southeast Asian heroin into the United States.

So far, the push-down/pop-up factor has played little role in the international cocaine market, for the simple reason that no government has yet pushed down in a significant way. Unlike marijuana- and opium-eradication efforts, in which aerial spraying of herbicides plays a prominent role, coca-eradication efforts are still conducted manually. The long anticipated development and approval of an environmentally safe herbicide to destroy coca plants may introduce an unprecedented push-down factor into the market. But even in the absence of such government pressures, coca growing has expanded rapidly during the past decade within Bolivia and Peru, and has expanded outward into Colombia, Brazil, Ecuador, Venezuela, and elsewhere. Moreover, once eradication efforts do begin, coca growers can be expected to adopt many of the same "guerrilla farming" methods adopted by marijuana and opium growers to camouflage and protect their crops from eradication efforts.

Beyond the push-down/pop-up factor, international source-control efforts face a variety of other obstacles. In many countries, governments with limited resources lack the ability to crack down on drug production in the hinterlands and other poorly policed regions. In some countries, ranging from Colombia and Peru to Burma and Thailand, leftist insurgencies are involved in drug production for either financial or political profit, and may play an important role in hampering government drug-control efforts. With respect to all three of the illicit crops, poor peasants with no comparable opportunities to earn as much money growing legitimate produce are prominently involved in the illicit business. In some cases, the illicit crop is part of a traditional, indigenous culture. Even where it is not, peasants typically perceive little or nothing immoral about taking advantage of the opportunity to grow the illicit crops. Indeed, from their perspective their moral obligation is not to protect the foolish American consumer of their produce but to provide for their families' welfare. And even among those who do perceive participation in the illicit drug market as somewhat unethical, the temptations held out by the drug traffickers often prove overwhelming.

No illicit drug is as difficult to keep out of the United States as heroin. The absence of geographical limitations on where it can be cultivated is just one minor obstacle. American heroin users consume an estimated six tons of heroin each year. The sixty tons of opium required to produce that heroin represent just 2–3 percent of the estimated 2–3,000 tons of illicit opium produced during each of the past few years. Even if eradication efforts combined with what often proves to be the opium growers' principal nemesis—bad weather—were to eliminate three-fourths of that production in one year, the U.S. market would still require just 10 percent of the remaining crop. Since U.S. consumers are able and willing to pay more than any others, the chances are good that they would still obtain their heroin. In any event, the prospects for such a radical reduction in illicit opium production are scanty indeed.

As Peter Reuter argues elsewhere, . . . interdiction, like source control, is largely unable to keep illicit drugs out of the United States. Moreover, the past twenty years' experience has demonstrated that even dramatic increases in interdiction and source-control efforts have little or no effect on the price and purity of drugs. The few small successes, such as the destruction of the Turkish-opium "French Connection" in the early 1970s, and the crackdown on Mexican marijuana and heroin in the late 1970s, were exceptions to the rule. The elusive goal of international drug control since then has been to replicate those unusual successes. It is a strategy that is destined to fail, however, as long as millions of Americans continue to demand the illicit substances that foreigners are willing and able to supply.

THE COST OF PROHIBITION

The fact that drug-prohibition laws and policies cannot eradicate or even significantly reduce drug abuse is not necessarily a reason to repeal them. They do, after all, succeed in deterring many people from trying drugs, and they clearly reduce the availability and significantly increase the price of illegal drugs. These accomplishments alone might warrant retaining the drug laws, were it not for the fact that these same laws are also responsible for much of what Americans identify as the "drug problem." Here the analogies to alcohol and tobacco are worth noting.

There is little question that we could reduce the health costs associated with use and abuse of alcohol and tobacco if we were to criminalize their production, sale, and possession. But no one believes that we could eliminate their use and abuse, that we could create an "alcohol-free" or "tobacco-free" country. Nor do most Americans believe that criminalizing the alcohol and tobacco markets would be a good idea. Their opposition stems largely from two beliefs: that adult Americans have the right to choose what substances they will consume and what risks they will take; and that the costs of trying to coerce so many Americans to abstain from those substances would be enormous. It was the strength of these two beliefs that ultimately led to the repeal of Prohibition, and it is partly due to memories of that experience that criminalizing either alcohol or tobacco has little support today.

Consider the potential consequences of criminalizing the production, sale, and possession of all tobacco products. On the positive side, the number of people smoking tobacco would almost certainly decline, as would the health costs associated with tobacco consumption. Although the "forbidden fruit" syndrome would attract some people to cigarette smoking who would not otherwise have smoked, many more would likely be deterred by the criminal sanction, the moral standing of the law, the higher cost and unreliable quality of the illicit tobacco, and the difficulties involved in acquiring it. Nonsmokers would rarely if ever be bothered by the irritating habits of their fellow citizens. The antitobacco laws would discourage some people from ever starting to smoke, and would induce others to quit.

On the negative side, however, millions of Americans, including both tobacco addicts and recreational users, would no doubt defy the law, generating a massive underground market and billions in profits for organized criminals. Although some tobacco farmers would find other work, thousands more would become outlaws and continue to produce their crops covertly. Throughout Latin America, farmers and gangsters would rejoice at the opportunity to earn untold sums of gringo greenbacks, even as U.S. diplomats pressured foreign governments to cooperate with U.S. laws. Within the United States, government helicopters would spray herbicides on illicit tobacco fields; people would be rewarded by the government for informing on their tobacco-growing, -selling, and -smoking neighbors; urine tests would be employed to identify violators of the anti-tobacco laws; and a Tobacco Enforcement Administration (the T.E.A.) would employ undercover agents, informants, and wiretaps to uncover tobacco-law violators. Municipal, state, and federal judicial systems would be clogged with tobacco traffickers and "abusers." "Tobacco-related murders" would increase dramatically as criminal organizations competed with one another for turf and markets. Smoking would become an act of youthful rebellion, and no doubt some users would begin to experiment with more concentrated, potent, and dangerous forms of tobacco. Tobacco-related corruption would infect all levels of government, and respect for the law would decline noticeably. Government expenditures on tobacco-law enforcement would climb rapidly into the billions of dollars, even as budget balancers longingly recalled the almost ten billion dollars per year in tobacco taxes earned by the federal and state governments prior to prohibition. Finally, the State of North Carolina might even secede again from the Union.

This seemingly far-fetched tobacco-prohibition scenario is little more than an extrapolation based on the current situation with respect to marijuana, cocaine, and heroin. In many ways, our predicament resembles what actually happened during Prohibition. Prior to Prohibition, most Americans hoped that alcohol could be effectively banned by passing laws against its production and supply. During the early years of Prohibition, when drinking declined but millions of Americans nonetheless continued to drink, Prohibition's supporters placed their faith in tougher laws and more police and jails. After a few more years, however, increasing numbers of Americans began to realize that laws and policemen were unable to eliminate the smugglers, bootleggers, and illicit producers, as long as tens of millions of Americans continued to want to buy alcohol. At the same time, they saw that more laws and policemen seemed to generate more violence and corruption, more crowded courts and jails, wider disrespect for government and the law, and more power and profits for the gangsters. Repeal of Prohibition came to be seen not as a capitulation to Al Capone and his ilk, but as a means of both putting the bootleggers out of business and eliminating most of the costs associated with the prohibition laws.

Today, Americans are faced with a dilemma similar to that confronted by our forebears sixty years ago. Demand for illicit drugs shows some signs of abating, but no signs of declining significantly. Moreover, there are substantial reasons to doubt that tougher laws and policing have played an important role in reducing consumption. Supply, meanwhile, has not abated at all. Availability of illicit drugs, except for marijuana in some locales, remains high. Prices are dropping, even as potency increases. And the number of drug producers, smugglers, and dealers remains sizable, even as jails and prisons fill to overflowing. As was the case during Prohibition, the principal beneficiaries of current drug policies are the new and old organized-crime gangs. The principal victims, on the other hand, are not the drug dealers, but the tens of millions of Americans who are worse off in one way or another as a consequence of the existence and failure of the drug-prohibition laws.

All public policies create beneficiaries and victims, both intended and unintended. When a public policy results in a disproportionate magnitude of unintended victims, there is good reason to reevaluate the assumptions and design of the policy. In the case of drug-prohibition policies, the intended beneficiaries are those individuals who would become drug abusers but for the existence and enforcement of the drug laws. The intended victims are those who traffic in illicit drugs and suffer the legal consequences. The unintended beneficiaries, conversely, are the drug producers and traffickers who profit handsomely from the illegality of the market, while avoiding arrest by the authorities and the violence perpetrated by other criminals. The unintended victims of drug prohibition policies are rarely recognized as such, however. Viewed narrowly, they are the 30 million Americans who use illegal drugs, thereby risking loss of their jobs, imprisonment, and the damage done to health by ingesting illegally produced drugs; viewed broadly, they are all Americans, who pay the substantial costs of our present ill-considered policies, both as taxpayers and as the potential victims of crime. These unintended victims are generally thought to be victimized by the unintended beneficiaries (i.e., the drug dealers), when in fact it is the drug-prohibition policies themselves that are primarily responsible for their plight.

If law-enforcement efforts could succeed in significantly reducing either the supply of illicit drugs or the demand for them, we would probably have little need to seek alternative drug-control policies. But since those efforts have repeatedly failed to make much of a difference and show little indication of working better in the future, at this point we must focus greater attention on their costs. Unlike the demand and supply of illicit drugs, which have remained relatively indifferent to legislative initiatives, the costs of drug-enforcement measures can be affected—quite dramatically—by legislative measures. What tougher criminal sanctions and more police have failed to accomplish, in terms of reducing drug-related violence, corruption, death, and social decay, may well be better accomplished by legislative repeal of the drug laws, and adoption of less punitive but more effective measures to prevent and treat substance abuse.

COSTS TO THE TAXPAYER

Since 1981, federal expenditures on drug enforcement have more than tripled—from less than one billion dollars a year to about three billion. According to the National Drug Enforcement Policy Board, the annual budgets of the Drug Enforcement Administration (DEA) and the Coast Guard have each risen during the past seven years from about $220 million to roughly $500 million. During the same period, FBI resources devoted to drug enforcement have increased from $8 million a year to over $100 million; U.S. Marshals resources from $26 million to about $80 million; U.S. Attorney resources from $20 million to about $100 million; State Department resources from $35 million to $100 million; U.S. Customs resources from $180 million to over $400 million; and Bureau of Prison resources from $77 million to about $300 million. Expenditures on drug control by the military and

the intelligence agencies are more difficult to calculate, although by all accounts they have increased by at least the same magnitude, and now total hundreds of millions of dollars per year. Even greater are the expenditures at lower levels of government. In a 1987 study for the U.S. Customs Service by Wharton Econometrics, state and local police were estimated to have devoted 18 percent of their total investigative resources, or close to five billion dollars, to drug-enforcement activities in 1986. This represented a 19 percent increase over the previous year's expenditures. All told, 1987 expenditures on all aspects of drug enforcement, from drug eradication in foreign countries to imprisonment of drug users and dealers in the United States, totalled at least ten billion dollars.

Of course, even ten billion dollars a year pales in comparison with expenditures on military defense. Of greater concern than the actual expenditures, however, has been the diversion of limited resources—including the time and energy of judges, prosecutors, and law-enforcement agents, as well as scarce prison space—from the prosecution and punishment of criminal activities that harm far more innocent victims than do violations of the drug laws. Drug-law violators account for approximately 10 percent of the roughly 800,000 inmates in state prisons and local jails, and more than one-third of the 44,000 federal prison inmates. These proportions are expected to increase in coming years, even as total prison populations continue to rise dramatically.[1] Among the 40,000 inmates in New York State prisons, drug-law violations surpassed first-degree robbery in 1987 as the number one cause of incarceration, accounting for 20 percent of the total prison population. The U.S. Sentencing Commission has estimated that, largely as a consequence of the Anti-Drug Abuse Act passed by Congress in 1986, the proportion of federal inmates incarcerated for drug violations will rise from one-third of the 44,000 prisoners sentenced to federal-prison terms today to one-half of the

[1] The total number of state and federal prison inmates in 1975 was under 250,000; in 1980 it was 350,000; and in 1987 it was 575,000. The projected total for 2000 is one million.

100,000 to 150,000 federal prisoners anticipated in fifteen years. The direct costs of building and maintaining enough prisons to house this growing population are rising at an astronomical rate. The opportunity costs, in terms of alternative social expenditures foregone and other types of criminals not imprisoned, are perhaps even greater.[2]

During each of the last few years, police made about 750,000 arrests for violations of the drug laws. Slightly more than three-quarters of these have not been for manufacturing or dealing drugs, but solely for possession of an illicit drug, typically marijuana. (Those arrested, it is worth noting, represent little more than 2 percent of the thirty million Americans estimated to have used an illegal drug during the past year.) On the one hand, this has clogged many urban criminal-justice systems: in New York City, drug-law violations last year accounted for more than 40 percent of all felony indictments—up from 25 percent in 1985; in Washington, D.C., the figure was more than 50 percent. On the other hand, it has distracted criminal-justice officials from concentrating greater resources on violent offenses and property crimes. In many cities, law enforcement has become virtually synonymous with drug enforcement.

Drug laws typically have two effects on the market in illicit drugs. The first is to restrict the general availability and accessibility of illicit drugs, especially in locales where underground drug markets are small and isolated from the community. The second is to increase, often significantly, the price of illicit drugs to consumers. Since the costs of producing most illicit drugs are not much different from the costs of alcohol, tobacco, and coffee, most of the price paid for illicit substances is in effect a value-added tax created by their criminalization, which is enforced and supplemented by the law-enforcement establishment, but collected by the drug traffickers. A

report by Wharton Econometrics for the President's Commission on Organized Crime identified the sale of illicit drugs as the source of more than half of all organized crime revenues in 1986, with the marijuana and heroin business each providing over seven billion dollars, and the cocaine business over thirteen billion. By contrast, revenues from cigarette bootlegging, which persists principally because of differences among states in their cigarette-tax rates, were estimated at 290 million dollars. If the marijuana, cocaine, and heroin markets were legal, state and federal governments would collect billions of dollars annually in tax revenues. Instead, they expend billions on what amounts to a subsidy of organized crime and unorganized criminals.

DRUGS AND CRIME

The drug/crime connection is one that continues to resist coherent analysis, both because cause and effect are so difficult to distinguish and because the role of the drug-prohibition laws in causing and labelling "drug-related crime" is so often ignored. There are four possible connections between drugs and crime, at least three of which would be much diminished if the drug-prohibition laws were repealed. First, producing, selling, buying, and consuming strictly controlled and banned substances is itself a crime that occurs billions of times each year in the United States alone. In the absence of drug-prohibition laws, these activities would obviously cease to be crimes. Selling drugs to children would, of course, continue to be criminal, and other evasions of government regulation of a legal market would continue to be prosecuted; but by and large the drug/crime connection that now accounts for all of the criminal-justice costs noted above would be severed.

Second, many illicit-drug users commit crimes such as robbery and burglary, as well as drug dealing, prostitution, and numbers running, to earn enough money to purchase the relatively high-priced illicit drugs. Unlike the millions of alcoholics who can support their habits for relatively modest amounts, many cocaine and heroin addicts spend hundreds and even thousands of dollars a week. If the drugs to which they are

---

[2] It should be emphasized that the numbers cited do not include the many inmates sentenced for "drug-related" crimes such as acts of violence committed by drug dealers, typically against one another, and robberies committed to earn the money needed to pay for illegal drugs.

addicted were significantly cheaper—which would be the case if they were legalized—the number of crimes committed by drug addicts to pay for their habits would, in all likelihood, decline dramatically. Even if a legal-drug policy included the imposition of relatively high consumption taxes in order to discourage consumption, drug prices would probably still be lower than they are today.

The third drug/crime connection is the commission of crimes—violent crimes in particular—by people under the influence of illicit drugs. This connection seems to have the greatest impact upon the popular imagination. Clearly, some drugs do "cause" some people to commit crimes by reducing normal inhibitions, unleashing aggressive and other antisocial tendencies, and lessening the sense of responsibility. Cocaine, particularly in the form of crack, has gained such a reputation in recent years, just as heroin did in the 1960s and 1970s, and marijuana did in the years before that. Crack's reputation for inspiring violent behavior may or may not be more deserved than those of marijuana and heroin; reliable evidence is not yet available. No illicit drug, however, is as widely associated with violent behavior as alcohol. According to Justice Department statistics, 54 percent of all jail inmates convicted of violent crimes in 1983 reported having used alcohol just prior to committing their offense. The impact of drug legalization on this drug/crime connection is the most difficult to predict. Much would depend on overall rates of drug abuse and changes in the nature of consumption, both of which are impossible to predict. It is worth noting, however, that a shift in consumption from alcohol to marijuana would almost certainly contribute to a decline in violent behavior.

The fourth drug/crime link is the violent, intimidating, and corrupting behavior of the drug traffickers. Illegal markets tend to breed violence—not only because they attract criminally-minded individuals, but also because participants in the market have no resort to legal institutions to resolve their disputes. During Prohibition, violent struggles between bootlegging gangs and hijackings of booze-laden trucks and sea vessels were frequent and notorious occurrences. Today's equivalents are the booby traps that surround some marijuana fields, the pirates of the Caribbean looking to rip off drug-laden vessels en route to the shores of the United States, and the machine-gun battles and executions carried out by drug lords—all of which occasionally kill innocent people. Most law-enforcement officials agree that the dramatic increases in urban murder rates during the past few years can be explained almost entirely by the rise in drug-dealer killings.

Perhaps the most unfortunate victims of the drug-prohibition policies have been the law-abiding residents of America's ghettos. These policies have largely proven futile in deterring large numbers of ghetto dwellers from becoming drug abusers, but they do account for much of what ghetto residents identify as the drug problem. In many neighborhoods, it often seems to be the aggressive gun-toting drug dealers who upset law-abiding residents far more than the addicts nodding out in doorways. Other residents, however, perceive the drug dealers as heroes and successful role models. In impoverished neighborhoods, they often stand out as symbols of success to children who see no other options. At the same time, the increasingly harsh criminal penalties imposed on adult drug dealers have led to the widespread recruitment of juveniles by drug traffickers. Formerly, children started dealing drugs only after they had been using them for a while; today the sequence is often reversed: many children start using illegal drugs now only after working for older drug dealers. And the juvenile-justice system offers no realistic options for dealing with this growing problem.

The conspicuous failure of law-enforcement agencies to deal with this drug/crime connection is probably most responsible for the demoralization of neighborhoods and police departments alike. Intensive police crackdowns in urban neighborhoods do little more than chase the menace a short distance away to infect new areas. By contrast, legalization of the drug market would drive the drug-dealing business off the streets and out of the apartment buildings, and into legal, government-regulated, tax-paying stores. It would also force many of the gun-toting dealers out of business, and would convert others into legitimate businessmen. Some, of course, would turn to other types of criminal activities, just as some of the bootleggers did following Prohibition's repeal. Gone, however, would be the unparalleled financial temptations that lure so many people from all sectors of society into the drug-dealing business.

THE COSTS OF CORRUPTION

All vice-control efforts are particularly susceptible to corruption, but none so much as drug enforcement. When police accept bribes from drug dealers, no victim exists to complain to the authorities. Even when police extort money and drugs from traffickers and dealers, the latter are in no position to report the corrupt officers. What makes drug enforcement especially vulnerable to corruption are the tremendous amounts of money involved in the business. Today, many law-enforcement officials believe that police corruption is more pervasive than at any time since Prohibition. In Miami, dozens of law-enforcement officials have been charged with accepting bribes, stealing from drug dealers, and even dealing drugs themselves. Throughout many small towns and rural communities in Georgia, where drug smugglers en route from Mexico, the Caribbean, and Latin America drop their loads of cocaine and marijuana, dozens of sheriffs have been implicated in drug-related corruption. In New York, drug-related corruption in one Brooklyn police precinct has generated the city's most far-reaching police-corruption scandal since the 1960s. More than a hundred cases of drug-related corruption are now prosecuted each year in state and federal courts. Every one of the federal law-enforcement agencies charged with drug-enforcement responsibilities has seen an agent implicated in drug-related corruption.

It is not difficult to explain the growing pervasiveness of drug-related corruption. The financial temptations are enormous relative to other opportunities, legitimate or illegitimate. Little effort is required. Many police officers are demoralized by the scope of the drug traffic, their sense that many citizens are indifferent, and the fact that many sectors of society do not even appreciate their efforts—as well as the fact that many of the drug dealers who are arrested do not

remain in prison. Some police also recognize that enforcing the drug laws does not protect victims from predators so much as it regulates an illicit market that cannot be suppressed, but can be kept underground. In every respect, the analogy to Prohibition is apt. Repealing the drug-prohibition laws would dramatically reduce police corruption. By contrast, the measures currently being proposed to deal with the growing problem, including better funded and more aggressive internal investigations, offer relatively little promise.

Among the most difficult costs to evaluate are those that relate to the widespread defiance of the drug-prohibition laws: the effects of labelling as criminals the tens of millions of people who use drugs illicitly, subjecting them to the risks of criminal sanction, and obliging many of these same people to enter into relationships with drug dealers (who may be criminals in many more senses of the word) in order to purchase their drugs; the cynicism that such laws generate toward other laws and the law in general; and the sense of hostility and suspicion that many otherwise law-abiding individuals feel toward law-enforcement officials. It was costs such as these that strongly influenced many of Prohibition's more conservative opponents.

PHYSICAL AND MORAL COSTS

Perhaps the most paradoxical consequence of the drug laws is the tremendous harm they cause to the millions of drug users who have not been deterred from using illicit drugs in the first place. Nothing resembling an underground Food and Drug Administration has arisen to impose quality control on the illegal-drug market and provide users with accurate information on the drugs they consume. Imagine that Americans could not tell whether a bottle of wine contained 6 percent, 30 percent, or 90 percent alcohol, or whether an aspirin tablet contained 5 or 500 grams of aspirin. Imagine, too, that no controls existed to prevent winemakers from diluting their product with methanol and other dangerous impurities, and that vineyards and tobacco fields were fertilized with harmful substances by ignorant growers and sprayed with poisonous herbicides by government agents. Fewer people would use such substances, but more of those who did would get sick. Some would die.

The above scenario describes, of course, the current state of the illicit drug market. Many marijuana smokers are worse off for having smoked cannabis that was grown with dangerous fertilizers, sprayed with the herbicide paraquat, or mixed with more dangerous substances. Consumers of heroin and the various synthetic substances sold on the street face even severer consequences, including fatal overdoses and poisonings from unexpectedly potent or impure drug supplies. More often than not, the quality of a drug addict's life depends greatly upon his or her access to reliable supplies. Drug-enforcement operations that succeed in temporarily disrupting supply networks are thus a double-edged sword: they encourage some addicts to seek admission into drug-treatment programs, but they oblige others to seek out new and hence less reliable suppliers; the result is that more, not fewer, drug-related emergencies and deaths occur.

Today, over 50 percent of all people with AIDS in New York City, New Jersey, and many other parts of the country, as well as the vast majority of AIDS-infected heterosexuals throughout the country, have contracted the disease directly or indirectly through illegal intravenous drug use. Reports have emerged of drug dealers beginning to provide clean syringes together with their illegal drugs. But even as other governments around the world actively attempt to limit the spread of AIDS by and among drug users by instituting free syringe-exchange programs, state and municipal governments in the United States resist following suit, arguing that to do so would "encourage" or "condone" the use of illegal drugs. Only in January 1988 did New York City approve such a program on a very limited and experimental basis. At the same time, drug-treatment programs remain notoriously underfunded, turning away tens of thousands of addicts seeking help, even as billions of dollars more are spent to arrest, prosecute, and imprison illegal drug sellers and users. In what may represent a sign of shifting priorities, the President's Commission on AIDS, in its March 1988 report, emphasized the importance of mak-

ing drug-treatment programs available to all in need of them. In all likelihood, however, the criminal-justice agencies will continue to receive the greatest share of drug-control funds.

Most Americans perceive the drug problem as a moral issue and draw a moral distinction between use of the illicit drugs and use of alcohol and tobacco. Yet when one subjects this distinction to reasoned analysis, it quickly disintegrates. The most consistent moral perspective of those who favor drug laws is that of the Mormons and the Puritans, who regard as immoral any intake of substances to alter one's state of consciousness or otherwise cause pleasure: they forbid not only the illicit drugs and alcohol, but also tobacco, caffeine, and even chocolate. The vast majority of Americans are hardly so consistent with respect to the propriety of their pleasures. Yet once one acknowledges that there is nothing immoral about drinking alcohol or smoking tobacco for non-medicinal purposes, it becomes difficult to condemn the consumption of marijuana, cocaine, and other substances on moral grounds. The "moral" condemnation of some substances and not others proves to be little more than a prejudice in favor of some drugs and against others.

The same false distinction is drawn with respect to those who provide the psychoactive substances to users and abusers alike. If degrees of immorality were measured by the levels of harm caused by one's products, the "traffickers" in tobacco and alcohol would be vilified as the most evil of all substance purveyors. That they are perceived instead as respected members of our community, while providers of the no more dangerous illicit substances are punished with long prison sentences, says much about the prejudices of most Americans with respect to psychoactive substances, but little about the morality or immorality of their activities.

Much the same is true of gun salesmen. Most of the consumers of their products use them safely; a minority, however, end up shooting either themselves or someone else. Can we hold the gun salesman morally culpable for the harm that probably would not have occurred but for his existence? Most people say no, except perhaps where the salesman clearly knew that his product would be used to commit a crime. Yet in the case of those who sell illicit substances to willing customers, the providers are deemed not only legally guilty, but also morally reprehensible. The law does not require any demonstration that the dealer knew of a specific harm to follow; indeed, it does not require any evidence at all of harm having resulted from the sale. Rather, the law is predicated on the assumption that harm will inevitably follow. Despite the patent falsity of that assumption, it persists as the underlying justification for the drug laws.

Although a valid moral distinction cannot be drawn between the licit and the illicit psychoactive substances, one can point to a different kind of moral justification for the drug laws: they arguably reflect a paternalistic obligation to protect those in danger of succumbing to their own weaknesses. If drugs were legally available, most people would either abstain from using them or would use them responsibly and in moderation. A minority without self-restraint, however, would end up harming themselves if the substances were more readily available. Therefore, the majority has a moral obligation to deny itself legal access to certain substances because of the plight of the minority. This obligation is presumably greatest when children are included among the minority.

At least in principle, this argument seems to provide the strongest moral justification for the drug laws. But ultimately the moral quality of laws must be judged not by how those laws are intended to work in principle, but by how they function in practice. When laws intended to serve a moral end inflict great damage on innocent parties, we must rethink our moral position.

Because drug-law violations do not create victims with an interest in notifying the police, drug-enforcement agents rely heavily on undercover operations, electronic surveillance, and information provided by informants. These techniques are indispensable to effective law enforcement, but they are also among the least palatable investigative methods employed by the police. The same is true of drug testing: it may be useful and even necessary for determining liability in accidents, but it also threatens and undermines the right of privacy to which many Americans believe they are entitled. There

are good reasons for requiring that such measures be used sparingly.

Equally disturbing are the increasingly vocal calls for people to inform not only on drug dealers but also on neighbors, friends, and even family members who use illicit drugs. Government calls on people not only to "just say no," but also to report those who have not heeded the message. Intolerance of illicit-drug use and users is heralded not only as an indispensable ingredient in the war against drugs, but also as a mark of good citizenship. Certainly every society requires citizens to assist in the enforcement of criminal laws. But societies—particularly democratic and pluralistic ones—also rely strongly on an ethic of tolerance toward those who are different but do no harm to others. Overzealous enforcement of the drug laws risks undermining that ethic, and encouraging the creation of a society of informants. This results in an immorality that is far more dangerous in its own way than that associated with the use of illicit drugs.

THE BENEFITS OF LEGALIZATION

Repealing the drug-prohibition laws promises tremendous advantages. Between reduced government expenditures on enforcing drug laws and new tax revenue from legal drug production and sales, public treasuries would enjoy a net benefit of at least ten billion dollars a year, and possibly much more. The quality of urban life would rise significantly. Homicide rates would decline. So would robbery and burglary rates. Organized criminal groups, particularly the newer ones that have yet to diversify out of drugs, would be dealt a devastating setback. The police, prosecutors, and courts would focus their resources on combatting the types of crimes that people cannot walk away from. More ghetto residents would turn their backs on criminal careers and seek out legitimate opportunities instead. And the health and quality of life of many drug users—and even drug abusers—would improve significantly.

All the benefits of legalization would be for naught, however, if millions more Americans were to become drug abusers. Our experience with alcohol and tobacco provides ample warnings. Today, alcohol is consumed by 140 million Americans and tobacco by 50 million. All of the health costs associated with abuse of the illicit drugs pale in comparison with those resulting from tobacco and alcohol abuse. In 1986, for example, alcohol was identified as a contributing factor in 10 percent of work-related injuries, 40 percent of suicide attempts, and about 40 percent of the approximately 46,000 annual traffic deaths in 1983. An estimated eighteen million Americans are reported to be either alcoholics or alcohol abusers. The total cost of alcohol abuse to American society is estimated at over 100 billion dollars annually. Alcohol has been identified as the direct cause of 80,000 to 100,000 deaths annually, and as a contributing factor in an additional 100,000 deaths. The health costs of tobacco use are of similar magnitude. In the United States alone, an estimated 320,000 people die prematurely each year as a consequence of their consumption of tobacco. By comparison, the National Council on Alcoholism reported that only 3,562 people were known to have died in 1985 from use of all illegal drugs combined. Even if we assume that thousands more deaths were related in one way or another to illicit drug abuse but not reported as such, we are still left with the conclusion that all of the health costs of marijuana, cocaine, and heroin combined amount to only a small fraction of those caused by tobacco and alcohol.

Most Americans are just beginning to recognize the extensive costs of alcohol and tobacco abuse. At the same time, they seem to believe that there is something fundamentally different about alcohol and tobacco that supports the legal distinction between those two substances, on the one hand, and the illicit ones, on the other. The most common distinction is based on the assumption that the illicit drugs are more dangerous than the licit ones. Cocaine, heroin, the various hallucinogens, and (to a lesser extent) marijuana are widely perceived as, in the words of the President's Commission on Organized Crime, "inherently destructive to mind and body." They are also believed to be more addictive and more likely to cause dangerous and violent behavior than alcohol and tobacco. All use of

illicit drugs is therefore thought to be abusive; in other words, the distinction between use and abuse of psychoactive substances that most people recognize with respect to alcohol is not acknowledged with respect to the illicit substances.

Most Americans make the fallacious assumption that the government would not criminalize certain psychoactive substances if they were not in fact dangerous. They then jump to the conclusion that any use of those substances is a form of abuse. The government, in its effort to discourage people from using illicit drugs, has encouraged and perpetuated these misconceptions—not only in its rhetoric but also in its purportedly educational materials. Only by reading between the lines can one discern the fact that the vast majority of Americans who have used illicit drugs have done so in moderation, that relatively few have suffered negative short-term consequences, and that few are likely to suffer long-term harm.

The evidence is most persuasive with respect to marijuana. U.S. drug-enforcement and health agencies do not even report figures on marijuana-related deaths, apparently because so few occur. Although there are good health reasons for children, pregnant women, and some others not to smoke marijuana, there still appears to be little evidence that occasional marijuana consumption does much harm. Certainly, it is not healthy to inhale marijuana smoke into one's lungs; indeed, the National Institute on Drug Abuse (NIDA) has declared that "marijuana smoke contains more cancer-causing agents than is found in tobacco smoke." On the other hand, the number of joints smoked by all but a very small percentage of marijuana smokers is a tiny fraction of the twenty cigarettes a day smoked by the average cigarette smoker; indeed, the average may be closer to one or two joints a week than one or two a day. Note that NIDA defines a "heavy" marijuana smoker as one who consumes at least two joints "daily." A heavy tobacco smoker, by contrast, smokes about forty cigarettes a day.

Nor is marijuana strongly identified as a dependence-causing substance. A 1982 survey of marijuana use by young adults (eighteen to twenty-five years old) found that 64 percent had tried marijuana at least once, that 42 percent had used it at least ten times, and that 27 percent had smoked in the last month. It also found that 21 percent had passed through a period during which they smoked "daily" (defined as twenty or more days per month), but that only one-third of those currently smoked "daily" and only one-fifth (about 4 percent of all young adults) could be described as heavy daily users (averaging two or more joints per day). This suggests that daily marijuana use is typically a phase through which people pass, after which their use becomes more moderate.

Marijuana has also been attacked as the "gateway drug" that leads people to the use of even more dangerous illegal drugs. It is true that people who have smoked marijuana are more likely than people who have not to try, use, and abuse other illicit substances. It is also true that people who have smoked tobacco or drunk alcohol are more likely than those who have not to experiment with illicit drugs and to become substance abusers. The reasons are obvious enough. Familiarity with smoking cigarettes, for instance, removes one of the major barriers to smoking marijuana, which is the experience of inhaling smoke into one's lungs. Similarly, familiarity with altering one's state of consciousness by consuming psychoactive substances such as alcohol or marijuana decreases the fear and increases the curiosity regarding other substances and "highs." But the evidence also indicates that there is nothing inevitable about the process. The great majority of people who have smoked marijuana do not become substance abusers of either legal or illegal substances. At the same time, it is certainly true that many of those who do become substance abusers after using marijuana would have become abusers even if they had never smoked a joint in their life.

DEALING WITH DRUGS' DANGERS

The dangers associated with cocaine, heroin, the hallucinogens, and other illicit substances are greater than those posed by marijuana, but not nearly so great as many people seem to think. Consider the case of cocaine. In 1986 NIDA reported that over 20 million Americans had tried cocaine, that 12.2 million had consumed it at least once during 1985, and that nearly 5.8 million had used it within the past month. Among those between the ages of eighteen and twenty-five, 8.2 million had tried cocaine, 5.3 million had used it within the past year, 2.5 million had used it within the past month, and 250,000 had used it weekly. Extrapolation might suggest that a quarter of a millon young Americans are potential problem users. But one could also conclude that only 3 percent of those between the ages of eighteen and twenty-five who had ever tried the drug fell into that category, and that only 10 percent of those who had used cocaine monthly were at risk. (The NIDA survey did not, it should be noted, include people residing in military or student dormitories, prison inmates, or the homeless.)

All of this is not to deny that cocaine is a potentially dangerous drug, especially when it is injected, smoked in the form of crack, or consumed in tandem with other powerful substances. Clearly, tens of thousands of Americans have suffered severely from their abuse of cocaine, and a tiny fraction have died. But there is also overwhelming evidence that most users of cocaine do not get into trouble with the drug. So much of the media attention has focused on the small percentage of cocaine users who become addicted that the popular perception of how most people use cocaine has become badly distorted. In one survey of high school seniors' drug use, the researchers questioned recent cocaine users, asking whether they had ever tried to stop using cocaine and found that they couldn't. Only 3.8 percent responded affirmatively, in contrast to the almost 7 percent of marijuana smokers who said they had tried to stop and found they couldn't, and the 18 percent of cigarette smokers who answered similarly. Although a similar survey of adult users would probably reveal a higher proportion of cocaine addicts, evidence such as this suggests that only a small percentage of people who use cocaine end up having a problem with it. In this respect, most people differ from monkeys, who have demonstrated in experiments that they will starve themselves to death if provided with unlimited cocaine.

With respect to the hallucinogens such as LSD and psilocybic mushrooms, their potential for addiction is virtually nil. The dangers arise primarily from using them irresponsibly on individual occasions. Although many of those who have used one or another of the hallucinogens have experienced "bad trips," others have reported positive experiences, and very few have suffered any long-term harm.

Perhaps no drugs are regarded with as much horror as the opiates, and in particular heroin, which is a concentrated form of morphine. As with most drugs, heroin can be eaten, snorted, smoked, or injected. Most Americans, unfortunately, prefer injection. There is no question that heroin is potentially highly addictive, perhaps as addictive as nicotine. But despite the popular association of heroin use with the most down-and-out inhabitants of urban ghettos, heroin causes relatively little physical harm to the human body. Consumed on an occasional or regular basis under sanitary conditions, its worst side effect, apart from addiction itself, is constipation. That is one reason why many doctors in early twentieth-century America saw opiate addiction as preferable to alcoholism, and prescribed the former as treatment for the latter when abstinence did not seem a realistic option.

It is important to think about the illicit drugs in the same way we think about alcohol and tobacco. Like tobacco, many of the illicit substances are highly addictive, but can be consumed on a regular basis for decades without any demonstrable harm. Like alcohol, most of the substances can be, and are, used by most consumers in moderation, with little in the way of harmful effects; but like alcohol, they also lend themselves to abuse by a minority of users who become addicted or otherwise harm themselves or others as a consequence. And as is the case with both the legal substances, the psychoactive effects of the various illegal drugs vary greatly from one person to another. To be sure, the pharmacology of the substance is important, as is its purity and the manner in which it is consumed. But much also depends upon not only the physiology and psychology of the consumer, but also his expectations regarding the drug, his social milieu, and the broader cultural environment—what Harvard University psychiatrist Norman Zinberg has called the "set and setting" of the drug. It is factors such as these that might change

dramatically, albeit in indeterminate ways, were the illicit drugs made legally available.

CAN LEGALIZATION WORK?

It is thus impossible to predict whether legalization would lead to much greater levels of drug abuse, and exact costs comparable to those of alcohol and tobacco abuse. The lessons that can be drawn from other societies are mixed. China's experience with the British opium pushers of the nineteenth century, when millions became addicted to the drug, offers one worst-case scenario. The devastation of many native American tribes by alcohol presents another. On the other hand, the legal availability of opium and cannabis in many Asian societies did not result in large addict populations until recently. Indeed, in many countries U.S.-inspired opium bans imposed during the past few decades have paradoxically contributed to dramatic increases in heroin consumption among Asian youth. Within the United States, the decriminalization of marijuana by about a dozen states during the 1970s did not lead to increases in marijuana consumption. In the Netherlands, which went even further in decriminalizing cannabis during the 1970s, consumption has actually declined significantly. The policy has succeeded, as the government intended, in making drug use boring. Finally, late nineteenth-century America was a society in which there were almost no drug laws or even drug regulations—but levels of drug use then were about what they are today. Drug abuse was considered a serious problem, but the criminal-justice system was not regarded as part of the solution.

There are, however, reasons to believe that none of the currently illicit substances would become as popular as alcohol or tobacco, even if they were legalized. Alcohol has long been the principal intoxicant in most societies, including many in which other substances have been legally available. Presumably, its diverse properties account for its popularity—it quenches thirst, goes well with food, and promotes appetite as well as sociability. The popularity of tobacco probably stems not just from its powerful addictive qualities, but from the fact that its psychoactive effects are sufficiently subtle that cigarettes can be integrated with most other human activities. The illicit substances do not share these qualities to the same extent, nor is it likely that they would acquire them if they were legalized. Moreover, none of the illicit substances can compete with alcohol's special place in American culture and history.

An additional advantage of the illicit drugs is that none of them appears to be as insidious as either alcohol or tobacco. Consumed in their more benign forms, few of the illicit substances are as damaging to the human body over the long term as alcohol and tobacco, and none is as strongly linked with violent behavior as alcohol. On the other hand, much of the damage caused today by illegal drugs stems from their consumption in particularly dangerous ways. There is good reason to doubt that many Americans would inject cocaine or heroin into their veins even if given the chance to do so legally. And just as the dramatic growth in the heroin-consuming population during the 1960s leveled off for reasons apparently having little to do with law enforcement, so we can expect a levelling-off—which may already have begun—in the number of people smoking crack. The logic of legalization thus depends upon two assumptions: that most illegal drugs are not so dangerous as is commonly believed; and that the drugs and methods of consumption that are most risky are unlikely to prove appealing to many people, precisely because they are so obviously dangerous.

Perhaps the most reassuring reason for believing that repeal of the drug-prohibition laws will not lead to tremendous increases in drug-abuse levels is the fact that we have learned something from our past experiences with alcohol and tobacco abuse. We now know, for instance, that consumption taxes are an effective method of limiting consumption rates. We also know that restrictions and bans on advertising, as well as a campaign of negative advertising, can make a difference. The same is true of other government measures, including restrictions on time and place of sale, prohibition of consumption in public places, packaging requirements, mandated adjustments in insurance policies, crackdowns on driving while under the influence, and laws holding bartenders and hosts responsible for the drinking of customers and guests. There is even some evidence that government-sponsored education programs about the dangers of cigarette smoking have deterred many children from beginning to smoke.

Clearly it is possible to avoid repeating the mistakes of the past in designing an effective plan for legalization. We know more about the illegal drugs now than we knew about alcohol when Prohibition was repealed, or about tobacco when the anti-tobacco laws were repealed by many states in the early years of this century. Moreover, we can and must avoid having effective drug-control policies undermined by powerful lobbies like those that now protect the interests of alcohol and tobacco producers. We are also in a far better position than we were sixty years ago to prevent organized criminals from finding and creating new opportunities when their most lucrative source of income dries up.

It is important to stress what legalization is not. It is not a capitulation to the drug dealers—but rather a means to put them out of business. It is not an endorsement of drug use—but rather a recognition of the rights of adult Americans to make their own choices free of the fear of criminal sanctions. It is not a repudiation of the "just say no" approach—but rather an appeal to government to provide assistance and positive inducements, not criminal penalties and more repressive measures, in support of that approach. It is not even a call for the elimination of the criminal-justice system from drug regulation—but rather a proposal for the redirection of its efforts and attention.

There is no question that legalization is a risky policy, since it may lead to an increase in the number of people who abuse drugs. But that is a risk—not a certainty. At the same time, current drug-control policies are failing, and new proposals promise only to be more costly and more repressive. We know that repealing the drug-prohibition laws would eliminate or greatly reduce many of the ills that people commonly identify as part and parcel of the "drug problem." Yet legalization is repeatedly and vociferously dismissed, without any attempt to evaluate it openly and objectively. The past twenty years have demonstrated that a drug policy shaped by exaggerated rhetoric designed to arouse fear has only led to our current disaster. Unless we are willing to honestly evaluate our options, including various legalization strategies, we will run a still greater risk: we may never find the best solution for our drug problems.

CHAPTER   11

STREET CRIME AND GANGS

INTRODUCTION

According to Emile Durkheim, one of the founders of sociology, all societies are confronted with the problem of criminality. The problem is universal because crimes and their punishment are needed to remind everyone (law-abiding citizens and criminals alike) of the importance of the society's rules. Crime serves the important function of defining and reinforcing the proper conduct essential to a coherent social order.

Durkheim's provocative thesis that crime is necessarily universal has attracted much interest and many critics. All societies may need an occasional criminal who is punished as a reminder to everyone to obey the rules, but this symbolic need cannot explain why crime rates skyrocket from time to time, forcing many law-abiding citizens to pay a high price for the misdeeds of their fellow citizens. There have been several crime waves in the history of the United States, and the 1990s is proving to be one of those periods of alarming statistics. According to the 1990 "crime clock" of the Department of Justice, a violent crime is committed every seventeen seconds and a property crime every two seconds. In 1990 over one million citizens were victims of aggravated assault, and the murder rate (94 per 100,000) reached an all-time high. Major portions of most large cities are not safe for evening walks or a night trip to the local restaurant. One in every 119 registered motor vehicles was stolen in 1990, at an estimated cost of $8 billion.[1] The law-abiding car owners, of course, pay higher insurance premiums to cover the costs of auto theft. According to the National Crime Survey of 1989, approximately 25 million American households were "touched by crime."[2] Millions of Americans respond to their fear of being victims of crime by purchasing guns, dogs, triple lock systems, and electronic alarms. Durkheim may be right; some crime may be normal for all societies. But could crime in the United States be reaching abnormal proportions?

There is no simple answer to Durkheim's argument. One reason is that there are many kinds of crime and some are more alarming than others. People are most alarmed about the offenses that the FBI reports as felonies: murder, forcible rape, robbery, aggravated assault, burglary, and auto theft. There is no generic criminal who is committing all of these offenses, but one source of fear is the street gang.

---

[1] U.S. Department of Justice, *Uniform Crime Reports, 1990* (Washington, D.C.: U.S. Government Printing Office, 1990), pp. 7, 23, 39.

[2] U.S. Department of Commerce, *Statistical Abstract of the United States* (Washington, D.C.: U.S. Government Printing Office, 1991), p. 182.

Sociologists have been making systematic observations of street gangs since the 1920s, when Frederick Thrasher studied 1,313 gangs in Chicago. Journalists have also had a longstanding interest in gangs. In recent years the perception is widespread that the gang problem is getting worse in the United States. Several factors contribute to this new sense of alarm: expanded drug smuggling; greater availability and use of deadly high-powered weapons; greater poverty and unemployment in the inner cities, which breeds a pervasive sense of hopelessness; and an increasingly casual attitude toward violence. In the past few years gang homicides have reached an all-time high in such cities as Los Angeles, Chicago, and Washington, D.C.

One currently popular strategy for fighting street crime is the program known as Crime Stoppers. Dennis Rosenbaum, Arthur J. Lurigio, and Paul J. Lavrakas provide a brief description of the Crime Stoppers program and assess its impact on the crime problem. These three sociologists contend that tougher policing of the streets will never be sufficient. Police officers can maintain order only when they have the support of the community's citizens.

Mike Royko disagrees. A veteran reporter in Chicago, Royko is familiar with city dwellers' fears of gangs. His response to the threat of gangs is to allow the police more authority to crack down on suspicious youngsters. C. Ronald Huff, who examines the problem of gangs in two Ohio cities, takes a broader view. Note Huff's approach to reliable and valid information, and the line of reasoning that leads him to conclusions strikingly different from Mike Royko's.

27. ENHANCING CITIZEN PARTICIPATION AND SOLVING SERIOUS CRIME

DENNIS P. ROSENBAUM, ARTHUR J. LURIGIO, and PAUL J. LAVRAKAS

A NATIONAL EVALUATION OF CRIME STOPPERS PROGRAMS

Fear of crime and a widespread perception that the crime problem in the United States cannot be handled by the police alone has spurred a number of citizen-based programs to facilitate crime reporting and prevention (see DuBow, McCabe, and Kaplan, 1979; Feins, 1983; Lavrakas, 1985; McPherson and Silloway, 1980; Roehl and Cook, 1984; Rosenbaum, 1986, 1988). One of the most visible and popular crime control programs in the United States is "Crime Stoppers." Variously known as "Crime Solvers," "Secret Witness," and "Crime Line," these self-sustaining programs utilize the mass media, the commu-

From *Crime and Delinquency*, Vol. 35(3) 1989, pp. 401–420. Copyright © 1989 Sage Publications, Inc. Reprinted by permission of Sage Publications, Inc.

Dennis P. Rosenbaum: Associate Professor of Criminal Justice at University of Illinois in Chicago. Arthur J. Lurigio: Assistant Professor of Psychology and Member of the Research Faculty at the Center for Urban Affairs and Policy Research, Northwestern University. Paul J. Lavrakas: Associate Professor in the Medill School of Journalism and Northwestern University Survey Laboratory, Northwestern University.

This article is based on research funded under Cooperative Agreement #NIJ-83-CX-K050 between Northwestern University and the National Institute of Justice, U.S. Department of Justice. Parts of this research were supported by funds from the Medill School of Journalism, Northwestern University. Any opinions expressed are those of the authors and do not necessarily reflect the official position of the National Institute of Justice.

nity, and law enforcement in an unprecedented way to involve private citizens in the fight against serious crime. Based on the premise that many individuals are unwilling to provide information to the police about criminal activity, either because of apathy or fear of retaliation (MacAleese and Tily, 1983), Crime Stoppers provides *cash rewards* as an incentive (typically ranging from $100 to $1,000), and offers *anonymity* to persons who come forth with details that lead to the arrest and/or indictment of suspected criminals.

During nearly a full decade following their initial implementation, no empirical research had been done to describe these programs or to examine critically their usefulness or impact. This article summarizes the results of the first and only national evaluation of Crime Stoppers. The research employed several different methodologies to explore a series of basic questions relating to program operations and effects.

BACKGROUND

Crime Stoppers programs are designed to encourage citizen participation in the process of solving difficult felony crimes. Solving serious crimes is an onerous task that constantly challenges law enforcement. There are many factors that limit the effectiveness of police performance. Of paramount importance is the ability of witnesses and callers to provide reliable information about the identity of suspects. Without basic information from people who know about the crime incident, the probability of solving any particular offense is drastically reduced (Skogan and Antunes, 1979). Stated differently, only a small percentage of arrests can be attributed to police-initiated contacts, whereas most arrests are the result of citizen-initiated contacts. Clearance rates are low (about 1 in 5 felony crimes) because detectives usually do not have the necessary "leads" from the community. Researchers estimate that even doubling or tripling the number of detectives would have virtually no effect on clearance rates (Eck, 1982). Indeed, a number of police studies demonstrate that traditional strategies of policing, which typically ignore the fundamental role of citizens in the prevention and control of crime, have been unsuccessful (Eck and Spelman, 1987; Kelling, 1988). Consequently, researchers, policymakers, and practitioners have called for increased citizen participation and responsibility in the fight against crime (see Lavrakas, 1985; Rosenbaum, 1986). The fundamental problem is that citizen participation in anticrime programs (or even participation in crime reporting activities) remains very low. Hence the search for innovative appeals to the citizenry has lead to the development and marketing of Crime Stoppers programs throughout the country.

The History and Nature of Crime Stoppers

Recognizing the critical role of the private citizen in solving crime, Greg MacAleese, a police officer in Albuquerque, New Mexico, started the first Crime Stoppers program in 1976. Although the Albuquerque program was preceded by other similar programs in the early 1970s that used cash rewards and anonymity as their primary incentives (see Bickman et al., 1977), Officer MacAleese was the first to feature the media in a central role. Since 1976, Crime Stoppers programs have appeared rapidly across the United States and have been touted as one of the nation's most cost-effective anticrime measures. The concept has spread quickly to Canada, Puerto Rico, New Zealand, Australia, and Great Britain. The precipitous growth of Crime Stoppers in the past few years is revealed by program statistics. In 1978, there were only 5 Crime Stoppers programs in the United States. Today there are an estimated 700 operational programs accepting calls, and new programs are emerging on

a continual basis (Crime Stoppers International, 1988).

The proper functioning of Crime Stoppers hinges upon the joint cooperation and concerted efforts of its various elements, which include representatives of the community, the media, and the police department. Each program's board of directors—reflecting the community's contribution through the formation of a nonprofit corporation—is responsible for setting policy, coordinating fund-raising activities aimed at public and private contributors, and formulating a system of reward allocation. The media play a major role in educating the public about the program's objectives, general operations, and achievements. Moreover, they serve to publicize the details of unsolved offenses by presenting a reenactment or narrative description of a selected "Crime of the Week." Anyone with information about this crime is encouraged to call Crime Stoppers, and if a suspect is arrested as a direct result of the information, the caller is likely to receive a cash reward. Law enforcement personnel who staff the program process the crime information reported by anonymous callers and direct it to detectives for further investigation. The police coordinator also functions in a variety of other capacities, which include such tasks as selecting the "Crime of the Week," drafting press releases and radio feeds, consulting in the production of televised crime portrayals, keeping records and statistics on program performance, and serving as the liaison with the board of directors, the media, and the investigators.

The Scope of the National Evaluation

The National Institute of Justice, interested in the possibility that Crime Stoppers might be an effective new strategy for controlling crime and enhancing citizen participation, elected to fund a national evaluation of these programs in 1984. The primary impetus for funding the evaluation was the notion that if Crime Stoppers helps to solve crimes by involving citizens in crime-reporting activities, then communities should be encouraged to implement the program. In addition, it was believed that existing or prospective programs may benefit from information regarding the factors that enhance or limit program success.

Given that Crime Stoppers programs had never been formally evaluated or researched, there were many unanswered questions. Three basic questions were proposed as a guiding framework for the national evaluation: First, how does Crime Stoppers work in both theory and practice? Second, what are the advantages and disadvantages of Crime Stoppers programs to law enforcement agencies and the community? Specifically, is there any evidence of effectiveness in stimulating citizen participation, solving felony crimes, and/or lowering community crime rates? How important are monetary rewards in gaining citizen participation, and is the size of the reward a big factor in caller satisfaction? Also what are the legal and social ramifications of pursuing this type of crime control strategy? Third, what are the policy implications of this research for existing or new programs? What factors limit or facilitate program productivity? The present article provides a summary of the major findings and conclusions in these areas.

RESEARCH METHODS

Three complementary methodologies were used in the national evaluation—telephone surveys, mail questionnaires, and case studies, with the latter involving different methodologies at particular sites. These methodologies are described below.

Telephone Screening Survey

Telephone interviews were conducted in February and March of 1984 with 602 locations to identify and characterize all known Crime Stoppers programs on a number of dimensions, including the size of the population served, type of program (e.g., citywide versus countywide) and current status (e.g., planned, operational, or discontinued).

Police Coordinator Survey

Police coordinators from operational programs identified in the screening survey were mailed a 42-page questionnaire covering the law enforcement, media, and community aspects of the programs. Of the 443 known operational programs in the United States and Canada that were sent this survey, 203 coordinators (or 46%) completed and returned the questionnaire after two extensive follow-up efforts. The survey was designed to yield information about the coordinator's background and experience, program development and support, day-to-day operating procedures, program records and statistics, reward setting and distribution practices, and program relations with the media, law enforcement, and the board of directors.

Board of Directors Survey

A board of directors mail questionnaire was completed by 37% of the chairpersons representing 123 separate programs. This survey examined all major aspects of the board's functions and responsibilities, including the composition and performance of the board, fund-raising strategies, and ratings of the program.

Media Executive Survey

A national mail survey of 235 news media executives was conducted to gather independent information about the media's perception of, and involvement in, Crime Stoppers. Two samples were drawn. The first was a representative sample of media organizations listed by Crime Stoppers Coordinators as participants in their programs. A total of 136 (25%) of the surveys were returned from newspapers, radio stations, and television stations. The second sample was drawn randomly from media outlets listed in the annual industry yearbook listing all operating media organizations in the United States. A total of 99 (13%) completed surveys were returned. The complete media survey findings are described in Lavrakas, Rosenbaum, and Lurigio (1990).

Case Studies

The day-to-day operations and processes of Crime Stoppers programs were examined firsthand through site visits of seven programs with diverse characteristics (e.g., urban versus suburban versus rural settings, single versus multijurisdictional coverage, high versus low productivity). The methodologies used included in-person interviews, observations, and reviews of program records and documents. In addition, two specialized case studies were conducted: An "Impact Study" in Indianapolis, Indiana, to measure the impact of a new Crime Stoppers program on residents, police officers, and businesspersons; and a "Reward Experiment" in Lake County, Illinois, to ascertain the effects of different reward amounts on callers' perceptions of the program and willingness to cooperate in the future. The methods and results of the Impact Study are reported in Lurigio and Rosenbaum (1989). The Reward Experiment is described here.

Lake County's program was selected for the Reward Experiment because (a) it was not yet operational and the board of directors was willing to permit an experimental intervention; (b) it represented a moderately large population (i.e., at least 300,000) and therefore was expected to receive enough calls to generate the data in a timely manner; and (c) it was based in a community that is comparable to many American communities served by Crime Stoppers in terms of its crime rate, media coverage, and size of the service area. Our sample was restricted to "run of the mill" cases that varied in seriousness. Extremely unusual or serious cases were excluded (e.g., kidnappings, murder, rape, and large narcotics cases).

A randomized experimental design was employed, with cases randomly assigned to one of three reward conditions. Staff at the new program estimated an average reward size of $250 per case, which was maintained by assigning cases to one of three reward sizes: low reward ($100), medium ($250), and moderately high reward ($400). When an anonymous informer called the program coordinator and was told the amount of the reward, the coordinator asked the caller about his or her willingness to participate in a short caller satisfaction survey. Callers who consented to participate (100%) were then interviewed immediately by a trained interviewer who asked them about their satisfaction with the reward size, their perception of the fairness of the compensation, their beliefs about the effec-

tiveness of Crime Stoppers, and their likelihood of calling the program again. The caller's anonymity was strictly maintained. A total of 44 interviews were completed.

MAJOR FINDINGS

Program Description

Standardization. Crime Stoppers is a highly standardized program. Although programs differ dramatically in their degree of success, virtually all Crime Stoppers programs are made up of the same key participants—a program coordinator (usually within the police department), detectives who investigate the cases, a board of directors representing the community, one or more media outlets, and citizen callers who provide tips. Furthermore, all programs offer rewards and anonymity to callers, even though the reward amounts and criteria for determining rewards vary from program to program.

Distinguishing Features. Some of the most distinguishing features of Crime Stoppers programs are associated with the population density of the areas being served. The nature of any particular program is determined by the resources and needs of the surrounding community. For example, the amount and type of media participation in Crime Stoppers vary as a function of the size of the population being served. As shown in Table 1, programs serving small areas rely most heavily upon radio and weekly newspapers to publicize Crime Stoppers, whereas programs serving larger populations are most likely to utilize VHF/UHF television as their primary media outlet. The larger urban or countywide programs tend to capitalize on the full range of media available to them, including daily newspapers, weekly newspapers, radio, and cable television.

Networking. Program "networking" has developed at the local, state, regional, national, and international levels. In their initial stages of operation, two-thirds of the programs surveyed reported that they had received either "a lot of help" or "quite a bit of help" from existing programs. Moreover, there is a widespread practice of sharing services and resources among multi-

TABLE 1. Size of Population Served by Type of Media Participation in 1984

| | Type of Media | | | | | | | | | |
| | Daily Newspaper | | Weekly Newspaper | | Radio | | VHF/UHF Television | | Cable Television | | |
Size of Population	% with	Ave. #	% with	Ave. #	% with	Ave. #	% with	Ave. #	% with	Ave. #	N[a]
Less than 50,000	51	.75	59	1.25	73	1.83	15	.22	35	.41	61
50,000 to 99,999	73	1.11	59	1.52	75	3.48	52	.86	23	.39	47
100,000 to 249,999	86	1.44	58	1.50	86	4.75	69	1.19	36	.44	38
250,000 or larger	75	3.34	61	3.18	80	7.50	89	2.68	36	.55	46

[a] Average sample size.

jurisdictional programs. Nearly half (49%) reported that they share a phone line, coordinator, media outlet, and/or board of directors with another community (i.e., a separate law enforcement jurisdiction). An average of between 7 and 9 communities participated in each sharing group.

Rewards. Monetary rewards are utilized as a major incentive to encourage citizen participation in Crime Stoppers. Table 2 shows that reward amounts vary greatly depending on whether the incident is a "Crime of the Week," a personal crime, a narcotics crime, or a property crime. Larger programs tend to offer larger rewards for the same types of crime. Many criteria are used to determine reward size, but 9 out or 10 programs reported that the severity of the crime was the primary determinant. Many other factors were cited, but there was no agreement about their relative importance. Boards generally handled reward decisions on a case-by-case basis, and used a variety of standards that sometimes conflicted with one another. For example, the crime may be very serious, but the informant provided low-quality information, was marginally cooperative, and lacked credibility from previous incidents.

TABLE 2. Average Reward Size (in dollars) by Type of Crime and Size of Population Served

| | Type of Crime | | | | |
Size of Population	Personal[a] Crimes	Narcotics	Property[b] Crimes	Crime of Week	N[c]
Less than 50,000	289	177	171	165	61
50,000 to 99,999	406	146	139	344	47
100,000 to 249,999	394	271	203	676	38
250,000 or larger	400	253	178	774	46
Overall average	379	207	171	505	192

[a] Includes homicide, rape, robbery, and assault.
[b] Includes burglary, theft, and auto theft.
[c] Average sample size.

Perceptions and Attitudes About Crime Stoppers

Crime Stoppers was found to be highly visible and well received by a national random sample of media executives. In total, 90% of the media executives surveyed were aware of the program, even though a substantial majority was not participating in Crime Stoppers at the time of our study. Furthermore, nearly two-thirds of the respondents reported that their organization would be "very likely" to participate if a local program were to start. However, the results may not be representative of all media executives because of the relatively low response rate.

Those participating in Crime Stoppers held even more favorable attitudes about the program. The enthusiasm for the program was very strong among police coordinators, the board of directors, and participating media executives, and the vast majority of each group viewed the program as "quite successful."

Public sentiment about Crime Stoppers has been mixed. Although most interested parties have expressed favorable attitudes toward Crime Stoppers, some journalists, defense attorneys, civil libertarians, and legal scholars have expressed misgivings about the programs (Rosenbaum and Lurigio, 1985). Our site visits and fieldwork produced a number of anecdotal observations regarding the legal and moral issues surrounding the program. Because of their overriding importance to the future of Crime Stoppers as an anticrime strategy, these public concerns are summarized below.

Legal and Societal Issues. Given the program's focus on the use of anonymous callers and sizable reward payments, a variety of concerns have been registered about its purpose, organizational arrangement, modus operandi vis-à-vis the courts, and long-term effects on society. Legal battles have captured the most attention and have focused on some important judicial questions: (a) Does pretrial media publicity (via Crime Stoppers reenactments and other coverage) prejudice the jury and entitle the defendant to a "change of venue"? (b) Can a witness's testimony be prejudiced by pretrial publicity about the facts of the case? (c) Should a witness's testi-mony be rendered credible (and therefore admissible) if he or she has been paid a sizable reward before (and sometimes after) giving testimony? (d) Should the Crime Stoppers program be forced to disclose the identity of a confidential informant? In addition, many of the legal and civil cases have focused on the alleged adverse effects of the program on the suspect (or sometimes the caller), including claims of false arrest and imprisonment, defamation of character, invasion of privacy and other civil rights, breach of contract (e.g., failure to pay the tipster), illegal fund-raising activities, and so on. Recent court cases have addressed many of these issues and, so far, Crime Stoppers has survived most of the tests.[1]

Outside the courtroom, critics have voiced concern about the long-term impact of Crime Stoppers on society. The fundamental concerns are these: (a) Will large sums of money and anonymity encourage citizens to make false accusations, violate civil rights, and distrust their neighbors? Will Crime Stoppers encourage "snitching" and invasions of privacy rather than a building of community bonds? (b) Should society pay citizens to do something that is generally considered their civic duty, that is, to report criminal conduct to the police? In addition, will such payment undermine people's intrinsic motivation to participate in civic activities without monetary compensation? These are difficult questions and empirical research has been unable to provide any clear-cut answers (see Rosenbaum and Lurigio, 1985).

Finally, there is some concern among journalists about the intensive role of media organizations as coproducers and advocates of the Crime Stoppers program. The most basic question is whether this level of involvement with law enforcement weakens the press's ability to function as the watchdog of governmental agencies and the police in particular. Although some of the top media outlets have chosen not to get involved, hundreds of media organizations see no problem with their participation.

---

[1] Judge Richard W. Carter of the Arlington, Texas, Municipal Court is the General Counsel for Crime Stoppers International, Inc. and is an excellent source of information on court cases in this general topic area.

Effectiveness of Crime Stoppers

"Hard" evidence of program effectiveness in controlling crime (i.e., evidence that allows us to make strong causal inferences because of a strong design) was not obtained in this project because of the national character of the evaluation. However, a number of empirical and anecdotal observations can be cited that pertain to the question of crime control.

Program Records.   To document their ability to "solve" crime, program staff have typically recorded several key statistics. As shown in Table 3, 570 programs have collectively solved more than 213,000 felony crimes, recovered more than $1.3 billion in stolen property and narcotics, and convicted more than 43,000 criminals. Nevertheless, there is little reason to believe that Crime Stoppers programs will immediately or substantially reduce the overall crime rate in most communities. While numerous crimes are solved through these programs, these successes amount to only a small fraction of the total volume of serious crimes committed each year in most communities.

In budgeting terms, Crime Stoppers may be considered a cost-effective program by taxpayers. Funding for most programs is provided by private contributions. For every crime solved, Crime Stoppers recovers an average of $6,593 in stolen property and narcotics. Nationally, a felony case was solved for every $77 spent in caller reward money. This figure, however, is difficult to interpret without comparable data on alternative crime control strategies.

Solving Dead-End Cases.   The available anecdotal evidence suggests that Crime-Stoppers programs are able to solve certain felony cases that are unlikely to be solved through traditional criminal investigations or by devoting a "reasonable" amount of law enforcement resources. The program was developed specifically to handle "dead-end" cases, and indeed Crime Stoppers has repeatedly "cracked" cases that have remained unsolved after a significant investment of investigative time. Success in these cases is believed to be the result of widespread media coverage, the promise of anonymity, and/or opportunity for a sizable reward. Nonetheless, controlled research is needed to provide a more rigorous test of this hypothesis.

Stimulating Citizen Participation

Crime Stoppers is intended to stimulate citizen participation in the fight against crime, both in the private and public sectors. In addition to a regular commitment from media organizations, the program seeks to encourage citizen involvement as callers, contributors, and active members of the board of directors. Media spots that offer rewards and anonymity are considered critical for increasing citizen involvement. Some observations about the extent of community involvement and the success of the media are described below.

Base of Support.   Thousands of calls received from anonymous callers and millions of dollars in paid rewards are clear indicators of commu-

TABLE 3. International Crime Stoppers Statistics

Felony crimes solved	213,094
Stolen property and narcotics recovered	$1,330,998,871
Average amount recovered per case	$6,246
Defendants tried	45,262
Defendants convicted	43,839
Conviction rate	97%
Rewards paid	$17,023,467

Source: Crime Stoppers International, 1989.
Note: Based on cumulative statistics reported by 570 programs through December 31, 1988.

nity support and citizen participation in Crime Stoppers. Nevertheless, as with many crime control programs, the base of community involvement appears to be concentrated in certain subgroups of the population who have the needed resources (see Rosenbaum, 1987). Specifically, financial support comes primarily from the business community (although telethons and other broad community appeals are being used increasingly as fund-raising techniques). In addition, the majority of anonymous tips—especially those that are perceived as useful—come from either the criminals themselves or "fringe players" (i.e., persons who associate with the criminal element). Program coordinators in our national sample estimated that 41% of the callers are "fringe players," 25% are "criminals," and only 35% are "good citizens." Fringe players were seen as providing the best leads for solving crimes.

Reward Effects. As noted earlier, a randomized experiment in Lake County, Illinois, was conducted to explore how callers would respond to different reward sizes, which were randomly determined. A one-way analysis of variance was performed to test the effects of reward size on informants' reactions. The results were consistent across all dependent variables: Reward size had no effect on informants. That is, callers in the low, moderate, and moderately high reward conditions did not differ in their satisfaction with

the reward, the perceived fairness of the reward, their belief in the effectiveness of Crime Stoppers, their intentions to use the program again, and other related measures. The results are shown in Table 4. With a few rare exceptions, even callers in the low-reward group (who receive only $100) reported that they were "very satisfied" with the amount of compensation.

We also tested the hypothesis that persons who had a low income or criminal history, or who directly attributed their participation to money (rather than anonymity), would be more disappointed by smaller rewards. To examine the hypothesis that rewards would have a differential effect depending on the informant's motive for calling the program, interaction terms were created and tested in a multiple regression framework. The results indicated that reward size did not interact with the informants' motives or their financial status to determine reactions to the reward payments. In summary, this experiment suggests that reward size is not a strong determinant of informant satisfaction or willingness to utilize the program for *typical* Crime Stopper cases.

Factors Associated with Program Productivity

Accurately assessing the performance of Crime Stoppers is currently a difficult task because of

TABLE 4. Caller Responses as a Function of Reward Size: A Randomized Experiment (Means with Standard Deviations in Parentheses)

Reward Size	Satisfaction with Reward	Perceived Fairness of Compensation	Perceived Effectiveness of Crime Stoppers	Likely to Call Crime Stoppers Again	N
Low ($100)	6.75 (3.39)	.75 (.45)	3.83 (.39)	3.67 (.89)	12
Moderate ($250)	7.35 (2.87)	.82 (.39)	3.62 (.50)	3.65 (.79)	17
Moderately high ($400)	7.93 (2.79)	.71 (.47)	3.73 (.46)	3.60 (.83)	15
Between-groups F value	0.52	0.25	0.72	0.02	

measurement problems. There were several identifiable limitations of record-keeping practices among programs. For example, most Crime Stoppers programs did not maintain a full range of basic statistics on productivity and effectiveness, and there was limited standardization of measurement across programs because of definitional problems. Also the commonly employed measures of "cases solved" and "property recovered" were biased in favor of large programs (i.e., those serving populations of 250,000 or more) and programs with a high volume of narcotics cases. There was a shortage of valid and reliable measures of program activities and effects at the time of our study.

Program coordinators were asked to supply data on program productivity, and several of these measures were judged acceptable for use in the evaluation after they were adjusted for local crime rates and/or population size. Specifically, program productivity was measured by the number of calls received (per 100,000 population), the quality of calls (as indicated by the number of cases forwarded to investigators), the number of suspects arrested (per 1,000 Part 1 crimes), and the number of cases cleared or solved (per 1,000 Part 1 crimes). The productivity results are summarized below. Separate multiple regression analyses were performed for each component of the program. Where relationships between variables are cited the reader can assume that the standardized regression coefficients are significant at the .05 level or less. Field observations are also included in this summary.

Program Coordinator Role. With regard to the law enforcement component, the best predictors of program productivity at the national level were the program coordinator's level of effort and job satisfaction. Coordinators who work more hours, make more public speaking engagements, and report more job satisfaction were involved in more productive Crime Stoppers programs than those reporting less activity and satisfaction. However, if a causal relationship exists, it is unclear whether the coordinator's effort or perceptions affect program productivity, or whether the influence operates in the reverse direction.

Field observations suggest that the job of program coordinator is very complex and demanding. It requires knowledge of public relations, criminal investigations, mass media, and program management, as well as other special skills (e.g., public speaking). These observations are consistent with the widely held belief that failure to select the right person for this job will greatly limit the success of the program.

Working with Detectives. Field observations indicated that the forwarding of *quality* (i.e., workable) information from Crime Stoppers to detectives is the key to arrest and also determines the credibility of the program among detectives. Some Crime Stoppers programs suffer from the problem of "underscreening" cases, whereby the staff pass along to detectives any little piece of information that they receive from the caller without making a judgment about its quality. This information often has little or no investigative value. Other programs suffer from "overscreening" cases, whereby the staff not only eliminate useless "tips," but take on the role of investigator and do everything except make the arrest.

The location of a Crime Stoppers program within the police department affects the program's relationship with investigators. Programs that are not located within the criminal investigations bureau are more likely to experience an uphill struggle for acceptance. Some operational and attitudinal problems can be attributed to inadequate training regarding program procedures and strategies for all police personnel from civilian volunteers to the police chief.

Media Outlets. The number of media outlets that participate in a Crime Stoppers program did not affect the level of program performance. However, programs that received more special coverage (e.g., front page or news-hour coverage) and those who reported more cooperative relationships with the media enjoyed greater success. The importance of establishing a consistently cooperative relationship with the media in the early phases of program development was emphasized by program coordinators as a means to prevent problems and maximize success.

Media competition for exclusive handling of Crime Stoppers is a problem in several cities. While 29% of the programs surveyed reported exclusive arrangements with the media, fierce competition for the program often occurs in larger urban areas with network television markets.

Board of Directors. The level of effort exhibited by the board of directors was the predominant factor in determining its level of success. The more time and energy invested by board members, the more success the program experienced with its critical task of fund-raising.

Ratings of Program Components. When program components were compared using multiple regression analysis, ratings of media cooperativeness were consistently more important for predicting program success than were ratings of the police coordinator or the board of directors (see Table 5). This finding does not necessarily suggest that media cooperation is the key to success, but only that program participants with successful programs gave higher ratings to their media component than participants with less successful programs.

Community Context. Productivity was the highest in communities with the lowest crime rates and areas with medium-sized populations (i.e., 100,000 to 250,000 people) (see Table 6). Perhaps communities of this size have sufficient resources to implement a well-staffed program and/or have a concerned, vigilant citizenry.

SUMMARY AND CONCLUSIONS

Crime Stoppers is a very popular and rapidly growing program for combating crime. Although this strategy has been adopted internationally over a relatively short period, its future in the United States appears to depend on two uncertain factors: its ability to survive the onslaught of legal challenges over the next few years and its ability to garner continued support and cooperation from the mass media.

With respect to their effectiveness in solving crimes, Crime Stoppers programs can cite impressive cumulative statistics, including the number of felony arrests, the number of persons convicted, and the amount of stolen property and narcotics recovered. Nevertheless, these data are not likely to reflect communitywide reductions in crime, unless one posits a general deterrent

effect due to mass media coverage. To date, this type of evaluation has not been performed.

Single dramatic cases of successful arrests and convictions are often more compelling to the public than dry aggregate statistics. Crime Stoppers is a highly visible program with a special appeal to the media, law enforcement, and community leaders. Furthermore, from strictly a crime-control perspective, this strategy may be effective at solving specific types of "dead-end" cases where additional citizen input is essential and at reaching segments of the population that are not attracted to traditional community crime prevention programs that encourage uncompensated overt participation. That is, Crime Stoppers is likely to appeal to persons who prefer to remain private, who are fearful of retaliation, who prefer/need monetary compensation, or who have other motives for not serving as a public witness. In neighborhoods characterized by drug wars and gang activity, the Crime Stoppers tip line may become a useful vehicle for citizens to "fight back" in an environment of extreme fear and limited options. On the other hand, critics fear that such programs will undermine the social fabric of our society by encouraging distrust among neighbors and discouraging participation in civic responsibilities without monetary compensation (see Rosenbaum and Lurigio, 1985).

Our randomized experiment on rewards suggests that reward size may not be as important to callers as most people believe. The results suggest that the usual advice of "when in doubt, pay more" may not be appropriate or necessary. Even $100 appears sufficient to keep most callers satisfied, regardless of the circumstances of the case.

Future Research

This national study is, to our knowledge, the first and only social scientific inquiry directed at Crime Stoppers programs. Although the present research constitutes an important first step toward understanding the nature and effects of this program, our knowledge is still very limited. Many of the observations and conclusions reached here are tentative and require further substantiation through controlled research. At this point, we do not know the independent and

TABLE 5. Program Productivity as a Function of Overall Success Ratings for Each Program Component (standardized regression coefficients)

Program Component Being Rated	Calls Received[a]	Calls Investigated[a]	Suspects Arrested[a]	Crimes Cleared[a]	Funds Raised[b]
		Productivity Measures (Dependent Variables)			
Police coordinator[c]	.19	.13	.25*	.17	.20
Board of directors[d]	−.28*	−.13	−.01	.04	.20
Media outlets[e]	.34**	.27*	.27*	.23*	.05
Overall program[f]	.32**	.35**	.37**	.43***	−.04
Proportion of variance explained (R^2)	.29	.26	.41	.41	.07

[a] Per 1,000 Part 1 crimes reported to the police.
[b] Total funds in the corporation's bank account per 100,000 population.
[c] Overall coordinator performance rating by board of director's chairperson.
[d] Combined board performance rating by coordinator and board chairperson.
[e] Combined media cooperativeness rating by coordinator and board chairperson (averaging separate ratings of each media type).
[f] Overall program success rating by coordinator.
*$p < .05$; **$p < .01$; ***$p < .001$.

TABLE 6. Program Productivity as a Function of Size and Type of Population Served

	Calls Received[a]	Calls Investigated[a]	Suspects Arrested[a]	Crimes Cleared[a]	Funds Raised[b]	N[c]
	Productivity Measures					
Size of population						
Less than 50,000	118	122	39	63	$37838	61
50,000 to 99,999	382	247	53	50	$11012	47
100,000 to 249,999	616	280	128	173	$ 9519	38
250,000 or larger	234	136	20	49	$ 547	46
Type of population						
Mostly urban residents	350	151	62	67	$13811	48
Mostly suburban residents	244	166	32	36	$12102	30
Mostly rural residents	273	69	68	52	$ 7754	13
Mixed	355	223	66	114	$24514	97

[a] Per 1,000 Part 1 crimes reported to the police.
[b] Total funds in the corporation's bank account per 100,000 population.
[c] Average sample size.

combined effects of monetary rewards and promises of anonymity on social behavior (see Rosenbaum and Lurigio, 1985). These are basic psychological incentives for citizen participation that deserve more careful study because they can have both prosocial and antisocial implications. Because Crime Stoppers offers an unprecedented role for the mass media in the area of crime control, the factors that constrain and facilitate this relationship should be closely examined, along with the effects of media coverage over extended periods of time. The legal implications of Crime Stoppers also deserve more careful scrutiny by legal and criminal justice scholars. Some of these issues will receive adequate attention in the courtroom, but often a more detached scholarly analysis, supplemented by research data, can help to identify the most appropriate course of legal action for our society.

Finally, the national character of this evaluation precluded the possibility of measuring the effects of the program on crime clearances. A controlled experiment would be necessary to determine whether Crime Stoppers is more cost-effective than conventional investigative techniques for solving particular types of crime. Researchers will need to examine the number of cases solved under each strategy, the average amount of time required to solve these cases, and the level of resources needed to achieve these results.

References

Bickman, L., J. Edwards, P. J. Lavrakas, and S. Green. 1977. *National Evaluation of Program Phase 1 Summary Report: Citizens Crime Reporting Projects*. Washington, D.C.: U.S. Department of Justice, Law Enforcement Assistance Administration.

Crime Stoppers International. 1988. *The Caller* (no. 53, April). Albuquerque, N.M.

———. 1989. *The Caller* (No. 61, January issue). Albuquerque, N.M.

DuBow, F., E. McCabe, and G. Kaplan. 1979. *Reactions to Crime: A Critical Review of the Literature*. Washington, D.C.: Government Printing Office.

Eck, J. E. 1982. *Solving Crime: The Investigation of Burglary and Robbery*. Washington, D.C.: Police Executive Research Forum.

Eck, J. E., and W. Spelman with D. Hill, D. W. Stephens, J. R. Stedman, and G. R. Murphy. 1987. *Problem Solving: Problem-Oriented Policing in Newport News*. Washington, D.C.: Police Executive Research Forum.

Feins, J. D. 1983. *Partnerships for Neighborhood Crime Prevention*. Washington, D.C.: Department of Justice, National Institute of Justice.

Kelling, G. L. 1988. *What Works: Research and the Police*. Washington, D.C.: Government Printing Office.

Lavrakas, P. J. 1985. "Citizen Self-Help and Neighborhood Crime Prevention Policy." In *American Violence and Public Policy*, ed. Lynn A. Curtis. New Haven, Conn.: Yale University Press.

Lavrakas, P. J., D. P. Rosenbaum, and A. J. Lurigio. 1990. "Mass Media, Law Enforcement and the Community: Understanding Relationships Through Crime Stoppers." In *The Media and Criminal Justice Policy*, ed. R. Surette. Springfield, Ill.: Charles C Thomas.

Lurigio, A. J., and D. P. Rosenbaum. 1989. "The Effects of Mass Media on Crime Prevention Awareness Attitudes and Behavior: The Case of Crime Stoppers." *American Journal of Community Psychology*.

MacAleese, G., and H. C. Tily. 1983. *Crime Stoppers Manual*. Albuquerque, N.M.: Crime Stoppers International.

McPherson, M., and G. Silloway. 1980. *Program Models: Planning Community Prevention Programs*. Minneapolis: Minnesota Crime Prevention Center.

Roehl, J. A., and R. F. Cook. 1984. *Evaluation of the Urban Crime Prevention Program*. Washington, D.C.: Department of Justice, National Institute of Justice.

Rosenbaum, D. P., ed. 1986. *Community Crime Prevention: Does It Work?* Beverly Hills, Calif.: Sage.

———. 1988. "The Theory and Research Behind Neighborhood Watch: Is It a Sound Fear and Crime Reduction Strategy?" *Crime and Delinquency* 33:103–134.

28.   GANG RIGHTS OFTEN WRONG THE INNOCENT

MIKE ROYKO

When I asked the woman for her name, her response was one of sheer terror. "I *can't* give you my name. Do you think I want that gang coming after my kid?"

That's what she had called about. She lives on the North Side in one of the neighborhoods where gangs are running wild, shooting each other and, as often as not, innocent bystanders.

In recent days, a baby has been killed. So was a woman shopper sitting in her car and a couple of nice teenagers who were on a porch minding their own business. And several others. The list is getting so long that we might consider putting up a wall of names similar to the Vietnam Memorial.

So the frightened woman asked: "When are the police going to do something about this?"

The answer, unfortunately, is that the police can't do much more than they're doing. And about all they can do is try to arrest the cold, young killers after they have shot someone. That's small comfort to the dead or their families.

It isn't that the police wouldn't like to do more. But thanks to the zeal of various lawyers, civil libertarians and judges, the gangbangers now laugh at the cops.

A few years ago, they didn't laugh much. They didn't have time to even giggle. That's when the police gang unit hassled them on sight. Any time they stuck their heads out the door, they ran the risk of being hauled in and charged with disorderly conduct.

It was only a misdemeanor, almost always dropped in court. But it kept them hopping and looking over their shoulders, which prevented some shootings and resulted in a lot of weapons being confiscated.

But lawyers went to federal court and persuaded a judge that this was harassment and a terrible violation of the gangbangers' constitutional rights. It probably was a violation, although I'm not sure how terrible it was. A bullet in an infant's head is far more damaging than a few hours in a police lockup.

So the federal judge said that the police could no longer violate the rights of some vicious punk who might have an Uzi hidden under his jacket.

Then there was the time Mayor Jane Byrne decided that the Cabrini-Green housing complex shouldn't be the country's biggest outdoor shooting gallery. Kids were dropping like bowling pins as the gangs went after each other.

So Byrne flooded the place with cops. They seized guns and dope, locked up punks and the body count promptly dropped to zero.

But the cry went up from lawyers, street workers and gangbangers' mothers that Byrne was turning Cabrini-Green into a police state. After I wrote a column saying Byrne's approach was necessary, I made a talk at the U. of I.'s Chicago campus and was picketed and jeered by several academics who said I must be some kind of fascist.

One of them was later accidentally killed in a gang shooting.

More recently, we've had efforts to get the gangs, the dope dealers and other slobs and menaces out of public housing.

The police and Vince Lane, the smart and hard-nosed head of the housing authority, would make surprise raids which disrupted and scattered the gang squatters, the dope squatters and other undesirables.

This was an effective tactic. Decent people could actually get on an elevator without winding up in the shaft.

But it offended the civil libertarians, and Lane's approach had to be modified. So now decent people have been restored their right to triple-lock their doors and be afraid to walk in their own hallways.

From *Chicago Tribune*, June 7, 1990. Reprinted by permission of Tribune Media Services.

So all I could tell that frightened lady who phoned me was, that if she could afford it, move.

If she couldn't, she should not let her teenage son sit on his own front steps. And if he did sit on the steps to dive for cover any time a car slowed.

I wonder about something. I know the ACLU lawyers and the other do-gooders have their hearts in the right place.

But do they ever go to the funerals?

29. YOUTH GANGS AND PUBLIC POLICY

C. RONALD HUFF

Recent studies (Klein and Maxson 1985, Chin 1986, Hagedorn 1988, Fagan 1988) have demonstrated that youth gangs in the United States have developed new, often violent organizational forms. The electronic and print media in many large and medium-sized American cities almost routinely carry accounts (often distorted) of "drug gangs," "Jamaican posses," "drive-by shootings," and other gang-related phenomena. However, research on these emerging/re-emerging gangs has been relatively rare, and studies that include interviews with gang members, as well as the use of official data, have been even more rare. This article summarizes one such study, an analysis of gangs in Ohio, and presents some public policy recommendations designed to address both the prevention and the control of youth gangs.

THE STUDY

The research on which this article is based took place from April 1986 to May 1988. The research project included in-depth case studies of youth gangs in Cleveland and Columbus, as well as secondary surveys of Ohio's five other large cities (Cincinnati, Toledo, Dayton, Akron, and Youngstown).

Data for the study were collected via the following methods:

1. Interviews with gang members, former gang members, police officers, representatives of community and social service agencies, and school officials in Cleveland and Columbus. To ensure a more representative sample of gang members, some of the interviews were conducted with gang members who had not been apprehended. These interviews generally took place either in members' housing projects or neighborhoods or in neutral locations. They were facilitated by trusted intermediaries who arranged them and accompanied the researchers.[1] Some of these interviews were recorded on audio tape while others, to reduce the interviewees' apprehensions, were summarized by handwritten notes.

2. Field observations of police operations targeting youth gangs and youth violence.

From *Crime and Delinquency*, Vol. 35 (4) October 1989, pp. 524–537. Copyright © 1989 Sage Publications. Reprinted with permission of Sage Publications, Inc.

C. Ronald Huff is Director, Program for the Study of Crime and Delinquency, and Professor of Public Policy and Management, Ohio State University.

[1] I am especially indebted to Akil Ogbanna, a caseworker with the Home Detention Project of the Cuyahoga County Juvenile Court (Cleveland), and the staff of the Youth Outreach Project (Columbus) for facilitating these interviews, which would otherwise have been impossible.

3. Analyses of secondary data from the Cleveland and Columbus police departments concerning arrests believed to be gang-related.

4. Surveys of all 88 county juvenile courts in Ohio, as well as the 7 chiefs of police of Ohio's largest cities and the principals of 66 junior and senior high schools (35 in Cleveland and 31 in Columbus).

PRINCIPAL FINDINGS

The surveys of school principals in Cleveland and Columbus revealed a moderate level of concern about gangs; little consensus on how to deal with the problem; and much agreement on the role of law enforcement, which is perceived as vitally important in controlling gang behavior in the two cities (law enforcement is viewed as having the primary responsibility).

The surveys of police chiefs of the largest cities in Ohio indicate that several chiefs currently acknowledge some problems with gangs; nearly all state that gangs have been a problem in the past, and all estimate that offenses by youth gangs represent less than 1% of all crime and less than 2% of all juvenile crime.

The case studies confirmed that youth gangs exist in both Cleveland and Columbus. During the course of this study, the primary and secondary data identified more than fifty separately named gangs in Cleveland, some of which undoubtedly were "splinter groups" or "groupies" rather than truly separate and unique gangs. Many of these gangs have either dissipated or merged with each other, leaving fifteen to twenty separate, viable gangs. In Columbus, the study identified more than twenty separately named gangs. However, with the same qualifications noted above, the number of truly separate, viable gangs at present is approximately fifteen. Cincinnati, though not a case study site, also has experienced youth gang problems during the course of this research, including incidents involving the neo-Nazi "Skinheads."

In terms of racial and ethnic identity, it is probable that about 90% of the members of Cleveland and Columbus gangs are black, while the remaining 10% are white and Hispanic. The study identified two Hispanic gangs (on Cleveland's west side). Statewide, police chiefs surveyed also reported that gang membership was more than 90% black, according to their own information.

The age of gang members ranges approximately from ten to thirty (with the most common age range being 14–24), and the larger gangs are stratified by age and sophistication. That is, until one is 16 or 17 years old, he is likely to be in a junior division of the gang. These divisions have their own leadership structures.

Several female "gangs" were identified in Cleveland and Columbus. However, upon closer investigation, these "gangs" were actually more similar to "groupies" whose identity was closely tied to that of male gang allies. Gang membership in Ohio is more than 90% male, according to data generated by this study.

Gangs in Columbus and Cleveland originated in the following ways:

1. Breakdancing/"rappin'" groups evolved into gangs as a result of intergroup conflict involving dancing, skating, and/or "rappin'" competition. This competition would sometimes spill over into the parking lots of skating rinks, where members frequently had concealed weapons in their cars.

2. Street corner groups similarly evolved into gangs as a result of conflicts with other "corner groups." These groups were more typical of distinctive neighborhoods, such as housing projects. In Cleveland, these groups had a much longer history than in Columbus, although that history has been uneven. Nonetheless, both cities have histories of street corner groups and "street hustling" that predate the current generation of street gangs.

3. Street gang leaders already experienced in gang life moved to Ohio from Chicago or Los Angeles. These more sophisticated leaders were often charismatic figures who were able to quickly recruit a following from among local youths.

Despite rumors to the contrary, this study produced no solid evidence that any Ohio youth gang is a "chapter" or direct affiliate of a gang in any other city (Chicago, Detroit, or Los Angeles in particular). It is likely that this confusion stems from the "out of state" identities of some gang leaders who moved to Ohio from other states. For the most part, this reflects our society's extensive geographic mobility, coupled with our historic tendency to blame "outsiders" for local problems rather than focus on the root causes (especially poverty and unemployment). However, in the past year Ohio's cities have witnessed the immigration of "crack" cocaine traffickers from Detroit, Los Angeles, and even Jamaica.

Members of the gangs identified in this study are overwhelmingly drawn from the "urban black underclass" described so well by Wilson (1987) and by Duster (1987). This is true of both Cleveland and Columbus, though for somewhat different reasons. Cleveland, a more heavily industrialized "rust belt" city, has been adversely impacted by the loss of many of its manufacturing jobs and the high unemployment rates it has experienced in the 1980s. Table 1 reflects changes in the poverty status of Cleveland families (including those with children under 18 years of age) from 1970 to 1980, while Table 2 presents the unemployment trend and the loss of manufacturing jobs during that period. Tables 3 and 4 present similar data for Columbus, widely known for its stable, "high-tech," service-oriented economy.

What is compelling about these tables is this: An economically and socially marginal youth who has dropped out of or been expelled from school, and/or is without job skills, is in deep trouble in either Cleveland or Columbus. In Cleveland, he is competing for a rapidly shrinking pool of manufacturing jobs (more than 36,000 of these jobs were lost between 1970 and 1980 alone) and cannot qualify for other jobs. In Columbus, there never were that many manufacturing jobs (in 1970 Columbus had less than one-half as many manufacturing jobs as Cleveland), and the jobs that exist require higher levels of education and job skills. To make matters worse, the military, a traditionally available alternative career path for the poor, is increasingly inaccessible due to the higher quality of applicants generated by an economy with relatively few attractive entry-level positions for unskilled workers.

As these tables reveal, poverty is increasingly victimizing families with children under 18 years of age. With little income to buy the flashy clothes and other consumer goods advertised throughout our society, a poor minority youth may find the "illegitimate opportunities" (Cloward and Ohlin 1960) available through gangs, crime, and drug sales more compelling than the legitimate options available to him.

TABLE 1. Poverty Status of Families (Cleveland), 1970–1980

	Year		Change 1970–1980	Percent of Change 1970–1980
	1970	1980		
Number of families	184,645	143,588	−41,057	−22.2
Number of families below poverty level	24,817	26,926	2,109	8.5
Percent of families below poverty level	13.4%	18.8%		5.4
Families below poverty level with children under 18 years	18,227	21,754	3,527	19.4
Percent of families below poverty level with children under 18 years	9.9%	15.2%		5.3

Source: U.S. Bureau of the Census.

TABLE 2. Total Unemployment and Loss of Manufacturing Jobs (Cleveland), 1970–1980

	Year		Change 1970–1980	Percent of Change 1970–1980
	1970	1980		
Civilian labor force	303,146	240,538	−62,608	−20.7
Unemployed	15,730	26,359	10,629	67.6
Unemployed as percent of civilian labor force	5.2%	11.0%		5.8
Work force employed by manufacturing	107,477	71,055	−36,422	−33.9
Manufacturing workers as percent of civilian labor force	35.5%	29.5%		−6.0

Source: U.S. Bureau of the Census.

The gangs identified in this study correspond to several loosely knit typologies:

1. Informal, *hedonistic gangs* whose focal concerns seem to be "getting high" (usually on alcohol and/or marijuana and other drugs) and "having a good time." These gangs occasionally engage in some minor property crime, but tend not to be involved in violent personal crime.

2. *Instrumental gangs* whose focal concerns are more economic and who commit a higher volume of property crimes for economic reasons. Most of these gang members also use alcohol and marijuana; some use "crack" cocaine. In addition, some *individual* members of these gangs sell drugs, but this is not an organized *gang* activity.

3. *Predatory gangs* that commit robberies, street muggings, and other crimes of opportunity

TABLE 3. Poverty Status of Families (Columbus), 1970–1980

	Year		Change 1970–1980	Percent of Change 1970–1980
	1970	1980		
Number of families	128,594	136,625	8,031	6.2
Number of families below poverty level	12,551	16,482	3,931	31.3
Percent of families below poverty level	9.8%	12.1%		2.3
Families below poverty level with children under 18 years	9,096	13,265	4,169	45.8
Percent of families below poverty level with children under 18 years	7.1%	9.7%		2.6

Source: U.S. Bureau of the Census.

TABLE 4. Total Unemployment and Loss of Manufacturing Jobs (Columbus), 1970–1980

	Year		Change 1970–1980	Percent of Change 1970–1980
	1970	**1980**		
Civilian labor force	227,330	279,727	52,397	23.0
Unemployed	8,647	17,894	9,247	106.9
Unemployed as a percent of civilian labor force	3.8%	6.4%		2.6
Work force employed by manufacturing	50,270	43,709	−6,561	−13.1
Manufacturing workers as a percent of civilian labor force	22.1%	15.6%		−6.5

Source: U.S. Bureau of the Census.

(including at least one known group rape). Members of these gangs are more likely to use highly addictive drugs such as "crack" cocaine, and these drugs contribute significantly to their labile, assaultive behavior. Members of these gangs may also sell drugs to finance the purchase of more sophisticated weapons. Although this study produced no hard evidence that any of these gangs is currently a "drug distribution network," they represent a ready-made "target of exploitation" for organized crime or other criminal groups.

Gang members actually spend most of their time engaging in exaggerated versions of typical adolescent behavior (rebelling against authority by skipping school, refusing to do homework, and disobeying parents; wearing clothing and listening to music that sets them apart from most adults; and having a primary allegiance to their peer group instead of their parents or other adults). They appear to "drift" into and out of illegal behavior, as described by Matza (1964), and the frequency and seriousness of their law-violating behavior appear to fit the three loose gang typologies above. The older the members of a gang, the more they seem to drift toward criminality and away from typical adolescent focal concerns.

Law-violating activities committed by youth gangs during the course of this study include theft, auto theft, intimidation and assault in school and on the street, robbery, burglary, rape, group rape, drug use, drug sales, and even murder. To be sure, the more serious the offense, the less frequently it occurs, but gang members do commit all of the above—and more. As one gang member said during his interview, "People may say there's no gangs 'cause they don't see no colors, but if they be robbin' people, shootin' people, and killin' people, they still a gang" (Field notes 1987).

While three of Ohio's largest cities have youth gangs, until recently only one (Columbus) had officially acknowledged their existence. This research, along with other national studies, suggests that cities experiencing problems with gangs pass through distinct and recognizable stages, and both Cincinnati and Cleveland (until recently) could best be characterized as being in the "official denial" stage. For a variety of reasons, not the least of which is protection of a city's "image," political leaders and others in key leadership roles are reluctant to acknowledge the existence of gangs.

Columbus's emergence from its own denial stage was probably accelerated by several gang-related incidents in 1984 and 1985, including: (1) a challenge issued by a gang leader on a local television news show, followed by his death several days later in a "drive-by shooting" carried out by a rival gang; (2) a gang-related assault on the governor's daughter; and (3) a gang-related assault on the mayor's son.[2]

Official denial of gang problems appears to facilitate victimization by gangs, especially in the public schools. School principals in several Ohio cities are reluctant to acknowledge "gang-related" assaults for fear that such problems may be interpreted as negative reflections on their management abilities. This "political paralysis" appears to encourage gang-related assaults and may send the wrong signals to gang members, implying that they can operate with impunity within the vacuum it creates.

Contrary to much "common wisdom," teachers who demonstrate that they care about a youth and then are firm but fair in their expectations are rarely, if ever, the victims of assault by gang members. Rather, it is those teachers who "back down" and are easily intimidated who are more likely to be the victims of assault. During two years of interviews, *not one* gang member ever said that a teacher who insisted on academic performance (within the context of a caring relationship) was assaulted. Such teachers are respected far more than those perceived as "weak," and "weakness" generally represents a quality to be exploited by gang members in an almost Darwinian fashion, much as they select targets on the street.

On the other hand, *overly* aggressive behavior directed at gang members appears to backfire. Interviews reveal that gang members have an intense dislike for police officers who use unnecessary "strong-arm" tactics in making arrests or questioning them, for example. Gang members indicated that they feel nothing but anger and

vengefulness when a police officer behaves "unprofessionally" and that they will seize any subsequent opportunity to "get even."

When asked what they think an officer should do when "baited" in front of other gang members or onlookers, gang members typically respond that an officer should "be professional," perhaps "laugh at him" and walk away rather than fight when challenged. Gang members admit grudging respect for such officers, and this respect appears to be even greater for officers who demonstrate some personal concern for gang members (asking how they're doing when they see them on the streets or admonishing them to stay out of trouble, for example).

Having moved through its "denial stage" rather quickly, Columbus reacted by implementing a comparatively well-balanced, two-pronged approach to the gang problem: (1) active and aggressive enforcement against gang leaders and hard core gang members via the Youth Violence Crime Section, a special 18-officer unit in the Columbus Police Department; and (2) prevention directed at marginal gang members and would-be members via the Youth Outreach Project, supported by United Way, the Columbus Public Schools, and the Columbus Department of Parks and Recreation. Columbus's approach is perhaps as well-balanced and well-coordinated as any in the nation, though much remains to be accomplished. Two keys to its effectiveness are its unique centralization of all four major gang control functions (intelligence, prevention, enforcement, and investigation) in one police unit (the Youth Violence Crime Section) and that unit's close cooperation with the schools, the courts, the prosecutor's office, the Youth Outreach Project, and other community agencies.

An unanticipated consequence of court-ordered busing in Cleveland and Columbus has been exacerbation of gang conflict in certain schools. Prior to mandatory busing, the gangs that existed were largely neighborhood, "turf"-oriented gangs. As a result of busing, there are now rival gangs at the same schools. Schools were not planned and organized with security in mind and do not readily lend themselves to such concerns. As a result, intimidation and assaults have occurred in certain schools where rival gangs find themselves together.

---

[2]It appears that one of the factors often responsible for moving cities out of the "denial" stage is, unfortunately, a highly publicized assault or homicide involving a highly visible "V.I.P." in the community (e.g., the governor's daughter and the mayor's son in Columbus; an affluent Asian woman in the Westwood theater district of Los Angeles; a Honolulu police officer). Generally, the victimization of the poor has not been sufficient to cause this issue to "bubble up" on the political agendas of most American cities.

Busing, along with the ready availability of automobiles and improved freeway systems in our metropolitan areas, has also provided gang members with vastly increased geographic mobility. Gang members described in detail the planning and execution of auto thefts in suburban shopping malls far away from their own homes, for example. The implications for law enforcement are clear: to effectively contain these gang-related offenses, police must have some centralized unit or, at the very least, must share intelligence on gang members and their activities. Whether a department has a gang unit, a juvenile bureau, or a highly decentralized organizational structure, it must identify and be able to recognize gang leaders and members who criss-cross the metropolitan area at will and who may show up at citywide events, such as rock concerts, to "shake down the squares" from the suburbs (intimidate and rob suburbanites coming into the city for such events).

Finally, busing has dramatically changed the meaning of "neighborhood." Forerunners of the current gangs in Cleveland and Columbus were neighborhood street corner groups and "turf"-oriented gangs who fought one another over turf, ethnic and racial conflict, and other issues. Interviews with gang members in both Cleveland and Columbus revealed that "neighborhood" no longer conveys the same kind of meaning, nor does it seem to have much importance to these youths. If still in school, they attend schools with pupils from various neighborhoods. Gang membership is no longer confined to the neighborhood, but involves confederates recruited at school, at skating rinks, and elsewhere throughout the city.

PUBLIC POLICY RECOMMENDATIONS

Youth gangs may best be viewed as a symptom of underlying social and economic problems that go far beyond the usual alienation found in youth subcultures in Western nations. The existence of an urban underclass, with its attendant socially disorganized and fragmented living conditions, gives rise to many social pathologies and the gang problem is just one of them. Primary pre-

vention should be heavily emphasized in any strategy addressing youth gangs, yet it is probably the most neglected type of intervention. As a number of police officers have said during this study, "Simply arresting them and locking them up is not the whole answer. We have to figure out a way to reach young kids *before* they get involved with these gangs" (Field notes 1988). Given the obstacles confronting poor and minority inner city youths, primary prevention programs must address both economic opportunity and neighborhood and family social structures.

For this reason, a two-stage strategy for states is recommended. This strategy, which will require federal assistance, is as follows:

1. In Phase One, a state would commission a study to identify *by zip code* those areas of our cities producing disproportionate numbers of commitments to prisons, youth correctional facilities, and mental health facilities, as well as those generating high numbers of public assistance recipients.[3] The total cost of these indicators of social and economic pathology would then be listed for each zip code area. These zip code areas, though not synonymous with "neighborhoods,"[4] would constitute the target areas for special primary prevention efforts.

2. In Phase Two, the state would issue a Request for Proposals for innovative primary prevention approaches to the multiple problems of these zip code areas. Such proposals

---

[3]This idea was formulated after learning that the Ohio Department of Youth Services had conducted an internal study analyzing commitments by zip codes. The idea seemed worthy of broader application across multiple social control "systems" (crime, welfare, mental illness, etc.), since zip code information is one of the few common denominators among state government databases, if not the only one.

[4]There are several problems inherent in using zip code information; among other things, zip code areas are not uniformly defined, and the populations of those areas are nonuniform. Therefore, any application of this strategy would necessitate some further efforts to standardize these indicators of social pathology on the basis of population size for the purpose of comparing seriousness and developing priority "targets."

would address methods of strengthening families and social institutions, improving job opportunities, and otherwise reducing the overwhelming obstacles confronting area residents. Our current failures in these areas of our cities are costing us a great deal of money and even more in human misery and wasted lives. This approach could offer some hope for innovation.

Schools and teacher preparation programs in our colleges and universities should move purposefully to develop teachers who are capable of teaching about and discussing situational ethics in general classrooms. Ethics should not be a special, isolated course, but rather should be integrated at appropriate points during the day as it relates to student dilemmas, student behaviors, history lessons, etc. This proposal is not meant to violate the separation of church and state; the instruction should not be in religion. Rather, it is analogous to the British "Lifeline" series on situational ethics. Other programs, such as Quest, that focus on values and ethics in the school context should also be considered.

Also, schools and teacher preparation programs should heed the findings of this study with respect to gangs' impact in schools. Teachers (and perhaps principals) need to have better assertiveness training and deeper understanding of some guiding principles such as Glasser's Reality Therapy, which emphasizes holding students accountable for their behavior.

As *preventive* measures, states should consider establishing statewide intergovernmental task forces on gangs, organized crime, and narcotics. The enormous profits to be made by selling drugs will be difficult for poor youths to resist. Some of the gangs that now exist may also be easy targets for exploitation by organized crime seeking new narcotics markets. If prevention is to be successful, it will require statewide coordination.

In addition, each large city should establish a local task force that brings together the following components (where they exist): juvenile bureau, youth gang unit, narcotics unit, organized crime unit, school security division, youth outreach project or other social service coordinating pro-

gram, and juvenile court. Information must be shared on a regular basis if prevention efforts are to be successful in dealing with the potential drug/gang connection.

The increased mobility of gang members requires that police agencies reassess their organizational structures and strongly consider establishing some citywide unit for monitoring gangs and collecting intelligence information. Ideally, the four major gang control functions identified above should be centralized in that unit as much as possible.

Police should be aggressive but professional in dealing with gangs. Gangs must learn that they cannot operate with impunity and that their sense of "invisibility" (which may be a carryover from the well-documented sense of invisibility described by many black citizens in a white-dominated society) is a false one. These aggressive police actions should, however, be targeted solely at the leaders and hard-core members. The marginal members and "wanna be's" can be influenced to redirect their behavior in more positive ways.

For leaders and hard-core gang members who are found delinquent (or, if adults, are found guilty of crimes), but who do not pose threats to public safety, the courts should consider the use of intensive probation supplemented by either random, unannounced visits and telephone monitoring or by electronic monitoring. The purpose of this sanction would be to break up street gangs by requiring that hard-core members and leaders be at home unless they are at school, at work, etc.

School boards should develop very clear policies forbidding weapons of any kind to be brought into schools, and these policies should be explained to all students and enforced without exception. Also, there should be a close working relationship between the schools and the local police, and students should be informed that schools are not "islands" where unlawful behavior is both "invisible" and immune from arrest and prosecution. Weapons offenses, violent assaults, and other serious offenses should be reported to the police.

Schools must make it clear to all that their first obligation is to ensure an environment conducive to learning, and that means one free from intimidation and assault. In some urban schools, administrative concern with school "image" and the administrators' careers, along with some of the other dynamics of official denial, seem to take precedence over the protection of children.

Traditionally, the school was a place that gang members treated with some respect—a sort of "neutral zone" where gang warfare was largely taboo. In part, this reflected tradition and neighborhood loyalties toward neighborhood schools. The demise of neighborhood schools seems to have significantly dissipated this sense of respect. It also has greatly complicated after-school extracurricular activities, since many students who might want to participate in those activities may have difficulty finding transportation home afterward. Finally, it has reduced the school's perceived importance as a neighborhood center where other kinds of activities occur (parent effectiveness training, continuing education classes, GED classes, job skills workshops, etc.), since the "common denominator" is no longer as clear to many residents.

Urban communities need to re-establish strong neighborhood-based centers and programs to tie the residents of inner city areas together in the pursuit of their common concerns. To rebuild a sense of community and collective responsibility, we must begin at the family and neighborhood levels.

Finally, several programs now operating in Ohio and elsewhere offer positive examples of programmatic efforts to address the hopelessness and despair confronting the urban underclass. These include Cleveland's "Scholarship in Escrow" Program. This program was begun because of a concern that about half of all students were dropping out of school, in part because they could see no tangible (i.e., job-related) benefits of a high school diploma. They often had siblings who *had* completed high school, but to no apparent avail; they still had no jobs and none of them could afford college or job training programs.

To counter this lack of incentive, the "Scholarship in Escrow" Program was created by a partnership between the Cleveland Public Schools and representatives of the private sector in metropolitan Cleveland. The program essen-

tially creates a trust fund ($16 million thus far) for all students enrolled in grades 7–12 and credits each of their accounts with ten dollars for every C, twenty dollars for every B, and forty dollars for every A earned in school. The money goes into a scholarship fund, where it earns interest. Each student earning money for grades receives a certificate (somewhat like a stock certificate) indicating the amount earned. Students who graduate from Cleveland public high schools have up to eight years to use their scholarship monies at any Pell Grant-certified college or technical school. The program is based on two rationales: (1) If wealthy families can create trust funds for the future of their children, why cannot we as a society create trust funds for *all* kids? and (2) Since their *future* income will be highly correlated with their educational achievement, why not pay kids for doing well in school now, as an intermediate reinforcement? The program is in its first year of operation, and thus far the superintendent reports that about half of the eligible students are earning money; the other half are earning nothing.

Youth gangs are symptomatic of many of the same social and economic problems as adult crime, mental illness, drug abuse, alcoholism, the surge in homelessness, and multi-generation "welfare families" living in hopelessness and despair. While we are justly concerned with the replacement of our physical infrastructure (roads, bridges, sewers) our *human* infrastructure may be crumbling as well. Our social, educational, and economic infrastructures are not meeting the needs of many children and adults. Increases in the numbers of women and children living in poverty (the "feminization" and "juvenilization" of poverty) are dramatic examples of this recent transformation.

To compete with the seductive lure of drug profits and the grinding despair of poverty, we must reassess our priorities and reaffirm the importance of our neighborhoods by putting in place a number of programs that offer hope, education, job skills, and meaningful lives. It is worth the cost of rebuilding our human infrastructure since it is, after all, our children whose lives are being wasted and our cities in which the quality of life is being threatened.

References

Chin, Ko-lin. 1986. "Chinese Triad Societies, Tongs, Organized Crime, and Street Gangs in Asia and the United States." Ph.D. dissertation, Wharton School, University of Pennsylvania, Philadelphia.

Cloward, Richard A., and Lloyd E. Ohlin. 1960. *Delinquency and Opportunity: A Theory of Delinquent Gangs.* New York: Free Press.

Duster, Troy. 1987. "Crime, Youth Unemployment, and the Black Urban Underclass." *Crime & Delinquency* 33:300–316.

Fagan, Jeffrey. 1988. "The Social Organization of Drug Use and Drug Dealing among Urban Gangs." Paper presented at the Ohio Conference on Youth Gangs and the Urban Underclass, Ohio State University, Columbus, May 1988. Forthcoming in *Criminology.*

Field notes. 1987. Interview with anonymous juvenile gang member, Cleveland.

Field notes. 1988. Interview with anonymous police officer, Columbus.

Hagedorn, John M. 1988. *People and Folks: Gangs, Crime and the Underclass in a Rustbelt City.* Chicago: Lake View Press.

Klein, Malcolm W., and Cheryl L. Maxson. 1985. "Rock Sales' in South Los Angeles." *Sociology and Social Research* 69:561–65.

Matza, David. 1964. *Delinquency and Drift.* New York: Wiley.

Wilson, William Julius. 1987. *The Truly Disadvantaged.* Chicago: University of Chicago Press.

CHAPTER 12

WHITE-COLLAR CRIME

INTRODUCTION

White-collar crime has gained increasing attention in the last quarter-century. Many highly publicized episodes of white-collar crime have been reported in the press. These stories call attention to the fact that highly respectable people, many of them from "good" families and highly educated, somehow end up on the wrong side of the law. Vice President Spiro Agnew pleaded "no contest" to allegations of bribes amounting to hundreds of thousands of dollars; senior executives at E. F. Hutton wrote at least $4 billion in overdrafts on accounts in four hundred banks; Hitachi executives carried out an elaborate scheme to steal trade secrets from IBM; Ivan Boesky used inside information to make hundreds of millions of dollars on the stock market illegally, then turned witness against Michael Milken, who had fraudulently made $1.5 billion and pleaded guilty to felony charges that brought him a sentence of ten years in a federal penitentiary and fines of $600 million.

These instances of white-collar crime are among the more publicized episodes of respectable thievery. Though virtually all bank robberies make the evening news, most white-collar crime goes unreported. Millions of dollars are lost each year in insurance fraud, for example, yet such cases rarely make the newspapers. The magnitude of white-collar crime is enormous. Justice Department officials estimate that a minimum of $200 billion is stolen each year by white-collar criminals, compared to a cost of a mere $11 billion for the work of violent blue-collar criminals.[1]

The sociologist Edwin Sutherland coined the term "white-collar crime." Data for his original study of seventy large corporations were obtained from newspapers, court records, and the proceedings of regulatory agencies. These sources were all in the public record, yet Sutherland's study was so controversial in the 1940s that the publisher demanded the deletion of all names from the book. The uncut version was finally published in 1983.

Sutherland's pioneering work failed to make a distinction between criminal activities for private self-interest and criminal activities for corporate interests. When so-called respectable people commit crimes for their own profit in the course of their occupations, their illegal activities are now called "occupational crimes"; crimes they commit on behalf of their corporations are called "corporate crimes." The bank clerk who embezzles money and the doctor who defrauds insurance companies and government agencies are committing occupational crimes. Corporation executives who misrepresent their products in advertising, evade corporate taxes and environmental regulations, and collude with executives of other firms to fix prices are engaged in corporate crime.

The management practices of Thomas Jones at the Northrop Corporation constitute a clear case of corporate crime. Thomas and a large cast of supporting characters inside the corporation and at high levels of government in several nations were able to cut one corrupt deal after another for several decades. The corruption was not confined to a few rogue employees. The investigative reporter John Hanrahan points out that the board of directors, other executives, and political leaders were fully aware of Jones's scandalous practices. Large-scale deceptions involving overseas payoffs, illegal political contributions, and falsified tests were carefully organized and orchestrated as a corporate strategy. Hanrahan's detailed account of wrongdoing in a major American company is more than the story of Mr. Jones; it is a case history of corporate culture and symbiotic ties with political institutions that protect illegal conduct.

The distinction between corporate crime and occupational crime is more difficult to make in the case of the S & L crisis, for at least two reasons. First, some of the financial misdeeds seem to have been motivated by personal greed as well as corporate advancement. It is difficult to determine whether Charles Keating's scandalous conduct, for example, was motivated by a desire to maintain an extravagant lifestyle or whether it was an organizational strategy involving many levels of decision making. Perhaps it was both. Second, the magnitude and complexity of the S & L crisis are unprecedented. The amount of money ($500 billion and counting), the range of organizations (hundreds of federal and state agencies), and the number of people involved (thousands of bankers, consultants, regulators, politicians) make the S & L crisis the

---

[1] Ted Gest, "Stealing $200 Billion 'the Respectable Way,'" *U.S. News & World Report*, May 20, 1985, pp. 83–85.

largest financial scandal in American history. We have selected three essays to allow readers an opportunity to sample views on this perplexing topic. The S & L crisis allows students to study two conflicting tendencies in the organizational culture of the capitalist system. On the one hand, capitalism places high value on aggressive striving

for profits; people who take big risks are celebrated. On the other hand, excessive concern for profits is denounced as greed and can bring the risk taker into conflict with the law. Some financial celebrities who are now in the penitentiary are part of the $500 billion S & L story.

30. THE DEVIL AND MR. JONES

JOHN HANRAHAN

Thomas V. Jones arrived at the Shoreham Hotel in Washington, D.C., on the evening of December 8, 1989, three weeks before he stepped down as the chief executive officer of the Northrop Corp., to receive his industry's equivalent of Hollywood's Oscar for Lifetime Achievement. For the 69-year-old executive, it was an occasion to reflect upon his 47 years in the aerospace industry—37 of them at Northrop—and to drink in his colleagues' tributes. More than the head of one of the country's major defense contractors, Jones was an architect of America's military-industrial machine, a man described by the *Los Angeles Times* as the "last of the aerospace Titans."

His record of achievements was impressive. During his 29-year reign, Northrop's sales increased more than 20-fold, from $263 million in 1959 to $5.8 billion in 1988. Jones, who had close ties to former President Ronald Reagan, helped Northrop win contracts totaling about $36 billion during the U.S. arms build-up of the 1980s. A player on the international stage, he frequently

met with many of the world's top foreign leaders, contacts that helped Northrop become a major worldwide supplier of military aircraft.

Presented at the Shoreham ceremony with the National Aeronautic Association's prestigious Wright Brothers Memorial Trophy, Jones was lauded as a "visionary, bold designer, planner, engineer and manager" who has "significantly enhanced the defense and air transportation capacity of the United States."

This flattering portrait was, of course, incomplete. As those who follow the defense industry know all too well, there is a dark side to Jones's legacy. In February 1990, just two months after Jones relinquished his CEO post to longtime company executive Kent Kresa, Northrop pleaded guilty to 34 felony counts of falsifying test results on key components for air-launched cruise missiles and AV-8B Harrier jets and was fined $17 million, perhaps the largest penalty ever imposed on a defense contractor. In a plea-bargaining deal, the government dropped 141 other criminal counts against Northrop and agreed to discontinue an investigation into allegations that Northrop falsified tests and used irregular purchasing procedures on the MX missile guidance system. Fraud allegations relating to the B-2 stealth bomber were also dropped.

Even now, up to seven grand juries throughout the country reportedly are investigating alle-

From *Common Cause Magazine*, November/December 1990, pp. 12–19. Copyright © 1990 Common Cause Magazine. Reprinted with permission.

John Hanrahan, a Washington writer, was formerly senior editor of Common Cause Magazine.

gations that Northrop has engaged in bribery, deliberate overcharging and falsifying test results. The allegations touch on nearly every major weapon Northrop has recently worked on, including not only the B-2 but the F-20 Tigershark fighter plane, the F/A-18 Hornet fighter attack jet and Tacit Rainbow (a top-secret anti-radar missile). Northrop also remains a target of the continuing "Ill Wind" grand jury probe into defense consulting practices.

Northrop and Jones, who will remain on the company's board until 1992, also face a continuing congressional investigation of questionable payments Northrop made to South Korean agents during attempts to sell F-20s to that country in the mid-1980s. In addition, Northrop is fighting several civil lawsuits filed by shareholders, former and current employees and the Justice Department, charging the firm with fraud and other improprieties.

This unenviable record leads critics to depict Northrop as one of the nation's most lawless military contractors. Rep. John Dingell (D-Mich.) chairman of the House Energy and Commerce oversight and investigations subcommittee, which has pursued numerous allegations of wrongdoing at Northrop, says Jones has presided over "a continuing criminal enterprise." Rep. Jim Slattery (D-Kan.) vows not "to vote for another dime for the Northrop company" until Jones is completely severed from the corporation.

How have Jones and his company managed to survive—and prosper—for so long? The answer to that question lies in the unique relationship that binds the Pentagon to its chief contractors—a factor amply clear in various Northrop investigations.

THE KOREAN CONNECTION

Last September, nine months after being honored by his peers in Washington, Thomas Jones abruptly resigned as Northrop's board chairman, a post he'd continued to occupy after his departure as CEO. The same day the public learned of an international arbitrator's ruling that in the mid-1980s Northrop had paid $6.25 million to South Korean businessmen in an effort to tempt the government in Seoul to buy the company's F-20 fighter plane. The arbitrator said Jones himself appeared to have been involved in the scheme.

The roots of the scandal go back to the late 1970s, when President Jimmy Carter limited U.S. arms transfers to third world hot spots. The administration opposed overseas sales of highly sophisticated fighters—such as the F-16 made by General Dynamics—but favored the sale of intermediate fighters, which are a technological rung below the country's most advanced aircraft. To Jones, this policy created a new business opportunity: Northrop would design and manufacture an updated intermediate fighter for sale to third world countries hungry for improved air power. Although no Defense Department funds were available for research and development of the plane, Jones decided to take the risk, ultimately sinking $1.2 billion into the F-20 Tigershark.

Jones figured his most likely customer would be Taiwan since Northrop already had sold the country hundreds of aircraft, including a large number of F-5s, the F-20's predecessor. But the Carter administration, reportedly fearful of jeopardizing relations with the People's Republic of China, blocked the sale. When Ronald Reagan moved into the White House, Jones's hopes were renewed. Unfortunately for Northrop, Reagan also decided that relations with China were too important to allow the sale of the F-20 to Taiwan.

With the loss of his top sales prospect, Jones scrambled for a buyer. He approached a number of foreign leaders as well as the U.S. Air Force, but not a single order was placed.

One major prospect was South Korea. The key to Northrop's sales strategy was to hire individuals who had access to top officials in Seoul's government. In March 1983 the company retained the services of Jimmy K. Shin, who was born in Korea but lived in Hawaii as a naturalized U.S. citizen. Shin in turn got Northrop to hire Park Chong Kyu, a former security chief for the government of South Korea, in August 1984. (Park died of liver cancer in December 1985.)

Shin and Park were described in memos by Northrop Vice President James Dorsey as businessmen "with a great deal of experience in doing business in ROK [Republic of Korea]" whose "contacts within the business community and in the upper levels of governmental activities in ROK will be invaluable."

Dorsey's reports portray the pair as the sort of pin-striped lobbyists who populate Washington, a characterization that's less than faithful to the facts.

Consider the résumé of Jimmy Shin. One of his principal business activities was as former part owner of the S Palace, a Honolulu bar. Raided in 1975 by the police, who shut down its illegal gambling operation, the bar reportedly employed young Korean women who were paid $50 a month, plus room and board, and were fired or sued if they married.

Attorneys for Northrop, who later investigated the company's efforts to sell the F-20 to Korea, claim that Shin's own lawyer, George Hong, told them during the course of an interview with Shin that his client is a liar with "an unsavory reputation both in Korea and in Honolulu."

This was the "business consultant" Northrop hired in 1983 at an annual salary of $102,000. Apparently pleased with its choice, the company renewed Shin's contract in 1984 and again in 1985. In 1987, when Northrop conducted an internal probe of the company's Korean operation, Shin admitted "he knew nothing about airplanes."

Shin's colleague in the Northrop deal, Park Chong Kyu, was nicknamed "Pistol Park," a reference to his love for guns. According to the *Wall Street Journal*, Park was "a well-known Mr. Fixit with many powerful friends." In 1980, for example, Park stood accused of obtaining more than $2 million in illegal real estate holdings and was placed under house arrest. His confinement didn't last long. Back in 1973, Park had reportedly hidden Chun Doo Hwan in his home when Chun was being sought by the military for his alleged involvement in a coup attempt. In 1980 Chun, by then the nation's president, pardoned Park, who went on to serve in the National Assembly.

Like Shin, Park owned a disreputable night club. Park's Safari Club in Seoul was known for gambling and women, and for business deals that sometimes involved Korean government officials. Once, when life at the club seemed dull, Park livened it up by pulling out his pistols and blasting the mirrors behind the bar.

As Northrop's field rep for the F-20, Park received a seemingly modest annual salary of $78,000—but that was only part of the story.

To promote the F-20, Shin later told Northrop's attorneys, he and Park spent $90,000 entertaining Korean government officials at hostess bars and restaurants. While Shin's contract limited his expenses to $200 a day, he said he was willing to absorb the loss because of the huge sales commissions he and Park anticipated.

Those commissions were to come through another Northrop representative in Korea, the Dong Yang Express Group, a transportation and tourism company controlled by Park. DYE's agreement with Northrop meant potential commissions of up to $55 million for Park and his associates, with Shin taking 25 percent.

As Park was signing on as a consultant, Northrop made an unusual business decision for a defense contractor. In July 1984 the aerospace company entered into a joint venture to build and own a deluxe hotel in downtown Seoul with a South Korean tourist and leasing firm, Asia Culture Travel Development Company. Northrop would invest $6.25 million. From all appearances, the deal had nothing to do with the F-20 but, curiously enough, the travel company was controlled by none other than Park Chong Kyu.

Northrop's $6.25 million contribution to the hotel project was "actually diverted to develop a slush fund to bribe various Korean officials" to buy the F-20, Rep. Dingell said during one of his subcommittee's many recent hearings on Northrop. And Jones appeared to be "personally involved in the scheme," Dingell said.

NOWHERE HOTEL

Details of the alleged scheme began to surface in 1987, when the executive committee of Northrop's board retained a private law firm to conduct an internal investigation.

Two lawyers from the firm interviewed Shin in January 1987 at a session described in a memo obtained by Dingell's subcommittee. Shin claimed a plan was hatched during a March 1984 meeting in Tokyo involving Shin and Park and two of Northrop's executive vice presidents, James Dorsey and Welko Gasich. According to the memo, Park "proposed to Dorsey and Gasich that he needed a 'lobby fund' of approximately $5 million as a payoff fund for various people" to sell the F-20.

Dorsey and Gasich were interested, Shin said, according to the interview memo, but told Park they could proceed only if they had some "legal documentation" to cover up the slush fund. Park then suggested an arrangement in which Northrop would put up an amount equal to the value of his Seoul nightclub. Dorsey and Gasich "indicated it was a good idea," the memo states, and suggested Park draw up a proposal. Some time later, Donald Foulds, a Northrop vice president, signed the agreement.

Five months after the Tokyo meeting, a Northrop subsidiary deposited $6.25 million in a Hong Kong bank account controlled by the travel company. Three weeks later, according to a recent decision by the International Court of Arbitration, an aide to Park withdrew the entire amount and distributed $3 million to Park, $2 million to Park's brother-in-law, who was chairman of Dong Yang, and $1 million to Shin. The aide kept the rest for himself. Whether any of this money subsequently went to any Korean government officials is still the subject of grand jury and congressional investigations.

Meanwhile, back at Northrop's headquarters in California, executives involved in the deal apparently were keeping the company's board of directors in the dark.

O. Meredith Wilson, chairman of the board's executive committee, says the hotel venture was first brought to the board's attention during a meeting on July 18, 1984. Testifying before Dingell's subcommittee in September 1988, Wilson said board members were concerned about "who they were dealing with." Jones later reported back to the board, Wilson said, saying he "was assured by a Korean . . . that they were sound people in Korea." Wilson testified that there were other things the board was not told at the time: The deal had already been signed, a fact he wouldn't learn for another six months, and the Seoul nightclub had been assessed at far less than the $6.25 million Northrop invested.

Wilson says information about the appraisal and other facts remained unknown to the board until the private law firm was retained in 1987.

Jones had reason to give Park high ratings. It was Park, after all, who had arranged for Jones to meet privately with President Chun Doo Hwan in Los Angeles in 1984 and in Honolulu in 1985. Chun at first seemed interested in buying the F-20, but apparently lost interest in October 1984, when a Tigershark crashed in Korea during a test flight arranged by Park. Chun, who left the presidency in February 1988, acknowledged discussing the F-20 with Jones but denied having received any money from Northrop relating to it.

By early 1986, Northrop's executives began to realize they had a problem. First, the Korean government made it clear it wasn't going to buy the F-20. Second, Northrop Vice Chairman Frank Lynch revealed that the hotel project had no licenses, no blueprints, no permits. The executive committee directed Lynch to retrieve Northrop's $6.25 million, but by then, of course, the money was long gone.

The board members got more bad news. Shin and others involved in the F-20 and hotel deals wrote to Jones and other Northrop officials threatening to go public with embarrassing details of the $6.25 million transaction unless they received some additional payments. Park's brother-in-law demanded Northrop pay $16.5 million to end its agreements with Dong Yang and the travel company.

In June 1986 Northrop sent $1.5 million to a Dong Yang account in Winnetka, Ill. International arbitrator Wolfgang Kuhn subsequently determined $500,000 of this went to Park's brother-in-law, $500,000 to Shin and $500,000 to another Korean who claimed he had worked on F-20 promotion.

Shin's attorney wrote to Northrop in early 1987, Kuhn found, threatening to sue Northrop for terminating his client's consulting contract unless the company retained Shin to recover the $6.25 million and paid him a 30 percent commission.

By this point, the situation was completely out of control. Claiming that funds relating to a legitimate business transaction had been stolen by Korean con men, Northrop filed lawsuits in Korea and Hawaii and initiated arbitration proceedings both in Korea and with the International Court of Arbitration. Both arbitration panels ruled against Northrop earlier this year; the lawsuits are pending.

The Korean arbitrator, while not determining what the $6.25 million was to be used for, found much to criticize in Northrop's business methods, noting, "It is unimaginable that officers of Northrop . . . would remit funds to an unknown Hong Kong passbook account without setting up some sort of internal control."

Arbitrator Kuhn was more explicit. He wrote that the $6.25 million "was paid in order to induce Mr. C. K. Park to use his influence to market the F-20." Kuhn was "convinced" that Dorsey, Foulds and Gasich—"and probably Mr. Jones"—knew of and approved Park's request for money to market the F-20.

"This is not a situation where low ranking officers colluded to defraud Northrop, but where Northrop acted, probably illegally, through its top management," Kuhn concluded. He said the $6.25 million payment appeared to violate both Korean and U.S. anti-corruption laws.

Though his term was not due to expire for eight months, Jones resigned as chairman the day Kuhn's decision became public. Northrop insists there was no connection.

Jones is lucky. Colleagues who were involved in the Korean deals are gone from the company, including Dorsey, Gasich and Foulds. Securities and Exchange Commission (SEC) documents also reveal that Jones was reprimanded by the company's board "regarding his management style in connection with Northrop's efforts to sell the F-20 to the government of South Korea." Company officials declined to elaborate.

Despite the arbitrator's rulings, the executives' departures and Jones's reprimand, Northrop maintains its innocence. Company spokesperson Tony Cantafio says, "We've said in the past and continue to say that we invested in a hotel, and we were defrauded by a group of Koreans." Jones, who seldom grants press interviews, did not respond to a request for comment.

He may have to talk eventually should two federal grand juries return indictments in their probes of events surrounding the Korean hotel deal and F-20 sales efforts.

Northrop ultimately lost its $1.2 billion investment in the F-20, in addition to still being out the $6.25 million it paid Park and the others. It long since has canceled the F-20 program; not a single F-20 was ever sold.

THE WATERGATE CONNECTION

The Korean debacle wasn't the first time Jones and his company faced allegations of employing shady middlemen to handle questionable financial transactions.

Congressional investigators and federal prosecutors found that shortly after Jones took over as CEO in 1960 he created a political slush fund that made illegal corporate campaign contributions to President Richard Nixon and other presidential candidates.

According to a Watergate prosecutor's memo, in the early 1960s Jones and Northrop Vice President James Allen decided to create "a convenient means to generate sizable corporate funds for purposes that for one reason or another could not be accounted for publicly."

In this case the middleman was William Savy, a French national and former intelligence operative. Savy's annual "consulting fee" was $180,000; he used 70 to 80 percent of the money to promote Northrop's aircraft in Europe and sent the rest to Allen for his use, after channeling it through secret bank accounts in Luxembourg and Switzerland. Allen told Watergate prosecutors illegal campaign payments included $15,000 to Lyndon Johnson in 1964, $15,000 to Nixon in 1968 and $5,000 to Nixon's 1968 opponent, Hubert Humphrey.

Jones and Allen didn't get caught, however, until they secretly funneled as much as $175,000 to Nixon's reelection campaign in 1972.

In February 1972 Jones met with three Republican fundraisers, including Herbert Kalmbach, Nixon's personal attorney. Memos from the special prosecutor's office show that although the executive was prepared to donate $50,000 to the campaign, Kalmbach "made clear to Jones that persons in his position were expected to be able to deliver $100,000." Anonymity could be guaranteed, Jones was told, to anyone who gave before April 7, 1972, the date a new campaign contribution law was to take effect—even though both the old law *and* the new one prohibited corporate donations.

Following the meeting with Kalmbach, Jones and Allen decided to send Savy corporate funds totaling $120,000, ostensibly as consultant fees. The Northrop executives told Savy to write 20 checks of $5,000 each on his Luxembourg bank account and send them to various GOP fundraising committees in March 1972.

Sometime later Jones told Kalmbach he could make additional funds available for "unforeseen campaign contingencies." In July 1972, when White House officials needed hush money for the Watergate burglary defendants, Kalmbach approached Jones again. Jones—not knowing what the money was intended for—personally delivered $50,000 to Kalmbach. (Kalmbach put the figure at $75,000.)

By the mid-1970s Jones was neck deep in investigations over campaign contributions, including two on Capitol Hill. Finally the Senate Watergate Committee held hearings and the special prosecutor filed charges. Despite cover-up attempts—special prosecutor's office memos say Jones, Allen and other Northrop officials backdated documents to make their campaign contributions appear to be legitimate personal donations—Northrop, Jones and Allen were charged with making illegal corporate donations.

Faced with a possible five-year prison sentence, Jones pleaded guilty in 1974 to one felony count and was fined $5,000. Allen also pleaded guilty and was fined $1,000, while Northrop was fined $5,000.

In its own internal investigation the following year, Northrop turned up further questions concerning both domestic and overseas payments by the corporation. One scheme was tied to Frank DeFrancis, Jones's most trusted lawyer with a reputation in international circles as counsel for the West Germany Embassy and the Italian government.

Hired by Northrop in 1967 and given a 15-year, $1.5 million contract in 1973, DeFrancis was instructed to report only to Jones—and never in writing.

DeFrancis established a Swiss company, Economic and Development Corp. (EDC), in 1971. The company, according to a later congressional investigation, was to market Northrop's aircraft by using influential European government officials and politicians as lobbyists. On paper, EDC was controlled by Swiss nationals who had no connection to Northrop, providing a comforting layer of deniability to all concerned. This questionable scheme was perfectly legal under U.S. law at the time. When EDC's existence became public in the mid-'70s, Jones told his board that because of EDC's setup, he was unaware of who its agents were or what they did to earn commissions of $1.2 million paid to EDC by Northrop.

In 1975 Northrop's executive committee reprimanded Jones for his "heavy share of the responsibility for the irregularities and improprieties" in the illegal campaign contributions and payments to foreign officials. The same year the SEC, after investigating tens of millions of dollars paid by Northrop to consultants and government officials in Europe, the Mideast and elsewhere, finally slammed the door on Northrop. Jones signed a consent decree with the agency, pledging that Northrop's employees would refrain from bribing foreign officials. In 1977 Congress passed the Foreign Corrupt Practices Act, banning overseas bribery by U.S. firms. (Federal grand juries are now deciding whether Northrop's $6.25 million payment to the South Koreans in 1984 violated the law.)

Before his death last year, DeFrancis went on to become a Maryland state official and race track mogul.

A convicted felon who had been excoriated by his own board, Jones nevertheless emerged from the 1970s still at Northrop's helm.

CREATIVE ACCOUNTING

During the 1980s, with its foreign sales declining but with the Reagan defense buildup in full swing, Jones's company came to depend more heavily on Pentagon contracts, which today account for 90 percent of its annual sales. As Northrop's Pentagon sales increased, so did its problems with criminal investigations and civil suits.

A major example is the B-2 stealth bomber. Former employees allege that as prime contractor for the B-2, Northrop cheated the government out of upwards of $13 billion.

In a civil suit and congressional testimony, Jean-François Truong, who spent three years as a financial controller at Northrop's plant in Pico

Rivera, Calif., said Northrop used two sets of financial records for the B-2 as part of a plan "calculated to deceive" the government and inflate the amount of money it would receive.

"There were the actual charges contained in the operating set," Truong told Dingell's subcommittee, "and then there was one prepared by the [Northrop] finance department for the Air Force to see. In the operational set, the frauds were exposed but quickly covered up by financial reports which were fabricated."

Northrop's alleged fraud was not committed by a few rogue employees, Truong said, but was "the result of a well-thought-out, organized and orchestrated corporate plan to make the money first and some sort of product later."

Truong says that he and the seven other controllers at the plant all were told to falsify the financial records destined for the Pentagon. When Truong refused to comply with the order, his manager fabricated the data himself because, he said, "he needed his job." Truong then went directly to his manager's boss, who "told me to be a 'team player.'"

Truong marched his concerns up the corporate ladder. Dissatisfied with the responses of middle managers, Truong approached Ken Berchtold, Northrop's vice president for finance, who was directly responsible for the B-2 program. Truong testified that Berchtold "seemed very uncomfortable when I told him that I was resigning unless Northrop took urgent corrective action and reported the truth about how far out of control B-2 finances were." Truong said Berchtold "indicated that he did not realize that there was a problem with the accounting system. He stated that he would get back to me. Two days later, [Northrop] security came, locked my cabinets and walked me out."

Amazingly, even though Defense Department personnel, including the Defense Contract Audit Agency, had offices within Northrop's plant, Truong says his work was "never audited" by anyone from the Pentagon.

Even more serious is Truong's charge that the Air Force eventually realized that Northrop's accounting system had been painting a false picture but allowed Northrop to get away with it.

And because the Air Force went along with Northrop, the Justice Department—while labeling the company's B-2 accounting system a "farce"—contended in a 1988 memo that it had to drop a criminal investigation of certain B-2 matters. (Others relating to Northrop and the B-2 are still being pursued by a federal grand jury.)

Truong and four other former Northrop employees have filed a civil fraud suit charging Northrop under the federal False Claims Act with unlawfully demoting or firing them for blowing the whistle. Under the act, plaintiffs are entitled to 15 to 25 percent of any damages the government recovers.

The employees' lawyer, Herbert Hafif, disputes the Justice Department's 1988 claim that it couldn't prosecute Northrop for fraud in the B-2 program. In a letter to Dingell's subcommittee, Hafif wrote it was "depressing to see that the resources of the United States government" could not be applied to "the greatest single fraud in U.S. history."

Northrop spokesperson Cantafio refutes the allegations. "We're being accused of defrauding the government of more than has actually been spent on the B-2. We find no substance to the allegations that Northrop knowingly overcharged the government on the B-2." He declined to discuss Truong's specific charges.

Meanwhile, taxpayers are once again taking it on the chin. The B-2's price tag, until recently a staggering $532 million per plane, is now put at $865 million by the Pentagon. A recent Congressional Budget Office study says that if fewer B-2s are bought and production stretched out, the cost of a single bomber could more than double to $1.95 billion.

FRIENDLY RELATIONS

Why has the Pentagon so often forgiven Northrop's reckless behavior? The symbiotic relationship between defense contractors and the Pentagon provides a clue. Often in defense procurement, a single major contractor is set up to build a weapon system or provide key components. To replace a contractor caught in wrongdoing would cause huge costs as well as delays the Pentagon feels would jeopardize military preparedness. Add to this the "revolving door" between the Pentagon and the defense industry, and you have a system ill equipped to criticize even its most corrupt contractors.

This web once again protected Northrop when it pleaded guilty last February to charges of falsifying tests on air-launched cruise missiles and Harrier jets.

The Justice Department had started a probe in 1987 of allegations that Northrop had knowingly used the wrong fluid in gyroscopes mounted inside air-launched cruise missiles. The proper fluid would allow the gyros to function at a temperature as cold as 65 degrees below zero. The fluid Northrop used couldn't be guaranteed beyond 40 degrees below zero, prosecutors said. The allegations meant that the nation's 1,715 cruise missiles, each carrying a 200-kiloton nuclear warhead, might be unreliable when exposed to extremely low temperatures—a contention Northrop says has not been borne out by subsequent tests.

When Mark Richard, deputy assistant attorney general in the Justice Department's criminal division, testified before Dingell's subcommittee in July, he said "evidence showed that since at least 1983, and probably before that time, Northrop knew it was using the wrong fluid. . . . Northrop confirmed these findings in 1982, 1983 and 1987, but never once disclosed the findings to the Air Force or to Boeing, the prime contractor."

After the Justice Department investigation was a year old, Richard said, Northrop finally admitted it had used the wrong fluid but "sought to minimize this breach of contract and did not offer to change the fluid." Instead, "by threatening to hold up delivery on parts for the Harrier jet, Northrop successfully persuaded the Navy to modify the contract so that the Northrop gyros had to be guaranteed only down to minus 40 degrees Farenheit. The Navy agreed to this change without notifying our investigators."

Northrop received added legal cover by obtaining similar waivers from the Defense Electronic Supply Center in Ohio and from an Air Force engineer at Robins Air Force Base in Georgia.

Richard testified that by granting the waivers the Navy and the Air Force—which both have air-launched cruise missile programs—undermined the government's ability to prosecute Northrop's faulty work on the gyro fluid.

In summer 1989 the company was indicted on 175 counts relating to the Harrier jet and cruise missiles. But before the indictment was settled, a deal was struck during plea bargaining: The government would drop several other Northrop criminal probes (including one into the guidance system for the MX missile) and a host of charges in the indictment if Northrop admitted to a few. Among the charges dropped were allegations that Northrop had knowingly used the wrong fluid in the gyroscopes. Given the waivers, Richard said, the Justice Department figured it couldn't successfully prosecute the gyro fluid charges.

The Navy similarly twice lowered its standards for Northrop's vibration testing on the Harrier jet stabilization system, Richard said, even after Northrop had falsified documents claiming to have met the higher standards.

Dingell slammed the Navy and the Air Force for lowering their standards to accommodate Northrop, saying, "These actions virtually tore the guts out of the prosecutor's case." Nevertheless, in the end Northrop pleaded guilty to 34 felony counts, admitting it had falsified test results on more than 110 guidance and stabilization systems for the cruise missile and the Harrier jet.

Ten Harriers have crashed in the last year, but the Air Force says none was due to a failure of a Northrop component.

Northrop's Cantafio told *Common Cause Magazine* that the charges shouldn't damage the corporation's reputation because they involve "only one small unit" (the Precision Products Division, or PPD) of the aerospace giant. When Northrop officials learned about allegations of improper testing, new CEO Kent Kresa told a congressional committee in October, "we fired the plant manager and three of his employees . . . [and] shut down the plant completely." Kresa termed the Northrop wrongdoing "a tragedy" that top management didn't know about but should have.

Despite Northrop's guilty plea, the Air Force's Suspension and Debarment Board—which had suspended the PPD at the time of the indictment—moved to lift the suspension. Federal prosecutors involved in the Harrier jet and cruise missile prosecutions, however, embarked on a campaign to bar Northrop from future defense contracts. They wrote to the board that the company showed "little if any remorse or willingness to admit that it has had serious problems with its management on critical weapons systems"—and had reinstated two top managers even though they had knowingly provided the wrong flight data transmitters for the cruise missile at least since 1983.

Northrop's falsified tests on the Harrier jet came back to haunt the Pentagon when officials disclosed in September that a key Northrop sensor had begun to fail sooner than expected. Since the Marines were using the Harriers in the Iraqi-Persian Gulf crisis, the parts had to be replaced quickly. Even though Northrop's PPD made the short-lived parts in the first place—and was still under suspension for the test falsifications—the Navy appeared ready to pay Northrop $300,000 for replacement sensors because no other company made them.

Members of Congress were irate. Government Operations Committee Chairman Rep. John Conyers (D-Mich.), who called hearings on the issue before his legislation and national security subcommittee, said he would pressure Defense Secretary Richard Cheney to "personally ensure that Northrop does not make a dime off this forced procurement." Northrop's Kresa subsequently offered to provide the replacements at no charge.

In spite of everything, top Pentagon officials continue to support Northrop.

In an amazing display of forbearance, John Betti, the under secretary of defense for acquisition, praised Northrop before Dingell's subcommittee in July. (Tom Jones had also been invited to the hearing, but refused for the fourth time in recent years.) Betti said Northrop is performing well, adding, "The proper management and control processes, procedures and disciplines are in place . . . [and] they are being adhered to."

Confronted with a laundry list of Northrop's proven and alleged criminal activities, Betti noted he had been on the job less than one year and wasn't familiar with many of the charges. In any case, he added, Northrop has corrected its most serious problems. Nowadays, he concluded, Northrop is a "responsible" contractor.

Subcommittee members were incredulous. Pointing to Betti's description of Northrop as

"presently responsible," Rep. Gerry Sikorski (D-Minn.) said the phrase applied to Northrop about as much as it would to a convicted bank robber "who is standing outside a bank with a gun."

HARD TIMES

These are not Northrop's glory days. The company faces continuing lawsuits and criminal investigations, ongoing congressional investigations and proposed cuts in defense spending. Its own marketing strategies haven't helped.

Northrop also is reeling from several recent financial blows, including its $1.2 billion loss on the F-20 Tigershark and heavy losses on some of its fixed-price contracts. Sales fell by $600 million between 1988 and '89, and shares of the company's stock, which traded at $56 in late 1985, plunged to $16.

Northrop's future looks even more uncertain, with the winding down of the Cold War, since more than 90 percent of the company's sales are to the military and the B-2 represents half of its military-related revenue. Earlier this year Defense Secretary Cheney reduced the Pentagon's B-2 order from 132 to 75. Congressional efforts to kill the B-2 nearly succeeded this summer and fall.

On top of this a new Air Force report released in October castigated Northrop as being poorly managed and having poor cost-accounting procedures on many prime contracts and subcontracts. Brig. Gen. Robert Drewes, who led the study of the various Northrop programs, blamed Northrop's problems on an undisciplined "corporate culture."

In March the Air Force, citing poor management performance, declined to renew Northrop's contract to build a key guidance component for the MX missile. Instead, the $135 million contract went to Rockwell International.

Though his company is hurting, Jones's own financial condition is rosy. As CEO in 1989 he drew a salary of $795,721. Now a consultant, he will receive fees from Northrop of $360,000 in 1990, $300,000 in 1991 and $240,000 in 1992. By remaining a board member until early 1992, Jones will get another $21,000 annually. He owns 2.4 million shares of Northrop's common stock, which is worth about $50 million. His retirement plan will add $920,685 a year to his bank account.

Jones's fatal flaw apparently was an inability to heed his own good counsel. Jones shared his views in a 1976 *New York Times* op-ed column, where he wrote: "It is wrong to believe that, regardless of performance, a defense company has the right to exist simply because it serves national security; a defense company must earn its way by the manner in which it serves that national security. . . . If the procurement process does not insist on the responsibility of individual companies, it will weaken the defense industry as a whole and ultimately the security of the nation it serves."

---

31. BANK ROBBERY ON A GRAND SCALE

RICHARD MORAN and JOSEPH ELLIS

Until recently, the most memorable comment on bank robbery was made by the legendary stickup man Willy Sutton. When asked why he robbed banks, Sutton explained, "Because that's where the money is." But the recent savings-and-loan scandal has produced a worthy rival in the quotation sweepstakes. Testifying before Congress, the California S & L commissioner observed, "The best way to rob a bank is to own one."

It is time we realized the enormous cost imposed on society by corporate criminals. Until this new breed of bank robbers showed up, there never was a robbery that bankrupted a bank. According to the Justice Department, the average take from a bank job is less than $3,000. Although Willy Sutton, John Dillinger, Bonnie and Clyde, and Jesse James have grabbed all the notoriety, the truth is, they don't amount to a hill of beans when compared to their modern-day counterparts.

Over the next 30 years the cost of bailing out the S & L industry is estimated at between $300 billion and $473 billion. During the next decade, every American taxpayer will be forced to contribute between $2,000 and $3,000 to finance the losses. The savings-and-loan scandal is the most costly crime in recorded history.

The fact is, most of these banks failed not because of deregulation, bad loans, or shifting commercial real estate markets, but because they were either bled dry by a bunch of pin-striped bandits or bankrupted by gamblers who took illegal risks with depositors' money.

A recent Government Accounting Office study found that criminal activity played a central role in the 26 most costly thrift failures. Of the 11,319 S & L bankruptcies referred to the Justice Department for possible prosecution, criminal behavior is believed to have played a significant role in 80 percent of them.

The illegal strategies and criminal techniques employed are much too complex to describe in detail here. Essentially they involved siphoning funds, illegal risk taking, and covering up. Siphoning, or bleeding-dry, was the most common and lucrative method employed. Top management paid themselves exorbitant salaries in violation of federal regulations, purchased luxury homes, boats, and cars, and arranged sweetheart deals for friends and relatives. In short, they robbed their own banks.

In defiance of federal laws and regulations, savings-and-loan managers made illegal high-risk acquisition, development, and construction loans, often requiring no down payment and re-

From *Christian Science Monitor*, December 22, 1989, p. 18. *Richard Moran is professor of sociology, and Joseph Ellis is dean of the faculty at Mount Holyoke College in Holyoke, Mass.*

lieving the developer of liability if the project went broke. If successful the bank would receive huge profits. If unsuccessful, the taxpayers would foot the bill, since all deposits up to $100,000 are insured by the federal government. It's a "heads I win, tails you lose" investment strategy.

And, finally, the executives and managers covered up. They inflated their net worth by financing the purchase of their own stock. They sold land back and forth to each other at inflated prices, thereby creating false increases in total assets. They "cooked" the books, hiding theft, fraud, and insolvency.

If you are having trouble seeing these bank executives as real criminals, consider that the Mafia has been doing the same thing for years. Once gangsters gain a foothold in a legitimate business, they too milk it dry by siphoning off cash, building up large credit lines from suppliers, and then liquidating inventories. When they pull out, all that remains is a shell of a company with creditors holding the bag. They leave be-

hind a snarled network of paper which makes it difficult and costly to prosecute. When the Mafia does this it is called a "bust-out." When bank managers do it, it is called an insolvency.

While it is true that deregulation of the banking industry created an atmosphere in which corporate crime flourished, this argument serves only to explain how the thievery got so out of hand. It does not excuse the executives' behavior or make it any less criminal. After all, prohibition explains how the mob was able to grow and prosper. And street crime can be traced to the conditions in the ghetto. Drug trafficking, auto theft, prostitution, take your pick, they all can be explained by pointing to the environment in which they are nourished.

Willy Sutton stole from banks the old-fashioned way—he robbed them. The new breed of bank robbers steal sums of money that Sutton never imagined in his most larcenous dreams. Yet very few of them will ever see the inside of a prison, even though they have perpetrated the greatest heist in American history.

---

32. THE GREAT BANKS ROBBERY

JAMES K. GLASSMAN

Vernon, Texas (pop. 12,000), is an oil and cotton center near the Oklahoma border. The hometown S & L, Vernon Savings and Loan, was started in 1960 by R. B. Tanner, a tough old bird who had been a bank examiner during the Depression and knew the importance of making loans to borrowers who would actually repay them. He built Vernon slowly and carefully, and by the end of 1981 his S & L, though fairly small, was probably the soundest in the country, with $82 million in assets and just $90,000 in overdue loans.

From *The New Republic*, October 8, 1990, pp. 16–21. Reprinted with permission.

As Tanner was building his little thrift, another native of Vernon, a hustler named Don Dixon, was getting rich building Spanish-style houses with signature red tile roofs all over the Dallas suburbs, all the while griping about how lenders kept borrowers like him on a short leash. Dixon decided he too wanted to be a lender, especially after Congress passed a law allowing S & Ls to put loads of high-risk real estate development loans on their books. In 1982 Dixon (who, with his beard, gold chains, and shirt open to the navel, looked a lot like the country singer Kenny Rogers) talked Tanner, then sixty-five, into selling him Vernon Savings and Loan. As James Ring Adams describes it in *The Big Fix*, at the first board meeting after the deal, Dixon asked his directors, including Tanner, to approve the purchase of a $125,000 three-foot-tall bronze sculpture of a squatting Indian for his office. Tanner realized Dixon was not his kind of banker and resigned from the board.

Over the next five years Dixon took in hundreds of millions of dollars in deposits, guaranteed by the Federal Savings and Loan Insurance Corporation (FSLIC), and used the money to make horrendous loans. Under Tanner, Vernon had only 0.1 percent of its loans in default. Federal regulators worry seriously when the proportion reaches 4 percent, and 10 percent generally means insolvency. When Vernon closed its doors on March 20, 1987, some 96 percent of its loans had gone bad. Worse, the S & L had $1.6 billion in assets, so FSLIC had a huge clean-up on its hands. A month later the government filed a civil racketeering suit against Dixon and thirteen of the S & L's officers, claiming they had looted Vernon of more than half a billion dollars. The suit said, among other things, that they had made loans of up to $90 million each to friends without "any reasonable basis for concluding the loans were collectible." In return for booking these bad loans, the S & L's officers were paid more than $22 million in bonuses over four years (Dixon himself got $4.5 million of that), plus $4 million in salary.

Dixon had his wife, her sister, and his stepdaughter on the payroll. According to lawsuits filed by the federal government, Vernon S & L bought a $2 million beach house for Dixon's use in Del Mar, California, and provided another $200,000 to furnish it. Dixon had a fleet of six aircraft at his disposal. During one eighteen-month period he billed Vernon for $561,874 in personal living expenses, including $36,780 for flowers, $37,339 for phone calls, $4,420 for pool service, $386 for pet services, and $44,095 for out-of-pocket incidentals. The Dixons built another house in Rancho Santa Fe, California, and flew to London to consult an interior decorator and buy $489,000 in furnishings.

For his walls, Dixon bought $5.5 million in Western art, also courtesy of the S & L. And since Dixon was a car buff, Vernon set up a subsidiary in La Jolla, California, to sell Ferraris and Rolls Royces. At a 1988 bankruptcy hearing Dixon pleaded that he should be able to keep his personal Vernon-financed car because it had four doors and served as "the family Ferrari." But the peak of Dixonian indulgence was something Don's wife, Dana, called "Gastronomique Fantastique," a two-week tour the Dixons and their friends took in October 1983 of the best restaurants of France, paid for by Vernon Savings and Loan. In a document found by regulators, Dana assiduously recorded the details of every meal. They dined at seven restaurants rated three stars by the *Guide Michelin*, supping on pressed duck, truffle soup, and minced kidneys. "It was truly a dream trip," she wrote, "hardly to be imagined by most, and barely to be believed even by those of us who experienced it first hand . . . a flying house party . . . of pure unadulterated pleasure."

The excesses at Vernon—the risky loans to developer-cronies, the nepotism, and the truffle soup—provide a perfect metaphor for the savings and loan crisis. How did we get here? Through a combination of deregulation, short-sighted home-district politics, changing cultural values, macroeconomics, and the deposit-insurance system. About the first four sources of the crisis, there's not much we can do, but eliminating, or sharply curtailing, deposit insurance is a smart solution.

Usually when businesses do what Vernon and other S & Ls did, they go broke, bankrupting their owners and leaving suppliers, bank creditors, and sometimes the IRS holding the bag. But the bulk of an S & L's creditors are its depositors, the people who lent their money to it for safekeeping. When it goes broke the depositors aren't left holding the bag because, ever since 1932, the federal government has guaranteed that if an insured S & L can't pay a depositor back, FSLIC (meaning, in effect, the U.S. Treasury) will. So after five years of high living and wild lending at Vernon, FSLIC had to commit to $1.3 billion to pay off depositors—more than 200 times what Dixon paid R. B. Tanner to buy the thrift.

Vernon was not an aberration. In the early 1980s developers like Dixon and Charles Keating Jr., men without the slightest bankerly inclination, bought small S & Ls and pumped them up with thousands of government-guaranteed deposits in $100,000 increments. The S & Ls acquired the deposits not from local savers but from rich investors, who shopped the nation for the highest interest rates. Brokers had no need to find well-run S & Ls as havens for their clients' cash, since FSLIC guaranteed all deposits, even in miserable thrifts like Vernon.

Brokered deposits were a grotesque distortion of the original purpose of deposit insurance. In 1932, when FSLIC and the Federal Deposit Insurance Corporation (FDIC) were established, the idea was to encourage small savers to get their cash out from under the mattress and into S & Ls and banks, where the money could be used to invest in homes and businesses. Deposit insurance made sense then because banks were failing at a rapid clip, and runs were common. The guarantees were tailored to the little guy: the limit on insurance was $2,500 per deposit. And S & Ls, in return for using nearly all of their deposits to provide mortgage loans to homebuyers, were allowed to pay slightly higher rates on their deposits than banks.

But in general S & Ls and banks struck the same deal with the feds fifty-eight years ago: the government would insure depositors against loss, and S & Ls and banks would agree to keep enough capital (that is, enough of their own money) in the vaults as a buffer against bad loans and hard times. At the time Franklin D. Roosevelt and the American Bankers Association, among others, anticipated a fundamental problem posed by deposit insurance: it gave savers no incentive to put their money in a sound S & L or bank. In fact, in most cases, depositors are better off choosing a bad S & L—since bad S & Ls, more desperate for funds, usually pay higher interest rates on deposits. In theory, government regulators could put S & Ls and banks out of business if the regulators felt that their loan losses were cutting too deeply into capital reserves, or if they behaved so recklessly that their capital was apt to disappear in the future. Thanks to the niceties of S & L and bank accounting practices, however, a good deal of subjectivity entered into the regulators' decisions. In many cases, it's difficult to say exactly when a loan goes bad.

In addition, powerful political forces mitigated the efforts of regulators blowing the whistle. This country has the most decentralized banking system in the world—more than 16,000 separate institutions, most of which tend to be very influential within their own communities. Members of Congress believe they must pay attention to the needs of the fellow who runs the hometown S & L, who, if he isn't a big contributor, is at least a big local employer and sustainer of small borrowers. So in the 1970s and early 1980s, when S & Ls got into trouble as a result of macroeconomic forces (not, at that point, because of reckless lending or big spending of the Dixonian sort), instead of letting the thrifts with the worst problems fail, Congress and the administration decided to change the rules. Congress was looking out for the interests of powerful home-district S & Ls while the Reaganites were following their deregulation agenda.

The theme of the new deregulatory laws, passed in 1980 and 1982, was that S & Ls should be allowed to grow their way back to health by making new, far riskier investments—like land-acquisition and construction loans to commercial real estate developers, junk bonds, and Ferrari dealerships. As a result, instead of a few dozen badly managed, or unlucky, thrifts going out of business at a cost to the taxpayers of $20 billion or $30 billion, we're now faced with more than 1,000 failing at a cost ten to twenty times as high.

But the S & L mess is also the result of a major cultural event: the disappearance in American life of the stigma against borrowing. In the 1980s, the go-go years of Reaganism, debt continued to create anxiety, but not in the old way. You no longer worried about whether you could pay back the loan, but whether you had borrowed enough to enjoy the good things in life before it was too late (meaning before someone cut off your line of credit). Debt allowed new heroes like Donald Trump, Ron Perelman, and Carl Icahn to acquire great American institutions, icons like the Plaza Hotel, Revlon, and TWA. The more speculative the venture, the more alluring. Few borrowers had experienced the Great Depression, and they vaguely sensed that, whatever happened, they would be bailed out like Chrysler and Lockheed. No one went flat broke in America, at least no one who started with something. Borrowing was where the tax deductions were, and it would let you buy a house in Mamaroneck for $3,000 a month or a BMW for $600.

Swept up in a competitive frenzy, bankers, who used to hem and haw while supplicants knelt to ask for money, started stuffing the dough into the pockets of anyone who would take it. In the past there was a dynamic at work in which lenders, in their reluctance to lend, would transfer a burden of guilt to borrowers: "Here's the money, my friend. But make sure you return it in the condition you received it." The dynamic disappeared when the lenders made it clear that the borrowers were doing them a favor: "Please," said a piece of junk mail I received a few years ago, "accept this line of credit, up to $10,000, to use as you wish." They didn't even seem to care if you gave it back. The great old white-shoe banker, George Moore, former chairman of Citibank, wrote in his memoirs: "If you let the credit men, the analysts, run the bank, you won't have any customers; if you let the salesmen run the bank, you go bankrupt." In the '80s, S & Ls let the salesmen run the bank.

The roots of this cultural change go deep. In the boom years after World War II the thrift business had been an easy game. You took in deposits at between 4 and 5 percent, thanks to interest ceilings, and lent it out at between 6 and 8 percent. Then, in the late '60s and '70s, several events conspired to raise banks' borrowing costs. The first was the Vietnam War (plus the War on Poverty), which Presidents Johnson and Nixon decided to finance with government bonds instead of taxes. With the government a more prominent issuer of debt, interest rates rose, as they always do when the competition for investors' funds increases. Then, after the Arab oil embargo of 1973, there was inflation. Saving became a game for suckers. If you put your money in a passbook account, you'd earn 5 percent; with inflation running 10 percent, the value of your principal was being whittled away. So Americans started taking money out of banks and spending it—buying things before their prices rose some more, in the process pushing inflation even higher.

Then it got worse. Some depositors were taking their money out of S & Ls and banks and putting it into investments, like money market funds (invented in 1972), that earned higher

rates of return. Finally, in 1980, with the strong backing of the White House, Congress passed the Depository Institutions Deregulatory Act, based on the noble sentiment that "all depositors, and particularly those with modest savings, are entitled to receive a market return on their savings." In fact, the purpose of the law was to stop banks and thrifts from bleeding to death. It raised the limit on federal insurance from $40,000 to $100,000 per account (the figure had been as low as $10,000 as recently as 1950), and it phased out interest-rate ceilings over a six-year period, ending in 1986. Banks and S & Ls now could offer higher interest to depositors and get the money to keep operating, but the cost of deposits—the cost of a bank's own borrowing— soared. In the mid-'70s, it was not unusual for a bank to pay no interest at all on most of its deposits. The S & Ls, by tradition, had been lending long (thirty-year home mortgages) and borrowing short (passbook savings accounts, which could be withdrawn on short notice). In 1981, most S & Ls were suffering "negative spreads" on their mortgages, not even counting overhead costs. So, as the old joke goes, they tried to make it up on volume.

Having solved the liquidity crisis (thrifts running out of money), Congress was faced with a profitability crisis (thrifts stuck with long-term loans that weren't paying enough interest to cover the cost of short-term deposits). Again, the proper response would have been to let the regulators shut down S & Ls whose capital was depleted; the insurance bill would have been fairly low, and a stronger generation of thrifts would have emerged.

Instead Congress, again with the strong support of the White House, decided to let S & Ls go into entirely new businesses: instead of forcing them to make loans only to people buying homes, let them lend to developers with big dreams. Or let them use their deposits to buy assets that get even better returns than conventional loans, like Michael Milken's junk bonds or what regulators euphemistically called "direct investments" (equity interests in hotels and shopping centers). In 1982, in the face of 250 S & L failures, Congress passed a bill sponsored by Senator Jake Garn, a Utah Republican who then headed the Senate Banking Committee, and Representative Fernand St. Germain, a Rhode Island Democrat who chaired the House Banking Committee. The Garn–St. Germain bill had such overwhelming support that it was approved without a recorded vote. It liberated the thrifts and then murdered them.

Most of the executioners showed up promptly after the bill sailed through. Like Don Dixon, they were wheeler-dealer real estate operators, who saw S & Ls as a source of unlimited funds (those guaranteed deposits) for their own ventures and those of their pals. Real estate was hot at the time, thanks to tax-law changes that allowed owners to depreciate their properties quickly, generating big up-front tax losses. Only circumspect lenders stood in the way of enormous profits, so, the developer figured, why shouldn't I become a lender myself? Regulators say there is a pattern among failed thrifts: a change of ownership between 1982 and 1984 (with the buyer often a developer or someone fronting for a developer) and spectacularly fast growth in assets—mostly real estate loans supported by lots of $100,000 brokered deposits.

With the hustlers coming out of the woodwork, many of the smart old-line bankers figured that this was a terrific opportunity to bail out of what they correctly saw as an increasingly difficult business. Thus in 1983 Don Crocker sold his California thrift, the small and mildly profitable Lincoln Savings and Loan, to Charles Keating, an Arizona homebuilder with a shady past. With help from Milken and his crew from the Beverly Hills office of Drexel Burnham Lambert, Keating bought Lincoln for $51 million, an astronomical price, nearly twice the thrift's net worth and three times what Lincoln's stock was fetching on the open market. To Keating it seemed worth it. He saw Lincoln as the perfect vehicle to enhance his personal wealth and prestige—and for a time, he was right.

Like Dixon, Keating pumped up his S & L using brokered money. In five years it grew sixfold, to $5.5 billion in deposits. And Lincoln pulled out of the traditional business of S & Ls almost entirely. Lending to home-buyers represented less than 2 percent of Lincoln's business. Meanwhile investments in junk bonds—high-interest debt issued by corporations, usually in conjunction with a leveraged buyout—went

from zero to $779 million. As usual, Milken benefited from the leverage: he helped Keating buy a $51 million thrift and then sold him junk bonds costing fifteen times the purchase price, thus reaping huge fees. Milken would repeat this little trick several times with other S & Ls, and they too would find when the debt bubble burst in 1989 that junk bonds were not particularly profitable.

Thanks to Garn–St. Germain, Keating and Milken and dozens of other operators were able to give a whole new meaning to thrifts. They became a way to help corporate raiders buy established companies, for speculators to build monuments to themselves (like Keating's Phoenician resort, probably the most spectacular hotel bust of all time), and for new thrift operators to get rich using other people's money. Keating, for example, hired his son as a senior officer at the age of twenty-six, a meteoric rise from busboy and waiter at a country club.

Keating, Dixon, and other S & L operators understood the importance of political connections. Stephen Pizzo, Mary Fricker, and Paul Muolo point out in *Inside Job* that Dixon had a yacht, the 112-foot *High Spirits*, which was anchored on the Potomac and used by House Majority Whip Tony Coelho for eleven fund-raising parties for the Democratic Congressional Campaign Committee in 1985 and 1986. The cost to the DCCC for those parties was zero; cost to Vernon S & L, $48,450. (After bank examiners discovered the set-up, the DCCC dutifully repaid Vernon.)

In late 1986 regulators finally understood what was happening at Vernon (which they affectionately called "Vermin"), declared its loans in default, and pegged its net worth at minus $350 million. As John Barry describes it in *The Ambition and the Power*, with time running out, Dixon turned to Coelho, who in turn contacted Majority Leader Jim Wright, who in another week would become Speaker of the House. Dixon told Wright that the regulators were trying to put him out of business immediately, but if he had a week or so he could work out a sale. Over Christmas Wright called Edwin Gray, the chairman of the Federal Home Loan Bank Board and the chief S & L regulator, and told him, "Ed, I don't know anything about Vernon Savings and

Loan or Don Dixon. . . . But he tells me he's got a buyer and needs one week to dispose of his business himself, and he says regulators want to close him down today. I wonder if you could look into it." The Speaker's intervention was too late. Regulators put Dixon out of business the very day of the phone call.

Keatings variation on the theme has received broader notice. He tried to keep regulators off his back by orchestrating donations to the campaign treasuries and political committees of twenty-four members of Congress, including five senators—Republican John McCain of Arizona and Democrats Alan Cranston of California, Dennis DeConcini of Arizona, John Glenn of Ohio, and Don Riegle of Michigan, the chairman of the Senate Banking Committee. The five put pressure on Gray and other top officials to keep Lincoln open in 1987, and it was not until 1989 that a regulator discovered that its net worth was minus $948 million and getting worse. It will cost at least $2 billion to clean up the mess, and the U.S. and California eventually filed civil and criminal charges against Keating and his associates. The Keating Five are currently being investigated by the Senate Ethics Committee.

But it wasn't their relationship with politicians that helped Keating, Dixon, and other S & L owners elude regulators; it was the nature of bank accounting, coupled with that inexhaustible supply of brokered, insured deposits. Many of the S & Ls that crashed used these two clever techniques: 1. Capitalized interest. A developer comes to an S & L with an idea for a speculative venture that will cost, say, $50 million. The S & L lends him the $50 million, plus legal and other "soft costs" (another $2 million or so), plus four "points" (the S & L's own fee for setting up the loan), plus interest at, for example, 14 percent for two years ($14 million). That comes to $68 million, up front. (Imagine buying your house with a loan from the bank covering 100 percent of the principal, all the closing costs and interest for two years.) The S & L, under accounting rules, can book the points as profit for itself immediately, and it can book the interest at a rate of $7 million a year. So in the first year the S & L records $9 million in income, even though none of the $9 million came from the developer. It all came from the S & L itself. You can see

where this sort of thing can lead—a $68 million loan for a $50 million project (and usually a risky one, at that) can go bad in a hurry. But since the developer doesn't have to pay interest out of his pocket for two years, the regulators can't tell whether the loan is in default until it's far too late. Even then, S & Ls would hide such loans by selling them to each other at inflated prices in a daisy-chain network.

2. Land flips. The idea here, perfected by Empire Savings and Loan Association of Mesquite, Texas, was to buy and sell vacant land, with the help of sleazy cohorts, sometimes turning the property over several times a day at higher and higher prices. The value of the land, on paper, would soar, and with the help of other S & Ls that were in on the deal and of compliant and negligent private appraisers, the property could end up trading hands for ten times its original price. (The Government Operations Committee cited one example in which a 3.6-acre piece of land was bought for $156,816 and eventually sold three months later for $1,724,976 with a loan from Empire of $1,879,250.) Doing the lending along the way, Empire would pick up points, between 6 and 18 percent of the purchase price, and book them as profit. The money for buying the land came from brokered deposits; eventually 85 percent of Empire's deposits, which grew from $17 million in 1982 to $309 million in 1984, came through brokers. The flips also inflated the asset side of Empire's balance sheet, making it the fastest-growing S & L in America.

The loans usually matured in six months to a year. Then Empire would come in with a construction loan that would repay the previous debt and cover closing costs, building costs, fees for the S & L, interest, and even the expenses in promoting the condos that would eventually (maybe) be built on the land. After two years of glory, Empire was shut down in 1984 at an ultimate cost to FSLIC of $163.8 million, at the time the biggest payoff in the insurance agency's fifty-year history. It would later seem a pittance.

It's important to understand that the money that Empire and the other go-go S & Ls lent out did not disappear off the face of the earth. It went to developers, who rented bulldozers and bought sheetrock and Porsches, and eventually went broke. The money helped fuel a boom in the West at a time when oil prices were falling. The problem today is that the money is already spent. The developers can't pay back the S & Ls, and the S & Ls can't pay back the savers, so the federal government has to step in. The government has been loath to do so, for two reasons: first, it means shutting down S & Ls owned by politically connected people, and, second, it means shelling out a lot of cash, which the government doesn't have.

In February 1986 the General Accounting Office estimated that FSLIC needed $22.5 billion in new capital so that it could shut down failing thrifts and pay their depositors. The administration asked for $15 billion, with the money coming from S & L insurance premiums rather than tax dollars. But the bill was held up in Congress for months, by Wright and others. The bill returned in the spring of 1987, and again House members opposed it. Finally, on July 29, 1987, a year and a half after the GAO report, Congress passed a compromise, giving FSLIC $10.8 billion—far too little, far too late.

So the next year FSLIC came up with a new solution: to "sell" failing thrifts to rich buyers for practically no money; to give these buyers, including billionares like Ron Perelman and Robert Bass, big tax breaks; and then to guarantee their S & Ls against losses down the road (using money that FSLIC figured Congress would appropriate after the presidential election). FSLIC and the Federal Home Loan Bank Board, which regulates S & Ls, desperate to unload the thrifts, started making quick and dirty deals. These deals either went sour, leaving the taxpayer to clean up the mess, or ended up making their new owners millions. For an investment of $171 million, for example, Pereleman earned more than $250 million in tax benefits and profits the first year. Just last month a congressional review found that the sale of 100 of these thrifts in 1988 will cost the taxpayers $71 billion.

By 1989 all of these scams and dilatory tactics had run their course, and Congress had to accept the task of putting up cash to shut down S & Ls and pay off deposits. But calling on taxpayers to foot the bill directly would cause political problems, so the Treasury floated thirty- and forty-year bonds to raise the first chunk of bailout money. The main effect of these bonds—and the

ones that will certainly follow—has been to increase competition for the limited funds of investors and thus raise interest rates for all of us. Forget all that talk of a $2,500 bill coming to each taxpayer for his or her share of the S & L bailout. The cost is more insidious, showing up in mortgage rates and interest on installment loans and increased costs for businesses that want to expand.

There's a second effect: throughout most of the '80s S & Ls did spread cash around, especially to commercial real estate developers. As a result, the centers of many American cities became overbuilt with office towers and the suburbs overbuilt with garden apartments and condos. This overbuilding has contributed to our current real estate slump and to severe losses for more traditional commercial lenders, the banks. The banks, in turn, have tightened up their lending policies, partly because their capital is being depleted by bad loans and partly because they fear the wrath of regulators who don't want to be blamed for another S & L disaster. So now, even good credit risks can't get loans, slowing down business in general and creating, at best, regional recessions.

There's certainly enough blame to go around in the S & L scandal: to Congress, for writing new laws, pressuring regulators, and starving FSLIC to keep insolvent thrifts alive; to the White House, for mindlessly pushing deregulation on an industry that wasn't ready for it and for doing its best to hold down the number of bank examiners; to the greedy, shortsighted industry itself; and, of course, to S & L operators, many of whom will be spending their retirement years in prison. But the culprit that's most productive to address is the policy of insuring deposits in S & Ls with the full faith and credit of the federal government.

The government simply can't continue to insure every account in each of this country's banks and S & Ls. It doesn't have the money. In fact, the great untold scandal is that ever since the failure of Continental Illinois Bank in 1982, federal insurance has covered *all* accounts—even those greater than $100,000. Today such deposits total $3 trillion, and the FDIC (which, in the 1989 S & L reform bill, swallowed up FSLIC) has assets totaling no more than one-half of 1 percent of that amount. What needs to be done immediately is to abandon the current policy and replace it with a limited insurance system. Federal deposit insurance should cover no more than, say, $50,000 per depositor—instead of $100,000 per account. I consider that an intermediate step on the way to phasing out deposit insurance altogether within two years. If small savers want total protection, they should put their money in U.S. Treasury securities, or into money market funds that invest only in federal bonds. The latter is a very simple alternative that didn't exist when FSLIC was founded.

Without federal insurance, depositors would demand that a reckless S & L pay them very high interest rates, or they would refuse to deposit their funds there. It's true that most people today aren't able to judge whether an S & L "deserves" their deposits, but they would learn very quickly, just as they've learned which cars are the safest and which stereo speakers produce the best sound. And consumers will have one obvious clue: an S & L that offers to pay high interest rates will almost always be a riskier bet for a depositor, just as a corporation that's forced to pay higher interest on its bonds is riskier. If there's still concern about the little guy, here's a simple solution: make deposit insurance a means-tested entitlement. It would be available only, for instance, to families whose income is less than $40,000 a year. Let the rich fend for themselves.

Finally, I am not advocating more deregulation. Federal regulators should still play a role in assuring the stability of individual banks and S & Ls, in much the same way that the FDA and FTC stand watch over the quality of consumer products. We should retain strict capital requirements and toughen accounting rules. But deposit insurance, which gives reckless banks, in effect, a direct pipeline to the U.S. Treasury to meet their operating expenses, must go.

Although a limited-insurance system wouldn't prevent unscrupulous bankers from making bad loans, it would prevent them from using federally backed money to grow their way out of their problems. It would also end one of the more egregious examples of state capitalism's tendency to privatize profits and socialize losses. The frightening truth is that there is no more discipline over S & Ls today than there was at the start of the '80s. Congress and the White House have been too busy pointing fingers to find a solution, and Federal Reserve Board chairman Alan Greenspan says he's waiting for a report from the Treasury on deposit insurance. So far that report is eighteen months in the making, and I don't have high hopes for it.

Unfortunately deposit insurance is an idea with a lot of political force behind it. Liberal politicians like it because it has a generous, populist quality, and conservative apologists for financial interests like it because it has the effect of lowering the interest rates that banks and S & Ls have to pay on their deposits. And a specious argument left over from the panic years of the '30s continues to have appeal—the notion that without deposit insurance, there would be uncontrollable "runs" on banks. In fact, spontaneous mass withdrawals are a rarity. Consider, for instance, money-market funds; they're uninsured by the federal government, yet they've never been hit with runs. More frequently, when investors grow suspicious of the stability of a financial institution, they pull their money out slowly over time. And even if a run does occur, the Fed can always open its "discount window" to the target of withdrawals, providing unlimited funds on an emergency basis, in the same way it stood by to help brokerage firms when the stock market plummeted in October 1987.

Abolishing deposit insurance is not a totally riskless solution to the S & L crisis, but it is the only step that will keep people like Don Dixon and Charles Keating out of the banking business. If the government continues to insure the deposits of poorly run institutions, allowing gamblers to double their debts at the roulette table, it will ensure something else: a financial disaster that will make this one look tame.

33. REVIEW OF *INSIDE JOB: THE LOOTING OF AMERICA'S SAVINGS AND LOANS*

GUS TYLER

Bankers and burglars have two things in common. First, they are both in business to enrich themselves. Second, they do so by laying their hands on "other people's money."

There are also two differences: First, we trust bankers but do not trust burglars. Second, when people lose money because of the action of burglars, the government does not make good the losses; but, when people lose money because of the action of bankers, the government does make good the losses.

After reading *Inside Job*, many will conclude that it was a mistake to differentiate between bankers and burglars: neither is to be trusted and neither deserves a government bailout. As the subtitle of the book suggests ("The Looting of America's Savings and Loans"), the bankers under ethical indictment are the thieves who moved in on the Savings and Loans, the once stolid institutions that accumulated local deposits from thrifty citizens to enable other hard-working citizens to buy homes. In the good old days, the banker was perceived to be a pillar of the community—concerned, conservative, conscientious, and conscience-ridden.

Then came deregulation and, with it, degradation—of banks, bankers, and many of those in government whose sworn duty it was to protect the people against theft. In a few short years—from 1982 to the present—a coterie of crooks

From *Challenge*, January/February 1990, pp. 61–64. Reprinted with permission of the publisher, M. E. Sharpe, Inc., 80 Business Park Drive, Armonk, New York 10504. Stephen Pizzo, Mary Fricker, and Paul Muolo, *Inside Job: The Looting of America's Savings and Loans*. New York: McGraw Hill, 1989.

Gus Tyler is Assistant President of the International Ladies' Garment Workers' Union, New York.

pulled off what must be the greatest heist in history to the tune of something between $300 billion and $500 billion. And, those who will pay the price for the crime will not be, with a few exceptions, the perpetrators but "the people," the taxpayers of the nation.

Inside Job is the sad story of how government policy encouraged larceny, then stymied efforts to halt the thievery, and then turned to the taxpayers to make whole the damage inflicted by the multimillionaire bankrobbers. In a cartoon, it would be Uncle Sam standing behind Willie Sutton saying: "Go to it, son. I'm behind you."

The insurance of bank deposits goes all the way back to the early days of Roosevelt. It was a risky business, of course, as is all insurance. But the risk was well worth taking. Small depositors were protected. Banks were run by reasonably responsible people, known by the folk in their community. As often as not, relationship between banker and depositor and banker and borrower was on a first name basis. What is more, the S & L was regulated. There was a cap on the rate of interest paid to depositors; there were clearly defined limits on the kind of things into which the bank could put its loans.

Fundamentally, the function of the S & L was clearly defined: an intermediary who made it possible for folk who wanted a guaranteed and safe return on investments to provide cash for neighbors who wanted to borrow to buy a residence.

Then came deregulation—in three steps. First, under Carter, ceilings on interest rates were lifted. Savings and Loans began to compete against one another to attract funds by offering higher interest rates. Second, the limit on deposits, once $40,000, was lifted to $100,000, encouraging brokered deposits—a development that was crucial in the corruption of the S & Ls. Then came the Garn–St. Germain Act of 1982 liberating the S & Ls from their "home financing" turf and allowing them to throw around their money with reckless abandon.

Although each of these very definable moves in the direction of deregulation contributed to the corruption of the S & Ls, what was most important in poisoning the ambience was the mood emanating from the White House that regulation per se was evil. In effect, this meant that whatever regulations might still remain should really be overlooked as a nonsensical nuisance of a liberal-minded past. The modicum of regulation that the legislature still allowed to survive would be killed by the executive—through simple nonfeasance.

FEWER COPS, LESS CONTROL

A perfect example of White House attitude toward regulation was a conference between Ed Gray, superconscientious head of the Federal Home Loan Board (FHLB) and Connie Horner, assistant to David Stockman at the Office of Management and Budget. Gray, flooded by massive mis- and malfeasance, asked for 1400 more examiners. "You want *more* examiners?" asked Horner. By Gray's account, "She told him that it wasn't a matter of money but of philosophy. The administration's philosophy was one of deregulation. That meant *fewer* regulators, not more." To sharp-eyed crooks it was clear that the law was lax and the cops were off the streets. This was their hour to go in for the big kill—and they did.

The first caper in the big scam is "cash-for-trash." The key player is the deposit broker loaded with millions, perhaps billions, of dollars in cash. He seeks out a bank that is money hungry, often a rather small S & L. He offers big, fabulous, incredible deposits—with a proviso. The bank must extend loans to borrowers recommended by the broker. The deal is cut.

The borrowers appear promptly, quite ready to pay the high interest rates one would expect to pay on money deposited in the bank with the expectation of high returns. These borrowers are "straw men," dummies for depositors who are now getting their money and other people's money back from the bank.

The borrowers have no intention of paying back the loan nor of servicing the debt. Why should they? If the bank goes bankrupt, the deposits are insured. So the depositor gets back his money and he also gets the sum he borrowed from the bank.

What do the borrowers do with the money? They buy land. They set up casinos. They finance shopping centers. But mainly, they appreciate the value of their holdings—by selling their properties at inflated prices to co-conspirators who sell it again at higher prices, establishing bloated values for properties that they can then use as collateral for borrowing more money.

In one hardly believable operation, the swindlers set up an assembly line for purchase and sale and repurchase and resale of properties so that in just so many moments they could multiply values by so many millions.

Crucial to such operations was some systematic way to avoid detection by regulators. The simplest thing to do, of course, was to buy the regulator outright or with promise of vice-presidency (or something like that) in a bank. In an ambience where the regulator himself or herself felt that the administration preferred nonenforcement, it was easy to accept a gratuity for overlooking rather than overseeing.

A DEVILISH GIMMICK

Not all inspectors were buyable, of course. So some other gimmick had to be invented to outwit the federal ferrets. The device to do so was devilishly simple. When banks got the word that an inspector was on the way (information they were obviously able to get from "insiders" of agencies) the bank-to-be-reviewed sold its bad debts to other banks. That cleared the bank's barrel of its rotten apples. When the inspection was over, the bank bought back the bad debts it had sold to its corresponding bank. In this way, banks swapped bad debts in timely fashion to elude the notice of prying feds.

Where did all the money come from for this multi-million, multi-billion dollar operation? Some of it came, of course, from cash-rich persons eager to get an extra point or two of interest on their insured deposits. They were honest folk who, like most depositors, never ask how their money is being used so long as the return is good. Why should they ask? The deposit is insured.

If they had asked, there would have been ready answers. For each outstanding dollar there was collateral—at least, on paper. How was a naive depositor to know that those highly valued properties were, in many instances, absolutely worthless—the puffed-up corpus of papered capers.

But not all the monies involved came from the pocket of unknowing innocents. One of the major players was—the Mafia.

It was not the intention of the authors—three first-rate investigative reporters with a keen knowledge of the banking business—to uncover a conspiracy, let alone one that involved the Mafia. The curiosity of the investigators was aroused by what was happening—of all places—in Guerneville, California, hometown of the tiny Centennial Savings and Loan. The editor of the local *Russian River News*, Stephen Pizzo, and the news editor, Mary Fricker, were piqued into curiosity when the sleepy little bank announced that it was going to spend $13 million in cash for a construction company. Pizzo wondered how it was possible for the bank to spend seven times its worth on such a purchase.

The nosey newspeople soon discovered that Centennial was "awash with money" and flooded with visitors from Las Vegas, Boston, Holland. They came from afar, they left with bundles, yet "the thrift's financial statements recorded phenomenal growth."

Question led to question. Where did the money come from? Where did it go? How could bank executives "justify these extravagant salaries, benefits, perks, planes, luxury cars, boats, trips?"

The newspeople put their questions in print. The President of Centennial, high-living Erv Hansen, exploded. He told an associate of Pizzo: "You tell your partner he better stop sticking his nose where it doesn't belong or I'll do to him what I did to that San Diego reporter." Pizzo paid heed because, he writes, he had "already discovered that some of the customers buzzing around Centennial's loan window had organized crime backgrounds."

A NATIONAL CRIME

What began as a purely local affair became a national investigation when the editor of *The National Thrift News* came upon Pizzo's story. Associate Editor Paul Muolo was dispatched to California to look into the Centennial affair. He found that it was a template for what was going on in other thrifts that had come to the attention of his paper.

As the national jigsaw puzzle was pieced together, certain names turned up over and over again in one part of the country after another. "Each of the Big Five New York families—Gambino, Genovese, Lucchese, and Columbo— turned up along with the lesser families such as the Civellas from Kansas City, the Peter Milano gang in Los Angeles, Carlos Marcello in New Orleans, Santo Traficante in Tampa, and others." The authors concluded that "some form of coordinated operation existed . . . The Mafia was actively looting the S & Ls."

For the "wise guys" of organized crime, the deregulation of the thrifts came at exactly the right time. They needed some new way to borrow money that they never intended to repay. For many years, organized crime figures looked upon the Teamster's Central States Pension Fund as their favorite money cow. When the Labor Department cracked down on the Teamsters, the mob had to look elsewhere. That "elsewhere" was the thrift industry after deregulation.

Thrifts could be taken over—through front men, of course—and then used to receive big deposits, grant easy loans, and, most importantly, to launder dirty money. *Inside Job*, a book that often reads like a how-to for swindlers, describes how to launder money:

Buy an asset (a piece of property or a business, for instance) with a loan from a thrift. Repay the loan over a period of time with dirty money. Once the loan was paid off, sell the asset and the money was laundered. (Or default on the loan and let the thrift repossess the property. Either way, you had an explanation for the origin of the money if anyone should ask.)

A twist that would allow you to both launder money and steal some from the thrift at the same time was to borrow more on the asset than you paid for it (and more than it was worth) and then default on the loan, claiming you lost money on the project. The money in your possession would then clearly be the product of the defaulted loan and, therefore, laundered. Plus, you'd have the extra money you had made by over-encumbering the asset (which the thrift would repossess and have to dispose of.)

For the mob, deregulation provided a laundry that paid you to do your wash. Why not? The "wise guys" owned the laundry and, in due time, the taxpaying sucker would foot the bill.

As first-rate journalists, the authors summon fact after fact, name after name, date after date to support their contentions. They do not assert; they prove.

Because they know the facts, they reject the popular explanation that the S & Ls went under—by the dozens—because of the collapse in the domestic oil industry. While the drop in petroleum price was undoubtedly a contributing factor, it was not the primary reason for the crisis in the thrifts. S & Ls were in trouble before the trouble with oil. They had to fall into deeper trouble no matter what happened with oil because burglars who once robbed banks with guns now looted banks with loads of lucre.

HERO TO THE RESCUE

While *Inside Job* is mainly about villains and their villainy, there are also a few heroes. Mainly, there is Ed Gray.

If the authors of *Inside Job* had tried to invent an Ed Gray to play the role of the good guy, they could not have done better than life itself. Gray seems to have been chosen out of central casting to play the part of a modern Mr. Smith in Washington. The stocky, congenial, plain-spoken Gray, an old friend and associate of Ronald Reagan, and a lobbyist for the U.S. League of Savings, a dear friend of Ed Meese, and a local bank executive—with some background in Washington—was asked by the chairman of the League, Leonard Shane, to be prepared to be named chairman of the Federal Home Loan Board. Gray assented.

In the next four years, the League turned against Gray. They did everything to get rid of him—FBI investigations, charges of over-ex-

tended expense accounts, gossip about homosexuality, rumors about health and resignation, pressure on the top to dump him. The League had made a mistake; Gray turned out to be an honest man.

If the book were turned into a movie, which it might well be, the title could be "Gray versus the Gang," with the gang being many of his old buddies.

One of the final ploys to get rid of Gray was an offer to him to take a super-paying job in the banking world. The offer, according to the authors, was made by Charles Keating, head of the holding company that owned Lincoln Savings of Irvine, California. Gray—with meager salary and personally in debt—turned down the lucrative temptation.

Early on, Gray wanted to act against Keating's Lincoln Savings. It was clear that the institution was insolvent. But for Gray to take over the bank (and other banks in a similar circumstance) his agency had to have the money with which to do it. The funds were lacking. He appealed to Congress for swift action so he could take Lincoln (and others) out of the hands of the plunderers. But Congress didn't react—or act.

The prolonged struggle that ensued between Gray and Democratic House leader Jim Wright is a revealing and revolting commentary on American politics. Wright's constituents—some Texas thrifts—charged that Gray was harrassing them, that he would bring on a crisis, that he was power-hungry, and that he ought to be dismissed or, at least, stopped. Wright listened to his constituents and withheld from Gray the money necessary to shut down the thieving thrifts. Had Gray been able to act in a timely fashion, American taxpayers would have been saved billions of dollars.

At a later point, when Gray managed matters to give the district offices of the FHLB the authority to shut down insolvent thrifts, the San Francisco branch of the FHLB moved to act against Lincoln. A self-appointed caucus of Senators, including some distinguished liberals, actively intervened to keep federal hands off Keating's kingdom.

When Keating was asked whether his remarkable political clout was due to the very sizable campaign contributions he made, he answered:

"I want to say in the most forceful way I can: I certainly hope so."

THE END IS YET TO COME

At several points in the book, the authors suggest that their narrative is still not ended. There are continuing indictments, trials on the calendar, further investigations.

As this review is written, the House Banking Committee is conducting hearings, unearthing information that goes even beyond the scandalous data contained in the book. There is the involvement of auditors and accounting firms, of the Federal Home Loan Bank Board in the days after Gray, of "cops" who joined the "robbers."

For those who wish to understand the background of these current revelations, reading *Inside Job* is a must. The book may well turn out to be an *Uncle Tom's Cabin* for our time—a story to stir the wrath of a nation in crusade to liberate the thrifts from the corrupt control of organized and unorganized crime.

CHAPTER 13

THE HOMELESS

INTRODUCTION

Journalists and sociologists have many ways to label social problems, and sometimes the labels overlap. Consider the case of the homeless. As a description of a social condition that faces hundreds of thousands, perhaps millions of Americans, homelessness can be considered a social problem in its own right. As a topic of inquiry and public policy, it has generated many expert surveys, television specials, and news stories. But many social commentators look at homelessness in terms of other social problems. It demonstrates, for example, the problems of mental patients who have been "deinstitutionalized." Others see homelessness as a failure of the nation's housing policy. Still others approach homelessness as a case study in the problems of poverty. And finally, some sociologists and journalists look at homeless people as social deviants who are pursuing an alternative lifestyle. All of these perspectives deserve careful thought. Homelessness is a complex topic that defies a simple explanation.

On one level, homelessness is a matter of personal hardship and a struggle to survive under extraordinary circumstances. James North depicts the private troubles that these people of the street constantly face in their daily search for food and shelter. At the level of public policy are such macro forces as the supply of low-cost housing units and the demand for manual skills in the job market. In the 1980s and 1990s, both have been in decline throughout the country. The consequence is a sharp rise in the number of people who can find neither work nor an affordable home.

The macro forces of declining housing stock and changing employment opportunities do not tell the whole story. Several micro issues—in particular, mental illness, alcoholism, and other forms of substance abuse—are also significant. Scott Shuger provides a valuable journalistic account of these personal problems.

Another aspect of the problem is the difficulty of determining how many people are homeless. In the late 1980s the estimates ranged from 300,000 to 3 million. It is difficult to count the homeless when the experts disagree on just who they are. Richard Appelbaum and Peter Dreier challenge some of the methods used by sociologists and government officials. They are especially critical of the methods used by Peter Rossi and James Wright in their Chicago Homeless Study. Rossi and Wright develop their methodology in the concluding essay. The reader must sort out this controversy. Establishing the "facts" is always an important part of studying any social problem. In the case of the homeless, the facts never speak for themselves. This fundamental difficulty complicates the task of developing causal inferences and proposing appropriate solutions. In various ways several essays in this chapter attempt to link evidence, causes, and solutions. The private and public issues involved in homelessness are so complex and so important that they demand thoughtful consideration of the key elements with which these authors build their arguments.

34. A SURVIVAL GUIDE FOR THE HOMELESS . . . FROM SOMEONE WHO LEARNED IT THE HARD WAY

JAMES NORTH

Otis Thomas, who was homeless himself for two years, has some specific, practical, detailed advice for anyone who is trying to survive on Chicago's streets this winter.

"First, get your papers in order," he says emphatically. "Birth certificate, social security card, other ID. You're going to need them to apply for

From *Chicago Tribune*, December 18, 1989.

general assistance, that $154, and to get into some shelters. You should also try to get some kind of mailing address."

Clothing is the second priority. "Decent shoes. Waterproof, leather. Preferably ankle length. Two pairs of socks. Long drawers, heavy pants. You'll want layers of clothes. Two heavy shirts. Jacket, cap, scarf, gloves."

Otis Thomas puts his hard-won street lore to use often. He works today as a night supervisor at the REST shelter for 60 homeless men, in the basement of the People's Church on Lawrence Avenue in Uptown. He has also been prominent in efforts to organize the estimated 40,000 or more people in the Chicago area who have no homes. Nationwide, the number of homeless people is estimated to be growing at 25 percent a year.

There are other components to his survival kit:

- "An info sheet, with addresses of shelters, the Salvation Army, other places where they'll feed you.
- "A friend who can take you in for a day or two now and then, so you can get yourself a shower, and keep yourself from a state of total depression.
- "A bus pass, if you can get one. You can keep warm riding the Els and buses. Otherwise, you have to hang out at the bus stops and ask people for their used transfers.
- "Addresses of the day labor agencies, so you can try to get work and put together the security rent deposit and the first month's rent that you'll need to get an apartment."

Otis Thomas discovered a whole new world when he fell into the ranks of the homeless back in 1986. He was raised in Chicago, went to Hyde Park High School, and worked steadily at a series of solid working class jobs until his last employer, a beer distributor, went out of business. He had been a helper on the delivery trucks.

Thomas was in his mid-40s. He is an athletic man, balding, with a graying beard, who sounds something like actor Bill Cosby, a man strong enough to put gentleness into his voice. "I was sitting up in a McDonald's in Uptown," he remembers, "and I realized that I only had seven cents in my pocket. I put my head in my hands and I said, 'Oh, my God, how can this be happening to me?'"

His mother still lived in the Chicago area, in a small apartment. "But I couldn't go stay with her," he says, "because that would have meant that I was saying to her that she had failed . . . that she had not raised me to live on my own."

Otis Thomas does not abuse alcohol or drugs,

so he was able to observe the catastrophe keenly even as he lived through it. He learned about a side to Chicago that he had never known existed. He learned that many people who work at the big hotels and restaurants downtown pass food to homeless people out the back doors, and allow them to erect makeshift shelters in the maze of dumpsters and alleyways in places like Lower Wacker Drive. "You'll find that the lower strata working people down there—sympathetic bellhops, janitors—take care of the poor," he says. He learned that most homeless people cannot be identified on sight, that those who are obviously mentally ill or usually intoxicated are a minority. "You might go into a McDonald's and see a guy sitting there with a coffee cup," he says. "But if you look up close, he's got a top on it. It's really empty. He might have grabbed it before they cleared the table. He's pretending. He doesn't want the security guard to put him out into the cold."

Thomas developed a mental map of the shelters around the city, places where up to 300 people sleep on cots in vast rooms, and he learned their different schedules and customs. One major refuge that pushes its religion especially annoyed him, even though he considers himself a religious man. "They force you to attend their services before they give you a bed," he says. "And they don't even have experienced preachers, just the new ones that are still coming out of their eggshells."

He learned which libraries and public buildings he could nod off in during the day. "You have to fold your coat over and put your arms around you," he says, "to make sure that no one picks your pockets." He found that he was sleeping a lot during the day. He said he later learned that it was a symptom of depression.

He learned which public bathrooms he could use for a quick wash. He learned which El stations to avoid when he rode the trains day and night to stay warm. "If you take the Dan Ryan to, I think, the end at 95th Street, you have to go out of that station and pay another fare to get back in," he cautions. He learned that certain grocery stores throw out stale bread at certain times of night, so he and other homeless people waited in the back alleys.

He learned that Saturdays and Sundays are

the worst days to be homeless, because some of the agencies that provide a warm place to hang out are closed. "Sunday is the time to go downtown, get away from the static, sit up in the movie house all day and catch up on your sleep," he says.

He learned an unusual way to shoplift food. "If I was really hungry, I would go into a store, slip open a loaf of bread, and take out a couple of pieces. Take a package of lunch meat, pull out a slice, fold it when no one was looking, eat it quickly. . . ." He imitated the furtive gestures with some embarrassment.

After a few months on the street, his depression got worse. "Your hygiene goes. You can't always wash your hands before you eat. If you're hanging out in a Walgreen's, trying to keep warm, you can't stand yourself—you *know* you stink. Someone will pass . . . you know he smelled you . . . you turn, and meet him eye to eye. . . ."

He learned that many homeless people work at the day labor agencies, where they earn the minimum wage or not much more. (The Chicago Coalition for the Homeless, citing a July, 1988, University of Chicago study, estimates that 20 percent of the homeless here are working.)

He learned that other homeless people make money less formally. Many of those who sell newspapers in the middle of the busier boulevards, or on the expressway ramps, are homeless. Others move purposefully through the alleys, following familiar routes, collecting used aluminum cans and other trash for recycling centers; they can earn $5 to $10 a day. Still others make their way out to O'Hare International Airport, where they can garner a few dollars returning luggage carts for 25 cents apiece.

HOMELESS, NOT HELPLESS

Today Thomas shares his street knowledge with the homeless men he supervises at the REST center. The church basement is spare, and there is always a slight odor of disinfectant. The 60 cots are lined up in neat rows. At 10 p.m., the men start filing in. Thomas greets them, usually wearing his "Homeless, Not Helpless" button. As the newcomers thumb through their wallets

for IDs, snapshots of their families sometimes flash by.

Some of them banter with Thomas; one younger man asks if his stockbroker called earlier. But others are too worn out to talk much after the long days of tramping up and down the streets. Thomas and the volunteers who help him ask who will need to be awakened earlier than the normal hour of 6 a.m. to go off to work. Some men come in visibly intoxicated; the shelter's staff occasionally will turn away someone who is abusive or hard to handle.

The REST shelter is one of the more genuinely integrated settings in the Chicago area. The "guests"—Thomas and the staff use the word without irony—include blacks, whites, Latinos and American Indians. There is no pattern in the eating or sleeping arrangements, except for what one wag, who works during the day as a short order cook, describes as the "snoring sections." One night, he gestured around the room and informed a newcomer, "The baritones sleep up here, the tenors over in that corner, the basses back there."

The men politely thank the volunteers who ladle out the soup and serve the other donated food, and take seats at tables. Thomas explains, "They used to have to eat on their cots, but that's not dignified. At the tables, they can sit around, talk, relax. Coming here should be like coming home to them."

After dinner, some of the men stretch out on their cots before the lights go out at 11. On certain nights, a substance abuse counselor meets with a group of them. Some read books, especially Bibles. One regular guest, a younger black man, reads his school books; he is studying to be a paralegal.

THE $24 QUESTION

Thomas has firm ideas about how to end homelessness. One evening after lights out, he sat watchfully outside the sleeping room and sketched out his philosophy. Clearly, he says, the first need is affordable housing. To a homeless man, two monetary figures are significant: $154, the amount most of them get each month from general assistance, and $130, the rent at the cheapest residential-type hotel in the Uptown area ("If you can get a room," Thomas adds). The $24 difference between those two figures leaves no room to maneuver for even the most ascetic miser.

Chicago, right in line with the trend nationwide, each year is losing 1,000 units of Single Room Occupancy (SRO) housing. The cumbersome term is a euphemism for low-income dwellings, many of which used to be more pungently described as "flophouses." Those units might not have been featured in *Better Homes and Gardens*, but they provided lodging for people who had had a bad break, a spell of unemployment, say, and needed a breather. Gentrification and drastic cuts in federal spending on housing during the Reagan years reduced the number of units at the lower end of the rental scale. Otis Thomas and other advocates say that homelessness will not end until the missing units are replaced.

Thomas interrupts his talk to welcome a latecomer into the shelter. The man asks to be awakened at 4 a.m. so he can get to his day labor job. Thomas tells him, "I saved you a bed on the other side of the room, away from that knucklehead who gets up ten times a night."

He returns to the larger issue of homelessness, and its profound effects on its victims. He believes that after as few as three months many homeless people can lose so much self-confidence that they would find it hard to reintegrate themselves into society even if enough affordable housing became available. Gesturing toward the men sleeping in the next room, he says: "Nobody gets eight hours in there. In the morning, they have to go right back out into the cold, even if there's six feet of snow. You start to wonder why you're being punished by God. The average guy in there prays at night. 'God, give me strength,' he prays. The average guy in there has thought about suicide. . . ."

Otis Thomas favors what he calls a step-by-step process to restore confidence and rebuild lives. "They have to start doing things for themselves again," he says. "Instead of waiting until 10 at night, they should be able to get back into the shelter at 4 if they're not working. There should be a little library here for them. The guys who can cook should do the dinner. There should be a laundry; there should be a job bank. We should have a sewing machine, to mend clothes. To stay here, I should have to do my share.

"But I don't know of any shelters that are run by the homeless themselves."

Yet even as the homeless stream into the shelter each week, there is a trickle out, of those who make it back into the mainstream or at least to its shores. Some are able to support themselves— and find a permanent residence—with day labor jobs; others find work in factories or restaurants. In Thomas' case, his activism brought him to the attention of officials in an advocacy group for the homeless. They alerted him to the job opening as supervisor at the REST shelter.

Thomas says that relearning self-reliance is particularly important for the men who must confront their dependence on alcohol and drugs. But he complains that many rehabilitation programs have long waiting lists. "Some of the guys are told to come back in 6 weeks, 12 weeks . . . Who wants to wait when I know what my problem is?"

Thomas' philosophy explains why he does not always give to panhandlers. "If I see somebody on the streetcorner, I assume he wants a drink," he says. "There are shelters where he can stay; there are places where he can eat; so he doesn't need money for that. It's not drugs, because he'll never panhandle enough for them. He *might* need bus fare, but he could just ask somebody for a used transfer. . . ."

Thomas paused, reflecting. "But maybe he *is* hungry. So what I might do is talk to him, invite him someplace to have a cup of coffee, a sandwich. Make sure he really eats. See what his situation is. Try to see what I can do to help him break out of that dependency cycle. Talk to him as a person."

35. HOMELESS: A PRODUCT OF POLICY

TODD SWANSTROM

Homelessness has captured the attention of policy makers and citizens across the nation. But the politics of compassion has focused attention on the homeless themselves and not on the causes of their plight.

The problem is not to explain why people are poor but to explain why poverty, in the 1980's, has taken the form of homelessness. It simply won't do to claim, as Ronald Reagan did in an interview before leaving office, that most people are homeless by choice. Nor can it be argued that homelessness has been caused by de-institutionalizing mental patients, since most de-institutionalization occurred in the late 1960's.

The primary cause of homelessness in the 1980's is an inadequate supply of housing, especially at the bottom of the rental market. And government policy is deeply implicated.

Evidence for the shortage of low income housing abounds. Vacancy rates in New York, San Francisco, and Boston recently have averaged 1 to 2 percent (5 percent is considered normal). Homelessness is only the most visible component of the undersupply problem. In New York City, more than 300,000 people are doubled up with friends and relatives.

Market theory assumes that supply automatically meets demand. But from 1974 to 1983, when low income families were spending more and more on rent, the supply of low rent housing units fell 8 percent.

Contrary to popular notions, Federal housing policy does not favor low income renters. In 1986, homeowner tax deductions totaled $42.4 billion, with more than 95 percent of the benefits going to those in the upper income range. Mean-

while, funding for housing under the Department of Housing and Urban Development fell two-thirds, from $30.2 billion in 1981 to $10 billion in 1986—the largest budget cut for a Cabinet-level department in the Reagan Administration.

Between 1981 and 1986, H.U.D.-subsidized housing starts fell from 144,348 to only 17,080 units. The Reagan Administration, instead of subsidizing production of new units, subsidized individuals with vouchers that would supposedly help them find housing on the private market. Jack Kemp, the new Secretary of H.U.D., says he is eager to solve the problem of homelessness; he should, however, avoid a rigid adherence to the Reagan approach, which is unworkable in many metropolitan areas.

Housing vouchers work only if the problem is affordability, not supply. In crowded metropolitan markets, the increasing demand for housing by voucher holders does not address the supply problem and may only result in escalating rents. In New York City, three out of every four vouchers are returned because the holder cannot find an affordable apartment that meets Federal standards.

Why isn't the housing supply responding to increased demand? The reasons are complex, but many have to do with local government policy. Overly stringent and discriminatory building codes, for example, increase quality but unfortunately decrease the supply of low income housing.

The most serious interferences in the market are zoning controls. Some prohibit the construction of multifamily apartments in areas zoned for residential use. Their effect is to prevent the market from responding to the demand for rental housing—especially low income housing.

In order to boost their tax bases, cities often cater to gentrification, disregarding the effects on the supply of low rent housing. White collar professionals in cities have taken many former low

Todd Swanstrom is professor of political science at the State University of New York.

income housing units off the market. New York City, for example, has given away billions in tax incentives for housing rehabilitation and new construction, but almost all of it has gone for luxury housing. Those tax incentives aided the destruction of the city's single room occupancy units. Since 1970, one million units have been lost nationwide—a major cause of homelessness.

Instead of attacking the causes of homelessness, we are spending billions of dollars on shelters. Building shelters, however, is like putting pots in the living room to catch dripping water without fixing the roof.

Homelessness is caused by a shortage of low rent housing—a shortage that is caused by misguided public policies. We know what needs to be done; what is lacking is the political will to do it.

36.   CENSUS COUNT NO HELP TO HOMELESS

RICHARD P. APPELBAUM and PETER DREIER

When it comes to federal policy, numbers count a great deal. The 1990 census, which plans the first-ever national count of people on streets and in shelters, will help determine the funding of programs for America's rapidly growing homeless population over the next decade.

We believe the census will severely undercount the homeless, pulling the rug out from under the few programs that presently exist. We are worried because all past efforts to accurately count the homeless have failed miserably.

The number of homeless people has become a political football. The Bush administration, like its predecessor, does not like to think of the problem as too big or too costly. Small problems require small numbers, and small numbers apparently require large studies.

Since a 1984 Department of Housing and Urban Development study placed the national

From *Chicago Tribune*, August 8, 1989. Reprinted with permission of Richard P. Applebaum.

Richard P. Appelbaum is chairman of the Department of Sociology at the University of California at Santa Barbara, and co-author of "Rethinking Rental Housing." Peter Dreier is director of housing for the Boston Redevelopment Authority and writes frequently on housing policy.

homeless figure at barely one-tenth of the National Homeless Coalition's figure of 2 to 3 million, millions of dollars, dozens of studies and countless interviewers have all sought to count the homeless. All of these efforts have failed. These undercounts have made it possible for the Bush Administration to justify small-scale programs that do not address the fundamental problem.

Why are all efforts to count the homeless doomed to failure?

Part of the answer is political: a deliberate effort on the part of the federal government to downplay the seriousness of the problem through statistical sleight of hand. Although HUD's 5-year-old figures continue to provide the official federal estimate of homelessness, two Congressional hearings that examined HUD's methods in detail found these figures worthless.

Other studies have attempted to correct HUD's mistakes, without success. One study is especially important, because its methods provide a model for the upcoming census. Unlike the HUD study, which relied on the opinion of "experts," the well-funded Chicago Homeless Study tried to actually count all the homeless in selected areas of the city on two early morning occasions.

The interviewers, who for security reasons included an off-duty police officer, scoured a random sample of blocks, asking the people they encountered wandering the streets if they had a place to sleep. Few were willing to talk to the interviewers, much less admit to being homeless: only 23 people on the first occasion, and 30 on the second.

These minuscule numbers were then projected to the parts of the city that were not surveyed, yielding a citywide homeless figure of only 2,000–3,000 people, considerably lower than even HUD's conservative estimate of 20,000. The prestigious *Science* magazine has since uncritically reported these doubtful results, giving further credence to the belief that the homeless can be accurately counted if only enough money is spent.

That belief has led the Census Bureau to get into the act. Next March 20, on "Street and Shelter Night," census takers will fan out across the United States in an effort to secure a one-time "hard" national count of the homeless. City governments will be asked to provide the Census Bureau with a list of shelters and street locations where the homeless congregate. Census takers will briefly interview the homeless they find in the shelters. And later, in the early morning hours, count the people they encounter in the streets.

Census officials admit there are numerous obstacles to an accurate count by this method, not the least of which is limited funding. Like all other previous attempts, the census count will be limited only to the visible homeless. The Census Bureau proposes to turn exclusively to local government officials for guesses of where they are to be found, ignoring homeless people outside the most obvious areas.

If the HUD study failed to locate numerous people while relying on shelter providers and others close to the homeless, how can the Census hope for success in relying on less well-informed government officials? Safety considerations pose another problem in counting, since census takers will be asked to avoid unsafe locations such as tunnels, cars and abandoned buildings.

The many homeless people who sleep in such places will therefore be ignored.

Finally, the street and shelter census will completely ignore those homeless people who are doubled-up with friends and relatives. The regular household census, which will be done two weeks later, will not make up for this deficiency, since many experts believe it is virtually impossible to get accurate information about illegal tenants.

While the Census Bureau admits that its count is not exhaustive, homeless advocates fear that whatever number they come up with will become the "official" number used for policy-making. In the words of the National Coalition for the Homeless, "everyone will be clamoring for the release of this 'scientific' count; as we know, anything is possible in the numbers game."

In that game, there are clear winners and losers. Researchers get large grants and build their careers as experts on homelessness. The federal government saves billions of dollars by "proving" that there really aren't all that many homeless people out there who require federal assistance. The major losers are the homeless themselves, including a growing number of the working poor and children, who are not only denied their mere existence, but the very programs they require to survive.

In our view, the one number that really does matter is the number of dollars the federal government spends on housing assistance for the poor. That number can be easily counted. It now stands at only $7 billion, a fifth the amount that was spent at the beginning of the decade. Today, less than one-third of America's 33 million poor people receive any kind of governmental housing assistance at all. That means that there are millions of poor people at risk of being homeless tomorrow should they be hit with a rent increase, domestic violence or a layoff.

If the Bush Administration is serious about the tragedy of homelessness, it will forget about counting the uncountable, and start putting money into housing programs until there is no need for homeless shelters.

37.   WHO ARE THE HOMELESS?

SCOTT SHUGER

For anyone living in a city, the dilemma unfolds dozens of times a day: There he is, between me and my immediate goal—The Man With The Styrofoam Cup, asking me a simple question: "Spare some change?" That question lights off others of my own that go unspoken: "What does this guy do with the money?" "How much does he make a day?" "Doesn't begging like this make him feel awful?" "Why doesn't it make him feel awful enough to stop and get a job?" "How did he get in this fix?" "Is he really in a fix, or is he taking me for a sucker?" "Why should I give to this guy rather than the other beggars on the block?" "Or do they think I can give to them all?"

"Spare some change?" comes up because I am in a limited way accessible to The Man With The Styrofoam Cup. My questions come up because he is in a radical way inaccessible to me. To most of us, the homeless are a visible mystery. Perhaps some of the most hardened among us would prefer them to be invisible. But the rest of us would prefer them to be less of a mystery. We want to help, yes, but we want our efforts to go where they will make a difference. For that to happen, we have to know what we're up against.

HYPE FOR THE HOLIDAYS

Although there have been some harder-edged stories on the homeless, the main message the media delivers about them is that despite their predicament, they're just like us. In a news spe-

cial, Tom Brokaw stated that the homeless are "people you know." Robert Hayes, director of the National Coalition for the Homeless, told *The New York Times* that when he is contacted by television news programs or congressional committees looking at homelessness, "they always want white, middle-class people to interview." A recent study that examined the national print and broadcast coverage given the homeless between November 1986 and February 1989 discovered that a quarter of the homeless people featured in stories were children. That was equal to the number of those identified as unemployed and three times the number identified as substance abusers. Only 4 percent of the stories attributed the plight of the homeless to their personal problems.

A recent publication of the Better Business Bureau reported, "Many of those living in shelters or on the street are no different from those with a place to live. . . . Being on the street is often something out of their control." In a *New York Times* op-ed piece, Rep. Charles Schumer wrote that "the slightest misstep or misfortune—a temporary layoff, a large medical bill, a divorce—could send [a low-income] family onto the streets. Indeed that's exactly what's been happening." The concrete examples of the homeless Schumer cited are a working mother of eight whose eldest is an honor student, and a 63-year-old woman forced to retire from her job as a waitress because of arthritis. In another *Times* op-ed piece entitled "The Homeless: Victims of Prejudice," two Ivy League law students said that the homeless people they met during a summer of intern work included a Broadway playwright, a highly decorated World War II veteran, and an ex-professional basketball player. Not to mention "pregnant women who lost the race to stay one step ahead of the housing marshal, students trying to study in noisy shelters, and average families working diligently to save enough money for an apartment."

From *The Washington Monthly*, March 1990, pp. 38–49. Copyright © 1990 The Washington Monthly Company, 1611 Connecticut Avenue, N.W., Washington, D.C. 20009; (202) 462-0128. Reprinted with permission from The Washington Monthly.

Scott Shuger is an editor of The Washington Monthly.

Jonathan Kozol, in his book on homeless families, *Rachel and Her Children*, features: a couple who, after their house burns down, lose their five children to foster homes and are reduced to panhandling; a 35-year-old woman, a college graduate who worked for many years before medical complications wiped out her savings, forced her to lose her home, ended her marriage, made her give up her kids, and left her sleeping on the beach; and a teacher, who when the heater in her building failed, was "in a matter of weeks . . . reduced from working woman and householder to a client of the welfare system." To the question "Why are they without homes?" Kozol responds, "Unreflective answers might retreat to explanations with which readers are familiar: 'family breakdown,' 'drugs,' 'culture of poverty,' 'teen pregnancies,' 'the underclass,' etc. While these are precipitating factors for some people, they are not the cause of homelessness. *The cause of homelessness is lack of housing.*" (Italics in the original.)

Last December, the Salvation Army came out with a special TV commercial to boost its Christmas campaign for the homeless in New York City: *On the sidewalk in front of a wrought-iron fence, framed by a shopping bag on one side and a suitcase on the other, there's a mother and her child together in a sleeping bag, their white skins reflecting the street lights. As a man carrying a briefcase walks by, the child sits up; you can see her long blonde hair now. The mother kisses the girl and pulls her back down, hugging and patting her as they drift back to sleep.* "Home for the Holidays," the ad's caption says.

Honor students and playwrights, college graduates sleeping on the beach, mothers and daughters sleeping in the park—this is what I can read about or see on TV. But this is not what I see in Washington. Where in all this is the Man With The Styrofoam Cup?

Although real homeless people are all around me every day, I've been vulnerable to the more idealized representations of the press because my approach to street people has been typical of the white middle class: Usually, I stare straight ahead and walk on by, my head full of those skeptical questions. Sometimes, something—an excess of change, a particularly good day, or just a weariness of skepticism—would make me stop

and give some money. But no matter what, there was one thing I would never, ever, do: Talk to these people. Recently, however, I decided to break that nervous middle class habit. I resolved to talk to the homeless, to ask them some of the questions I had been keeping to myself in all the years of walking right by.

NIGHTS OF WINE AND POSES

I first put my new approach into effect one night last winter. On the stretch of Connecticut Avenue just above Dupont Circle, it was cold and rainy, and the panhandlers were huddled in bunches near the entrances of the restaurants on the block. With most of the dinner crowd already gone, the best pickings were over for the day. That left only pedestrians like me.

Two men come up to me, styrofoam cups in hand: "Spare some change?" Both men are unsteady on their feet and hard to understand, with 100-proof breath. I make a donation and learn that the tall black man is named Mike and the short one is K.C. I ask them how long they've been on the streets, and they tell me six months. They've both had jobs in construction. Mike says he used to work as a bartender until he lost his job because of his drinking. When I ask where they stay at night, Mike says that the owner of an art gallery across the street lets them sleep in the lobby of the building. Mike says they get to bathe every two days at a shelter in Alexandria.

"What do you do with the money you get?" I ask. Mike gives me a thumb-to-the-lip bottle motion. Then he shrugs his shoulders in embarrassment. "I got to go to a program. An in-patient program so I cain't get out so I cain't mess up. I got to clean my act up."

Mike is very polite, calling me "sir" frequently and saying "excuse me" to every passerby. K.C. is a little closer to the edge of his personal envelope tonight. When a couple turns into the restaurant behind us, he snaps at them, "If you don't eat all your food, bring a doggy bag for us."

Some surveys say that an inordinate number of the District's homeless are veterans. So I ask, "Were either of you guys in the service?" "I was on the Ho Chi Minh Trail," replies Mike. "I was over there in Korea," says K.C. "Quit telling the man lies," scolds Mike. I ask K.C. where and when. "I'm trying to 'member man. I'm shell-blocked," he says. "I ain't no dummy. Now hold it. All I know is I was in the 101 Screaming Eagles Fort Campbell Kentucky. Basic Training Fort Dix. But where I was, I can't remember. I got shell-blocked. I've been shot up and all that shit, but I'm still alive."

Before I can pursue this, a completely drunk or stoned black woman comes over. She's in her late twenties, I'd guess. Her head is covered by a tight bandana and her eyes are only slits. Without saying anything, she greets Mike with a French kiss that lasts about ten seconds. Then she spends at least that long sticking her tongue in his ear. Even so, she's hanging on to Mike as much for navigation as for affection. "Sandra, this is him," Mike says, pointing towards me.

"I'm Chocolate," says Sandra. "That's Memphis and that's um, Black." Mike shrugs his shoulders in embarrassment again. Just then, a younger guy, more drugged than drunk, charges toward us. This guy is really revved up on something. He starts shouting at me from 25 feet away. He's in his late teens, early twenties, with a fighter's build and a bull neck. "That's my girlfren'—what you all doing to her?" He pushes the other three behind him and gets in my face. "Who do you see on this corner first? What's wrong? You gonna help us out?"

As I start to leave, Mike offers his hand. His handshake is solid. I bet the rest of him was too, several thousand drinks ago. "Give me your address," demands Sandra. "Can I go home with you tonight?" It was somewhere between pitiful and sexual. "I don't want no shelter. I want to go to your house. I want to sleep in a bed, a real righteous bed."

A block away I cross paths with two guys standing out of the rain under the overhang of a closed lunch stand. Both in their twenties, one white, the other black. It quickly becomes apparent that all they have in common is this dry spot of sidewalk. The white guy, who tells me his name is Wayne, asks me for some change, telling me he got laid off from a construction job. The black guy, without introducing himself, quickly tries to take over. "Hey, I'm in a situation too. I'm a starving artist, and nobody's giving me

nothing. I don't have a job. But I'm a millionaire, I know that inside. That my art is worth money, OK? But I know I'm gonna make it. All I got to do is go to New York. I've been trying for four years to get back there. I just need enough money to go to New York. The only thing I need is like 150 bucks."

I ask him if he ever tries finding work in the want ads. "Everybody keeps saying that, man! The paper is to get you to buy it or look at it. They're still making money off you! Hey, see all these stores out here? Every one of them got a loan to get what they've got. Well, I need a loan. If I had a loan for about $10,000, I'd be a multimillionaire, man, because my art is fuckin' baaad. That's the only way I'm gonna make it—if I get a fuckin' loan."

Wayne hasn't said a word during this rap. But when the starving artist, now pretty agitated, nervously walks to the corner to search out better possibilities than me, Wayne rolls his eyes and says to me out of the corner of his mouth, "It don't take nobody no four years to get back to New York, I'm sorry." Wayne is not wildly drunk, but now that I'm standing close to him I can tell he's pretty numbed up. Wayne is one of the truly unsheltered homeless. In good weather he sleeps in the park just opposite the Q street Metro exit. In bad weather he sleeps under the portico of an attorney's office or in a nearby building that's under construction. He has shoulder-length light-blond hair coming down from under his ball cap, a moustache, and the beginnings of a beard. About four years ago, he came to this area from Texas with his family. Then his mother died and his father started a housepainting company in Virginia. Wayne used to work there. I ask him why he quit. This was, after all, the decision that finally put him on the street. I figure there had to be a pretty dramatic reason. All Wayne comes up with is this: "I just couldn't deal with it, too many Spanish workers—they can't speak English because most of them are illegal immigrants—and being the boss's son."

The artist comes back. "Can you give me a buck or 50 cents, man, so I can get on the subway?" he asks me. As I give him two quarters, I notice that he's wearing a Burberry scarf. After he leaves, Wayne says, "I don't like him. He's a con artist. I'm watching right now to see if he gets on the subway." He doesn't.

Wayne turns his attention back to me. "I used to be in trouble all the time until I got my head cleared. Put it this way," he chuckles, "I got a few tatoos from prison." Wayne says his conviction for knifing a guy in a Texas bar fight is a problem when he's looking for work. "That's why I go for jobs that are under the table."

HOPE FOR SOME HOMELESS

In my travels around Washington, I rarely see homeless women on the street. But there are places outdoors where they congregate. One such spot is a steep stretch of Belmont Street in the northwest quadrant of the city. Walking north on 14th Street and turning onto Belmont any evening at around 5:30, you will gradually become aware of a pilgrimage—first just a few shadows moving through the uneven light, but eventually a line of them making the daily trek up to the top of the hill. Most of the shadows are families, virtually all black, living in temporary housing for the homeless. There are very few men, either by themselves or attached to a family group. I fall in step with the shadow families, curious to see what could have this drawing power.

At the top of the hill is the one-time Pitts Hotel, a ramshackle building now operated as a shelter for homeless families. Parked out front under the archway is a gleaming yellow Rolls Royce, District license plate 347. A man standing next to it tells me that it belongs to the building's owner, Cornelius Pitts. The people file by it without taking much notice. The building has room for only 50 or so families, but every day the District's Department of Human Services deposits four additional busloads of shelter residents—mostly families—at the foot of the hill so that they can get a cooked meal.

Watching the women come and go on Belmont, you can't avoid the feeling that they are fighting some powerful obstacles in addition to the lack of a permanent place to live. Many seem tired and cranky, snapping at their children and cuffing them for transgressions that are hard to see in this light. "I'm not here because I'm all

drugged up," says a plump woman with four kids in tow, hurrying down the hill to make the last bus. "I work as a nurse's assistant at D.C. General, and the truth is"—her voice lowers—"I had to leave where I was living because my friend was beating on me."

Despite these dark overtones, the longer I watch and listen, the more I become aware of the many hopeful signs on Belmont Street. As a group, these women seem fairly straight. Straight enough for Tom Brokaw. They stand in stark contrast to street hustlers like K.C. or the artist. Although the meals and the pick-up buses run on such a tight schedule that most of the women are in too much of a hurry to talk to me, those who do tell me that they are working, leaving their kids with babysitters during the day. A gregarious teenage mother of an 11-month-old tells me her biggest complaint: these daily crosstown voyages for food have left her baby with a persistent cold. A soft-spoken woman with three kids tells me that she has just gotten herself on a list downtown for housing placement; she hopes that in a few more weeks the city will be able to locate a place for her. Most of the women are dressed neatly, and some of the kids are in adorable get-ups: Bows in hair and party shoes for the girls, superhero jackets and team ballcaps for the boys. Obviously, many of these people are using their meager means for the right things; given more sustenance, most of them would only do more of the same. Yes, for the Belmont families, it seems that housing *would* be a big part of the answer.

HEARTBREAK HOTEL

At Mt. Carmel House, a homeless women's shelter in Washington's Chinatown, you can meet the people the Belmont Street women are trying not to become. Ann, for instance—a sad-eyed 41-year-old black woman who has come to this women's shelter straight from a stint at the detox unit at D.C. General. Ann discovered she couldn't handle alcohol after many years of what she calls "trial and error." Before booze derailed her life, she was a data clerk at the Veterans' Administration. But now she's lost her job, and her 18-year-old daughter lives with Ann's mother.

Or there's Marsha, a black woman in her twenties whose five years on cocaine and one year of living on the streets have somehow left her eyeballs and her teeth the same yellow color. This time last year, she was pawning anything she could get her hands on and working as a prostitute to raise drug money. A high-school dropout who was sexually abused by her father, Marsha has a daughter by a man she used to live with; she no longer has any contact with him and the authorities have taken the child away. Last November, Marsha got shot in the head by "some crackhead going around in the streets shooting for the hell of it. I should have gone to the doctor right away," she says. "But I wouldn't go to the doctor until I'd done all my cocaine first."

Celeste Valente, who's been a social worker at Mt. Carmel House for eight years, says that the shelter's 40-odd resident population now includes more younger women than it used to. There's been a decrease in the mentally ill clientele (now 30 percent of the population, down from 80 percent a few years ago) and an increase in drug addicts (almost all those in the shelter who are not mentally ill are substance abusers). Valente guesses that "more than 80 percent of the women who come here have been raped or were the victims of incest."

Another woman living at Mt. Carmel is Virginia, who's spent the last year in shelters—four in all. She's white, in her forties, with "done" hair, pink lipstick, and rouged cheeks. Her handbag says "Maui" on it. She could easily pass for a suburbanite down here doing volunteer work. In fact, she now volunteers a couple of nights a week at a nearby dinner program. "When I was working," Virginia remembers, "I gave about $1,500 of my United Way funds to the House of Ruth [another women's shelter in Washington]. And when I became homeless, that's the first place I went." Virginia's father was career Army. She was born in Austria. She has a literature degree from Georgetown. "I had the life," she says.

Here it seems I've come across a person worthy of Jonathan Kozol, the Salvation Army, and all the other "it could happen to anyone" theorists. But there's a difference they might not like. Virginia's an alcoholic. And she spent a long time in what she describes as a "sick" relationship with a sexually abusive man. After she was laid off from her job managing an engineering office, she stayed in her apartment, watched TV, and drank for eight months. "I drank copious amounts of beer," she tells me, "three six-packs to a case a day."

KARMIC CROSSED WIRES

During the eighties, Lafayette Park, just across Pennsylvania Avenue from the White House, became a campground for homeless squatters. Indeed, some people have lived there for most of the decade, conducting what they call a "peace vigil." The vigil is often on the itinerary of school classes visiting from out of town. The peace squatters have positioned themselves along the south edge of the park, where their placards about Hiroshima and nuclear freeze face the president's front door. Sixties-like, they give themselves new names like "Sunrise." One vigiler I talk to, who's lived here for three years, used to work as an art restorer before joining the scene he describes as a "karmic crossfire." He doesn't want to live anywhere else. He supports himself by performing three nights a week in a "folk rock" band. The rest of the time he's out in the park, sometimes sleeping in his jury-rigged plastic shelter, sometimes cooking up a stew, or greeting pedestrians with lines like, "Peace, brother. Thanks for smiling"—whether the guy is smiling or not.

But some of the homeless in Lafayette Park are conducting more private vigils. Take the man on the park bench, hands on knees, open bottle of beer at his feet, just staring intensely at the White House. With the green of his poncho and the way his eyes are bulging, he looks like a frog on a lily pad. "I'm here to talk to George," he tells me. When he sees my fatigue pants, he goes to Red Alert. "Are you Marine Corps, FBI, Secret Service? Are you wearing a tape recorder?" I reassure him. He's so close to jumping out of his skin that I worry about what would happen if he were to notice the two men in uniform on the White House roof. "Yeah, George is a good man," the guy on the bench says, continuing to stare straight ahead. "I don't have nothing against him. He's a naval aviator and all that.

When he went out to San Francisco after that earthquake, I talked to him." I asked the man if he flew out there to do that. "Nope," he says, never taking his eyes off his quarry, "talked to him by Telstar."

The Telstar man has plenty of company in Washington. Near my office, for instance, there is the tall, helmeted man who keeps a guardpost at the corner of Q and Connecticut. When you get close to him, you can see that he's wearing a flannel West German army uniform. He's sort of handsome and he has that straight-from-the-diaphragm voice and ramrod posture so valued in drill instructors. His long reddish brown hair runs in a thin, tight braid down his back. Tucked in his helmet and pointing straight up are three toothbrushes, looking like periscopes.

When I ask him his name, he replies, "General. U.S. General. None of that Noriega thing for me." I notice that he's wearing a Top Gun squadron patch; he tells me where he got it: "The Surgeon General distributed it to the field artillery and ballistics command and the dominions of trade. Top Gun. Miramar California. I took the training out there about eight weeks ago. It was about the failure to inform people at the White House. And to maintain gun standards, computer standards, or surgical standards."

When I ask General what he's doing at this corner, he tells me, "This is the field marshal air combat warning post here for the businesses and the banks. This post is the way that the military has become involved about the levering of the topmost business developments." What's he watching out for? The answer comes back instantly: "The Turks." As to how long he'll be in this assignment, General guesses about 40 years. "It should improve sometime in the nineties as far as the Motorola business is concerned. Eventually I will tend towards Walkman business. How the General maintains his districting or vector businesses is highly dependent upon Walkman skills."

General does not know he's homeless. When I ask him where he goes at night and in bad weather, he tells me that he confers with the president. He readily distinguishes himself from panhandlers, whom he dismisses as "people who have no ownership interests or no mortgage or paper interests." However, in a way, he does have his own version of "Spare some change?" As I'm leaving, he says to me, "You should bring me a banknote so that the interests you represent can be represented here."

THE GRATE SOCIETY

Under an overpass in Foggy Bottom just east of the Potomac and just north of the exclusive Watergate apartment complex are some steam grates that have long served as a thermal oasis for the homeless. The night I walk by is chilly, so the grates are pretty full. When I approach, several of the men there ask me for change. The hot air rushing out of this hole in the ground produces a loud hum you have to shout over. The steam itself provides a two-part sensation: first your face gets hit by a pleasant rush of warmth, then your nose gets hit by the stench of stale booze. Booze that's soaked through clothes, that's soaked through skin, that's soaked through lives.

There are nine or ten men at the grate this night. It's an interracial group. Some are huddled at the edges, some just racked out across it. The two men who asked me for money talk to me a lot, but some of the others never even look in my direction.

One man tells me he's been out here for two years, another says eight. The liveliest talker is a young black guy named Tony. In his mid-twenties, he's handsome and, in an alcoholic sort of way, articulate. Tony points to a woman coming our way. "Here comes my girlfriend. That's why I'm out here, because of her." A black woman weaves towards us. She's really drunk. She plops down sullenly at the edge of the grate, no use for anybody. "I met her in July when I came out the Navy," Tony says, unaccountably thrilled to see her.

Tony says he's not really homeless because he can stay with his aunt at 14th and Euclid. But it's real late and he's still out here drinking.

Tony says he was in the Navy for eight years. "Aviation. Backseater in F-14s. I was a second lieutenant. I worked in the Indian Ocean on the *Nimitz*. Just got out in July. I'm going back. I'm in the reserves." There's a pause. "I was supposed to been back—I'm not going to lie to you. I'm AWOL. When I came out of high school and went to the Navy, I started out as an NCO—a noncommissioned officer. I was an NCO all the way. I went to school in Annapolis. When I go back, they may drop me down to like E-4. After I get out of the brig. I see Navy cars go by here every day. They're MPs, man, I know they lookin' for me.

"I want to re-up for maybe four more years. And then come back and get me a job at one of these airports as an aviator or air traffic controller. But it's gonna be a while for me now because last Saturday night, some girl stabbed me in my chest. And all I got is one lung now." As he's telling me this, Tony's unbuttoning his shirt. He shows me a Band-Aid just under his clavicle. It's not a very elaborate dressing, and I don't see any signs of actual injury. "I just got out of the hospital. And today two guys tried to jump on me." Tony shows me his punching hand. The knuckles on it are very swollen. "So it's gonna be a while—maybe another two months—until I go back."

Tony says the Navy sent him here on shore leave to bury his grandmother. "That's when I met Karen," he tells me, nodding toward the poor woman who just joined us. "Took a liking to her. And she turned my head around." He says Karen used to drive trucks in the Army, that she was in Vietnam. He says she's 38. She looks 58. Tony reaches between his knees into the red plastic milk crate he's sitting on and pulls out a white plastic flask. Gin, he tells me. A pint a day. Pointing at the others, he explains, "They drink that hard stuff."

Tony's story was fascinating, but it wasn't true. You can't start out in the service as an NCO, and "second lieutenant" is not a rank in the Navy.

The old man at my feet, whom Tony introduces as Jimmy, "the granddaddy of the grates," mumbles at me. In the slurred words of a lifelong drunk he tells me that he's worked as a tow-truck driver at an Amoco station for 18 years. But, he says, "See those," pointing at some of Georgetown's poshest apartments, "I don't make enough money to rent no apartment for $250 a month. So I stay here." Jimmy's incredibly dirty. He never looks up at me. His attention is riveted on a little pack of picture cards he keeps riffling through. They're not baseball cards, although

they're that size. Because they're predominantly pink, I assume they're pornographic. When Jimmy hands me one, I see they're not. They're pictures of food. The card in my hand is "Shrimp with Greens."

The closest thing to an American monument to homelessness is the shelter run by the Community for Creative Non-Violence (CCNV) in the former Federal City College building at the intersection of 2nd and D in downtown Washington. This is the building that the federal government agreed to lease to homeless advocate Mitch Snyder in 1984 after Snyder led a 51-day fast. Housing 1,400 homeless—1,265 men and 135 women—it's the largest shelter in the country, perhaps in the world. CCNV's literature calls it "a national model."

Since its inception, the CCNV shelter has received over $13 million in combined federal and D.C. appropriations, and another $500,000 in corporate donations. I wanted to get an idea of what that money is buying. To do that, I decided to take my idea of talking to the homeless one step further by going to the shelter and asking for help.

SHELTER SKELTER

I showed up at CCNV late on a Saturday afternoon in January, dressed in my worst clothes and having not washed or shaved for days. In front of the building, Saturday night is already well underway. Thirty or so men are standing on the porch and along the sidewalk, talking loudly and taking regular pulls from the brown paper bags they all seem to have. One of the louder guys is a gapped-toothed man in a purple parka. He's shouting out at anybody walking by and going through a loud review of the lunch he had at some soup kitchen: "Uhhhh-uhhhh, barbecue chicken! I'm telling you, they got *down*. . . ."

When they're not drinking and cursing, the men spend a lot of time spitting. The sidewalk is phlegm-spotted. It's hard to find a dry spot on the steps to sit on. Almost as soon as I do, I attract the attention of disastrously drunk man who until then had been working full-time trying to keep from impacting the sidewalk. He's lurching about furiously, like a man on the deck of a storm-blown ship. He finally makes it over next to me. Even sitting down, he's weaving. He mumbles something to me I can't make out. The second time, I catch it: "Do you have five cents?" When I say I don't, he repeats the question. Then he mumbles something else, "What's in the bag?" For authenticity, I have a paper bag with me. The drunk grabs my arm and tries to pull me towards him. "What's in the bag?" "Nothing for you," I tell him, moving away. This catches Purple Parka's attention. From his perch, he looks down at me and barks, "Talk to the man like that and I'll bust yo' ass on the sidewalk."

When a woman comes to the front of the building with some stuff to donate, Purple Parka comes down and swarms all over her, putting his arm around her and trying to take her through a door where she doesn't want to go. "Be sociable," another man tells him. "You not on the staff." Parka snaps back, "I ain't yo' nigger." When a girl with a pretty hairstyle walks by, he shouts at her, "I want your hair!" She replies, "You gonna buy me some more?"

I move down to the wooden benches near one corner of the building. From here, I can see something that I couldn't before. Behind a van across the street, two guys are fighting. They must be pretty drunk; the pace doesn't let up a bit even when one guy slams the other's head into the van.

There's a constant stream of men coming in and out of the building. A beer can in a paper sack is practically part of the uniform. A few weeks before tonight, *Newsweek* ran a picture of the area where I'm sitting now. In the shot, the CCNV building and grounds looked spic-and span. The three guys now on the bench to my right, sharing a joint, weren't there. And neither were the two women and one guy on the sidewalk right in front of me, passing a reefer between them. A young black guy dressed in the immaculate fashion of followers of Muslim leader Louis Farrakhan—black suit, bow tie, highly polished shoes—comes over to the trio. I expect him to tell them to put the joint out. But instead he takes off his Walkman and lends it to one of the women. She closes her eyes and sways to the music, continuing to take her tokes. A guy yells down to the group from the balcony, "You know she be horny when she smokes that shit!"

So far, out of the hundred or so people I've seen at CCNV, I'm the only white. That's why I notice when three white guys come out of the building. They're walking down the ramp when a tall man with one of those Eraserhead hairdos that's high and flat on top and shaved bald all around the sides suddenly comes up in their faces and edges them towards the wall. He says something to them and then they sheepishly continue on their way. Eraserhead has now joined Purple Parka out front as one of CCNV's unofficial greeters. He's got a pocket square tucked into his sports jacket, and is wearing a fancy-looking watch and four rings.

I go inside to find out what prospects there are for getting put up for the night. I'm told that the shelter is full until Tuesday, but that a van will eventually come to take me to one of the city's emergency shelters. I decide to wait in the lobby. Over the next couple of hours there I see a lot.

Residents continue to stream in and out of the building. (There is no sign-in or sign-out. The building is open most of the time. Between midnight and 4 a.m. the front door is opened for five minutes every half hour.) About a third of the people I see are carrying Walkman sets. At least half are carrying beer or liquor. The stuff's usually in a paper bag, but several people, Eraserhead among them, are carrying beer in plastic cups. Later, a CCNV spokesman named Lawrence Lyles tells me that CCNV policy is that "we allow people to have beer and hard stuff, but not illegal drugs. As long as they maintain themselves. This is the residents' house. If you were home, you'd drink a little beer, wouldn't you?" But more than a few of the residents are not maintaining themselves. Drunks—weaving, falling-down drunks—are a common sight in the lobby. Some of them get up the steps only because they are carried up. Only once does a staff member ask anybody what he's carrying in. And when the resident laughs off the question, the staff member doesn't pursue it. What I see supports what an experienced city social worker tells me later: "There are drugs in CCNV. The place is out of control."

Conversation here tends to be animated, often hostile. "If all you needed to live was a teaspoon of water," one man snaps at another, "I wouldn't give it to you." Another man explains in a loud voice why he wants a stiletto. "Because if I miss you one way, I'll cut you coming back." "Look," says one laughing guy to his friend, pointing to a bearded, wasted white man whose eyes are set on infinite, "Charlie Manson is on parole."

A handsome man with longish gray-black hair comes down to get his mail. He's carrying two books, the first I've seen here. He's neatly dressed in a completely coordinated Army camouflage uniform. In this scene, he looks as solid as a rock. He's walking towards me as he finishes his letter. "They say they will give me money if I go to a psychiatrist," he tells me, his face lit up now by a scary smile. "But I will stay here instead!"

Even in this chaos, there are some touches fit for a public service announcement. An older black man asks a feeble-looking white man about how he's mending since he got hit by a car. He listens patiently as the man shows him his injuries and explains what medical appointments he has set up in the days ahead. A lady gives a man in a wheelchair a spin he clearly enjoys.

At about 8 p.m., one of the staff members very politely informs the few of us who've been waiting for transportation that there will be no van run tonight. He quickly goes on to tell us that there's room at one of the city's newest emergency shelters. And it's within walking distance, over at the Department of Employment Services just around the corner.

On my way there, I fall in with two other guys, Tom and James, headed for the same place. They are both refreshingly clean-cut and substance-free. We all shake hands and quickly hit it off. The DES shelter is actually in the employees' parking garage underneath the building. It's well heated, and the nice lady volunteer who checks us in issues us like-new Army cots and a tuna sandwich apiece. There are about 50 people already on cots when we arrive—the place is full. The three of us help each other set up our cots. Tom takes a shower and brings some cups and water back from the bathroom to make up some Kool-Aid he's brought with him. He shares it with James and me and gives us each a cookie, too. The shelter atmosphere is pretty much like that of a barracks; there's plenty of "smokin' and jokin'" but the drunks are mostly down

for the count. The roving armed guard probably helps.

The three of us talk among ourselves. Tom's a white guy with a bushy moustache. He just got out of jail—during a routine traffic stop the day before, he got arrested on an old warrant for driving without a license. He made bail, but he's from Virginia, and without a license or car (it got impounded), and low on money, he has no way to get back. And he has no place to stay here. His court date is next month, and he figures he will get some jail because, as he puts it, "this isn't the first time."

James is black and works in the kitchen at the Marriott in Crystal City. He's wearing an Army jacket, from his days as a parachute rigger in the Airborne. This is his first day on the streets. He had been living with his girlfriend, but they had a fight. James works on the side as a party DJ. At one of these parties, a girl gave him her phone number to give to a friend of his, but James's girlfriend discovered it in his jacket and went nuts, throwing James out of the house and all of his stuff down the stairs. I ask James if there isn't a family member he can stay with until this boils over. "I tried staying with my mother," he answers, "but she had too many restrictions—she won't give me a key, she won't let me in past 11 at night, and there's no TV downstairs. I'm a party animal."

Lying back on my cot, I spend a long time staring at the garage ceiling, trying to figure out James's logic. Why would somebody clean and employed choose this—and tomorrow night maybe something much worse—over coming in at 11 to a house with only one TV? Would "people you know" do that?

CONSPICUOUS DYSFUNCTION

The Depression taught most Americans that there are plenty of ways to become poor that aren't one's fault. By now this is a lesson well learned. Perhaps too well learned. Americans tend to believe that homelessness is exclusively a social problem, a system failure. This idea goes hand-in-hand with the traditional liberal notion that the solution to the problem is simply the provision of housing and jobs. While there is something to this, it's not *the* solution—as I found out for myself, there's too much else going on with the homeless.

Allowing for the possibility of some overlap, here's how I would roughly classify the homeless people I met: At least three-quarters were (current or recovering) substance abusers, three-quarters were unattached men, and about a third seemed to some degree mentally ill. But there is another important factor I observed in about half of the homeless people I talked to—one that takes a little explaining. I call it the "X-factor" because I'm not having much luck figuring it out.[1]

Ronald Reagan once came in for a lot of well-deserved criticism for saying that anybody who is homeless is so only because he chooses to be. That's a ridiculous notion. Sleeping in the park in the winter, being chronically sick and disoriented—nobody chooses *that*. But just the same, people like the New York artist, Wayne from Texas, and James are carrying something around in their heads that's separating them from opportunities and propelling them towards ruin. The artist has his incoherent put-down of the classifieds. Wayne has his equally confused contempt for the work at his father's business, and James has his odd standards about acceptable living conditions. Here are some other examples of the X-factor I came across in talking to the homeless:

• One of the beggars I frequently see is a 24-year-old black guy who goes by the street name "Quickness." He can usually be found around Dupont Circle either zoned out or trying to be. He tells me that he originally came to Washington to sell PCP, but he got caught

and spent three years in jail. He's been on the streets for the seven months since he got out. When I ask him what he wants out of life, he tells me "money." His parents are back in Florida, and they know he's up here, but he won't go back to them and he won't even tell them he's homeless. Quickness prefers staying in the streets to that.

• A fiftyish man whom I often see late at night begging near my office, an articulate man who appears sane and drug- and alcohol-free, tells me that he served in submarines in the Navy and then worked at the Nuclear Regulatory Commission. He says that he lost his job at the NRC because of differences with his bosses. Later, he landed a job stuffing envelopes for a political organization, but he quit because he didn't agree with the material he was mailing and went back to the streets, where he makes about $2 an hour (it turns out that's the typical figure for a Washington beggar).

• A young woman I met who splits her begging between Dupont Circle and Georgetown tells me that she recently failed the Civil Service exam. I ask her if she has tried to get into a job training program. "I feel that I don't have the time for that. I just want something right now. Something I can just walk into and get right then and there."

All of these people fail the Bill Shade test. Bill is the only single male homeless person I met who I am convinced is actively trying every day to become unhomeless. Bill was working in construction when he got burned out of his apartment. Most of what Bill collects from begging he turns over to the woman who takes care of his daughter. Once I was talking to Bill when I noticed the Help Wanted sign behind his head. He read my mind: "I already went in there, but they want a girl to work behind the counter." So instead he sweeps the sidewalk in front of the shop. He works odd jobs whenever he can. He cleans up around the bank where he sleeps. He puts quarters in expired parking meters to save people he doesn't know from paying the $15 ticket. He's hoping to get the funds together to move back to Baltimore with his daughter. If reading this story makes you feel like helping a

---

[1] It's interesting to compare my description of the homeless population based on my own experience with what you can find in print elsewhere. Most respected policy studies and surveys are now saying that about a third of the homeless are mentally ill, a third are substance abusers, and a third are "other." That is, they find less substance abuse than I did, about the same amount of mental illness, and tend to leave the rest of the population an undifferentiated mystery while I think some of that remainder is in the grip of X-factor thinking.

single homeless person directly, call me or write me about Bill Shade.

I'm finding it hard to articulate the troublesome mental baggage that hampers the New York artist or Quickness, say, but not Bill Shade. It's not, contra the Reagan camp, mere laziness—these people work much harder every day then most just to keep from freezing to death. It's something more like a twisted sense of pride—a sense of personal specialness tweaked so ridiculously high that anything—even sleeping outside and begging for food—is viewed as better than forms of compromise that you and I would readily accept, like fitting in at work, getting a job out of the newspaper, or coming home at 11. For all I can tell, some of this odd thinking is the extreme rationalization so common in alcoholics and substance abusers, and some is a sign of a treatable organic thought disorder, like mild schizophrenia. But I'm also convinced that some of the homeless I met who evinced the X-factor were neither mentally ill nor addicts. What do we make of them?

If you've raised children in the seventies and eighties, then you know how the emphasis on rampant instant gratification and conspicuous consumption of such television fare as "Dallas," "Lifestyles of the Rich & Famous," and "L.A. Law" can distort your children's desires and expectations. Sometimes being "tough"—emphasizing setting goals and working hard to achieve them, etc.—brings kids around on this. But many parents have experienced the bewilderment that comes when that doesn't work. How do we reach Johnny? How do we bring him down to earth so that he can make a good life for himself? Parents can use up a decade or more wrestling with such questions, often without arriving at an answer. Well, maybe the bewilderment I feel in the face of the foregoing examples is similar, with a similar cause. But about two or three times more extreme. It seems that some of the homeless have just soaked up way too much of our culture's obsession with "too much, too soon."

There can be all the low-cost housing in the world, and an untreated paranoid won't set foot in it, and an untreated schizophrenic might burn it down. (Dr. E. Fuller Torrey, a psychiatrist who is an expert on the homeless mentally ill, told me that he has encountered both outcomes.) And a drug addict will spend the rent money on crack. So homelessness is in large measure a mental health problem and a drug problem that defies the conventional liberal answers of housing and jobs. But notice this about the X-factor homeless: They aren't likely to be people for whom jobs and housing alone would be the answer, either. Once a man decides to eat only caviar, he will turn down bread as fervently as an ordinary man turns down poison. If low-cost housing were made available to the New York artist (and for all I know, it already has been), but there was no $10,000 loan, how would he pay the rent? If he were offered a nonglamorous job to make the rent, would he take it?

There certainly seem to be homeless people who are nearly like you and me, save for some intervening bad breaks. Many of the women on Belmont Street appear to fit that bill, as does Bill Shade. So for people like these, fixing the bad break—making jobs and housing available—*is* what's called for. But media depictions to the contrary, there are more homeless people—the untreated mentally ill, the addicted, and those with the X-factor—*who are not like us.* As a result, if they are ever to realize secure and steady lives, they will require different kinds of help.

Traditional liberals don't want to admit such differences—and that's wrong—because they want us to help all the homeless—that's right. Neoconservatives admit the differences (right) because they don't want to help them all (wrong). The correct position is to admit the differences among the homeless while strenuously working to help them all. If conservatives need to care more, liberals need to *see* more. It's a cruel joke to pretend that an untreated mentally ill person is better off in the streets than he would be if he were compelled somehow to take medication, or to pretend that Quickness would hold down a job with the same tenacity as Bill Shade. To make real progress in the fight against homelessness, we must first be honest about who the homeless are.

38.   THE URBAN HOMELESS: A PORTRAIT OF URBAN DISLOCATION

PETER H. ROSSI and JAMES D. WRIGHT

Few of our contemporary social problems rival homelessness in the public attention received in this decade.[1] There are ample and obvious reasons for this attention, for the plights of the homeless easily evoke sympathy and concern. In a society that places so high a value on the concept of home and devotes so much attention to housing and its accoutrements, the vision of being without a home is clearly a frightening one, bound to evoke sympathy for persons so afflicted.

The high level of concern about homelessness has not produced much in the way of empirically adequate knowledge about the extent of homelessness and the conditions that produce it. Estimates of the size of the national homeless population vary from about a quarter million to upward of 3 million;[2] equally wide variations exist in the estimates for specific cities and states. The sources of homelessness are also not understood in any detail. Is homelessness primarily a housing problem, an employment problem, a condition created by deinstitutionalization of the chronically mentally ill, a manifestation of the breakdown of family life, a symptom of the inadequacies of our public welfare system, or a combination of these and other factors? To be sure, there have been many dramatic and moving descriptive accounts of the plight of homeless persons, but these do not cumulate to precise knowledge about the extent and character of the problem of homelessness.

Reasonably valid data on homelessness is unquestionably difficult to obtain. National statistical series contain little or no information on the homeless population. The U.S. census essentially counts the homed population; conventional surveys are ordinarily derived from samples of households and therefore miss those without conventional dwellings.[3] This article de-

From *Annals of the American Academy of Political and Social Science*, Vol. 501, January 1989, pp. 132–142. Copyright © 1989 Sage Publications, Inc. Reprinted with permission of Sage Publications, Inc.

Peter H. Rossi, S. A. Rice Professor of Sociology, is acting director of the Social and Demographic Research Institute at the University of Massachusetts, Amherst, and the recipient of the Common Wealth Award for contributions to sociology. His latest work is Down and Out in America, *a monograph on homelessness and extreme poverty. James D. Wright is the Charles and Leo Favrot Professor of Human Relations in the Department of Sociology at Tulane University. He has authored or coauthored more than 80 scholarly papers; among his 11 books the most recent is* Homelessness and Health, *coauthored with Eleanor Weber.*

[1] The rather sudden welling up of concern can be indexed by the number of listings under "homelessness" in the *Reader's Guide to Periodical Literature* (New York: H. A. Wilson, 1976, 1983–85). In 1975, there were no listings; in 1981, 3; in 1982, 15; in 1983, 21; and in 1984, 32.

[2] U.S. Department of Housing and Urban Development, *A Report to the Secretary on the Homeless and Emergency Shelters* (Washington, D.C.: Office of Policy Development and Research, 1984); U.S. Department of Health and Human Services, *Helping the Homeless: A Resource Guide* (Washington, D.C.: Government Printing Office, 1984); U.S. General Accounting Office, *Homelessness: A Complicated Problem and the Federal Response,* 1985.

[3] The 1980 population census included some partial attempts to enumerate persons living in shelters and in public places, such as train and bus stations, but this effort did not cover all places where homeless persons might be found nor did the census cover all cities. U.S. Department of Commerce, Bureau of the Census, *Persons in Institutions and Other Group Quarters, 1980 Census of Population,* pub. PC80-2-4D (Washington, D.C.: Government Printing Office, 1984). Virtually all

scribes the findings from research using an adaptation of modern sample-survey methods, a study that is the first to provide reasonable valid data on the homeless of a major city, Chicago.[4]

A major significant obstacle to the study of the homeless is the lack of an agreed-upon definition of homelessness.[5] On the most general level, the homeless can be defined as those who do not have customary and regular access to a conventional dwelling or residence. But what is a conventional dwelling or residence, and what is customary and regular access? There is a continuum running from the obviously domiciled to the obviously homeless, with many ambiguous cases to be encountered along that continuum. Any effort to draw a line across that continuum, demarcating the homed from the homeless, is of necessity somewhat arbitrary and therefore potentially contentious.

These definitional ambiguities are not simply scholastic issues. A definition of homelessness is, *ipso facto,* a statement as to what should constitute the floor of housing adequacy below which no member of society should be permitted to fall. It is equally obvious that the number and existential conditions of the homeless depend in no small part on how the phenomenon is defined.

In dealing with these definitional problems, we have found it useful to distinguish between

---

survey- or census-based estimates omit homeless persons, and most pass over institutionalized persons as components of such estimates, leading to corresponding underestimates of poverty-impacted populations.

[4] A full account of the methodology and the findings can be found in Peter H. Rossi, Gene A. Fisher, and Georgianna Willis, *The Condition of the Homeless of Chicago* (Amherst: University of Massachusetts, Social and Demographic Research Institute; Chicago: University of Chicago, National Opinion Research Center, 1986).

[5] On the definitional problem, see Edward Baxter and Kim Hopper, *Private Lives, Public Spaces: Homeless Adults on the Streets of New York City* (New York: Community Service Society of New York, Institute for Social Welfare Research, 1984); Steven Crystal, *Chronic and Situational Dependence: Long-term Residents in a Shelter for Men* (New York: Human Resources Administration of the City of New York, 1982).

(1) the literally homeless, persons who clearly do not have access to a conventional dwelling and who would be homeless by any conceivable definition of the term; and (2) precariously, or marginally, housed persons, with tenuous or very temporary claims to a conventional dwelling of more or less marginal adequacy. This distinction, of course, does not solve the definitional problem, although it does more clearly specify subpopulations of likely policy interest.

METHODOLOGY USED IN THE CHICAGO STUDY

Most conventional quantitative social research methods depend on the assumption that persons can be enumerated and sampled within their customary dwelling units, an assumption that fails by definition in any study of the literally homeless. The strategy devised for the Chicago study therefore departed from the traditional sample survey in that persons were sampled from nondwelling units and interviews were conducted at times when the distinction between the homed and homeless was at a maximum. Two complementary samples were taken: (1) a probability sample of persons spending the night in shelters provided for homeless persons—the shelter survey; and (2) a complete enumeration of persons encountered between the hours of midnight and 6 a.m. in a thorough search of non-dwelling-unit places in a probability sample of Chicago census blocks—the street survey. Taken together, the shelter and street surveys constitute an unbiased sample of the literally homeless of Chicago, as we define the term.

Our research classified persons as literally homeless if they were residents of shelters for homeless persons or were encountered in our block searches and found not to rent or own a conventional housing unit.

In the street surveys, teams of interviewers, accompanied by off-duty Chicago police officers, searched all places on each sampled block to which they could obtain access, including all-night businesses, alleys, hallways, roofs and basements, abandoned buildings, and parked cars and trucks.[6] All persons encountered were queried to determine whether they were homeless, and they were interviewed if found to be homeless.

We believe the Chicago Homeless Study to be the first attempt to apply modern sampling methods to the study of the homeless, and, as such, it provides the first scientifically defensible estimates of the size and composition of the homeless population in any city.

ECONOMIC, SOCIAL, AND DEMOGRAPHIC CHARACTERISTICS OF THE LITERALLY HOMELESS

Being homeless is predominantly a male condition; three out of four—76 percent—of the homeless were men, in sharp contrast to the proportion of the Chicago adult population that is male, 46 percent.[7] Blacks and Native Americans constituted considerably more than their proportionate share of the homeless, with whites and Hispanics proportionately underrepresented. Although the average age of the homeless—40 years—was not far from that of the general adult population, there were proportionately fewer of the very young—under 25—and the old, or those over 65. Nor were the homeless very different from the general population in educational attainment, the typical homeless person being a high school graduate.

The modal homeless person was a black male high school graduate in his middle thirties. Average characteristics, however, obscure an important fact, namely, that the homeless population is somewhat heterogeneous. Especially significant was a minority of young black women—about 14 percent of the homeless—who were, typically, homeless with their young children and apparently in transition from unsatisfactory housing arrangements to establishing new households with those children. In addition, older males—over 40—tended to be white and were usually homeless for relatively long periods of time.

In the wealth of social and economic detail contained in our interview data, three salient characteristics of the homeless stand out: extreme poverty; high levels of disability resulting from poor physical and mental health; and high levels of social isolation, with weak or nonexistent ties to others.

Extreme Poverty

The literally homeless are clustered at the extreme lower boundary of the American population that is in poverty. Within the rather narrow income range found, there was some heterogeneity, as the differences between the various measures of central tendency show. The mode comprised the almost one in five—18 percent—who reported no income at all in the month prior to the survey; median income for the month was $99.85, and average, or mean, income for the same period was $167.39. Given that the 1985 poverty level for single persons under 65 was $5250, the official poverty level was 2.6 times the average annual income and 4.4 times the median annual income of Chicago's literally homeless.[8] On average, the literally homeless survive on substantially less than half the poverty-level income.

In Chicago there is almost no affordable housing at these levels of income. In 1985, the aver-

---

[6] Instructions to interviewers were to enter all places until they encountered locked doors or were forbidden—for example, by managers or proprietors—to go further. Police escorts were hired to protect interviewers. Cooperation rates were 81 percent in the shelter surveys and 94 percent in the street surveys. The majority of the shelter respondents not interviewed were not present at the time of interview, being temporarily out of the shelter for one reason or another.

[7] The percentage of women—24 percent—among the homeless is in stark contrast to the homeless, or skid row, population of Chicago as studied in the late 1950s, virtually all of whom were men. See Donald Bogue, *Skid Row in American Cities* (Chicago: University of Chicago, 1963).

---

[8] Poverty levels for households of various sizes and for various years are given in *The Statistical Abstract of the United States* (Washington, D.C.: Government Printing Office, 1986).

age monthly rental for SRO rooms, among the cheapest accommodations available for single persons, was $195,[9] $27 above the average monthly income of the homeless. At this level of extreme poverty, spending one's entire available income would still not be quite enough to afford the cheapest available housing, much less also cover the costs of food and other necessities. That the literally homeless manage to survive at all is a tribute to the laudable efforts of the shelters, soup kitchens, and charitable organizations that provide most necessities.

The homeless make some contribution to their own support. Although a very small percentage—4 percent—held full-time jobs, almost two in five had worked for some period over the previous month, mostly at casual, poorly paid part-time jobs. Remarkably, work and other economic activity was, on average, the source of 29 percent of total monthly income. Even more of a surprise, income transfer payments accounted for very little of their income, with only about a quarter—28 percent—receiving Aid to Family with Dependent Children (AFDC) or General Assistance (GA)—mostly the latter. Income transfer payments amounted to 30 percent of the total income; another 21 percent was accounted for by pension and disability payments, received by about one in five, or 18 percent.

Job histories of the literally homeless suggest that they have been among the extremely poor for years. On the average it was more than 4.6 years, or 55 months, since their last steady job, defined as full-time employment lasting three or more months; the median amount of time was 3.3 years, or 40 months. Interestingly, elapsed time since last steady job was very much greater than time currently homeless, the latter averaging about 22 months, with a median of 8 months.[10]

This suggests that many among the literally homeless were helped by their families and friends through relatively long periods of unemployment,[11] but that the patience, forbearance, or resources of these benefactors eventually ran out, with literal homelessness then added to chronic unemployment as a problem experienced daily.

Disability

Many disabling conditions plague the homeless, ones that would ordinarily make it difficult or impossible for a person to lead a full life—to obtain employment, participate in social life, or maintain relationships with others. Of course, disability is a matter of degree, so that it is difficult to calculate precise proportions; nevertheless, it is abundantly clear that the proportions among the literally homeless are much higher than in the general adult population.

More than one in four reported that they had some health problem that prevented their employment. Prominent among the conditions reported were mental illness, cardiovascular ailments, and gastrointestinal disorders. Likewise, more than one in three—37 percent—reported themselves as being in only "fair" or "poor" health, a level of self-reported ill health about twice that found in the general adult population, 18 percent. Behavioral indicators support these self-reports, with more than one in four reporting a hospital stay of more than 24 hours during the previous year.[12] High levels of alcoholism and drug abuse are also indicated by the one in three who reported stays in detoxification centers.

---

[9] Jewish Council on Urban Affairs, *SRO's, an Endangered Species: Single Room Occupancy Hotels in Chicago* (Chicago: Jewish Council on Urban Affairs and Community Emergency Shelter Organization, 1985).

[10] "Time currently homeless" is counted as months elapsed since last domiciled. Many homeless people have been homeless more than once; among those who had become homeless sometime in the year prior to the interview, 11 percent had had one or more homeless episodes in previous years.

[11] Research on recipients of General Assistance in Chicago documents that many of the extremely poor survive mainly through the goodwill of family and friends. See Matthew Stagner and Harold Richman, *General Assistance Profiles: Findings from a Longitudinal Study of Newly Approved Recipients* (Chicago: University of Chicago, National Opinion Research Center, 1985).

[12] For the self-reported health status of the U.S. adult population for 1982, see the first Special Report of the R. W. Johnson Foundation (1983). Additional data on the health status of the homeless are reported by P. W. Brickner et al., *Health Care of Homeless People* (New

Relatively high levels of mental illness are evident in the data. Almost one in four—23 percent—reported having been in a mental hospital for stays of over 48 hours, more than eight times the level found in the general population. Among those who had been in mental hospitals, three out of five, or 58 percent, had had multiple hospitalizations. Nearly one in five—16 percent—reported at least one suicide attempt.

In addition to the self-report data, two short scales were administered to measure psychiatric symptomatology.[13] On a scale measuring symptoms of depression, nearly half—47 percent—of the Chicago homeless registered levels suggesting a need for clinical attention, compared to about 20 percent in the national Health and Nutritional Examination Survey. On a second scale, measuring psychotic thinking, one in four showed two or more signs of disturbed cognitive processes; almost every item showed significantly higher levels of psychotic thinking than a comparison group tested in a New York City working-class neighborhood.

Contacts with the criminal justice system represent yet another, albeit qualitatively different, disability that is rather widespread. Such contacts at least indicate prior adjustment difficulties, some of a rather serious nature. Two of five—41 percent—had experienced jail terms of two or more days, 28 percent had been convicted by the courts and placed on probation, and 17

percent had served sentences of more than one year in state or federal prisons, presumably for felony offenses.

The cumulative incidence of these various disabilities is staggering. More than four out of five—82 percent—of the homeless either reported fair or poor health, or had been in a mental hospital or a detoxification unit, or received clinically high scores on the demoralization scale or on the psychotic-thinking scale, or had been sentenced by a court. A majority had had two or more such experiences or conditions. Although these data clearly do not sustain precise estimates of the degree of disability among the literally homeless, it is clear that the prevalence is several magnitudes above that encountered in the general adult population.

Social Isolation

A high degree of social isolation is also endemic among the homeless. Most—57 percent—have never married; of those ever married, most are separated or divorced, on either count in sharp contrast to the patterns of the general adult population.[14] The very few—9 percent—who are still with families are almost exclusively homeless women with dependent children.

The literally homeless are relatively isolated from extended family and from friends. Nearly nine in ten—88 percent—have surviving relatives and family members, but only three in five—60 percent—maintain even minimal contact with them—visiting, writing, talking with, or telephoning them at least once every two or three months. Similar low levels of contact with families of procreation—spouses, ex-spouses, or children—were also reported; 55 percent had such persons, but only one in three maintained contact with them. Overall, one in three reported no contact with any relatives and almost one in four reported no contacts with either relatives or friends.

Further evidence on strained relations with family and relatives was shown in replies to a

---

York: Springer-Verlag, 1985); James Wright et al., in *Research in Social Problems and Public Policy*, ed. M. Lewis and J. Miller (Greenwich, Conn.: JAI Press, 1987), 4:41–72.

[13] The first scale was a shortened version of the CES-D scale measuring symptoms of depression, developed by the Center for Epidemiological Studies of the National Institute of Mental Health for the national Health and Nutritional Examination Survey; the second was a shortened version of the Psychiatric Epidemiological Research Interview developed by Dohrenwend and associates. Barbara S. Dohrenwend et al., "Social Functioning of Psychiatric Patients in Contrast with Community Cases in the General Population," *Archives of General Psychiatry*, 40:1174–82 (1983); Bruce P. Dohrenwend et al., "Nonspecific Psychological Distress and Other Dimensions of Psychopathology," ibid., 37:1229–36 (1980).

---

[14] It is interesting that, despite their marital histories, more than half—54 percent—had children, but current contact with these children tended to be minimal.

sequence of questions on preferred living arrangements. We asked whether respondents would like to return to their families and whether their families would take them. Among the young homeless women, very few wanted to return; many of the young men would have liked to but believed they would not be welcome.

The social isolation of many of the homeless implies that they lack access to extended social networks and are therefore especially vulnerable to the vagaries of fortune occasioned by changes in employment, income, or physical or mental health.

AN INTERPRETATION OF HOMELESSNESS

The characteristics of the homeless as derived from the Chicago Homeless Study pertain only to the literally homeless and are not necessarily descriptive of the precariously homed. Indeed, there is some evidence that the latter may also be in extreme poverty but differ in other important respects. The Illinois GA rolls for the city of Chicago in 1985 contained about 100,000 individual recipients, most of whom were single-person households, largely male, and with annual incomes below $1848, the eligibility cutoff point. Given that GA monthly payments of up to $154 are by themselves insufficient to bring recipients above $1848 per year, we can consider GA clients as among the extremely poor. Because only few are literally homeless, we may regard the clients as reasonably representative of the precariously homed of Chicago or at least of some large portion thereof.

Stagner and Richman's study of those receiving GA in 1984 provides a description of this group showing them to be similar to the literally homeless in demographic composition.[15] Most— 68 percent—are male, 71 percent are black, and 91 percent are unmarried; they tend to be slightly younger—the average age was 34—than the literally homeless. GA recipients contrasted strongly with the literally homeless in three important respects. First, GA recipients are consid-

erably more integrated socially, with half living with relatives and friends and an additional 30 percent receiving financial assistance from such sources. Second, disability levels among GA clients are much lower. Far fewer—9 percent— have physical-health conditions that prevented employment or had been in mental hospitals, the latter amounting to 1 percent. Third, GA clients had work histories with shorter median periods—19 months—since their last full-time jobs.

There are undoubtedly other persons in Chicago, as poor or poorer, who are not on the GA rolls. Some of the precariously homed extremely poor participate in other income-maintenance programs such as AFDC or Supplemental Security Income (SSI), receive payments under Old-Age and Survivors Insurance (OASI) or other retirement plans, or are receiving unemployment benefits. It is difficult to estimate the total number of the extremely poor of Chicago, although the magnitude is at least 100,000 and possibly as many as 200,000 persons whose annual incomes from all sources are under $2000, 38 percent of the official poverty level. Most, if not all, of these extremely poor persons are at high risk of becoming literally homeless.

Considering jointly the special and distinctive features of the literally homeless in relation to the contrasting characteristics of other extremely poor persons, we offer the following interpretation of homelessness and some speculation about the forces that influence changes in the size of the homeless population.

At the base of our interpretation is the viewpoint that literal homelessness is primarily a manifestation of extreme poverty. Literal homelessness, or the proportion of persons being literally without conventional housing, is a function of extreme poverty, in a housing market that has an inadequate supply of very-low-cost housing to offer to single-person households. The incidence of literal homelessness falls very heavily on persons who are unaffiliated with households and upon those who have been extremely poor for long periods of time. The homeless therefore are the long-term very poor who have been unable to maintain supportive connections with—or have been rejected by—their parental families and friends and who have not been able for a

---

[15] Stagner and Richman, *General Assistance Profiles.*

variety of reasons to establish their own households.

Why the literally homeless have been extremely poor for so long, why they have been rejected, and why they have difficulty establishing such households are issues very likely connected with their disabilities. Persons with serious disabilities are likely to experience difficulty connecting with full-time lasting employment and also difficulty maintaining their shares in the webs of reciprocity that constitute the support structures of kin and friends. It should be noted that because their parental families and friends likely also are among the poor and have few resources to share with others, the burden of taking on the support of an additional adult is high. If the adult in question presents behavioral difficulties and a prospect of being dependent indefinitely, it is quite understandable why relatives and friends may be reluctant to take on a burden that would strain both resources and patience.

The literally homeless constitute only a very small fraction of the very poor, most of whom manage somehow to avoid literal homelessness. Using the size of the Chicago GA rolls, 100,000, as a conservative estimate of the magnitude of the very poor, the literally homeless constitute about 2.7 percent of the very poor. To understand literal homelessness properly and to predict its course, we need to know more about how most of the very poor manage to avoid that condition. We can speculate, on the basis of some knowledge, that they do so mainly by either overspending on housing or being subsidized by their families and friends.

Overspending on Housing

Some of the extremely poor may avoid literal homelessness by spending all or mostly all of their cash income on housing. These are persons who live in single-room-occupancy hotels or furnished rooms or share inexpensive apartments and who obtain food through food stamps or handouts from food kitchens; clothing from charitable sources; and medical care from free clinics and through Medicaid. To pursue this pattern of life consistently, one must also have a consistent source of income as provided by minimum OASI

payments, small pensions from other sources, GA, disability payments, and perhaps small remittances from relatives or ex-spouses. They must also live close to facilities that can provide free or low-cost meals, casual employment, and the other amenities.

We suspect that the reason why there were so few very old persons among the literally homeless is because even minimum OASI payments provide sufficient consistent income to enable retired persons or their surviving spouses to live alone or share dwellings with others. The same line of reasoning can explain why so few of the literally homeless were receiving disability payments: SSI recipients received enough consistent income from SSI payments to connect with the lowest end of the housing market. The homelessness literature is full of references to persons in extreme poverty who spend as much as they can on housing from their small pensions or other remittances but find that they do not have enough money to be in rented quarters all the time. Their small pensions or welfare checks can be stretched to cover, say, all but the last few days before the next check arrives. These are persons who are homeless on a part-time basis, supplementing their rented quarters by spending some nights in shelters or on the streets.

Private Subsidies

Most of the extremely poor avoid literal homelessness by being given housing and subsistence at little or no charge by their relatives—mainly parents and siblings—and friends. The households that provide these subsidies incur the marginal costs of adding another person to be housed and fed. Note that these costs may not be a severe financial drain on the household in question, especially if the person in extreme poverty provides some payments to the subsidizing household or shares in household chores. For example, adding another adult person to a household may not mean any additional rent outlay, nor may it be necessary to purchase any additional food, if the rations given to every household member are diminished in order to share with the additional member. But there are other, nonfinancial costs, including increased space pressures, reduced privacy, lower food quality and quantity, and increased wear and tear on facilities. In addition, there is also the potential for interpersonal conflict.

Private subsidies may be virtually the only way that extremely poor single persons can live on the income-maintenance payments to which they may be entitled. Illinois's GA payments of $154 per month are simply not enough to allow a recipient to enter the private housing market. AFDC payments to single-parent households, although more generous than GA, also fall short of providing enough to live on without additional income in kind or cash.

The foregoing suggests that the size of the literally homeless population is driven by those macro processes that affect the availability of low-skilled employment, the ability of poor families to help their less fortunate members, the market conditions affecting the supply of very low-cost housing for single persons, and the coverage of income-maintenance programs for disabled and single persons, as follows:

1. Changes in demand for low-skilled workers. The employment prospects for low-skilled workers can affect the number of literally homeless in two ways: directly, by influencing the job prospects for low-skilled single persons and hence their abilities to earn sufficient income to keep them from being extremely poor; and indirectly, by influencing the abilities of families to provide subsidies to their long-term unemployed peripheral adult members. A major difference between the description of Chicago's skid row in the late 1950s[16] and the portrait emerging from our 1985–86 study is that in the earlier period a strong market demand apparently existed for casual labor from which the homeless men living in the flophouses and cheap hotels could earn enough to pay their rents and buy food. Side by side with the flophouses on Madison Street in Chicago were employment exchanges for casual laborers. With the decline in demand for low-skilled casual labor such employment exchanges are no longer available.

2. Changes in the level of income-maintenance support for poor families and for poor single persons. The more generous the levels of welfare support, the more likely families are to put up with their long-term unemployed and disabled adult relatives. Many commentators on the homeless problem suspect that cutbacks in social welfare programs have led to an increase in homelessness. In this connection as well, the processes involved may work indirectly, by providing lower incomes to poor families and thereby lowering their abilities to subsidize their adult unemployed members, and directly, by lowering the coverage and real value of income-maintenance programs available to single persons. Income transfer payments over the past two decades have not kept pace with inflation. The recent rise in the size of the literally homeless population may be at least a partial reflection of the lowered real value of welfare payments and the consequent decreased ability of poor families on AFDC or other income-maintenance programs to subsidize their peripheral unemployed adult members. Similarly, the decline in the real value of GA payments implies a correspondingly decreased ability of single-person households in that program to afford rentals available at the bottom of the housing market.

3. Changes in the coverage of income-maintenance support programs for disabled persons, including admission into total-care institutions such as mental hospitals. The greater the coverage of disability payment programs, the more likely are disabled single persons to be able to afford low-cost housing for single persons. Hence the less likely are such persons to become homeless. Similarly, changes in the coverage of indoor support programs, such as mental hospitals, can also influence the numbers of persons who are literally homeless. In this view, being institutionalized may be regarded as a form of public subsidy for the maintenance of extremely poor persons. Deinstitutionalization forces such extremely poor persons either into the literally homeless group or into the privately subsidized poor.

4. Quantitative and qualitative changes in the supply of very low-cost housing. As low-cost

---

[16] Bogue, *Skid Row in American Cities.*

housing units for low-income families become short in supply or smaller in size, the greater becomes the burden imposed on such families by support for their long-term unemployed and disabled peripheral adult relatives. Similarly, the shorter the supply and the higher the cost of inexpensive housing for single-person households, the more likely single-person households are to be homeless. In city after city, the supply of low-cost housing for single-person households has experienced precipitous declines in the past decade. In Chicago, single-room occupancy capacity has been estimated to have declined by almost 25 percent in the period 1980–83. This trend almost surely has contributed heavily to the growth of the literally homeless experienced in the past decade.

5. Changes in the numbers of persons who are disabled in middle adulthood. Although disability levels in a population ordinarily may be only indirectly and weakly influenced by social policy, the special character of the disabilities of the literally homeless may be more amenable to such purposeful policy moves. Many of the homeless men are disabled mainly because of alcohol and, to a lesser extent, other substance abuse. Measures taken to reduce the amount of alcohol abuse during early adulthood, particularly among males, would do much to reduce the prevalence of disability in their middle years.

These macro processes suggest both short-term and long-term remedies for the extremely poor and the literally homeless in America. Short-term measures that would considerably ameliorate the condition of the homeless include measures that would increase the amount of income available to the extremely poor. In particular, more generous income-maintenance programs and wider coverage for disability programs would both help poor families to provide help to their long-term unemployed adult members and help such members directly. Indeed, one may even consider some of the possible programs as Aid to Families with Dependent Adults! The long-term measures would include increasing the supply of low-cost housing, particularly for single persons; providing more low-skilled employment opportunities in ways that would be accessible to the extremely poor; and measures designed to lower the prevalence of disabling conditions among young adult males. In the meantime, support for shelters, food kitchens, and other charitable organizations serving the literally homeless is necessary at least to lessen the extreme hardships imposed by that condition.

CHAPTER 14

HEALTH AND
MEDICAL CARE

INTRODUCTION

In the past quarter century two major issues have gained increasing personal and public attention: the promotion of good health habits and the persisting crisis in the health-care system. These are separate but related issues. For example, several major corporations are facing alarmingly high costs for their employees' health insurance. Some companies respond to this problem by sponsoring and promoting a physical fitness program. It is more cost-effective to prevent an illness than to try to get insurance companies to lower their premiums. Better health habits and adequate medical care are crucial issues at every level of society: individuals, families, communities, corporations, and nations. Today topics related to health and the provision of needed medical care are discussed at the kitchen table and debated in the halls of Congress.

The United States' health-care system is best described as a loosely structured arrangement that combines private enterprise with government support and regulation. Some self-employed people purchase their own health insurance, but most Americans are covered through their employers. Many elderly and retired persons receive partial coverage through a federal health insurance plan, Medicare. Persons in poverty are supported through Medicaid, a public assistance program financed by the federal government and the individual states. Not all poor persons receive benefits, though, because each state establishes its own eligibility standards within broad federal guidelines. Perhaps the most striking feature of the American health-care system is the fact that many people (approximately 38 million in 1990) are not covered by a private or government insurance plan. All citizens of Canada, England, Sweden, and many other industrial nations are covered by their nation's health-care system, but Americans are required to pay for their own health care if they have no employer who will pay the premiums for partial coverage.

There is considerable variability in the health care provided to the American people. On the private side, some companies offer generous insurance protection and others offer extremely limited coverage. Many people who are unemployed or marginally employed have no medical coverage at all. Given this uneven arrangement that favors some people and forgets others, it is not surprising that politicians, journalists, physicians, insurance executives, and a steady stream of experts associated with various think tanks began to write about the health-care crisis in the 1980s and 1990s.

One feature of health care in the United States that always receives considerable attention is its spiraling costs. For a variety of reasons, the costs of health care are beyond the capacities of ordinary households, the insurance companies, the corporations, and state and federal governments. Numerous studies have been conducted in efforts to analyze this problem and recommend strategies to reduce costs. But various recommendations, such as predetermined flat fees to hospitals and physicians for certain medical procedures, have failed to solve the problem. Vernon R. Loucks, Jr., has written a short opinion piece on this complex problem. His brief essay offers an excellent overview of the crisis Americans now face.

David Mechanic is one of the leading sociologists of medicine in the United States. His article "Promoting Health" provides an excellent introduction to the sociological approach to health as a social problem. Health is more than physical fitness; it is profoundly social. One's health is strongly influenced by the social context of one's life. This fact becomes dramatically apparent in the study of social class and various indicators of well-being. For many decades sociologists have documented a disparity between the rich and the poor. Poor people have higher rates of chronic illness, a shorter life span, and higher infant mortality than the affluent. Many factors contribute to this disparity, including differences in access to adequate health care and in lifestyle. Mechanic's central thesis is crucial to any comprehensive understanding of health and illness in a complex society: the social context of one's life is just as important as personal decisions about staying healthy.

39.   WHO'LL TAKE ON THE HEALTH CRUNCH?

VERNON R. LOUCKS, JR.

Neither government nor business leaders have even begun to summon up the courage and imagination necessary to fix the health care situation in this country. Our economy and our hospitals, let alone our people, can't stand this reticence much longer.

Projections made by my company show a dangerous gap between growth in demand for health care and the resources likely to be available to meet it.

Demand is likely to grow 65 percent by 2000 and 160 percent by 2010. The factors driving it include population growth and aging, some expanded access, new technologies and AIDS. To fill that demand, we would have to spend 16 percent of gross national product on health care in 2000 and 20 percent in 2010. Those investments are not likely, especially in view of concerns about other high priorities like education, housing, transportation and the environment.

The crunch between demand and resources is already painful, not just for the health care system but for those it is supposed to serve: 422 U.S. hospitals have closed in the last five years, 80 of them last year; 13 have closed in Chicago, most of them in medically underserved areas.

The situation worsens. In 1984, the first full year under Medicare's "prospective payment" system, 21 percent of hospitals reported losing money on their Medicare caseloads. By last year, it was 51 percent.

Resources that we are investing too often are being placed in the wrong areas. It's insane to be spending tens or hundreds of thousands of dollars on individual babies born addicted to drugs

From *Chicago Tribune*, June 7, 1990. Reprinted with permission of Baxter International.

Vernon R. Loucks, Jr. is Chairman and Chief Executive Officer of Deerfield-based Baxter International, which makes and markets health-care products and services.

when some prenatal education for their mothers would be far less expensive and much more humane.

To date, business and government "leadership" on all of this has been woefully tentative.

Large companies have talked about turning the problem over to the government through some sort of national health insurance. It's as if traditional celebrants of private-sector efficiency have decided all of a sudden that the government can do a better job than industry on this one.

At least three major federal panels are at work studying health policy. And from a position on the sidelines, President Bush says he is "committed to bringing the staggering costs of health care under control," which speaks only to the very surface of the matter.

The economy and effectiveness of the health care system can be improved in numerous ways. Just cutting out the one-third of all diagnostic tests that are probably unnecessary would save as much as $10 billion. With regard for humanity as well as economy, we should analyze the $20 billion in Medicare spending used in the last year of life. And by following "best demonstrated practices" in day-to-day management, even some very good hospitals can save 10 percent to 15 percent of their costs.

But no improvement will be made without definitive change in the way we direct and control health care spending. Four principles should be applied:

1. We need to focus on health outcomes as opposed to inputs. The United States has yet to do a good job of delineating exactly what we want out of our health system—prevention versus cure, long life versus happy and productive life. Until we face this question, we'll continue demanding more than we can afford.

2. We must invest heavily in an up-to-date fact

base on the use and effectiveness of health care resources. We certainly don't know today if we are getting our money's worth. Is $75,000 spent on Surgical Procedure X producing at least that much value in a continued happy, productive life? Some businesses, on behalf of their employees, have begun to analyze health services, hoping to encourage those that produce the greatest human returns. This is one area where study and reporting by state and federal government could be beneficial, but only with some private oversight to ensure relevance.

3. We need to think about systemwide effects, not discrete "chess moves." When a hospital serving a poor area closes, the people don't go away. The weight of their health needs is felt in other, surrounding hospitals. If local and regional interests, including businesses, do not step up to this problem, then a federal, probably less progressive, health system is inevitable.

4. We must be willing to make trade-offs. There's no end to what we could spend on health care if we tried to do everything possible for everyone who might want it done. Our objective is not immortality; it's the greatest possible number of years of healthy life. There's a point beyond which more care at today's levels of technology is cruel.

None of these principles is easy or automatic, but they are all practical and applicable. What's needed is leadership.

40. PROMOTING HEALTH

DAVID MECHANIC

Health promotion has become very fashionable. In a recent major conference in Berlin on this topic, speaker after speaker reiterated the need for more attention to improved lifestyles, particularly in such areas as smoking, drinking, nutrition, and exercise. The session then adjourned to dinner festivities, where little else was available but liquor and beer, salted snacks, and a variety of bratwursts. This instance would be unworthy of comment except that it typifies the enormous gap between our rhetoric and behavior, and helps identify the challenge that serious efforts at health promotion must face. The main point of this article is simple, but crucial: most behavior, either conducive or detrimental to health, is influenced as much or more by the routine organization of everyday settings and activities as by the personal decisions of individuals. Health education efforts that ignore this principle are destined to failure.

American society places high value on health, as reflected in public health attitudes, the more than half trillion dollars a year expended on health services, and the immense interest reflected in the media. Since the 1970s, there has been growing health consciousness and efforts to induce an increased sense of personal responsibility for physical fitness and improved behaviors in areas relevant for health, in part motivated by the uncontrollable escalation of medical care costs. Whether considering education campaigns relevant to cigarette smoking, alcohol and drug use, or those devoted to exercise, nutrition, and safety, it is evident that health promotion has become a growth industry. The threat of the AIDS epidemic, and its close link to personal sexual and drug-using behavior, reinforces the shared view that individuals play a major role in their own destinies and can shape their vitality, health, and longevity.

From *Society*, January/February 1990, pp. 16–22. Copyright © 1990 Transaction Publishers. Reprinted with permission of Transaction Publishers.

Eliminating noxious habits and other known risk factors has some impact on those affected. But health education campaigns are commonly ineffective, and when they succeed in changing behavior, they often do so only for a limited time. Yet the faith and potential persist. There have been some notable successes, for example, the impressive drop in cigarette smoking among men from 52 to 32 percent in the period 1965 to 1987. The comparable decrease for women, from 34 to 27 percent, is more disappointing, given the enormous effort and attention devoted to the smoking issue. In other areas such as alcohol consumption, drug use, excess weight, high risk cholesterol levels, and even blood pressure control, the progress achieved is even less impressive. In still other areas such as homicide, adolescent pregnancy, and suicide, we have made no progress at all over the past 40 years, or we are losing ground. The age-adjusted death rate for homicides increased from 5.4 to 9 deaths per 100,000 residents between 1950 and 1986.

It would be foolish to place too much faith in health education to contain these rates and mortality. The determinants of health risks are far too complex and forceful to succumb to ordinary efforts to inform the public and change its practices. Effective health promotion requires a deeper scrutiny of the structure of communities and the routine activities of everyday life, as well as stronger interventions than those characteristic of much that goes on. Current efforts still function largely at the margins.

Almost a hundred years ago, Émile Durkheim published his classic study of suicide, in which he examined how social constraints characteristic of varying groups and situations were linked with suicide rates. He identified two processes associated with suicide, but in somewhat different ways. First, a loosening of social constraints, whether characteristic of egoistic suicide or anomie, was associated with elevated suicide rates. Alternatively, a high level of social integration associated with a tradition of ritualistic suicide in response to duty could also lead to high rates.

Durkheim's insights on how group structures constrain individual behavior are important for developing appropriate strategies for change. The strength of the individual's ties to the immediate social context determines the scope of influence exercised over behavior. As the level of social integration diminishes, the group—whether family, neighborhood, or larger social entity—is less successful in enforcing its expectations. When group commitment and social integration are strong, the specific norms characteristic of the group and its normal settings shape the boundaries of permissible behavior and define the limits of deviance.

Most of the behavior we view as health-relevant is embodied in daily structures and routines. The regularity of daily functions, eating and sleeping habits, and routine exercise and levels of exertion are substantially programmed for us. The norms of our social contexts define the appropriateness of a wide range of risk behaviors, as well as the circumstances under which such behavior is permitted. Expectations and the shame of non-conformity impose standards for our efforts and motivate our achievements. These very basic group structures and processes account for much of the behavior we observe.

EXPLAINING HEALTH INDICATOR TRENDS

The relevance of social relationships for explaining patterns of morbidity and mortality is well documented. People's attachments consistently predict mortality in both sexes, even after adjusting for other known risk factors affecting death. The specific mechanisms, and how they function, are not well understood. But the ways in which individuals are tied to social structures, and how groups exercise influence, help explain a variety of seemingly unrelated findings in the health care literature.

Disease causation is multifaceted and complex, and there is a compelling need to separate selection from true causal factors, and to disentangle many interrelated factors. Yet, it is intriguing that such measures as socioeconomic status, marital status, religiosity, and church attendance are commonly associated with health outcome measures. A particularly important challenge is to understand, more clearly than we presently do, why poor health is associated with indices of low socioeconomic status. The fact that many subgroups of the population have favorable health experience despite low socioeconomic status suggests that poverty is not sufficient as an explanation. While the relationships noted above involve a variety of interpretative issues, they all have an underlying factor in common. In each case, those with the poorest health experiences come from disrupted social settings and are less constrained or protected by family and community expectations. Such indicators as marriage, religiosity, church attendance, community participation, and higher socioeconomic status may have varying meanings and impacts, but they all imply a certain conventionality and regularity in lifestyle. In contrast, high rates of morbidity and mortality among the divorced, among the socially alienated, among the lowest socioeconomic strata, and among disadvantaged minority groups in part reflect the loss of authority of the family and the neighborhood over behavior. Family disruption removes many of the living constraints that give daily life a predictable rhythm.

Women have benefited greatly from increased education and growing equality. But as some cultural constraints on women decrease with gender equality, women have the same opportunities as men for good and bad. Women drink and smoke more than in previous decades, and more commonly confront such problems as lung disease and alcoholism. Age-adjusted death rates among white women in the United States for cancer of the respiratory system increased from 4.6 per 100,000 in 1950 to 23.1 in 1986, surpassing the rate for breast cancer. Similarly, rates of death for COPD (chronic obstructive pulmonary disease) increased during this period from 2.8 to 13.3. The comparable change among black women was from 4.1 to 23.3 for respiratory cancer. Although the data are less complete, black female deaths are also rising for COPD. Ironically, these increases come during a period when deaths have declined substantially; the age-adjusted rate changes for all deaths among white women fell from 645 to 388 between 1950 and 1986, while the comparable rates for black women declined from 1107 to 588. The only other two major causes of death that have not substantially decreased are suicide and homicide. In fact, rates of death by homicide

among white women doubled between 1950 and 1986.

THE CONSTRAINTS OF CULTURE

In his book *Who Shall Live?* Victor Fuchs explains the huge differences in death rates between the contiguous states of Utah and Nevada by the fact that "Utah is inhabited primarily by Mormons, whose influence is strong throughout the state. Devout Mormons do not use tobacco or alcohol, and in general lead stable, quiet lives. Nevada, on the other hand, is a state with high rates of cigarette and alcohol consumption and very high indices of marital and geographical instability." As Fuchs points out, the states are comparable on many of the indices associated with mortality, such as income and schooling. They share many other similarities, as well, such as climate, urbanization, and concentration of health care resources. Fuchs is correct in a general sense, but Mormonism and its influence encompass a variety of features that not only affect health indices, but also are related to low rates of delinquency, crime and violence, high educational achievement, and a purposeful orientation. In these respects, Mormons are not unlike other cultural groups such as Jews, Chinese, and Japanese, who also perform well on many health and welfare indices.

Mormons and other groups with good health indices share a strong kinship structure that serves as a solid base for childhood socialization, a positive orientation to education, and an ethic that gives work a meaningful place in the group's value structure. The Mormon church teaches the importance of the family, parenthood, and family relationships, and encourages a strong orientation toward mastery of the environment, emphasizing active effort, accomplishment, and the acquisition of skills and education. As Thomas O'Dea notes in his book *The Mormons:*

Life is more than a vocation, more than a calling; it is an opportunity for deification through conquest, which is to be won through rational mastery of the environment and obedience to the ordinances of the church. This doctrine, permeating individual and community life, is expressed today in a configuration of attitudes clustering around activity and development. This configuration represents an important aspect of the individual's integration into the life of the Mormon group, for it relates the striving of individuals to collectively prescribed ends. Moreover, since it is taught by exhortation and example from early childhood, this set of attitudes becomes second nature to those brought up in the Mormon home and community environment.

Mormons have good health not simply because they value health and refrain from smoking and drinking. Mormons health derives in part incidentally from the daily routines that evolve out of the accepted patterns of everyday living, including family, work, and play.

The presence of a well-knit group structure that demands a person's loyalty and commitment is only an enabling factor. Also at issue are the particular values, goals, and preferences which are taught and rewarded. Early studies on medical care utilization that focused on ethnic groups in New York City found that ethnic exclusivity and cohesiveness resulted in greater skepticism of medical care. But a similar study among Mormons found that a comparable group structure may encourage high acceptance and use of medical services. Group structures provide a basis for influence. But the content of values shapes behaviors.

SOCIOECONOMIC STATUS, RACE, AND HEALTH

SES (socioeconomic status) and race are associated with almost every health index. These aggregate associations are important, but it is essential to understand specifically what factors associated with SES and race account for these relationships. Many subgroups in the population despite low income, limited education, and disadvantage perform well on many important measures of health and well-being. Immigrants to the United States early in this century had high rates of infant mortality relative to native-born whites. But as Odin Anderson noted:

Even though the Jewish group was foreign-born, lived in as crowded conditions as other foreign-born, bore just as many children . . . and enjoyed an income which was much lower than that of native-born whites, this group experienced the lowest infant mortality of all groups.

Some of this effect may have been due to breast feeding, which was more prevalent among Jewish mothers. But the concern for the health of children and resulting solicitude within traditional Jewish culture also has been commonly noted. As with Mormons, the strong family structure and emphasis on children and their development have not only contributed to health awareness, but also to educational and occupational achievement.

Health outcomes depend heavily on patterns of family life and social participation and how everyday activities and behavior are structured. The aggregate associations between SES and health summarize the product of many different processes pertinent to both. Effective action requires better understanding of the underlying patterns of relationships that result in these correlations.

CROSS NATIONAL CONSIDERATIONS

The United States and other developed countries have achieved relatively high levels of health and longevity, in contrast to most of the underdeveloped and developing nations. Factors essential to enhancing health and longevity may not be as apparent as in other regions of the world. The fact that large variations in health and mortality exist among poor nations allows us to better understand broad influences. Developing countries that have achieved levels of expectation of life at birth which approach those of developed nations are those that have succeeded in reducing fertility and infant mortality and in improving child health.

John Caldwell, in examining mortality patterns in the developing countries, has identified several areas with low per capita GNP (gross national product) but exceptional success in reducing infant mortality. In his analysis, he focuses on four states and countries—Kerala (India), Sri Lanka, Costa Rica, and Jamaica—each having low infant mortality relative to income. He also discusses such countries as China and Cuba, which have successfully reduced infant mortality through aggressive political organization leading to the establishment of an institutional infrastructure for maternal and infant health. For our immediate purposes, the former examples are not more important than the latter, although it is worth noting that there are alternative pathways to achieving varying health targets.

Health is multi-dimensional and an active, motivated population is especially important for achieving favorable health status. In this respect, Caldwell finds female schooling to be a particularly crucial element in the health equation. Those countries with the poorest mortality outcomes were Islamic countries, where there has been traditional resistance to contact between the sexes and strong constraints on the social participation of women outside the household. Some of these countries, compared to the poor nations achieving good health, are relatively affluent, such as Saudi Arabia, Libya, Iraq, Iran, and Oman. This reality suggests that a country's affluence is no more than a potential enabling factor. Female education is a complex indicator, particularly in light of the fact that in many of the countries studied, the levels of schooling under consideration are modest in Western terms. Caldwell puts great emphasis on the position of women, their levels of autonomy, and their political participation, factors which are all associated with female education. He notes the powerful combination of education and the accessibility of health facilities in reducing infant mortality. Education has also been an important predictor of health outcomes in Western countries, suggesting the value of examining its significance more closely. The relationship of education to various health behaviors and outcomes appears to be linear, even at relatively high educational levels.

WHY IS EDUCATION IMPORTANT?

Education is the single most important determinant of psychological modernity. Alex Inkeles, who has carefully studied this phenomenon, notes that:

Central to this syndrome are: (1) openness to new experience, both with people and with new ways of doing things such as attempting to control births; (2) the assertion of increasing independence from the authority of traditional figures, such as parents and priests, and a shift of allegiance to leaders of government, public affairs, trade unions, cooperatives, and the like; (3) belief in the efficacy of science and

medicine, and a general abandonment of passivity and fatalism in the face of life's difficulties; and (4) ambition for oneself and one's children to achieve high occupational and educational goals. Men who manifest these characteristics (5) like people to be on time and show an interest in carefully planning their affairs in advance. It is also part of this syndrome (6) to show strong interest and take an active part in civic and community affairs and local politics; and (7) to strive energetically to keep up with the news, and within this effort, to prefer news of national and international import over items dealing with sports, religion, or purely local affairs.

Inkeles argues that schooling establishes the attitudes and values and teaches the psychological dispositions essential to psychological modernity. He also suggests that this learning occurs incidental to the curricula. Such learning is, in part, a response to the structure of the classroom situation itself (e.g., the ordered sequence of activities and scheduling) and to modeling and other psychological processes. Inkeles' concerns are directed toward modernization in the developing countries, but it should be clear that the concept of psychological modernity applies to problems in developed nations, as well.

Schooling is particularly important because of its association with a wide range of psychosocial and interactional capacities including cognitive complexity, self-concept, active coping, self-efficacy, openness to information, and conceptual skills in managing information. Persons with more schooling have greater knowledge and are inclined to acquire more. When exposed to information, they assimilate it more readily and in greater quantities than the less educated. Joe Spaeth, in *Schooling and Achievement in American Society*, has argued that socioeconomic levels are indicators of cognitive complexity, and that children exposed to better educated models, whether parents or teachers, learn to cope actively with complex stimuli.

The foregoing suggests, at the very least, a two-stage process of enablement and action. Schooling establishes the conditions for positive health by encouraging active and informed orientations to the environment. It engenders an ability to use information in a way that better allows values and intentions to be implemented. But the active inclinations that schooling induces should be separated from the content of values or instruction that push these inclinations in one direction or another. Encouraging psychological modernity through schooling, shaping values and preferences in health-relevant directions, and providing accessible services necessary for effective prevention and care requires separate initiatives. Together, they provide a powerful combination for effective health outcomes.

PRACTICAL IMPLICATIONS

A difficulty with this type of analysis is that its focus on deeper dimensions of culture and social structure leaves the practitioner initially frustrated. Such practitioners understand how they might launch an anti-smoking or good nutrition campaign, but do not have a clue as to how they might initiate culture change or modify social structure. Admittedly, these are difficult challenges, requiring a relatively long time perspective. But if we think in this broader context, we can build more effective strategies that integrate our efforts in a synergistic way. The alternative is to accept the fragmented, and largely ineffective, individual efforts as the best we can do.

Processes of culture change require collective action, and depend on the principles by which social movements become established and innovations diffuse among populations. The process itself has several interrelated elements. First, there has to be an agenda, a set of ideas and practices that are seen as conducive to some valued goal. Second, there have to be credible innovators who serve as models for the adoption of the desired practices. Third, there has to be some motivating force, shared by the larger target population, that encourages taking up new practices. And fourth, there have to be reinforcers that sustain a new practice until it becomes part of the natural flow of everyday activities.

In many instances, there may be strong inducers and reinforcers working against change. Many of the behaviors detrimental to health are immediately rewarding, are often sustained by powerful economic interests that promote the noxious practice, or are so integrated into current cultural practices that they are repeatedly reinforced, often inadvertently, and are strongly re-

sistant to change. In the case of smoking, even the sustained and well-publicized efforts to reduce smoking pale in comparison to the well-financed and strategically targeted advertising campaigns promoting it.

Smoking, as noted earlier, constitutes a reasonable success story, particularly in the context of the intense advertising efforts of the industry. It is impossible to untangle the influences that reduced smoking, but it is clear that the culture has changed, as has individual behavior. Smoking has been prohibited in many public places and restricted in public transportation, in restaurants, and in workplaces. Perhaps even more important is that the norms have been modified sufficiently to put smokers on the defensive. It is no longer embarrassing to ask people not to smoke in social settings, and smokers are increasingly made to feel apologetic about their behavior. Such normative changes may not induce many people to give up smoking, but will probably change the frequency and context of smoking, making it easier for those who want to quit. Even more important is that young people are growing up in contexts where they sense growing disapproval of smoking, and this may work as a deterrent to initiating the behavior.

Other types of behavior, such as alcohol consumption, are so much a part of social occasions that there are strong inducers to drink even among those inclined not to. Drinking is inevitably associated with occasions of conviviality and recreation and serves as a lubricant for socialization. The patterning of alcohol use at parties, taverns, athletic events, and the like makes it inevitable that drinking and driving will be associated. While such devices as collecting car keys at teen-age parties or using designated drivers for partying groups may help at the fringes, the organization of social life still induces and sustains drinking and driving.

Nutrition offers another example where the patterning of eating behavior, the increasing prevalence of eating outside the home, and the growth of the fast-food industry encourage less-than-optimal practices. There is evidence of limited change in restaurant fare, including low-calorie, low-salt meals, more salads, and fish; the fact is that it takes considerable awareness and conscious effort to practice good nutritional behavior in these contexts. Any set of practices that must depend on vigilance and effort is not likely to be sustained consistently.

What has been briefly noted about smoking, drinking, or nutrition can be said about almost any common behavior detrimental to health. They flourish in contexts that routinely sustain them and usually require vigilance and conscious choice to resist. The challenge is to define points of leverage that change the balance of influences so that everyday activities favor more positive patterns. This requires coordinated programs that make efforts that are regulatory, technological, and educational.

Our culture generally resists regulation of personal choice. It is clear that the ease of access affects use. Self-service machines for cigarettes make them more accessible to youngsters; the age of drivers' licensing affects rates of injury and death; taxes on alcohol and cigarettes affect levels of consumption. In any instance, while there may be reluctance to prohibit access, regulatory alternatives for restricting accessibility still remain viable options. These restrictions are likely to have their largest effects on youth who should be the targets of such efforts in any case.

One important way of supporting good health practice independently of conscious positive health behavior is to incorporate it into the technology itself. We are all familiar with inflatable air bags and involuntary seat belts, the safe cigarette, low-salt food products, fire-proof garments, and the like. Such technical solutions to risk depend on cost and consumer acceptability. Much more could be done to develop technologies that promote health, as well as potential markets for such products. Industry is extraordinarily adaptive in responding to consumer wants; encouraging the development and expansion of health-promoting products and activities should be part of any long-range strategy.

Health educators seek interventions that will activate individuals to take responsibility for their health. This task is complicated by the fact that healthy behavior arises from different motives and processes. Health-relevant behaviors themselves are usually loosely associated and may in some instances be negatively correlated. Exercise and risk-taking are associated, both possibly influenced by an underlying activity factor.

But the evidence is consistent that well-integrated group settings that encourage behavior with positive health consequences have a broader impact on an individual's health. Affective processes are powerful reinforcers of cognitive processes as well. Studies of adolescents show that young people's perceptions of how much their parents care about them is more predictive of positive health behavior than specific admonitions or even parents' health behavior. Most parents care deeply about their children, and most parents, regardless of their own habits, want their children to avoid obviously dangerous behavior. Most people, at least on a cognitive level, understand the risks of smoking, drinking, and drug use, and most youngsters share such awareness. Feelings of acceptance and love in a context that defines these behaviors as damaging seem to help insulate youngsters from many unacceptable behaviors.

We live in a culture where health is an important shared value, and there is much readily available health information. Those with more conceptual skills assimilate information and use it more wisely than those who are deficient in such skills. These skills not only make complex information more understandable, but also give individuals the resources to plan and use information aggressively. Acquisition of conceptual skills is facilitated by group expectations and influences. We have no assurance that improving conceptual skills alone will necessarily enhance health, but such improvement has benefits that transcend health concerns. Improved general education may do more indirectly to promote the subcultures and health goals we seek than many of the public information campaigns designed to shape specific behaviors in a particular way.

The examination of some of the evidence concerning health-promotive processes suggests the importance of understanding how to bolster group influences in the direction of health-promotive values. Particularly crucial are the ways in which the structure of everyday expectations and activities pattern our lives. Individual motivation to enhance health is important, but many of the influences on behavior are less conscious and perhaps less obvious because they are routine. Health-promotive activities that must depend on persistent, conscious motivation are unlikely to succeed in the long run. But once imprinted on our habits and routines, these activities are likely to have their effects, regardless of our attention.

Readings Suggested by the Author

Anderson, Odin W. Infant Mortality and Social Cultural Factors: Historical Trends and Current Patterns. In E. G. Jaco, ed., *Patients, Physicians, and Illness: A Sourcebook in Behavioral Science and Health.* New York: Free Press, 1958.

House, James; Landis, Karl R.; and Umberson, Debra. Social relationships and health. *Science* 241 (1988).

Mechanic, David. Socioeconomic status and health: An examination of underlying processes. In John P. Bunker, Debra S. Gomby, and Barbara H. Kehrer, eds., *Pathways to Health: The Role of Social Factors.* Menlow Park, Calif.: Kaiser Family Foundation, 1989.

CHAPTER 15

MENTAL HEALTH

INTRODUCTION

From the Bible to Shakespeare, literature and history are filled with accounts of people who have suffered from mental torment that inhibited their capacity to conduct their everyday affairs. Every schoolchild in England and the United States learns that King George III was a mad and witless ruler. In the twentieth century, medicine and psychiatry have transformed madness and melancholy into "mental illness." Much controversy surrounds this modern transformation. For many decades the American Psychiatric Association established firm definitions of mental disorders as either "neurotic" or "psychotic." In recent years these terms and the sharp distinction they imply have fallen into disfavor. The term "neurosis" has been officially discontinued in favor of new labels such as "affective disorder," "anxiety disorder," and "disorders of impulse control." Some crit-

369

ics, most notably Dr. Thomas Szasz, insist that mental illness is a myth perpetrated by official agents of social control (physicians, clinical psychologists, social workers, judges) who use labels to regulate behavior they consider undesirable. At the other extreme, some physicians insist that various types of mental illness are best understood as physical conditions and should be treated by appropriate drugs.

It is difficult to define mental illness with any precision. Despite this difficulty, numerous studies conducted by psychologists and sociologists during the past three decades make bold claims about its prevalence in our society. A famous pioneering study in 1962 (the Midtown Manhattan Study) determined that only 18 percent of the people in New York City were "well"; another 58 percent displayed mild or moderate symptoms, and 23 percent were diagnosed as "impaired." According to the National Institute of Mental Health, during any six-month period 25 million people cope with some kind of mental disorder. The same agency estimates that one person in five suffers from some form of mental illness. These studies and others all seem to agree on one fundamental finding: millions of Americans are afflicted by the pain of mental illness, yet many do not receive adequate treatment. This condition constitutes a major social problem.

During the twentieth century a major cyclical change has occurred in the treatment of mentally disturbed people. For many decades private and public institutions housed the mentally ill. The trend toward reliance on institutional care for the mentally ill continued until the 1950s, when approximately 600,000 patients were in mental wards. In the 1960s the movement to deinstitutionalize the mentally ill began. This trend has led to the closing of most state mental hospitals and a sharp reduction in the number of persons in institutional settings. Richard Warner examines this major change in American policy and practice. His essay examines the American case through historical and comparative analysis. Warner is keenly aware of the larger social, political, and economic context in which the policies of deinstitutionalization have been implemented. His inferences about causation have sobering implications for solutions.

Arthur J. Lurigio and Dan A. Lewis provide a fine empirical study of what is actually happening in the lives of mental patients who are no longer confined to the routines of institutional life. Their descriptive analysis of 313 Chicago residents who spend their lives in two worlds—the mental hospital and the streets—is a bleak account of the conditions confronting hundreds of thousands of Americans who suffer from various mental disorders. Despite advances in medication and psychosocial therapy and occasional public alarm about the plight of the mentally ill, the United States approaches the twenty-first century with no effective solution in sight for the social problems of mental illness.

41. DEINSTITUTIONALIZATION: HOW DID WE GET WHERE WE ARE?

RICHARD WARNER

In surveying the American mental health scene more than three decades after the beginning of deinstitutionalization, we may be excused for the sense of disillusionment that accompanies the question, "How did we get where we are?" In the soup lines and the shelters for the homeless on skid row in any of the nation's large cities, a quarter to a half of the men suffer from severe mental illness, excluding alcoholism (Bachrach, 1984), and a substantially greater proportion of homeless women are found to be psychotic (Reich & Siegel, 1973). Homelessness itself may be seen as a consequence of poverty and high housing costs, but the large proportion of the homeless who are mentally ill must be regarded, in part, as a reflection of mental health policy in the post-deinstitutionalization era. New York City presents a grimly ironic situation in which some former state hospital patients have come full circle back to the institution that originally discharged them—but this time for shelter, not treatment. In response to a class action suit filed on behalf of the city's homeless, an empty state hospital building on Ward's Island has been opened as an emergency shelter. Over 80% of the residents have been found to be mentally ill, but the conditions are far worse than when the building was staffed as a hospital (Baxter & Hopper, 1982).

From *Journal of Social Issues*, Vol. 45(3) pp. 17–30. Reprinted with permission of The Society for the Psychological Study of Social Issues, PO Box 1248, Ann Arbor, MI 48106.

Richard Warner is Medical Director of the Mental Health Center of Boulder County, Colorado, and Associate Professor in the Departments of Psychiatry and Anthropology at the University of Colorado. He is the author of Recovery from Schizophrenia: Psychiatry and Political Economy.

If Dorothea Dix were to return from the grave and renew her pilgrimage through the nation's jails, she would find little to gratify her. Remembered in history and psychiatry for her successful, pioneering campaign to end the detention of the indigent insane in jails, and to establish and enlarge state mental hospitals, she would find much of her work undone. Up to 11% of the inmates of U.S. local jails are psychotic, and a similar proportion of those in state and federal prisons suffer from severe mental illness (Steadman, McCarty, & Morrisey, 1989; Warner, 1985). The conditions of detention for mentally ill offenders are, at best, barren and unstimulating, and at worst, degrading, dangerous, and inhumane. An entire floor of the ten-story Dade County Jail, for example, is given over to the detention of around 100 mentally ill inmates. The most floridly disturbed of these psychotic people are stripped naked and isolated; the feeding slots in the doors of their cells are sealed so that food cannot be hurled back at the corrections officers. Jail staff may be called to respond to half a dozen or more suicide attempts in the jail on a single night.

The problems noted here are not isolated instances of abuse or ill-managed systems of care; rather, they are aspects of a national mental health system that is failing to meet the needs of a very large proportion of the mentally ill. So many of the nation's schizophrenics and other chronically mentally ill citizens are homeless, in jail, in single room occupancy hotels, boarding homes (generally large, bare institutions), nursing homes (where the environment and unskilled care may be as bad as that of the old hospital back wards), or in hospitals, that no more than half of such people are living in what could be termed a domestic environment—that is, in their own residence or with family members (Torrey & Wolfe, 1986; Warner, 1985). Although only a minority of psychotic patients are being treated in hospitals, state mental health budgets often do not reflect the transfer of care to the community. Outpatient and community services in New York State, for example, receive only a quarter of the amount of funding allocated to state psychiatric hospitals (Torrey & Wolfe, 1986). Many mentally ill people in U.S. cities are left without treatment. The Government Commission on Mental Health Services for the District of Columbia reports that, in 1987, the city's public mental health system served 3,500 chronic mentally ill patients, 1,500 of whom were in long-term hospital care. The commission, however, knew of the existence of a further 500 chronic mentally ill people in jail, 800 in nursing homes, and 2,000 mentally ill homeless who were receiving virtually no treatment. Thus, little more than half of the identified chronic mentally ill in Washington, D.C., were receiving regular services.

Many of these problems may be attributed to the fact that the elimination of public hospital beds has been pushed much further in the U.S. than elsewhere in the industrial West. Table 1 illustrates the scale of the policy change. The per capita availability of public psychiatric beds in the U.S. declined more steeply between the mid-1960s and the mid-1970s, and reached a lower level than in any other Western industrial nation (World Health Organization, 1967–1977). Much of this change in public bed census is at-

tributable to the increasing privatization of psychiatric health care, but its effect on the chronic mentally ill, many of whom have no hospital-care health-insurance benefits, has been great. While this program of radical deinstitutionalization has had many negative effects because of lack of availability of community services (especially in the nation's large cities), it has also provided the opportunity, unmatched in the Western world, for the development of novel community treatment approaches and support programs for seriously disturbed patients. This opportunity, unfortunately, has only in isolated cases led to the development of comprehensive and reasonably effective community programs (Brook, Cortes, March, & Sundberg-Sterling, 1976; Mosher & Burti, 1989; Stein & Test, 1980). How did it come about that mental health policy took such a radical turn in the U.S.? Why, indeed, did deinstitutionalization occur at all in postwar Europe and North America, and what factors shaped its different national forms?

ANTIPSYCHOTIC DRUGS

The belief is widespread in American psychiatry that the antipsychotic drugs brought about the shift to the community in the mid-1950s by making possible the effective outpatient treatment of psychosis. Chlorpromazine ushered in a "therapeutic revolution" in the treatment of schizophrenia, argues Davis (1980) in the *Comprehen-*

TABLE 1. Psychiatric Hospital Beds per 10,000 Population in the Western Industrial Nations

Nation	1965	1968	1971	1974
Australia	27.1	24.3	21.6	20.7
Canada	35.9	30.2	26.2	21.8
France	20.5	21.9	23.0	—
Germany, West	17.7	18.2	18.7	17.8
Italy	22.4	21.8	20.9	20.9
Japan	13.3	16.8	18.0	18.4
Sweden	35.4	43.2	42.2	40.5
United Kingdom (England)	28.5	26.2	23.8	31.9
United States	31.1	32.0	24.1	14.2

Source: World Health Organization (1967–1977).

sive Textbook of Psychiatry. He goes on to claim that the "massive reduction in the number of hospitalized schizophrenic patients" following the introduction of the new drugs "is the most convincing proof of the efficacy of those agents" (p. 2257). Davis illustrates this point with the now familiar graph showing the rise and fall in the number of residents of U.S. public mental hospitals in recent decades, peaking in 1955 when chlorpromazine began to be widely used—the broken line in Figure 1. It is clear, however, that the figures relevant to this issue are not the *absolute* numbers of hospitalized patients, but the numbers as a proportion of the general population. A graph of the *rate* of mental hospital occupancy—the solid line in Figure 1—reveals a different picture. The rate of hospital use peaked in 1945 and never climbed as high again. While it is apparent that there has been a marked decline in the U.S. mental hospital population since the advent of the antipsychotic drugs, events in the first postwar decade were already altering patterns of psychiatric hospital use.

In contrast to the belief widely held in the U.S., many psychiatrists practicing in northern Europe in the postwar years observed that the advent of the antipsychotic drugs in 1954 often had little impact on hospital discharge rates (Shepherd, Goodman, & Watt, 1961). Odegard (1964), in Norway, and Norton (1961), in Britain, were among those whose hospital statistics revealed that much greater increases in hospital discharge rates occurred in the postwar years preceding the introduction of drug treatment than in the years that followed. Although there were isolated examples in the United States of these earlier changes in discharge policy, in the main the American experience matched the pattern of change in New York State recorded by Brill and Patton (1959). There, the postwar state hospital population increased by about 2,000 patients a year until 1955, but as large numbers of patients began treatment with the new drugs, the upward trend was converted into an annual decrease in population. Whatever the policy changes were that preceded the arrival of chlorpromazine, it is clear that their impact was considerably more noticeable in northern Europe than in North America. What were these changes?

THE POSTWAR SOCIAL PSYCHIATRY REVOLUTION

As early as 1945, changes were apparent in the care of the hospitalized mentally ill in Britain. At Netherne Hospital, near London, more open

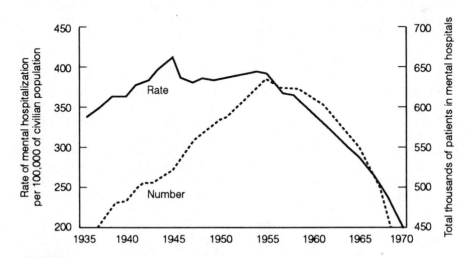

FIGURE 1

Resident patients in U.S. federal, state, county, and private psychiatric hospitals. Reprinted from Warner (1985, p. 81).

wards were created, patients were allowed greater freedom, restraints were abandoned, and in consequence, patients became less withdrawn, aggressive, and incontinent (Freudenberg, Bennet, & May, 1959). In 1949, Dingleton Hospital, in the Borders of Scotland, became the first completely open-door hospital; other British hospitals followed suit in 1953, becoming part of the open-door movement that was to sweep Europe. Day hospitals became widespread in Britain in the 1940s and 1950s, and in Amsterdam, home treatment for the mentally ill was established (Clark, 1974). Such changes were slower to develop in the U.S.: St. Lawrence Hospital, New York, became fully open-door in 1958, after drug treatment was well established (Langsley, 1981).

Within some European hospitals radical changes were occurring. Beginning in 1946, staff and patients worked together to create "therapeutic communities," in which the introduction of patient government and staff and patient role blurring served to erode traditional institutional authority. Developed initially for demoralized ex-soldiers, unemployed "drifters," and patients with character disorders, the therapeutic community idea was introduced, in due course, into hospital units for psychotic, brain-damaged, and elderly patients (Clark, 1974; Jones, 1968; Warner, 1985). The new therapeutic optimism was geared to early discharge, rehabilitation, and community treatment. Many patients lost their chronic institutional features and moved into group homes and hostels or returned to live with their families. Sheltered workshops prospered, first in Holland, and after 1960, in Britain (Clark, 1974).

Such revolutionary changes, in several areas preceding the introduction of chlorpromazine, explain why drug treatment seemed to have little effect in many hospitals. On wards where attention had been paid to the therapeutic environment, the new drugs were of limited benefit (Rathod & Bombay, 1958). This point is, perhaps, best illustrated by Odegard's data for the 17 psychiatric hospitals in Norway. Those hospitals that previously had a poor discharge record showed the greatest benefit from the introduction of drug treatment; those that already had higher discharge rates and were presumably us-

ing the newer social therapies showed no increase in the number of patients discharged and maintained in the community after the antipsychotic drugs arrived in 1954 (Odegard, 1964). Data such as these suggest that antipsychotic drug treatment is more effective for psychotic patients living in inadequate or stressful settings, and they help explain why the antipsychotic drugs had a more revolutionary impact on the locked back wards of U.S. asylums, where so many patients showed signs of severe deterioration due to institutionalism. Since the benefits of social therapy did not become so apparent in the U.S., drug treatment here has all too often been used as a substitute for, not a supplement to, adequate psychosocial care. The product is the revolving-door patient.

DEINSTITUTIONALIZATION IN THE UNITED STATES

Much of the truly rehabilitative thrust apparent in the early stages of deinstitutionalization in northern Europe (and which, to a great extent, has since been lost) was never a central feature of American deinstitutionalization. The rhetoric of community care—increased individual freedom and anticipated higher patient functioning—was present. Practice, however, did not generally mirror the rhetoric. A substantial proportion of those discharged from U.S. mental hospitals ended up in another, and sometimes worse, category of institution—nursing homes. Thus, although the number of patients in U.S. state and county mental hospitals declined from 504,604 in 1963 to 369,929 in 1969, the number of patients with mental disorders in nursing homes increased to such an extent that the total institutionalized population of the mentally ill was actually *higher* in 1969. The number of mentally ill in hospitals and nursing homes combined rose from 726,325 in 1963 to 796,712 in 1969 (Scull, 1977). Nor do these figures include patients discharged to yet another type of back ward in the community—the board-and-care home. Hundreds of thousands of patients across the country have been housed in these often huge, bare, and sordid inner-city establishments, frequently with inadequate or nonexistent psychiatric care (Lamb & Goertzel, 1972; Langsley, 1981). What accounts for these features of U.S. deinstitutionalization?

OUTDOOR RELIEF

Sociologist Andrew Scull (1977) has argued cogently that both the British and American deinstitutionalization movements have been powered by the postwar development of welfare programs that enable the indigent and the disabled to be maintained more cheaply outside an institution. This way of curtailing dependence on government support, sometimes termed "outdoor relief," had been sharply reduced in the mid-19th century in favor of institutional forms of support. By the end of World War II, however, escalating maintenance and replacement costs for the aging institutions, rising institutional staffing costs, and increased political pressure to provide more comprehensive relief of poverty combined to make noninstitutional forms of social insurance more attractive. Scull's argument is persuasive, but its weakness, as we shall see, is that it fails to account for national differences in the timing and style of the deinstitutional process. Odegard (1967), for example, makes it clear that the arrival of comprehensive social insurance in Norway came a decade after the onset of deinstitutionalization and made discharge possible for a second wave of psychotic patients—those categorized as "not cured."

In the U.S., it is apparent that the expansion of Social Security Disability Insurance (SSDI) and the introduction of Supplemental Security Income (SSI) in the 1960s did allow the discharge of mentally disabled people into the community. In addition, Medicaid stimulated massive growth in the nursing home industry by making possible the transfer of mentally ill patients to private institutional care (Mechanic, 1987). State legislators readily perceived that these shifts in the location of patient care would allow the transfer of a substantial part of the state costs to the federal budget. It is this feature of American government—shared federal and state fiscal responsibility—that has given U.S. deinstitutionalization many of its special features. The radical reduction in public hospital bed census (with

relatively little regard for the ultimate fate of the patients), the dramatic growth of private-sector institutions, the failure to fund community programs adequately (after the withdrawal of federal seed money)—all of these features may be seen as attempts to minimize state costs while maximizing the federal contribution, through Medicaid and support payments, toward the care of the mentally ill. Even the increased criminal justice costs resulting from the arrest and jailing of psychotic offenders for minor crimes do not significantly affect the state, being borne primarily by county budgets.

LABOR DYNAMICS

Disability payments and health insurance, however, do not explain all of the national differences in deinstitutional policy. Why, for example, was there a truly rehabilitative quality to the open-door movement in northern Europe during the postwar period but not in the U.S.? Why was there an earlier start for deinstitutionalization in northern Europe and a late start in Italy? The timing of the introduction of welfare reform does not coincide with these policy changes. To explain such variations we must look at differences in the perceived social value of the inmates of the institutions, and especially at the importance of their contribution to the labor force.

So acute was the labor shortage in postwar Britain that *The Times* of January, 1947, called for the selective immigration of half a million foreign workers, and one economist predicted "economic chaos" if 100,000 foreigners could not be recruited to work the coal mines. The government launched a propaganda campaign against nonproductive "spivs and drones," and the *Daily Mail* suggested that, if Scotland Yard were to round up "work dodgers," a million-and-a-half workers could be added to the labor force. By September of that year the Cabinet was discussing the possibility of closing down the football pools (a popular legal form of gambling) to force the redeployment of the women who processed the coupons into the labor-starved textile industry (Sinfield, 1981).

It is hard for those who have not lived through such a time to comprehend a labor shortage of these dimensions. Such sustained peacetime labor starvation had scarcely been seen in northern Europe since records began. Switzerland has experienced full employment on a similar scale through much of the 20th century (Mitchell, 1978); so has the USSR (especially Moscow and other large cities) from 1930 until recently (Ellman, 1979); and labor was in short supply in industrializing and expanding America during the first half of the 19th century (Boorstin, 1969). In each of these countries, at these times, psychiatric treatment developed truly rehabilitative qualities and achieved superior results in rates of recovery from serious mental illness (Warner, 1985). It seems reasonable to conclude that such a heavy demand for labor, extraordinary by recent Western standards, can be a stimulus to the rehabilitation of the marginally functional mentally ill. Contemporary observers agreed that this was true with respect to the postwar European social psychiatry revolution. British psychiatrist David Clark (1974) identified as major factors promoting the open-door movement, "the development of welfare states where the disabled (including the psychiatrically crippled) were supported in their homes [and] the development of full employment (in northern Europe at least) creating a demand for the labour of impaired people" (p. 23). Similarly, Odegard (1967) reported that, in Norway, "Since the war there has been a certain degree of overemployment, and it has been possible for hospitals to discharge to an independent existence even patients with a borderline working capacity and a questionable social adjustment" (p. 819).

In the U.S., current vocational rehabilitation efforts for the mentally ill are extremely limited (U.S. Department of Labor, 1979) and our concerns are principally focused, in these times of significant unemployment, on the benefits of work for the patient, not on the potential economic gains for society. Thus, it is easy to overlook the strategic importance that the labor of the mentally ill holds during periods of labor shortage. For example, the rehabilitation of schizophrenic patients alone in postwar Britain may have added as many as 30,000 workers to the labor force (Warner, 1983). The labor-force mobilization of the disabled during wartime offers another illustration of this point. One report shows that virtually none of the disabled workers in the San Francisco Bay area was unemployed in 1942–1943 (McGowan & Porter, 1967), and the employment of the mentally retarded in Britain and America is known to have increased from around 40% in the Great Depression to 80% or 90% during World War II (Tizard & O'Connor, 1950).

The importance of the labor market in stimulating the European social pyschiatry revolution is illustrated by an examination of postwar national unemployment statistics. According to Maxwell Jones (personal communication, 1978), one of the most prominent postwar British social psychiatrists and innovators, the countries that led the social psychiatry revolution were Britain, the Netherlands, Norway, and Switzerland. The postwar unemployment statistics (adjusted to render them more comparable) for these countries and other parts of Europe and North America are listed in Table 2 (Maddison, 1964; Mitchell, 1978). The four countries which were more psychiatrically progressive at that time are among those with low unemployment rates. Countries like the United States and Italy, where psychiatric innovations were delayed, had higher rates of unemployment.

Thus, two major political forces—the demand for labor and the opportunity for cost savings— each tending to produce somewhat different results, may be seen to be at work in shaping the postwar deinstitutional movement. Postwar full employment in northern Europe stimulated truly rehabilitative forms of social therapy, designed to bring marginally functional psychiatric patients into the labor force, even before the antipsychotic drugs were available. The introduction of disability support payments allowed patients to be discharged in the absence of employment opportunities, and the availability of antipsychotic drugs exaggerated this process by facilitating the transfer of patients to low-cost settings without the necessity for careful social design of their environment. In the United States, where the postwar labor shortage was never acute, rehabilitative efforts were generally weak; cost saving became the most important driving force and was amplified by the opportunity to shift state expenses to the federal budget. The sharp rise in unemployment in Britain be-

TABLE 2. Unemployment Rates (in Percent) in Northern Europe and North America

Year	High Unemployment Nations						Low Unemployment Nations					
	Belgium	Denmark	Germany	Italy	Canada	USA	France	Netherlands	Norway[a]	Sweden	Switzerland	UK
1950	6.3	4.1	7.2	8.7	3.6	5.2	1.4	2.0	2.7	1.7	0.5	2.5
1951	5.7	4.5	6.4	9.2	2.4	3.2	1.3	2.4	3.6	1.6	0.2	2.2
1952	6.8	5.9	6.1	9.8	2.9	2.9	1.3	3.5	2.4	1.7	0.3	2.9
1953	6.8	4.4	5.5	10.2	2.9	2.8	1.6	2.5	3.3	1.9	0.3	2.6
1954	6.2	3.8	5.2	8.7	4.5	5.3	1.6	1.8	2.2	1.8	0.2	2.3
1955	4.7	4.7	3.8	7.5	4.3	4.2	1.5	1.3	2.5	1.8	0.1	2.1

[a] All unemployment statistics, except for Norway, have been adjusted to render them comparable.
Sources: Maddison (1964) and Mitchell (1978).

ginning in the late 1960s helps explain the decline in British psychiatric rehabilitative programming after that time. The delay in the introduction of open-door policies and community treatment in Italian psychiatry until the 1960s may be seen as a reflection of the high postwar national unemployment rate in that country. The truly rehabilitative thrust of the Italian anti-institutional movement, when it did get under way, with its emphasis on the social integration of patients in the community and the development of worker cooperatives to enhance their employment (Scheper-Hughes & Lovell, 1987), may have a great deal to do with the explosive economic growth and labor shortage that occurred in the northern Italian provinces throughout the 1960s (Kogan, 1981). The subsequent failure of the rehabilitative policies of the democratic psychiatry movement to take hold in the southern provinces of Italy (Scheper-Hughes & Lovell, 1987) may well reflect the very different economic and labor-force conditions in those parts of the country.

CHANGING TIMES

An analysis, conducted by Warner (1983), of the relationship between mental hospital use and a number of social indicators in a sample of Western industrial nations revealed the shift in the importance of the labor market in shaping psychiatric institutional policy as postwar economic and political conditions have changed. Using a stepwise multiple regression procedure, Warner found that the number of public mental hospital beds provided (per capita of the population) in nine Western nations was positively associated with the national unemployment rate in 1965— unemployment explaining 40% of the variance ($p < .05$). By 1974, however, national unemployment rates had increased significantly and now explained only 1% of the variance in the provision of mental hospital beds. In that year, two new factors were associated with the number of beds—a large proportion of elderly people in the population (34% of the variance) and a low national infant mortality rate (36% of the variance)—(combined effect, $p < .05$).

These results suggest that labor-market forces become an important factor in psychiatric policy-making only when a significant labor shortage exists. (In 1965, national unemployment rates in five of the nine countries in the sample were below 2%.) When a large pool of healthy unemployed people exists, national mental hospital bed provision is determined, to a greater extent, by the number of demented elderly patients (for, in many countries, such patients are cared for in public institutions), and by the national commitment to comprehensive health and welfare provisions. The national infant mortality rate that, in economically advanced countries, may be taken as a fair indicator of the state's commitment to universally adequate health and welfare services, had become inversely related to mental hospital use by 1974. In the United States, for example, where health care is unevenly distributed (and infant mortality is relatively high), drastic cutbacks in mental hospital care have taken place. In Sweden, where health and welfare provisions are comprehensive (and infant mortality is low), psychiatric hospital care is extensive.

CONCLUSION

How did we get where we are? It may be argued that economic and political circumstances, more than professional philosophy or technological innovation, have shaped our mental health care system. We have the kind of system, in the United States, which might be expected to develop in a society with a sustained labor glut, with little political commitment to comprehensive health care, and with a governmental structure characterized by multiple levels of fiscal responsibility for the treatment, support, and control of the mentally ill.

How do we get where we want to go? Few economists of either right- or left-wing persuasion, however fervently they may wish for it, foresee the imminent development of full employment (in its literal sense) in postindustrial America. It is likely that the mentally ill will continue to be excluded from, or marginal to, the labor force. If we are to minimize the adverse consequences of this factor upon their rehabilitation, we must look for changes in national health care that would make psychiatric treatment available to all and that would concentrate fiscal responsibility at one level of government.

Multiple studies have now demonstrated that intensive community support and treatment of psychotic patients can drastically decrease the morbidity caused by illness, virtually eliminate the revolving-door syndrome, and yet cost no more overall than standard care (Stein, 1987). It would be feasible to develop a comprehensive network of such community support programs if we were to establish a mental health system in which, to use a popular phrase, "the dollar follows the patient"—that is, in which the savings derived from the prevention of hospital use are added to the funding of the community treatment program. An adequately funded, government-operated health maintenance organization offering comprehensive psychiatric care for severe conditions is one possible mechanism for achieving this end.

The Robert Wood Johnson Foundation is currently funding an innovative pilot project in South Carolina that is attempting to establish a program of this type on a limited scale. The state Division of Mental Health aims to develop a statewide prepaid health plan for Medicaid-eligible, chronically disabled psychiatric patients. Under the pilot plan, participating mental health centers will assume responsibility for the health and mental health care of these patients through the flexible use of Medicaid funds. The planners anticipate that the new funding mechanism will create incentives to expand comprehensive community support services in order to maintain the patients' psychiatric stability and physical health. For such a plan to work on a national level, it would be necessary to make Medicaid (or other governmental health insurance) available to all severely psychiatrically impaired people, and to ensure adequate funding of the program by both state and federal levels of government. However, this may not be politically feasible. Legislators at different levels of government would need to be persuaded that such comprehensive care would burden their budget no more than the combined expense of current health insurance, public hospital expenditures, and relevant criminal-justice costs.

Even if it were possible to prove this point and to establish a comprehensive state mental health care system, we would be left with an intractable political problem. When the economy is weak and the labor of the mentally disabled is not in demand, there will be a strong tendency for legislators to pare mental health funding down to lower and lower levels. Recent developments in British National Health Service funding illustrate this point. Until now, there has been no effective lobby to resist this trend. In the future, perhaps, the combined forces of the now well-established organization of relatives of the mentally ill (the National Alliance for the Mentally Ill) and the burgeoning consumer movement of psychiatric patients may exert a significant effect on the political process.

Through its radical deinstitutional policies, the United States, as we have seen, has developed a few, isolated models of humane, effective community care that have earned international attention. Current economic conditions limit the extent to which we can develop genuinely rehabilitative programs, but within these limits, we know how to do a passable job. Given the right funding mechanisms and fiscal incentives, our model programs could form the basis for a nationwide community treatment system that would reduce morbidity, mortality, and misery, and cost little more than our present patchwork of expensive, inefficient, and fragmentary services.

References

Bachrach, L. L. 1984. The homeless mentally ill and mental health services: An analytical review of the literature. In R. Lamb, ed., *The Homeless Mentally Ill: A Task Force Report of the American Psychiatric Association*, pp. 11–53. Washington, D.C.: American Psychiatric Association.

Baxter, E., and Hopper, K. 1982. The new mendicancy: Homeless in New York City. *American Journal of Orthopsychiatry* 52:393–408.

Boorstin, D. J. 1969. *The Americans*. Vol. 2, *The national experience*. Harmondsworth, Middlesex: Penguin.

Brill, H., and Patton, R. E. 1959. Analysis of population reduction in New York State mental hospitals during the first four years of large-scale therapy with psychotropic drugs. *American Journal of Psychiatry* 116:495–509.

Brook, B. D.; Cortes, M.; March, R.; & Sundberg-Sterling, M. 1976. Community families: An alternative to psychiatric hospital intensive care. *Hospital and Community Psychiatry* 27:195–197.

Clark, D. H. 1974. *Social therapy in psychiatry*. Baltimore: Penguin.

Davis, J. M. 1980. Antipsychotic drugs. In D. I. Kaplan, A. M. Freedman, and B. J. Sadock, eds., *Comprehensive Textbook of Psychiatry*, 3:2257–2289. Baltimore: Williams & Wilkins.

Ellman, M. 1979. *Social Planning*. Cambridge: Cambridge University Press.

Freudenberg, R. K.; Bennet, D. H.; and May, A. R. 1959. The relative importance of physical and community methods in the treatment of schizophrenia. In *International Congress of Psychiatry, Zurich, 1957*, pp. 157–178. Zurich: Fussli.

Jones, M. 1968. *Social Psychiatry in Practice*. Baltimore: Penguin.

Kogan, N. 1981. *A Political History of Postwar Italy: From the Old to the New Center-Left*. New York: Praeger.

Lamb, H. R., and Goertzel, V. 1972. The demise of the state hospital: A premature obituary? *Archives of General Psychiatry* 26:489–495.

Langsley, D. G. 1981. Community psychiatry. In H. I. Kaplan, A. M. Freedman, and B. J. Sadock, eds., *Comprehensive Textbook of Psychiatry*, 3:2836–2853. Baltimore: Williams & Wilkins.

McGowan, J. F., and Porter, T. L. 1967. *An Introduction to the Vocational Rehabilitation Process*. Washington, D.C.: U.S. Department of Health, Education, and Welfare, Vocational Rehabilitation Administration.

Maddison, A. 1964. *Economic Growth in the West*. New York: Twentieth Century Fund.

Mechanic, D. 1987. Correcting misconceptions in mental health policy: Strategies for improved care of the seriously mentally ill. *Milbank Quarterly* 65:203–230.

Mitchell, B. R. 1978. *European Historical Statistics, 1750–1970*, abridged ed. New York: Columbia University Press.

Mosher, L. R., and Burti, L. 1989. *Community Mental Health: Principles and Practice*. New York: Norton.

Norton, A. 1961. Mental hospital ins and outs: A survey of patients admitted to a mental hospital in the past 30 years. *British Medical Journal* 1:528–536.

Odegard, O. 1964. Pattern of discharge from Norwegian psychiatric hospitals before and after the introduction of the psychotropic drugs. *American Journal of Psychiatry* 120:772–778.

———. 1967. Changes in the prognosis of functional psychoses since the days of Kraepelin. *British Journal of Psychiatry* 113:813–822.

Rathod, N. H., and Bombay, M. B. 1958. Tranquillisers and patients' environment. *Lancet* 1:611–613.

Reich, R., and Seigel, L. 1973. The chronically mentally ill shuffle to oblivion. *Psychiatric Annals* 3:35–55.

Scheper-Hughes, N., and Lovell, A. M., eds. 1987. *Psychiatry Inside Out: Selected Writings of Franco Basaglia*. New York: Columbia University Press.

Scull, A. 1977. *Decarceration: Community Treatment and the Deviant—A Radical View*. Englewood Cliffs, N.J.: Prentice Hall.

Shepherd, M.; Goodman, N.; and Watt, D. C. 1961. The application of hospital statistics in the evaluation of pharmacotherapy in a psychiatric population. *Comprehensive Psychiatry* 2:11–19.

Sinfield, A. 1981. *What Unemployment Means*. Oxford: Robertson.

Steadman, H. J.; McCarty, D. W.; and Morrissey, J. P. 1989. *The Mentally Ill in Jail: Planning for Essential Services*. New York: Guilford.

Stein, L. I. 1987. Funding a system of care for schizophrenia. *Psychiatric Annals* 17:592–598.

Stein, L. I., and Test, M. A. 1980. Alternatives to mental hospital treatment: I. Conceptual model, treatment program, and clinical evaluation. *Archives of General Psychiatry* 37:392–397.

Tizard, J., and O'Connor, N. 1950. The employment of high-grade mental defectives: I. *American Journal of Mental Deficiency* 54:563–576.

Torrey, E. F., & Wolfe, S. M. 1986. *Care of the Seriously Mentally Ill: A Rating of State Programs.* Washington, D.C.: Public Citizen Health Research Group.

U.S. Department of Labor. 1979. *Sheltered Workshop Study.* Vol. 2, *Study of Handicapped Clients in Sheltered Workshops and Recommendations of the Secretary.* Washington, D.C.: U.S. Government Printing Office.

Warner, R. 1983. The effect of the labor market on mental hospital and prison use: An international comparison. *Administration in Mental Health* 10:239–258.

————. 1985. *Recovery from Schizophrenia: Psychiatry and Political Economy.* Boston: Routledge & Kegan Paul.

World Health Organization. 1967–1977. *World Health Statistics Annual.* Vol. 1, *1963–1977 Series.* Geneva.

42. WORLDS THAT FAIL: A LONGITUDINAL STUDY OF URBAN MENTAL PATIENTS

ARTHUR J. LURIGIO and DAN A. LEWIS

Our society's effectiveness in treating the chronic mentally ill is defined essentially by whether patients can survive independently of

From *Journal of Social Issues*, Vol. 45(3) pp. 79–90. Reprinted with permission of the Society for the Psychological Study of Social Issues, PO Box 1248, Ann Arbor, MI 48106.

Arthur J. Lurigio is currently Assistant Professor of Criminal Justice at Loyola University and Research Associate at the Center for Urban Affairs and Policy Research at Northwestern. Dan A. Lewis is Associate Director of the Center for Urban Affairs and Policy Research, and Chairman of the Graduate Program in Human Development and Social Policy at the School of Education and Social Policy, both at Northwestern University. Currently, he is the principal investigator of the Politics of School Decentralization Project funded by the Spencer Foundation in collaboration with the Chicago Urban League.

custodial, long-term care. Such survival depends on their ability to find income, maintain interpersonal relationships, and secure adequate housing. The successful transition from state or community-based institutions to autonomous adult life requires accomplishment of these critical tasks, which also reflect patients' symptomatology, well-being, and social integration.

This article describes an investigation of mental patients in the community and their movements into and out of state institutions. It examines the circumstances that surround psychiatric admissions, and the problems and obstacles patients confront in their struggle to manage outside of hospitals, board-and-care residences, and nursing homes. By looking beyond the bounds of controlled treatment settings, the study was able to achieve a more broadly representative view of patients' adjustment to daily life and to acquire a clearer understanding of why patients return to the hospital.

BACKGROUND

There is a growing consensus that the community mental health movement has not achieved its articulated aims. By the mid-1970s, the policy of deinstitutionalization was being assailed on all fronts (e.g., Gruenberg & Archer, 1979). Despite the initial optimism generated by efforts to extend mental health services beyond the hospital, it was fast becoming apparent that community care of mental patients was accompanied by new (and in some ways more insidious) problems of exclusion, neglect, and abuse. Mass media portrayals vividly depicted the casualties of deinstitutionalization, and decried the move "out of their beds and into the streets" (American Federation, 1975) and from "back wards to back alleys" (Trotter & Kutter, 1974).

In the wake of community mental health reform, most chronic patients are still being treated in either institutional settings (e.g., nursing homes) or community settings (Kohen & Paul, 1976; Rose, 1979; U.S. Department of Health, Education, and Welfare, 1980), both of which are characterized by shoddy care, poverty, stigma, and social isolation. Many mental patients today live in abject surroundings, do not receive mental health services, and have little chance of returning as a functioning member of society. This has led several observers to note that the conditions that patients currently endure in the community are more deplorable than the conditions they previously endured in the hospital (e.g., Tessler & Goldman, 1982). Faced with a grim life outside the institution, without the mainstays of families, jobs, and adequate housing, these individuals return repeatedly to the safe and predictable environment of the hospital. The pattern of recurring readmission has continued to escalate since the early 1960s, and 70% of all admissions to mental hospitals are now readmissions—a telling statistic that underlines the egregious failure of community mental health reform. The "revolving door" of the mental hospital continues to spin (Weinstein, 1983).

The Mental Health Policy Project

This paper is based on a longitudinal study of a random sample of 313 mental patients in Chicago, known as the Mental Health Policy Project. This project was a three-year study conducted at Northwestern University's Center for Urban Affairs and Policy Research, aimed at learning more about the people who utilize state mental health services in large urban settings. Some of the questions explored included the following: Who uses the hospital? What kinds of psychiatric problems lead to hospitalization? How do patients fare in the community regarding jobs and housing? What is the usual process for admitting patients to the institution? Do patients pose a threat to the community? Which patients are most likely to be rehospitalized? The goal of the project was to move beyond prior studies by telling the story of hospitalization and readmission almost entirely from the patients' viewpoint. Most of the data were qualitative and descriptive, based on patients' self-reports in semistructured interviews. Hence, there were only a few instances where quantitative or comparative analyses of the survey responses were performed.

Data were collected by interviewing a random sample of patients, in person, at three points in time. The first interview was shortly after admission while patients were hospitalized at one of four state-run psychiatric institutions serving Chicago. The second and third wave of interviews, at 6 and 12 months following their earlier admission, were conducted wherever we could locate patients, which included a wide variety of settings and circumstances. The interview schedule was designed to tap an extensive array of psychiatric, psychological, social, environmental, and familial factors. The study also analyzed Illinois Department of Mental Health records, and patients' arrests and criminal histories.

A complete description of the study is beyond the scope of this paper, but may be found in Lewis et al. (in press). Here, we summarize some of the major findings, and discuss their implications for current mental health policies and practice.

MAJOR FINDINGS

Patient Characteristics

A descriptive analysis of demographic characteristics showed that mental patients in the sample were disproportionately young (67% were between the ages of 18–34), black (55%), and male (63%). They were also predominantly poor, unemployed, and on welfare. The average income of the sample was approximately $400 per month, while half of the patients earned less than $300 per month. Moreover, 6% of the sample reported no monthly income, and nearly one-fourth (23%) stated that they earned less than $100 per month, whereas only 7% reported a yearly income of $12,000. Nearly half of the respondents (48%) had not completed high school; 21% indicated that they were presently married.

Patient Diagnosis

Diagnosis is often conceptualized as a critical variable in explaining patients' symptomatology and prognoses, and in guiding their treatment and reintegration. Hence the study examined the relationships between hospital diagnosis, patient demographics, and status at admission (voluntary or involuntary). The Department of Mental Health provided a primary admitting and discharge diagnosis for 95% ($N = 298$) of the total sample of mental patients interviewed at the hospital. An overwhelming majority were diagnosed as either schizophrenic (67%) or as having a major affective disorder (27%). Female patients were more likely than male patients to be diagnosed as having an affective disorder and less likely to be diagnosed as schizophrenic [$\chi^2(1) = 4.78, p < .05$]. Unmarried patients were more likely to be diagnosed as schizophrenic and less likely to be diagnosed as an affective disorder [$\chi^2(1) = 6.17, p < .05$]. There were no significant relationships between diagnosis and patient age or status at admission.

Black male patients were much more likely to be admitted as schizophrenic than were white male patients [$\chi^2(6) = 26.83, p < .001$]. Specifically, 75% of the black males were diagnosed as schizophrenic and only 14% were diagnosed as an affective disorder. In the nonblack racial groups (whites, Hispanics, and Orientals), the percentages in those diagnostic categories were much less disparate.

A comparison of hospital diagnoses with diagnoses made by independent clinicians who interviewed a subsample of the patients in the larger investigation showed that blacks (especially black males) were the single group most likely to be diagnosed as schizophrenic by both hospital staff and independent clinicians. The tendency to diagnose blacks as schizophrenic was nonsignificantly greater among hospital clinicians.

Involuntary Commitment

Before the advent of the patients' rights movement many persons were admitted to the state hospital involuntarily. Recent reforms have promised to provide due process for patients being institutionalized against their will, as well as to preserve the right of the hospital to commit patients who are a "danger to themselves or others." Findings showed that the actual implementation of such reforms did not always accomplish these objectives. In Illinois, the state mental hospital staff presently encourage voluntary admissions and discharge patients as expeditiously as possible. Involuntary commitment, once the mechanism by which dangerous or severely disabled patients were institutionalized for longer periods of time, is now rarely used. Only 3% of the sample in our study were committed involuntarily during the first admission. A variety of strategies was used to persuade or coerce patients to sign into the hospital voluntarily in order to circumvent the complex and protracted legal procedure that governs involuntary commitment. One result of this was an automatic cap on the time that patients could legally spend in the hospital. In short, due process was formally guaranteed, but seldom achieved.

Many of the admissions classified as voluntary belied patients' true sentiments regarding hospitalization. Indeed, when asked if "they wanted to go to the hospital," nearly half of the so-called voluntary patients responded that they did not desire to be admitted. The following illustrative comments were made by patients who were recorded as voluntary admissions: "I had to sign myself in or go to jail"; "I sign in voluntarily because I know they got me; there's no way out for me."

Some patients stated that they had been committed by the court before, but signed in voluntarily at their current admission in order to be released from the hospital more quickly. Other patients reported that their therapists told them they would be committed by the court if they refused to sign in voluntarily. Both the patients and therapists interviewed in this study revealed that a kind of bargaining occurs in which future privileges are exchanged for voluntary admissions. One therapist described his interaction with a patient this way:

We worked out a deal. He was supposed to go to court on Tuesday because he had been refusing to sign in voluntarily. I told him if he goes to court he runs the risk of being committed. I suggested that he consider signing in voluntarily and cooperating with us. I would speed up his discharge. He also wanted an off-grounds pass so he could pick up his check. I told him he could have one if he signed in voluntarily.

Patients who were dangerous to themselves or others or seriously debilitated by mental illness were not likely to be treated any differently from patients who were less threatening or less symptomatic. Of the numerous patients who reported violent behavior prior to their hospitalization, only 5 were involuntarily committed. There was no correlation between involuntary commitment and violent behavior. Patients who reported self-destructive behavior were also no more likely to be committed, for none of such patients in this study were involuntarily committed. Our findings show that the typical state mental hospital is no longer serving the function of confining dangerous or severely ill patients for longer periods of time.

Although our results show that some of the most troublesome and threatening patients in the mental health system are not being committed, they do not suggest that commitment court itself nor the laws that constrain it are an important source of the problem. It is true that some cases are dismissed in court, either because the hospital has not followed the legal procedure for the filing of petitions and certificates, or because hospital personnel present contradictory testimony regarding the dangerousness of the patient. However, this did not happen with any of the patients in this study, indicating that it is a relatively rare event, as is commitment itself.

In summary, relatively few patients are admitted involuntarily, largely because of the complicated and time-consuming nature of the process, which evolved as a way to protect patients from unnecessary commitments. Hospital staff have developed alternative coercive methods to sidestep the procedural regulations that impede involuntary admissions. In essence, the onerousness of involuntary commitment can be avoided, while patients can still be forced into the hospital by ostensibly more innocuous practices. Moreover, coerced voluntary admissions are frequently involved as part of the negotiations between patients and staff.

Hospital Admissions

Almost two-thirds (64%) of the sample had a history of prior psychiatric admissions. Approximately 5% were admitted to the hospital 15 or more times. The sex, race, and age of patients were not related to the number of prior hospitalizations on their records. Black males had the highest rates of readmissions, whereas white females had the lowest rates of readmissions. Married patients were less likely than unmarried patients to have been previously hospitalized. Half of the patients spent an average of less than two weeks in the mental hospital during any given admission.

For some patients, a hospital admission may be the last step in a series of futile attempts to get help for their problems. We investigated whether patients obtained help in the two months prior to their hospitalization at the beginning of the study and found that only about half of the sample (46%) received help. Older patients were significantly more likely than younger patients [χ^2 (2) = 10.27, $p < .01$] to report seeing a professional for treatment or counseling preceding their most recent admission to the hospital. There was a nonsignificant trend for patients with more previous admissions to be more likely to seek services before entering the hospital.

The greatest percentage of patients who reported seeking help (22%) were seeing a psychiatrist, on the average of two days per month for less than one hour a visit. The chief purpose of the visit was to obtain or adjust their medication. Only 6 patients in the sample availed themselves of a self-help group, a source of support that has become increasingly popular among other categories of people with problems in living. In short, most of the mental health resources for diverting patients from the hospital were not reaching the bulk of persons in the sample.

Predicting Hospitalization

Another goal of the research was to identify predictors of recidivism. The measures included a variety of demographic, psychiatric, psychological, social, environmental, and familial factors, which previous research and theories had suggested as potential correlates of readmission—all patient characteristics, rather than system characteristics or treatments. The outcome or criterion measure of recidivism was defined as the number of times patients were readmitted to the hospital during the one year of the study. Only two of the variables were found to be significant predictors of readmission: age ($\beta = -.023$, $p < .01$) and number of prior admissions ($\beta = .053$, $p < .01$). Younger patients and patients with a history of previous psychiatric hospitalizations were more likely to be reinstitutionalized.

These findings are consistent with earlier research showing no relationship between recidivism and demographics, diagnosis, patients' self-reports, and clinical rating scales. Again, as in several previous investigations, prior hospitalization was the strongest predictor of rehospitalization. The relationship between age and readmissions is consistent with the prototype of the young chronic mental patient. Being young may be associated with a higher risk for recidivism because of denial of illness, treatment noncompliance, poverty, severity of illness, higher prevalence of schizophrenia, alcohol and drug abuse, dearth of social support, and/or greater perceived dependence on the hospital.

Jobs, Income, and Housing

The data demonstrated that most mental patients were living an impoverished existence. For all demographic groups, at least two-thirds of the patients were not employed two months prior to hospitalization, and almost 40% stated that they "had not earned enough money to pay their bills." As a consequence, mental patients must rely heavily on others for financial assistance. More than half of the sample (56%) were receiving public aid, and more than one-third (37%) were entirely dependent upon their families to survive economically.

These state mental patients in Chicago were also quite transient; 42% indicated that they had moved at least once during the 6 months preceding their hospitalization. Adequate housing remained a problem for many, with more than 30% of the respondents reporting that they "worried a great deal about a place to stay." Although only 21% of the sample were currently married, the vast majority of patients stated that they "lived with someone" when they were out of the hospital. Many of these living arrangements, however, were not permanent, as demonstrated by the prevalence of homelessness among patients.

Homelessness

Prior studies have shown that homelessness is a serious problem for a substantial number of mentally ill persons. Recent estimates of the homeless population indicate that between one-third ("Abandoned," 1986) and one-half (Lipton, Sabatini, & Katz, 1983) of the homeless are chronically mentally ill. Investigations of specific shelters for the homeless have yielded even more striking data. For example, Bassuk, Rubin, and Lauriat (1984) studied the residents of a typical shelter in Boston, and found that 91% had a diagnosable mental disorder, although not necessarily a chronic one. Similarly, Fischer et al. (1986) reported that 80% of the homeless (in a sample drawn from missions in Baltimore) were diagnosed as having had a mental disorder at some point in their lives. In interpreting these statistics, it should be noted that the causal relationship between homelessness and mental illness can run in either direction, and that different studies of homelessness define a "mental disorder" in broader or narrower ways. Nonetheless, there is abundant evidence to show that homelessness is a major problem among the mentally ill (see "Abandoned," 1986).

We explored the relationship between homelessness, mental illness, and hospitalization. Although many respondents stated that a psychological or psychiatric problem precipitated their admission (28%), a notable proportion (20%) of these Chicago-area patients viewed "housing problems" as the primary reason for their hospitalization. Most of the patients (73%) in unstable living situations (nearly 20% of the total sample) reported that they came to the hospital as a means of securing shelter. The homeless patients returned to the hospital more frequently than patients with more stable housing [$t(311) = 2.37, p < .08$]. Readmission for these patients is not only a function of decompensation or demoralization (Rossi, Fisher, & Willis, 1986), but it is also a product of ebbing personal assets. The hospital is not seen as a place for treatment; rather, it is seen as a source of warmth, food, companionship, and social support: a "haven," "a roof over one's head," "a warm meal," and "a place to see friends."

The following case vignettes illustrate patients' utilization of the mental hospital as a desirable, expedient, and exploitable resource (cf. Lewis & Hugi, 1981).

Anne, a 35-year-old black woman, claimed that the cause of her hospitalization was "survival," that she "didn't have any place to live properly." She vehemently denied any mental illness: "Treatment has nothing to do with it. I really need security, independence, and survival. I don't have a mental illness or emotional problem."

Betty, a 41-year-old white woman, claimed that the only treatment she required was to have "speedy living arrangements" made for her.

George, a tough-looking man in his mid-thirties with a lengthy criminal record, was accused of rape by a female resident of the facility where he resided. George believed that the management of the facility would accept the woman's word over his and send him to prison. Therefore, he cut his wrist, claimed he wanted to commit suicide, and was promptly sent to the mental hospital.

Hannah, a 21-year-old white woman, wanted to leave her halfway house. "They [people at the halfway house] were asking me to find another place to live and I couldn't. They were tired of me and I was tired of them. So I told a staff member that I wanted to commit suicide and they sent me to the hospital."

Patient Criminality

Because poverty and unemployment are often associated with crime, we investigated the criminal behavior of mental patients, as have numerous prior studies (e.g., Cocozza, Melick, & Steadman, 1978; Durbin, Pasewark, & Albers, 1977; Rabkin, 1979; Teplin, 1984). Our data present a somewhat inconsistent and complicated pattern. Patients' arrest records revealed that approximately 20% were arrested during the period studied, but only 11% of the arrests were for violent crimes against persons. Patients were most likely to be arrested for criminal damage/trespass to land and for disorderly conduct, and least likely to be arrested for drug possession and prostitution. Half of the patients interviewed admitted that they engaged regularly in income-generating activities that "caused them trouble with the law" (e.g., shoplifting, selling drugs, panhandling).

The criminal histories of the mental patients were more extensive and serious than suggested by their recent arrests. More than one-third (36%) had prior records, and among those who had been arrested during the study, 75% had prior records. In contrast to their recent arrest records, their criminal histories showed that 26% of the patients' past arrests were for alleged violent offenses (e.g., robbery, battery, assault).

Mental patients commit crimes for a variety of reasons, and three distinct categories of criminal mental patients were identified (Lurigio, 1987). The first type (42% of patients who committed crimes) were individuals whose involvement in illegal acts was a consequence of their illness. Their criminal histories generally contained offenses such as disorderly conduct, criminal trespass to land, disturbing the peace, and public intoxication. These patients engaged in few deliberate or intentional activities designed to break the law, and spent much of their time residing in and relying on institutions. Criminal behavior was incidental to their mental disorder, and being symptomatic in public appeared to be their only "crime."

The second type of patients involved in crime resorted to criminal behavior as an act of survival or desperation. Their criminal histories showed a number of nonserious property offenses (e.g., petty theft, shoplifting) and prostitution, which supplemented their meager incomes or welfare support. Criminal activity within this group occurred in spurts: i.e., a high rate of activity within an abbreviated time period followed by continuous months of no arrests. This pattern suggests that this type of criminal patient may be resorting to crime during periods of heightened impoverishment or hardship. Their criminal intent was dubious, and it appeared unlikely that they had truly adopted a criminal lifestyle.

The third type of patients who commit crimes were those whose offenses raised a concern for public safety: residential burglary, assault, rape, and robbery. Their criminal histories were indistinguishable from criminals not mentally ill with respect to type of offenses and the frequency and persistence of criminal activity. Compared to the other two groups, patients in this group were substantially more likely to be sentenced to probation or prison terms, and were also more likely to be involved in substance abuse and drug sales. Their mental disorder seemed incidental or secondary to their criminality. In addition, they were the least seriously impaired by their mental illness.

Use of Aftercare Services

The feasibility of deinstitutionalization is dependent in large part on the availability and use of aftercare services. Although community services have developed greatly in the past 3 years, they have not supplanted the hospital as the hub of patient care (Kohen & Paul, 1976), and their rate of growth has not kept pace with the burgeoning number of patients requiring aftercare to recover and readjust following their hospitalization.

Our study profiled service use by discharged patients in Chicago, and explored the relationship between service use and readmissions to state institutions. The vast majority of discharged patients who received aftercare (80%) were referred to these agencies by a psychiatric hospital or the psychiatric unit of a general hospital. Most patients were likely to keep their initial appointments at the aftercare agency and to continue in aftercare for 6 months or longer. Nearly half (49%) of the patients had been in aftercare for

more than one year. Nevertheless, the use of aftercare, in general, was unrelated to readmissions during a 6-month period following a recent hospitalization; i.e., patients who participated in aftercare were no less likely to remain out of the hospital, compared to patients who did not participate in aftercare [$\chi^2 (1) = .28$, ns].

CONCLUSIONS

As the present findings reveal, the lives of mental patients are plagued by poverty, homelessness, inadequate aftercare services, and a dearth of community-based resources to prevent repeat hospitalizations. Although decidedly fewer patients are currently being committed involuntarily, many are being coerced into psychiatric institutions. The typical state mental patient in Chicago is an indigent, black male, without a job, without any interest in traditional treatment, without close family or community ties, and without any real hope of recovering fully from their disorder or emerging from the oppressive conditions of the underclass.

The plight of the urban mental patient appears less a result of psychiatric illness and more a by-product of poverty, stigmatization, disenfranchisement, and estrangement from family and friends. Some patients drift into illegal activities as a strategy for survival, and most return eventually to the refuge of the state hospital, which often represents their only stable environment and source of support. This is especially true of younger patients, who may find it overwhelming to grapple with the stressful demands and responsibilities of early adulthood.

The practical and policy implications of the research reported in this paper suggest that the most effective interventions for chronic patients would not be couched in psychiatric terms but rather in terms of decent housing, employment, and family relations. It seems likely that patients will not benefit much from more sophisticated treatments or medications in the absence of basic social and economic supports. We should be offering them viable avenues to move away from the periphery and closer to the mainstream of society. Mental illness can cripple a person's ability to cope with the same conflicts, problems, and demands that confront functioning members of the community. Our first responsibility is to alleviate their economic burdens through better public aid and housing opportunities. In addition, interventions should equip patients with the requisite skills to secure gainful employment and to reestablish important interpersonal relationships. Mental health care must begin to focus in large measure on helping patients master the basics of living outside the institution. This is the foremost challenge and obligation of both policymakers and service providers.

References

Abandoned. 1986, January 6. *Newsweek*, pp. 14–20.

American Federation of State, County, and Municipal Employees. 1975. *Deinstitutionalization: Out of Their Beds and into the Streets.* Washington, D.C.

Bassuk, E. L.; Rubin, L.; and Lauriat, A. 1984. Is homelessness a mental health problem? *American Journal of Psychiatry* 141:1546–1550.

Cocozza, J. J; Melick, M. E.; and Steadman, H. J. 1978. Trends in violent crime among ex-mental patients. *Criminology* 16:317–334.

Durbin, J.; Pasewark, R.; and Albers, D. 1977. Criminality and mental illness: A study of arrest rates in a rural state. *American Journal of Psychiatry* 134:80–83.

Fischer, P. J.; Shapiro, S.; Breakey, W.; Anthony, J.; and Kramer, M. 1986. Mental health and social characteristics of the homeless: A survey of mission users. *American Journal of Public Health* 76:514–524.

Gruenberg, E., and Archer, J. 1979. Abandonment of responsibility for the seriously mentally ill. *Milbank Memorial Fund Quarterly/Health and Society* 57:485–506.

Kohen, W., and Paul, G. L. 1976. Current trends and recommended changes in extended-care placement of mental patients: The Illinois system as a case in point. *Schizophrenia Bulletin* 2:575–594.

Lewis, D. A., and Hugi, R. 1981. Therapeutic stations and the chronically treated mentally ill. *Social Service Review* 55:206–220.

Lewis, D. A.; Wagenaar, H.; Riger, S.; Rosenberg, H.; Reed, S.; and Lurigio, A. J. In press. *Worlds of the Mentally Ill: How Deinstitutionalization Works in the City.* Carbondale: Southern Illinois University Press.

Lipton, F. R.; Sabatini, A.; and Katz, E. 1983. Down and out in the city: The homeless mentally ill. *Hospital and Community Psychiatry* 34:817–821.

Lurigio, A. J. 1987. Toward a taxonomy of the criminal mental patient. Unpublished manuscript, Center for Urban Affairs and Policy Research, Northwestern University.

Rabkin, J. 1979. Criminal behavior of discharged mental patients: A critical appraisal of the research. *Psychological Bulletin* 86:1–27.

Rose, S. M. 1979. Deciphering deinstitutionalization: Complexities in policy and program analysis. *Milbank Memorial Fund Quarterly* 57:429–460.

Rossi, P. H.; Fisher, G. A.; and Willis, G. 1986. *The Condition of the Homeless of Chicago.* Amherst: Social and Demographic Research Institute, University of Massachusetts.

Teplin, L. A. 1984. Criminalizing mental disorder: The comparative arrest rate of the mentally ill. *American Psychologist* 39:794–803.

Tessler, R. C., and Goldman, H. H. 1982. *The Chronically Mentally Ill: Assessing Community Support Programs.* Cambridge, Mass.: Ballinger.

Trotter, S., and Kutter, B. 1974, February 24. Back wards to back alleys. *Washington Post.*

Weinstein, A. S. 1983. The mythical readmission explosion. *American Journal of Psychiatry* 140:1443–1446.

U.S. Department of Health, Education, and Welfare. 1980. *The National Nursing Home Survey: 1977 Summary for the United States.* DHEW Publication no. PHS 79-1794. Washington, D.C.: U.S. Government Printing Office.

CHAPTER 16

AIDS

INTRODUCTION

In 1981 the Center for Disease Control reported the first case of acquired immune deficiency syndrome (AIDS). The first cases involved male homosexuals and did not attract much attention. But four years later the public was shocked to learn that the deadly disease had ravaged a celebrity actor, Rock Hudson. In the next few years Dr. C. Everett Koop, the surgeon general, generated considerable controversy by sending a booklet to every household in the United States explaining the risks of human immunodeficiency virus (HIV) and urging the use of condoms to prevent infection. The biggest media splash of the AIDS crisis occurred in 1991 with the news of Magic Johnson's affliction. Rock Hudson's case was widely publicized, but his homosexual background reinforced the impression that AIDS was a special problem of gay men. Magic Johnson's case was different. He is an athlete, unquestionably straight, and had acquired the HIV through a heterosexual relationship. Suddenly the AIDS crisis had shifted from gay men and intravenous drug users to the general population of heterosexual men and women.

By the 1990s most experts estimated that the AIDS epidemic had spread to 1 to 3 million Americans. In one decade it had moved through three distinct phases. AIDS began with active homosexual and bisexual men, who congregate in such cities as San Francisco, New York, and Chicago. The second AIDS wave spread to intravenous drug users, who were predominantly poor blacks and Hispanics. Most recently, HIV transmission has moved to straight men and women and to their children. Since the period from infection with HIV to AIDS symptoms ranges from a few years to a decade, it is difficult to determine the full extent of the AIDS epidemic. Whatever the precise statistics, the numbers continue to mount dramatically in the United States and other parts of the world. AIDS will remain a major social problem for the foreseeable future. Many aspects of AIDS can be examined as a social problem. One major problem has been the failure of public and private organizations to respond to the crisis once it was identified. People at all levels of government have proved reluctant to mobilize preventive strategies or to provide adequate medical care for the victims. Two investigators report that "New York City did not begin funding for AIDS until well into 1984, when there were already 1,700 cases."[1]

Second, AIDS has had a devastating impact on gay men and racial minorities. The AIDS crisis represents the larger failure of society to overcome poverty and discrimination. Third, AIDS provides a clear example of the American tendency to view most social problems as failures of individual responsibility (if you live a straight life and avoid drugs, you won't get AIDS), rather than as conditions that require public action.

AIDS places considerable strain on individuals who care for their AIDS-stricken loved one as well as on hospitals, hospices, and other health-care institutions. Two essays in this chapter explore various aspects of this problem. Marilyn Chase writes about the stressful overload that volunteers are facing in San Francisco. Brad Edmondson calls attention to the larger demographic problem of providing medical assistance to increasing numbers of chronically ill people. He sees parallels between the AIDS crisis of the 1990s and the emerging crisis of health care for an aging population.

Mark S. Kaplan addresses the question of how a thoughtful person sorts out the private affairs of responsible living and the public issues of the welfare of all citizens, including marginal people who are vulnerable to AIDS. Kaplan offers important insights on this question.

The last essay in this chapter is a powerful statement on the private crisis of AIDS patients who confront the ultimate questions of life and death. Kent L. Sandstrom gives us a vivid account of the intimate drama of persons with AIDS who continue to live their daily lives with a deep awareness that their social identities have undergone a profound transformation. At this existential level, there is little room for consideration of policy debates and economic trends. This personal crisis faces over one million Americans in the 1990s.

[1] Charles Perrow and Mario Guillen, *The AIDS Disaster* (New Haven, Conn.: Yale University Press, 1990), p. 2.

43. VOLUNTEERS' DISTRESS CRIPPLES HUGE EFFORT TO PROVIDE AIDS CARE

MARILYN CHASE

Thanks to an army of volunteers, [San Francisco] has lavished more humane and generous care on its AIDS sufferers than any other big city in the country. Volunteers have provided the ill and dying a multitude of free services, from counseling to hot meals to housecleaning, that would cost millions of dollars a year if provided by professionals. The city wears its tradition of volunteerism like a cloak of honor. The effort has become a model, as yet unmatched, for AIDS-care programs around the land.

But its heart and soul—cadres of dedicated volunteers—are suffering from battle fatigue or burnout, or from the disease itself, "The San Francisco model is near collapse," a city task force reported to Mayor Art Agnos recently.

New recruits, many of them female, are enlisting in insufficient numbers to cope with San Francisco's increasing number of AIDS sufferers. Of the city's population of 715,000, about 8,000 are AIDS patients. By 1993, the number is expected to nearly double to 15,000. Because improved medical care has prolonged the lives of patients, their need for other services is being prolonged, too. Yet the force of volunteer caregivers is shrinking.

EMOTIONAL TRAUMA

"Literally hundreds of thousands of hours have been voluntarily given to support the San Francisco model of community-based care," Lee Smith, president of Levi Strauss & Co.'s international division and a member of the mayor's task force, said in recent congressional testimony.

"But past and current volunteers cannot keep up with the burgeoning caseload."

A CONSUMING EFFORT

Five years ago, Mr. Parmley began his volunteer experience answering calls on the AIDS Foundation's hotline. To help deal with the many callers who had medical questions, he began compiling medical-journal reports into a thick reference book. Then he was drawn into foundation policymaking and educational and legislative campaigns. With his regular job he found himself putting in 70- and 80-hour weeks.

Home offered no respite. "My house became AIDS West," he says. Many patients gave him power of attorney to manage their finances and, he says, he found himself "making decisions for them with their doctors—and then burying them. It was too hard on me. I'd been taking care of over 50 people I'd lost. My life was work, taking care of people, and the foundation."

He developed severe pain, compounded by stress, from a pinched sciatic nerve. "I got to the point where I couldn't walk," he says. "I became very emotional, withdrawn." He quit his volunteer work a year ago, and since then has pursued hobbies and found new friends. He contemplates doing some volunteer work again. "But I don't think I'll ever return to the level of intensity I had in the past," he says. "Some of us have just spent too many years in it."

For most volunteers, stress works in subtler ways. For Bruce Werner, volunteering began as an antidote to his personal grief and led to a more generalized mourning. A 44-year-old employee of a large corporate travel agency, he began his volunteer work when his companion died of AIDS in 1984. "I was very depressed and suicidal," he says. "It was either volunteer or check out, and I didn't feel like checking out."

GUILT AND FRUSTRATION

For five years, he manned a phone at the AIDS Hotline, consoling others and buoying his own spirits at the same time. "It helped me. It was a support group," he says. Then his energy began to ebb, as his guilt mounted over being healthy amid the suffering.

"You get calls from people who've just been diagnosed, and think they're going to die in a year. You get calls from people who've been thrown out of their homes. You hear a lot of hard-luck stories. . . . It was getting very hard," he says.

"Sometimes you feel guilty because you don't experience illness and death as deeply" as the clients, he adds. "And you're frustrated because you can't do more." As a result, he says, "I started calling in sick, and that isn't like me. I needed to back off a bit. The exhaustion is real."

Mr. Werner finally took a year off. He plans to rejoin the volunteer corps. "I was raised a Calvinist," he says. "We're right up there where guilt is concerned." Now he describes himself as "numb, a tough old cactus."

Ruth Brinker, founder of a volunteer program, has quit doing volunteer work herself. The elegant, silver-haired widow began Project Open Hand in 1984. Now a brisk, industrial-style operation, it turns donated food into 1,500 meals a day for AIDS patients. Mrs. Brinker long did double duty as Open Hand's chief executive officer and as a volunteer delivery worker, making the rounds in her car every evening after a day of administration work. "It's very satisfying," she says of the volunteer duty. "People wait for [us] at the window. We get to provide a service that's vital to existence."

But stew and solace cannot fend off death. Every week for three years, a name or two on Mrs. Brinker's client list disappeared. "It had gotten so painful, with the accumulated deaths, that I needed to divorce myself, to put some distance between me and the clients," she says. "I have watched too many people die, people that I had gotten to know well and become fond of. Even now that I don't do deliveries, when I hear someone has gone, I feel a pang."

To conserve her energy and keep the program alive, she now sticks to office work, especially the enlistment of fresh volunteers from new sources such as churches and ethnic communities. "I'm committed to staying with this program until the end of the epidemic," she says. "It's so important. We just simply must continue."

Glenn Cooper tried to avoid burnout by making a practical contribution, scrubbing and sweeping instead of counseling. The 35-year-old manager of computer services for Morrison & Foerster, a San Francisco law firm, signed on with Shanti Project's corps of practical support volunteers, doing housework.

"I thought it wouldn't be as emotionally draining as doing other kinds of support," he says. "It turned out to be not so easy. I found myself becoming quite attached to people."

SAYING GOODBYE

Each Saturday, he headed to the house of a client to wash the laundry and scrub toilets and sinks. He recalls a client who, at first, was embarrassed to accept such help; eventually he became confused from the neurological complications of AIDS and utterly dependent on Mr. Cooper's services. "It was as if I became his mother," Mr. Cooper says. "I'd come in and clean. Babysitting was what we called it. I'd take his temperature, give his medication. By Christmas of 1988, during the holiday festivities, he was sinking fast. I got a call to go over if I wanted to say goodbye. I said goodbye and wiped the sink for the last time. If he knew me, he didn't acknowledge it. It was as if he was asleep."

Mr. Cooper had to withdraw from the work for several months. With his next client, he tried to stay more detached. But once again, his client's death brought a sense of desolation and displacement. "I went over to help pack up," he says. "It was awkward. I wanted to grab a broom, but his roommates were having a professional come in. I needed a sense of direction. So I packed up records and sheets. There certainly was, in an emotional sense, burnout."

After another hiatus, Mr. Cooper is now weighing his options. "I was thinking about running away from the emotional attachment," he acknowledges. "But I have framed pictures of these two gentlemen by my bedside. I have decided it's worthwhile."

If it is hard for the healthy to stay on their feet, it is even harder for those with AIDS who volunteer. Larry Hjort, 42 years old, was diagnosed with AIDS in 1986 and has been on disability from his job with a national medical organization since 1988. He recently started a second career as a trainer of emotional support volunteers at Shanti Project. He knows that if burnout doesn't limit his tenure, the virus will.

"A lot of people who used to volunteer are dead," he says bluntly. "How else can you say it? They got involved early in their diagnosis, or before they knew. Every month there's another obit for a former volunteer, and that hasn't helped. A lot of their friends get burned out. I've only done it for a year," he adds. "I don't know if I could hold up for four or five years. I doubt it."

"BRAVE EXPERIMENT"

The toll taken by burnout, amid a rising caseload, means that the demand for volunteer services outstrips supply right now. For the first time since its founding, Shanti Project has been unable to accommodate all the requests it gets for volunteer assistance. "We have these tremendous waiting lists," says Holly Smith, spokeswoman for Shanti, which needs to recruit 770 new volunteers this year, more than doubling its current rolls. "I'm concerned. But it [recruitment] has to succeed. The reality is, we're not going to be able to get the dollars to provide the service. That's the bottom line."

San Francisco's situation serves as a reminder to the rest of the country that volunteer care depends on a finite amount of human energy, says Robert Munk, an official of the AIDS Service Providers Association of the Bay Area, a coalition of 100 volunteer agencies. "People are living longer, so the total number of people with AIDS will continue for many years," he says. "These volunteer efforts are services that other communities are paying cash for. That's why the San Francisco model has cost less. But the day of reckoning is here; the crunch is at hand."

Given current fiscal strains, it seems improbable that sufficient financial aid will be forthcoming to pay professionals to do the work currently done gratis by volunteers here in San Francisco. But absent such cash infusions—or an outpouring of new volunteers that isn't in sight—the outlook for AIDS-care programs and their patients is dreary.

Many more may be condemned to wait out their days in general-hospital wards, further burdening an AIDS-care system already bursting at the seams. Elsewhere the outlook for comprehensive AIDS care is at least as grim. In cities with large numbers of AIDS patients, such as New York, Chicago, Dallas, Houston, and Miami, volunteer networks are less developed than San Francisco's. These cities already rely heavily on their public hospitals and emergency rooms as caretakers of last resort, and as burnout thins their already meager ranks of volunteers the care crunch will intensify.

June Osborne, dean of the University of Michigan School of Public Health and chairman of the National Commission on AIDS, says volunteers shouldn't be asked to make up for the nation's lack of comprehensive AIDS care. She calls San Francisco's volunteer system "a historic and heroic response . . . a brave experiment, but probably doomed from the start."

44.   AIDS AND AGING

BRAD EDMONDSON

In 1940, pneumonia was a life-threatening disease, most babies were born at home, and Americans could expect to live 63 years. Today, most pneumonia can be controlled by antibiotics, nearly all babies are born in hospitals, and the average American lives 75 years. Medicine has made astonishing progress in this century. But now it is confronting its economic limits.

Spending on health care has risen from 9 percent of the gross national product in 1980 to 12 percent today. It could reach 15 percent by 2000, according to the Health Care Financing Administration. Employer spending on health insurance has risen three times faster than wages since 1980, and stood at $140 billion in 1988, according to the U.S. Chamber of Commerce. Government spending added another $230 billion. And despite these costs, an estimated 37 million Americans are uninsured, according to the Washington, D.C.-based Employee Benefits Research Institute.

As we head into the 1990s, two of America's sacred cows are on a collision course. The doctor's oath to preserve human life is at odds with the corporate need to make a profit. A collision is inevitable because two demographic forces will drive the need for care to historic highs in the near future. The crunch will forever change American health care, and the institutions that pay for it.

The first demographic force is AIDS. AIDS, or acquired immuno-deficiency syndrome, is caused by a virus, so it spreads like any other viral epidemic—geometrically. The first 295 cases were reported to the Centers for Disease Control (CDC) in 1981, followed by 5,905 cases

in 1984, 25,471 in 1987, and an estimated 53,000 to 60,000 in 1990. The CDC estimates that between 800,000 and 1.3 million Americans are infected with the virus that causes AIDS—HIV. Most will eventually develop the disease, which is proving itself to be nearly 100 percent fatal.

Treating AIDS is an expensive proposition. According to a 1987 study by the Rand Corporation, the lifetime medical cost of an AIDS patient in his 30s is between $70,000 and $141,000. That is much more than the lifetime cost of treating someone in his 30s who has a heart attack ($67,000), digestive cancer ($47,000), or leukemia ($29,000). In the 1990s, treating AIDS will cost tens of billions of dollars each year.

By now, most Americans know that AIDS is deadly. Yet 88 percent don't know anyone who has the disease, according to the National Center for Health Statistics. That's because more than 90 percent of AIDS victims are homosexual men or drug users. They are highly concentrated in a few neighborhoods.

Half of all AIDS cases are in the New York City, Los Angeles, San Francisco, Miami, or Houston metropolitan areas. Half of all AIDS cases are treated by only 5 percent of hospitals. Just ten hospitals care for fully one-third of AIDS patients, according to the National Public Health and Hospital Institute.

At hospitals like San Francisco General and St. Vincent's in New York City, AIDS lives up to its reputation as a plague. But to most middle- and upper-class Americans, the disease remains remote. Those who are not at risk of catching AIDS tend to ignore it. But they ignore it at their peril, because AIDS has a lesson to teach. It is showing us how we need to prepare for the second demographic force: the aging of the American population.

Stress exposes the weak points of any system. The stress of AIDS has exposed the weak points of American health care: the lack of preventive medicine, a shortage of facilities to treat chronic

From *American Demographics*, March 1990, pp. 28–34. Copyright © 1990 *American Demographics*. Reprinted with permission of *American Demographics*.

Brad Edmondson is executive editor of American Demographics.

conditions, and no universal access to health insurance. These weak points are so troubling that Lee Iacocca and other top corporate leaders are now lobbying for legislation that would socialize medicine. They realize that if the flaws in our health-care system are not corrected, the plight of AIDS patients today will foreshadow the geriatric care all Americans will receive in the future.

THE LAST YEAR OF LIFE

Today, 13 million Americans have celebrated their 75th birthday. The number of Americans aged 75 and older will grow 26 percent between 1990 and 2000 and by another 26 percent between 2001 and 2020, according to Census Bureau projections. By 2040, baby boomers will push the numbers in this age group to fully 37 million.

Today, 1 American in 20 is aged 75 or older. In 2040, it will be at least 1 in 8. These census projections are conservative; they assume that recent declines in mortality will not continue. If mortality continues to decline at a rate of 2 percent a year, the number of 75-to-84-year-olds will be 25 percent greater in 2040 than the Census Bureau projects. The number of Americans aged 85 and older will be 83 percent greater, according to a report in the *Milbank Quarterly.*

Like AIDS deaths, the deaths of the very old are costly. That's because the elderly often need long-term care. Canadian men aged 45 to 64 spend an average of only 7 days in a nursing home in the year before their death, compared with 111 days for men aged 85 and older. For Canadian women, the average rises from 10 days for 45-to-64-year-olds to 173 days for those aged 85 and older, according to the records of the universal health insurance program in Manitoba, Canada. Overall, the deaths of those aged 85 and older cost 31 percent more than the deaths of those aged 75 to 84, and 79 percent more than those aged 65 to 74, according to a study reported in the *Milbank Quarterly.*

In the diverse health-care system of the U.S., costs are harder to track than in Canada. But there is evidence already that aging is stressing American hospitals. Patients aged 65 and older accounted for 31 percent of all discharges from

U.S. hospitals in 1987, up from 16 percent in 1965.

Both AIDS patients and the aged often need expensive drug therapies. Scientists now believe that those infected with HIV will live longer if they receive the drugs AZT, which keeps the virus from reproducing, and pentamidine, which helps prevent pneumonia. The median annual cost of these drugs is about $10,500 per patient. Giving them to every infected person would cost $10.2 billion, according to a 1988 study in the *Journal of the American Medical Association.* Similarly, many of the drugs used to treat the chronic conditions suffered by the elderly are also expensive. The anti-cancer drug Interferon costs more than $5,000 a year, for example.

The cost of care for chronic conditions has health administrators and insurers scrambling to get dying patients out of hospitals and back home or into hospices. Because AIDS victims and the aged both suffer from chronic, debilitating illnesses, both are heavy users of home health care and personal services. In New York City, volunteers from the Gay Men's Health Crisis provide many services for free. But as the nation ages, the need for these services is likely to overwhelm voluntary efforts.

Home-based services will be the fastest-growing segment of health care for decades to come. But as AIDS shows, dying at home is not what it used to be.

HOSPITALS VS. HOSPICES

San Francisco has gained a reputation as the city that cares about AIDS. At the earliest stages of the epidemic, volunteer groups like the Shanti Project, San Francisco AIDS Foundation, and Hospice of San Francisco emerged to provide care. Today, as the city's cumulative case load approaches 8,000, most of the funds for AIDS come from local taxes.

The goal of San Francisco's AIDS groups is to keep patients out of the hospital as long as possible. The result is that the cost of care for AIDS patients is much less in San Francisco than in other parts of the country. At San Francisco General Hospital, AIDS patients averaged a 12-day stay in 1984, costing $9,000, according to the

Journal of the American Medical Association. In the same year, New York City's AIDS patients averaged a 25-day stay costing $20,300, according to an article in the *New York State Journal of Medicine.*

One reason why San Francisco has managed the AIDS crisis so well is because most AIDS victims there are white, well-educated, and affluent homosexual men. In New York City, drug users account for most new cases, and the majority of AIDS victims are black or Hispanic. San Francisco's gay community has enormous political clout. New York City's junkies have no clout, no money, and no health insurance. When they get sick, they go to the hospital and stay there.

This relative lack of community care has created a health-care crisis in New York. St. Vincent's is jammed with AIDS patients who have nowhere to go, making it difficult to find beds for patients with other problems. City officials announced plans for an AIDS shelter last fall, but it may be a case of too little, too late: at one hospital in the Bronx, the share of emergency-room patients who tested positive for HIV jumped from 13 percent to 38 percent in the past year. The city's health commissioner estimates that the cost of treating AIDS over the next five years will approach $7 billion.

Community-based care cuts medical costs, and it allows the dying to make the most of the time they have left. But there's one catch: community care now depends on voluntary efforts, and often the volunteers aren't there.

AIDS reveals that community-based care doesn't work in our poorest communities. It raises the prospect of an aging America where the haves die at home surrounded by family or friends, while the have-nots die alone in human warehouses.

THE SOONER THE BETTER

In some important ways, AIDS patients are different from the dying elderly. Elderly Americans are partly protected by universal health insurance, for example. And the aged are usually better candidates for home health care than are drug addicts.

But the similarities between AIDS patients and the aged are greater than their differences.

Both face chronic, debilitating conditions like weight loss, dementia, depression, and infections. To stay at home, both depend on informal networks of relatives and friends. And like a growing number of the elderly, many persons with AIDS either live alone or depend on people who are also vulnerable to illness.

Most caregivers agree that the most humane, cost-effective way to treat the chronically ill is to provide home services and hospices rather than hospitals and nursing homes. Hospitals favor home health care because it eases overcrowding and boosts profits. "Self-interest will move them in that direction," says Dr. Mervyn Silverman, president of the American Foundation for AIDS Research. Most AIDS patients end up being supported by the public, and "I don't know too many hospitals that are making a killing on Medicaid," he told the *Healthcare Forum Journal.*

Insurers and employers also favor home health care because it promises to save them money. But while home health care is more humane and cost effective when it keeps AIDS patients out of the hospital, it may not work as well for the aged. Hospices and home care do not save money if they replace unpaid help, which is often the case with the elderly. One national study found that family members provided about ten hours of care a day to relatives who died at home. If paid help substitutes for this unpaid family care, home care may actually increase the cost of treating chronic conditions, says professor A. E. Benjamin of the University of California–San Francisco, in the *Milbank Quarterly.*

Those who push for home health care now may regret it later. The real cost of home care may be hidden because so many AIDS patients depend on public support. This means that employers and private insurers so far have dodged the full cost of AIDS. But everyone ages, and private insurers whose plans expand to cover home care could end up with an enormous liability.

AIDS shows that when childless, unmarried people develop a terminal disease, they need one of two things: an outpouring of support from their friends, or a health-care payer with deep pockets. As the ranks of childless and unmarried Americans continue to grow, rising costs will push the health-care system toward two solutions: increased support for nonprofit community care groups, and a national health-insurance system.

EVERYTHING, WITHIN LIMITS

The United States spends 12 percent of its gross national product on a health-care system that excludes millions of people, and which is threatened by AIDS and aging. In contrast, Canada provides care to everyone at 8.6 percent of its GNP. Other Western countries spend even less. Like Canada, they have national health insurance.

American businesses, some of whose competitors are based in Canada or Europe, are looking at health-care costs and seeing red. "I never thought I would be in favor of a government health policy, but there are some things the government must do," Robert Mercer told the *New York Times*. "We have to spread the burden."

Mercer isn't a socialist; he's the former chairman of Goodyear Tire and Rubber Company. A growing number of America's corporate captains now see national health care as a way to regain their competitive edge in the global marketplace.

Some employers think they can tame health-care costs by shifting more of the burden onto their employees. Others think they can cut costs by getting more involved. Caterpillar, Inc., administers its own health claims. Southern California Edison operates 10 clinics for its 57,000 employees.

But companies large and small have had little success with cost containment. General Electric's health-care costs per employee rose 17 percent in 1987 and 13 percent in 1988, and were projected to rise 20 to 25 percent in 1989, said Art Puccini, vice president for labor relations, in a speech last year. The company now spends just

under $1 billion a year on health care, despite aggressive cost-containment measures. The average cost of health care for companies with fewer than 100 employees rose more than 30 percent in 1987, according to a survey by the National Association of Manufacturers. Such costs are enough to make the most avid free-market boosters "reexamine [their] thinking and positions with respect to government-sponsored national health insurance," said Puccini.

The drive for universal health care is picking up speed at the state level. Hawaii already guarantees health care to all residents; a similar law takes effect in Massachusetts in 1992. Ohio is considering a state-run health plan. A New York proposal would require all businesses in the state to provide health insurance for their employees. At the federal level, Congress is considering a range of proposals, from full-scale national health care to minimum requirements on employers.

Revolutionary changes are on the horizon in the hospital industry as well. Financial pressure will force more than one-third of all hospitals to close or become specialized institutions by the turn of the century, according to the National Association for Hospital Development. Massachusetts already has a state board to decide which acute-care hospitals will be converted into nursing homes, mental hospitals, or drug treatment centers.

Epidemics expose fundamental strengths and weaknesses. The AIDS epidemic points the way to a new health-care system in which large general hospitals will be replaced by a variety of therapeutic environments. The health-services industry will continue to grow, but not by providing high-tech extensions of human life. The new focus will be on preventing problems, curing acute conditions, minimizing the effects of chronic disease, and accepting death with dignity.

45.   AIDS: INDIVIDUALIZING A SOCIAL PROBLEM

MARK S. KAPLAN

The failure of the U.S. Government to develop an effective policy to address the devastating and disproportionate impact of HIV-related (Human Immunodeficiency Virus) disease on the lives of minorities and the poor partly results from an individualistic social philosophy. This philosophy has pervaded and sustained constricted AIDS (Acquired Immune Deficiency Syndrome) policy formulations since the outbreak of the epidemic in 1981, when AIDS and HIV diseases were first associated with marginalized, oppressed, or feared groups.

Now the epidemic must also be seen in the United States as a phenomenon associated with social and developmental problems. By concentrating on the personal behavior of individuals, the underlying social and cultural forces associated with the changing configuration of the epidemic are all too often missed. According to the CDCs (Centers for Disease Control) black and Hispanic AIDS cases represent almost 42 percent of the total in the United States, although these ethnic groups make up only 18 percent of the population. At this writing, a black or Hispanic American is three times more likely than a white to develop AIDS. And while the life expectancy of an American white is about two years after diagnosis of AIDS, for a black or Hispanic, it is only 19 weeks. Of the approximately 1900 pediatric AIDS cases in the United States, 77 percent are black or Hispanic, while in New York City, of nearly 536 children with AIDS, 91 percent are from these groups. According to the Panos Institute, approximately 84 percent of

women with AIDS in New York City are black or Hispanic. AIDS is already the biggest single cause of death in New York City among black and Hispanic women aged 25 to 29, and by 1991, AIDS is likely to be the leading killer of women in their childbearing years.

A VALUE-CRITICAL ANALYSIS OF AIDS POLICY

This analysis parallels criticism by Irving Louis Horowitz, who feels that "[t]he human confrontation with the AIDS epidemic is at rock bottom a matter of values [rather] than of policies." Values are central to the AIDS policy domain. Values influence the selection and definition of a specific policy issue, goals, and objectives, as well as evaluation criteria. My intent is to make use of a mode of inquiry known as value-critical policy analysis. This mode of analysis seeks to unravel the underlying value systems of established policies, and the context nourishing these tacit assumptions. Value-critical policy analysis is also concerned with the social implications of value systems and their accompanying assumptions. This mode of inquiry provides a framework for considering the social problems arising from the underlying and ubiquitous assumptions governing HIV/AIDS policy formulations. An awareness of value systems places the policy enterprise in a wider context, perhaps alerting us to unthought-of consequences. Policy makers' failure to develop a positive response to the HIV/AIDS epidemic afflicting minority populations partly results from assumptions associated with the individualistic lifestyle paradigm of disease causality that pervades much of contemporary health research and practice. As with other diseases, current health policy assumes that individuals, through their behavior, exercise significant control over HIV infection.

The question of individual lifestyle as the cause of HIV infection reflects an inherently in-

From *Society*, January/February 1990, pp. 4–7. Copyright © 1990 Transaction Publishers. Reprinted with permission of Transaction Publishers.

Mark S. Kaplan is a National Cancer Institute Postdoctoral Fellow in the Institute for Health Promotion and Disease Prevention Research at the University of Southern California.

dividualistic bias. A disease could potentially be of the individual's own creation, but only in a very limited sense. HIV disease must not be seen exclusively as a self-induced condition. Rather, as Nick Freudenberg argues in the Spring 1988 issue of *Health/PAC Bulletin,* we must view HIV disease as a phenomenon that is "inseparably entwined in the social and political fabric of this country." As for evidence in support of this argument, in a recent speech to the International Child and Youth Care Conference, the President of the Panos Institute, Jon Tinker, said, ". . . in the United States and abroad, AIDS is increasingly becoming a disease of the poor and underprivileged." The poverty-related social complexion of the current AIDS/HIV phenomenon makes it necessary for policy makers and behavioral researchers to widen and even change traditional subjects of interest and to examine individual behavior in context or even shift the major interest to an exclusively structural or ecological orientation.

The individualistic paradigm remains firmly entrenched in prevention policy formulations aimed at HIV/AIDS, as well as other social problems. As Peter M. Hall comments in the *Journal of Applied Behavioral Science:*

Individualism has been and remains a powerful influence in our society. Not only is it one of our most cherished values, but it structures how we apprehend society and how we conceive and respond to social problems.

Individualism assumes and values that human beings are autonomous, responsible, creative, and active persons who should be free to develop their potentialities and abilities to the maximum extent, so long as they do not infringe upon others' rights.

Individualization of responsibility or personal accountability for HIV-risk behavior has contributed to a slow and weak response by policy makers and the public in confronting the AIDS problem. The reliance on conventional health education activities as the cornerstone of prevention policy as well as the main line of defense against the present social configuration of the AIDS epidemic has serious limitations. A value-critical analysis reveals the characteristically reductionist nature of the tacit assumptions associated with educational approaches.

What are these assumptions? First, conventional health education assumes that individuals are responsible for causing their own behavior. Second, it suggests that such behavior as dangerous sexuality and IV (intravenous) drug use are triggered by some cognitive deficit in an individual. Finally, the conventional approach assumes that such behavior can be altered by correcting the individual.

Jennie Naidoo, in *The Politics of Health Education,* criticizes the conventional health education approach on the following grounds: It "ignores health as a social problem; it wrongly assumes the existence of free choice; and it is ineffective in preventing [environmentally-induced] ill health." This criticism elicits the support of those who recognize the need to adopt an approach which considers systemic contributions to the HIV/AIDS epidemic.

AIDS POLICY IN A WIDER CONTEXT

Lifestyle theory is currently a central issue in the determination of AIDS prevention policy. This individualist paradigm took hold before the current concerns with HIV-related disease arose. Since the eighteenth century, there have been two distinct traditions in the evolution of health policy: the clinical heritage and the collective public health movement. The clinical heritage focused on curative interventions and the collective public health movement emphasized issues of disease prevention. The first public health movement, also known as the Great Sanitary Awakening (1840–1880), was spurred by the works of Rudolf Virchow, Friedrich Engels, and Edwin Chadwick. Chadwick, a disciple of Jeremy Bentham, and his colleagues labored for three years before bringing out in 1842 their monumental *Sanitary Condition of the Labouring Population in Great Britain.* In the report, Chadwick demonstrated with sound empirical epidemiology that disease was undeniably associated with economic status, habitation, and working conditions. The result of the report's findings led to the passage of the Public Health Act of 1848.

Health policy has undergone a major change since the mid–nineteenth century. The first public health revolution was concerned with the noxious social and physical environment. Its successor, the present-day public health revolution, is now concerned with the individual. Today, proponents link ill-health with misbehavior and unhealthy habits. To the lifestyle theorists, health promotion makes scientific and policy sense. By health promotion I refer to the lifestyle skills and individual competence to influence factors determining health. According to the British medical sociologist Michael Calnan, the individualistic tendencies of the current health promotion approaches to behavior-related disease (such as HIV/AIDS, lung cancer, and others) prevention policy make at least two important assumptions about the development of ill-health and how it should be controlled.

First, this approach relies on the medical model of disease causation and disease management, as it plays down the social and economic influences on health and emphasizes the individual as the fundamental unit of analysis. Second, the ideology of personal accountability presumes that individuals' responsibility for their behavior will be sufficient to lead to a major improvement in their health. The most salient underlying assumption holds that individuals have the power and autonomy to control their own spatio-temporal environment. Discussions of lifestyle behavior have largely ignored systemic influences, and instead focus almost exclusively on individual responsibility.

The individualistic lifestyle theory of disease causality and control is increasingly embraced by governments around the world. The United Kingdom and Canada took the initiative earlier in outlining the health problems facing the developed nations. British and Canadian policy makers emphasized their preventable nature and proposed individual-based preventive programs, such as health promotion. In 1974, the Federal Ministry of Health in Canada published the so-called Lalonde Report. (Marc Lalonde was then the Minister of National Health and Welfare.) This was followed in 1976 by the publication of *Prevention and Health: Everybody's Business* in the United Kingdom. The British Department of Health and Social Security stressed the need for individuals to take care of themselves by changing their lifestyles.

Following the British and Canadian lead, the U.S. Department of Health and Human Services released in 1979 the Surgeon General's Report on Health Promotion and Disease Prevention, *Healthy People*, heralded by some as the blueprint for the second public health revolution. The *Healthy People* report attempted a sweeping review of health in the United States and concluded with a lengthy series of recommendations designed to meet the problems of rising health care costs and those instances of morbidity and mortality that continue to command the attention of the medical profession. The thrust of the report was captured in the Secretary of Health and Human Services, Joseph Califano's, rousing introduction:

We are killing ourselves by our careless habits. . . . We are a long, long way from the kind of national commitment to good personal health habits that will be necessary to change drastically the statistics about chronic disease in America. . . . Americans can do more for their health than any doctor, any machine or hospital, by adopting healthy lifestyles.

As political scientists Deane Neubauer and Richard Pratt note, if Califano is correct, and if individuals do not transform their lifestyles, they will become dependent on medicine, the health-maintaining potential of which is limited. The only viable way for dealing with ill-health and the escalating cost of care is for the individual to make more intelligent lifestyle choices.

Individuals have some control over their lives. But it is a far cry from that to the current wisdom that "Just Say No to Drugs and Sex" will end the AIDS crisis. Most people's choices and behaviors are influenced by the conditions of the social relations they are caught up in. As sociologists William R. Arney and Bernard J. Bergen argue, discussing changes in lifestyles without first discussing the changes in social conditions which give rise to them, without recognizing that lifestyle is derivative, is misleading, and only blames the victims.

AIDS: AN ALTERNATIVE EXPLANATORY FRAMEWORK

What other limitations weaken the personal accountability lifestyle thesis? What alternative frameworks exist for connecting situational and environmental adversities, at-risk behavior, and HIV-related disease? Three issues demand consideration if we are to arrive at any possible answers. What is to be explained? What should the unit of analysis be? How will the explanation proceed? The answers to these questions are advanced as a prelude rather than the finished expression of an AIDS prevention doctrine or policy.

What needs to be explained is the transformation in the social complexion of the AIDS epidemic from a disease of gay white men to one that decimates minority populations, intravenous drug users, and their sexual partners. According to the United Nations International Narcotics Control Board, in some parts of Europe and the United States, more than half the AIDS sufferers contracted this disease through intravenous drug use. As Robert M. Swenson noted in a 1988 issue of *American Scholar*, in some areas of New York City, 80 percent of intravenous drug users are now infected with HIV. In July 1989, the CDC concluded that, of the 15,550 AIDS cases attributed to IV use, 80 percent are black or Hispanic. To control HIV disease in these populations, we might ask: What are the adverse social and material conditions associated with HIV transmission? Attention must be aimed at specifying the social constraints of large, economically depressed urban areas on the lives of the oppressed classes that make harmful behavioral choices appear optimal.

As for the proper unit of analysis in studying the HIV epidemic, the preponderance of the drug use literature focuses on the individual in explaining drug abuse and correspondingly targets most intervention efforts at the individual level. The phenomenon of drug abuse must be regarded as a social problem. The aim must be to place and relate the individuals and their behavior to the social and political context. There are powerful social forces which condition drug-taking phenomena. These include class structure, sexual divisions, and traditions of the local economy. Intravenous drug use must be examined in the context of the user's role and position in society.

Does community stress contribute to intravenous drug use? It is important to identify the social and psychological factors that are prevalent in the lower social classes that increase susceptibility to ill-health. In *Sociology in Medicine*, Mervyn W. Susser and colleagues note that "[e]conomic hardship, frustrated aspirations, chronic insecurity about jobs, frequent disruption of social ties, are all features of the lives of the working class and the poor." An adequate explanation of health-jeopardizing behavior must take proper account of these endemic stressors that influence the everyday life and material conditions of the poorer classes.

There are two different methods for developing explanations of the connection between IV drug use and AIDS: one can be called the empiricist, individual-level perspective which was described above, and the other, the materialist-realist approach. In contrast to the predominant individualistic perspective, the materialist strategy locates personal choice in the context of subcultures and their collective responses to adversities in the social and material environment.

The current exigencies of the HIV/AIDS epidemic call for an immediate educational campaign. Over the long haul, a broader public policy effort will have to be directed at the more general and complex problems of social organization which impact on the poor and minority communities, including health care, housing, education, food and nutrition, transportation, economics, employment, and urban design. To paraphrase S. M. Miller in *The Milbank Quarterly*, in the long run, reducing economic and social inequalities may be the only road to the achievement of a healthier and just society.

Readings Suggested by the Author

Adam, Barry D. 1989. The state, public policy, and AIDS discourse. *Contemporary Crises* 13.

Aggleton, Peter, and Homans, Hilary, eds. 1988. *Social Aspects of AIDS*. London: Falmer Press.

Crimp, Douglas, ed. 1988. *AIDS: Cultural Analysis/Cultural Activism*. Cambridge, Mass.: MIT Press.

Fee, Elizabeth, and Daniel M. Fox, eds. 1988. *AIDS: The Burdens of History*. Berkeley: University of California Press.

Neubauer, Deane, and Richard Pratt. 1981. The second public health revolution: A critical appraisal. *Journal of Health Politics, Policy and Law* 6.

Rodmell, Sue, and Alison Watt, eds. 1986. *The Politics of Health Education: Raising the Issues*. London: Routledge & Kegan Paul.

46.   CONFRONTING DEADLY DISEASE: THE DRAMA OF IDENTITY CONSTRUCTION AMONG GAY MEN WITH AIDS

KENT L. SANDSTROM

The phenomenon of AIDS (acquired immunodeficiency syndrome) has been attracting increased attention from sociologists. A number of observers have examined the social meanings of the illness (Conrad 1986: Sontag 1989; Palmer 1989), the social influences and behavior involved in its onset and progression (Kaplan et al. 1987) and the larger social consequences of the AIDS epidemic (Ergas 1987). Others have studied the "psychosocial" issues faced by individuals who are either diagnosed with the illness (Nichols 1985; Baumgartner 1986: Weitz 1989) or closely involved with someone who has been diagnosed (Salisbury 1986; Geiss, Fuller and Rush 1986; Macklin 1988).

Despite this growing interest in the social and psychosocial dimensions of AIDS, little attention has been directed toward the processes of social and self-interaction (Denzin 1983) by which individuals acquire and personalize an AIDS-related identity. Further, given the stigmatizing implications of AIDS, there has been a surprising lack of research regarding the strategies of stigma management and identity construction utilized by persons with this illness.

This article presents an effort to address these issues. It examines the dynamics of identity construction and management which characterize the everyday lives of persons with AIDS (PWAs). In doing so, it highlights the socially ambiguous status of PWAs and considers (a) the processes through which they personalize the illness, (b) the dilemmas they encounter in their interpersonal relations, (c) the strategies they employ to avoid or minimize potentially discrediting social attributions, and (d) the subcultural networks and ideologies which they draw upon as they construct, avow and embrace AIDS-related identities. Finally, these themes are situated within the unfolding career and lived experience of people with AIDS.

From *Journal of Contemporary Ethnography*, Vol. 19(3) October 1990, pp. 271–294. Copyright © 1990 Sage Publications, Inc. Reprinted with permission of Sage Publications, Inc.

METHOD AND DATA

The following analysis is based on data gathered in 56 in-depth interviews with 19 men who had been diagnosed with HIV (human immunodeficiency virus) infections. On the average, each individual was interviewed on three separate occasions and each of these sessions lasted from 1 to 3 hours. The interviews, conducted between July 1987 and February 1988, were guided by 60 open-ended questions and were audiotaped. Most interviews took place in the participants' homes. However, a few participants were interviewed in a private university office because their living quarters were not conducive to a confidential conversation.

Participants were initially recruited through two local physicians who treat AIDS patients and through a local self-help organization that provides support groups and services for people with HIV infections. Those individuals who agreed to be interviewed early in the study spoke with friends or acquaintances and encouraged them to become involved. The majority of interviews were thus obtained through "snowball" or chain-referral sampling.

By employing a snowball sampling procedure, we were able to gain fairly rapid access to persons with AIDS-related diagnoses and to discuss sensitive issues with them. However, due to its reliance on self-selection processes and relatively small social networks, this method is not likely to reflect the range of variation which exists in the population of persons with advanced AIDS-related infections. This study is thus best regarded as exploratory.

All respondents were gay males who lived in a metropolitan area in the Midwest. They varied in age, income, and the stage of their illness. In age, they ranged from 19 to 46 years, with the majority in the 28 to 40 age bracket. Six persons were currently employed in professional or white-collar occupations. The remaining 13 were living marginally on Social Security or disability benefits. Several members of this latter group had previously been employed in either blue-collar or service occupations. Seven individuals were diagnosed with AIDS, 10 were diagnosed with ARC (AIDS-related complex), and 2 were diagnosed as HIV positive but both had more serious HIV-related health complications (e.g., tuberculosis).

ON BECOMING A PWA: THE REALIZATION OF AN AIDS IDENTITY

For many of these men, the transformation of physical symptoms into the personal and social reality of AIDS took place most dramatically when they received a validating diagnosis from a physician. The following account reveals the impact of being officially diagnosed:

She [the doctor] said, "Your biopsy did come out for Kaposi's sarcoma. I want you to go to the hospital tomorrow and to plan to spend most of the day there." While she is telling me this, the whole world is buzzing in my head because this is the first confirmation coming from outside as opposed to my own internal suspicions. I started to cry—it [AIDS] became very real. . . *very real.* . . .

Anyway, everything started to roller coaster inside me and I was crying in the office there. The doctor said, "You knew this was the way it was going to come out, didn't you?" She seemed kind of shocked about why I was crying so much, not realizing that no matter how much you are internally aware of something, to hear it from someone else is what makes it real. For instance, the first time I really accepted being gay was when other people said "You are gay!" . . . It's a social thing—you're not real until you're real to someone else.

This quote illustrates the salience of social processes for the validation and realization of an identity—in this case, an AIDS-related identity. Becoming a PWA is not simply a matter of viral infection, it is contingent on interpersonal interaction and definitions. As depicted in the quote, a rather momentous medical announcement facilitates a process of identity construction which, in turn, entails both interpersonal and subjective transformation. Within the interpersonal realm, the newly diagnosed "AIDS patient" is resituated as a social object and placed in a marginal or liminal status. He is thereby separated from many of his prior social moorings. On the subjective level, this separation produces a crisis, or a disruption of the PWA's routine activities and self-understanding. The diagnosed individual is prompted to "make sense" of the meaning of his newly acquired status and to feel its implications for future conceptions and enactments of self.

PERSONALIZING THE ILLNESS: SELF-FEELINGS EVOKED BY AIDS

As he interprets and responds to the meaning of his condition, the diagnosed individual *personalizes* (Asher 1987) it, adjusting it to the distinctive features of his life (e.g., his work situation, family history, personal relationships, character traits, and access to resources). Certain self-feelings and psychic reactions are especially important in this personalizing process. For example, PWAs may feel anguished about the loss of their future, the loss of a highly valued job, or by a diminished sense of sexual desirability. They may also feel troubled by their loss of everyday skills or opportunities and their lack of involvement in normal interaction. The remarks shared by one interviewee are reflective of such sentiments:

Of course, I can't drive now and it is difficult to deal with the fact. That is a big loss, it really is . . . and also knowing that I can't go back to work. I'm getting used to not working but mentally it is a loss— your thinking is lessened. I don't have to give a quick answer anymore. When somebody would come up to me at work and ask a question, I would have the answer for them before they could even finish the question. Now that ability isn't there anymore. I had really enjoyed being able to do that.

These experiences of loss are typically accompanied by reactions of grief. Indeed, a few PWAs stressed that grief had become a predominant theme in their everyday lives. Most PWAs grieved about their loss of health, potential, and a normal life span. They also felt grief regarding the loss of previous sources of personal continuity and self-validation such as work, friendships, and sexual relationships.

Feelings of guilt can also be induced by an AIDS diagnosis. These feelings have several sources and dimensions. For instance, PWAs may feel guilty about the possibility that they infected their sexual partner(s). They may also feel guilty about the anguish, grief, or suffering

that their diagnoses provoke among partners, friends, or family members. Furthermore, they may experience identification guilt because they are members of groups which are stigmatized by cultural conceptions (Conrad 1986), media accounts (Seidman 1988) and conservative religious doctrines (Palmer 1989). These stigmatizing perspectives are sometimes internalized by PWAs and may lead them to (consciously or unconsciously) interpret their condition as a kind of punishment. Such a reaction is illustrated in the following remarks:

In the beginning, it [AIDS] triggered feelings that had to do with . . . well, I hesitate to say this but it was like I deserved this [illness]. This is exactly what I deserved! I've heard other gay men talk about the same thing like "God, we've tried to live such a decent life and we're being punished." We made that connection of somehow being punished . . . and even if we didn't come right out and say it was punishment or something, what we said or what I said was "Well, God's trying to tell us something here."

Finally, due to the fatality of this disease, being informed that one has AIDS can also elicit strong feelings of death anxiety:

After the doctor told me that I had Kaposi's sarcoma, I was really in bad shape. . . . I don't mean to be melodramatic but something inside me was saying "Holy shit, you're going to die! No, you're not going to just die but you're going to die very soon!"

An AIDS diagnosis can evoke powerful images of death which may result in shock, denial, panic, and despair. These reactions inhibit the ability of newly diagnosed individuals to understand the immediate effects of their condition, to cope more effectively with the symptoms associated with the illness, and to deal with the demands of their everyday lives. Also, feelings of severe death anxiety make it more likely for PWAs to oscillate between phases of denial, anger, bargaining, depression, and acceptance as they grapple with the prospective implications of their diagnosis (Nichols 1985).

In summary, emotions such as grief, guilt, and death anxiety emerge in response to the social and biographical ramifications of AIDS. These self-feelings become a vital part of the phenomenological experience of the diagnosed, influencing their interpretation and individuation of the meaning of their condition. Through these self-feelings, the illness is personalized and definitions of self are challenged, transformed, understood, and sustained.

The Liminal Situation of the PWA: Constraints and Opportunities

As an individual enters into and personalizes the status of being a PWA, he finds his life characterized by ambiguity. The manifestations and consequences of his HIV infection are unclear and unpredictable. He is uncertain about what specific symptoms will be triggered by his illness, how he will feel from day to day, how much longer he can expect to live, and whether or not he will be able to live with dignity (Weitz 1989).

In the social realm, the experience of the PWA is especially ambiguous. Given the fear and mystery that surround AIDS, responses of others to his diagnosis can range from avoidance, hostility, and rejection to empathy and support. Regardless of the specific reactions of others, a shift or rupture occurs in the individual's social location. The PWA is not only separated from his previous social anchorages but he is not clearly linked to any new ones. Also, given the diverse and competing social definitions of AIDS, he is not provided with a precise indication of his current status. The newly diagnosed PWA thus becomes situated as *liminal persona,* that is, he is "neither here nor there; he is betwixt and between the positions assigned by law, custom, convention and ceremonial" (Turner 1969, 95).

Most important, recently diagnosed PWAs encounter both the constraints and opportunities that go along with their liminal social situation. On one hand, their liminal location can intensify problematic self-feelings and provoke a sense of confusion about the implications of their illness. Further, the ambiguous social meaning of their condition makes it more difficult for them to enact an AIDS-related identity. That is, although PWAs are provided with a medical designation, they are [not] given a clear idea of what role or set of behavioral expectations correspond to this identity. They subsequently have few practical

guidelines for constructing a meaningful course of action.

In a more positive light, the liminal situation of PWAs can elicit a sense of power and opportunity. Feelings of empowerment can be derived from the mystery and danger associated with liminalty (Turner 1969). At the same time, a sense of opportunity can arise from the lack of conventions and guidelines applying to those with such a novel and ambiguous condition. In essence, since AIDS is a rather unique and vaguely understood phenomenon, PWAs are granted some room to improvise and maneuver when constructing a behavioral repertoire to go along with their medical identity. They are not simply constrained or captured by this identity. Instead, they are afforded a certain amount of power and opportunity to define what it means to be a PWA and to reshape the meaning of this identity in their social encounters. Nevertheless, in their ongoing efforts to construct and negotiate a viable identity, PWAs must grapple with a number of stigmatizing reactions and interpersonal dilemmas.

INTERPERSONAL DILEMMAS ENCOUNTERED BY PWAs

Stigmatization

Stigmatization is one of the most significant difficulties faced by people with AIDS as they attempt to fashion a personal and social meaning for their illness. The vast majority of our informants had already experienced some kind of stigma because of their gay identities. When they are diagnosed with AIDS, they usually encountered even stronger homophobic reactions and discreditation efforts. An especially painful form of stigmatization occurred when PWAs were rejected by friends and family members after revealing their diagnosis. Many respondents shared very emotional accounts of how they were ostracized by parents, siblings, or colleagues. Several noted that their parents and family members had even asked them to no longer return home for visits. However, rejections were not always so explicit. In many cases, intimate relationships were gradually and ambiguously phased out rather than abruptly or clearly ended.

A few PWAs shared stories of being stigmatized by gay friends or acquaintances. They described how some acquaintances subtly reprimanded them when seeing them at gay bars or repeatedly reminded them to "be careful" regarding any sexual involvements. Further, they mentioned that certain gay friends avoided associating with them after learning of their AIDS-related diagnoses. These PWAs thus experienced the problem of being "doubly stigmatized" (Kowalewski 1988), that is, they were devalued within an already stigmatized group, the gay community.

PWAs also felt the effects of stigmatization in other, more subtle ways. For example, curious and even sympathetic responses on the parts of others, especially strangers, could lead PWAs to feel discredited. One PWA, reflecting on his interactions with hospital staff, observed:

When they become aware [of my diagnosis], it seemed like people kept looking at me . . . like they were looking for something. What it felt like was being analyzed, both physically and emotionally. It also felt like being a subject or guinea pig . . . like "here's another one." They gave me that certain kind of look. Kind of that look like pity or that said "what a poor wretch," not a judgmental look but rather a pitying one.

An experience of this nature can precipitate a crisis of identity for a person with AIDS. He finds himself being publicly stigmatized and identified as a victim. Such an identifying moment can seriously challenge prior conceptions of self and serve as a turning point from which new self-images or identities are constructed (Charmaz 1980). That is, it can lead a PWA to internalize stigmatizing social attributions or it can incite him to search for involvements and ideologies which might enable him to construct a more desirable AIDS identity.

Counterfeit Nurturance

Given the physical and social implications of their illness, PWAs typically desire some kind of special nurturing from friends, partners, family members, or health practitioners. Yet displays of unusual concern or sympathy on the part of others can be threatening to self. People with AIDS may view such expressions of nurturance as counterfeit or harmful because they highlight their condition and hence confirm their sense of difference and vulnerability.

The following observation illustrates the sensitivity of PWAs to this problem:

One thing that makes you feel kind of odd is when people come across supportive and want to be supportive but it doesn't really feel like they are supportive. There is another side to them that's like, well, they are being nice to you because they feel sorry for you, or because it makes them feel good about themselves to help someone with AIDS, not because they really care about you.

PWAs often find themselves caught in a paradox regarding gestures of exceptional help or support. They want special consideration at times, but if they accept support or concern which is primarily focused on their condition, they are likely to feel that a "victim identity" is being imposed on them. This exacerbates some of the negative self-feelings that have already been triggered by the illness. It also leads PWAs to be more wary of the motivations underlying others' expressions of nurturance.

Given these dynamics, PWAs may reach out to each other in an effort to find relationships that are more mutually or genuinely nurturing. This strategy is problematic, though, because even PWAs offer one another support which emphasizes their condition. They are also likely to remind each other of the anomalous status they share and the "spoiled" features (Goffman 1963) of their identities qua PWAs.

Ultimately, suspicions of counterfeit nurturance can lead those diagnosed with AIDS to feel mistreated by almost everyone, particularly by caregivers who are most directly involved in helping them. Correctly or incorrectly, PWAs tend to share some feelings of ambivalence and resentment toward friends, lovers, family members, and medical personnel.

Fears of Contagion and Death Anxiety

Fears of contagion present another serious dilemma for PWAs in their efforts to negotiate a functional social identity. These fears are generated not only by the fact that people with AIDS are the carriers of an epidemic illness but also because, like others with a death taint, they are symbolically associated with mass death and the contagion of the dead (Lifton 1967). The situation may even be further complicated by the contagion anxiety which homosexuality triggers for some people.

In general, others are tempted to withdraw from an individual with AIDS because of their fears of contracting the virus. Even close friends of a PWA are apt to feel more fearful or distant toward him, especially when first becoming aware of the diagnosis. They may feel anxious about the possibility of becoming infected with the virus through interactions routinely shared with him in the past (e.g., hugging and kissing). They may also wish to avoid the perils of being stigmatized themselves by friends or associates who fear that those close to a PWA are a potential source of contagion.

Another dimension of contagion anxiety is reflected in the tendency of significant others to avoid discussing issues with a PWA that might lead them to a deeper apprehension of the death-related implications of his diagnosis. As Lifton (1967) suggested, the essence of contagion anxiety is embodied in the fear that "if I come too close to a death tainted person, I will experience his death and his annihilation" (p. 518).

This death-related contagion anxiety often results in increased strain and distance in a PWA's interactions with friends or family members. It can also inhibit the level of openness and intimacy shared among fellow PWAs when they gather together to address issues provoked by their diagnoses. Responses of grief, denial, and anxiety in the face of death make in-depth discussions of the illness experience keenly problematic. According to one respondent:

Usually no one's ever able to talk about it [their illness and dying] without going to pieces. They might start but it only takes about two minutes to break into tears. They might say something like "I don't know what to do! I might not even be here next week!" Then you can just see the ripple effect it has on the others sitting back and listening. You have every possible expression from anger to denial to sadness and all these different emotions on people's faces. And mostly this feeling of "what can we do? Well . . . Nothing!"

Problems of Normalization

Like others who possess a stigmatizing attribute, people with AIDS come to regard many social situations with alarm (Goffman 1971) and uncertainty (Davis 1974). They soon discover that their medical condition is a salient aspect of all but their most fleeting social encounters. They also quickly learn that their diagnosis, once known to others, can acquire the character of a *master status* (Hughes 1945; Becker 1963) and thus become the focal point of interaction. It carries with it "the potential for inundating the expressive boundaries of a situation" (Davis 1974, 166) and hence for creating significant strains or rupture in the ongoing flow of social intercourse.

In light of this, one might expect PWAs to prefer interaction contexts characterized by "closed" awareness (Glaser and Strauss 1968). Their health status would be unknown to others and they would presumably encounter fewer problems when interacting. However, when in these situations, they must remain keenly attuned to controlling information and concealing attributes relevant to their diagnosis. Ironically, this requirement to be dramaturgically "on" may give rise to even more feelings of anxiety and resentment.

The efforts of persons with AIDS to establish and maintain relationships within more "open" contexts are also fraught with complications. One of the major dilemmas they encounter is how to move interactions beyond an atmosphere of fictional acceptance (Davis 1974). A context of fictional acceptance is typified by responses on the part of others which deny, avoid, or minimize the reality of an individual's diagnosis. In attempting to grapple with the management of a spoiled identity, PWAs may seek to "break through" (Davis 1974) relations of this nature. In doing so, they often try to broaden the scope of interactional involvement and to normalize problematic elements of their social identity. That is, they attempt to project "images, attitudes and concepts of self which encourage the normal to identify with [them] (i.e., 'take [their] role') in terms other than those associated with imputations of deviance" (Davis 1974, 168).

Yet even if a PWA attains success in "breaking through," it does not necessarily diminish his interactional difficulties. Instead, he can become caught in an ambiguous dilemma with respect to the requisites of awareness and normalization. Simply put, if others begin to disregard his diagnosis and treat him in a normal way, then he faces the problem of having to remind them of the limitations to normalcy imposed by this condition. The person with AIDS is thus required to perform an intricate balancing act between encouraging the normalization of his relationships and ensuring that others remain sensitized to the constraining effects of such a serious illness. These dynamics promote the construction of relationships which, at best, have a qualified sense of normalcy. They also heighten the PWAs sense that he is located in an ambiguous or liminal position.

AVOIDING OR MINIMIZING DILEMMAS

In an attempt to avoid or defuse the problematic feelings, attributions, and ambiguities which arise in their ongoing interactions, PWAs engage in various forms of identity management. In doing so, they often use strategies which allow them to minimize the social visibility of their diagnoses and to carefully control interactions with others. These strategies including *passing, covering, isolation,* and *insulation.*

The particular strategies employed vary according to the progression of their illness, the personal meanings they attach to it, the audiences serving as primary referents for self-presentations, and the dynamics of their immediate social situation.

Passing and Covering

As Goffman (1963) noted in his classic work on stigma, those with a spoiled identity may seek to pass as normal by carefully suppressing information and thereby precluding others' awareness of devalued personal attributes. The PWAs we interviewed mentioned that "passing" was a maneuver they had used regularly. It was easily employed in the early stages of the illness when more telltale physical signs had not yet become apparent and awareness of an individual's diagnosis was [confined] to a small social circle.

However, as the illness progresses, concealing the visibility of an AIDS-related diagnosis becomes more difficult. When a person with AIDS begins to miss work frequently, to lose weight noticeably, and to reduce his general level of activity, others become more curious or suspicious about what ailment is provoking such major changes. In the face of related questions, some PWAs elected to devise a "cover" for their diagnosis which disguised troubling symptoms as products of a less discrediting illness.

One informant decided to cover his AIDS diagnosis by telling co-workers that he was suffering from leukemia:

There was coming a point, I wasn't feeling so hot. I was tired and the quality of my life was decreasing tremendously because all of my free time was spent resting or sleeping. I was still keeping up with work but I thought I'd better tell them something before I had to take more days off here and there to even out the quality of my life. I had already had this little plan to tell them I had leukemia . . . but I thought how am I going to tell them, what am I going to tell them, how am I going to convince them? What am I going to do if someone says, "You don't have leukemia, you have AIDS!"? This was all stuff clicking around in my mind. I thought, how could they possible know? They only know as much as I tell them.

This quote reveals the heightened concern with information control that accompanies decisions to conceal one's condition. Regardless of the psychic costs, though, a number of our informants opted for this remedial strategy. A commonly used technique consisted of informing friends, parents, or co-workers that one had cancer or tuberculosis without mentioning that these were the presenting symptoms of one's AIDS diagnosis. Covering attempts of this kind were most often employed by PWAs when relating to others who were not aware of their gay identity. These relationships were less apt to be characterized by the suspicions or challenges offered by those who knew that an individual was both gay and seriously ill.

Isolation and Insulation

For those whose diagnosis was not readily visible, dramaturgical skills, such as passing and covering, could be quite useful. These techniques were not so feasible when physical cues, such as a pale complexion, emaciated appearance, or facial lesion made the nature of a PWA's condition more apparent. Under these circumstances, negotiations with others were more alarming and they were more likely to include conflicts engendered by fear, ambiguity, and expressions of social devaluation.

In turn, some PWAs came to view physical and social isolation as the best means available to them for escaping from both these interpersonal difficulties and their own feelings of ambivalence. By withdrawing from virtually all interaction, they sought to be spared the social struggles and psychic strains that could be triggered by others' recognition of their condition.

Nonetheless, this strategy was typically an unsuccessful one. Isolation and withdrawal often exacerbated the feelings of alienation that PWAs were striving to minimize in their social relationships. Moreover, their desire to be removed from the interactional matrix was frequently overcome by their need for extensive medical care and interpersonal support as they coped with the progressive effects of the illness.

Given the drawbacks of extreme isolation, a number of PWAs used a more selective withdrawal strategy. It consisted of efforts to disengage from many but not all social involvements and to interact regularly with only a handful of trusted associates (e.g., partners, friends, or family members). Emphasis was placed on minimizing contacts with those outside of this circle because they were likely to be less tolerant or predictable.

PWAs engaging in this type of selective interaction tried to develop a small network of intimate others who could insulate them from potentially threatening interactions. Ideally, they were able to form a reliable social circle within which they felt little need to conceal their diagnosis. They could thereby experience some relief from the burden of stigma management and information control.

BUILDING AND EMBRACING AN AIDS IDENTITY

Strategies such as passing, covering, isolation, and insulation are used by PWAs, especially in the earlier stages of their illness, to shield themselves from the stigma and uncertainty associated with AIDS. However, these strategies typically require a high level of personal vigilance, they evoke concerns about information control, and they are essentially defensive in nature. They do not provide PWAs with a way to reformulate the personal meaning of their diagnosis and to integrate it with valued definitions of self.

In light of this, most PWAs engage in more active types of *identity work* which allow them to "create, present and sustain personal identities which are congruent with and supportive of the[ir] self-concept[s]" (Snow and Anderson 1987, 1348). Certain types of identity work are especially appealing because they help PWAs to gain a greater sense of mastery over their condition and to make better use of the behavioral possibilities arising from their liminal condition.

The most prominent type of identity work engaged in by the PWAs we interviewed was embracement. As Snow and Anderson (1987) argued, embracement refers to "verbal and expressive confirmation of one's acceptance of and attachment to the social identity associated with a general or specific role, a set of social relationships, or a particular ideology" (p. 1354). Among the PWAs involved in this study, embracement was promoted and reinforced through participation in local AIDS-related support groups.

Support Groups and Associational Embracement

People facing an existential crisis often make use of new memberships and social forms in their efforts to construct a more viable sense of self (Kotarba 1984). The vast majority of respondents in this study became involved in PWA support groups in order to better address the crisis elicited by their illness and to find new forms of self-expression. They typically joined these groups within a few months of receiving their diagnosis and continued to attend meetings on a fairly regular basis.

By and large, support groups became the central focus of identity work and repair for PWAs. These groups were regarded as a valuable source of education and emotional support that helped individuals to cope better with the daily exigencies of their illness. At support group meetings, PWAs could exchange useful information, share feelings and troubles, and relate to others who could see beyond the negative connotations of AIDS.

Support groups also facilitated the formation of social ties and feelings of collective identification among PWAs. Within these circles, individuals learned to better nurture and support one another and to emphasize the shared nature of their problems. Feelings of guilt and isolation were transformed into a sense of group identification. This kind of *associational embracement* (Snow and Anderson 1987) was conveyed in the comments of one person who proclaimed:

I spend almost all of my time with other PWAs. They're my best friends now and they're the people I feel most comfortable with. We support one another and we know that we can talk to each other any time, day or night.

For some PWAs, especially those with a troubled or marginal past, support group relationships provided an instant "buddy system" that was used to bolster feelings of security and self-worth. Recently formed support group friendships even took on primary importance in their daily lives. Perhaps because of the instability and isolation which characterized their life outside of support groups, a few of these PWAs tended to exaggerate the level of intimacy which existed in their newly found friendships. By stressing a romanticized version of these relationships, they were able to preserve a sense of being cared for even in the absence of more enduring social connections.

Identity Embracement and Affirmation

Most of the PWAs we interviewed had come to gradually affirm and embrace an AIDS-related identity. Participation in a support group exposed them to alternative definitions of the reality of AIDS and an ongoing system of identity construction. Hence, rather than accepting public imputations which cast them as "AIDS victims," PWAs learned to distance themselves from such designations and to avow more favorable AIDS-associated identities. In turn, the process of *identity embracement* was realized when individuals proudly announced that they were PWAs who were "living and thriving with the illness."

Continued associations with other PWAs could also promote deepening involvement in activities organized around the identity of being a person with AIDS. A case in point is provided by a man who recounted his progression as a PWA:

After awhile, I aligned myself with other people with AIDS who shared my beliefs about taking the active role. I began writing and speaking about AIDS and I became involved in various projects. I helped to create and promote a workshop for people with AIDS. . . . I also got involved in organizing a support group for family members of PWAs.

As involvement in AIDS-related activities increases, embracement of an AIDS-centered identity is likely to become more encompassing. In some cases, diagnosed individuals found themselves organizing workshops on AIDS, coordinating a newsletter for PWAs, and delivering speeches regularly at schools and churches. Virtually all aspects of their lives became associated with their diagnosis. Being a PWA thus became both a master status and a valued career. This process was described by a person who had been diagnosed with ARC for two years:

One interesting thing is that when you have AIDS or ARC and you're not working anymore, you tend to become a veteran professional on AIDS issues. You get calls regularly from people who want information or who want you to get involved in a project, etc. You find yourself getting drawn to that kind of involvement. It becomes almost a second career!

This kind of identity embracement was particularly appealing for a few individuals involved in this study. Prior to contracting an AIDS-related infection, they had felt rejected or unrecognized in many of their social relationships (e.g., family, work, and friendships). Ironically, their stigmatized AIDS diagnosis provided them with an opportunity for social affirmation. It offered them a sense of uniqueness and expertise that was positively evaluated in certain social and community circles (e.g., public education and church forums). It could even serve as a springboard for a new and more meaningful biography.

Ideological Embracement: AIDS as a Transforming Experience

Support groups and related self-help networks are frequently bases for the production and transmission of subcultural perspectives which controvert mainstream social definitions of a stigma. As Becker (1963) argued, when people who share a deviant attribute have the opportunity to interact with one another, they are likely to develop a system of shared meanings emphasizing the differences between their definitions of who they are and the definitions held by other members of the society. "They develop perspectives on themselves and their deviant [attributes] and on their relations with other members of the society" (p. 81). These perspectives guide the stigmatized as they engage in processes of identity construction and embracement.

Subcultural perspectives contain ideologies which assure individuals that what they do on a continuing basis has moral validity (Lofland 1969). Among PWAs, these ideologies were grounded in metaphors of transformation which included an emphasis on *special mission* and *empowerment*.

One of the most prominent subcultural interpretations of AIDS highlighted the spiritual meaning of the illness. For PWAs embracing this viewpoint, AIDS was symbolically and experientially inverted from a "curse" to a "blessing" which promoted a liberating rather than a constricting form of identity transformation. The following remarks illustrate this perspective:

I now view AIDS as both a gift and a blessing. That sounds strange, I suppose, in a limited context. It sounds strange because we [most people] think it's so awful, but yet there are such radical changes that take place in your life from having this illness that's

defined as terminal. You go through this amazing kind of *transformation*. You look at things for the first time, in a powerful new way that you've never looked at them before in your whole life.

A number of PWAs similarly stressed the beneficial personal and spiritual transitions experienced as a result of their diagnosis. They even regarded their illness as a motivating force that led them to grapple with important existential questions and to experience personal growth and change that otherwise would not have occurred.

For many PWAs, *ideological embracement* (Snow and Anderson 1987) entailed identity constructions based on a quasi-religious sense of "special mission." These individuals placed a premium on disseminating information about AIDS and promoting a level of public awareness which might inhibit the further transmission of this illness. Some felt that their diagnosis had provided them with a unique opportunity to help and educate others. They subsequently displayed a high level of personal sacrifice and commitment while seeking to spread the news about AIDS and to nurture those directly affected by this illness. Most crucially, their diagnosis provided them with a heightened sense of power and purpose:

Basically I feel that as a person with ARC I can do more for humanity in general than I could ever do before. I never before in my life felt like I belonged here. For the most part, I felt like I was stranded on a hostile planet—I didn't know why. But now with the disease and what I've learned in my life, I feel like I really have something by which I can help other people. It gives me a special sense of purpose.

I feel like I've got a mission now and that's what this whole thing is about. AIDS is challenging me with a question and the question it asks is: If I'm not doing something to help others regarding this illness, then why continue to use up energy here on this earth?

The idea of a "special mission" is often a revitalizing formulation for those who carry a death taint (Lifton 1967). It helps to provide PWAs with a sense of mastery and self-worth by giving their condition a more positive or redemptive meaning. This notion also gives form and resolution to painful feelings of loss, grief, guilt and death anxiety. It enables individuals to make use of these emotions, while at the same time transcending them. Moreover, the idea of special mission provides PWAs with a framework through which they can moralize their activities and continuing lives.

Beliefs stressing the empowering aspects of AIDS also served as an important focus of identity affirmation. These beliefs were frequently rooted in the sense of transformation provoked by the illness. Many of those interviewed viewed their diagnosis as empowering because it led them to have a concentrated experience of life, a stronger sense of purpose, a better understanding of their personal resources and a clearer notion of how to prioritize their daily concerns. They correspondingly felt less constrained by mundane aspects of the AIDS experience and related symptoms.

A sense of empowerment could additionally be derived from others' objectification of PWAs as sources of danger, pollution, or death. This was illustrated in the remarks of an informant who had Kaposi's sarcoma:

People hand power to me on a silver platter because they are afraid. It's not fear of catching the virus or anything, I think it is just fear of identification with someone who is dying.

The interactional implications of such attributions of power [were] also recognized by this same informant:

Because I have AIDs, people leave me alone in my life in some respects if I want them to. I never used to be able to get people to back off and now I can. I'm not the one who is doing this, so to speak. They are giving me the power to do so.

Most PWAs realized their condition offered them an opportunity to experience both psychological and social power. They subsequently accentuated the empowering dimensions of their lived experience of AIDS and linked these to an encompassing metaphor of transformation.

SUMMARY AND CONCLUSIONS

People with AIDS face many obstacles in their efforts to construct and sustain a desirable social identity. In the early stages of their career, after receiving a validating diagnosis, they are confronted by painful self-feelings such as grief, guilt, and death anxiety. These feelings often diminish their desire and ability to participate in interactions which would allow them to sustain favorable images of self.

PWAs encounter additional difficulties as a result of being situated (at least initially) as liminal persons. That is, their liminal situation can heighten negative self-feelings and evoke a sense of confusion and uncertainty about the social implications of their illness. At the same time, however, it releases them from conventional roles, meanings, or expectations and provides them with a measure of power and maneuverability in the processes of identity construction.

In turn, as they construct and negotiate the meaning of an AIDS-related identity, PWAs must grapple with the effects of social reactions such as stigmatization, counterfeit nurturance, fears of contagion, and death anxiety. These reactions both elicit and reinforce a number of interactional ambiguities, dilemmas, and threats to self.

In responding to these challenges, PWAs engage in various types of identity management and construction. On one hand, they may seek to disguise their diagnoses or to restrict their social and interactional involvements. PWAs are most likely to use such strategies in the earlier phases of the illness. The disadvantage of these strategies is that they are primarily defensive. They provide PWAs with a way to avoid or adjust to the effects of problematic social reactions, but they do not offer a means for affirming more desirable AIDS-related identities.

On the other hand, as their illness progresses and they become more enmeshed in subcultural networks, most PWAs are prompted to engage in forms of identity embracement which enable them to actively reconstruct the meaning of their illness and to integrate it with valued conceptions of self. In essence, through their interactions with other PWAs, they learn to embrace affiliations and ideologies which accentuate the transformative and empowering possibilities arising from their condition. They also acquire the social and symbolic resources necessary to fashion revitalizing identities and to sustain a sense of dignity and self-worth.

Ultimately, through their ongoing participation in support networks, PWAs are able to build identities which are linked to their lived experience of AIDS. They are also encouraged to actively confront and transform the stigmatizing conceptions associated with this medical condition. Hence, rather than resigning themselves to the darker implications of AIDS, they learn to affirm themselves as "people with AIDS" who are "living and thriving with the illness."

References

Asher, R. 1987. Ambivalence, moral career, and ideology: A sociological analysis of women married to alcoholics. Ph.D. diss., University of Minnesota.

Baumgartner, G. 1986. *AIDS: Psychosocial factors in the acquired immune deficiency syndrome.* Springfield, Ill.: Charles C Thomas.

Becker, H. S. 1963. *Outsiders.* New York: Free Press.

Charmaz, K. 1980. The social construction of pity in the chronically ill. *Studies in Symbolic Interaction* 3:123–45

Conrad, P. 1986. The social meaning of AIDS. *Social Policy* 17:51–56.

Davis, F. 1974. Deviance disavowal and the visibly handicapped. In L. Rainwater, ed., *Deviance and Liberty*, pp. 163–72. Chicago: Aldine.

Denzin, N. 1983. A note on emotionality, self, and interaction. *American Journal of Sociology* 89:402–9.

Ergas, Y. 1987. The social consequences of the AIDS epidemic. *Social Science Research Council/Items* 41:33–39.

Geiss, S.; Fuller, R.; and Rush J. 1986. Lovers of AIDS victims: Psychosocial stresses and counseling needs. *Death Studies* 10:43–53.

Glaser, B. S., and Strauss, A. L. 1968. *Awareness of Dying.* Chicago: Aldine.

Goffman, E. 1963. *Stigma.* Englewood Cliffs, N.J.: Prentice Hall.

———. 1971. *Relations in public.* New York: Harper & Row.

Hughes, E. C. 1945. Dilemmas and contradictions of status. *American Journal of Sociology* 50:353–59.

Kaplan, H.; Johnson, R.; Bailey, C.; and Simon, W. 1987. The sociological study of AIDS: A critical review of the literature and suggested research agenda. *Journal of Health and Social Behavior* 28:140–57.

Kotarba, J. 1984. A synthesis: The existential self in society. In J. Kotarba and A. Fontana, eds., *The Existential Self in Society*, pp. 222–23. Chicago: Aldine.

Kowalewski, M. 1988. Double stigma and boundary maintenance: How gay men deal with AIDS. *Journal of Contemporary Ethnography* 7:211–28.

Lifton, R. J. 1967. *Death in Life.* New York: Random House.

Lofland, J. 1969. *Deviance and Identity.* Englewood Cliffs, N.J.: Prentice Hall.

Macklin, E. 1988. AIDS: Implications for families. *Family Relations* 37:141–49.

Nichols, S. 1985. Psychosocial reactions of persons with AIDS. *Annals of Internal Medicine* 103:13–16.

Palmer, S. 1989. AIDS as metaphor. *Society* 26:45–51.

Salisbury, D. 1986. AIDS: Psychosocial implications. *Journal of Psychosocial Nursing* 24(12):13–16.

Seidman, S. 1988. Transfiguring sexual identity: AIDS and the contemporary construction of homosexuality. *Social Text* 19/20:187–205.

Snow, D., and Anderson, L. 1987. Identity work among the homeless: The verbal construction and avowal of personal identities. *American Journal of Sociology* 92:1336–71.

Sontag, S. 1989. *AIDS and Its Metaphors.* New York: Farrar, Straus & Giroux.

Turner, V. 1969. *The Ritual Process.* Ithaca, N.Y.: Cornell University Press.

Weitz, R. 1989. Uncertainty and the lives of persons with AIDS. *Journal of Health and Social Behavior* 30:270–81.

CHAPTER 17

ABORTION

INTRODUCTION

Social problems can never be understood and resolved in narrow scientific terms of evidence and the logic of causal inference. Social problems are defined on the basis of values; and values cannot be reduced to evidence or the logic of causal explanation. The same evidence may lead to two radically divergent interpretations, because the two positions are based on conflicting values. No social problem illuminates the significance of values more vividly than the current abortion controversy. During the past quarter century two clashing groups have taken absolutist positions that allow no room for compromise. "Right to life" and "freedom of choice" have become rallying cries for partisans, to whom the question is an either/or proposition: either the unborn have a right to life *or* women have a right to control their own bodies.

Women throughout the world have been inducing abortions for thousands of years.

But in Western societies since the mid–nineteenth century—not earlier—the Catholic church and some governments have opposed abortion and made its practice illegal. For many years in the United States, abortions were prohibited by state laws. In the 1960s increasing pressure from women's groups and the medical profession led to more liberal state laws that expanded the reasons a woman could obtain an abortion (her health, fetal deformity, rape). Pressure to liberalize the abortion laws reached a climax in 1973 with the Supreme Court's decision in *Roe* v. *Wade*. The Court ruled that a state could not restrict a woman's freedom to have an abortion during the first six months of pregnancy if that was her choice; to do so would infringe her right to privacy. *Roe* v. *Wade* was a sweeping decision that gave a woman and her physician ultimate control over the matter of abortion. This decision set off a firestorm of controversy between advocates of choice, who argued for the rights of women, and those who would deny that choice in the interest of protecting the rights of the fetus. Arguments of ethics, law, and medicine raged in every forum of public discourse. While the rhetoric of debate continued, the realities of increasing abortions further inflamed the debate. Depending on one's point of view, women were either regaining a freedom too long denied or committing murder. By the late 1980s, 1.5 million women were terminating their pregnancies each year. It has been estimated that one of every four pregnancies will end in an abortion. As women continue to exercise their legal right to abortion, millions of Americans are convinced that the choice they are making is immoral.

In terms of both rhetoric and realities, the abortion controversy involves many issues: changing sex roles, overpopulation, access to health care by the poor, the quality of life for children and their parents. This chapter does not pretend to resolve these issues. Lynn M. Morgan's essay calls attention to various cultural definitions of social birth, which is distinct from biological birth. Morgan also notes other important cultural values in the United States that are part of the abortion debate: tolerance and freedom of private choices within the family. Katha Pollitt and Rosalind Petchesky examine important themes in the abortion debate as feminists define the issues. What are the value assumptions that focus the premises as well as the conclusions of these two essays? Finally, are feminist values in alignment or in tension with broader values of American society?

Hyman Rodman, Betty Sarvis, and Joy Walker Bonar have examined recent trends in court decisions, public opinion, and medical technology. They do not see the current clashing of absolutes as a deadlock that will continue indefinitely; they see significant movement toward a compromise position. This conclusion rests on reported observations of change, not a deductive argument from value assumptions about the beginning of human life or the rights of women. The authors do not recommend the terms of a compromise, but they predict that compromise will be reached. Does this prediction rest on an understanding of American values, trends in medical technology, or shifts in public opinion?

47. WHEN LIFE BEGINS—A CULTURAL PERSPECTIVE

LYNN M. MORGAN

Abortion is not only a moral and religious issue, it is a cultural issue. People from other cultures hold different beliefs about when a fetus or young child becomes a person.

If we agree that cultural diversity is one of America's strengths, then we should be content with existing laws, which can accommodate a range of cultural traditions. In hopes of giving us another way of thinking about the abortion issue, anthropologists have looked at how other cultures have resolved the question of when life begins. They have found such enormous variations that the terms of the United States abortion debate look rather circumscribed in comparison.

Roe v. Wade, the 1973 Supreme Court decision legalizing abortion during the first two trimesters of pregnancy, dismayed pro-life activists, because the court determined that the fetus does not become a person under the law until viability, in the last three months of pregnancy. The court's decision would also have shocked the Chippewa Indians of North America. To them, even a barely formed embryo was a person. If a Chippewa woman miscarried—at any stage of pregnancy—the fetus would be washed, wrapped, buried, and mourned.

The Manus of the western Pacific named all miscarried fetuses and exchanged gifts in their honor. To the Chippewas and the Manus, induced abortion was unthinkable. Fortunately, American pro-life forces do not take their position to these extremes. If they did, they would insist that we name and hold funeral services for a miscarried or aborted fetus.

The customs practiced by the Chippewas and Manus are relatively rare. Far more common are cultures where life begins sometime *after* birth.

From *The Christian Science Monitor*, May 5, 1989, p. 19. Reprinted with permission.

Lynn M. Morgan is assistant professor of anthropology at Mount Holyoke College, in South Hadley, Mass.

Many societies separate biological birth from social birth. The infant does not become a person until days, weeks, or even months after it is born. It becomes a person when it is named or unveiled, or when some other culturally significant ceremony is performed.

Biological birth is thus less important than social birth. There is no cultural equivalent of the elated telephone call, engraved birth announcement, or photograph to record the memorable event. Neighbors are not allowed to see the newborn or mother. The infant must "prove" during the time between biological and social birth that it deserves personhood; first by managing to survive outside the womb, and then by showing it has the vigor, health, and emotions of a "person." Only if the newborn survives is it ready to be born socially and welcomed into the community.

The Todas, living in south India, keep their newborn indoors for three months. They do not publicly announce the child's sex or name. The sun must not touch the child's face. After three months, the relatives hold a "face opening" ceremony. They bring the infant outdoors with its head covered, to be unveiled when the first bird sings. Until the ceremony is performed, the infant is not considered a person, its death not a significant social event.

Likewise among the Ashanti in West Africa, where many children die young, a newborn is thought to be in limbo between the human and spirit worlds. Parents learn through bitter experience not to become emotionally attached to newborns. After seven days, a naming ceremony severs the infant's ties to the spirit world and ties it to the social group. If the child dies before the ceremony, it is considered the death of a spirit-child. There is no mourning. This is analogous to an early miscarriage in the U.S.

Pro-choice activists in the U.S. do not go to this extreme. No one suggests that legal or moral rights of personhood should be postponed until after birth, or that infanticide should be permitted. Biological birth marks social birth; the guarantees of personhood apply to all born children. On this, pro-choice as well as pro-life advocates agree.

The U.S. is a pluralistic country, but it's not a melting pot. It is more like a rich stew where the flavors never meld. An estimated 10,000 Ashanti live in New York City alone. With such cultural diversity in the U.S., it is not surprising that we cannot agree about when life begins.

Yet American law does set limits. Life begins somewhere between conception and birth—not earlier, not later. We already have sufficient legislation to protect this American consensus: The 14th Amendment of the Constitution guarantees the rights of personhood from the moment of birth, and other laws prohibit induced third-trimester abortion and infanticide. This range is as close as we can come to agreement while still respecting the cultural and religious differences among us.

To legislate further the definition of when life begins would be to violate one of our most deeply held American values: tolerance for the beliefs of those who migrate to our shores. The impasse over abortion could be solved only at the expense of cultural diversity. Let's leave the law the way it stands, and leave the finer distinctions to parents, who have the greatest stake in making the best choice in their pregnancies.

48. A NEW ASSAULT ON FEMINISM

KATHA POLLITT

Some scenes from the way we live now:

- In New York City, a pregnant woman orders a glass of wine with her restaurant meal. A stranger comes over to her table. "Don't you know you're poisoning your baby?" he says angrily, pointing to a city-mandated sign warning women that drinking during pregnancy can cause birth defects.

- In California, Pamela Rae Stewart is advised by her obstetrician to stay off her feet, to eschew sex and "street drugs," and to go to the hospital immediately if she starts to bleed. She fails to follow this advice and delivers a brain-damaged baby who soon dies. She is charged with failing to deliver support to a child under an old criminal statute that was intended to force men to provide for women they have made pregnant.

- In Washington, D.C., a hospital administration asks a court whether it should intervene and perform a Caesarean section on Angela Carder, seriously ill with cancer, against her wishes and those of her husband, her parents and her doctors. Acknowledging that the operation would probably shorten her life without necessarily saving the life of her 25-week-old fetus, the judge nonetheless provides the order. The Caesarean is performed immediately, before her lawyers can appeal. Angela Carder dies; so does her unviable fetus. That incident is subsequently dramatized on *L.A. Law*, with postfeminist softy Ann Kelsey arguing for the hospital; on TV the baby lives.

- In the Midwest, the U.S. Court of Appeals for the Seventh Circuit, ruling in *UAW* v. *Johnson Controls*, upholds an automotive battery plant's seven-year-old "fetal protection policy" barring fertile women (in effect, all women) from jobs that would expose them to lead. The court discounts testimony about the individual reproductive lives and plans of fe-

From *The Nation*, March 26, 1990, pp. 409–418. Copyright © 1990 The Nation Company, Inc. Reprinted with permission.

male employees (many in their late 40s, celibate and/or with completed families), testimony showing that no child born to female employees had shown ill effects traceable to lead exposure and testimony showing that lead poses a comparable danger to male reproductive health. The court accepts testimony that says making the workplace safe would be too expensive.

All over the country, pregnant women who use illegal drugs and/or alcohol are targeted by the criminal justice system. They are "preventively detained" by judges who mete out jail sentences for minor crimes that would ordinarily result in probation or a fine; charged with child abuse or neglect (although by law the fetus is not a child) and threatened with manslaughter charges should they miscarry; and placed under court orders not to drink, although drinking is not a crime and does not invariably (or even usually) result in birth defects. While state legislatures ponder bills that would authorize these questionable practices by criminalizing drug use or "excessive" alcohol use during pregnancy (California Senator Pete Wilson is pushing a similar bill at the federal level), mothers are arrested in their hospital beds when their newborns test positive for drugs. Social workers increasingly remove positive-testing babies into foster care on the presumption that even a single use of drugs during pregnancy renders a mother ipso facto an unfit parent.

What's going on here? Right now the hot area in the developing issue of "fetal rights" is the use of drugs and alcohol during pregnancy. We've all seen the nightly news reports of inner-city intensive care units overflowing with crack babies, of Indian reservations where one in four children are said to be born physically and mentally stunted by fetal alcohol syndrome (F.A.S.) or the milder, but still serious, fetal alcohol effect. We've read the front-page stories reporting studies that suggest staggering rates of drug use during pregnancy (11 percent, according to *The New York Times,* or 375,000 women per year) and the dangers of even moderate drinking during pregnancy.

But drugs and alcohol are only the latest focus of a preoccupation with the fetus and its "rights" that has been wandering around the *Zeitgeist* for the past decade. A few years ago, the big issue was forced Caesareans. (It was, in fact, largely thanks to the horrific Angela Carder case—one of the few involving a white, middle-class woman—that the American College of Obstetricians and Gynecologists condemned the practice, which nonetheless has not entirely ceased.) If the Supreme Court upholds the *Johnson Controls* decision, the next battleground may be the workplace. The "save the babies" mentality may look like a necessary, if troubling, approach when it's a matter of keeping a drug addict away from a substance that is, after all, illegal. What happens if the same mentality is applied to some 15 million to 20 million highly paid unionized jobs in heavy industry to "protect" fetuses that do not even exist? Or if the list of things women are put on legal notice to avoid expands to match medical findings on the dangers to the fetus posed by junk food, salt, aspirin, air travel and cigarettes?

Critics of the punitive approach to pregnant drug and alcohol users point out the ironies inherent in treating a public-health concern as a matter for the criminal justice system: the contradiction, for instance, of punishing addicted women when most drug treatment programs refuse to accept pregnant women. Indeed, Jennifer Johnson, a Florida woman who was the first person convicted after giving birth to a baby who tested positive for cocaine, had sought treatment and been turned away. (In her case the charge was delivering drugs to a minor.) The critics point out that threats of jail or the loss of their kids may drive women away from prenatal care and hospital deliveries, and that almost all the women affected so far have been poor and black or Latino, without private doctors to protect them (in Florida, nonwhite women are ten times as likely to be reported for substance abuse as white women, although rates of drug use are actually higher for whites).

These are all important points. But they leave unchallenged the notion of fetal rights itself. What we really ought to be asking is, How have we come to see women as the major threat to the health of their newborns, and the womb as the most dangerous place a child will ever inhabit? Why is our basic model "innocent" fetuses that would be fine if only presumably "guilty" women refrained from indulging their "whims"? The list of dangers to the fetus is, after all, very long; the list of dangers to children even longer. Why does maternal behavior, a relatively small piece of the total picture, seem such an urgent matter, while much more important factors—that one in five pregnant women receive no prenatal care at all, for instance—attract so little attention? Here are some of the strands that make up the current tangle that is fetal rights.

THE ASSAULT ON THE POOR

It would be pleasant to report that the aura of crisis surrounding crack and F.A.S. babies—the urge to do *something,* however unconstitutional or cruel, that suddenly pervades society, from judge's bench to chic dinner party to 7 o'clock news—was part of a massive national campaign to help women have healthy, wanted pregnancies and healthy babies. But significantly, the current wave of concern is not occurring in that context. Judges order pregnant addicts to jail, but they don't order drug treatment programs to accept them, or Medicaid, which pays for heroin treatment, to cover crack addiction—let alone order landlords not to evict them, or obstetricians to take uninsured women as patients, or the federal government to fund fully the Women, Infants, and Children supplemental feeding program, which reaches only two-thirds of those who are eligible. The policies that have underwritten maternal and infant health in most of the industrialized West since World War II—a national health service, paid maternity leave, direct payments to mothers, government-funded day care, home health visitors for new mothers, welfare payments that reflect the cost of living—are still regarded in the United States by even the most liberal as hopeless causes, and by everyone else as budget-breaking giveaways to the undeserving, pie-in-the-sky items from a mad socialist's wish list.

The focus on maternal behavior allows the government to appear to be concerned about babies without having to spend any money, change any priorities or challenge any vested interests. As with crime, as with poverty, a complicated, multifaceted problem is construed as a matter of freely chosen individual behavior. We have crime because we have lots of bad people, poverty because we have lots of lazy people (Republican version) or lots of pathological people (Democratic version), and tiny, sickly, impaired babies because we have lots of women who just don't give a damn.

Once the problem has been defined as original sin, coercion and punishment start to look like hardheaded and common-sensical answers. Thus, syndicated columnist and *New Republic* intellectual Charles Krauthammer proposes locking up pregnant drug users en masse. Never mind the impracticality of the notion—suddenly the same Administration that refuses to pay for drug treatment and prenatal care is supposed to finance all that plus nine months of detention for hundreds of thousands of women a year. Or its disregard of real life—what, for example, about the children those women already have? Do they go to jail, too, like Little Dorrit? Or join the rolls of the notorious foster care system? The satisfactions of the punitive mind-set sweep all such considerations aside. (Nor are liberal pundits immune from its spell. Around the same time Krauthammer was calling for mass incarceration, Mary McGrory was suggesting that we stop wasting resources—*what* resources?—on addicted women and simply put their babies in orphanages.)

THE NEW TEMPERANCE

While rightly sounding the alarm about the health risks and social costs of drugs, alcohol and nicotine, the various "just say no" crusades have so upped the moral ante across the board that it is now difficult to distinguish between levels and kinds of substance use and abuse and even rather suspect to try. A joint on the weekend is the moral equivalent of a twenty-four-hour-a-day crack habit; wine with meals is next door to a daily quart of rotgut. The stigmatizing of addicts, casual users, alcoholics, social drinkers and smokers makes punitive measures against them palatable. It also helps us avoid uncomfortable questions about why we are having all these "substance abuse" epidemics in the first place.

Finally, it lets us assume, not always correctly, that drugs and alcohol, all by themselves, cause harm during pregnancy, and ignore the role of malnutrition, violence, chaotic lives, serious maternal health problems and lack of medical care.

SCIENCE MARCHES ON

We know a lot more about fetal development than we did twenty years ago. But how much of what we know will we continue to know in ten years? As recently as the early 1970s, pregnant women were harassed by their doctors to keep their weight down. They were urged to take tranquilizers and other prescription drugs, to drink in moderation (liquor was routinely used to stop premature labor), to deliver under anesthesia and not bother to breast-feed. Then too, studies examined contemporary wisdom and found it good. Today, those precepts seem the obvious expression of social forces: the wish of doctors to control pregnancy and delivery, a lack of respect for women and a distaste for female physiological processes. It was not the disinterested progress of science that outmoded these practices. It was another set of social forces: the women's movement, the prepared-childbirth movement and the natural-health movement.

What about today's precepts? At the very least, the history of scientific research into pregnancy and childbirth ought to make us skeptical. Instead, we leap to embrace tentative findings and outright bad science because they fit current social prejudices. Those who argue for total abstinence during pregnancy have made much, for example, of a recent study in *The New England Journal of Medicine* that claimed women are more vulnerable than men to alcohol because they have less of a stomach enzyme that neutralizes it before it enters the bloodstream. Universally unreported, however, was the fact that the study included alcoholics and patients with gastrointestinal disease. It is a basic rule of medical research that results cannot be generalized from the sick to the healthy.

In a 1989 article in *The Lancet*, "Bias Against the Null Hypothesis: The Reproductive Hazards of Cocaine," Canadian researchers reported that studies that found a connection between cocaine use and poor pregnancy outcome had a better

than even chance of being accepted for presentation at the annual meeting of the Society for Pediatric Research, while studies that found no connection had a negligible chance—although the latter were better designed. While it's hard to imagine that anyone will ever show that heavy drug use or alcohol consumption is good for fetal development, studies like this one suggest that when the dust settles (because the drug war is officially "won"? because someone finally looks at the newborns of Italy, where everyone drinks moderate amounts of wine with food, and finds them to be perfectly fine?) the current scientific wisdom will look alarmist.

MEDIA BIAS

The assumptions that shape the way researchers frame their studies and the questions they choose to investigate are magnified by bias in the news media. Studies that show the bad effects of maternal behavior make the headlines, studies that show no bad effects don't get reported and studies that show the bad effects of paternal behavior (alcoholic males, and males who drink at conception, have been linked to lower I.Q. and a propensity to alcoholism in offspring) get two paragraphs in the science section. So did the study, briefly mentioned in a recent issue of *The New York Times,* suggesting that housewives run a higher risk than working women of having premature babies, stillbirths, underweight babies and babies who die in the first week of life. Imagine the publicity had it come out the other way around! Numbers that back up the feeling of crisis (those 375,000 drug-taking pregnant women) are presented as monolithic, although they cover a wide range of behavior (from daily use of cocaine to marijuana use during delivery, which some midwives recommend, and for which one Long Island woman lost custody of her newborn for eight months), and are illustrated by dire examples of harm that properly apply only to the most hard-core cases.

THE "PRO-LIFE" MOVEMENT

Antichoicers have not succeeded in criminalizing abortion but they have made it inaccessible to millions of women (only sixteen states pay for poor women's abortions, and only 18 percent of counties have even one abortion provider) and made it a badge of sin and failure for millions more. In Sweden, where heavy drinking is common, relatively few F.A.S. babies are born, because alcoholic women have ready access to abortion and it is not a stigmatized choice. In America antichoice sentiment makes it impossible to suggest to a homeless, malnourished, venereally diseased crack addict that her first priority ought to be getting well: Get help, then have a baby. While the possibility of coerced abortions is something to be wary of, the current policy of regulation and punishment in the name of the fetus ironically risks the same end. Faced with criminal charges, pregnant women may seek abortions in order to stay out of jail (a Washington, D.C., woman who "miscarried" a few days before sentencing may have done just that).

As lobbyists, antichoicers have sought to bolster their cause by interjecting the fetus-as-person argument into a wide variety of situations that would seem to have nothing to do with abortion. They have fought to exclude pregnant women from proposed legislation recognizing the validity of "living wills" that reject the use of life support systems (coma baby lives!), and have campaigned to classify as homicides assaults on pregnant women that result in fetal death or miscarriage. Arcane as such proposals may seem, they have the effect of broadening little by little the areas of the law in which the fetus is regarded as a person, and in which the woman is regarded as its container.

At a deeper level, the "pro-life" movement has polluted the way we think about pregnancy. It has promoted a model of pregnancy as a condition that by its very nature pits women and fetuses against each other, with the fetus invariably taking precedence, and a model of women as selfish, confused, potentially violent and incapable of making responsible choices. As the "rights" of the fetus grow and respect for the capacities and rights of women declines, it becomes harder and harder to explain why drug addiction is a crime if it produces an addicted baby, but not if it produces a miscarriage, and why a woman can choose abortion but not vodka. And that is just what the "pro-lifers" want.

THE PRIVILEGED STATUS OF THE FETUS

Pro-choice activists rightly argue that antiabortion and fetal-rights advocates grant fetuses more rights than women. A point less often made is that they grant fetuses more rights than 2-year-olds—the right, for example, to a safe, healthy place to live. No court in this country would ever rule that a parent must undergo a medical procedure in order to benefit a child, even if that procedure is as riskless as a blood donation and the child is sure to die without it. (A Seattle woman is currently suing the father of her leukemic child to force him to donate bone marrow, but she is sure to lose, and her mere attempt roused *Newsday* science writer B. D. Colen to heights of choler unusual even for him.) Nor would a court force someone who had promised to donate a kidney and then changed his mind to keep his date with the organ bank. Yet, as the forced-Caesarean issue shows, we seem willing to deny the basic right of bodily integrity to pregnant women and to give the fetus rights we deny children.

Although concern for the fetus may look like a way of helping children, it is actually, in a funny way, a substitute for it. It is an illusion to think that by "protecting" the fetus from its mother's behavior we have insured a healthy birth, a healthy infancy or a healthy childhood, and that the only insurmountable obstacle for crack babies is prenatal exposure to crack.

It is no coincidence that we are obsessed with pregnant women's behavior at the time that children's health is declining, by virtually any yardstick one chooses. Take general well-being: In constant dollars, welfare payments are now about two-thirds the 1965 level. Take housing: Thousands of children are now growing up in homeless shelters and welfare hotels. Even desperately alcoholic women bear healthy babies two-thirds of the time. Will two-thirds of today's homeless kids emerge unscathed from their dangerous and lead-permeated environments? Take access to medical care: Inner-city hospitals are closing all over the country, millions of kids have no health insurance and most doctors refuse uninsured or Medicaid patients. Even immunization rates are down: Whooping cough and measles are on the rise.

THE "DUTY OF CARE"

Not everyone who favors legal intervention to protect the fetus is antichoice. Some prochoicers support the coercion and punishment of addicts and alcoholics—uneasily, like some of my liberal women friends, or gleefully, like Alan Dershowitz, who dismisses as absurd the "slippery slope" argument (crack today, cigarettes tomorrow) he finds so persuasive when applied to First Amendment issues. For some years now bioethicists have been fascinated by the doctrine of "duty of care," expounded most rigorously by Margery Shaw and John Robertson. In this view, a woman can abort, but once she has decided to bear a child she has a moral, and should have a legal, responsibility to insure a healthy birth. It's an attractive notion because it seems to combine an acceptance of abortion with intuitive feelings shared by just about everyone, including this writer, that pregnancy is a serious undertaking, that society has an interest in the health of babies, that the fetus, although not a person, is also not property.

Whatever its merits as a sentiment, though, the duty of care is a legal disaster. Exactly when, for instance, does the decision to keep a pregnancy take place? For the most desperately addicted—the crack addicts who live on the subway or prostitute themselves for drugs—one may ask if they ever form any idea ordinary people would call a decision, or indeed know they are pregnant until they are practically in labor. Certainly the inaccessibility of abortion denies millions of women the ability to decide.

But for almost all women the decision to carry a pregnancy to term has important, if usually unstated, qualifications. What one owes the fetus is balanced against other considerations, such as serious health risks to oneself (taking chemotherapy or other crucial medication), or the need to feed one's family (keeping a job that may pose risks) or to care for the children one already has (not getting the bed rest the doctor says you need). Why should pregnant women be barred from considering their own interests? It is, after all, what parents do all the time. The model of women's relation to the fetus proposed by the duty of care ethicists is an abstraction that ignores the realities of life even when they affect the fetus itself. In real life, for instance, to quit one's dangerous job means to lose one's health insurance, thus exposing the fetus to another set of risks.

It is also, even as an abstraction, a false picture. Try as she might, a woman cannot insure a healthy newborn; nor can statistical studies of probability (even well-designed ones) be related in an airtight way to individual cases. We know that cigarettes cause lung cancer, but try proving in a court of law that cigarettes and not air pollution, your job, your genes or causes unknown caused *your* lung cancer.

Yet far from shrinking from the slippery slope, duty of care theorists positively hurl themselves down it. Margery Shaw, for instance, believes that the production of an imperfect newborn should make a woman liable to criminal charges and "wrongful life" suits if she knows, or should have known, the risk involved in her behavior, whether it's drinking when her period is late (she has a duty to keep track of her cycle), delivering at home when her doctor advises her not to (what doctor doesn't?) or failing to abort a genetically damaged fetus (which she has a duty to find out about). So much for that "decision" to bear a child—a woman can't qualify it in her own interests but the state can revoke it for her on eugenic grounds.

As these examples show, there is no way to limit the duty of care to cases of flagrant or illegal misbehavior—duty is duty, and risk is risk. Thus, there is no way to enshrine duty of care in law without creating the sort of Romania-style fetal-police state whose possibility Dershowitz, among others, pooh-poohs. For there is no way to define the limits of what a pregnant woman must sacrifice for fetal benefit, or what she "should have known," or at what point a trivial risk becomes significant. My aunt advised me to get rid of my cats while I was pregnant because of the risk of toxoplasmosis. My doctor and I thought this rather extreme, and my husband simply took charge of the litter box. What if my doctor had backed up my aunt instead of me? If the worst had happened (and it always does to someone, somewhere), would I have been charged with the crime of not sending my cats to the Bide-A-Wee?

Although duty of care theorists would impose

upon women a virtually limitless obligation to put the fetus first, they impose that responsibility *only* on women. Philosophy being what it is, perhaps it should not surprise us that they place no corresponding duty upon society as a whole. But what about Dad? It's his kid too, after all. His drug and alcohol use, his prescription medications, his workplace exposure and general habits of health not only play a part in determining the quality of his sperm but affect the course of pregnancy as well. Cocaine dust and smoke from crack, marijuana and tobacco present dangers to others who breathe them; his alcoholism often bolsters hers. Does he have a duty of care to make it possible for his pregnant partner to obey those judge's orders and that doctor's advice that now has the force of law? To quit his job to mind the children so that she can get the bed rest without which her fetus may be harmed? Apparently not.

The sexist bias of duty of care has already had alarming legal consequences. In the Pamela Rae Stewart case cited at the beginning of this article, Stewart's husband, who had heard the doctor's advice, ignored it all and beat his wife into the bargain. Everything she did, he did—they had sex together, smoked pot together, delayed getting to the hospital together—but he was not charged with a crime, not even with wife-beating, although no one can say that his assaults were not a contributing cause of the infant's injury and death. In Tennessee, a husband succeeded in getting a court order forbidding his wife to drink or take drugs, although he himself had lost his driver's license for driving while intoxicated. In Wyoming, a pregnant woman was arrested for drinking when she presented herself at the hospital for treatment for injuries inflicted by her husband. Those charges were dropped (to be reinstated, should her baby be born with defects), but none were instituted against her spouse.

It is interesting to note in this regard that approximately one in twelve women are beaten during pregnancy, a time when many previously nonviolent men become brutal. We do not know how many miscarriages, stillbirths and damaged newborns are due, or partly due, to male violence—this is itself a comment on the skewed nature of supposedly objective scientific research. But if it ever does come to be an officially recognized factor in fetal health, the duty of care would probably take yet another ironic twist and hold battered pregnant women liable for their partner's assaults.

The Broken Cord, Michael Dorris's much-praised memoir of his adopted F.A.S. child, Adam, is a textbook example of the way in which all these social trends come together—and the largely uncritical attention the book has received shows how seductive a pattern they make. Dorris has nothing but contempt for Adam's birth mother. Perhaps it is asking too much of human nature to expect him to feel much sympathy for her. He has witnessed, in the most intimate and heartbreaking way, the damage her alcoholism did, and seen the ruin of his every hope for Adam, who is deeply retarded. But why is his anger directed only at her? Here was a seriously alcoholic woman, living on an Indian reservation where heavy drinking is a way of life, along with poverty, squalor, violence, despair and powerlessness, where, one might even say, a kind of racial suicide is taking place, with liquor as the weapon of choice. Adam's mother, in fact, died two years after his birth from drinking antifreeze.

Dorris dismisses any consideration of these facts as bleeding-heart fuzzy-mindedness. Like Hope on *thirtysomething,* Adam's mother "decides" to have a baby; like the martini-sipping pregnant woman Dorris badgers in an airport bar, she "chooses" to drink out of "weakness" and "self-indulgence."

Dorris proposes preventive detention of alcoholic pregnant women and quotes sympathetically a social worker who thinks the real answer is sterilization. Why do alcoholic Indian women have so many children? To up their government checks. (In fact, Bureau of Indian Affairs hospitals are prohibited by law from performing abortions, even if women can pay for them.) And why, according to Dorris, do they drink so much in the first place? Because of the feminist movement, which has undermined the traditional temperance of reservation women.

The women's movement has had about as much effect on impoverished reservation dwellers as it had on the slum women of eighteenth-century London, whose heavy binge drinking—and stunted babies—appalled contemporary observers. That Dorris pins the blame on such an improbable villain points to what fetal rights is really about—controlling women. It's a reaction to legalized abortion and contraception, which have given women, for the first time in history, real reproductive power. They can have a baby, they can "kill" a baby, they can refuse to conceive at all, without asking permission from anyone. More broadly, it's an index of deep discomfort with the notion of women as self-directed social beings, for whom parenthood is only one aspect of life, as it has always been for men. Never mind that in the real world, women still want children, have children and take care of children, often under the most discouraging circumstances and at tremendous emotional, economic and physical cost. There is still a vague but powerful cultural fear that one of these days, women will just walk out on the whole business of motherhood and the large helpings of humble pie we have, as a society, built into that task. And *then* where will we be?

Looked at in this light, the inconsistent and fitful nature of our concern about the health of babies forms a pattern. The threat to newborns is interesting when and only when it can, accurately or fancifully, be laid at women's doorstep. Babies "possibly" impaired by maternal drinking? Front-page stories, a national wave of alarm. A *New England Journal of Medicine* report that 16 percent of American children have been mentally and neurologically damaged because of exposure to lead, mostly from flaking lead paint in substandard housing? Peter Jennings looks mournful and suggests that "all parents can do" is to have their children tested frequently. If the mother isn't to blame, no one is to blame.

In its various aspects "fetal rights" attacks virtually all the gains of the women's movement. Forced medical treatment attacks women's increased control over pregnancy and delivery by putting doctors back in the driver's seat, with judges to back them up. The *Johnson Controls* decision reverses the entry of women into high-paying, unionized, traditionally male jobs. In the female ghetto, where women can hardly be dispensed with, the growing practice of laying off or shifting pregnant women around transforms women, whose rates of labor-force participation are approaching those of men, into casual labor-

ers with reduced access to benefits, pensions, seniority and promotions. In a particularly vicious twist of the knife, "fetal rights" makes legal abortion—which makes all the other gains possible—the trigger for a loss of human rights. Like the divorce-court judges who tell middle-aged housewives to go out and get a job, or who favor fathers in custody disputes because to recognize the primary-caretaker role of mothers would be "sexist," protectors of the fetus enlist the rhetoric of feminism to punish women.

There are lots of things wrong with the concept of fetal rights. It posits a world in which women will be held accountable, on sketchy or no evidence, for birth defects; in which all fertile women will be treated as potentially pregnant all the time; in which courts, employers, social workers and doctors—not to mention nosy neighbors and vengeful male partners—will monitor women's behavior. It imposes responsibilities without giving women the wherewithal to fulfill them, and places upon women alone duties that belong to both parents and to the community.

But the worst thing about fetal rights is that it portrays a woman as having only contingent value. Her work, her health, her choices and needs and beliefs, can all be set aside in an instant because, next to maternity, they are all perceived as trivial. For the middle class, fetal rights is mostly symbolic, the gateway to a view of motherhood as self-sacrifice and endless guilty soul-searching. It ties in neatly with the currently fashionable suspicion of working mothers, day care and (now that wives are more likely than husbands to sue for it) divorce. For the poor, for whom it means jail and the loss of custody, it becomes a way of saying that women can't even be mothers. They can only be potting soil.

The plight of addicted and alcohol-impaired babies is indeed a tragedy. Finally, we are forced to look at the results of our harsh neglect of the welfare and working poor, and it's only natural that we don't like what we see. We are indeed in danger of losing a generation. But what about the generation we already have? Why is it so hard for us to see that the tragedy of Adam Dorris is inextricable from the tragedy of his mother? Why is her loss—to society, to herself—so easy to dismiss?

"People are always talking about women's duties to others," said Lynn Paltrow, the A.C.L.U. lawyer who successfully led the Pamela Rae Stewart defense, "as though women were not the chief caregivers in this society. But no one talks about women's duty of care to them-*selves*. A pregnant addict or alcoholic needs to get help for *herself*. She's not just potentially ruining someone else's life. She's ruining her own life.

"Why isn't her own life important? Why don't we care about her?"

49.   GIVING WOMEN A REAL CHOICE

ROSALIND PETCHESKY

The abortion conflict refuses to go away. From a Supreme Court Justice to the popular press, a chorus of voices in the United States in 1989 declared abortion "the most politically divisive domestic legal issue of our time." Today it stands squarely in the middle of politics, signifying one's position on a liberal–conservative continuum and signaling shifts in institutional power arrangements. The question is *why* the abortion debate persists, why it becomes such a charged site for struggles over not only changes in family, gender and sexual relations in American society and their cultural meanings but over the terms of public disorder.

During the past decade of legal abortion in the United States—a period of heightened political conservatism—advocates of women's reproductive freedom have faced a complicated paradox. Women's "right" to abortion remains, at least at this writing, embedded in the formal apparatus of the law and, depending on the wording of the questions, commands remarkably consistent and continuous support in national public opinion polls. Moreover, neither antiabortion

From *The Nation*, May 28, 1990, pp. 732–735. Copyright © 1990 The Nation Company, Inc. Reprinted with permission.

Rosalind Petchesky is director of women's studies at Hunter College. This article is adapted from the new introduction to the revised edition of her book Abortion and Woman's Choice.

crusades, innumerable court challenges, bureaucratic regulations, curtailment of Medicaid funding in all but a handful of states, a moratorium on all federal research on abortifacients, clinic harassment nor bombings have made a significant dent in abortion *practice*; about 1.5 million women a year in the United States still persist in getting abortions. This pattern shows that access to abortion will continue to be perceived by women as a necessity, if not a "right," so long as pregnancies occur in women's bodies.

Yet all around the edges of this little kernel of "right," tempers flare, firebombs destroy medical offices, antiabortion "rescue" squads harass patients and providers, and litigations pit pregnant women against vengeful spouses and irate male fetal advocates. Perhaps most serious of all, fetuses (and babies) have become icons of popular culture beside which pregnant women languish in disrepute. This cultural guerrilla warfare against abortions (and the women who get them) has created a climate hospitable to the ultimate undoing of *Roe* v. *Wade*, an aim supported by many of the conservative judges with whom the Reagan Administration had by 1988 filled the country's highest courts. In *Webster* v. *Reproductive Health Services* a plurality of the Supreme Court, without actually rescinding the abortion right, was, in Justice Harry Blackmun's dissenting words, opening the door to "more and more restrictive" state regulation that will impede its "meaningful exercise."

This radical shift seems strange in light of the

failures of antiabortion forces in the past decade in conventional political arenas. Since 1977, when the Hyde Amendment curtailing federal funding of abortions was passed, not a single major piece of antiabortion legislation has got through Congress. Particularly after the 1986 elections, when the Democrats recaptured the Senate, it became clear that the prospects for antiabortion legislative initiatives were null. And despite Presidents Reagan and Bush, who have strongly voiced antiabortion rhetoric, the Republican Party itself is not a bastion of antiabortion sentiment. Many Republican politicians now view the "pro-life" position as a distinct liability at the polls.

But in retrospect these failures appear negligible relative to the most effective political gain of the antiabortion movement in this period: the election of two Presidents committed to appointing conservatives who would pass the litmus test to the federal and Supreme Court benches. The real question is not how we tally up "pro-life" gains and losses in electoral and legislative contests but rather how "antiabortion" came to be a sign for a whole range of conservative values. In contrast with their limited gains in formal institutional politics, antiabortion forces have registered a seismic impact on symbolic politics, that is, on cultural and political discourse, media imagery and popular perceptions. More than ever, abortion is the fulcrum of a much broader ideological struggle in which the very meanings of the family, the state, motherhood and young women's sexuality are contested.

Abortion in the United States is still overwhelmingly a phenomenon of young, unmarried women, the majority of them teenagers or in their early 20s. Eighty-two percent of all women getting abortions in 1987 were unmarried, and nearly all were either working or attending school. Two-thirds had family incomes under $25,000 a year, and two-thirds were white, even though abortion rates are higher for black and Latino women. In other words, we are talking about young, single women who are working or students, most of them poor or working class— women who are trying to stay in school, develop their skills *and* maintain sexual lives before taking on marriage and childbearing. These facts more than any others—in a society still imbued

with racist and patriarchal values about gender and sex—explain why women's abortion access, despite continued formal legality, is so fiercely contested.

Abortion in the 1970s and 1980s is the consequence, not cause, of complex and mostly positive changes in young women's lives since 1960: higher rates of employment and college attendance, later age at marriage (meaning inevitably more premarital sex) and lower birthrates. The Alan Guttmacher Institute has published comprehensive studies showing that, while other developed countries have experienced similar trends and show similar levels of adolescent sexuality, the United States has "much lower rates of contraceptive use and much higher rates of childbearing, abortion and pregnancy" (especially among teenagers but also among older women) than nearly any other developed country. These more disturbing trends are also the result of complicated social conditions peculiar to the United States: first, the "absence of a unified system of primary health care provision," of which contraceptive services would be an integral and routine part; second, the severe social inequalities in this country, giving many poor young women little reason to plan or hope; and third, the "deep-seated ambivalence toward sexuality" in American culture, in which the glorification of rape and the refusal to advertise condoms can exist side by side.

But these complicated social dynamics are difficult to see. How much simpler to blame young women for "promiscuity" and for "using abortion as a method of birth control," or to blame feminism, and abortion as its main signifier, for subverting the family. What disturbs many people about changes in family life over the past two decades is not that abortion is legal, but that teenagers seem lax and out of control; that sex seems out of control; that mothers are not home when they used to be (to take care of people and police teen sex); that fathers seem to be losing authority over wives and daughters; and that, for perhaps a majority of women at some time in their lives if not for good, having sex and raising children are perceived and experienced outside dependence on men. Indeed, the possibility of lesbian sexuality and lesbian motherhood as viable alternatives presents itself in a more open way than ever in modern history. I suspect that more people share fears about these trends than the small number who actively oppose a woman's right to get an abortion. Thus on one level "moral" opposition to abortion is a response to certain real dimensions of young and poor women's empowerment that many people find threatening.

When I was a teenager in Tulsa, Oklahoma, in the late 1950s and early 1960s, the abortion experience was of course steeped in shame, but it had little to do with harm to the fetus. My generation of young middle-class women knew nothing about the fetus. Like the pregnancy scare and "unwed motherhood," abortion meant shame only because it connoted sex—you'd "done it" without the sanctity of marriage. White teenagers' sexuality in this historical milieu was mediated through an ingenious custom called petting, which was class-, race- and gender-specific and followed definite heterosexist codes. Sex was something you did secretly, in dark parked cars, and you did it only up to a certain point. Built into the very definition of the petting culture as a sexual practice was its own denial; along with shotgun marriages and homes for unwed mothers, it hid the reality of white middle-class women as sexual beings.

The 1970s and 1980s, without in any sense having brought us a "sexual revolution," caused changes in the *signs* of white female teenage sexuality. Birth control and abortion services, widely available without age or marital restrictions, have helped to make the young white woman's sexuality visible, thereby undermining historical race and class stereotypes of "nice girls" and "bad girls." The local abortion clinic represents the existence of her sexual identity independent of marriage, of paternal authority, perhaps of men; and so in a sense it connotes white feminism. This is an important missing piece of the story, and it is why the clinic becomes a target—of bombs and government regulation as well as of prayers—and why, for ardent antiabortionists, the solution of "more effective contraception" so misses the point. The clinic symbolically threatens white patriarchal control over "their" young women's sexual "purity," and thus becomes a target of white patriarchal wrath.

For the one-third of abortion clinic patients who are women of color, both the experience of abortion and the meanings of antiabortion resentment have been different from their meanings for white women. One is struck by the absence, in crowds of Operation Rescue demonstrators, of people of color; except for an occasional black preacher and his followers, it is overwhelmingly a white Christian movement. One senses that, whatever misgivings black and Latino people may have about abortion and the white feminists whom they perceive as leading the pro-choice movement, they are aware of the underlying racism of the antiabortion campaign. The denial of abortion funding and access is clearly racist in its consequences: Poor women are disproportionately women of color and are more likely to suffer deaths or injuries from illegal or botched abortions.

However, many black women have been reluctant to get involved in activities supporting women's abortion rights. To the extent that such activities are associated with white feminist aspirations to "sexual freedom," they may conflict with black women's experiences in several different ways. First, the sense of a collective past in which black women were systematically raped and sexually demeaned by white racists, having constantly to "prove" their "virtue," may make it difficult or painful for many black women to identify with a movement whose emphasis is "sexual liberation." Second, the abortion issue may simply pale next to the daily onslaught of life-and-death crises caused by inadequate health care; child and infant mortality rates twice as high as those for whites; death rates from childbirth four times, and from hypertension seventeen times, those of white women; and the decimation of families by AIDS, drugs and poverty.

People of color have often, and sometimes justifiably, been wary of those promoting abortion and birth control as more interested in racist eugenics or population control than in health. But racism can also take the form of white pronatalism. The pronatalism of the so-called right-to-life movement is not so much about numbers as it is about a patriarchal conception of women's roles as childbearers, mothers and wives. Yet a populationist note is also audible in the continued refrains about adoption as an "alternative to abortion." These appeal to commonly voiced concerns about the "shortage of babies to adopt," and this shortage, it is well known, specifically involves *white* babies. As Patricia Williams notes in the Autumn 1988 issue of *Signs*, while black people were bought and sold under slavery, now "it is white children who are bought and sold, [and] black babies have become 'worthless' currency to adoption agents—'surplus' in the salvage heaps of Harlem hospitals." What, one wonders, do antiabortionists intend should become of the approximately 500,000 additional nonwhite babies who would be born if hypothetically all abortions were to stop? Whether their solution is adoption by white upscale baby consumers (making poor women conscripted surrogate mothers) or increased poverty and suffering (since they oppose the level of social spending needed to help poor mothers raise their own babies), it is a patently racist and class-biased fantasy.

After seventeen years of legal abortion in the United States, feminists have learned that mere legality, even a constitutional right in terms of individual privacy, is perfectly compatible with a wide range of constraints on abortion access, particularly for poor women, rural women, women of color and young teenagers. Legality does not assure women material means, moral support or political legitimation in their abortion decisions. It certainly does not guarantee funding, conveniently located services, protection from harassment and intimidation at the clinic door or a uniform standard of good treatment once inside. Through a series of bureaucratic tactics and an official rhetorical stance, the neoconservative state under Reagan and Bush has continued to seek restrictions on women's access to abortion. In so doing, it has attempted to accommodate antiabortion politics to the formal doctrine of liberal privacy.

State-sponsored restrictions on abortion access take a variety of forms, but they are harshest for poor women, who suffer from the cutoff of federal and state funds and a shortage of public services, and for teenage women, who in many states and localities are hindered by parental consent or notification requirements. Since no doctor or facility is *required* to provide abortions

in a market-dominated medical economy, they are in fact unavailable in many locales. Eighty-two percent of U.S. counties, particularly in rural areas, are without any abortion providers at all. Well before the *Webster* decision public hospitals, upon which most poor and rural women rely for their health care, increasingly refused to provide abortion services, accounting for only 13 percent of induced abortions in 1985. To whatever extent such policies affect the actual number of women getting abortions, they frame the meaning of abortion as an individual and social experience.

The struggle to achieve women's reproductive freedom cannot succeed in the long run if conducted as a civil liberties struggle for individual privacy. At bottom it is a deeply cultural and social conflict for which formal legality provides at best a thin protective cover. What is lost in the language of liberal privacy is the concept of social rights, familiar in most European social democracies: that society has a responsibility to ameliorate the conditions that make either abortion or childbearing a hard, painful choice for some women, and that the bearers of this right are not so much isolated individuals as they are members of social groups with distinct needs.

That is why a feminist politics of reproductive rights cannot rest solely on the notion of privacy. The real paradox—and tragedy—of the past seventeen years of legal abortion is not that although the majority of people believe in "individual choice," politicians and judges do not listen. Rather, it is that the majority believe in "individual choice"—the language of privacy—but fail to connect this belief to the social changes and affirmative public efforts needed to make such choice real for *all* women. A full reproductive rights agenda must involve access not only to abortion services and funds but to adequate prenatal care, maternal, infant and child health services, child care, housing, sex education without stigma, drug treatment and, of course, universal health insurance. While antiabortionists clamor for the rights of fetuses and embryos, we live in a society in which one-fifth of children, more than one-fourth of all black children and one-third of all poor children have no health coverage at all. As Gloria Joseph wrote in 1981, "Given these realities of health care [as] seen by Black people, White women must understand why Black women do not devote their full energies to the abortion issue. The emphasis has to be on total health care." Until privacy or autonomy is redefined in reference to social justice provisions that can give it substance for the poorest women, it will remain not only a class-biased and racist concept but an antifeminist one, insofar as it is premised on a denial of social responsibility to improve the conditions of women as a group.

Happily, a new political movement based on a broader array of forces than feminism has yet known is beginning to emerge under the vocal leadership of black feminists active in the reproductive rights struggle. Perhaps the most besieged clinic in the country is the Atlanta Feminist Women's Health Center. The center's former health education director, Dazon Dixon,

herself black, tells a story about a young black client trying to maneuver through Operation Rescue pickets and television cameras so she could enter the clinic for an abortion:

When a young looking, blonde and blue-eyed white man screamed charges at her that the Rev. Martin Luther King Jr. would "turn over in his grave for what she is doing" and that she was contributing to the genocide of African-Americans, she broke. She stopped, stared him in his eyes with tears in hers, then quietly and coolly said, "You're a white boy, and you don't give a damn about me, who I am or what I do. And you even know less about Martin Luther King or being Black. What you have to say to me means nothin', not a damn thing." He was silenced and she walked on.

That young women's voice foretells the future, not only of abortion politics but of feminism in America.

50. THE ABORTION QUESTION

HYMAN RODMAN, BETTY SARVIS, and JOY WALKER BONAR

Opposing positions on the abortion question are so sharply different and so strongly held that it is difficult to develop a satisfactory abortion policy. The abortion laws in many countries represent an attempt at compromise between opposing positions, but the compromises do not please the partisans on either side of the abortion debate. The controversy therefore continues in the media, in the legislatures, in the courts, in the streets, and sometimes in the abortion clinics.

Although we often refer to pro-choice and pro-life positions as though they are monolithic, the situation is far more complex. Some people,

From *The Abortion Question*, 1987, pp. 157–172. New York: Columbia University Press. Reprinted with permission.

for example, want to prohibit abortion except when the woman's life is threatened by the pregnancy. Some also accept one or more other justifications for a legal abortion—e.g., threats to the woman's physical or mental health, a pregnancy resulting from rape or incest, the likelihood of fetal deformity, and the woman's social and economic circumstances. Some want to accept abortion without the requirement of justifications, and hence would like to see the repeal of all laws pertaining to abortion (see Callahan 1977).

Partisans sometimes feel so strongly about their positions that communication is impossible because they are on completely different wavelengths. Research and clinical findings are often shaped to conform to preconceived beliefs. One psychiatrist assures us that guilt never accompanies abortion and another that it always does

(Sarvis and Rodman 1974:106). The dark and choppy waters surrounding the abortion question make for difficult sailing. Shaping abortion policy is difficult and seems endlessly controversial. In recent years, however, a few glimmers of light have appeared. One hope for calmer waters, as this chapter will make clear, stems from several developments that lead toward greater acceptance of early abortion and lesser acceptance of late abortion. Another hope on the horizon is the development of new contraceptive and abortifacient drugs.

UNDERLYING MORAL DIFFERENCES

The major opposing groups in the abortion controversy have adopted terms that aptly summarize their position and the irresolvable essence of their moral differences. One side is pro-choice. Its cohorts insist they are not pro-abortion. They often make it clear that they are against abortion and would like to reduce the number of abortions through improved sex education and family planning programs. But since they recognize that there will still be unwanted pregnancies, they accept abortion as a last resort, and they deplore any attempt to eliminate that choice from a pregnant woman.

The other side is pro-life. Its supporters recognize the difficulty of the woman with an unwanted pregnancy. Although they are ambivalent in their support of improved sex education and family planning programs, they want to prevent unwanted pregnancies or to help women with unwanted pregnancies. But they are not prepared to accept abortion because they believe that it is the killing of human life. It is only when the pregnant woman's life is endangered that they may be willing to accept abortion.

Although the above attempt to summarize opposing positions is oversimplified, it is a reasonable account of the principal arguments. The pro-choice groups decry the enlarged pictures of human fetuses that pro-lifers sometimes show. And the pro-life groups understandably pay less attention to the trials and tribulations of women with unwanted pregnancies, and decry the pictures of women who have died at the hands of illegal abortionists.

In the United States, until the early 1970s, restrictive abortion laws forced many woman into illegal abortion and its attendant dangers. As a result, there were dramatic appeals to change the laws, including exaggerated estimates of the number of illegal abortions and deaths resulting from them. This led to revised laws that made abortion legal, at least under some conditions.

Currently, the legal status of abortion has made possible a growing number of abortions and leads to occasional cases of an aborted fetus that lives for a while and that may have been viable (Tunkel 1979). As a result, there are now dramatic appeals to restrict abortions, including exaggerated accounts of the human characteristics of the embryo and fetus and exaggerated estimates of the number of late abortions.

LAW AND PRIVATE MORALITY

By separating private morality from the law it becomes possible to accommodate differing moral positions and to respect (or at the least not to prosecute those who adhere to) these positions. The Wolfenden Report of 1957, which dealt with homosexuality in Britain, strongly urged the separation of law and private morality: "There must remain a realm of private morality and immorality which is . . . not the law's business" (Wolfenden Report 1957). This argument, of ancient vintage, produced major changes in British law in 1967, including a liberalization of the abortion law. The argument was also influential in bringing about passage of the revised Canadian abortion law in 1969. Although the percentage of Roman Catholics in Canada is much higher than in the United States, the voice of the Catholic hierarchy in Canada has been muted and has better accepted the separation of law and private morality (de Valk 1974).

If we could clearly and consensually distinguish universal values from group-specific values, or public morality from private morality, we might have a route toward a resolution of the abortion controversy. Thus, the 1957 Wolfenden Report accepted the idea that homosexuality was in the domain of private rather than public morality. Similar ideas in many countries influenced the liberalization of laws on birth control and divorce, and in these areas the Roman Catholic Church has accepted the distinction between moral law and civil law (de Valk 1974:29–32). There has been a general movement in the Western world to sever the tie between traditional religious morality and the law on sexual behavior. As a result we commonly hear that "the state has no business in the bedrooms of the nation" (Pierre E. Trudeau, quoted in de Valk 1974:57), and there is a growing—but certainly not universal—acceptance of sexual behavior as private morality.

On abortion, however, it is much more difficult to get moral consensus. The Roman Catholic hierarchy is not prepared to deal with abortion in the same way that it deals with birth control and divorce. In most developed nations, birth control and divorce clearly are in the realm of private morality, but there is no such moral consensus on abortion. This is due to a fundamental difference. For pro-life partisans, human life is at stake when we deal with abortion. Thus a pro-choice statement that abortion reduces maternal mortality or morbidity, or reduces the suffering of unwanted children, has a hollow sound when it strikes against the idea that each abortion represents the killing of an innocent human life. The abortion controversy therefore persists, and the separation of law and private morality does not seem to be a route that is available to resolve the controversy.

ATTEMPTED COMPROMISES

Given the absolute position that abortion is the killing of a human being and the absolute position that a woman has a right to control her own body and her own childbearing, there can be no compromise and no debate—only opposing partisans who talk past each other. But although the moral debate is irresolvable, the legal and judicial worlds have had to make policy decisions about abortion.

Some suggest that the best way out of the legal and moral difficulty is to write no law regarding abortion, and to deal with it like any other medical procedure. In that way no legal justifications (such as health or eugenic indications) that might be objectionable to Roman Catholics or others are specifically acknowledged. This was the American situation prior to the mid–nineteenth century. Such a solution is, of course, tantamount to placing abortion in the realm of private morality, and separating private morality from the law. It effectively treats abortion in a permissive fashion, without any need for special justifications or procedures. In consequence, this approach is not acceptable to pro-life partisans and it does not resolve the legal and moral controversy.

Legislatures and courts have used two kinds of compromises in deciding difficult abortion questions: (a) permitting abortion only for certain reasons and forbidding all other abortions; (b) permitting abortions up to a certain gestation time and forbidding later abortions. We shall briefly discuss each of these compromise solutions, and indicate how they point the way toward future directions in abortion policy.

JUSTIFICATIONS FOR ABORTION

Under this compromise, abortion is forbidden unless there are certain reasons or justifications for it. The moral principle that underlies this compromise is that the embryo and fetus have rights, but not the right to life in the same sense that a human being has. As a result, abortion is not legally available unless it can be justified. One widely accepted justification is the preservation of the pregnant woman's life. Other justifications are illustrated by the British law, passed in 1967: justifications for abortion include danger to the woman's life or health, pregnancy due to criminal assault, a threat of fetal deformity, and socioeconomic reasons. According to proposals made by the American Law Institute (1962:189–190) justifications include danger to the woman's physical or mental health, the threat of severe fetal deformity, and pregnancy due to rape, incest, or other felonious intercourse. Several states in the United States adopted some of these legal justifications between 1967 and 1970. The law in Canada, passed in 1969, is a good example of the "justifications" compromise. It bans abortion unless justified on the grounds of protecting the woman's life or health. There is no time limit in the gestation period after which abortion is forbidden, and thus the Canadian law is a pure case of a "justifications" approach.

GESTATION TIME

Another compromise is to permit abortion up to a particular time in the gestation process and to forbid abortions after that time. The principle that underlies this compromise is that the embryo and fetus represent developing human life. Up to a certain point the embryo or fetus is judged not to be sufficiently developed to warrant protection, and no justification for abortion is needed. Beyond that point, however, the embryo or fetus is judged to have developed sufficiently to be worthy of protection, and abortions are not permitted after that time (except to save the pregnant woman's life). Alternatively, a justifications approach may be applied during a time period between permissive early abortion and prohibited late abortion.

The process of biological development, from the zygote at conception to the baby at birth, is conceptualized and subdivided in many ways. Distinctions are made by days or weeks of gestation, by months or trimesters, or by using conception, implantation, quickening, viability, and birth as anchoring points. One can refer to the development of various organs or to the development of the cerebral cortex as the critical processes.

There is no absolutely clear point in the development process at which we can agree that biological development has reached the point where the fetus should be protected from an abortion. Legal policies on abortion are therefore somewhat arbitrary and often contentious. Some insist that the uncertainty calls for a moral choice in favor of human life, with abortion prohibited from the earliest possible time in the gestation period. Others insist that the moral imperative of a woman's right to make decisions about reproduction and childbearing call for a policy that permits legal abortion until the latest possible time in the gestation period. The earliest possible time in the gestation period is fertilization and the latest possible time is birth, and there are opposing partisans in the abortion debate who have adopted these radically different points as the cornerstone of their policy. Research findings in medicine, however, and new technological developments, are narrowing the range of policy choices about abortion.

MEDICAL ADVANCES

Advances in medical technology have been increasing the survival rate of premature infants of low birth weight. These techniques, used before and during labor, and after delivery (Beard, 1981; Campbell 1985), are having an impact on medical and ethical thinking about fetal viability. Neonatal intensive care units, with respirators and drug treatment, have lowered the age of viability to about 24 weeks, and infants of even lower gestational age[1] have a chance of surviving with aggressive medical intervention. These advances have changed the possibilities for fetal viability and have become part of the debate on abortion law and policy. From the 1960s to the 1980s the point of viability decreased from about 28 weeks to about 24 weeks gestational age (Stubblefield 1985). More than 50 percent of the premature infants at these gestational ages are able to survive with state-of-the-art medical care.

The neurological outcome for these infants is not always favorable; many premature infants kept alive through aggressive treatment survive with major handicaps such as mental retardation or cerebral palsy. But the outcome is often positive, with normal functioning or only minor handicaps. Strong (1983) summarizes several reports on infants weighing 500 to 1,000 grams at birth. The reports range from approximately 5 to 30 percent with a normal neurological outcome among infants who survive, and they range from 7 to 30 percent who survive with a major handicap. Aggressive medical treatment is expensive and the outcome for very low birth weight and very low gestational age infants is not very good. These medical advances therefore raise difficult ethical and social policy questions about whether to pursue aggressive care, when to do so, and for how long (Milligan, Shennan, and Hoskins 1984).

---

[1] In this chapter, we use gestational age and weeks of gestation to refer to the time since the last menstrual period (LMP). This is in accord with conventional use—for example, Stubblefield (1985:161) and Centers for Disease Control (1985:35)

LEGAL CONSIDERATIONS

Medical advances lowering the threshold of fetal viability have implications for the legal situation in the United States. The U.S. Supreme Court, in its *Roe* v. *Wade* decision, refers to the developing fetus and its potential life; viability is the critical point at which a state may prohibit abortion (unless the woman's life or health is threatened). Medical advances in caring for premature infants have influenced many hospitals and physicians to eschew late abortions. The occasional birth of a live infant resulting from a late abortion, and criminal charges brought against a few physicians for contributing to the subsequent death of the infant, have also made late abortions more difficult to obtain. Approximately half of all abortions take place during the first 8 weeks of gestation (i.e., 8 weeks since the last menstrual period), and approximately 85 to 90 percent during the first 12 weeks LMP. Only about 1 percent take place at 21 weeks or later (CDC 1985).

Amniocentesis, to determine numerous fetal diseases, cannot be carried out until the sixteenth week of gestation. Amniotic fluid is withdrawn and fetal cells are cultured, providing a prenatal diagnosis by the eighteenth to twentieth week. If the threshold of fetal viability were lowered to 18 or 20 weeks, many abortions based on information from amniocentesis would be denied. If the threshold were lowered further, a larger number of abortions would be denied. Many medical researchers, however, are not hopeful about the prospects for lowering the threshold of viability below 22 to 23 weeks, unless some sort of artificial womb were developed. Medical developments in neonatal care therefore do not rule out legal abortions performed up to about 21 weeks' gestation. Moreover, recent advances in prenatal testing are making it possible to diagnose fetal abnormalities much earlier in pregnancy.

Justice O'Connor's dissenting opinion in *Akron* (1983) has drawn much attention. She questions the reliance on "stages" of pregnancy that was adopted in *Roe* and believes that the trimester approach "cannot be supported as a legitimate or useful framework for accommodating the woman's right and the State's interests." This is because of changing medical technology and because "the *Roe* framework is inherently tied to the state of medical technology that exists whenever particular litigation ensues." O'Connor's *Akron* dissent, however, is more fundamental than the problem posed by advancing medical technology:

In *Roe*, the Court held that although the State had an important and legitimate interest in protecting potential life, that interest could not become compelling until the point at which the fetus was viable. The difficulty with this analysis is clear: *potential* life is no less potential in the first weeks of pregnancy than it is at viability or afterward. At any stage in pregnancy, there is the potential for human life. . . . Accordingly, I believe that the State's interest in protecting potential human life exists throughout the pregnancy.

Justice O'Connor's dissent in *Akron* has increased speculation that *Roe* will eventually be overturned. However, we should not conclude that O'Connor wants to overturn *Roe*. True, she does stress the existence of potential life throughout the pregnancy and she states that medical science is pushing the point of viability toward conception. When she says that the *Roe* framework "is clearly on a collision course with itself," she is referring to a collision between a principle that limits states' rights to regulate abortion and a principle that extends states' rights. O'Connor states the first principle in her *Akron* dissent. "As the medical risks of various abortion procedures decrease, the point at which the State may regulate for reasons of maternal health is moved further forward to actual childbirth." The second principle—prohibiting abortion from the time of fetal viability—pushes the potential ban on abortion "further back toward conception." The first principle has curtailed state regulations for reasons of maternal health through the sixteenth week of gestation. The second principle has extended prohibitions due to fetal viability to 21–23 weeks.

The O'Connor collision is not as serious as it has at times been portrayed. First, there is still a good deal of space between 16 and 21 weeks.

Second, it is likely that one principle will take precedence over the other, thereby avoiding a collision. Will the first principle or the second principle take precedence?

FIRST SOLUTION

One possible solution to the abortion question, a solution that may eventually dampen the controversy, will be the easy acceptance of early abortions and the prohibition of late abortions. The outlines of such a solution are already visible in many countries throughout the world. Although there is still much controversy in the United States about induced abortion at any stage of pregnancy, most abortions take place early, and it is now virtually impossible to obtain an abortion during the last trimester of pregnancy or even during the latter part of the second trimester.

The solution we are predicting assumes that most nations will permit abortion during the early weeks of gestation without a need to justify the abortion. It also assumes that abortions will be forbidden or will be difficult to obtain later on during pregnancy. Evidence of such developments can be found in many nations. For example, Czechoslovakia, Denmark, and Hungary have permissive abortion policies during the first 12 weeks of gestation, with more stringent requirements afterwards. The dividing line is 18 weeks in Sweden, 90 days in Italy, and 10 weeks in France (Rodman and Trost 1986).

In Canada, even early abortions must be justified, and each abortion must be approved by a hospital abortion committee. This procedure, however, is not working well (Badgley Report 1977). As Rodman says:

The members of therapeutic abortion committees do not see the woman whose abortion is at issue; they rely strictly upon the written record. Thus, depending upon the willingness of the woman's physician to tailor the record to the justification permitted by law, and the willingness of the therapeutic abortion committee to interpret the law broadly, the woman may or may not be approved for an abortion. As a result of this bureaucratic procedure, there are great inequities in how the law is implemented from province to province, from locality to locality, and from hospital to hospital. (1981:234)

These procedures contribute to very substantial delays in obtaining an abortion in Canada, adding to the risk of an abortion. They are not likely to survive for much longer. Their survival thus far has been aided by physicians who circumvent the legal requirements for abortion (Badgley Report 1977; Rodman 1981).

Another reason for moving away from a justifications approach is found in the U.S. experience under reform laws, during the 1960s and early 1970s. Making judgments about whether an abortion is legally justified on medical or psychiatric grounds is subjective and difficult. Physicians often make these judgments based on their ideological beliefs. They may grant permission for otherwise illegal acts or withhold permission for legal acts based on deeply held values rather than on legal considerations. Under such circumstances, the medical role is uncomfortable; some physicians become the mechanism for circumventing restrictive laws. It is demeaning to patients and to physicians to go through the charade of paying lip service to the law while circumventing it.

Along with developments in a more permissive direction for early abortions, there are developments toward greater restriction for later abortions. Technological advances making it possible to sustain a fetus outside the mother's body at earlier gestational ages are contributing toward these restrictions. Further, improvements in contraceptive technology and in the delivery of contraceptive information and services will very likely reduce the number of unwanted pregnancies and the demand for abortion. Once a monthly or a post-coital pill is developed, the demand for induced abortion as presently practiced will decrease still further. Finally, advances in embryology and fetology, including advances in diagnosing and treating fetal disease, will increase the pressure for early abortion and against later abortion.

Whether through changes in law or in medical practice, abortion policy is heading toward our predicted "first solution": easy-to-get early abortions, hard-to-get late abortions. The dividing line between early and late abortion, of course, is critical. Because of the present inability of prenatal testing to diagnose many fetal abnormalities until about the eighteenth to twentieth week of gestation, there are reasoned suggestions to draw the line at about 20 or 21 weeks.

Not only would such a voluntary limit respond to the sense of repugnance generated by late abortions, it would also take account of the growing ability of medicine to push the point of viability back below 24 weeks. That latter point is not trivial. As many commentators have noted, any significant change in the time of viability could seriously challenge an important aspect of the *Roe* v. *Wade* decision. (Callahan 1985:163)

There are also reasoned suggestions to sever the tie between fetal viability and a woman's right to an abortion. "We need to refocus the right to abortion as one not defined by the fetus or by technological advances, but rather one that is tied to women's constitutional right to privacy, autonomy and bodily integrity" (Benshoof 1985:163). In many countries, however, the direction of abortion policy is toward finding a compromise between a woman's right to an abortion and the state's right to provide some degree of protection to the developing fetus.

New prenatal techniques are making it possible to diagnose fetal abnormalities much earlier than heretofore. This will relieve some of the pressure that is generated by tying the legality of abortion to fetal viability. One technique, chorionic villus sampling, makes diagnosis possible by 9 or 10 weeks' gestational age. A catheter, guided by ultrasound, is inserted into the uterus through the cervix, and it aspirates a small amount of the tissue surrounding the fetus. Many medical centers are undertaking clinical trials with the technique, comparing its accuracy and safety with amniocentesis. Initial reports suggest that the technique is more likely to lead to spontaneous abortion than is the case with amniocentesis, but that complication rates decrease with physicians' experience (Hogge, Schonberg, and Golbus 1986; Elias et al. 1986). If the risks are eventually shown to be low, chorionic villus sampling may replace amniocentesis as the diagnostic procedure of choice (see McGovern, Goldberg, and Desnick 1986). Such a development would greatly reduce the need for late abortions in cases of fetal abnormality.

We predict that the dividing line between early and late abortion will eventually turn out to be approximately 12 weeks. Induced abortion prior to that time will be readily accepted by a very large majority of the public; after that time, abortion will be severely restricted, and perhaps legally available only to preserve the pregnant woman's health or life.

SECOND SOLUTION

A second possible solution to the abortion controversy will stem from the development of new contraceptive technology. New drugs, still under investigation, offer promise of a once-a-month pill or of a post-coital pill. Like menstrual extraction and IUDs, these new drugs would offer protection before it can be determined whether the woman is pregnant. They hold out the promise of menstrual regulation or of abortifacient action in the first few days of pregnancy, thus fitting neatly into the movement toward early abortion. These drugs, taken once a month, or taken by the woman after sexual intercourse, could become the preferred method of the future. They would be simple, safe, and effective; they would not require continuous use; they would not interfere with the act of coitus; and they would be available for the woman to use at her own convenience. Unfortunately, such drugs are still experimental. But current research efforts suggest that such an ideal contraceptive, or at least improved contraceptives, will be available for widespread use by the first decade of the twenty-first century.

One morning-after pill, currently available for use in England and Germany, indicates the possibilities for the future. The pill, developed by A. Albert Yuzpe of the University of Western Ontario, contains norgestrel and ethinyl estradiol. Four pills are taken over a 12-hour period, and treatment must begin within 72 hours after intercourse (Johnson 1985). The method apparently works by interfering with the implantation of the fertilized ovum. Because of short-term side effects, such as vomiting and nausea, and the possibility of long-term side effects, it is not used on a regular basis. It is recommended for emergencies—for example, if a hole is found in a diaphragm or condom, if withdrawal is mistimed, or under other circumstances that lead to an unprotected act of sexual intercourse. In addition to its use in England and Germany, some use is also made of the method in other European countries. In the United States it is used as a treatment for rape in some pilot projects at college health centers. This post-coital pill is not the ideal contraceptive of the future and it is not the solution to the abortion controversy, but it is a harbinger of drugs yet to come.

One drug that offers promise for the future, known as RU 486, was developed by scientists at Roussel Uclaf, a pharmaceutical company in Paris. It inhibits the action of progesterone in the uterus, thus interfering with implantation and contributing toward the onset of menstruation. An account of the development of this drug is provided by Spitz and Bardin (1985). Initial research suggests that the drug is effective in inducing menses even after implantation has occurred. Several organizations are carrying out research in France, Sweden, the United States, and other countries to determine the most effective method of treatment. One possibility being explored is a once-a-month pill that would induce or assure menses, but the optimal dose and timing has not yet been determined. As Spitz and Bardin (1985:261) say, "RU 486 is still in early clinical trials. Although the results are promising, a once-a-month contraceptive pill using RU 486 is still far from reality. Many problems remain to be resolved." Among other things, the seriousness of side effects must be carefully evaluated. Whether RU 486 actually turns out to be an ideal or useful monthly pill remains to be seen. But it is an example of a new type of drug that will ultimately have major implications for contraceptive and abortion practice and policy.

One result of the widespread use of such a drug, with either contraceptive action preventing fertilization or with contragestive action during the first few days after fertilization, could be a substantial reduction in the fiery controversy engendered by the abortion debate.

CONCLUSION

Abortion policy has been plagued by rancorous controversy. The controversy did not end during 1966 to 1973, when various states enacted reform and repeal laws. Nor did the controversy end with the U.S. Supreme Court's *Roe* decision of 1973. Rather, with each major change, the controversy increased. Partisans who lost one battle sought other areas in which to press their fight. Thus, after *Roe*, anti-abortion advocates chipped away at various programs and policies in an effort to block access to abortion. Attempt to pass a federal anti-abortion statute or constitutional amendment failed. Efforts to end the use of public funds to subsidize abortions for medically indigent patients were successful at the federal level and showed considerable success at the state level. The battles continue, with much intensity, and with new efforts to sway public opinion and legislators' votes. Thus we have bombings of abortion clinics and vigils to protect them. We have local referenda on abortion. We have a variety of media and publicity campaigns. Hopes and fears about what may happen are at an all-time high. When it comes to abortion policy, one person's solution is another person's problem. We are going to see new weapons in the abortion war and new arenas in which battles are fought.

In the face of rising tension and controversy, how can one predict that peace will eventually settle on the land? The "definitive" *Roe* decision did not end the war. How can we be so sanguine as to believe that the end is now in sight?

The answer, we believe, can be seen in developments already taking place. One single event will not end the war; rather, a series of developments will gradually quell the intensity of the controversy. Intense debates about alcohol and contraception have diminished, with only pockets of resistance to a public policy that permits the sale of alcohol and contraceptives and the delivery of contraceptive services. We predict that abortion will eventually share the same fate.

In sum, we predict that ultimately U.S. policy will permit early abortions and prohibit late abortions, and that the intensity of the abortion controversy will subside by the first decade of the twenty-first century. It is difficult to predict what the dividing line may be between early and late abortion, and we may find that the dividing line (in medical practice if not also in law) changes over time. Our prediction is that, ultimately, early abortions up to approximately 12 weeks' gestation will be readily available without the need for justification. Beyond that time, abortions would be legally available only when continuing the pregnancy threatens the pregnant woman's life or health, or perhaps also for severe problems of fetal development. This policy would confirm the reasoning of *Roe* v. *Wade* and it would acknowledge and anticipate medical advances by changing the dividing line between readily available abortions and hard to get abortions from approximately 21 weeks gestational age to 12 weeks.

We also predict (as do many others) that new contraceptive or contragestive drugs will substantially decrease the number of unintended pregnancies and the need for surgical abortion. Moreover, medical advances will make it possible to diagnose many fetal abnormalities earlier. These developments fit neatly into the movement toward early abortions. With the development of a once-a-month or morning-after pill, women will be able to regulate their menstrual cycle without knowledge of whether a pregnancy has occurred.

Perhaps we need to emphasize that we are making a prediction about the direction in which abortion policy is heading; we are not making a policy recommendation. We are not saying that 12 weeks' gestation is the ideal dividing line between early and late abortions. Rather, based on medical advances and legal developments, we predict that the eventual dividing line in the United States will be approximately 12 weeks' gestation. Although such a resolution may not appear satisfactory from the current perspective of either pro-choice or pro-life groups, we think that by the first decade of the twenty-first century it will be accepted as reasonable and relatively noncontroversial public policy.

References

Akron v. *Akron Center for Reproductive Health et al.* U.S. Supreme Court, Nos. 81–746 and 81–1172 (June 15, 1983).

American Law Institute. July 20, 1962. *Model Penal Code*, 2d ed. Philadelphia: American Law Institute.

Badgley Report. 1977. *Report of the Committee on the Operation of the Abortion Law* (Robin F. Badgley, chairman). Ottawa: Minister of Supply and Services.

Beard, R. W. 1981. Technology in the care of mother and baby: An essential safeguard. In R. Chester, Peter Diggory, and Margaret B. Sutherland, eds., *Changing Patterns of Childbearing and Child Rearing*, pp. 1–12. London: Academic Press.

Benshoof, Jane. 1985. Late abortion and technological advances in fetal viability: Reasserting women's rights. *Family Planning Perspectives* 17:162–163.

Callahan, Daniel. 1985. Late abortion and technological advances in fetal viability: Some moral reflections. *Family Planning Perspectives* 17:163–164.

Callahan, Daniel. 1977. Abortion: A summary of the arguments. In Robert M. Veatch, ed., *Population Policy and Ethics: The American Experience*. New York: Irvington.

Campbell, Alastair V. 1985. Viability and the moral status of the fetus. In Ciba Foundation Symposium 115, *Abortion: Medical Progress and Social Implications*, pp. 228–243.

CDC (Centers for Disease Control). 1985. *Abortion Surveillance: Annual Summary, 1981*. Atlanta: U.S. Department of Health, Education, and Welfare, Public Health Service.

de Valk, Alphonse. 1974. *Morality and Law in Canadian Politics: The Abortion Controversy*. Montreal: Palm.

Elias, Sherman, Joe Leigh Simpson, Alice O. Martin, Rudy Sabbagha, Allan Bombard, Barbara Rosinsky, and Lora D. Baum. 1986. Chorionic villus sampling in continuing pregnancies. I. Low fetal loss rates in initial 109 cases. *American Journal of Obstetrics and Gynecology* 154:1349–1352.

Hogge, W. A., S. A. Schonberg, and M. S. Golbus. 1986. Chorionic villus sampling: Experience of the first 1000 cases. *American Journal of Obstetrics and Gynecology* 154:1249–1252.

Johnson, Jeanette H. 1984. Conception—the morning after. *Family Planning Perspectives* 16:266–270.

McGovern, Margaret M., James D. Goldberg, and Robert J. Desnick. 1986. Acceptability of chorionic villi sampling for prenatal diagnosis. *American Journal of Obstetrics and Gynecology* 155:25–29.

Milligan, J. E., A. T. Shennan, and E. M. Hoskins. 1984. Prenatal intensive care: Where and how to draw the line. *American Journal of Obstetrics and Gynecology* 148:499–503.

Rodman, Hyman. 1981. Future directions for abortion morality and policy. In Paul Sachdev, ed., *Abortion: Readings and Research*, pp. 229–237. Toronto: Butterworths.

Rodman, Hyman and Jan Trost, eds. 1986. *The Adolescent Dilemma: International Perspectives on the Family Planning Rights of Minors.* New York: Praeger.

Sarvis, Betty and Hyman Rodman. 1974. *The Abortion Controversy.* 2d ed. New York: Columbia University Press.

Spitz, Irving M. and C. Wayne Bardin. 1985. Antiprogestins: Prospects for a once-a-month pill. *Family Planning Perspectives* 17:260–262.

Strong, Carson. 1983. The tiniest newborns: Aggressive treatment or conservative care? *Hastings Center Report*, February, pp. 14–19.

Stubblefield, Phillip G. 1985. Late abortion and technological advances in fetal viability: Some medical considerations. *Family Planning Perspectives* 17:161–162.

Tunkel, Victor. 1979. Abortion: How early, how late, and how legal? *British Medical Journal* 2:253–256.

Wolfenden Report. 1957. *Report of the Committee on Homosexual Offences and Prostitution* (Sir John Wolfenden, chairman). London: HMSO.

CHAPTER **18**

STRATIFYING THE CLASSROOM

INTRODUCTION

Equal opportunity is a value deeply rooted in American life. Abraham Lincoln articulated that value eloquently in his first annual address to Congress when he described the American mission: "to lift artificial weights from all shoulders; to clear the paths of laudable pursuit; to afford all an unfettered start, and a fair chance in the race of life." The public schools of the United States have often been portrayed as crucial institutions of equal opportunity. Schools are the places where children begin their journey toward fulfillment of the American dream.

Visions of public education as an avenue of equal opportunity for all students regardless of race, social class, gender, or creed have been challenged by sociologists who have made systematic observations of teachers and students in the classrooms and corridors of public schools. A close study of schools and what students experience in them reveals sharply stratified arrangements in which students are divided according to their ability. The educational practice of "tracking" has been adopted by most public schools in this century.

Educators often defend the practice of grouping students by their ability as the best way to serve both slow learners and the gifted. But many researchers refute this claim. They point out that students in the lower tracks suffer from the stigma of being labeled as low achievers and are forced to endure watered-down instruction by the weakest teachers. Critics also point out the overwhelming proportions of lower-class and minority students in the lower tracks, whereas the higher tracks have larger proportions of white students from middle- and upper-class homes. Schools become miniature stratification systems that parallel the structures found in the larger community.

In the 1980s and 1990s many educators were troubled by the pernicious implications of the tracking system. It seemed already to have doomed lower-track students

to failure in school and beyond in the workplace. New models of education were developed that emphasized cooperative learning among heterogeneous groupings of students: the fast learners would help the slow, and all would benefit. Some educators insist that *all* students be defined as "gifted." The advocates of these new models of education claim that research demonstrates that all students achieve more under the cooperative-learning system.

Joan Beck is skeptical about the new approaches. She sees the problem in zero-sum terms: the benefits gained by the slower students come at the expense of the gifted students. Sheila Tobias examines the broader issues of tracking and summarizes numerous problems that trouble many educators. No quick answers are available, but educators and the public must keep Abraham Lincoln's vision of America in mind if this nation is ever to have a school system that affords "all an unfettered start, and a fair chance in the race of life."

51.   LET BRIGHT PUPILS MOVE AHEAD, EVEN IF IT SEEMS UNFAIR

JOAN BECK

Is it unfair to group public school children by ability? To allow some youngsters to move ahead faster, to learn more than others?

What if the children in the faster classes are more likely to be white and middle class and

most of those learning less are minorities and poor? Is tracking by ability then unacceptable racial segregation?

When the goal of providing all children equality of education conflicts with the goal of helping all children learn up to the level of their abilities, which should take precedence?

Support for ability grouping—by 1st grade reading sections, by subject matter, by across-the-board tracking, even by special schools for the gifted and talented—rises and falls as much in response to political pressures as academic rationales.

Now, opposition to grouping is growing, largely reflecting the desperate concern for helping poor, minority youngsters at risk of academic failure. Some school systems are dismantling existing track systems. Other educators are even talking about phasing out the popular magnet schools so their resources can be diverted to struggling neighborhood schools.

Opponents of ability grouping make several strong arguments. It can be difficult, for example, to identify all the "gifted," "talented" and "bright." Formal tests are often inadequate. Teacher judgments can be biased by family background, behavior and appearance. Some bright children will be missed because they don't fit compliant, middle-class stereotypes or have difficulty speaking English.

Further, children left behind in slower tracks or groups suffer a serious loss of self-esteem and from a lack of brighter classmates and role models from whom to learn. Because the "bright" groups move ahead faster, slower youngsters can't ever catch up and are stuck forever in the academic pits.

Bright kids draw the best teachers and the most resources, opponents charge. Slower youngsters get dull drill, plodding lessons, inexperienced teachers.

Some of the school systems backing away from ability grouping have found an ally and an excuse in the Carnegie Foundation. Last year, a report by its Council on Adolescent Development strongly condemned tracking as "one of the most divisive and damaging school practices in existence."

The Carnegie report cited "the psychic numbing" children in the lower tracks experience from a "dumbed-down" curriculum, the widening gap in achievement between faster and slower groups and the increased racial isolation of ability groupings.

Instead, it proposed that schools deal with students of widely diverse academic abilities by teaming them together in cooperative learning projects in which brighter students help slower classmates and "students receive group rewards." The report also advocates using capable students to tutor others.

Such proposals do irreparable injustice and harm to bright children, who are just as entitled as other youngsters to an education appropriate to their abilities. Yet the smarter children are, the more likely their classes will leave them bored and unchallenged, with their great potential unfulfilled.

Bright children already know most of what they are expected to learn during an average school year, studies show. To expect them, as Carnegie does, to spend much of their class time helping slower learners is an inexcusable waste of their irreplaceable learning time. They need the challenge of new ideas and new material and opportunities to learn at the accelerated speed most comfortable for them.

To expect them to sustain a love of learning while marking time waiting for slower students to catch up, if ever, is like asking Michael Jordan to be challenged by playing basketball indefinitely at a local "Y."

Bright children are much more likely to be middle class than minority poor. (Some incalculable part of intelligence is assumed to be inherited and fostering their children's learning is one mark of successful middle-class families, white or minority.)

But the remedies lie in protecting all children's developing brains through good prenatal care and using proven early learning techniques to increase intelligence long before 1st grade—not in holding smart youngsters back.

Instead of treating high intelligence and talent as a sort of shameful secret, schools should be doing everything they can to find giftedness and learning potential in all children, to nourish it, cherish it and encourage it—especially in youngsters from families that lack the resources to do so themselves.

Bright children aren't entitled to more resources or better teachers than other youngsters. But they are due an equal share—and an education that is a good match for their abilities.

Educators who refuse to acknowledge the special needs of high-ability children—because of a preoccupation with at-risk youngsters, a misreading of research on the gifted or a lopsided focus on equality instead of excellence—need to look ahead to the nation's next century.

The new drugs, genetic therapies, inventions,

energy solutions, transportation and housing systems, economic improvements, foreign policy strategies, government and business expertise, environmental leadership and human rights advocacy will have to come from today's children. We can't afford to make their schooling a holding-back operation—whatever the motivation.

---

52.   TRACKED TO FAIL

SHEILA TOBIAS

No one who has ever read Aldous Huxley's anti-utopian novel, *Brave New World*, can forget the book's opening scene, a tour of the "Hatchery and Conditioning Centre." There human embryos in their first hours of existence are transformed into Alphas, Betas, Gammas, Deltas and Epsilons—the five social classes that collectively meet the economy's manpower needs. Arrested in their development, the Gamma, Delta and Epsilon embryos are programmed *in vitro* for a lower-class future. After "birth," whatever individuality remains with these preordained proletarians will be conditioned out of each child, until there is no one in this brave new world who does not grow up accepting and even loving his bleak servitude.

Huxley's totalitarian embryology may seem fanciful to us, but his real message was political, not technological. Huxley understood, as he wrote in the foreword to the 1946 edition of *Brave New World*, that any "science of human differences" would enable the authorities to assess the relative capacities of each of us and then assign everybody his or her appropriate place in society. Huxley's vision of the modern state, with its desire for social control, implies that the discovery that ability can be measured will suggest that it *should* be. Similarly, the knowledge that people can be sorted by ability will lead irresistibly to the belief that they ought to be.

Today, many educators contend that a "science of human differences" does exist in the form of standardized tests for intelligence and ability. And, as Huxley foresaw, the pressures have grown to put these discriminating instruments to use. Education in this country is becoming a process of separating the "gifted" from the "average," the "intelligent" from the "slow"—one is tempted to say, the wheat from the chaff. From an early age, children are now ranked and sorted (a process known variably as tracking, ability grouping or screening) as they proceed through school. Those who test well are encouraged and expected to succeed and offered the most challenging work. Those who do not, get a watered-down curriculum that reflects the system's minimal expectations of them.

All this is a far cry from the vision of schooling that America's founding educators had in mind. Horace Mann, the father of American public education and the influential first secretary of the Massachusetts board of education from 1837 to 1848, thought public education would be "the great equalizer" in a nation of immigrants. For over a century now, Mann's egalitarian vision, translated into educational policy, has helped millions of immigrants to assimilate and to prosper here. But this vision is now threatened by a competing view of individual potential—and worth. We are becoming a society where test-taking skills are the prerequisites for a chance at getting a good education, and where hard work, hope and ambition are in danger of becoming nothing more than meaningless concepts.

From *Psychology Today*, September 1989, pp. 54–60. Reprinted with permission. © 1989 Sussex Publishers, Inc.

Sheila Tobias is the author of Breaking the Science Barrier, Succeed With Math *(1987) and* Overcoming Math Anxiety *(1978).*

A poor showing on tests was once a signal to all concerned—child, teacher, parents—that greater effort was needed to learn, or to teach, what was required. It didn't mean that a child *couldn't* learn. But the damaging assumption behind testing and tracking as they are now employed in many schools is that *only* those who test well are capable of learning what is needed to escape an adult life restricted to menial, dead-end jobs. This new message imparted by our schools is profoundly inegalitarian: that test-measured ability, not effort, is what counts. What many students are learning is that they are *not* equal to everybody else. Gammas, Deltas and Epsilons shouldn't even try to compete with Alphas. Alphas are better, *born* better, and it is impossible for others to catch up. What's tragic about this change is not just that it's unjust—but that it's untrue.

A LIFETIME OF TESTING

In a private Los Angeles primary school, a 4-year-old is being taught to play a gamelike test he is going to have to pass to show that he is ready for kindergarten. This is the first in an endless series of evaluations that will determine who he is, what he can learn and how far he will go in school. Just before the test begins, the counselor hands him the red plastic cube he will use. But he doesn't need her cube. He has taken this test so often, as his parents drag him around for his preschool admissions screenings, that when the time comes to play, he pulls his *own* bright red cube out of his pocket. Whether or not he is ready for this particular school, he is more than ready for the test.

Each year after this child's admission to kindergarten, he will take "norm-referenced tests" to show his overall achievement against those of his age group and "criterion-referenced tests," which examine the specific skills he is supposed to have learned in each grade. Even if he and his parents are not told his test scores (a practice that varies from school to school), ability-grouping in elementary school will soon let him know where he stands. "By the second or third grade," says Susan Harter, a psychology professor at the University of Denver who studies social develop-

ment in children, "children know precisely where they stand on the 'smart or dumb' continuum, and since most children at this age want to succeed in school, this knowledge profoundly affects their self-esteem."

The point is that today "smart or dumb" determinations are made very early. "Those who come to school knowing how to read or who learn very quickly are pronounced bright," says Jeannie Oakes, author of *Keeping Track: How Schools Structure Inequality*. "Those for whom reading is still a puzzle at the end of the first grade are judged slow." And these early decisions stick. As children proceed through the elementary grades, more and more of their course work is grouped by ability. By ninth grade, 80% to 90% of students are in separate classes determined by whether they are judged to be "fast," "average" or "slow."

MAGNIFYING OUR DIFFERENCES

Tracking in all its variants is rarely official policy, and the validity and fairness of standardized testing have long been under fire. Nevertheless, both tracking and testing are becoming more common. As a result, argues University of Cincinnati education professor Joel Spring (in unwitting resonance with Huxley), education in America has become a "sorting machine."

Moreover, the stunting effects of this machine may remain with students for a lifetime. "Adults can remember well into middle age whether they were 'sharks' or 'goldfish' in reading," says Bill Kelly, professor of education at Regis College in Denver. Students learn whether they have good verbal skills or mathematical ones. They learn whether or not they are musically or mechanically inclined, and so on. There are millions of adults who carry with them the conviction that they "can't do math" or play an instrument or write well. And it may all be the result of assessments made of them and internalized as children—long before they had any idea of what they wanted from life. Their sense of inadequacy may prevent them from exploring alternative careers or simply narrow their experiences.

Why are testing and tracking on the rise? Oakes, who has studied more than 13,000 junior- and senior-high-school students, their schools and their teachers, suggests that the answer has several components. They range from the focus on educational excellence during the last decade to widespread public confidence that testing is an accurate, appropriate way of gauging educational potential. Oakes also believes that testing and tracking comprise a not-so-subtle effort to resegregate desegregated schools. But they reflect as well a preference among teachers for "homogeneous groupings" of students, which are easier to teach than classes composed of students of varying abilities.

Whatever the motives, Oakes is convinced that the basic premise of the whole system is wrong. There is no way, she says, to determine accurately the potential of young or even older children by standardized tests. One key reason: Such examinations are always fine-tuned to point out differences, not similarities. They eliminate those items that everyone answers the same way—either right or wrong. Thus, small differences that may or may not measure ability in general are amplified to give the test makers what they want, namely ease of sorting. Test results, then, will make any group of individuals appear to be more different than they really are.

Benjamin Bloom, Distinguished Service Professor Emeritus of Education at the University of Chicago, agrees. "I find that many of the individual differences in school learning are man-made and accidental rather than fixed in the individual at the time of conception," he writes in his book *All Our Children Learning*. "When students are provided with unfavorable learning conditions, they become even more dissimilar." Bloom concedes that some longitudinal studies show that between grades 3 and 11, for example, children's rank in class remains virtually the same. But this is not because intelligence is fixed, he argues. It is the result of the unequal, unsupportive education the schools provide. So long as schools think there is little they can do about "learning ability," says Bloom, they will see their task as weeding out the poorer learners while encouraging the better learners to get as much education as they can.

WATERED-DOWN EDUCATION

Research generated by Oakes and others supports Bloom, revealing that placement in a low track has a corroding impact on students' self-esteem. Worse yet, because there are real differences not just in level but in the *content* of what is being taught, tracking may in fact contribute to academic failure.

Students in low-track courses are almost never exposed to what educators call "high-status knowledge," the kind that will be useful in colleges and universities. They do not read works of great literature in their English classes, Oakes's team found, and instead of critical-thinking skills and expository writing, low-track students are taught standard English usage and "functional literacy," which involves mainly filling out forms, job applications and the like. In mathematics, high-track students were exposed to numeration, computational systems, mathematical models, probability and statistics in high school. "In contrast," writes Oakes, "low-track classes focused grade after grade on basic computational skills and arithmetic facts" and sometimes on simple measurement skills and converting English to metric.

More generally, Oakes's team also found that high-track classes emphasize reasoning ability over simple memorization of disembodied facts. Low-track students, meanwhile, are taught by rote, with an emphasis on conformity. "Average" classes—the middle track—resembled those in the high track, but they are substantially "watered down."

Is this discriminatory system the only way to handle differences in ability among students? One innovative program is challenging that notion. Called "accelerated learning," it is the creation of Henry M. Levin, a professor of education and economics at Stanford University. Levin, an expert on worker-managed companies, decided to apply the principles of organizational psychology to an analysis of the crisis in education. He began with a two-year study, during which he surveyed the literature on education and looked at hundreds of evaluations of at-risk students at elementary and middle schools, Fully one-third of all students, he estimated, were "educationally disadvantaged" in some way, were consigned to a low track and were falling farther and farther behind in one or more areas. These children needed remedial help, but that help, Levin writes, treated "such students and their educators as educational discards, marginal to mainstream education." For them, the pace of instruction was slowed to a crawl and progressed by endless repetition. The whole system seemed designed to demoralize and fail everyone who was a part of it. As Levin told one reporter, "As soon as you begin to talk about kids needing remediation, you're talking about damaged merchandise. And as soon as you have done that, you have lost the game."

To try to change the game, Levin designed and is helping to implement the Accelerated Schools Program. Now being tested in California, Utah, Missouri and (this fall) Illinois, the project accepts that elementary school children who are having academic problems *do* need special assistance, but it departs radically from traditional tracking in every other respect. First, Accelerated Schools are expected to have all their students learning at grade level by the time they reach the sixth grade. In other words, the remedial track exists only to get students off it. Collectively, the teachers and administrators at each school are allowed to design their own curricula, but they must create a clear set of measurable (and that means testable) goals for students to meet each year they are in the program. Finally, it is expected that the curriculum, whatever its specifics, will be challenging and fast-paced and will emphasize abstract reasoning skills and a sophisticated command of English.

Levin's program reflects the current administration's view that business practice has much to contribute to schooling. Levin wants schools to find a better way to produce what might be called their product—that is, children willing and able to get the quality education they will need in life. To do this, he recognizes that schools must offer better performance incentives to students, teachers and administrators. "Everyone benefits from the esprit de corps," explains Levin, "and the freedom to experiment with curriculum and technique—which we also encourage—is an incentive for teachers." By insisting

upon school and teacher autonomy, the regular attainment of measurable goals and the development of innovative, engaging curricula, Accelerated Schools also hope to erase the stigma associated with teaching or needing remediation. The early results of this six-year test program are encouraging: The Hoover Elementary School in Redwood City, CA, one of the first schools to embark on the project, is reporting a 22 percentile increase in sixth-grade reading scores, actually outperforming state criteria. Both Levin and Ken Hill, the district superintendent, caution that these results are preliminary and the improved scores could be due to many factors other than the Accelerated Schools Program. But regardless of the program's measurable impact, Hill sees real changes in the school. "Teachers are now working with the kids on science projects and developing a literature-based reading program. There's a positive climate, and all the kids are learners."

Another alternative to tracking is what Bloom calls "mastery learning." He believes that it is the rate of learning, not the capacity to learn, that differentiates students with "high" or "low" abilities. This is a critical distinction, for we are rapidly approaching the day when all but the most menial jobs will require relatively complex reasoning and technical skills.

In a mastery class, children are given as much time as they need to become competent at a certain skill or knowledge level. Teachers must take 10% to 15% more time with their classes and break the class down into small groups in which the fast learners help their peers along. In time, the slower students catch up both in the amount of knowledge acquired and in the rate at which they learn. Though slow students may start out as much as five times slower than their classmates, Bloom says, "in mastery classes, fast and slow students become equal in achievement and increasingly similar in their learning rates."

At present, fewer than 5% of the nation's schools are following either of these promising strategies, estimates Gary Fenstermacher, dean of the University of Arizona's College of Education. He is a firm believer that de-tracking in some form must be the educational wave of the future. "There are ethical and moral imperatives for us to do whatever we can to increase the equality of access to human knowledge and understanding," he says.

SECOND CLASS AND DROPPING OUT

Until society responds to those ethical and moral imperatives, however, the educational system, with its testing, tracking and discriminatory labeling, will continue on its questionable course. Today, around 25% of America's teenagers— 40% to 60% in inner-city schools—do not graduate from high school, according to Jacqueline P. Danzberger of the Institute for Educational Leadership in Washington, DC. Most of the attrition occurs by the third year of high school, and many educators believe increased testing is a contributing factor.

Norman Gold, former director of research for the District of Columbia's public school system, says school dropouts are linked to the raising of standards (with no compensatory programs) in the late 1970s and the end of "social promotions"—the habit of routinely allowing failing students to move to a higher grade. "Studies show," he says, "that the risk of dropping out goes up 50% if a child fails one school year." Neil Shorthouse, executive director of Atlanta's Cities in Schools, which enrolls 750 teenagers on the point of dropping out, agrees. "Most of these kids quit school," he says of his students, "because they repeatedly get the message that they are bad students, 'unteachables.' "

Ending social promotions was long overdue. What purpose is served by graduating high-school students who can't read, write or do simple arithmetic? But schools have done little to help these failing students catch up. The present system is continuing to produce a whole class of people, particularly inner-city blacks and Hispanics, who have little economic role in our society. High school, Gold observes, has become an obstacle course that a significant number of young people are unable to negotiate. "We expect them to fail. We have to have greater expectations, and equally great support."

These failing students are missing what John Ogbu, an educational anthropologist at the Uni-

versity of California, Berkeley, calls "effort optimism," the faith that hard work will bring real rewards in life. Ogbu's ethnographic studies of black and Hispanic schoolchildren in Stockton, CA, suggest that one reason today's inner-city children do poorly in tests is that "they do not bring to the test situation serious attitudes and do not persevere to maximize their scores." The fault lies neither with their intelligence, Ogbu argues, nor with the absence of the "quasi-academic training" that middle-class children experience at home. Rather, it is their lower caste status and the limited job prospects of their parents that lower their sights. Tracking formalizes this caste humiliation and leads to disillusionment about school and what school can do for their lives.

WHO IS "SMART"? WHO WILL "SUCCEED"?

The consequences of increased testing and tracking are only now beginning to be felt. First there is personal trauma, both for students who do reasonably well but not as well as they would like, and for those who fail. "When a child is given to understand that his or her worth resides in what he or she achieves rather than in what he or she is, academic failure becomes a severe emotional trauma," David Elkind writes in *The Child and Society*.

But the most severe consequence may be what only dropouts are so far demonstrating—an overall decline in Ogbu's effort optimism. Its potential social effects extend well beyond the schoolroom. Intelligence and ability, says writer James Fallows, have become legally and socially acceptable grounds for discrimination, and both are measured by the testing and tracking system in our schools. Doing well in school has thus come to be the measure of who is intelligent and who has ability. Beyond that, Fallows writes, our culture increasingly accepts that "he who goes further in school will go further in life." Many of the best jobs and most prestigious professions are restricted to those with imposing academic and professional degrees, thus creating a monopoly on "positions of privilege."

At a time when our economy requires better-educated workers than ever before, can we afford to let abstract measures of ability curtail the educational aspirations and potential accomplishments of our children? Quite aside from questions of national prosperity, do we really want to become a culture whose fruits are not available to most of its citizens? Despite income disparities and more classism than many observers are willing to admit, there has always been the *belief* in America that success, the good life, is available to all who are willing to work for it. But with our current fixation on testing and tracking, and what Fallows calls credentialism, we may be abandoning that belief and, with it, the majority of our young people.

CHAPTER 19

MARKET CHOICE VERSUS THE COMMON SCHOOL

INTRODUCTION

In the nineteenth century such visionary educational leaders as Horace Mann led the common school movement. They envisioned a common school in every community where children of all social classes and religious backgrounds could come together for an equal opportunity to be educated. The common schools would have a common curriculum that taught youngsters reading, writing, arithmetic, history, the civic virtues, and the ethic of hard work. This common curriculum was intended for all Americans. But on weekends and evenings children could go with their parents to church or synogogue for special religious instruction according to the customs of the family. Some religious groups (especially Roman Catholics, some Lutherans, and evangelical Protestants) have chosen to create alternative church schools, and other private boarding and day schools are available to children whose parents can pay their tuition, but the vast majority of youngsters in the past 150 years have attended public schools. The common school is a major American institution that has served each generation of young citizens for two centuries.

Though the public school is a well-established institution in the United States, it is not above criticism. In fact, during the past decade public schools have been repeatedly attacked from all quarters: the press, politicians, business leaders, and college professors. In 1983 the United States Department of Education published a scathing report about the inadequacy of American schools titled *A Nation at Risk*. This report opened a floodgate of criticism. American schools suffered from low test scores, high teenage pregnancy rates, drugs, and violence, and they produced illiterate graduates. By the early 1990s everyone seemed to agree that America's public schools were failing. The crisis of American public schools had become a major social problem.

In the early 1980s the first wave of school reform was initiated by state governors who promoted new plans to regulate the school system with mandatory tests for students and teachers, new graduation requirements, a "return to basics," and "no pass, no play"

rules for high school athletes. By the late 1980s it was apparent that these reforms had not stemmed the rising tide of mediocrity in the classrooms.

Further reforms were needed in the public school system. The next step for school reform challenged a basic feature of the system: the notion that children must attend the school in the district or community where they live. This geographic restriction denied parents the opportunity to choose other schools they might consider more promising for their youngsters. The new reforms recommended an open-market approach that would give parents choices for their children. Joe Nathan's essay summarizes some of the key arguments in favor of choice. Dennis Evans challenges the claims made by advocates of choice. James Q. Wilson reviews the most important book published on the topic, John E. Chubb and Terry M. Moe's *Politics, Markets, and America's Schools*. Chubb and Moe criticize the existing system and promote a new reform that relies on the principles of the marketplace. The debate is hardly finished, but thoughtful civic leaders everywhere are probing for a new approach to the public school problem for the twenty-first century.

53.   INTERDISTRICT PROGRAMS OFFER
"EXPANDED OPPORTUNITIES"

JOE NATHAN

While public-school choice programs will not solve all of our schools' problems, well-designed plans can help provide the freedom educators seek, the expanded opportunities many students need, and the dynamism the public-education system requires.

As interest in choice has grown, however, a number of misconceptions about this strategy have developed. Unless educators and policymakers reexamine these myths, a powerful tool for educational improvement will be misused.

The rationale for choice is based primarily on economic and market metaphors. Wrong. Although use of controlled competition may encourage improvements, there are in fact several other important justifications for choice among public schools. Among these, a key rationale is the recognition that there is no one best school for all students or all educators.

In the early 1970's, the St. Paul Board of Education helped a group of parents and educators, including myself, create a K–12 public school that developed individual plans for all students, used an adviser-advisee system, combined classroom work with community service, and required demonstrated competence rather than accumulation of credits for graduation. The school won a federal award as a "carefully evaluated, proven innovation worthy of national replication."

But while some teachers and students flourished at this school, others wanted less flexibility, and this group convinced the board to establish a second, more traditional school.

Though parents and educators in the two programs disagreed on how schools should be organized and instruction provided, both schools educated students effectively. Both enrolled a cross-section of the city's population, and both are still open 17 years later.

The lesson of St. Paul's experience holds true around the country. And the view that no one system works best for everyone is not inconsistent with "effective schools" research. An effective school requires a clear philosophy and a staff committed to its goals—and part of the strength of the finest public alternative schools is the distinctive character of their programs. Effective schools are not identical schools.

Choice may undercut efforts to promote equity. To the contrary, a second rationale for more choice rests on the value of expanding opportunities for all students.

The crucial question here is whether, by adopting choice plans, policymakers will narrow affluent families' educational advantage. The rich already have choice of schools: They can send their children to private schools or pay tuition to another public-school district; they can move to an exclusive suburb and send their children to a "public" school where the price of admission is the ability to purchase an expensive home and pay high real-estate taxes.

These arguments are a familiar element of debates about educational-voucher plans, in which tax funds would pay for students to attend public, private, and parochial schools.

For many people, choice among *public* schools is an acceptable compromise. In Minnesota, for example, a number of groups that oppose vouchers—such as the Minnesota PTA, League of Women Voters, Elementary and Secondary Principals, and Association of Alternative Programs—endorsed Gov. Rudy Perpich's proposals for more public-school choice.

Some opponents of choice contend that expanding opportunity may be fine in theory, but in practice it will be the most affluent and in-

---

From *Education Week*, April 19, 1989, pp. 24 & 32. Reprinted with permission of the author.

formed who use choice systems for their children. But sound plans attract students from all backgrounds.

Programs in New York's East Harlem and in Cambridge, Mass., show that choice can help produce systemwide improvements, including significant gains in achievement and motivation for black and Hispanic students from low-income groups. Each of these districts has made *every* school at certain levels an option. Both systems provide two critical features: parent information and counseling, and transportation to schools.

Minnesota's experience also is encouraging. Many of the students who have used our "postsecondary options" and "second chance" programs come from low-income families. And the percentage of minority students who signed up for open enrollment in 1988–89 is slightly higher than the percentage of minorities in overall enrollment.

Many young people from low-income backgrounds will not reach their potential if they all are required to attend schools with a single instructional philosophy. Some will blossom, for example, in a strict traditional school, or one that emphasizes performing arts along with basic skills. Others will do better in a Montessori program.

Charles Glenn, director of the Massachusetts education department's office of educational equity, has noted that "choice can do much to promote equity. It does so by creating conditions which encourage schools to become more effective . . . by allowing schools to specialize and thus to meet the needs of some students very well rather than all students at a level of minimum adequacy, and by increasing the influence of parents over the education of their children in a way which is largely conflict-free."

There is little, if any, research showing that public-school choice has a positive impact. Mary Anne Raywid of Hofstra University, who has spent more than a decade studying choice plans, reports otherwise. From her research, she concludes that providing families with options among public schools can have dramatic positive results.

Ms. Raywid cites more than 120 studies indicating that when families have the opportunity to select among different kinds of public schools, students' academic achievement and attitudes improve. Graduation rates have also risen.

In addition, Ms. Raywid has found that parents allowed to choose among different schools are more involved, supportive, and satisfied.

While research on Minnesota's programs is limited, it is encouraging. More than 12,000 students have taken advantage of the state's postsecondary-options law, adopted in 1985. Many of them were not doing particularly well in high school; hundreds had dropped out in frustration or boredom. But such young people are earning grades as high or higher than those of college freshmen in rigorous courses at postsecondary institutions.

Another choice law, enacted in 1987, enables youngsters who are not succeeding in one district to attend public school in another district. This law has been used by several thousand students, about half of whom are returning to school after having dropped out.

And Minnesota's choice policies have helped stimulate improvement for students who decide to stay in a district, as well as for those who transfer. The number of Advanced Placement courses offered has quadrupled since high-school students gained the right to attend postsecondary institutions. More than 30 high schools have created new cooperative courses with universities since the program began.

The primary beneficiaries of school choice are parents and students. In well-designed choice plans, educators benefit along with parents and students: They are given the time and freedom to create distinctive programs.

Ms. Raywid's research shows much higher morale among educators who have helped develop alternative approaches or worked in nontraditional public schools than among educators in conventional programs. They have been empowered; their ideas are respected.

This outcome helps explain why choice plans complement "school-based management" programs—and why neither choice nor school-based management is sufficient by itself. With choice only, a school may try to implement many different approaches—open, fundamental, Montessori, language-immersion, performing arts—

at one time; the result is a bland mediocrity satisfying almost no one.

And school-based management without choice can lead to frustrating conflicts. What happens when some parents, teachers, and students do not like the established program?

While choice within a district may be acceptable, interdistrict choice is a bad idea. Some of the strongest proponents of interdistrict choice are parents and youth workers from rural areas. They have testified about being "captives" in certain districts; they have asked for alternative programs or advanced-mathematics or science courses—funding of which would require modest decreases in athletic budgets—only to be called "elitist."

Participants in Minnesota's second-chance program, which has enabled thousands of youngsters who were not doing well in one school to attend another outside their district, have said that the new opportunity changed their lives.

And certain legal limits shape the overall impact of interdistrict choice in Minnesota: The programs cannot have a negative effect on desegregation, and districts may not select students on the basis of previous grades or behavior.

But what works in Minnesota may not be appropriate in other states, as Governor Perpich has noted. After examining the results of choice in Minnesota, Massachusetts, East Harlem, and elsewhere, other states and districts should determine how it can best be applied to help solve their most pressing problems.

Nevertheless, all proposals are not equally effective. To increase the likelihood of success, all plans should:

- Clearly state goals and guidelines for schools;
- Provide information and counseling to help parents select among various programs;

- Avoid "first come, first served" admissions procedures and prohibit admissions on the basis of past achievement or behavior;
- Offer opportunities for building-level educators at a range of schools to help create distinctive programs, rather than concentrate resources on a few schools;
- Make transportation within a reasonable area available for all students;
- Require that dollars follow students;
- Implement racial-balance procedures that promote integration;
- Continue oversight and modification.

Choice is an alternative to spending money. Both liberal and conservative governors are proposing public-school choice plans because choice reinforces other education-improvement efforts. Expanding educator and parental choice encourages better use of existing funds, but it also costs money. So do providing time for staff and program development, and arranging parent information and transportation. While these costs need not be staggering, they are real.

Seventy percent of the public thinks parents should be able to select among public schools. Chris Wilcox agrees. A Minnesota student who had not succeeded in one public school, Chris used the state's new laws to attend an alternative school and a local community college.

He recently wrote that choice "gave me the chance to personalize my education and the confidence that I can make something of myself and control my own destiny."

There are millions of youngsters like Chris who will benefit from well-designed public-school choice plans. Let's move ahead thoughtfully but decisively.

54. THE MYTHOLOGY OF THE MARKETPLACE IN SCHOOL CHOICE

DENNIS L. EVANS

The acclaim being accorded the notion of "parental choice" of schools is but one more example of the sad truth that public education ranks right up there with popular music, sartorial styles, and TV stardom in terms of susceptibility to faddism. The hypnotic appeal of the "quick fix" leads us to uncritically create a new orthodoxy out of any program or platform that promises progress. And the greater the promise, the greater the alacrity of our acceptance.

The proponents of choice have been beguiled by an a priori assumption that the virtues of competition in the marketplace can be made applicable to any organizational endeavor, including the education of our children. When voices such as those of the President and the gurus of corporate America extol choice and competition as forces that will dramatically alter public education, it is admittedly difficult to resist their siren call. But its "flag and apple pie" appeal notwithstanding, the notion that parental choice and the resultant competition among schools will lead to lasting generational progress in public education is flawed in several significant ways. Those flaws emanate from the mythology surrounding the choice issue. Some of the most pervasive myths include:

Competition leads to quality. The proponents of choice assume that a cause-and-effect relationship exists between competition and quality in the marketplace, and that a similar dynamic would work with schools. In the business world, however, the relationship between competition

and quality is a function of profit. If a company can show a greater profit by providing a cheaper, lower-quality product (planned obsolescence!) or service ("no frills"), that is exactly what it will do. The company is not in business to give the consumer the best possible product or service at the lowest possible price; to the contrary, it will attempt to improve its profit margin by any method that will work.

Competition only allows the consumer, on occasion, to save some money. But the product or the service may still remain shoddy. We accept as fact the notion that "you get what you pay for." When you truly want a high-quality product or service, you must be willing to pay more for it. If you are not concerned with quality, you will look for the cheapest product. Thus it is that we have fine restaurants and fast food; first class and coach; Mercedes and Yugos. Competition impacts pricing far greater than it does the quality of a product.

Corporate America knows best. Beyond the mythology that promotes competition as a panacea, there is a related mentality that pervades discussions, not just of school choice, but of school reform in general. It is based on the same reasoning that led to the legendary phrase, attributed to a former G.M. board chairman, that "what's good for General Motors is good for the country."

Some of the most strident voices criticizing public education, and proposing choice options, come from corporate America. Why do we have faith that the gospel according to Xerox has substantive meaning for education? Why do we put our trust in emanations from a corporate boardroom regarding what should occur in a classroom? For every success story in the business world we can also point to an Edsel, an Eastern, or a Lincoln Savings.

If we are so enamored of the corporate model,

From *Education Week*, October 17, 1990, pp. 32–34. Reprinted with permission of the author.

Dennis L. Evans is a high school principal in Newport Beach, Calif., and an instructor in the administrative-credential program of the University of California at Irvine.

then perhaps we should consider a Chrysler-type bailout for our schools; give the schools everything they need financially and then see if they can "turn a profit." To coin a phrase, "What's good for Chrysler is good for the schools."

Parents will make wise choices. It certainly makes political sense to extol the wisdom that parents will supposedly manifest if they are given the opportunity to shop for schools. What evidence exists to support that politically attractive myth? Are these the same parents who are so lacking in discrimination in other areas of the marketplace? On what basis do these parents make decisions regarding the choice of automobiles, television sets, dishwasher detergent, and political candidates?

The proponents of choice will obviously avoid expressing concerns regarding the ability of parents to make independent and wise choices. But some have begun asking pertinent questions, such as whether or not parents given school choice may need some type of consumer-protection safeguards. Do we really believe that most parents are prepared to make substantive decisions matching the "learning style" of their child with the broad array of choice options the concept's advocates foresee? Is it not more reasonable to assume that marketing, packaging, and advertising will dictate school choice?

Certainly, most parents will be highly motivated to make a wise choice of schools. Unfortunately, good intentions are no guarantee of good decisions.

Lay decisionmakers are superior to professionals. Parental choice is but one of the many manifestations of our populist distrust of professionals. It is a distrust that causes us to accept the mythology that all educational decisionmaking would be best served if the public were to make the decisions. That mythology is based, in part, on the fallacious notion that the schools are "selling" something and that the public as "consumer" knows best. But the practice of lay control of public education is much more deeply founded than mere infatuation with the marketplace.

In public education, we have doggedly maintained the colonial tradition of lay school boards. And indeed, in places like Chicago, we have extended that anachronism to give neighborhood councils the authority to make educational-policy decisions. Is it not somewhat ironical, at a point in time when the family unit is in great disarray, when parental authority over the behavior of children has reached a nadir, when "latch key" children are legion, that we remain willing to hand over the destiny of all of our children to that same "public"?

If, for the sake of argument, we accept the view of the critics and the politicians that public education is in need of massive reform, would it not make sense to critically assess the role that lay decisionmakers have had in leading public education into this crisis? It may be heretical to suggest that lay legislators and school-board members are not the best sources for educational decisionmaking, or that neighborhood-council members would do well to concentrate on their own children, but perhaps we have reached a point when heresy is what is needed. We cannot afford to continue to use "the Little Red Schoolhouse" as our model for the governance of public education.

Those who challenge the bandwagon hysteria and hoopla that surround parental choice will likely be labeled as elitists, obstructionists, or even worse, "professional educators." But the fact remains that we are not merely dealing with automobiles or copying machines. We are debating the destiny of our children. And that is far too vital an issue to allow the zealots, the politicians, the corporations, or even our most sacrosanct traditions to stifle inquiry, discussion, and dissent.

55. MULTIPLE CHOICE TEST—A REVIEW OF *POLITICS, MARKETS, AND AMERICA'S SCHOOLS*

JAMES Q. WILSON

Social scientists who write about public policy occasionally manage to catch up with popular wisdom. More rarely, they manage to improve on it. John Chubb and Terry Moe, two political scientists, have done both in this extraordinary book about our public schools. Their volume brings to completion a story begun a quarter century ago, when serious scholars first began to ask what effect schools, and the money we spend on schools, have on our children.

In 1966 the U.S. Office of Education released what quickly became known as the Coleman Report, after its senior author, James S. Coleman. Charged by law with measuring "the lack of equal educational opportunities" for blacks and other minorities, and drawing on a painstaking analysis of differences in school achievement among 575,000 pupils in 4,000 schools across the country, Coleman and his colleagues reported to a stunned Office of Education that virtually none of the obvious differences among schools—pupil-teacher ratios, per-pupil expenditures, the age and quality of physical facilities, the number of books in the library—explained differences in educational attainment. How much students learned seemed to be associated almost entirely with their family backgrounds and the backgrounds of their peers.

The inputs into schools—for example, money—did not have much effect on the outputs of those schools. Perhaps because the finding

was so contrary to the conventional wisdom, an embarrassed Office of Education released the report on the Fourth of July weekend, when not many reporters are in town and newspapers publish thin editions. But did the Coleman Report really disprove the conventional wisdom? To the extent that received opinion held that spending more on teachers and school facilities would improve educational attainment, the answer is yes: within the range of variation to be found in this country, spending more does not get you more. Other studies and further analyses of the original Coleman data, notably by Christopher Jencks, have pretty much confirmed that.

But in this matter there is another sort of received opinion: the opinion of typical parents. Before and after the Coleman Report, millions of American families decided where to live partly on the basis of the quality of the schools available to their children in various neighborhoods and suburbs. And having chosen a home, many of those parents promptly joined PTAs, lobbied school boards, and argued with principals, all with an eye toward improving school quality. Were these parents ignoramuses who needed only to read a 737-page government report, together with its 548-page statistical appendix, to learn the error of their ways? And having read these documents, would they have been well-advised to ignore schools in choosing a neighborhood and watch television instead of going to PTA meetings?

I think not. Certainly Coleman did not think so. Schools differ in quality, but the quality differences cannot be measured in terms of objective characteristics. The problem facing social scientists was to observe the intangible characteristics of schools. This means, alas, trying to measure the unmeasurable (or at least the very hard to measure). To accomplish this, one would probably have to settle for looking very closely at just a few schools.

From *The New Republic*, October 8, 1990, pp. 39–42. Reprinted with permission. John E. Chubb and Terry M. Moe, *Politics, Markets, and America's Schools* (Brookings Institution, 1990).

James Q. Wilson is the Collins Professor of Management and Public Policy at UCLA and the author, most recently, of Bureaucracy: What Government Agencies Do and Why They Do It *(Basic Books).*

This was done. In 1979 Michael Rutter and his colleagues in England reported on their close observation of several thousand children as they went through twelve secondary schools in working-class areas of London. They gathered much of the same data as Coleman and came up with much the same results; objective differences among schools with respect to such things as physical facilities were not correlated with differences in pupil achievements. But two intangible factors *were* correlated: the academic balance among students (the mix of gifted and not-so-gifted students within a school) and the ethos of the school. The ethos or the organizational culture associated with schools that produced better results was an atmosphere that emphasized the importance of learning, a consistent and effective pattern of discipline, the frequent use of praise, classroom sessions that were carefully planned in advance, and regularly assigned homework.

Rutter's findings were especially compelling because, unlike Coleman, who compared the educational attainments of many students at one point in time, Rutter followed a group of students as they progressed through school. This longitudinal design enabled him to state with more confidence that school ethos was not simply associated with good outcomes, it actually caused them. Many studies began to appear that reported very similar findings—so similar, indeed, that scholars began listing them as elements in what they called the "more effective schools" model. Parents were right to think that some schools did a better job than others, and they were not wasting their time when they tried to improve the atmosphere—the ethos—in the classroom.

Knowledge had advanced, but to what effect? How could government policy or school reformers produce, how could they plan, a desirable ethos in tens of thousands of classrooms? Good teachers make a difference, but by what observable characteristics can we identify good teachers? And once identified, how can we motivate them to use their talents to the fullest? Economist Eric Hanushek was able to show that good teachers improved educational attainment, but he could find no way of predicting who would be a good teacher. Certainly the number of courses taken or degrees received was no guide; for the purpose of producing a classroom ethos that was conducive to learning, teachers with a lot of training in education were not better equipped, on the average, than teachers without these credentials.

At this point, in 1982, Coleman (with Thomas Hoffer and Sally Kilgore) returned to the fray. In *High School Achievement*, he and his colleagues argued that, if you statistically hold constant the ability and family background of high school students, private and parochial schools do a better job of educating children than public schools. Just as the 1966 report outraged the civil rights establishment, the 1982 report incensed the educational establishment. Amid a welter of self-serving and ad hominem charges, one serious point was made: even if you control statistically for every measurable background factor (race, class, intelligence, parental aspirations, and so on), it is still possible that some unmeasured factor has led the easier-to-educate children to enter, disproportionately, the private and parochial schools. Thus, what appears to be the better educational outputs of these schools may in fact be the result of the superior pupil inputs to them. Coleman gave some powerful answers to this criticism, but he agreed that there was always a possibility—he thought it was remote—that selection bias was influencing his results.

This time, however, Coleman was clearly in step with public opinion. By the tens of thousands, parents were taking their children out of public schools and putting them into private or religious schools, confident that as a result their children would be better educated. So great has this movement been that today the typical private school is no longer the expensive, all-white New England boarding school but the inner-city, moderately expensive, integrated day school, and the typical Catholic school is no longer all-Catholic in its student body. In fact, the level of interracial and interclass contact is now higher in private and parochial high schools than it is in public ones.

Assuming (as I do) that Coleman's findings and popular opinion are correct, the policy implications are clear, and politically unpalatable: use income transfers or vouchers to facilitate the access of families to private and parochial schools. The voucher option, whereby school funds would go to parents who would then be able to spend them at any approved school, including private ones, has been widely discussed, but it is perceived by the public school establishment—teachers, principals, and school bureaucracies—as a threat to their existence. They are quite right. Worse, the voucher is hopelessly entangled in the debate over public support of religious schooling. Though there is a lot to be said for vouchers, they have acquired a stigma that makes the word, if not the concept, what politicians call a nonstarter.

There is another possibility, of course. We can devise some way of changing public schools so that they more nearly duplicate the success of private and parochial ones. Coleman, Hoffer, and Kilgore gave some clues as to what the change would entail, and they sounded very much like the effective-schools ethos described by Rutter and others: better discipline, a constructive learning environment, high expectations of performance, more homework, and so forth. But how do you do this? Educational reformers over the last decade or so have tried to accomplish this by mandate. If we require better educational attainment, then higher attainment will result. And so state after state has adopted rules requiring more and tougher subjects be taught, proficiency tests passed, and clearer goals enunciated.

Other reformers, worrying that improved educational achievement may not automatically follow from a law mandating it, have turned their attention to ways of improving and empowering teachers. If the classroom teacher is the key, then give him or her the pay, the freedom, the power, and the status necessary to unleash creative teaching. But that approach finesses the central issue. Which teacher is most likely to use more freedom and power constructively? Politically, if you empower any teacher, you must empower all; if you pay any teacher more, you must pay all more. And in many cases the power does not really go to teachers, it goes to teacher unions, notably the National Education Association.

Now come Chubb and Moe to ask the fundamental question: What is there, organizationally and politically, about some schools that makes them more effective? To find the answer, they

take much the same data that Coleman, Hoffer, and Kilgore used and supplement them with facts, gathered from questionnaires sent to principals, teachers, and staff members in the schools that had produced the data on student achievement. To deal with the vexing problem of separating the effects of student traits on achievement from the effects of schools on achievement, Chubb and Moe measure not the level of student achievement at one point in time, but the gain (or loss) in that achievement over a two-year period—from the sophomore to the senior year of the same high school students. An effective school is one in which a student with a given level [of] ability makes the greatest gain; an ineffective school is one in which a student with the same ability level (and family background) makes the least gain, or drops back.

Chubb and Moe find, as did Coleman, that the resources of the school make no difference in educational gains. Neither does race (after controlling for the socioeconomic status of the parents). What does make a difference is (naturally) student ability, parental status, and the status of one's student peers. So far, this is what Coleman and Rutter found. But Chubb and Moe discover in addition that, holding everything else constant, school organization makes a difference.

What is "school organization"? Chubb and Moe mean four things: school standards (having high graduation requirements and a strong emphasis on academic excellence); leadership (having a principal with a strong desire for control and a strong commitment to teaching); teacher quality (having many teachers who were highly rated by their principals and who have a large amount of influence, low rates of absenteeism, and strong feelings of efficacy and harmony with others); and educational practice (having a high proportion of students in academic "tracks," a lot of homework, and effective classroom discipline). In short, Chubb and Moe took the elements of an effective school ethos as observed in close-up studies of a few schools and derived ways of measuring their presence in a quantitative study of many schools.

So far, no surprises. Now the big question. Why are some schools able to acquire the effective-school ethos, an ethos that alone, after controlling for ability and social class, is worth an extra half-year of educational attainment for a typical sophomore? The answer given by Chubb and Moe is the distinctive and most controversial feature of their study: other things being equal, good schools are better because they are less bureaucratic, and they are less bureaucratic because they are less subject to democratic controls.

They are emphatically not making an argument against democracy as such, only against the version of democracy that has been used to govern public education. As the United States has arranged matters, public schools are accountable to elected bodies that are responsive to the demands of relevant constituencies, or at least to the more insistent of these demands. Those constituencies are taxpayers (who want economy), organized teachers (who want security), civil rights groups (who want integration), educational reform groups (who want specific programs adopted or changed), and politicians (who want power). Moreover, democratic control as practiced here means that there will be a single school system in each large city (and sometimes one for a collection of cities). Thus, the school administrators must manage large organizations, and this can only be done by adopting uniform rules and issuing standard operating procedures.

The need to satisfy the constraints of outside constituents and the requirements of large-scale management leads to the creation of a system designed to minimize the amount of discretion, or autonomy, exercised by any given school in the system. But topheavy, centralized management, which is rational from the point of view of school administrators, is irrational from the point of view of school principals and teachers. Education is a complex, labor-intensive, highly discretionary activity carried on in small, low-visibility settings (that is, classrooms). If it were a business, no management consultant would dream of suggesting that the performance of such tasks would be improved by putting day-to-day control of the enterprise in the hands of the top executives. A centralized school bureaucracy does not exist to serve the needs of parents and pupils. No matter how well-intentioned the top executives, they are managing an organization that, by law, must be more sensitive to the demands of legislators, judges, and special-interest groups than to the demands of pupils and parents (assuming it had some way of measuring them).

But there exists another version of democracy: the democracy of client power. It is the democracy of the marketplace, where each consumer "votes" with his or her purchases, leaving other consumers free to vote with theirs. To the extent that the organization gets its resources from consumers, it must be attentive to their preferences; the alternative is failure. Moreover, if there are no economies of scale—in education, there probably are few—then there is no organizational advantage to having a large bureaucracy to manage the school. Under these circumstances, school systems will delegate a great deal of authority to lower-level managers, principals, or headmasters. This difference helps to explain why the New York City public school system has a bureaucratic overhead made up of about 6,000 officials, while the Catholic schools of the New York City archdiocese, which teach about a quarter as many pupils, have a central staff of twenty-five.

The data gathered by Chubb and Moe are consistent with this theory. More effective schools are those that have fewer administrative constraints. Many of these schools are private or parochial. But even among public schools, the more effective ones tend to be the less constrained ones. Not surprisingly, the less constrained public schools tend to be small and located in suburban rather than urban areas. Lest the reader assume that this is restating the obvious, recall that the more effective public schools are smaller and suburban even *after* the effect of money resources, social class, and student ability have been noted.

At this point the typical academic book would end with a restatement of findings and a call for more research. Not this book. In their final chapter, the most interesting in the book, Chubb and Moe set forth a plan for improving public schools in a way that draws on their own findings. The plan involves creating more choice. Unlike many choice plans, however, their plan operates on the supply side as well as on the demand side. In their view, the schools cannot be improved by imposing more requirements or regulations; that just adds to the cumbersomeness of the bureaucratic constraints. Nor can they be improved by decentralization or school-based management; these efforts to make schools smaller will not work unless they also make the schools accountable to parents.

Briefly, Chubb and Moe propose the following: any organization that creates a school that meets minimum state criteria will be certified as a school. The applying organization can be (and in most cases will be) an existing public school, but private organizations will be eligible to apply as well. Every student will be free to attend any public school in the state. Free transportation will be supplied, to the extent possible, so that a theoretical choice will be an actual one. For each pupil enrolled, the school will receive a set fee—a scholarship—from the state, paid for with tax revenues. The amount of that fee will be set by the state to take into account differences among children: children with learning disabilities, for example, or those with conduct disorders, would get more to pay for the extra attention and care they require.

Each school will set its own admission requirements, selecting (on a nondiscriminatory basis) those applicants it wants. Each school will also be free to expel students that it cannot handle. The governance of a given school will be up to that school; it can be run by the principal, by a teachers' collective, by a parent organization, by a local elected body, or even by a union. Statewide teacher tenure laws would be abolished, though individual schools could create tenure systems if they wished. Teachers would be free to join unions, but the unions would bargain with individual schools, not with a district or a system. The state would continue to set teacher certification standards, but (Chubb and Moe hope) the standards would be minimal, akin to what now apply to private schools. There would be no statewide assessment of educational attainment: parents and parents alone would judge how well the schools are doing. Schools that did well in the eyes of parents would retain or increase their enrollments and thus their revenues. Schools that did poorly would lose revenue and go out of business.

It may seem as though the authors wish to privatize schooling, but that is not the case. Private schools that wished to remain wholly private would continue to operate as they do now.

Public schools would still be public, in the sense that they would be supported with tax revenues and subject to state certification requirements. The public system might or might not allow religious bodies to form public schools (though Chubb and Moe prefer that they be permitted). The significant change is the introduction of choice, with meaningful consequences for both the suppliers and the consumers of education.

All of this is controversial, but none of this is unreasonable or farfetched. The proposal is consistent with the authors' rigorous research and in line with what is now being tried in Minnesota, Cambridge (Massachusetts), and East Harlem (New York City). The best parallel is East Harlem, where, in District Four, 14,000 students chose among dozens of schools, many with a distinctive character that can be inferred from their names—East Harlem Career Academy, Academy of Environmental Science, and the Jose Feliciano Performing Arts School (to name but a few). Several schools were created and run by public school teachers; many share buildings with other schools. Each school controls its own admissions and loses money if it does not attract pupils. According to Chubb and Moe, teachers and parents alike are enthusiastic and pupil achievement scores have risen dramatically.

Can the East Harlem experiment be made effective statewide? Chubb and Moe think so. Indeed, they think that unless it is, it will collapse when the handful of visionaries who began it either leave or fall on hard times. The forces arrayed against this choice plan (and almost any choice plan) are formidable—teacher unions (but not individual teachers who have been in a choice program), state departments of education, local school boards, and some intellectuals who persist in thinking, despite the nearly unanimous evidence to the contrary, that some combination of money and regulations will change the schools and that any choice plan is "undemocratic," by which they mean, of course, not centrally governed.

Though the Chubb-Moe plan is consistent with the Chubb-Moe evidence, that is not the same as saying that the evidence proves that the plan will work. Only experience can prove which reforms, if any, will work as intended. Moreover, skillful as the authors have been in analyzing their data, their findings are not invulnerable to the criticisms leveled at Coleman's comparison of public and private schools. No matter how many statistical controls one employs, no matter how conservative one's methodology may be, there is always the chance that the differences between more and less effective public schools are not the result of organizational factors, but of human factors (student motivation, teacher attitudes, community support) that have escaped measurement. It is hard to create an effective public agency, so hard that one may be tempted to attribute the consequences to chance and circumstance rather than to plan and intention.

Still, no important change would ever take place if we waited until the evidence were conclusive. Entrepreneurship and prudent risk-taking are as important in public management as they are in private management. Whatever one's reservations about the studies done so far, they already constitute a far greater body of credible evidence than was available to those who created the public school, who sought to integrate segregated schools, who imposed on the schools the myriad regulations governing special-needs education, proficiency testing, or teacher certification. By comparison to a pro-choice plan, those earlier ideas were shots in the dark.

SCHOOL DROPOUTS

INTRODUCTION

Problems of poverty in the United States have changed dramatically in the past three decades. In the 1960s most persons below the poverty line were elderly; today they are children. Infants born into circumstances of poverty face many obstacles in their early years. By the time they enter school, many of them will be defined as "students at risk"; few of them will graduate with their classmates. Children of poverty often have difficulty with their academic work. Their families show little interest in reading, writing, or participating in cooperative problem solving. Many of these youngsters have low self-esteem, limited social skills, and little exposure to tasks of cognitive complexity.

First-grade children begin their educational journey with 108 months of schooling ahead of them. Early in this extended period of formal learning a sharp division starts to emerge: many of the students of poverty fall behind and many of the students of affluence surge ahead. By the time students reach early adolescence, in the seventh and eighth grades, the predictable pattern of failure for many low-income youngsters is all too apparent. They have experienced repeated failure and lost all interest in putting out the extra effort to catch up. Educators now face a dilemma. Do they try to keep low-achieving students in school by lowering their standards for academic work and behavior or do they press for high standards and let the unmotivated students flounder and drift away? Neither choice is acceptable. Some educators are experimenting with new learning environments that provide a third alternative: keeping all students in school and providing stimulating and challenging opportunities that generate high motivation to succeed. There are a few American schools where such exciting things are happening, but only a few.

Investigations of the general patterns of poverty and schooling in America by journalists, social scientists, and educators all lead to similar conclusions. The number of poor children has been increasing for several years. Most schools have not been able to reverse the tendency of low-income students to drop out before graduation. School dropouts face harsh economic problems, since they are prepared for only marginal employment. Their children are likely to perpetuate the problem. For a variety of reasons, schools have not been able to break the cycle of poverty, low achievement in school, and dropping out. So poverty is perpetuated from one generation to the next in a prosperous nation that seems to be drifting toward a two-tier society of haves and have-nots.

The three essays in Chapter 20 address various aspects of the problem of poverty and schooling. James P. Markey, an economist, examines the grim statistics on children who drop out of school. He sees the importance of staying in school, but does not simplify the issue by suggesting that a high school diploma will automatically solve a young person's employment problems. Jackson Toby, a sociologist, sees little point in forcing disinterested adolescents to stay in school if they are undermining the work of teachers and serious students. For Toby the problem is not dropping out, it is staying in and ruining the learning environment for others. Two journalists, Sally Reed and R. Craig Sautter, provide an overview of the problem and some current educational strategies to remedy the situation. These three essays call attention to a major challenge confronting leaders and educators in the late twentieth century: to design successful learning environments for an increasing number of children of poverty who must attain new levels of academic achievement and sophisticated job skills.

56. THE LABOR MARKET PROBLEMS OF TODAY'S HIGH SCHOOL DROPOUTS

JAMES P. MARKEY

Among the Nation's unemployed, about 3 of 8 are young persons age 16 to 24. The high unemployment rates among youth reflect the problems often encountered by these new entrants to the job market. Without a doubt, the youth facing the greatest difficulties are the 4 million high school dropouts. Many dropouts do not participate in the job market at all; of those who do, 1 of 4 are unemployed.

THE DROPOUT PROBLEM

Education has long been recognized as vital in building an able and skilled work force, and the 20th century has seen a tremendous rise in the educational level of the U.S. population. At the beginning of this century, only 10 percent of male students received a high school diploma. During the 1950's, more than half of all students graduated from high school.[1] By the late 1960's, data from the National Center for Educational Statistics put high school completion rates at about 75 percent, where they have since remained.[2] This apparent halt in the rising trend of

high school completions has resulted in heightened awareness of the dropout problem. Currently, there is debate on the appropriateness of using high school completion rates (and the derived dropout rate) as a means of estimating the magnitude of the dropout problem. The adequacy of estimates obtained from other methods is also questioned given that the range of reported dropout rates extends from 14 percent to 25 percent.[3] However, regardless of the measure chosen, there is little conclusive evidence to suggest that there has been significant improvement in the dropout situation over the last two decades.

Information on dropouts is obtained from several sources, including the administrative records of local school districts, longitudinal surveys of youth/student cohorts, and the Current Population Survey (CPS).[4] This article assesses the labor market behavior of young high school dropouts, relying heavily on data from the CPS. Each October, a supplement to the regular CPS asks questions regarding the school enrollment status of household members, including the year they last attended school and the highest grade completed. Separate data are tabulated for high school graduates and high school dropouts[5] and for two groups of special interest—recent dropouts (those who dropped out of school between October of the previous year and the current October) and recent graduates (those who completed high school during the current calendar year).

From *Monthly Labor Review*, June 1988, pp. 36–43. Reprinted with permission.

James P. Markey is an economist in the Division of Labor Force Statistics, Bureau of Labor Statistics. The author thanks Robert J. McIntire and Bernard R. Altschuler, Office of Employment and Unemployment Statistics, Bureau of Labor Statistics, for constructing the computer programs used in this study.

[1] Jerald G. Bachman, Swayzer Green, and Ilona D. Wirtanen, *Youth in Transition*, vol. 3 (Ann Arbor: University of Michigan, Institute for Social Research, 1971), p. 4.

[2] Unpublished data from the U.S. Department of Education, Center for Education Statistics, Washington, D.C.

[3] For a discussion of the different dropout measures and the debate surrounding the dropout problem, see Chester E. Finn, Jr., "The high school dropout puzzle," *Public Interest*, Spring 1987, pp. 3–22; and "School dropouts: The extent and nature of the problem," Briefing Report to Congressional Requesters, GAO/HRD-86-106BR (U.S. General Accounting Office, June 1986).

[4] Data in this article were derived primarily from the October Current Population Survey (CPS). The CPS is

The number of recent dropouts has averaged about 700,000 a year for the last 20 years, although it was at its lowest level, 562,000, in 1986.[6] The 1978 high of 839,000 roughly mirrors the population peak of baby-boomers. The following tabulation shows the number of recent dropouts, 1967–86:

	Recent Dropouts (thousands)		Recent Dropouts (thousands)
1967	614	1977	832
1968	610	1978	839
1969	661	1979	812
1970	712	1980	759
1971	657	1981	713
1972	734	1982	668
1973	790	1983	597
1974	813	1984	601
1975	737	1985	612
1976	749	1986	562

---

a monthly survey of approximately 60,000 households conducted and tabulated for the Bureau of Labor Statistics by the Bureau of the Census. Most analysis in this article relates to persons 16 to 24 years of age in the civilian noninstitutional population. Because it is a sample survey, estimates derived from the CPS may differ from actual counts that could be obtained from a complete census. Therefore, estimates based on a small sample should be interpreted with caution. For further information on sampling reliability, see *Students, Graduates, and Dropouts, October 1980–82,* Bulletin 2192 (Bureau of Labor Statistics, 1983).

[5] In this article, the term "high school dropouts" refers to individuals who are not enrolled in school and have not completed 4 years of high school. The term is somewhat of a misnomer, as this group contains a small proportion of persons who never attended high school. In October 1986, 14 percent of the "high school dropouts" had left school before ever attending high school. No attempt is made to analyze this small group separately.

[6] Data refer to recent graduates and dropouts age 16 to 24. In addition, an average of 86,000 persons 14 and 15 years of age dropped out of school annually over the same period. While the data presented on dropouts refer to persons who had not completed high school when surveyed, a number of dropouts do return to school or obtain high school equivalency certificates at a later date. Estimates of returnees are as high as half of all dropouts. For further information, see Andrew J.

The recent dropouts of 1986 were nearly equally divided among young men (53 percent) and young women (47 percent), which was typical of the last two decades. Although the dropout problem is often represented as primarily a problem among minority youth, only 16 percent of recent dropouts in 1986 were black, a proportion representative of black high school enrollment, while 80 percent were white.[7] Since 1973, when data were first tabulated for Hispanics (most Hispanics are counted as white), a disproportionate number of dropouts have been of Hispanic origin. Most recently, 23 of 100 recent dropouts were Hispanic, although Hispanics account for only 9 percent of the enrolled high school population.

In October 1986, there were about 4 million young high school dropouts, representing nearly 1 of 8 of the 16- to 24-year-olds.[8] To better understand this sizable group, this article first explores the phenomenon of dropping out of school before analyzing the labor market behavior and performance of young dropouts.

DROPPING OUT: FACTORS AND REASONS

Several factors have been theorized to explain what influences a youth's decision to drop out of high school. Reliable indicators of who will com-

---

Kolstad and Jeffrey A. Owings, *High School Dropouts Who Changed Their Minds about School* (U.S. Department of Education, Center for Education Statistics, April 1986).

[7] This was the first year in which blacks did not make up a disproportionate share of recent dropouts. Because of the relatively small size of the black youth population, the 1986 anomaly may be a result of sampling error, and not indicative of a change in the past trend.

[8] These figures are not intended as a dropout rate, but only as an indication of the prevalence of dropouts in the 16- to 24-year-old population. See footnote 3 for references on the distinction among these and other measures of the dropout problem.

TABLE 1. Median Family Income By Type of Family in Which 16- to 24-Year-Old Recent High School Dropouts and Graduates Reside, October 1985

Type of Family and Income[1]	High School Dropouts	High School Graduates	
		Enrolled in College	Not Enrolled in College
All families (thousands)	450	1,457	968
Percent with income less than $10,000	40.9	5.7	14.7
Median family income	$12,064	$34,171	$22,659
Married-couple families (thousands)	231	1,190	699
Percent with income less than $10,000	23.4	2.9	8.8
Median family income	$21,249	$37,593	$26,575
Families maintained by women (thousands)	183	206	226
Percent with income less than $10,000	68.0	21.0	33.8
Median family income	$6,764	$17,966	$12,323

[1] Data refer only to those families reporting income.

plete high school appear to be family background characteristics, such as income and parental education, and an individual's performance on intelligence tests and demonstrated reading skill.[9] Studies have found that dropouts are more likely to score lower on ability tests and to come from families with relatively low income and education.

Data from the October 1985 supplement to the CPS were used to look at two background variables for recent graduates and dropouts: family income and parental education. Because it lacks the necessary longitudinal capacity, the CPS cannot identify the parental education and family income of dropouts and graduates prior to their leaving school, but a reasonable proxy for the two variables is found by using data for recent graduates and dropouts who were still living with their parents when surveyed.[10] (Thus, the discussion in this section excludes recent

graduates and dropouts who were living on their own.)[11]

As one might expect, family income differed significantly for recent dropouts and high school graduates. Median income was $12,100 for families of recent dropouts, $22,700 for families of

cluded may be a very small number of individuals who are not sons or daughters of the householder, but are otherwise related (such as a sister or a cousin). The householder, a proxy for the dropout's or graduate's parent, is the person (or one of the persons) in whose name the housing unit is owned or rented. In married-couple families, the term "householder" is replaced by "reference person," but is defined identically. In cases of joint ownership or rental partnership by husband and wife, the reference person is self-designated, invariably the husband. Although several simplifying assumptions have been made, the data are believed to accurately portray the characteristics of the specified population.

[11] Only a small percentage of dropouts are on their own. For example, in October 1985, 91 percent of recent high school graduates and 74 percent of recent high school dropouts were living with their parents.

[9] Bachman and others, *Youth in Transition*, chap. 3.

[10] This group is identified as recent graduates and dropouts who are relatives of the householder. In-

TABLE 2. Distribution of 16- to 24-Year-Old Recent High School Dropouts and Graduates by the Educational Attainment of the Householder in the Family in Which They Reside, October 1985

[In percent]

Type of Family and Educational Attainment of Householder	High School Dropouts	High School Graduates	
		Enrolled in College	Not Enrolled in College
All families[1]	100.0	100.0	100.0
Less than 4 years of high school	55.1	10.3	32.0
4 years of high school	26.7	35.5	46.3
1 to 3 years of college	13.6	22.9	12.7
4 years of college or more	4.7	31.4	9.0
Married-couple families	100.0	100.0	100.0
Less than 4 years of high school	53.5	10.1	33.9
4 years of high school	27.4	34.3	43.9
1 to 3 years of college	11.3	21.7	13.3
4 years of college or more	7.8	33.9	8.9
Families maintained by women	100.0	100.0	100.0
Less than 4 years of high school	59.9	11.7	23.5
4 years of high school	24.2	41.7	55.3
1 to 3 years of college	15.9	30.6	11.9
4 years of college or more	(2)	16.0	9.3

[1] Includes a small number of families maintained by men.

[2] Less than 0.5 percent.

recent high school graduates not enrolled in college, and $34,200 for families of college-enrolled recent high school graduates.[12] These income differences are explained, in part, by the distribution of family types for each group. For example, dropouts are more likely to come from families maintained by women, whose incomes, on average, are less than half those of married-couple families. (See table 1 page 465).

A second factor, parental education, has also been suggested as influencing the dropout's decision. More than half of the recent dropouts were in families where the householder[13] had completed less than 12 years of school; only 10 percent of college-enrolled recent graduates were in such families. (See table 2.) Dropouts are also more likely to live in families maintained by women, and these women tend to have relatively low levels of both educational attainment and income.

These findings support previous studies that show parental education and family income as factors associated with dropping out of high school. While the findings do not establish a causal relationship, they help identify youths

---

[12] Median income figures are tabulated from data collected on the CPS control card. This method yields estimates that lack a high degree of precision, but allows for intergroup comparisons.

[13] A householder is the person (or one of the persons) in whose name the housing unit is owned or rented. See footnote 10.

who are "at risk" of dropping out. The data also suggest differences in the familial backgrounds of graduates and dropouts which will not be changed by obtaining a high school diploma, and which must be recognized when formulating programs dealing with the employment problems facing young dropouts.

In addition to the familial background factors, responses obtained from dropouts on their reasons for leaving school add vital information to their portrait. Data on reasons for leaving school are available from the Center for Education Statistics' longitudinal survey of high school sophomores and seniors, begun in the spring of 1980.[14] The survey categorized reasons for dropping out as school-related, family-related, or other (the categories are not mutually exclusive; dropouts could give more than one reason). Among the other reasons, "offered job and chose to work" was listed separately and is of special interest in this analysis. The following tabulation shows the percent of dropouts, by reason, from the Center for Education Statistics' survey:

	Male	Female
Had poor grades	35.9	29.7
School not for me	34.8	31.1
Married or planned to get married	6.9	30.7
Was pregnant	—	23.4
Had to support family	13.6	8.3
Offered job and chose to work	26.9	10.7

For young women, the decision to leave school is primarily related to school or family matters. Many listed marriage or pregnancy as the reason for dropping out; only 11 percent listed "offered job and chose to work." In view of their low labor force participation after leaving school, it appears that work-related factors play a minor role in the decision of young women to drop out. Marital status and childbearing appear to be important factors. For many young men, the reasons given for dropping out of school suggest an implicit choice of work over further studies. For

example, in addition to school-related reasons, "offered job and chose to work" and "had to support a family" figured prominently.

In analyzing data on the reasons for leaving school, it is important to note that "*post hoc* explanations provided by dropouts may be somewhat questionable because of the complexity of the dropout phenomenon and the natural tendency for persons to rationalize behavior which might be regarded by others as evidence of failure."[15] However, data on the reasons for dropping out of school provide insight into the post-school behavior of dropouts. And the labor force behavior of dropouts, both female and male, is inextricably linked to the reasons and causes of dropping out.

FEMALE DROPOUTS

Between October of 1985 and 1986, more than a quarter of a million young women dropped out of high school. Only a little more than half of them were in the labor force in October 1986, continuing the historical pattern of comparatively low labor force participation among young female dropouts. About 20 years earlier, the participation rate for 16- to 24-year-old female dropouts was just 38 percent. Their participation has steadily increased over the last two decades, reaching 50 percent in 1986. However, their rate was still dramatically below the 77-percent rate for 16- to 24-year-old women who had ended their studies with a high school diploma.

Children and Marriage. Childbearing and marriage would seem to be two important factors in explaining the low labor force participation of female dropouts. A special tabulation of the March 1987 CPS data provided a look at the relationship between marital status, presence of children, and labor force participation of 16- to 24-year-old female high school graduates who did not go to college[16] and dropouts. As expected, the presence of children had a negative effect on the participation of both groups. However, regardless of marital or maternal status,

---

[14] Samuel S. Peng, *High School Dropouts: Descriptive Information from High School and Beyond*, Bulletin NCES 83-221b (Washington: U.S. Department of Education, National Center for Education Statistics, November 1983).

[15] Peng, *High School Dropouts*, p. 4.

[16] All analyses regarding high school graduates refer to those individuals with 4 years of high school education only, unless otherwise specified.

TABLE 3. Labor Force Participation Rates of 16- to 24-Year-Old Female High School Dropouts and Graduates by Marital Status, Presence of Children, Race, and Hispanic Origin, March 1987

| Marital Status and Presence of Children | Dropouts | | | | Graduates[1] |
	Total	White	Black	Hispanic Origin	
Total	46.1	47.7	37.9	35.1	77.4
With no own children	59.5	62.4	40.6	58.0	87.1
With own children	35.6	35.5	36.3	21.2	60.0
Married, spouse present	39.5	37.9	(2)	22.8	67.9
With no own children	51.4	47.9	(2)	(2)	81.5
With own children	35.5	34.7	(2)	18.4	58.4
Other marital status[3]	50.0	55.4	35.7	45.4	82.9
With no own children	61.6	66.9	36.5	65.3	88.8
With own children	35.8	36.8	35.1	25.1	62.4
Maintaining families with own children	32.8	35.1	28.2	(2)	61.3

[1] Data refer to graduates who completed 4 years of high school only.
[2] Data not shown where base is less than 75,000.
[3] Refers to single, widowed, divorced, or separated women.

dropouts have significantly lower rates of participation than do graduates. (See table 3.)

The presence of children has, by far, the greatest impact on the labor force participation of young female dropouts. Regardless of marital status, just over one-third of the dropouts who were mothers were in the labor force. Marital status, however, affects young women's dependence on family and government for financial support. About 44 percent of unmarried mothers lived with relatives, and many received government assistance. Using data from the Center for Human Resource Research's longitudinal study of young women age 14 to 24 that was begun in 1979, Frank L. Mott and Nan L. Maxwell found that about 32 percent of white dropouts with children and 74 percent of black dropouts with children received government assistance from at least one of the following programs: Aid to Families with Dependent Children, food stamps, and Supplemental Social Security.[17]

Among female dropouts with children, labor force participation rates vary substantially by race and ethnicity. For example, Hispanic dropouts have significantly lower rates than do their white or black counterparts. (See table 3.) Cultural attitudes regarding marriage, childrearing, and paid employment may help explain the variations in participation. Although both white and black dropout mothers have similar participation rates, they exhibit distinctly different marital patterns—only 1 of 10 black mothers was married, compared with about 6 of 10 white mothers and Hispanic mothers. (See table 4.) The high proportion of unmarried black dropouts explains, to some extent, the large percentage of black mothers receiving government assistance, compared with white mothers. This marital pattern also results in nearly half of all black dropout mothers living with relatives, and about 40 percent maintaining their own families.

Even when they do not have children, black female dropouts seem to have a very tenuous attachment to the labor force. Fewer than half of them were in the labor force in March 1987, in contrast to about 60 percent of their white or Hispanic counterparts.

[17] Frank L. Mott and Nan L. Maxwell, "School-age mothers: 1968 and 1979," *Family Planning Perspectives*, November/December 1981, p. 290.

TABLE 4. Distribution of 16- to 24-Year-Old Female Dropouts, by Marital Status, Presence of Children, Race, and Hispanic Origin, March 1987

Marital Status and Presence of Children	Total	White	Black	Hispanic Origin
Total female dropouts:				
Number (thousands)	2,024	1,577	391	454
Percent	100.0	100.0	100.0	100.0
Married, spouse present	37.2	44.1	10.2	45.8
Other marital status[1]	62.8	55.9	89.8	54.2
With no own children:				
Number (thousands)	887	714	144	171
Percent	100.0	100.0	100.0	100.0
Married, spouse present	21.1	23.7	9.7	26.9
Other marital status[1]	78.9	76.3	90.3	72.5
With own children:				
Number (thousands)	1,137	863	247	283
Percent	100.0	100.0	100.0	100.0
Married, spouse present	49.8	61.1	10.5	56.9
Other marital status[1]	50.2	39.0	89.5	43.1
Maintaining own family	28.1	23.8	42.9	24.4
Living with relatives	22.2	15.3	46.6	18.7

[1] Refers to single, widowed, divorced, or separated women.

Unemployment. The poor labor market performance of female dropouts is also exemplified by their high unemployment rates. In October 1986, the jobless rate for female dropouts age 16 to 24 was 30.4 percent, about 2½ times the rate for women this age who had ended their education with a high school degree.

From data collected in the October 1986 CPS supplement, a special tabulation was constructed to compare female dropouts and graduates as they go through the transition period during the 4 years after leaving high school. Using cross-sectional data, the following tabulation [See next column.] shows the effect of time out of school and age on the unemployment rates of dropouts and graduates.

Unemployment rates for both groups show some decline with age and time out of school, although for dropouts the jobless rate remains exceptionally high. The unemployment rate was 34 percent for current-year dropouts, compared with 20 percent for 1986 high school graduates

	Unemployment Rates	
	Dropouts	Graduates
Last attended high school:		
Current year (1986)	33.7	20.3
1 year ago	40.3	14.3
2 years ago	31.8	16.6
3 years ago	36.5	8.2
4 years ago, or longer	26.4	10.8
Age in 1986:		
16–17	37.1	—
18–19	35.9	15.9
20–21	27.8	12.7
22–24	28.2	11.2

not enrolled in college. The gap between graduates' and dropouts' unemployment rates was smallest immediately after leaving school.

MALE DROPOUTS

Because of their strong labor force attachment, the labor market problems of male dropouts have often received more analytical attention than those of female dropouts. Numerous studies of the "youth employment problem" identify young male dropouts as the group most adversely affected by a slack youth labor market.[18] Job competition for full-time employment is keen, with dropouts competing not only among themselves, but also with high school graduates who did not go to college. The employment problems of black youth dropouts are often viewed as approaching crisis proportions.

The occupational distribution of young male dropouts suggests that they compete with male high school graduates who did not attend college. Among both groups, about two-fifths of the employed 16- to 21-year-olds were machine operators, fabricators, or laborers; about one-fourth were employed in precision production, craft, and repair jobs; and 1 of 7 was in service occupations. Such competition between graduates and dropouts often puts the dropout at a distinct disadvantage. In the extreme, the use of the high school diploma as an employment screening device could prevent the qualified dropout from even being considered by the employer.

The occupational distribution of high school dropouts is also noteworthy because of the small proportion (14 percent) employed in service occupations. A popular stereotype portrays employed youth as low-paid, often part-time workers in service occupations. However, male dropouts are more likely to work full time in the goods-producing sector as operators, fabricators, or laborers, and as precision production, craft, or repair workers. The sector's lagging performance does not promise very strong employment prospects for the recent dropouts who, in the past, have found jobs in mining, manufacturing, and construction.[19]

The jobless rates for high school dropouts and graduates provide some indication of the labor market performance of these competing groups. In October 1986, more than 1 of 5 male dropouts were unemployed, compared with 1 of 10 high school graduates. Among dropouts, the jobless rate for blacks (44 percent) was much higher than that for whites (18 percent) and Hispanics (15 percent). However, the most useful measure of the labor market success of male dropouts and high school graduates may be the employment-population ratio—that is, the employed as a proportion of the civilian noninstitutional population. This measure focuses on the more clear-cut and analytically important distinction between employment and "nonemployment" (this category includes those unemployed and those not in the labor force), particularly for out-of-school young men, for whom it is sometimes difficult to distinguish between being outside the labor force and being unemployed.[20] In October 1986, the employment-population ratio was 56 percent for recent male dropouts, and 70 percent for recent high school graduates. Although the employment-population ratios for dropouts generally increase with age and time out of school, the gap between graduates and dropouts remains fairly constant. Using cross-sectional data for October 1986, the following tabulation illustrates the impact of the age and time out of school variables on employment-population ratios:

	Employment-Population Ratios	
	Graduates	Dropouts
Last attended school:		
Current year (1986)	69.4	47.6
1 year ago	81.1	58.5
2 years ago	80.9	61.0
3 years ago	87.0	64.8
4 years ago, or longer	87.7	73.6
Age in 1986:		
16–17	—	44.2
18–19	73.7	63.0
20–21	83.1	68.2
22–24	88.3	74.1

[18] See Richard B. Freeman and David A. Wise, eds., *The Youth Labor Market Problem: Its Nature, Causes, and Consequences* (Chicago: National Bureau of Economic Research, 1982); and Richard B. Freeman and Harry J. Holzer, eds., *The Black Youth Employment Crisis* (Chicago: National Bureau of Economic Research, 1986).

[19] Thomas Nardone, "Decline in youth population does not lead to lower jobless rates," *Monthly Labor Review*, June 1987, pp. 40–41.

[20] For a discussion of the distinction between unemployment and out of the labor force, see Kim B. Clark

Both aging and time out of school give young men a chance to mature and gain valuable work experience as they pass through a "moratorium period," where employment is often of secondary importance.[21] However, over the last two decades there has been an alarming downtrend in employment-population ratios of out-of-school youth, particularly for young black dropouts. It is no longer clear whether the normal increase in such ratios that is typically associated with aging will be enough to integrate these black dropouts into the labor force during their prime working years.[22]

Nonemployment of Out-Of-School Youth. While quite sensitive to cyclical changes over the last 15 years, the employment-population ratio of male dropouts and high school graduates has trended downward—although more moderately for high school graduates. From October 1973 (1 month prior to a business cycle peak) to October 1986 (4 years into an expansion), the employment-population ratio of black dropouts fell 25 percentage points, while the white and the Hispanic ratios declined only 7 and 8 percentage points, respectively. Similarly, the decline in the employment-population ratio for black graduates was more severe than that for their white or Hispanic counterparts.

While low employment-population ratios among dropouts demonstrate that a large proportion are not working, that measure alone does not capture the underlying dynamics of the labor force activity of dropouts. It is important to know whether low employment-population ratios are a result of frequent, short spells of nonemploy-

ment or a product of extended periods of nonemployment. A study sponsored by the National Bureau of Economic Research identifed long spells of nonemployment as the primary cause of low employment-population ratios of out-of-school black youth.[23] Analysis of CPS work experience data confirm the existence of long periods of nonemployment among a sizable proportion of dropouts. During 1986, 17 percent of men age 20 to 24 with less than 4 years of high school had no work experience at all; 25 percent had worked 26 weeks or less. By comparison, about 40 percent of the black dropouts reported no employment whatsoever for the year. Since 1974 (when data were first available), the proportion of black dropouts with no work experience during the year has increased dramatically. This is also true among high school graduates, where blacks clearly had the highest incidence of and greatest rise in nonemployment. The following tabulation shows the proportion of 20- to 24-year-old male graduates and dropouts with no work experience during selected calendar years:

	Total	White	Black	Hispanic Origin
Graduates:				
1974	5.3	4.6	9.0	9.2
1979	5.4	3.7	15.2	8.7
1982	9.6	7.2	22.9	9.5
1986	6.7	4.8	15.7	8.9
Dropouts:				
1974	10.4	9.1	15.1	8.8
1979	12.4	9.3	23.9	9.4
1982	19.6	14.9	40.1	14.3
1986	16.8	11.8	39.7	9.6

There has also been a slight polarization in the distribution of weeks of work for the dropouts who do work. The proportion working 50–52 weeks rose from 46 percent in 1979 to 50 percent in 1986, while the percentage working 26 weeks or less also increased slightly. (See table 5.) Black dropouts, however, have shown a decrease in the proportion working full year, as

---

and Lawrence H. Summers, "The dynamics of youth unemployment," in Freeman and Wise, eds., *The Youth Labor Market Problem: Its Nature, Causes and Consequences*; and Christopher J. Flinn and James J. Heckman, "Are unemployment and out of the labor force behaviorally distinct labor force states?" *Journal of Labor Economics* 1, no. 1 (1983).

[21] Paul Osterman, *Getting Started* (Cambridge, Mass.: MIT Press, 1980), p. 27.

[22] Richard B. Freeman and Harry J. Holzer, "The black youth employment crisis: Summary of findings," in Freeman and Holzer, eds., *Black Youth Employment Crisis*.

---

[23] John Ballen and Richard B. Freeman, "Transitions between employment and nonemployment," in Freeman and Holzer, eds., *Black Youth Employment Crisis*.

TABLE 5.   Distribution of 20- to 24-Year-Old Male High School Dropouts with Work Experience by Number of Weeks Worked, Race, and Hispanic Origin, 1979 and 1986
[in percent]

Weeks Worked	Total		White		Black		Hispanic Origin	
	1979	1986	1979	1986	1979	1986	1979	1986
Total with work experience	100.0	100.0	100.0	100.0	100.0	100.0	100.0	100.0
50–52 weeks	45.6	49.6	47.2	53.3	37.7	28.1	47.2	58.9
40–49 weeks	16.7	12.4	17.5	12.2	13.4	10.8	13.4	9.1
27–39 weeks	14.4	9.3	13.8	9.8	17.7	6.6	17.7	9.9
1–26 weeks	23.8	28.8	21.2	24.6	31.2	54.5	22.1	21.9
14–26 weeks	13.7	16.0	12.7	13.9	13.9	27.5	15.6	11.3
1–13 weeks	10.2	12.7	8.5	10.7	17.3	26.9	6.5	10.6

well as a large increase in the number working half a year or less.

Young high school dropouts face a difficult time in today's labor market. Unemployment rates are high, especially among black dropouts. Only half of all female dropouts are in the labor force at any time, and many of these young women have the additional responsibility of motherhood, often without a spouse. A surprisingly small proportion of male dropouts are employed, with many experiencing long periods of nonemployment.

In a labor market demanding increasingly higher skill levels, school dropouts face declining employment opportunities. Further, they must compete with high school graduates for these limited jobs. The data suggest that dropouts are less likely to achieve success in the labor market than are high school graduates. However, it would be misleading to infer that the employment problems of dropouts would be solved solely by obtaining a high school diploma. While the importance of education cannot be overstated, there are differences in the family background and personal characteristics of dropouts and graduates that affect labor market success. These differences cannot be overcome simply by obtaining a diploma.

57. OF DROPOUTS AND STAY-INS: THE GERSHWIN APPROACH

JACKSON TOBY

In 1922 Yale professor George S. Counts published one of the first scholarly studies of youngsters who left high school without graduating. He referred to them as "children of high school age not in school"; the word "dropout" had not yet been coined. Counts deplored his finding that the children of middle-class and native-born parents were more likely than the children of the poor and of immigrants to graduate from American public high schools. He probably felt, correctly, that poverty forced most of the dropouts of the first two decades of the twentieth century to leave school whether they wished to withdraw or not. Largely the children of immigrants, they took low-paid jobs to help support their families. In that era, less than one-fifth of all adolescents stayed in high school until graduation.

Today, however, it is widely believed that everyone should graduate from high school—and not too long after turning eighteen. As a result, "dropout" is now a pejorative in the United States. In the early twentieth century, less stigma was placed on adolescents who chose not to stay in school, but instead to leave school to work. The choice that adolescents then made could reflect a personal commitment, whether to further education or to employment.

The experience of the Gershwin brothers reflects these alternate commitments. George Gershwin left the High School of Commerce in May 1912, four months short of his sixteenth birthday, to take a job as a song plugger on Tin Pan Alley. His brother Ira, by contrast, graduated from the most selective public high school in New York City, Townsend Harris Hall, and went on to the City College of New York. Their different paths, of course, converged in the field of popular music. The success of each ought still to be instructive to us, and should cause us to rethink our approach to the dropout problem.

Today's situation obviously differs from the one that confronted adolescents in the Gershwins' era. Most American adolescents now graduate from high school, unlike their counterparts of three generations ago. Those who drop out, although still disproportionately from poor families, are no longer motivated primarily by poverty. The existence of a welfare safety net that includes Aid to Families with Dependent Children (AFDC), Medicaid, food stamps, and Supplemental Security Income has reduced the financial pressure on the children of poor families to leave school. Indeed, there are often financial reasons for youngsters to remain enrolled. Between the ages of sixteen and twenty-one, children of AFDC families are eligible for benefits if they are enrolled in school, but not if they have dropped out. Similarly, in calculating a family's eligibility for benefits the Social Security Act excludes the part-time earnings of dependent children enrolled in school. As interviews with dropouts consistently confirm, most school dropouts leave the system because they lack interest in what the schools are designed to teach.

DROPOUTS IN OTHER LANDS

In the United States the word "dropout" carries stigma; that is, it evokes disapproval and pity. Especially in big-city school districts with large minority enrollments, administrators have become increasingly frantic about symptoms of student apathy: absenteeism, class cutting, and dropping out altogether.

Even in communities with low dropout rates, principals are concerned about dropouts. They

From *The Public Interest*, No. 95 (Spring 1989), pp. 3–13. Copyright © 1989 by National Affairs, Inc. Reprinted with permission of the author.

Jackson Toby is professor of sociology and director of the Institute for Criminological Research at Rutgers University.

want *every* student to remain in school until graduation and will do almost anything to cajole students to do so if they appear to be at risk of dropping out. For example, in 1987 the principal of a middle-class New Jersey high school (from which more than 95 percent of the students graduate) obtained a federal grant of $108,000, which he used to pay marginal students to stay in school. Each of the 130 students identified as a potential dropout was offered a $25-a-week reward for acceptable behavior. In order to earn the money, students were expected to attend every day, to be on time, to do the assigned homework, and to bring books and writing implements to class. Only seventy accepted the challenge in 1987–1988, and each week fewer than half actually earned the $25.

The American desperation about "dropouts" is not shared by all developed countries. Consider Sweden and Japan, countries at least as committed to education as the United States. There is no Swedish word for "dropout." The closest term is literally translated as "school-tired." The implicit assumption is that youngsters who get tired of school need a rest. Consequently it is acceptable for Swedish secondary-school students to withdraw from school for a semester or so to recuperate. The Swedish attitude is not very different from the American attitude toward college students who wish to take time off to clarify their goals. Swedes expect most tired students to return to school eventually; not only Swedes but Scandinavians in general treat education as a lifetime activity. Many Scandinavians start work before completing their educations and return to school later, usually part-time.

Unlike the Swedish language, Japanese does have a word for "dropout," but dropouts are rare in Japan. Nonetheless, schooling there is compulsory only through ninth grade, and both public and private high schools charge tuition. A family with a child in a public high school spends about 5 percent of its income on school expenses; the figure for private high schools is 10 percent. Japanese families often incur additional expenses to educate their children, because a substantial minority of Japanese high school students—perhaps a third—attend private tutoring sessions after school and on weekends.

The Japanese assume that school is a full-time, six-day-a-week, ten-month-a-year task for young people. Students are expected to study extremely hard by American standards, because they and their parents believe that their futures depend on graduating not merely from high school but from a *good* high school. A good high school is one that can prepare students for admission to the most selective universities. Prestigious high schools select entering students by competitive examinations; on the basis of these examinations, students are admitted or rejected by the high schools of their choice. Some students refuse admission to lesser high schools, choosing instead to study for an additional year and retake the examinations after diligent private work. In Japan, then, an important type of dropping out actually reflects a commitment to high educational achievement.

Few Japanese youngsters fail to go to high school or leave it to enter the labor force. These few, however, are expected to (and do) find jobs, although not very good ones. In Japan, adults and children alike understand that educational achievement leads to occupational success. That is one reason why 94 percent of junior high school graduates attend high school, and 88 percent of them complete it.

RECONSIDERING UNIVERSAL HIGH SCHOOL EDUCATION

It is easy to see why Americans today believe that everyone should graduate from high school at age eighteen, despite the success of a George Gershwin. If Gershwin were starting out today as a fifteen-year-old dropout, he might not manage to become a song plugger and to gain needed musical experience. Social norms and child-labor laws have changed. Americans now tend to think that the place of teenagers is in school, not at a full-time job.

Furthermore, one can concede that George Gershwin should not have been pressured to remain in high school (and that American popular music would have been worse off if he had been) without wanting to legitimize dropping out. This is because George Gershwin had exceptional talent and a pretty good idea of what he wanted to do with his life. That a genius can realize his potential without formal education, it could be argued, does not mean that the great majority of youngsters can afford to follow his example. On the other hand, successful dropouts are by no means unique; they include not only film stars like Clark Gable and professional athletes like Muhammad Ali, but also many entrepreneurs, such as Marion Isbell, the founder of the Ramada Inn motel chain. As long as some dropouts do conspicuously well, however atypical they may be, youngsters who dislike school will not believe that a high school dropout is necessarily doomed to dead-end jobs or a life of crime.

Of course, potential Gershwins who leave high school in order to pursue some special interest are far different from youngsters who drop out of school without *any* goals, academic or non-academic. When aimless youngsters leave high school, they do not leave for a job on Tin Pan Alley—or even to work at McDonald's—but to hang out on street corners, perhaps selling crack, smoking it, or both. For this reason, many people believe that it is best to bribe such youngsters to stay in school for their own good, or to force them to stay by raising the statutory age for compulsory school attendance. At least school will keep them off the streets, and it may even make them minimally literate.

Seductive as this line of reasoning is, it is ultimately unpersuasive, because it fails to recognize that education depends on cooperation between students and teachers. When children are young, such cooperation is commonplace, especially when their parents believe in education and encourage effort. But teenagers pose a bigger problem. The best way to obtain their cooperation is to convince them that education is worthwhile. That is the secret of Japanese schools. Japanese adolescents willingly work long and hard in high school, because they believe that their future depends on educational achievement.

THE STAY-IN PROBLEM

Some years ago, when interviewing Joe, a young inmate in a New Jersey reformatory, I asked him about his school experiences. "I liked school," he said.

I was surprised. Most of the delinquents I had known hated school and did poorly in their schoolwork. "What did you like about it?" I asked. He told me about sitting in the lunchroom with his gang and having food fights, about "making out" in the halls with his girlfriends, about smoking in the boys' room, about harassing a young, inexperienced teacher so much that she left teaching the following year. "What about your classes?" I asked. "Did you like them?"

"Yeah," he replied. "I liked gym." I persisted. Did he like English, math, or anything else in the curriculum? "No," he replied, smiling. "They weren't in *my* curriculum."

Joe wasn't a dropout. But from the point of view of the other students in the school that he attended before his arrest for car theft, it might have been better if he *had* dropped out. He stayed in simply because his high school made negligible academic demands upon him. He never did any homework. He frequently cut classes. He skipped school when he felt that there was something more important to do. In short, he stayed in for the wrong reasons. One Joe in a high school is bearable. However, when the Joes constitute a constituency to be reckoned with, schools have a "stay-in" problem.

In inner-city neighborhoods, this happens almost as a matter of course. Children living in female-headed households supported by public welfare are not necessarily uninterested in school. But research shows that parental encouragement has a powerful effect on educational performance and aspiration, and youthful unwed mothers, preoccupied with their own problems, rarely encourage their children to do well in school—much less help them with homework. Such children suffer from a second handicap: their friends too are likely to be uninterested in school. Without parental or peer support for learning, these adolescents are as likely to curse and threaten teachers and other students as to study.

Maybe it is understandable when they drift into crime, promiscuity, and drug and alcohol abuse. But what are teachers and principals to do about it? One inner-city principal decided that apathetic or hostile adolescents should not be permitted to distract the real students. In December 1987 Joe Clark, principal of Eastside

High School in Paterson, New Jersey, suspended sixty students who, according to Clark, had been in high school for four or five years, were not attending classes regularly, and had no hope of graduating. Some were more interested in drugs than in history or English. "I'm tired of parasites . . . who don't want to better themselves," said Clark. "Go out and get a job." Clark had the support of most Eastside students, but the Paterson Board of Education and the press considered his action high-handed.

The stay-in problem is a chronic challenge to inner-city schools, but suburban schools also have youngsters who have become "school tired." One response to stay-ins in both types of schools is to degrade the curriculum by emphasizing entertainment. Courses that are peripheral to the central academic mission of school have proliferated, covering such subjects as driver education, science fiction, and pottery making. Well-taught, such courses might help interest students in reading and writing. But that would require making serious intellectual demands on students, including the Joes—something schools are afraid to do. The bottom line is that the desire to keep students enrolled leads schools to offer courses, and especially electives, that have precious little education value for anybody.

When New Jersey Governor Thomas Kean proposed in his January 1989 State of the State address that the legislation requiring two and one-half hours of physical education a week be amended, he was addressing an aspect of this problem. Governor Kean thought it reasonable to allow local school boards to schedule gym as often as they saw fit—or even to make gym an elective. "We require as much phys. ed. as English and more than math, science, art, and history," the Governor said. Furthermore, Department of Education studies showed that given the time consumed by changing clothes, the amount of exercise during physical education classes was not contributing much to youth fitness. To the Governor's surprise, Senator Matthew Feldman, Chairman of the State Senate Education Committee, protested: "In inner-city neighborhoods, a day without physical education will trigger an exodus from our high schools."

Senator Feldman wanted to cater to school-tired stay-ins in order to hold down the dropout rate, without much consideration of the consequences for students more receptive to learning. Aside from the academic consequences, the presence of students like Joe in schools increases the levels of violence, drug abuse, theft, and general disruption. A decade ago the Safe Schools Study, a national survey of violence and vandalism in 642 public secondary schools, demonstrated that schools with above-average proportions of academically uninterested students were also schools with high rates of attacks against teachers and students.

Such a correlation between poor academic performance and school violence does not, by itself, prove causation. It might be that kids from poor neighborhoods or from racial and ethnic minorities make schools dangerous. But excellent and safe schools can be found in such neighborhoods despite minority clienteles. Dunbar High School in Washington, D.C., for example, had high academic standards between 1870 and 1955, even though its students were black children whose tested aptitudes and economic circumstances were modest. During that period Dunbar sent the majority of its graduates on to college. Its alumni included the first black Cabinet member, a United States Senator, and distinguished judges. What was Dunbar's secret? Students chose to attend it, attracted by its reputation and willing to conform to its stringent curricular requirements. In 1955, however, Dunbar stopped recruiting students from all over the Washington metropolitan area, and instead enrolled local students regardless of whether they wanted to attend. Dunbar soon developed the disciplinary and academic problems that might be expected in a school serving a population on the lowest socioeconomic level in America.

It is not where students come from that determines the climate of a school, but how hard they are willing to work and what they aim to do.

MISTAKING THE SYMPTOM FOR THE CAUSE

The implications of this logic horrify most Americans: in order for schools to be safer and more concerned with education, some kids *ought* to drop out. Those who are horrified fear that dropping out leads to drug abuse and criminality. Studies, after all, show a higher incidence of many types of antisocial behavior among dropouts than among high school graduates. But dropping out may simply be a symptom of deeper, pre-existing problems that lead independently to unemployment, drug abuse, and crime. The evidence is that dropping out of school has less serious consequences than is generally believed.

Two excellent studies—one a national study conducted by the Survey Research Center at the University of Michigan, the other a California study—tracked youngsters for four years, beginning when they started the ninth grade. Whether they dropped out during those four years or remained in school until graduation, they were monitored carefully. In one study, official arrest records and self-reported crimes were tabulated; in the other, only self-reported offenses. The dropouts did indeed have higher delinquency rates than the graduates. But their antisocial behavior began long before they dropped out. In the national study, their delinquency rates did not increase after they dropped out; in the California study, delinquency actually declined somewhat after the students left. On the other hand, delinquency rates for students who stayed in school until graduation actually rose over the four years.

These findings are buttressed by the fact that arrests of juvenile offenders are not appreciably greater during the summer or other holiday periods than when schools are in session. America would probably not experience a crime epidemic even if the dropout rate increased.

THE GEORGE AND IRA GERSHWIN APPROACH

Although George Gershwin did not follow his brother's path of academic achievement, he did pursue excellence. Leaving school early did not cause him to think of himself as a failure, and his family neither pitied nor condemned him. He and Ira set high standards for the transition from childhood to adulthood, but they did not suppose that going to school continuously was the

sole way to make that transition. In the tradition of George and Ira Gershwin, I favor giving fifteen-year-olds the responsibility for choosing between really studying in a real school and doing something else, like working.

A school counsellor should say something like this to a prospective dropout: "You probably ought to stay in school and learn what you have to learn in order to get a fulfilling job and to be a good citizen. But I understand that students can get awfully tired of school. And a few, a very few, might be able to make it in the world without a high school education. Okay, withdraw for the time being, but keep in touch. Let us help you with job referrals and counseling—and maybe with part-time courses when you want them. If you make it, great. If you eventually decide that you want to come back to school full-time, no sweat. The door will be wide open for you—even in the middle of a semester."

There is one catch. Schools have to be able to give good educations. And in order for schools to do so, students must work hard. They must attend regularly, do homework, and pay attention in class. Those who balk at making prospective dropouts choose between a more onerous school experience than they now have and leaving school altogether should keep in mind that students would make the choice in consultation with parents or other relatives. Most families, even pretty demoralized ones, would urge children to stay in school when offered a clear choice. The problem today is that many families don't get a clear choice; the schools attended by their children unprotestingly accept tardiness, class cutting, inattention in class, and truancy. A child can drop out of such a school psychologically, unbeknownst to his family, because enrollment doesn't even mean regular attendance. In effect, prospective dropouts choose whether to fool around inside school or outside school. That is why making schools tougher academically, with substantial amounts of homework, might have the paradoxical effect of persuading a higher proportion of families to encourage their kids to opt for an education.

But what are the risks? If high school attendance were up to students and their families, how high would the dropout rate go? No one knows for sure, but there are clues suggesting that it would not increase much. Professor James Coleman and his colleagues demonstrated in their "High School and Beyond" study of a thousand American high schools that students were less likely to drop out of Catholic schools than out of public schools, even though the Catholic schools had stricter academic and behavioral requirements. It is possible that the Catholic schools attracted better students to begin with, but Coleman's analysis showed that the dropout rate was lower in Catholic schools than in public schools for youngsters with comparable socioeconomic characteristics, including minority youngsters. Surprisingly, it appears that schools where anything goes are not the schools that kids want to attend.

Another clue is the effect of various school-attendance laws. Five states (Arkansas, Louisiana, Maine, Mississippi, and Washington) require attendance only until age fifteen or less; four states (Hawaii, Ohio, Oregon, and Utah) require attendance until age eighteen or high school graduation; most other states require attendance until age sixteen. If legal compulsion were decisive, sixteen- and seventeen-year-olds ought to be much less likely to attend school in Washington than in Hawaii. In fact, the variation in attendance for sixteen- and seventeen-year-olds is small on average, only 5 percent more of the age cohort remains in school in states in which attendance is mandated for older students. Apparently, most kids go to school not because the law makes them but because they, their parents, and their friends value education. If so, making high schools more demanding and letting students choose whether to attend will drive away only a few students—whom the schools are well rid of anyway.

One virtue of the Gershwin approach is that a bad choice is less likely to be irrevocable than under present circumstances. Dropouts will not have burned their bridges. They will be treated as presumptive returnees and therefore as quasi-members of the school community who might benefit from school services. Even George Gershwin might have benefited from an evening course in music theory at his high school. The more usual dropout might need help in preparing for job interviews, or in learning how to cope with problems that arise on the job. Open lines of communication would increase the likelihood that dropouts would return to school if their dreams failed to come true.

Another advantage of the Gershwin approach is that it can only raise the academic performance of high school students. The low academic standards of American schools are a national disgrace; they were revealed anew in a recent report showing how poorly the math and science knowledge of American thirteen-year-olds compared with that of adolescents in Korea, Canada, Spain, the United Kingdom, and Ireland. Raising academic standards appreciably, however, is not feasible without simultaneously legitimating dropping out. Otherwise, schools would be either failing to enforce their standards or stigmatizing and irrevocably banishing students who are unwilling or unable to be diligent. The Gershwin approach avoids both horns of this dilemma.

When George Gershwin's name is mentioned, the last association that comes to mind is "high school dropout." But what about fifteen-year-old kids who *wrongly* think they are like George Gershwin? In the face of an unrealistic dream, American society should say, "Pursue excellence in the field that attracts you. If acting, sports, or business doesn't work out for you, come back to school and give yourself a second chance." This strategy is best because no one knows in advance who will profit more from formal education than from other endeavors. In addition, our national preoccupation with getting everyone through high school is wrecking the educational system, especially in inner-city neighborhoods—where good schools can save kids from catastrophe.

Even today, there are good schools, but they are suburban schools, private schools, and selective public schools. Efforts to prevent dropping out at all costs condemn children who attend inner-city high schools to an education that is form without substance. The Gershwin approach is more democratic; it dares to insist that all high schools should be excellent.

58. CHILDREN OF POVERTY: THE STATUS OF 12 MILLION YOUNG AMERICANS

SALLY REED and R. CRAIG SAUTTER

It is 9 a.m. on a November morning, and Terrence Quinn, principal of Public School 225 in Rockaway, Queens, New York, is serving breakfast. But he's not in the school cafeteria. He's in the lobby of a ramshackle welfare hotel where homeless parents and their children have come to seek shelter. With a social worker in tow, Quinn has cruised the hotel corridors, knocking on doors, inviting what is an ever-changing group of parents to share coffee and break bagels and doughnuts with him while he tries to persuade them to send their children to his elementary school six blocks—and a world—away.

Quinn first tried his pied piper approach to drawing poor children into his school in November 1988, and he repeats the effort periodically. His aim is to make the parents and children feel welcome in his school. Last spring, Jacqueline, a sixth-grader who had lived at the hotel, was selected as the school's valedictorian. One month before the official announcement, she entered Quinn's office and asked to speak to him in private.

"Can someone on welfare actually be the valedictorian?" she asked.

Quinn reassured Jacqueline, a youngster who has overcome many obstacles. Each day millions of others like her are trying to do likewise. And it's not fair. While the last decade became known in the media for its rampant greed, it left millions of poor people (and their children) literally out in the cold. The outcomes are heartbreaking. Why should a child such as Jacqueline feel so humiliated and ashamed of her predicament?

Jacqueline doesn't know it, but she's not alone. We've all been numbed by the horror stories we've heard of late—stories of homeless families sleeping in cars and of crack babies abandoned to hospital nurseries. Meanwhile, the mind-boggling statistics paint a dreadful picture of what life in this nation is like for far too many children. Once you gather all the figures—from conferences, from government agencies, and from scores of reports—the result is frightening. As a nation we're talking about setting goals for fire safety while a wildfire rages out of control all around us. What can educators, politicians, and individual citizens do? People's lives are at stake, and we can't wait any longer.

WAR WITHOUT END

A generation after president Lyndon Johnson declared an official War on Poverty, nearly one-fifth of America's youngest citizens still grow up poor; often sick, hungry, and illiterate; and deprived of safe and adequate housing, of needed social services, and of special educational assistance. Millions of these youngsters are virtually untouched by the vast wealth of the nation in which they begin their fragile and often painful lives.

It didn't take long to lose the War on Poverty. Only a decade after president Johnson's bold declaration, his antipoverty offensive had been lost for millions upon millions of children. By 1975, after the cutback of the Great Society programs by the Nixon and Ford Administrations and after spiraling inflation hit the economy, the interests of children slid lower on the list of economic priorities than even the interests of the elderly. The youngest Americans became the poorest Americans.

During the Great Depression, most Americans were poor. At the end of World War II, about one-third were still poor, but the industrial output of the U.S. was rapidly expanding. By August 1964, when the first antipoverty legislation was enacted, 32 million Americans (about 15% of

From *Phi Delta Kappan*, June 1990, pp. K1–K11. Reprinted with permission of the authors.

Sally Reed and R. Craig Sautter are writers and editors based in Chicago.

the population) were materially impoverished. About 13 million of those poor people were children. More of them were elderly.

The one front that has at least received sustained reinforcements since the War on Poverty was scaled back is the fight to improve the lot of the elderly poor. By 1990, 90% of the elderly poor were receiving significant benefits through Social Security cost-of-living adjustments, through housing assistance, through Medicaid, and through other federal and state safeguards.

As a result of this triumph of social policy for senior citizens, many child advocates, including educators and politicians, insist that we can do the same for our most vulnerable citizens, our children. This persistent band is finally making progress toward changing the way society treats youngsters who are the innocent victims of accidents of birth or family misfortune.

But the scale of the problem is overwhelming. Over the past 15 years the incidence of poverty among children has increased and become complicated in ways that portend catastrophic consequences, not only for the children themselves, but also for our schools, our economy, and our social well-being.

Since 1975 children have been poorer than any other age group. By 1989 young people accounted for 39.5% of America's poor. The official U.S. poverty rate for all citizens in 1989 edged slightly downward to 13.1%—only a 2% decline from the Johnson era. Yet in raw numbers more Americans are poor today than before the War on Poverty. Nearly 40 million people of all ages live in families with income levels below the official poverty line of $7,704 for a family of two, $9,435 for a family of three, and $12,092 for a family of four. The current poverty rate is higher than during the worst recession years of the 1970s.

Actually, the real crisis for children and families is even worse than it first appears. Income for the average poor family in 1988 was $4,851 *below* the poverty line. For poor families headed by females, that gap was $5,206. Levels of family income this low mean that some serious family needs—such as food, clothing, medicine, early learning assistance, and housing—are not being met. The result for the children of these families is sickness, psychological stress, malnutrition, underdevelopment, and daily hardship that

quickly takes its toll on their young minds and bodies.

Even though the postwar baby boom has long since subsided, nearly as many young people are poor today as when the War on Poverty was launched. However, the percentage today is higher. More than 12.6 million U.S. youngsters—nearly 20% of all children under the age of 18—are poor. Thus one in five American children goes to bed hungry or sick or cold.

And when these children wake each day, they face little prospect that the economic plight of their families will improve enough to make their lives better. Often they internalize the bleakness of their situation and blame themselves for it. Their lives become bitter and humorless or filled with anxiety and fear. Of course, many poor children retain their dignity, and their character is tempered by the Spartan battle for subsistence. But millions of others, permanently damaged, are unable to recover and fall victim to the vicious social pathology of poverty.

And the future seems even grimmer. U.S. Secretary of Education Lauro Cavazos has estimated that, by the year 2000, "as many as one-third of our young people will be disadvantaged and at risk."

Some American youngsters will never even have the chance to see the turn of the century. As has happened in other wars, they will perish. More than 10,000 children in the U.S. die each year as a direct result of the poverty they endure. Often they die during the first weeks of their lives because simple and inexpensive prenatal health care was unavailable to their mothers.

The U.S. has the highest rate of child poverty among the industrialized nations, nearly three times that of most other economically advanced nations. Moreover, the Children's Defense Fund, a leading Washington-based child advocacy group, has sadly noted that only the U.S. and South Africa, among the advanced industrial nations, do not provide universal health coverage for children and pregnant women and do not provide care to foster early development.

THE YOUNGER, THE POORER

And the picture gets worse. The younger a child is in America today, the greater are his or her chances of being poor. According to the U.S. Census Bureau, the Americans most likely of all to be poor are those age 3 and under. Officially, 23.3% of this age group are poor. During the early years so critical to development, nearly one-fourth of U.S. children lack medical, nutritional, and early-learning assistance. Thus many poor children are needlessly condemned to physical and psychological deficiencies for the rest of their lives.

Further down the road, the social cost of this neglect will almost certainly be extravagant. Physical and mental damage that could have been prevented by inexpensive prenatal check-ups or by nutritional programs in early childhood haunts our society in expensive educational, medical, welfare, and correctional costs that can reach into the hundreds of thousands of dollars. For example, 11% of children end up in special education classes because of cognitive and developmental problems, many of which could have been prevented by prenatal care. Even a pragmatist can count. The willful neglect of America's poor children is not only immoral; it is just plain stupid.

Children of poverty who make it through their earliest years relatively unscathed face new hardships later on. Nearly 22% of 3- to 5-year-olds are poor. Then, after six years of material want, most poor children enter school and make their first significant contact with a social institution. Indeed, the largest group of poor children ranges between the ages of 6 and 11. More than four million of these children—19.9% of the age group—continue to grow up in unremitting destitution.

Schools should be equipped to help these children gain skills to cope with and ultimately to escape from their economic circumstances. But far too many schools fail far too many poor children. And poor communities tend to get stuck with poor schools as patterns of taxation make a bad situation worse.

Only as children enter their teenage years—and begin to confront a new set of social and biological problems—does the poverty rate actually dip. But even among young people between the ages of 12 and 17, more than 16% live below the poverty line. That figure is higher than the poverty rate for the general population.

The Carnegie Council on Adolescent Development has emphasized that, between the ages of 10 and 15, young people are extremely volatile. For poor teens, the match is even closer to the fuse, since these youngsters are often beseiged by problems of school failure, pregnancy, substance abuse, and economic stress.

These young people suffer not only the immediate physical and psychological damage of economic and social adversity; the long-term effects of their childhood deprivation and neglect also manifest themselves in a growing complex of social ills. One-fourth of young black men are reported to have trouble of some kind with correctional authorities. Illiteracy among poor dropouts is endemic. And the personal tragedy of broken homes and a future of perpetually low-paying jobs feeds young black men into the drug trade—and the morgue. The popular appeal of Jesse Jackson's slogan, "Up with Hope," demonstrates just how many young people are growing up in the hopelessness that poverty breeds.

YOUNG FAMILIES, POOR CHILDREN

Then there is the matter of family circumstances. Almost 50% of all U.S. children living in a family headed by a person 25 years of age or younger are poor. One-third of all children living in a family headed by a person 30 years of age or younger are poor. In fact, while the nation's overall poverty rate slowly declined from 1967 to 1987, the poverty rate for children living in a family headed by a person 30 years of age or younger shot up from 19% to 35.6%.

Likewise, if a child lives in a family headed by a woman, the chances are better than 50/50 that the child is poor. More than 56% of families headed by single black women are poor. The poverty rate for families headed by Hispanic women is 59%. Yet single-parent families do not necessarily cause poverty. Half of the nation's poor children live with both parents.

Contrary to popular perception, child poverty is not a phenomenon confined to the inner cities. Fewer than 9% of America's poor people live in the nation's core cities. The largest number of poor people still live in semi-isolation in towns and hamlets across the country. About 17% of these people are hidden in rural America. Just as in the inner cities, poverty rates in some rural areas have reached 50% and higher. And some rural regions have been poor for generations. Surprisingly, 28% of America's poor struggle amidst the affluence of suburban communities, shut out from most of the benefits that their neighbors enjoy. Westchester County, New York, one of the 11 wealthiest suburban areas in the country, now has more than 5,000 homeless people looking for shelter.

Another inaccurate perception about poverty is that being poor is directly related to race. Two-thirds of poor Americans are white. The Children's Defense Fund calculates that one white child in seven is poor. However, the *rate* of poverty is considerably higher for minorities, who are fast becoming majority demographic groups in the 10 largest states. Four out of nine black children are poor; three out of eight Hispanic children are poor. Poverty in America knows no racial boundaries, no geographic borders. The only common denominator for the children of poverty is that they are brought up under desperate conditions beyond their control—and, for them, the rhetoric of equal opportunity seems a cruel hoax, an impossible dream.

THE FLIP SIDE OF PROSPERITY

During the "get-rich-quick" decade of the 1980s, when the number of U.S. billionaires quintupled, child poverty jumped by 23%. More than 2.1 million children tumbled into poverty as the stock market first soared, then plummeted, and finally rebounded. The bull market, with its leveraged buyouts, $325 billion savings-and-loan ripoffs, tax cuts for the wealthy, and junk bond scams, did little to drive up the value of children on the domestic agenda.

"The story of child poverty has become a story of American decline," a congressional staffer who works on poverty-related legislative issues recently lamented. "People have a vague sense that we are doing something wrong nationally, that we are going to be in trouble in the near future. The plight of children is related to this feeling. In addition to being immoral, our treatment of children is profoundly shortsighted. It is economically and socially shortsighted to allow

children to grow up with unhealthy bodies and lousy educations and poor nutrition and inadequate health care. We all know that, but now it looks like it will kill us in the 21st century."

What makes matters worse is that the poor are getting poorer. According to the U.S. House of Representatives' Select Committee on Children, Youth, and Families, the income gap between families with the highest incomes and those with the lowest was wider in 1988 than in any year since 1947. The poorest 20% of families received less than 5% of the national income, while the wealthiest 20% received 44%, the largest share ever recorded. Maurice Zeitlin, a sociologist at the University of California, Los Angeles, recently concluded that the richest 1% of families own 42% of the net wealth of all U.S. families—a staggering proportion that has changed little since the 19th century. This super-rich elite owns 20% of all real estate, 60% of all corporate stock, and 80% of family-owned trusts. These huge disparities make the familiar excuses about budget deficits and tax burdens standing in the way of helping children seem feeble at best.

The vast and ongoing transformation of the U.S. economy from manufacturing to service jobs and from local to global markets has also harmed poor families. When the unemployment of the recession of the 1980s finally began to ease, many of the new jobs were service jobs that paid half as much as manufacturing jobs. According to Michael Sherraden, a professor at Washington University in St. Louis, "The overwhelming reality is that most new jobs being created today are very low-skilled service jobs with low pay and no benefits, not high-tech jobs."

Statistics from the U.S. Department of Labor show that, although the unemployment rate has fallen steadily since 1983, the poverty rate has remained high. Since 1983 unemployment has dropped by 4%. Meanwhile, the overall poverty rate has fallen only 2%—and has actually increased for children.

WORKING HARDER, GETTING POORER

U.S. Census Bureau figures reveal that nearly half of the heads of all poor households are employed. In 1988 the proportion of poor heads of households who worked full-time increased by 1.8%. But that was accompanied by a decline in the average earnings of full-time male workers. A low minimum wage offers one explanation for this stubborn trend. For example, full-time work at the minimum wage by the head of a family of three leaves that family $2,500 below the poverty line.

In nearly 42% of poor households headed by females, the women are employed. About 10% work full-time, year-round. And 87% of poor children live in a family in which at least one person is employed at least part of the time. However, from 1979 to 1987 income for young families with children dropped by nearly 25%.

"The public has a misconception about who the poor are," Sherraden observes. "Most people who live below the poverty line are not welfare recipients and members of the underclass. They are people who have jobs or are members of a household in which someone has a job." He adds, "What kind of message are we delivering if people work hard and still do not make it?"

Some of the workers in poor families are children and teenagers. In 1989 the U.S. Department of Labor discovered 23,000 minors working in violation of the Fair Labor Standards Act. In fact, child labor violations have doubled in the last five years. Most such violations have involved young teenagers working too many hours or under unsafe conditions. Unlike the sweatshops of the past, many violators of child labor laws today are hamburger joints and fast-food establishments. Many teenagers work long hours because they must do so in order to survive, not because they are trying to buy designer jeans or are exploring future careers in food services. And, as teachers know, working often becomes a reason for classroom failure.

CUTBACKS AND REDUCTIONS

To add to an already bad situation, government cutbacks and the perpetual budget crisis have increased children's woes. The House Select Committee on Children, Youth, and Families found that, since 1970, the median grant through Aid to Families with Dependent Children (AFDC) has fallen 23%, from $471 to $361 in constant dollars. In 1987 AFDC reached only

56% of children in poverty, a lower proportion than in 1964 when the first volley was fired in the War on Poverty.

"Child poverty is Ronald Reagan's legacy to the 1990s," according to Rep. George Miller (D-Calif.), who chairs the Select Committee on Children, Youth, and Families. Between 1980 and 1988, during President Reagan's military build-up, the U.S. government spent $1.9 trillion on national defense, while cutting $10 billion from programs aimed at protecting poor children and families.

According to the Center for the Study of Social Policy, AFDC benefits and food stamps for a family of four amounted to only 66.3% of the 1988 poverty line, down from 70.9% in 1980. Meanwhile, participation in the food stamp program has declined 14% since 1982.

At the same time, federal assistance for low-income housing tumbled 76% when adjusted for inflation. In *The Same Client: The Demographics of Education and Service Delivery Systems*, a recent report from the Institute for Educational Leadership, Harold Hodgkinson concluded that many dropouts and school failures can be attributed directly to such basic factors as the high cost of housing that eats up most of a family's available and limited income. Children living on the edge of homelessness are prevented from finding the stability that usually makes successful schooling possible.

"If low-income children were living in economically and socially secure housing with some rent protection, there is little doubt that most of them could stay out of poverty and in school, while their parents stay on the job and off welfare," Hodgkinson advised in the report. He argued that national housing strategies to increase the availability and reduce the cost of housing are essential, if we wish to limit poverty. So are preventive social strategies that help people who are facing financial emergencies to stay out of poverty.

NO PLACE TO CALL HOME

Poor housing or no housing—those seem to be the options facing most poor children. Homeless children are one more distressing by-product of the new poverty that plagues this nation. The

U.S. Department of Education estimates that 220,000 school-aged children are homeless and that 65,000 of them do not attend school. About 15,600 homeless children live in publicly operated shelters, 90,700 live in privately operated shelters, 55,750 stay with relatives or friends, and 63,170 live "elsewhere." The greatest number of homeless children live in Los Angeles, New York, Chicago, Minneapolis, and Houston. Homelessness among children in the nation's capital has increased by a factor of five in recent years.

A report from the General Accounting Office estimated that, on any given night, 186,000 children who are not actually homeless are "precariously housed," living on the verge of homelessness. The Department of Health and Human Services calculates that, over the course of a year, as many as one million youngsters under age 18 lack a permanent home or live on the streets.

Despite the $1.7 billion in federal funds expended through the Stewart B. McKinney Homeless Assistance Act of 1987 and the millions more spent through the Runaway and Homeless Youth Act of 1974, homelessness continues to grow—a disturbing reminder that not all is well in the land of the free.

The future also looks bleak for those categories of young people who no longer live at home, according to the House Select Committee on Children, Youth, and Families. Its late 1989 report, *No Place to Call Home: Discarded Children in America,* concluded that by 1995 nearly a million children no longer living with their parents will cause serious problems for the schools. The study found that between 1985 and 1988 the number of children living in foster care jumped by 23%, while federal funding for welfare services for children rose only 7%.

Foster children are only one of the categories of displaced children, most of whom come from poor families. The number of children in juvenile detention centers rose 27% between 1979 and 1987, while funding fell from $100 million to $66.7 million. The number of children in mental health facilities also soared by 60% between 1983 and 1986. Meanwhile, federal block grants for mental health services declined by $17 million.

Drug and alcohol abuse by parents contributed to these dangerous trends. From 1985 to 1988 the number of children born with drug exposure quadrupled, reaching 375,000 in 1988. Add to that the number of abused or neglected children, which climbed 82% between 1981 and 1988. Of course, not all of these children are poor, but needy children fall into these categories much more frequently than their not-needy counterparts.

Rep. Miller warned that the nation's schools could be "overwhelmed" by such problems in the 1990s. He noted that teachers, counselors, and social workers are already overworked and that none of them "receives the training needed to deal with the complex and difficult problems confronting children and families today."

Clearly, no social problem operates in isolation. Poverty breeds personal and social disintegration. Difficulties in the areas of health, housing, and education are all linked. For example, significant numbers of homeless children suffer a wide range of health disorders. Many risk hearing loss because of untreated ear infections. That in turn leads to serious learning problems. In many homeless shelters, such infectious diseases as tuberculosis and whooping cough run rampant among uninoculated youngsters. Poverty is more than a social label; it is a disease that weakens and often destroys its victims.

HEALTHY GOALS, UNHEALTHY RESULTS

At first glance, it seems that the U.S. has a comprehensive health-care system. For example, we spent $551 billion on health care in 1987. But 37 million Americans, including more than 12 million children, have no health insurance. Uninsured children have a 20% greater chance of poor health and are less likely to have proper immunization against infectious diseases.

Nearly half of all poor children do not receive benefits from Medicaid, despite recent congressional action ordering states to provide more extensive coverage to poor children and pregnant mothers. The National Commission to Prevent Infant Mortality has found that the U.S. ranks 20th among the nations of the world in infant mortality and has urged Congress to take over Medicaid to insure that it reaches *all* infants and pregnant mothers.

This year the Pepper Commission, a bipartisan group of congressional representatives, urged a massive overhaul of the national health system, which is "in total crisis." Among other reforms, the commission called for universal protection for poor children and families. But the $66 billion a year price tag has scared off many potential supporters.

One pregnant woman in four receives no prenatal care during the critical first trimester. Such a mother is three to six times more likely to give birth to a premature, low-birth-weight baby who will be at risk for developmental disability or even death. Ultimately, 10.6 of every 1,000 newborns in the U.S. die—the highest rate in the developed world.

In 1980 Dr. Julius Richmond, then surgeon general of the U.S., published a list of 20 health-care goals for infants and children to be achieved by 1990. Like the recent list of educational goals promulgated by President Bush and the National Governors' Association, the health-care targets were ambitious and essential to heading off social and economic crisis. But by late 1989 the American Academy of Pediatrics, an organization of 37,000 experts on children's medical health, concluded that only one of the 20 goals had been achieved.

That one success was in reducing neonatal mortality: the death rate for infants in the first 28 days after birth has dropped from 9.5 to 6.4 deaths per 1,000. However, other goals, such as improving birth weights and prenatal care and narrowing the gap between racial groups in infant mortality, remain unfulfilled. The mortality rate for black infants is still twice that for white infants, about the same as it was 26 years ago; the infant mortality rate for the entire U.S. population stands at 10.1%, while the rate for African-Americans is 17.9%. (By contrast, the infant mortality rate in Japan is just 4.8%.) Moreover, surviving black infants have nine times more chance than white infants of being neurologically impaired.

Dr. Myron Wegman of the University of Michigan School of Public Health, who conducted the study for the pediatricians, discov-ered the existence of two separate medical nations within this land. One nation is prosperous, with the latest in health technology and knowledge at its disposal; the other nation is deprived, with death rates and health problems that match those commonly found in the Third World. Dr. Wegman blamed government cuts in health programs and social services during the Reagan Administration for a slowdown that prevented reaching the goals.

IMPACT ON SCHOOLS

What do the mountains of statistics and a heritage of damaged lives mean for educators in the public schools? Surveys of teachers have found disturbing news. The Metropolitan Life Insurance Company's annual *Survey of the American Teacher* discovered that in 1989 American teachers were greatly alarmed at the health and social problems of their students.

Other surveys show that teachers worry about constant pupil turnover, about students' health problems, and about students' preoccupation with family problems. Once again, such concerns are more common among teachers of children from low-income families. Guidance counselors report that, even at the elementary level, they find themselves "dealing with one crisis after another" in a child's life.

Teachers also report that they are seeing more children with learning disabilities. In fact, over the last 10 years the number of children diagnosed as learning disabled has increased 140%— to about 1.9 million children. While educators argue over the meaning of the term and debate possible reasons for the increase, veteran teachers claim that they have never before seen so many children with problems of comprehension and basic skills in their classes.

According to Verna Gray, a veteran teacher in the Chicago schools, poverty leads to more problems than just the lack of the basic academic skills needed to succeed in school. "Many of these youngsters don't have any self-esteem or even the belief that they can achieve," she notes.

The effects on the schools of increasing numbers of children living in poverty may not be completely clear, and the details are certainly debatable. But no one disputes that there are serious effects—or that the effects are negative.

WHAT SOCIETY MUST DO

No single individual or group can successfully tackle all the factors that contribute to child poverty. The lack of jobs that pay a decent wage, for example, is the biggest contributor to poverty in small towns, cities, and suburbs. Clearly, this is a national problem that can be addressed only by a comprehensive economic policy that gives top priority to the creation of jobs that pay a living wage. A number of family experts believe that an even greater increase in the minimum wage than the one recently passed by Congress is essential to help the working poor escape a lifetime of poverty.

Some effective programs already exist to deal with almost every aspect of the cycle of child poverty. But the programs that work have never been properly funded. Head Start is the classic example. Head Start was created by the antipoverty legislation of the 1960s, and a number of studies have documented its positive impact. One study found that nearly 60% of the Head Start graduates were employed at age 19, compared to just 32% of a control group. Only 49% of the control group had graduated from high school, while 67% of the former Head Start students had earned high school diplomas. Nearly 40% of the Head Start graduates had taken some colleges courses, while just 21% of the control group had taken any coursework beyond high school.

Such statistics add up to lives and money saved. One dollar invested in Head Start saves $7 in later social services that are not needed. Numbers of this kind have convinced many, but Head Start, which celebrates its 25th birthday this year, still serves only one in five eligible students.

That situation might be about to change. There are hopeful signs that some basic services for poor children could improve in the next few years if the federal government reasserts its leadership in child care, health coverage, and education.

Major political players are lining up in favor of a vastly extended support system for early care and education. The National Governors' Association has made early childhood learning a top goal, and President Bush's education budget called for a modest increase of $245 million for Head Start. Most important, the mammoth child-care bill hammered out by Congress over the last two years will bolster Head Start by as much as $600 million over the next five years. At press time, only a veto by President Bush, who wishes to shift to the states more of the burden of funding the program, can block what has become the most important piece of antipoverty legislation in the last 25 years.

Educators worry that, as the number of children in poverty grows, education for those children—without sharp increases in funding for Chapter 1 and Head Start—can only get worse, not better. Susan Frost, executive director of the Committee for Education Funding, says that "there is no alternative to Chapter 1 and Head Start, which are estimated to serve only one-half and one-fifth respectively of eligible children." The needs of such children, she adds, are not going to be met by restructuring.

Meanwhile, there is growing public support for offering a wider array of social and health services in the schools. In September 1989 a survey by the Washington Post and ABC News found widespread support for a variety of nontraditional services in the schools: the dissemination of information about birth control, counseling for psychiatric and drug-related problems, more nutrition information, and so on. Likewise, the 21st Annual Gallup Poll of the Public's Attitudes Toward the Public Schools (published in the September 1989 *Kappan*) found 74% of the public willing to spend more tax dollars to screen children for health programs, 69% willing to spend more money for Head Start, and 58% willing to spend more for day care for young children whose parents work.

WHAT SCHOOLS CAN DO

The prevalence of child poverty in the U.S. is enough to make any educator shudder—and not just because of the damage to the children. All too often the public schools are given the burden of overcoming economic and social inequities, usually without adequate resources to confront these difficult problems. Indeed, children who have been maimed by such new social epidemics as homelessness and crack use by pregnant women are already testing the resources and tolerance of the schools. Many reformers believe that, instead of another add-on program, the schools need a coordinated and concerted societal effort to deal with these problems.

Still, all across the nation, educators are struggling to meet the crisis with innovative solutions and more of their legendary dedication. The many examples of their efforts fall into two major categories: mobilizing parents and integrating community and health resources into the school.

PARENT INVOLVEMENT

Some educators are reexamining the roles parents can play in the schools. But poor parents face significant obstacles to becoming involved. According to the National Committee for Citizens in Education, "A parent who speaks limited English or who was herself a school dropout is unlikely to volunteer as a member of a school improvement council. A poor parent who has no automobile may not be able to send his child to a better public school located outside the attendance area—even when the option is available—unless transportation is provided by the school district. These barriers to full participation can be removed with training, encouragement, and resources that insure equal access."

Nevertheless, many educators are putting their energies into parent solutions—and getting results.

- The Center for Successful Child Development, known as the Beethoven Project, is a family-oriented early childhood intervention program at the Robert Taylor Homes, a public housing project on the south side of Chicago. Sponsored by the Chicago Urban League and by the Ounce of Prevention Fund, the Beethoven Project opened in 1987. Some 155 families now benefit from a variety of educational, social, and medical services for young children who will ultimately enroll in the Beethoven Elementary School.
- In Missouri, Parents as Teachers combines an early childhood component with an education

program for parents. It began as a pilot program in 1981, and today all 543 Missouri school districts are required to provide certain services to families, including parent education, periodic screening through age 4 to detect developmental problems, and educational programs for those 3- and 4-year-olds who are developmentally delayed. The program is not restricted to poor children, but it can catch their problems early, and results have been encouraging.

- James Comer, director of the School Development Program at Yale University, is working with 100 inner-city schools across the country to create management teams made up of parents, teachers, and mental health professionals. The aims are to improve the teachers' knowledge of child development, to involve parents, and to provide children with community resources normally found outside the school.
- In California and Missouri a new approach, known as the Accelerated Schools Program, is trying to change parents' attitudes toward their children. The Accelerated Schools Program attempts to raise parents' expectations about what their children can do, while it also focuses on giving literacy training to the parents. The goal is to empower parents so that they can become involved in their children's education. The program currently operates in two schools in California and in seven schools in Missouri.

A number of researchers and scholars have endorsed the idea of parent involvement. For example, Harold Stevenson of the University of Michigan released a study in 1989 that found that, contrary to popular belief, black and Hispanic mothers are keenly interested in their children's education and want to be involved despite the economic and social barriers to their doing so.

Parents can play a key role in many aspects of a school, providing a sense of community that can nurture as well as protect children in a school setting. During a cold Boston winter, for example, parents noticed that some children at David A. Ellis School in Roxbury did not have warm jackets. The parents established a clothing exchange to make sure that the children were warm on their way to school.

"The parents are part of the everyday life of the school," says Owen Haleem of the Institute for Responsive Education (IRE) at the Boston University School of Education. Two years ago the IRE organized a Schools Reaching Out Project. In January 1990 it organized a national network to increase parent and community involvement in urban public schools serving low-income communities. Known as the League of Schools Reaching Out, the network now includes 37 schools in 19 urban school districts.

"New relationships with low-income parents must be fashioned in order to break the link between poverty and school failure," according to Don Davies, president of the IRE. Two schools were part of a two-year pilot study of ways to develop these new relationships. The David A. Ellis School in Roxbury and Public School 111 in District 2 on the west side of Manhattan each converted one classroom near the principal's office into an on-site parents' center and initially paid a full-time "key teacher" to serve as a link between the school, the students' families, and the community. P.S. 111 offered classes in English as a second language (ESL) for Spanish-speaking parents and organized a lending library for educational toys and games. Parents at Ellis School offered ESL and formed a support group to study for the high-school-equivalency exams. Both schools send trained parents and community members to visit other parents at home and organize collaborative projects between teachers and parents.

The IRE pilot study was modeled, in part, on a similar program in Liverpool, England, where each school has a coordinator of social services. The IRE programs at P.S. 111 and at Ellis School try to combat the idea that parents need only to come to school for meetings. According to Haleem, "Our goal was to work with regular public schools to build fundamentally different relationships with low-income parents." And both schools have recorded achievement gains, which, Haleem notes, may not be connected to the parent involvement program. But then again they might be.

To some child advocates, *family* literacy is the key both to involving parents and to improving student achievement. A Department of Defense study conducted in the 1980s found that the most important variable in determining the educational attainment of 16- to 23-year-olds was the educational level of their mothers. Indeed, Thomas Sticht of Applied Behavioral and Cognitive Sciences, Inc., in San Diego argues that federal programs need to work with families.

Next year the Department of Education will spend $10,477,00 for Even Start, a program of financial assistance to local agencies that conduct projects in family-centered education. Privately funded and family-centered literacy projects, such as the Kenan Family Literacy Project in Louisville, Kentucky, also teach basic skills to parents while their children attend a preschool. Operating in seven schools in Kentucky and North Carolina, the Kenan Family Literacy Project teaches parents to read and to teach their children to read. This program was a model for the Foundation for Family Literacy, initiated by First Lady Barbara Bush.

For poor children whose parents remain uninvolved, schools may have to come up with other answers. An increasing number of social scientists argue that just one relationship between an adult and a disadvantaged child in stressful conditions can make a significant difference.

Public/Private Ventures, a nonprofit organization based in Philadelphia, examined five programs involving adults in the community and at-risk students. It found that the bonds that formed between the generations helped the youngsters weather crises, gave them a sense of stability, and improved their sense of their own competence.

SCHOOLS AS SOCIAL CENTERS

Indeed, many educators feel that they'll be able to address the needs of poor children only if the community works with the schools.

"The most urgent task is to regenerate families deep in the inner cities," Roger Wilkins, a professor of history at George Mason University, argued in the *New York Times* last year. "While employment, early childhood education, and child-care programs are critical parts of such an effort, it is essential that the public schools become the focus of special remedies," Wilkins asserted. "In addition, the schools would become centers of the community for the children they serve and for their parents and grandparents."

Indeed, more and more schools are designing programs that link social services and academic programs. But such ventures require schools and communities to overcome the instinct to protect their own turf and to agree to work together as one entity.

A number of states—including New York, Oregon, South Carolina, and Florida—have initiated new efforts to coordinate services for children. The problem is that child services are so spread out. In California, for example, 160 state programs for children operate out of 45 agencies. Schools must organize the services in ways that funnel them directly toward the complex needs of poor youngsters.

One initiative that helps not only poor children but all children coming of age today was started by Edward Zigler, Sterling Professor of Psychology and director of the Bush Center in Child Development and Social Policy at Yale University. Zigler has touted "Schools for the 21st Century"—schools that function as community centers, linking a host of family-support services to help children overcome social, psychological, and health problems. The approach includes home visitations, assistance for parents with infants, day care for 3- to 5-year-olds, before- and after-school care for school-age children, teen pregnancy prevention programs, and adult literacy classes. Zigler's program began in Independence, Missouri, and has spread to five states.

One educator who agrees that the school needs to take on a broader role in the lives of children is Allan Shedlin, Jr. In 1987 the Elementary School center that Shedlin directs called for a reconceptualization of the elementary school as the locus of advocacy for all children.

"Traditional sources of support for the child—the family, the neighborhood, schools, social and religious organizations, nutritional and health care programs—are fragmented or do not exist at all for many children," says Shedlin. School has become the only agency that deals with every child, every day. Thus the school

should serve as the center of advocacy for children.

The National School Boards Association (NSBA) argues that school officials cannot wait until all the desired elements are in place before taking action, and it suggests a number of remedies. Schools should:

- establish a local policy to help all children learn—perhaps by means of counseling programs, tutoring programs, or parent involvement;
- examine the needs of a community and determine whether parents need day-care services, health services, job skills, or the help of volunteers;
- develop a demographic profile of the school system—find out whether families are in poverty and whether there are single-parent families, migrant families, immigrant families—and communicate this information to all people in the school system;
- define and identify all youth at risk—considering such factors as student absenteeism, poor grades, low test scores in math or reading, chemical dependency, boredom, and family mobility;
- follow student progress in school by keeping comprehensive records;
- evaluate programs that have already been implemented;
- give administrators and teachers flexibility in helping students at risk and make use of student mentors, faculty advisors, teaching teams, and tutoring;
- involve parents in children's schooling; and
- work with local businesses, agencies, and organizations to develop and fund programs.

Carol Pringle didn't believe that she could wait any longer to help the poor children in her Seattle community. In April 1989 the mother of three and former schoolteacher organized a two-room schoolhouse called First Place. It is now one of a dozen programs in the country designed for homeless children. Technically it is a nonprofit agency, but it works in cooperation with the Seattle School District, which provides buses each day to round up children (kindergarten through grade 6) from homeless shelters all over the city.

Two salaried teachers and a number of volunteers have adapted the regular school curriculum for this new clientele. But the school also finds shoes for the children and, in addition to basic academics, provides breakfast, lunch, and a safe environment. Students stay an average of four to five weeks, but some attend for only a single day. They come from shelters for battered women or live with mothers who can't afford housing. Some are from families that move constantly in an effort to find work.

Other school systems have different programs. The Harbor Summit School in San Diego is near the St. Vincent de Paul Joan Kroc Center. The Tacoma (Washington) School District and the Tacoma YWCA run the Eugene P. Tone School.

However, some school officials believe that homeless children should not be placed in separate programs, Yvonne Rafferty, director of research with Advocates for Children, claims that all children should be in regular programs. New York City prohibits any separate programs for homeless children, and Minneapolis tries to provide homeless children with transportation to their former school.

Essentially the solution to the problem of schooling for homeless children is a state responsibility. The McKinney Act of 1987 grants money to states to develop plans so that homeless children can gain access to the schools.

Like Carol Pringle, Carol Cole couldn't wait any longer. Just as the first wave of crack babies was hitting the school systems across the nation, she was hard at work creating a special program for such children. The Salvin Special Education School in Los Angeles is a two-year-old program designed to aid children born to crack-addicted mothers. Eight 3- and 4-year-olds work with three teachers, who give the children as much individual attention as possible. The school has a pediatrician, a psychologist, several social workers, and a speech and language specialist. According to Cole, the home lives of the children are "chaotic." Salvin School reaches only eight children at a time. But 375,000 drug-exposed babies are born annually.

A survey released by the NSBA in February 1990 found that urban school districts face an "awesome challenge" in trying to provide more social services when federal aid for such programs has declined in real dollars. The survey of 52 urban school districts found that the proportion of resources devoted to attacking social and health programs puts "a severe strain on local school districts' budgets, draining their coffers."

Jonathan Wilson, chairman of the NSBA Council of Urban Boards of Education, argues that local resources are running dry. If urban schools are to improve their performance, he maintains, they need dramatic hikes in state and federal funding and in Chapter 1.

In the end the Children's Defense Fund calculates that the key investments to help rescue children from poverty are not prohibitively expensive. The CDF estimates that universal health care for children and pregnant women is a relatively inexpensive prevention measure and is a far better social policy than trying to remediate social ills later. In addition, the CDF figures that the costs of eliminating poverty and child poverty are not as high as many people think. Good nutrition, basic health care, and early education can make a big difference.

"We must shed the myth that all poor children need massive, long-term public intervention," Marian Wright Edelman told those attending the annual meeting of the CDF in Washington, D.C., in March 1990. "Certainly, some children are so damaged that they need such help," Edelman allows. "But millions of poor children need only modest help. They need child care, not foster care; a checkup, not an intensive-care bed; a tutor, not a guardian; drug education, not detoxification; a scholarship, not a detention cell. But it has been hard to get them what they need—even when we know what to do and when it saves us money."

According to CDF estimates (based on 1987 figures), the cost of eliminating child poverty is $17.22 billion; the cost of eliminating poverty in families with children, $26.874 billion; the cost of eliminating poverty among all persons, $51.646 billion. That last figure is equivalent to only 1% of our gross national product. Eliminating poverty in families with children would cost only about 1.5% of the total expenditures of federal, state, and local governments combined.

Indeed, if the nation's largest bankers are capable of writing off billions of dollars in debts owed by developing nations, if the U.S. Congress can almost nonchalantly commit $325 billion dollars to bailing out the unregulated and marauding savings-and-loan industry, if the public can live with military excesses and a variety of foreign affairs ventures, then surely we can renegotiate the terms of the escalating human debt embodied by the children of poverty.

Congress, the states, and local communities must rewrite the options of opportunity for all our children, but especially for our poor children. We must be willing to write the checks that guarantee poor children a real chance of success from the moment they are conceived until the moment that they receive as much education as they can absorb. Only then will the tragedy of children deprived from birth of a dignified life be banished forever from this land.

CHAPTER 21

POPULATION GROWTH AND
THE ENVIRONMENT

INTRODUCTION

At the time of the Roman Empire, the earth's population had reached 200,000. It took 2 to 5 million years to reach this number of people. By 1800, world population had multiplied 5,000 times to reach 1 billion. The second billion had arrived by 1930, and thirty years later the population had reached 3 billion. By 1975 the number was 4 billion, and it leaped to 5.3 billion by 1990. Some demographers—people who study trends in human populations—are predicting 6 billion people by the turn of the century, and no one can predict the ultimate ceiling of this upward curve. The human population may have been slow in starting to expand, but population growth in the last half-century is often described as a population explosion. What do such numbers mean? Is the world's population growth out of control? Are our children doomed to live in a world of depleted resources and a poisoned environment? What should individuals and governments do to control population? We cannot give quick and final answers to these questions, but this chapter examines the issue of the impact of population expansion on the environment and the negative effects of environmental changes on humans.

Demographers examine changes in human populations (both growth and decline) as the outcomes of three fundamental factors: births, deaths, and migration. The total number of births per year in a population tells us less than the number of births per 100,000 population (the birth rate); similarly, the mortality rate tells us the number of deaths per 100,000 population. Migration comprises both immigration (the movement of people into a society) and emigration (the movement of people out of a society). These three causes of population change are highly complex, because they are influenced by many other factors. Birth rates, for example, are affected by such factors as wealth, war, environment, and the social values about family life.

No single pattern describes population changes in all societies, past and present. Historically, many societies have maintained stable populations for centuries because death rates balanced birth rates. Women had many children, but few survived to adulthood and fewer still lived to old age. Some societies feel the pressure of too many people because their crops fail and they have so few other resources that they cannot buy food on the world market. This situation occurred in Ireland during the great potato famine of the nineteenth century and currently confronts several African nations, where millions of productive acres become desert each year and their people face starvation. Sometimes the pressure of a growing population can be relieved through migration. Between 1820 and 1920, for example, millions of Europe-

ans emigrated to the United States, Canada, South America, and Australia. These variations on population change are instructive for the future. If past and present population patterns are diverse, then it is likely that future patterns will also vary among the world's societies. This chapter does not suggest that population change is one problem with one solution.

This chapter looks at the crucial issue of how human populations relate to the ecosystem. As the world's population continues to explode at the end of the twentieth century, many commentators worry about the negative impact of increasing numbers of people on a finite environment. What are the causes and consequences of a growing population on the good earth where all humans must adapt to available resources and to one another in viable communities and societies? R. Paul Shaw questions any suggestion that population growth has a direct impact on the environment and holds that causal relations are so complex that no one factor can be singled out for blame where environments and societies deteriorate. Jodi Jacobson offers a gloomy forecast of a new and growing problem in human history: the massive displacement of people who have destroyed their ecosystems. She introduces a new term, "environmental refugees," which threatens to apply to tens of millions of people in the late twentieth century and beyond. Paul and Anne Ehrlich place most of the blame for the deterioration of the environment on that small portion of the human population who happen to be rich.

There is no simple causal relationship between the growth of human populations and various social and environmental problems. But any study of environmental deterioration must assess issues of population expansion as well as economic factors and the lifestyles of various social classes. Human populations have often been out of sync with their ecosystems. Most demographers ponder these issues and hope that we have time to develop new policies that will be in greater harmony with the good earth.

59.   POPULATION GROWTH: IS IT RUINING THE ENVIRONMENT?

R. PAUL SHAW

Years ago, on a hot summer day in Beirut, I visited a beach where poor people and refugees flocked like lemmings. It was overcrowded, the beach facilities were non-existent, and it was filled with litter.

The beach had all the earmarks of an "overpopulation problem," something I took seriously as a United Nations Population and Development adviser to the Arab world.

Sitting there, I thought back to my classroom days at Berkeley and the University of Pennsylvania where I had been taught about the perils of rapid population growth. In his famous "Essay on Population," nineteenth century British economist Thomas Malthus warned that unfettered reproduction of our species would outstrip food supply, produce misery and vice, and bring the demise of humanity. I also recalled the words of Professor Kingsley Davis, a distinguished demographer now at Stanford University, that "in subsequent history the twentieth century may be called the century of world wars or the century of the population plague." Even Robert McNamara, then head of the World Bank, advocated

From *Populi*, Vol. 16 (2) 1989, pp. 21–29. Reproduced with permission by The United Nations Population Fund.

R. Paul Shaw is a senior population economist, United Nations Fund for Population Activities (UNFPA). The views expressed in this article are those of the author and do not necessarily reflect the official position of UNFPA.

that "excessive population growth is the greatest single obstacle to the economic and social advancement of most societies in the developing world."

I wondered if the same reasoning applied to places like Lebanon, Syria and Jordan where population was soaring, environments were littered with waste, and the poor were packed into urban slums and refugee camps.

What happened next was unforgettable. Only 40 feet away, at water's edge, a giant explosion lifted a plume of water high into the air. I wasn't the only one to leap to my feet, ears ringing.

Instantly I realized what was happening. It wasn't a terrorist attack. Behind me, young militiamen were hurling sticks of dynamite over beachgoers' heads into the ocean. The reason soon became apparent: a fishing boat moved in to collect the stunned marine life.

No wonder Lebanon's coastal waters were being depleted so rapidly. Before living there, I had been told the problem was one of overfishing because of overpopulation. But this, and other experiences, brought home that the number of inhabitants in the country clearly played a minor part. I learned that the civil strife, lawlessness, mismanagement of resources, and misuse of technology were the major factors in the destruction of the country's marine life.

I suspected the same kinds of factors were responsible for the dismal conditions on the beach—conditions easily open to misinterpretation as simply consequences of population growth.

Now, a decade later, I often recall my experiences in Lebanon when I contemplate the concern throughout the world over environmental degradation. Global population growth is being singled out as a major cause of polluted rivers and oceans, denuded lands, depleted forests, and so on.

According to the United Nations Population Fund's annual report for 1988, "Increasing human demands are damaging the natural resource base. High fertility and rapid population growth are contributing to the process." This position, shared by the Geneva-based World Commission for Environment and Development and the International Union for the Conservation of Nature, has produced extremely supportive reactions in the press, from governments and agencies specializing in population.

Other organizations, like the Washington-based Worldwatch Institute and the Population Crisis Committee, have been far more forceful, arguing that population programmes are a panacea for solving poverty and worldwide environmental degradation.

Yet there are powerful dissenting views. Dr. Barry Commoner, an eminent environmentalist at Queens College, New York, told a 1988 United Nations meeting of experts "the theory that environmental degradation is largely due to population growth is not supported by the data." Many experts at the meeting agreed with him. In fact, the University of Maryland's Dr. Julian Simon takes the position that unconstrained population growth is, in fact, a primary resource, something to be welcomed, not discouraged.

Then there are scores of critics, past and present, who have found holes in the Malthusian spectre. They have counterargued that scientific soil management and crop production can help offset the consequences of population growth by achieving greater production with fewer resources and less waste.

Opinions clash on this extremely important issue because there is widespread misunderstanding about the nature of causes involved. There are two kinds, ultimate and proximate. When damage to the environment is assessed in terms of ultimate factors it becomes evident to Western population experts that many fundamental causes of deteriorating world ecology originate in their "own backyard," having little to do with rampant Third World population growth. None the less, when we realize the insolubility of these root causes, then rapid population growth—a proximate, confounding cause—takes on significance.

Commoner hit home on ultimate causes when he said that polluting technologies and levels of affluence—not overpopulation—were largely responsible for the planet's environmental ills. This is evident when we trace the origins of municipal and industrial waste. In 1985, developed countries were responsible for three quarters of the world's 2.5 billion metric tons of waste. Yet, these nations contained less than one quarter of the world's population.

Developed countries are the big polluters because they are principal originators and users of high-tech manufacturing and chemicals. As Commoner observed, the richer the country, the more natural products—soap, wood, cotton, paper, leather—are replaced by synthetic, petrochemical products—detergents, synthetic fibers and plastics. In agriculture, organic fertilizers have been displaced by chemical ones, and natural methods of pest control, such as crop rotation, have been replaced by pesticides. In transportation, convenient truck freight is being favoured over more costly, less polluting rail freight. In commerce, reusable goods have been replaced by throwaways such as plastics which will be around 100 years from now—and longer.

Developed countries also dominate the production and testing of military technologies, producing the most lasting pollutants known to humanity—nuclear wastes. Expenditures in this domain topped $900 billion in 1988, more than worldwide expenditures on health or education, and more than 10,000 times the budget of the United Nations Environment Programme.

Equally important, income levels are such that wealthier nations consume, and discard, relatively great quantities of polluting products. The Paris-based Organization for Economic Cooperation and Development surveyed 20 industrial countries to find that municipal and industrial waste per person per year is about 1.6 tons on average. This is approximately 10 times the level in less developed countries. Poverty in these countries not only limits the amount and type of consumption per capita, but also motivates for more judicious use of resources and conservation.

Overloading the environment with carbon monoxide, lead, ozone and trash is just one form of environmental degradation. There is another—one attributable to acts of overt destruction and related neglect. Humanity's warfare is one of the most important ultimate causes! As a gauge of direct damage, consider the little cited but devastating environmental legacy of the Vietnam War. Between 1955 and 1975 the war produced more than 25 million craters (20–90 feet wide), leveled and denuded 1 million hectares of forest, and rendered at least 5 million acres unproductive because of Agent Orange pesticides and other chemicals.

No amount of deforestation in Brazil, desertification in the Sahel, or water pollution in the Nile can compare with the cumulative effects of war. Ecosystems have been pulverized in an endless variety of countries. Recent examples include hundreds of billions of dollars of damage in Lebanon, Iran, Iraq, the province of Eritrea in Ethiopia, nations bordering South Africa, Afghanistan, even Bangladesh. This kind of environmental degradation has little to do with rapid population growth.

As a gauge of indirect damage, consider how war impacts on the stability of socio-economic environments. Africa is a case in point. Between 1955 and 1985, countries in the region experienced more than 200 attempted coups d'état, most involving ethnic conflict, where tribal or national interests strive to control reins of state power. Such conflicts continuously distort production and preservation activities in agriculture. For example, more than 8 million peasants have fled their villages to escape terror and violence in Ethiopia, Mozambique, the Sudan and Uganda. This chaos has upset fragile systems of transport and marketing, suspended the maintenance of irrigation and land systems, and forced people to migrate to places that cannot possibly sustain larger populations. In such cases, population pressure, or communities unable to sustain themselves, are only the visible tip of the iceberg.

Of course, warfare also actively demolishes planning environments, or the very projects designed to combat population pressure. In one instance, a large-scale, environmentally sensitive agricultural project was crippled in the Moroccan Sahel just as tomato crops were ripening.

Then there are the environmental effects of cold war, involving exploitation and aggression between groups. British ecologist Paul Harrison has observed that a high proportion of forestry efforts fail in Africa because they exclude local communities. Many projects have been established on land expropriated from local villages. On perceiving exploitation by elitist or ethnically different groups, the locals have sabotaged plantations by illegal grazing, tree-felling and encroachment.

Some observers see population pressure as the culprit. Deeper analysis, however, reveals that intergroup conflict often victimizes weaker groups, thereby producing "population pressure" on artificially constrained resources.

The most disadvantaged, especially those in countries of sub-Saharan Africa, Asia and Latin America, are also forced by poverty, debt and a struggle for survival into "hands-on" environmental degradation. They denude public lands of shrubs and trees for firewood, and they overtax the productive capacity of soils by planting and harvesting too frequently. When rural areas can no longer support them, these people flee to urban areas where overcrowded slum and squatter settlements cannot possibly handle more human waste. By 1985, the United Nations estimated that approximately 1.3 billion people were living in such poverty-stricken conditions.

Is it reasonable to expect that reducing population growth will improve the lot of these people, thus paving the way for a rejuvenated environment?

A great many studies have sought to establish a causal relationship between population growth and poverty but often without success. The fact is, there is no assurance that fertility reduction per se can turn the poverty/environment relationship around without other necessary factors being present.

Yet, debate over the relationship between population and poverty has been fruitful in other ways—it has uncovered the ultimate causes at work, which I have referred to. In most less developed countries, these involve institutions and policies that have distorted the social, economic, political and physical environments where the poor live.

In some nations, land mismanagement policies and commercialization schemes have eaten up public lands or developed them for real estate. It is when poor ethnic groups are pushed out or large-scale mechanization schemes displace small-scale farmers to less productive lands that poverty and overuse promote environmental degradation.

The same applies to deforestation of many areas of the world for development of new farmland, extraction of raw materials or for new living space.

It was apparent to me when I was a United Nations adviser to the Arab world that environments are equally vulnerable to distortion when governments concentrate their development funds in relatively well-off enclaves instead of poor parts of their countries. Colonial as well as post-colonial government expenditures on health, education and infrastructure have been disproportionately channeled to some urban-industrial centres. This imbalance has entrenched inequalities among rural people, retarded economic growth of their communities, spurred migration from villages to cities, and transformed urban centres into cauldrons of environmental degradation.

Significant efforts to correct these imbalances have been rare. Moreover, governments have fared poorly at redistributing city populations and urbanward migrants through the creation of intermediate-size cities (countermagnets) or land resettlement schemes. Rather than put all the blame on population growth for undermining urban planning, we should also look to mismanagement of regional development funds. These have produced overconcentrations of people in places unable to accommodate them.

Another factor with powerful distortionary effects involves food pricing policies, such as those existing in Egypt or Thailand, aimed at lowering agricultural prices to keep urban consumers happy. A classic example is keeping wheat prices down to ensure cheaper bread. On several occasions I have been embroiled in debate with Third World government officials on the extent to which such policies contribute to rural stagnation by depressing prices at which farmers can

sell their produce and destabilizing farm family incomes. My own research has revealed that by widening the rural/urban income gap, these policies have accelerated the rural exodus, again promoting urban congestion and related environmental degradation. Rural environments have suffered as well. As farm families have abandoned their land, traditional methods of caring for soils have gone with them, involving irrigation, desalination, and age-old techniques to combat desertification.

Finally, a host of complex intercountry connections are impacting on the environment with unintended negative consequences. For example, it may seem far-fetched to talk of trade protectionism as an indirect cause of environmental stress. Yet, the persistently high level of agricultural trade protection, practised for decades by developed countries, is a case in point. The World Bank reckons that governments of North America and Western Europe spend about $200 billion a year to protect their domestic agriculture. Japan, for example, supports rice production up to eight times the world price, and the U.S. heavily subsidizes wheat and dairy production. Such policies have been working for decades to deprive less developed countries of crucial income from agricultural exports. Direct losses have been estimated at around $30 billion per year, undermining farm profits and perpetuating poverty, whether population is reduced or not. These factors compromise the development of poorer countries, sap motivation to maintain and care for agricultural lands, and promote urban migration and subsequent environmental degradation.

Examples of this kind may be obvious to planners with developing country experience. But they are often overlooked, for it is the tip of the iceberg that receives the greatest attention when large congested populations and environmental degradation appear together. From there it is but a short step to correlate the two, failing to recognize they are joint products of deeper forces.

Does all this imply that increasing population has no real relationship to environmental degradation? If ultimate causes are understood and can be controlled, then proximate causes—like population growth—diminish in significance. For example, were all technologies to be stripped of their polluting elements, the number of users of those technologies would be irrelevant as a factor in global pollution. The answer to our question is contingent, therefore, on prospects for altering ultimate causes. This brings us to an ironic twist.

Though environmentalists such as Commoner are correct about major players in global degradation, the view that population growth impacts on the environment *is* relevant because ultimate causes are highly resistant to change.

To illustrate, efforts to reduce air emissions may have made major headway in the case of lead, but there has been little progress implementing more costly emission controls for sulphur dioxide, carbon monoxide, nitrogen oxides and volatile organic compounds. The same applies to water pollutants including fecal coliform, dissolved oxygen, nitrates, phosphates and suspended sediments. These discouraging examples are particularly significant for one reason—they come from rich countries most able to afford research and action programmes to minimize polluting technologies.

Unlike wealthy countries, the costs to develop and install non-polluting technologies are well outside the reach of poorer countries. Indeed, Commoner's own assessment of global poverty leads him to conclude that poor countries will make a far greater effort to introduce the cheapest technologies (more output and jobs at least cost) than the more expensive non-polluting technologies. To think otherwise in a world plagued by $1,200 billion debt seems wishful. The World Commission on Environment and Development, with representatives from 21 different nations, cited similar reasons for pessimism in its 1987 report.

It is this kind of situation that gives population growth lots of opportunity to exacerbate world environmental degradation.

Here is a likely scenario of what may happen over the next 40 years. Less developed countries will be responsible for more than 90 percent of the world's new population. This alone will increasingly shift the responsibility for global waste generation toward poorer countries. In addition, as levels of living and consumption rise in these countries, their inhabitants will generate more municipal and industrial wastes per capita.

Calculations show that these developments—population growth, access to polluting technologies, and higher consumption levels—will interact to raise global waste generation from approximately 2.5 billion metric tons in 1985 to more than 4.5 billion tons by 2025. Whereas poorer countries contributed only 25 percent to global waste in 1985, they will have likely contributed more than 50 percent by 2025!

Failure to tackle ultimate factors will also jeopardize a preoccupation of poorer countries—to work toward supportable populations for sustainable development. The relationship between sustainable development, population, and natural resources can be illustrated as follows: Imagine that a small tractor is pulling a wagon containing a few people up a hill. Suppose we want to add more people and/or speed up the tractor beyond its current resource capacity. To sustain more people and greater speed, rich country economists would advocate fitting a bigger engine to the tractor. And they would likely have easy access to the money, technical know-how and future fuel resources to do so.

In poorer countries, one could advocate the same thing—as many development economists do. Major problems announce themselves, however. Foremost is poverty, or scarce indigenous capital to devise, operate, and maintain the bigger engine. Another problem is massive international indebtedness. Merely paying $100 billion interest on the debt each year is beyond the capacity of most poor countries. Yet another problem concerns limitations of rich country altruism. On average, residents of these countries give only one third of 1 percent of their income to poor countries, leaving little hope that foreign aid will make a notable dent on poverty or indebtedness.

Continuing our analogy, to merely maintain the pulling capacity and speed of existing engines in less developed countries is a major challenge. Here the idea of working toward sustainable populations and development, as advocated by UNFPA, makes sense.

Unsustainable populations are evident when governments are unable to assure continued human resource investments, such as school enrollments, employment creation, provision of health services, and housing. If we increase the energy demand on the tractor by loading additional people on the wagon, speed will not be maintained and the engine will likely collapse.

Again, population growth should not be construed as the ultimate problem here, but as a proximate exacerbating one. In the absence of effective development and technological progress on a "grander scale," it is correct to say that an excess of births over deaths cannot help but contribute to unsustainable development and thus add stress on the environment.

The moral of this story is not an encouraging one. Ultimate causes are far more to blame for environmental degradation than proximate ones. Yet, the intractable fundamental factors are rarely addressed.

By default then, proximate agents gain importance. This signifies that inaction to reduce population will worsen environments in poorer countries, and that global spillover effects can be anticipated as these nations increasingly adopt polluting technologies from the West and generate consumption-rated wastes.

Yet, there is no evidence to demonstrate that limiting population growth by itself, without other positive development factors being taken into account, will actively lift the veil of poverty or regenerate environments. Population policy, however, can buy invaluable time while we figure out how to dismantle the ultimate causes.

60. ENVIRONMENTAL REFUGEES: NATURE'S WARNING SYSTEM

JODI L. JACOBSON

More than two years after an explosion at a nuclear reactor in the Ukraine spewed clouds of radiation from Kiev to Krakow, Soviet officials have announced plans to demolish the adjacent town of Chernobyl. This death warrant extinguished any hope of returning home for the city's 10,000 former residents. Because the world's worst nuclear disaster has permanently contaminated their home town, they will be forced to settle elsewhere.[1]

These people are refugees, though not by any standard definition. According to widely accepted doctrine, refugees are people who decide to seek asylum out of fear of political, racial or

From *Populi*, Vol. 16 (1) 1989, pp. 29–32. Reprinted with permission of United Nations Population Fund.

Jodi L. Jacobson writes on population and environmental issues.

[1] "Plan to Raze Chernobyl Reported," *New York Times*, 9 October 1988.

religious persecution, or who leave their homes because of war, civil strife or economic difficulties.

This conventional notion, however, leaves out a new and growing class—environmental refugees.

Throughout the world, vast areas are becoming unfit for human habitation. These lands are being despoiled either through long-term environmental degradation or by brief but catastrophic events. Unsustainable land-use practices, for example, have reduced the ability of ecosystems to support life—"carrying capacity"—throughout the Third World. On the other hand, high-risk technologies have sometimes resulted in accidents, such as the Chernobyl explosion, that leave whole regions uninhabitable for extended periods.

The number of refugees in need of protection and assistance under traditional classifications, now more than 13 million, is mounting daily because of wars and insurrections, repressive political systems and deteriorating economic conditions, particularly in the Third World.

Most governments as yet do not recognize environmental decline as a legitimate cause of refugee movements, choosing instead to ignore the issue. Neither the United States State Department nor the United Nations High Commissioner for Refugees, for example, collects data on this problem. Yet the number of environmental refugees—estimated by the author to be at least 10 million—rivals that of officially recognized refugees and is sure to overtake this latter group in the decades to come. Moreover, those nations that have been the traditional haven for refugees are increasingly trying to restrict this form of immigration.[2] This absence of public awareness and understanding of the decline in the earth's habitability only exacerbates the problem.

The degradation of agricultural land is the most widespread threat to habitability worldwide. But other factors, including the gradual poisoning of land and water by toxic wastes, and the effects of natural disasters made worse by human activity, are adding to the ranks of environmental refugees. Moreover, the expected rise of the sea level because of global warming threatens to reduce the planet's habitable area on a grand scale, perhaps forcing the evacuation of low-lying cities and agricultural land throughout the world.

To judge by what populations will put up with before they flee an environmental hazard, society's standards concerning habitability are fairly lax. People are willing to tolerate a broad range of threats to health and longevity. Witness the fact that, throughout the world, densely populated cities plagued by air and water pollution are the rule rather than the exception. And, in many countries, millions have built homes in areas prone to avalanches and floods.

For every environment refugee, then, there are thousands whose lives are compromised each day because of unhealthy or hazardous conditions. Because migration is a last resort, the rising number of environmental refugees should

be seen as an important indicator of the extent and severity of worldwide environmental deterioration.

Long-term declines in habitability occur in stages, themselves often the result of imperceptible changes. Before too long in the process, health may become threatened. Malnutrition is found throughout Africa and Asia where land degradation has cut crop yields. Increased cancer rates, for example, are associated with the high levels of toxic chemicals in some parts of the United States.

In the final stages of decline, a town, city, or region may become virtually uninhabitable. For example, desertification—the impoverishment of land from human activities and natural stresses—has irreparably damaged millions of hectares of once-productive land and made refugees out of millions of sub-Saharan African farmers in this decade alone.

Now it looks as if rising seas will supplant encroaching deserts and other forms of land degradation as the major threat to habitability in the not-too-distant future. This will result from global warming, primarily the result of fossil fuel use in industrial countries. The Third World will suffer the greatest and most immediate impact of the rise in sea levels that will occur because of the thermal expansion of the oceans and the melting of the icecaps. The 1 metre increase in sea level projected over the next century will displace millions of people in the delta regions of the Nile and Ganges rivers, for instance, exacerbating land scarcity in the already densely populated nations of Egypt and Bangladesh. Protecting shorelines and wetlands, not to mention the infrastructures and water supplies of coastal cities, will require billions of dollars, perhaps even more than many well-off nations will be able to pay.

Unfortunately, while more and more land is rendered uninhabitable each year, population is increasing by 90 million annually—most of it in areas already in advanced stages of environmental degradation. All will need food, water, clothing and shelter. One certain result of their struggle for these necessities will be further pressures on the earth's ecosystems and their ability to support human life.

Agricultural lands are degrading on every

---

[2] U.S. Committee for Refugees, *World Refugee Survey, 1987 in Review* (Washington, D.C.: American Council for Nationalities Service, 1988).

continent. This deterioration is most acute and its impact is greatest in those Third World countries where the majority of the people are farmers. Soil erosion may cost Canada some $U.S.5 billion annually in reduced yields, but Canadians do not starve. By contrast, sharply deteriorating land resources in Africa imperil the lives of millions.[3]

Throughout the Third World, subsistence farmers eke out a living on land that is depleted of nutrients, stripped of topsoil, and no longer able to withstand natural stresses such as drought or heavy rain.

Lacking official recognition, most environmental refugees go uncounted. Many fleeing land degradation are not classified as environmental refugees because they simply move on to cultivate ever-more marginal lands. In Africa, thousands end up in the relief camps that are now regular fixtures on that continent. Others move to urban areas: the massive shift from rural regions to cities that has occurred in the Third World since mid-century is due in large part to the complex of factors underlying land degradation.

Desertification, the most severe form of land degradation, is most acute in the arid and semi-arid regions. A United Nations Environment Programme survey estimated that a total of 4.5 billion hectares around the world—fully 35 percent of the earth's land surface—are in various stages of desertification. These areas are home to more than 850 million people, many of whom are at risk of having their homes and livelihoods foreclosed by land degradation.[4]

Of all continents, Africa, a land where poor soils and variable rainfall pose a harsh climate for agriculture, has spawned the most environmental refugees. Most come from the Sahel, a belt that spans several agro-ecological zones and stretches west to east across some nine countries from Mauritania and Senegal on into the Sudan. Desertification is accelerating in the Sahel, the world's largest area to be threatened by the wholesale loss of arable land. As the region's habitability declines, the movement of people increases: in the last 20 years the area's urban population has quadrupled.[5]

Land degradation is also undermining habitability north of the Sahel. Larger human and cattle populations have exceeded the carrying capacity of arid lands in Algeria, Egypt, Libya, Morocco and Tunisia. In Algeria, for example, desertification has begun to undercut the economy. In Morocco, high population densities on arid lands are leading to desertification. Irrigation canals, roads, and oases are threatened by drifting sand and shifting dunes.[6]

In the southern part of the continent, deforestation, soil erosion and the depletion of water supplies have driven tens of thousands of environmental refugees from their farmlands to other rural areas, into towns and cities, or into relief camps.

In India, what seem to be self-reinforcing drought conditions have also taken hold. Between 1978 and 1983, western Rajasthan and parts of eastern India were gripped by serious drought. Thousands of farmers whose crops had failed for years on end began moving out of these areas by mid-1983 to neighbouring Haryana and Madhya Pradesh. Many moved to the huge

---

[3] Standing Committee on Agriculture, Fisheries and Forestry, *Soil at Risk: Canada's Eroding Future*, a report on soil conservation to the Senate of Canada (Ottawa, 1984).

[4] United Nations Environment Programme, *General Assessment of Progress in the Implementation of the Plan of Action to Combat Desertification* (New York, 1984); figure on earth's total land surface from James H. Brown, *Biogeography* (St. Louis: C. V. Mosby, 1983); United Nations Environment Programme, *Sands of Change: Why Land Becomes Desert and What Can Be Done About It*, Environment Brief no. 2 (1988); and H. E. Dregne and C. J. Tucker, *Desert Encroachment*, Desertification Control Bulletin no. 16 (1988). See also

Peter D. Little, ed., *Lands at Risk* (Boulder, Colo.: Westview Press, 1987), and M. B. K. Darkoh, "Socioeconomic and Institutional Factors Behind Desertification in Southern Africa," *Area* 19, no. 1 (1987).

[5] United Nations Environment Programme, *Sands of Change;* for information on the ecology of the Sahelian region, see Harrison, *Greening of Africa;* and James Brooke, "Some Gains in West Africa's War on the Desert," *New York Times,* 13 September 1987.

[6] United Nations Environment Programme, *Desertification Control in Africa: Actions and Directory of Institutions* (Nairobi, 1985).

coastal city of Madras, where the influx caused lines for such basic commodities as water.[7]

In Latin America and the Caribbean, land degradation results from the combination of highly inequitable land distribution and rapidly growing populations. Latin America is home to some of the world's biggest cities in large part because of migration from rural areas. Millions of poverty-stricken farmers facing decades of agricultural neglect and land degradation throughout the mountains and the plains of South America fill the urban shantytowns of Sao Paulo, Rio de Janeiro, Mexico City, Lima and La Paz. In many countries, particularly in Central America, the response to enduring poverty and environmental decline has been civil war and (often illegal) migration to the United States.[8]

Agriculture is the backbone of developing economies. Yet throughout the Third World, farmers have been forced by financial and population pressures to adopt short-cut methods that are leading to long-term land degradation. By interfering with important natural cycles and overusing fragile, barely stable ecosystems, they are creating a self-reinforcing cycle of land deterioration. When the countryside is no longer able to produce a crop, the farmers along with the rest of the rural populace are forced to move on. Whether they end up in cities or relief camps, or cultivating marginal lands, these people constitute a growing class of environmental refugees.

---

[7] Mary Anne Weaver, "India: 'Greening' of a Bad Drought," *Christian Science Monitor,* 25 May 1983; United Nations Environment Programme, *Sands of Change;* J. Bandyopadhyay and Vandana Shiva, "Drought, Development, and Desertification," *Economic and Political Weekly,* 16 August 1986; Jayanta Bandyopadhyay, "Political Ecology of Drought and Water Scarcity," *Economic and Political Weekly,* 12 December 1987; Steven R. Weisman, "India's Drought Is Worst in Decades," *New York Times,* 16 August 1987; and Anthony Spaeth, "Harshest Drought in Decades Devastates India's Crops, Slows Economic Growth," *Wall Street Journal,* 19 August 1987.

[8] Lester R. Brown and Jodi L. Jacobson, *The Future of Urbanization: Facing the Ecological and Economic Constraints,* Worldwatch Paper 77 (Washington, D.C.: Worldwatch Institute, May 1987).

UNNATURAL DISASTERS

When an earthquake in Colombia or a flood in India causes hundreds of deaths and leaves thousands homeless, society accepts these losses as unfortunate accidents of fate. These natural disasters are second only to land degradation as a factor in the growing number of environmental refugees. But more people are being killed or displaced by avalanches, cyclones, earthquakes and floods than ever before, and close examination of the environmental backdrop against which these events occur suggests a strong human component.

"Unnatural disasters"—normal events whose effects are exacerbated by human activities—are on the rise. Human pressures on forests, soils and land have rendered ecosystems less resilient, less able to cope with natural fluctuations. Ultimately they collapse under otherwise normal stresses, creating and magnifying disasters such as landslides and floods.

At the same time, competition for land and natural resources is driving more people to live in these marginal, disaster-prone areas, leaving them more vulnerable to natural forces. Hence, millions of Bangladeshis live on "chars," bars of silt and sand in the middle of the Bengal delta, some of which are washed away each year by ocean tides and monsoon floods. Millions of Nepalis live in the areas most likely to be hit by earthquakes. And thousands of slum dwellers in the cities of Latin America perch on deforested hillsides prone to mudslides in heavy rain.

Human-induced changes in the environment can turn a normal event into a catastrophe. The deterioration of major watersheds in many Third World countries, for example, increases the number of devastating floods. The floods in Bangladesh and the Sudan in 1988 are cases in point.

Similarly, degradation of the Nile watershed contributed to the flooding in the Sudan. The headwaters of the Blue Nile are in the highlands in Ethiopia, where a rich and diverse agriculture developed thousands of years ago. Today, the highlands constitute 90 percent of the arable land, supporting 88 percent of the country's population and 60 percent of its livestock. But deforestation and poor soil husbandry, coupled with rapid population growth, have undermined the nation's agricultural base.[9]

Some "natural" tragedies are the result of development strategies that blatantly disregard their impact on the environment. In 1983, a cyclone in the Philippines that normally might have caused fewer than 100 fatalities killed thousands. Floods caused by the tropical storm were far more numerous and severe than in the past.

Toxic chemicals and hazardous waste pose another mounting threat. We now see a small but growing number of refugees from land poisoned by hazardous wastes. Once confined to industrial countries, the inherent conflict between disposal of toxic wastes and human habitation is spreading around the world.[10]

The rapidly growing volume of hazardous waste in industrialized nations, coupled with high disposal costs, has led some companies to export their industrial residues to the Third World, threatening a new wave of chemical illnesses and refugees. It costs from \$U.S.250 to \$U.S.350 per ton to dispose of hazardous municipal and industrial wastes in the United States, for example, but some developing countries will accept such wastes for as little as \$U.S.40 per ton.[11]

Local conditions and lack of monitoring of waste treatment mean that a large proportion of these imported wastes will end up in the local environment. Frequent rains and poor soils in tropical areas hasten the migration of chemical wastes into groundwater supplies. Thousands of tons of United States and European wastes have already been shipped to Africa and the Middle East.

Industrial society has developed a chemical dependency. More than 80,000 synthetic and organic compounds are commonly used worldwide in homes and by agriculture and industry. Modern chemicals usually offer an economic quick fix. Pesticides increase food production. Chemical-based plastics lower the cost of consumer items by replacing expensive metals. Almost every manufactured product and every manufacturing process involves the use of chemical compounds. Global production of organic chemicals alone increased from about 1 million tons a year in the 1930s to about 250 million tons in 1985 and is now doubling every 7 or 8 years.[12]

But chemicals exact a high cost. Producing and using them often entails releasing large quantities of hazardous wastes into the environment. Residues from pesticides, herbicides and fungicides end up in rivers, bays and aquifers. Exhaust from cars and factories pollutes the air. Industrial wastes buried in landfills seep into groundwater and poison soils. Eventually, these waste products can affect biological productivity and human health. In some areas, the toxic hazards have forced people to move.

Chemical contamination can be sudden—the result of a rail accident, for instance. Or it can result from the insidious penetration of toxic substances into the atmosphere, the food chain or water supplies. Although toxic wastes pose a pervasive threat to the environment, until recently few countries had laws regulating their disposal. As a result, many companies found it easier and cheaper to discard their wastes into landfills, waterways or the atmosphere. The disposal of chemical wastes in landfills over the past several decades has created enormous problems for communities throughout the world, which are faced with the choice of expensive clean-ups or contamination of their environment by leaking toxics. Put another way, many of today's contaminated communities are being forced to pay for the toxic sins of the past.

In the United States, dumping wastes into landfills that were later topped off and used for other purposes, such as housing developments, became commonplace. Today thousands of toxic

[9] Hans Hurni, "Degradation and Conservation of the Resources in the Ethiopian Highlands," *Mountain Research and Development* 8, nos. 2–3 (1988).

[10] United Nations Environment Programme, *Hazardous Chemicals*, Environment Brief no. 4 (Nairobi, 1988); see also Sandra Postel, *Defusing the Toxics Threat: Controlling Pesticides and Industrial Waste*, Worldwatch Paper 79 (Washington, D.C.: Worldwatch Institute, September 1987).

[11] Wendy Grieder, United States Environmental Protection Agency (EPA), quoted in Nathaniel Sheppard, Jr., "U.S. Companies Looking Abroad for Waste Disposal," *Journal of Commerce*, 20 July 1988.

[12] Ibid.

waste sites are festering sores in towns and cities throughout the country.

Love Canal was one such community. But it proved to be just the tip of the toxic iceberg. Thousands of other sites across the country are contaminated. Throughout the world, moreover, urban residents have long tacitly accepted the reality of living with higher levels of pollution in their immediate environment, particularly in the air they breathe. Automobiles, power plants and industrial plants are the biggest contributors to air pollution. Where pollution control technology is unavailable and regulations are unenforced, as in Eastern Europe and the Soviet Union, both regions where the post-war rush to industrialize was given precedence over environmental protection, emissions have made atmospheric pollution so bad as to render whole regions virtually uninhabitable.

Pollution poses grave threats to agriculture and human health throughout the Eastern European nations. The Polish Government, for example, recently declared the village of Bogomice and four others "unfit for human habitation" because of the extremely high levels of heavy metals in the air and soil deposited by emissions from nearby copper smelting plants. The government is encouraging villagers from this region to resettle elsewhere by offering compensation.[13] Likewise, in the Soviet Union, the quality of air, soil, water, and forest resources is in rapid decline.

Sudden accidents, such as a rail crash, fire or explosion, can instantaneously confer upon thousands of people the status of environmental refugee. In the 19 years leading up to 1978, there were 7 major chemical accidents worldwide, killing a total of 739, injuring 2,647, and forcing 18,230 from their homes. All but one occurred in industrialized countries.[14]

Among the worst examples of an accident in the industrial world was the 1976 explosion at a small chemical plant in Seveso, Italy, that sent a cloud of smoke and high toxic dioxin particles wafting over the countryside. Since 1978, the number and severity of toxic disasters has in-

creased, with more of these in the Third World. In the next 8 years, there were 13 major chemical accidents. The numbers tell the tragedy: 3,930 dead, 4,848 injured and nearly 1 million evacuated.[15]

Higher wage costs and tighter controls on production and disposal of hazardous chemical materials in industrial nations, along with the development of a global market for chemical products, have sent some multinational firms scurrying to build plants in developing nations. Experience shows that such investments can be a mixed blessing. Although they gain some jobs and revenue from the chemical industry, most developing countries have neither laws controlling toxic chemicals nor the technical and institutional capacity to put them into force. The general lack of controls makes incidents of contamination more likely.[16]

The toxic leak in 1984 at Bhopal, India, was perhaps the worst example of this trend. A Union Carbide pesticide plant accidentally released a cloud of deadly methyl isocyanate over the town, killing about 2,500 and sending more than 200,000 fleeing for their lives. As many as 100,000 people are still suffering side effects, such as blurred vision, disabling lung diseases, intestinal bleeding, and neurological and psychological disorders. Nuclear reactor accidents have the most pervasive and long-lasting consequences of any industrial catastrophe. Chernobyl was the worst reactor accident in history. But the fact remains that an even more serious disaster could occur at any time at one of the reactors in a densely populated area.

THE THREAT OF INUNDATION

Among the various environmental problems that cause the displacement of people from their hab-

---

[13] United Nations Environment Programme, *Hazardous Chemicals*.
[14] Ibid.

[15] Jane H. Ives, ed., *The Export of Hazard* (Boston: Routledge & Kegan Paul, 1985); and Postel, *Defusing the Toxics Threat*.
[16] Robert C. Cowen, "Man-made Gases Increase the Chance of Major Weather Change," *Christian Science Monitor*, 30 June 1988; and warming projections from "The Greenhouse Effect, Climate Change, and Ecosystems," in B. Bolan et al. (eds.), *Scope 29* (Chichester: John Wiley, 1986).

itats, none rivals the potential effects of sea-level rise as a result of human-induced changes in the earth's climate. A 1 metre rise in ocean levels worldwide, for example, may result in the creation of 50 million environmental refugees from various countries—more than triple the number in all recognized refugee categories today.

Most scientists are in agreement that global warming is under way, caused by the accumulation of "greenhouse gases" primarily because of fossil fuel use in industrial countries. The uncertainties lie in just how much higher the earth's average temperature will go, and how quickly the increase will take place. Recent estimates predict that a global temperature increase of 1.5 to 4.5 degrees Celsius can be expected as early as 2030, rising to as much as 5 degrees by 2100.[17]

Small increases in the earth's average temperature because of the greenhouse effect will lead to a rise in the global sea level for two reasons. First, as atmospheric temperatures rise, so too will the average temperature of the oceans. Because of this heat transfer, the waters of the earth will expand. Second, higher temperatures will also cause polar ice to melt, further raising the level of the sea. Large masses of ice, such as the West Antarctic sheet, may break off, displacing water and further raising sea level.[18]

If correct, the predicted temperature changes would precipitate a rise in sea level of 1.4 metres to 2.2 metres by the end of the next century. (In comparison, global sea-level rise has probably not exceeded 15 centimetres over the past century.) Such an increase will affect people and infrastructure around the globe. Yet, while sea-level rise due to global warming is induced largely by the industrial world, developing countries stand to suffer the most immediate and dramatic impacts.[19]

Where will those displaced by rising seas go? Moving further inland, millions of environmental refugees will have to compete with the local populace for scarce food, water and land, perhaps spurring regional clashes—for example, tensions between Bangladesh and its large neighbour to the west, India, are likely to heighten as the certain influx of environmental refugees from the former rises. Eventually, the combination of rising seas, harsher storms and degradation of the Bengal delta may wreak so much damage that Bangladesh as it is known today may virtually cease to exist.

Egypt's habitable area is even more densely populated than Bangladesh. By 2100, sea-level rise will range between 257 and 332 centimetres, inundating up to 26 percent of Egypt's habitable land and affecting an equal percentage of both population and domestic economic output. Several shallow, brackish lakes along the coast, accounting for 50 percent of the nation's fish catch, would also be endangered.[20]

In 2100, cartographers will likely be drawing maps with new coastlines for many countries as a result of sea-level rise. They may also make an important deletion: by that year, if current projections are borne out, the Maldives may have been washed from the earth. The small nation, made up of a series of 1,190 islands in atolls, is nowhere higher in elevation than 2 metres. A mean sea-level rise of equal height would submerge the entire country.

Developed nations, heavily reliant on the burning of fossil fuels over the past century, must assume the primary responsibility for global warming and its consequences. And while they are in a far better financial position than developing countries to undertake the remedial technological measures necessary to save coastal areas and inhabited land (thereby mitigating the problem of environmental refugees), these

[17] James G. Titus, United States Environmental Protection Agency, "Causes and Effects of Seal-level Rise," presented to the First North American Conference on Preparing for Climate Change: A Co-operative Approach, Washington, D.C., 27–29 October 1987; Erik Eckholm, "Significant Rise in Sea-level Now Seems Certain," *New York Times,* 18 February 1986; and Ann Henderson-Sellers and Kendall McGuffie, "The Threat from Melting Ice Caps," *New Scientist,* 12 June 1986.
[18] Titus, "Causes and Effects."

[19] Ibid.; Population Reference Bureau, *1988 World Population.*
[20] Goemans and Vellinga, "Low Countries and High Seas"; United States coastline figure from *The 1988 Information Please Almanac* (Boston: Houghton Mifflin, 1987).

actions will cost them dearly. The Netherlands, for example, will have to spend at least $U.S.5 billion by 2040 shoring up dikes and increasing drainage capacity to save their delta region. Large though these expenditures are, they are trivial compared with what the United States, with more than 19,000 kilometres of coastline, will have to spend to protect its territorial integrity.

CONCLUSIONS

Environmental refugees have become the single largest class of displaced persons in the world. They fall into three broad categories: those displaced temporarily because of a local disruption such as an avalanche or earthquake; those who migrate because environmental degradation has undermined their livelihood or poses unacceptable risks to health; and those who resettle because land degradation has resulted in desertification or because of other permanent and untenable changes in their habitat. Although precise numbers are hard to fix due to lack of data, it appears that this last group—the permanently displaced—is both the largest and the fastest growing.

Until sea-level rise overtakes it, land degradation will remain the single most important cause of environmental refugees—more than 10 million by conservative estimates. Land degradation occurs in stages, moving from moderate to severe desertification, for example. Thus it produces refugees in both of the last two categories.

Refugees from land degradation often migrate from region to region cultivating one plot of marginal land after another, exacerbating the problem and moving on when the land no longer produces enough to meet basic needs. Others fill Third World cities. Across Africa, Asia and Latin America, the swelling ranks of such refugees are signalling a large-scale decline in the carrying capacity of agricultural lands worldwide. At some point this land will become so damaged that it is not economically or technically feasible to restore it to original levels of productivity.

Current trends are likely to worsen over the next few decades unless society acts to combat the problems underscored by the creation of environmental refugees. More and more land will be rendered unproductive or uninhabitable whether through desertification, toxic pollution or unnatural disasters. By the middle of the next century, the combined number of environmental refugees from all these problems and the inevitable rise in sea levels because of global warming will probably exceed the number of refugees from all other causes by a factor of six.

The vision of tens of millions of persons permanently displaced from their homes is a frightening prospect, one without precedent and likely to dwarf even past and current wars in its impact on humanity. The growing number of environmental refugees today is already a rough indicator of the severity of global environmental decline. This yardstick may be imprecise but its message cannot be clearer.

61. TOO MANY RICH FOLKS

PAUL R. EHRLICH and ANNE H. EHRLICH

There is a widespread misapprehension that the population problem centres in the poor countries. In the popular view, the "population problem" is being caused by Indian peasants, African herders, macho Latin American men, and the like. And a casual glance at demographic statistics might easily persuade the unsophisticated that this is correct. The population growth rate in Kenya is over 4 percent, which if unchanged would double the population in only 17 years. The average growth rate for the less developed world (excluding China) is 2.4 percent (doubling time 29 years), and travelers virtually anywhere in the developing world are greeted by huge numbers of children under the age of fifteen, who make up roughly 40 to 50 percent of the population.

In contrast, rich nations have either very slow growth rates (well under 1 percent), have reached zero population growth (ZPG), or in some cases such as West Germany and Hungary actually have shrinking populations. So, one might assume that, if Bangladeshis and Rwandans would just learn to use condoms, everything would be just fine.

Of course, nothing could be further from the truth. Rapid population growth, and overpopulation itself, do create serious problems for poor countries; indeed, they explain why most of them seem unable to escape poverty.

But population growth and overpopulation among the rich are creating a lethal situation for the entire world. It is the rich who dump most of the carbon dioxide and chlorofluorocarbons into the atmosphere. It is the rich who generate acid rain. And the rich are "strip-mining" the seas and pushing the world towards a gigantic fisheries collapse. The oil staining the shores of Prince William Sound was intended for the gas-guzzling cars of North America. The agricultural technology of the rich is destroying soils and draining supplies of underground water around the globe. And the rich are wood-chipping many tropical forests in order to make cardboard to wrap around their electronic products.

It is not crude numbers of people or population density per se that should concern us; it is the *impact* of people on the life support systems and resources of the planet. That impact can be conceived as the product of three factors: population size (P); some measure of affluence or consumption per capita (A); and an index of the environmental damage done by the technologies used to supply each unit of affluence (T). The entire population-resource-environment crisis can be encapsulated in the equation:

$$I = P \times A \times T \ (I = PAT)$$

The $I = PAT$ equation explains (in very simplified terms) why the industrialized nations, regardless of comparative population size or density (people per square kilometre), must be considered to have much more severe population problems than any poor nation. Unfortunately, nations do not even try to keep statistics on the average per capita environmental impact of their citizens; and it would be difficult to calculate precisely if they did.

In order to make reasonable comparisons of affluence per person, we have chosen a surrogate statistic: per capita use of commercial energy. This is a rather reasonable surrogate, since much environmental damage is done in the processes of extracting and mobilizing energy, and even more is done by its use. Per capita commercial energy use oversimplifies by combining the A

From *Populi*, Vol. 16 (3) 1989, pp. 21–24. Reprinted with permission by United Nations Population Fund.

Paul R. Ehrlich is professor and Anne H. Ehrlich is senior research associate, Department of Biological Sciences, Stanford University, Stanford, California. This essay is based in part on P. R. Ehrlich and A. H. Ehrlich, The Population Explosion *(New York: Simon & Schuster, 1990).*

and T factors into a single unit of per capita impact, but that cannot be avoided. Generally, there is no convenient way to separate A and T using national statistics.

But the legitimacy of using the surrogate can be seen by considering how societies handle energy. Hundreds of thousands of birds and sea mammals killed at Prince William Sound in Alaska, the death of lakes and forests in eastern North America and northern Europe from acid precipitation, and roughly three-quarters of the contribution to global warming that is due to carbon dioxide released in burning fossil fuels, all follow from the mobilization of energy to power overdeveloped societies. Global warming, entrained by huge releases of carbon dioxide, the acidification of ecosystems resulting from emissions of sulphur and nitrogen oxides from factories, power plants, and automobile exhausts, are examples of damage caused by energy use. That damage is no respecter of wealth or national boundaries; its consequences are visited on the poor as much as the rich who enjoy the benefits of using the energy.

Energy is also used in paving over natural ecosystems to create superhighways and parking lots to serve automobiles; energy is required to produce the plastic and paper and aluminium cans that clog landfills and festoon highways and seashores; energy powers the boats that slaughter whales and deplete fisheries; energy is used to produce pesticides and cool the offices of Arizona developers as they plan the further unsustainable suburbanization of the American desert Southwest; energy warms the offices of oil company officials in Anchorage as they plan the "development" of the Alaskan National Wildlife Refuge.

Energy is being used to pump aquifers dry around the world to support a temporary increase in grain production, and energy lets us fly in jet aircraft 30,000 feet above the circular irrigation patterns created by the pumping—energy that caused environmental damage when oil was pumped out of the ground and now is causing environmental damage as jet exhausts are spewed into the atmosphere. And, of course, energy damages when used to mine ores, win metals from those ores, and use those metals and other energy-intensive materials to manufacture

automobiles, aircraft, TVs, refrigerators, and all the other paraphernalia of civilization.

Poor people don't use much energy, so they don't contribute much to the damage caused by mobilizing it. The average Bangladeshi is not surrounded by plastic gadgets, the average Bolivian doesn't fly in jet aircraft, the average Kenyan farmer doesn't have a tractor or a pickup, the average Chinese does not have air-conditioning or central heating in his apartment. Of slightly over 400 million motor vehicles in the world in 1980, 150 million were in the United States, 36 million in Japan, 24 million in Germany, 1.7 million each in India and China, and 0.18 million in Nigeria.

So statistics on per capita commercial energy use are a reasonable index of the responsibility for damage to the environment and the consumption of resources by an average citizen of a nation. By that measure, a baby born in the United States represents twice the disaster for Earth as one born in Sweden or the USSR, three times one born in Italy, 13 times one born in Brazil, 35 times one in India, 140 times one in Bangladesh or Kenya, and 280 times one in Chad, Rwanda, Haiti, or Nepal.

These numbers can be somewhat misleading in several respects. Both Sweden and the Soviet Union use about half as much energy per capita as Americans. But the Swedes use it much more efficiently to produce a roughly equal standard of living, whereas Soviet energy use is much less efficient, and their standard of living is considerably less than half that of the United States (and much more pollution is produced).

In most developing countries, including the last six named above, people overwhelmingly depend for energy on locally cut fuelwood, not commercially sold fossil fuels, hydropower, or charcoal, so their actual energy consumption is understated. The average Indian is certainly not eight times richer than a citizen of Chad or Haiti!

Nevertheless, as a rule of thumb, the concept is useful. There are more than three times as many Indians as Americans, so, as a rough estimate, the United States contributes about 10 times as much to the deterioration of Earth's life support systems as does India. By the same standard, the United States has 300 times the negative impact on the world's environment and resources as Bangladesh, and Sweden is 25 times more dangerous to our future than Kenya. These statistics should lay to rest once and for all the myth that population pressures are generated principally by rapid population growth in poor nations.

There is another way to look at the disproportionate negative impact of rich nations on civilization's future. The entire planet is now grossly overpopulated by a very simple standard. The present 5.3 billion people could not be supported if humanity were living on its income—primarily solar energy, whether captured by plants in the process of photosynthesis or by human-made devices such as solar heat collectors, solar electric cells, dams, or windmills.

Far from living on its income, however, civilization is increasingly dependent on its capital, a one-time bonanza of nonrenewable resources inherited from the planet. These resources include the fossil fuels, high-grade mineral ores, and most importantly, rich agricultural soils, underground stores of "ice-age" water, and biotic diversity—all the other species of planets, animals, and microorganisms—with which human beings share Earth.

In the process of depleting this capital, humanity is rapidly destroying the very systems that supply us with income. And people in industrial countries use a vastly disproportionate share of the capital. They are the principal depleters of fossil fuels and high-grade mineral ores. With less than a quarter of the world's population, citizens of rich nations control some four-fifths of its resources. They and the technologies they have spread around the world are responsible for more than their share of the depletion of soils and groundwater, and they have played a major role in causing the destruction of biodiversity, both within their national territories and elsewhere.

Overpopulation in industrial nations obviously represents a much greater threat to the health of ecosystems than does population growth in developing nations. The 1.2 billion people in the developed world contribute disproportionately to global warming, being responsible for about four-fifths of the injection of carbon dioxide into the atmosphere caused by burning fossil fuels. Most of the responsibility

for ozone depletion, acid precipitation, and oceanic pollution can be laid at the doorstep of industrial nations. So can the environmental consequences of much cash-crop agriculture, mining operations, and oil drilling and shipping worldwide. And industrialized nations share responsibility with developing countries for the roughly one-quarter of atmospheric CO_2 buildup caused by tropical deforestation.

While people in rich nations must shoulder responsibility for civilization's resource depletion and environmental deterioration, they are also in a better position to lead the way in making the necessary changes to improve the human predicament. Still-growing populations, after decades of slackening growth, could soon achieve zero population growth and begin shrinking. Rather than lament the shift to an "older" population, people in developed countries should celebrate and encourage the trend. The smaller the population (P), if per capita consumption or affluence (A) and technologies (T) remain the same, the less the environmental impact (I).

But the affluence and technology factors also can be more easily reduced in rich countries than in poor ones. Energy consumption could be substantially lowered through conservation in virtually all developed nations. Considerable progress in that direction was made in the United States, one of the world's more energy-wasteful nations, between 1977 and 1987, largely as a response to higher petroleum prices and growing dependency on imported oil. Unfortunately, the Reagan administration terminated or phased out most of the governmental incentives to conserve energy or develop alternative sources that had been put in place during the 1970s. By the late 1980s, Americans were reverting to their old bad habits, although the possibilities for energy conservation had only begun to be tapped. Far from lowering the standard of living, the changes that were implemented, as well as those that remain possible, reduce energy costs to consumers and substantially lessen pollution.

Beyond conservation, many fairly painless changes could be made in the energy mix of most developed nations that would markedly reduce the release of CO_2 to the atmosphere. By substituting natural gas for coal, for instance, CO_2 emissions could be cut by about 50 percent for the same energy benefit—and, again, less pollution. And renewable energy sources, especially solar-generated electricity, are increasingly practical substitutes for fossil fuels.

Apart from energy, most developed nations have ample room to shift to more environmentally benign technologies (thus reducing T). What is needed are economic incentives for manufacturers to take account of the costs of transport, distribution, use, and disposal of products, not just production costs, in making decisions. This could prove tricky, as corporations increasingly shift manufacturing processes to poor countries to avoid higher labor costs and environmental restrictions in the home countries. As the global economy becomes more and more integrated, international standardization of environmental regulations may become necessary.

If the overdeveloped nations of the world fail to reduce their environmental impacts, working as far as possible on all three factors—population, consumption, and technology—they can hardly expect the developing world to do so. And without reductions in CO_2 and other greenhouse emissions by the rich, growing energy use by the poor nations will accelerate the greenhouse buildup. The sheer size and growth rates of populations in developing nations, along with their altogether reasonable aspirations and plans for development, virtually guarantee such an acceleration.

To illustrate, suppose that China halted its population growth at about 1.2 billion (unlikely as that seems) and only doubled its per capita energy consumption, using its abundant supplies of coal. At that, its per capita consumption of energy would still be only 14 percent of the average American's; yet that apparently modest increase would cancel the benefits of Americans giving up all use of coal (currently supplying about 20 percent of U.S. energy) and not replacing it with a carbon-based fuel. Similarly, if India achieved success in ending its population growth at 2 billion, and doubled its per capita energy use to about 7 percent of present U.S. consumption, it too would offset the foregoing of U.S. coal. Unfortunately, Americans can only give up coal-burning once.

So, while the rich nations today are the primary culprits in generating global warming (and numerous other environmental problems), an alarming potential for greatly increasing these problems resides in the poor countries, largely because the P factor is both so large and still growing so fast. If poor nations are to have any chance at all to end their population growth humanely and to develop their economies, the rich must scale back their assaults on the planet's life-support systems.

Viewed in this light, the situation clearly requires co-operation among all nations in implementing solutions to the human predicament. If the habitability of Earth is to be preserved for all our descendants, we have no choice but to end and reverse population growth, limit our consumption of resources, replace damaging technologies with gentler ones, and attempt to design a better, more sustainable civilization.

Having pioneered in today's destructive development, it seems only appropriate for the rich countries to lead in setting things right—by moving toward population shrinkage.

CHAPTER 22

THE ENVIRONMENT AND
THE MARKET

INTRODUCTION

This book closes with two essays that address one of the most complex and urgent issues facing the next generation: How can citizens and their leaders generate needed wealth through free choices in the capitalist market yet at the same time constrain the wealth-producing system that is creating intolerable levels of pollution into our land, water, and air? In the past hundred years humans have modified the world's environment in such complex ways that new international strategies are required to address the problems we have created. Around the world chlorofluorocarbons emitted from factories and homes are creating a sizable hole in the protective ozone layer of the upper atmosphere. The massive burning of fossil fuels in autos, home furnaces, jet engines, and electrical power plants has contributed to a significant rise in the level of carbon dioxide in the atmosphere, trapping the heat absorbed from the sun's rays and raising temperatures throughout the world: the so-called greenhouse effect. Some critics dismiss these gloomy observations as the exaggerations of doomsayers; but at the end of the twentieth century thoughtful people everywhere are studying trends and warning signals that will not go away. In a mere hundred years the industrial nations have plundered and polluted the planet to an extent never before imagined. The next generation must set a new course to bring human communities into balance with the other parts of the ecosystem.

How can human societies develop appropriate strategies to restore the balance between humankind and the environment? For many decades the conventional answer to this question was government regulation. The logic seemed simple and straightforward. Private enterprise places its emphasis on profit and tends to neglect the negative consequences of the pollutants being dumped into landfills, rivers, and the air. Since most corporations neglect to clean up their mess, the government shall set environmental standards and regulate their operations through inspections and fines. This simplistic approach to the environmental crisis sees corporations as bad guys and government regulators as good guys.

We have selected two essays on the environmental crisis that avoid such simple notions. To be sure, there are greedy capitalists in the world who have destroyed forests, polluted rivers, and darkened the sky with ash. But how does one explain the fact that the Communist nations of Eastern Europe and the Soviet Union polluted their environments far more thoroughly than the capitalist nations of Western Europe and North America? There was no room on their agenda for regulation of polluters. Government regulation in capitalist societies has at least curtailed some of the worst abuses of pollution. The long-term solution, however, does not lie in an adversarial relationship between producers of goods and services and environmental interest groups.

It may help some people to understand the environmental problem by seeing images of filthy factories that need to be closed, but the complexities of the problem require a more sophisticated assessment of many factors that contribute to the unstable relationship between human groups and the environment. Murray Weidenbaum is a conservative economist who has devoted much of his career to challenging the wisdom of government regulation as a solution to social problems. He argues for a new set of strategies that emphasize incentives rather than punishments. T. H. Tietenberg links two global problems: poverty pushes many Third World nations to ravage their environments. Capital-rich countries need to work with Third World nations to devise joint policies that alleviate poverty and restore the environment at the same time. Tietenberg offers hope with a practical strategy that speaks to the concerns of all nations of the world.

62. PROTECTING THE ENVIRONMENT

MURRAY WEIDENBAUM

Every poll of citizen sentiment shows overwhelming support for doing more to clean up the environment. A public opinion survey by *The New York Times* and CBS News reported in 1983 that 58 percent of the sample agreed with the following statement: "Protecting the environment is so important that requirements and standards cannot be too high and continuing environmental improvements must be made regardless of cost."

Despite the continuation of such an overwhelming public mandate and a plethora of new laws and directives by the EPA (Environmental Protection Agency) plus hundreds of billions of dollars of compliance costs expended by private industry, the public remains unhappy with the results.

Unfortunately, environmental action is an extremely important example of not wishing to pay the piper. Those same citizens who want environmental improvements "regardless of cost" vociferously and adamantly oppose the location of any hazardous-waste facility in their own neighborhood. Nor are they keen on paying for the cleanup. Of course, they strongly favor cleaning up the environment, but each prefers to have the dump site located in someone else's backyard and to have the other fellow pay for it.

An example of this situation is the reaction of the enlightened citizens of Minnesota to a $3.7 million grant from the EPA to build and operate a state-of-the-art chemical landfill that could han-

From *Society*, November/December 1989, pp. 49–56. Copyright © 1989 Transaction Publishers. Reprinted with permission of Transaction Publishers.

Murray Weidenbaum is Mallinc Krodt Distinguished University Professor and director of the Center for the Study of American Business at Washington University. His most recent books include the third edition of Business, Government, and the Public, The Future of Business Regulation, *and* Public Policy toward Corporate Takeovers.

dle hazardous wastes with a high assurance of safety. In each of the 16 locations that the state proposed, the local residents raised such a fuss and howl that the state government backed off. Ultimately, the unspent grant was returned to the EPA.

The Minnesota experience is not exceptional. The EPA was also forced to stop a project to test whether the sludge from a municipal waste treatment plant could be used as a low-cost fertilizer. Public opposition was fierce, even though the EPA was going to use federally owned land and the sludge was expected to increase crop yields by 30 percent.

Since 1980, not a single major new disposal facility has been sited anywhere in the United States. According to a state-by-state review, the outlook for the future is "even more bleak," in large part because of the deteriorating emotional atmosphere surrounding any effort to locate a new dump site. As Peter Sandman of Rutgers University has pointed out, the public perceives environmental matters not only emotionally, but also morally. "Our society," he has written, "has reached near-consensus that pollution is morally wrong—not just harmful or dangerous . . . but wrong." Yet, the individuals who make up that same public are reluctant to personally assume the burdens associated with that strongly held view.

This ambivalent attitude toward the environment is not new. In 1969, the National Wildlife Federation commissioned a national survey to determine how much people were willing to pay for a cleaner environment. At a time of peak enthusiasm for environmental regulation, the public was asked, "To stop pollution destroying our plant life and wildlife, would you be willing to pay an increase in your monthly electric bill of $1?" The "no" vote won hands down, 62 percent to 28 percent (with 10 percent "not sure"). That study, we should recall, was taken before the big runup in utility bills. Perhaps not too surprisingly, the survey showed strong support for taxing business to finance environmental cleanup.

In other words, most Americans very much want a cleaner environment, but are willing neither to pay for it nor to inconvenience themselves. Americans try to take the easy way out—by imposing the burden on "someone else," preferably a large, impersonal institution.

It is much easier for Congress to express a desire for cleaner air or purer water than for an agency like the EPA to fulfill that desire. Vast sums of money have been spent for these purposes in recent years. From 1970 to 1986, Congress appropriated more than $55 billion for the operation of the EPA. The headcount of EPA employment rose from a few hundred in 1970 to over nine thousand in 1988. These numbers are dwarfed by the costs for the private sector to comply with government's rules on environmental cleanup. The U.S. Council on Environmental Quality estimated the total at more than $100 billion for 1988, and more than $750 billion for the preceding decade (in dollars of 1986 purchasing power).

These staggering outlays have not prevented critics from initiating an almost endless array of lawsuits whose main purpose is to get the EPA to act faster and to do more. Typical of the assaults on the EPA is this statement by Congressman James J. Florio of New Jersey: "They are not in charge. They do not have the resources by their own actions to get the work done, and they are more interested in cosmetics than anything."

The plaintive response of the EPA administrator at the time was that "EPA's plate is very full right now." That plate is being heaped higher on an almost daily basis. One of the EPA's newest responsibilities, for instance, is regulation of genetically engineered pesticides. Rapid scientific improvements permit the detection and, perhaps, regulation of ever more minute quantities of pollutants.

Meanwhile, John and Jane Q. Public are making the problem worse. In 1965, the average American disposed of three pounds of garbage a day. By 1985, that figure was up to four pounds each day and rising—in addition to wastes from agriculture, mining, industry, construction and demolition, sewage, and junked autos.

The EPA can claim important accomplish-

ments. Between 1970 and 1985, air pollution from vehicles fell by 46 percent for hydrocarbons, 34 percent for carbon monoxide, and 75 percent for lead. Rivers that were nearly devoid of life teem with fish once again. Lake Erie, so laden with pollutants in 1969 that a river feeding into it caught fire, has been revived.

Despite these successes, the EPA frequently falls short in meeting congressionally mandated goals for pollution cleanup. The hard fact is that the status quo in environmental policy is not sufficient. Congress continues to pass high-sounding legislation with unrealistic timetables and inflexible deadlines, while the EPA gets ever greater responsibility and private industry spends billions more on environmental compliance. In the words of the EPA's former administrator, William Ruckelshaus, "EPA's statutory framework is less a coherent attack on a complex and integrated societal problem than it is a series of petrified postures."

THE PUBLIC SECTOR DRAGS ITS FEET

Misperceptions of the villains in the pollution story abound. Many people fall into a common trap—that of associating polluters exclusively with business. Many companies do generate lots of pollution. But the same can be said about government agencies, hospitals, schools, and colleges.

The EPA lacks the enforcement power over the public sector that it possesses over the private sector. Reports of plant closings because of the high cost of meeting environmental standards are common. In contrast, there is no record of a single government facility closing down because it was not meeting ecological requirements.

It is not surprising that the GAO (General Accounting Office) says that performance of federal agencies in the disposal of hazardous waste "has not been exemplary." A GAO report issued in 1986 says that, of 72 federal facilities inspected, 33 were in violation of EPA requirements and 22 had been cited for Class 1 (serious) violations. Sixteen of the thirty-three facilities remained out of compliance for six months or more. Three had been out of compliance for more than three years. A follow-up report by the GAO in 1987 showed little further progress. Only four of eleven federal agencies had completed the identification of hazardous-waste sites and none had finished assessing the environmental problems they had uncovered. Of 511 federal sites failing to meet EPA standards, only 78 had been cleaned up.

A major offender is the DOD (Department of Defense), which now generates more than 500,000 tons of hazardous waste a year. That is more than is produced by the five largest chemical companies combined. The lax situation uncovered by the GAO at Tinker Air Force Base, in Oklahoma, is typical of the way in which many federal agencies respond to the EPA's directives: "Although DOD policy calls for the military services to . . . implement EPA's hazardous waste management regulations, we found that Tinker has been selling . . . waste oil, fuels, and solvents rather than . . . recycling."

The GAO reported that two of the five commercial waste sites receiving the base's wastes had major compliance problems. Also, personnel at Tinker Air Force Base were dumping hazardous wastes in landfills that themselves were in violation of EPA requirements. In one case, the EPA had been urging the Oklahoma Department of Health for several years not to renew a landfill's permit. In another instance, the State Water Resources Board was seeking a court order to close the site. Civilian agencies, including those in state and local governments, continue to be reluctant to follow the same environmental standards that they impose on the private sector.

Federal policy arbitrarily excludes one of the largest single sources of pollution from the EPA's effective jurisdiction: the runoff of pesticides and fertilizers from farms. The EPA reports that in six of the agency's ten regions, pollution from farms and urban streets is the principal cause of water quality problems. But pollution from these sources remains virtually unregulated.

Large quantities of agricultural pollution can be controlled fairly easily at low cost by using limited-till plowing techniques. In striking contrast, industrial pollution control has often been pushed to the limits of economic feasibility.

Congress follows a double standard: for urban and industrial pollution it requires the imposition of tough standards to qualify for permits to discharge wastes. For rural and farm pollution, the EPA is merely given money to study the problem.

Congress wants a cleaner environment. But so far it has not mustered the will required to impose the most modest pollution controls on a politically powerful group of constituents. Farm families also want a cleaner environment—but it is always nice to get someone else to pay for your desires.

ECONOMIC SOLUTIONS TO HAZARDOUS WASTE PROBLEMS

Turning to specific environmental problems, we can start with the controversy over the disposal of hazardous wastes. Instances of toxic-waste contamination at Love Canal, in New York State, and at Times Beach, Missouri, have brought a sense of urgency to the problem. The public mood on the subject of hazardous waste leaves little room for patience—but much opportunity for emotional response.

Emotionally charged responses are encouraged by the fact that even scientists know little about the effects on human health of many toxic substances such as the various forms of dioxin. The EPA can now measure levels of some substances in terms of parts per billion and occasionally per quadrillion, but even the experts still debate the significance of exposure at those rates. The scare headlines about chemical health hazards deal with exposures that are akin to the proverbial needle in the haystack. Actually, the needle-haystack comparison is much too modest. One part per billion is the equivalent of one inch in 16,000 miles, a penny in $10 million, four drops of water in an Olympic-size pool, or a second in 32 years.

The most severe reaction to dioxin reported so far by humans is a bad case of chloracne, a severe acne-like rash. The bulk of the available information on dioxin and other hazards is based on extrapolating from data on animal experiments, which is very tricky. Most tests on animals are conducted at extremely high concentrations of the suspected element, which do not reflect real-world conditions in which the animals (or humans) live. Scientists note that the massive doses that are fed the animals overwhelm their entire bodies. A level of exposure that is harmful to one type of animal may not be injurious to another. The lethal dose of the most toxic dioxin (2,3,7,8 TCDD) for hamsters is 5,000 times higher than that for guinea pigs. Extrapolating the results to humans involves even more conjecture. Still, our hearts must go out to the people in Times Beach, Missouri, and in Love Canal, New York, who have suffered financial and psychological damage from the emotional responses to the scare stories they have seen and heard so frequently.

In trying to avoid a repetition of these situations, the EPA has promulgated detailed regulations on how polluters must keep track of hazardous wastes and how they should dispose of them. Because of growing public concern over leaky and dangerous dump sites, Congress in late 1986 extended and expanded Superfund, the program designed to clean up hazardous-waste sites. The law requires companies and, ultimately, consumers, to pay $9 billion into Superfund by 1991. Yet, despite all this effort and attention, the problem of how to dump hazardous wastes is scarcely less serious than it was in 1980, before Congress passed the original Superfund law.

As it stands, the law provides for a large fund raised primarily through taxes on producers of chemical and petroleum products. The EPA uses this money to identify and clean up hazardous waste sites. But little progress is made because, as we noted earlier, there is a severe shortage of dump sites.

ECONOMIC INCENTIVES NEEDED

A more clearheaded view of waste disposal problems is needed in the United States. Because definitions vary among levels of government, estimates of the amount of hazardous waste disposed of each year in the United States range from 30 million to 264 million metric tons. Most of this waste is buried in landfills because incineration, the safest and most effective means of disposal, is nearly ten times as costly. Even so,

government and industry spend more than $5 billion each year to manage toxic wastes. The annual cost by 1990 is projected to reach $12 billion.

Many experts believe that using landfills is inherently unsafe, if for no other reason than that they are only storage sites. Moreover, there are not enough of them. The EPA estimates that 22,000 waste sites now exist in the United States, and fully ten percent of them are believed to be dangerous and leaking.

The result: not enough reliable environmentally safe places to dump toxic substances. Although the EPA wants to clean up as many landfills as possible, it has very little choice as to where to put the material it removes under the Superfund mandate. Taxpayers may wind up paying for the costly removal of waste from one site, only to find later on that they have to pay again for removing it from yet another dangerous site.

Meanwhile, legal fees mushroom. The litigation costs involving cleanup at the various Superfund sites are estimated to run somewhere between $3.5 billion and $6.4 billion.

Eventually, society will have to face the main reason for the scarcity of hazardous-waste sites—the "not in my backyard" syndrome. Sites for the disposal of toxic substances have joined prisons and mental hospitals as things the public wants, but not too close by.

The hazardous-waste disposal problem is not going to disappear unless Americans adopt less polluting methods of production and consumption. Until then, greater understanding is needed on the part of the public, as is a willingness to come to grips with the difficult problems arising from the production and use of hazardous substances. It will cost large amounts of money (probably in the hundreds of billions of private expenditures in the next decade) to meet society's environmental expectations. Spending money may be the easiest part of the problem. Getting people to accept dump sites in their neighborhoods is much more difficult.

The answer surely is an appeal not merely to good citizenship, but also to common sense and self-interest. In a totalitarian society, people who do not want to do something the government desires are simply forced to do so, with the threat of physical violence ever present. In a free society with a market economy, we offer to pay people to do something they otherwise would not do. The clearest example in modern times is the successful elimination of the military draft coupled with very substantial increases in pay and fringe benefits for voluntarily serving in the armed forces.

Individual citizens have much to gain by opposing the location of hazardous-waste facilities near them, and there is a basic logic to their position. It is not fair for society as a whole to benefit from a new disposal site, while imposing most of the costs (ranging from danger of leakage to depressed property values) on the people in the locality. But local resistance to dealing with hazardous wastes imposes large costs on society as a whole. Those costs are in the form both of inhibiting economic progress and having to ship waste from one temporary site to another.

Individual interests and community concerns can be reconciled by the use of economic incentives. The idea is to look upon environmental pollution not as a sinful act but as an activity costly to society and susceptible to reduction by means of proper incentives. After all, the prospect of jobs and income encourages many communities to offer tax holidays and other enticements to companies considering the location of a new factory—even though it may not exactly improve the physical environment of the region. Under present arrangements, however, there is no incentive for the citizens of an area to accept a site for hazardous wastes in their vicinity, no matter how safe it is.

Some areas might accept such a facility if the state government (financed by all the citizens benefitting from the disposal facility) would pay for something the people in that locality want but cannot afford—such as a new school building, firehouse, or library, or simply lower property taxes. Unlike an industrial factory, a hazardous-waste facility provides few offsetting benefits to the local residents in the form of jobs or tax revenues. Government can do a lot to improve environmental policy in other ways. The EPA could reduce the entire hazardous-waste problem by distinguishing between truly lethal wastes—which should be disposed of with great care—and wastes that contain only a trace or minute amounts of undesirable materials. To the

extent that this would require changes in legislation, the agency should urge Congress to make them.

The experience of a company in Oregon provides insights into why Congress needs to legislate common sense into the antipollution laws. The firm has been dumping heavy-metal sludges on its property for over 20 years. Company officials told the GAO that they automatically classify the material as hazardous. Why? Because it would be too costly and time-consuming to try to prove that it was not. The GAO learned from several industry associations that other companies, similarly uncertain and wanting to avoid expensive testing costs, simply declare their wastes to be hazardous, whether they really are dangerous or not. That is not the only example in which those complying with environmental regulations lose sight of the fundamental objectives to be met.

TACKLING FIRST THINGS FIRST

A 1987 EPA report concluded that the agency's priorities "do not correspond well" with its rankings by risk of the various ecological problems on its agenda. The agency's own study found areas of high risk but little regulatory effort. A key example is runoff of polluted water from farms and city streets.

Conversely, the study showed that areas of "high EPA effort but relatively low risks" included management of hazardous wastes, cleanup of chemical waste dumps, regulation of underground storage tanks containing petroleum or other hazardous substances, and municipal solid waste. The reason for this mismatch between needs and resources is obvious. The EPA's priorities are set by Congress and reflect public pressure more than scientific knowledge. Driven by the forces of environmental politics, the nation has repeatedly committed itself to goals and programs that are unrealistic. This has meant deploying regulatory manpower unwisely and diverting limited resources to concerns of marginal importance.

The results of this mismatch are substantial. Not all hazards are created equal. Some disposal sites are being filled with innocuous material while truly dangerous substances are or will be, for lack of space, dumped illegally or stored "temporarily." What would help is more widespread application of the legal concept known as *de minimus non curat lex*—the law does not concern itself with trifles.

Back in 1979, a federal circuit court supported the view that there is a *de minimus* level of risk too small to affect human health adversely. It cited that doctrine in turning down the claim that some "migration" of substances occurred from the packaging into the food product. In 1985, the FDA concluded that using methylene chloride to extract caffeine from coffee presented a *de minimus* risk. The substance is safe for its intended use. In 1987, the National Research Council recommended that the EPA apply a "negligible risk" standard across the board in determining how much of which pesticides can be permitted to show up in food.

CANCERPHOBIA MISALLOCATES RESOURCES

One approach to eliminating the gridlock in regulatory policy is to focus on the underlying public concern that is driving the pressures for more sweeping environmental and other social regulation. That concern is the worry about cancer. The regulatory waters have become badly muddied by the public's misconception of the causes of cancer. A widely held notion is that the environment is primarily responsible. There is, of course, a germ of truth to that belief.

It turns out that several years ago a distinguished scientist—John Higginson, director of the World Health Organization's International Agency for Research on Cancer—assigned the primary blame for cancer to what he labeled "environmental" causes. His highly-publicized finding that two-thirds of all cancer was caused by environmental factors provided ammunition for every ecological group to push for tougher restrictions on all sorts of environmental pollution.

Upon a more careful reading, it is clear that the eminent scientist was referring not to the physical environment but to the age-old debate of "environment" versus "heredity" as the main influence on human beings. In the case of cancer, he was identifying voluntary behavior—such as personal life-styles and the kinds of food people eat—as the main culprit responsible for cancer. Higginson specifically pointed out, "But when I used the term environment in those days, I was considering the total environment, cultural as well as chemical . . . air you breathe, the culture you live in, the agricultural habits of your community, the social cultural habits, the social pressures, the physical chemicals with which you come in contact, the diet, and so on." But that explanation has not slowed down the highly vocal ecology groups who latched on to a "catchy" albeit confused theme—the extremely carcinogenic environment in which Americans supposedly live.

More recently, one university scientist tried to add some objectivity to the cancer debate by quantifying the issue. Harry Demopoulos of the New York Medical Center examined why approximately 1,000 people die of cancer each day in the United States. About 450 of the deaths, or 45 percent, can be attributed to diet. Citing the work of Arthur Upton of the National Cancer Institute, Demopoulos noted that eating more fresh fruits and vegetables and curtailing fat consumption would be most helpful. Clearly, obesity is not the type of environmental pollution that justifies the EPA's increasingly onerous standards.

The second major cause of cancer deaths, according to Demopoulos, is the consumption of excessive quantities of distilled liquor and the smoking of high-tar cigarettes. These voluntary actions resulted in 350, 35 percent, of the cancer deaths. Again, this is not the environmental pollution that motivates most ecology activists.

A distant third in the tabulation of leading causes of cancer is occupational hazards, accounting for five percent of the total. Demopoulos believes that this category may have leveled off and be on the way down. He reasons that many of the occupationally induced cancers are due to exposures two or more decades ago, when scientists did not know that many chemicals were capable of causing cancer.

A fourth category, accounting for three percent, is caused by exposure to normal background radiation. The fifth and last category of causes of cancer (accounting for two percent) is preexisting medical disorders. These include chronic ulcerative colitis, chronic gastritis, and the like. The remaining ten percent of the cancer deaths in the United States are due to all other causes; it is noteworthy that air and water pollution and all the toxic hazards that are the primary cause of public worry are in this miscellaneous ten percent, not in the 90 percent. Government policy is unbalanced when the great bulk of the effort deals with a category of risk that is only some fraction of one-tenth of the problem.

Hard data can dissipate much of the fear and fog generated by the many cancer-scare stories that the public has been subjected to in recent years. Overall, cancer death rates are staying steady or coming down. The major exception is smoking-related cancer. For the decade 1974–1983, stomach cancer was down 20 percent, cancer of the cervix-uterus was down 30 percent, and cancer of the ovary was down eight percent.

Life expectancy is steadily increasing in the United States (to an all-time high of 75, for those born in 1985) and in most other industrialized nations, except the Soviet Union. This has led cancer expert Bruce Ames of the University of California to conclude, "We are the healthiest we have been in human history." This is no justification for resting on laurels. Rather, Ames's point should merely help lower the decibel level of debates on environmental issues and enable analysis to dominate emotion in setting public policy in this vital area.

A BIRTH CONTROL APPROACH TO POLLUTION

Over 99 percent of environmental spending by government is devoted to controlling pollution after it is generated. Less than one percent is spent to reduce the generation of pollutants. For fiscal 1988, the EPA budgeted only $398,000—or .03 percent of its funds—for "waste minimization." That is an umbrella term that includes recycling and waste reduction.

The most desirable approach is to reduce the generation of pollutants in the first place. Economists have an approach that is useful—providing incentives to manufacturers to change their production processes to reduce the amount of wastes created or to recycle them in a safe and productive manner.

As we noted earlier, the government taxes producers rather than polluters. By doing that, the country misses a real opportunity to curb actual dumping of dangerous waste. The federal Superfund law is financed with taxes levied on producers of chemical "feedstocks" and petroleum plus a surtax on the profits of large manufacturing companies and contributions from the federal Treasury. Thousands of companies outside of the oil and chemical industries wind up paying very little, whether they are large polluters or not. Contrary to widely held views, a great deal of pollution occurs in sectors of the economy other than oil and chemicals. The manufacture of a single TV set generates about one hundred pounds of toxic wastes.

Switching to a waste-end fee levied on the amount of hazardous wastes that a company actually generates and disposes of would be far more economically sound than the status quo. This more enlightened approach would require a basic correction in the Comprehensive Environmental Response, Compensation, and Liability Act (or "Superfund"), but it would be a very beneficial form of hazardous-waste "birth-control."

A GENERAL APPLICATION OF MARKET INCENTIVES

More generally, if the government were to levy a fee on the amount of pollutants discharged, that would provide an incentive to reduce the actual generation of wastes. Some companies would find it cheaper to change their production processes than to pay the tax. Recycling and reuse systems would be encouraged. Moreover, such a tax or fee would cover imports which are now disposed of in our country tax-free. In short, rewriting statutes, such as the Superfund law, so that they are more fair would also help protect the environment—and would probably save money at the same time.

Already, some companies are recycling as they become aware of the economic benefits. One chemical firm burns 165,000 tons of coal a year at one of its textile fibers factories, generating 35,000 tons of waste in the form of fly ash. The company recently found a local cement block company that was testing fly ash as a replacement for limestone in making lightweight cement blocks. The chemical company now sells the fly ash to the cement block manufacturer. What used to be an undesirable waste by-product has been turned into a commercially useful material. The companies are simultaneously conserving the supply of limestone.

A timber company, through its research, developed a new use for tree bark, the last massive waste product of the wood products industry. The firm designed a bark processor that made it the first domestic producer of vegetable wax, an important ingredient in cosmetics and polishes. A factory in Illinois had been creating a veritable sea of calcium fluoride sludge (at a rate of 1,000 cubic yards a month) as a by-product of its manufacture of fluorine-based chemicals. The company found that the sludge could be mixed with another waste product to produce synthetic fluorspar, which it had been buying from other sources. Recycling the two waste products now saves the firm about $1 million a year.

Incentives to do more along these lines could be provided in several ways. The producers could be subsidized to follow the desired approach. In this period of large budget deficits, that would, of course, increase the amount of money that the Treasury must borrow.

A different alternative is to tax the generation and disposal of wastes. The object would not be to punish the polluters, but to get them to change their ways. If something becomes more expensive, business firms have a natural desire to use less of the item. In this case, the production of pollution would become more expensive. Every sensible firm would try to reduce the amount of pollution tax it pays by curbing its wastes. Adjusting to new taxes on pollution would be a matter not of patriotism, but of minimizing cost and maximizing profit. The pollution tax approach appeals to self-interest in order to achieve the public interest.

Charging polluters for the pollution they cause gives companies an incentive to find innovative ways to cut down on their discharges. These fees would raise costs and prices for products whose production generates a lot of pollution. It is wrong to view this as a way of shifting the burden to the public. The relevant factor is that consumer purchasing is not static. Consumer demand would shift to products which pollute less—because they would cost less. To stay competitive, high-polluting producers would have to economize on pollution, just as they do in the case of other costs of production. Since pollution imposes burdens on the environment, it is only fair that the costs of cleaning up that pollution should be reflected in the price of a product whose production generates this burden.

Nine countries in Western Europe have adopted the "polluter pays" principle. In these nations, pollution control is paid for directly by the polluting firm or from the money collected from effluent taxes. The West German effluent-fee system, the oldest in operation, began before World War I. It has succeeded in halting the decline in water quality throughout the Ruhr Valley, the center of West Germany's iron and steel production. It is also serving as a model for a more recent French effort.

Practical problems make changes in pollution policy difficult in the United States. Both the regulators and the regulated have an interest in maintaining the current approach. Pollution taxes have little appeal in the political system, particularly in Congress. Many reject a pollution tax on philosophical grounds, considering pollution charges a "license to pollute." They believe that putting a price on the act of polluting amounts to an attitude of moral indifference towards polluters. The tendency to look at ecological matters as moral issues makes it difficult to adopt a workable approach.

Although economists are often accused of being patsies for the business community, environmental economics makes for strange alliances. So far, business interests have opposed the suggestions of economists for such sweeping changes in the basic structure of government regulation as using taxes on pollution. Despite the shortcomings of the present system of government regulation, many firms have paid the price of complying with existing rules. They have learned to adjust to regulatory requirements and to integrate existing regulatory procedures into their long-term planning.

As any serious student of business-government relations will quickly report, the debate over regulation is miscast when it is described as black-hatted business versus white-hatted public interest groups. Almost every regulatory action creates winners and losers in the business system and often among other interest groups. Clean air legislation, focussing on ensuring that new facilities fully meet standards, is invariably supported by existing firms that are "grandfathered" approval without having to conform to the same high standards as new firms. Regulation thus protects the "ins" from the "outs."

There are many other examples of regulatory bias against change and especially against new products, new processes, and new facilities. Tough emissions standards are set for new automobiles, but not for older ones. Testing and licensing procedures for new chemicals are more rigorous and thoroughly enforced than for existing substances. This ability to profit from the differential impacts of regulation helps to explain

why business shows little enthusiasm for the use of economic incentives and prefers current regulatory techniques.

The reform of regulation is truly a consumer issue. The consumer receives the benefits from regulation and bears the burden of the costs of compliance in the form of higher prices and less product variety. The consumer has the key stake in improving the current regulatory morass.

Suggested Readings

Ames, Bruce N. *Six common errors relating to environmental pollution.* Lousville: National Council for Environmental Balance, 1987.

Reese, Craig. *Deregulation and environmental quality.* Westport, Conn.: Quorum Books, 1983.

63.   THE POVERTY CONNECTION TO ENVIRONMENTAL POLICY

T. H. TIETENBERG

One of the treasures of Maine folklore is the well-known story of a thoroughly disoriented tourist. Enticed by unusually brilliant fall foliage, the tourist forsook the security of the well-marked main highways for some less traveled country roads. After an hour of driving, he was no longer sure he was even headed in the right direction. Seeing a Maine native mending a fence, he pulled over to seek assistance. When he heard

From *Challenge*, September/October 1990, pp. 26–32. Reprinted with permission of the publisher, M. E. Sharpe, Inc., 80 Business Park Drive, Armonk, New York.

Thomas H. Tietenberg is Chairman of the Department of Economics at Colby College, Waterville, Maine, and former President of the Association of Environmental and Resource Economists.

the tourist's destination, the native sadly shook his head and in his best Maine accent responded, "If I was goin' they-uh, I sure wouldn't start from he-uh!"

The underlying message of this story is both timely and relevant. Had we known long ago that human activities could seriously affect environmental life-support systems and could deny future generations the quality of life to which our generation has become accustomed, we might have chosen a different, more sustainable path for improving human welfare. The fact that we did not have that knowledge and therefore did not make that choice years ago means that the current generation is faced with making more difficult choices with fewer options. These choices will test the creativity of our solutions and the resilience of our social institutions.

As the scale of economic activity has proceeded steadily upward, the scope of environmental problems triggered by that activity has transcended both geographic and generational boundaries. Whereas the nation-state used to be sufficient for resolving environmental problems, that may no longer be the case. Whereas each generation of humans used to have the luxury of being able to satisfy its own needs without worrying about the needs of those generations to come, that may no longer be the case either.

The most difficult environmental problems of the 21st century will be global problems—global in scale and global in scope. Rising emissions of greenhouse gases might raise the global temperature sufficiently to cause climate modification, increased desertification, and a rise in the sea level sufficient to wipe out some low-lying countries. The decline in the stratospheric ozone level is expected to cause an increase in eye cataracts and skin cancer. The decline of biodiversity by deforestation and the extinction of species will limit the very gene pools that have been such a rich source of new medicines and new crops. The irony of this decline in biodiversity is that we are destroying these gene pools at a record rate at precisely that point in history when advances in biotechnology allow as to take maximum advantage of their existence.

NO MAN IS AN ISLAND

Problems like global warming, ozone depletion, and the loss of biodiversity require international cooperation, which is by no means a foregone conclusion. Global environmental problems can trigger very different effects on countries represented at the negotiating table. While low-lying countries could be submerged by a rise in sea level resulting from a warming trend, or arid nations could lose their marginal agricultural lands to desertification, other nations with traditionally intemperate climates may see agricultural productivity rise as warmer climates support longer growing seasons. To produce the desired effect, new international agreements must be enforceable, but this will be difficult as long as they infringe upon significant segments of society with legitimate claims to an alternative future. Perhaps the most legitimate such claim is advanced by those in abject poverty.

My feeling is that we will not be able to solve the environmental problems of the 21st century without solving global poverty as well. But how to accomplish the latter without worsening global environmental problems is one of the most important questions of our time. As Jim MacNeill, former director of the World Commission on Environment and Development, stated recently, "If current forms of development were employed, a five- to tenfold increase in economic activity would be required over the next fifty years to meet the needs and aspirations of a population twice the size of today's 5.2 billion, as well as to begin to reduce mass poverty."

Poverty is both a cause and an effect of many of the environmental problems to be confronted. The poor not only suffer disproportionately from the environmental damage caused by the better off, they have become a major cause of environmental decline. Survival strategies may necessarily sacrifice long-term goals simply to ward off starvation or death. Trees needed to provide moisture and nourishment for the soil over the long run may be cut down to provide immediate income or warmth. Highly erodible land may be brought into necessarily temporary cultivation simply because the only realistic alternative is starvation.

The world's poor are caught in a downward spiral. At the local level they have limited access to land or productive assets. At the national level they are held at bay by corruption and development policies that discriminate against the poor. Globally their situation is worsened by rising debt burdens, falling export prices for the products they sell, and the flight of capital that could be used to create jobs and income.

As we sit in our comfortable surroundings it is easy to think of absolute poverty as a thing of the past, but that view is wrong. DEAD WRONG! In September 1988, current World Bank President Barber Conable assessed the situation for his governing board: "Poverty on today's scale prevents a billion people from having even minimally acceptable standards of living. . . . In sub-Saharan Africa more than 100 million people—one in four—do not get enough to eat." Agricultural productivity per capita has been declining in Africa since 1967 and in Latin America since 1981. The World Bank reports that from

1979 to 1983 life expectancy fell in nine African countries. In Zambia twice as many children died from malnutrition in 1984 than in 1980. In its 1989 annual report, the United Nations Children's Fund (UNICEF) concluded "at least half a million young children have died in the last 12 months as a result of slowing down or the reversal of progress in the developing world."

The chief determinant of well-being is income. Income can purchase food, health services, education. What are the trends in incomes? As Inter-American Development Bank President Enrique Iglesias said in September 1988, "The per capita income of the average Latin American is 9 percent lower today than it was in 1980. This is average. In some countries the standard of living has slipped back to where it was twenty years ago."

The picture is not totally bleak. Success against poverty is possible. Asian countries have done well in the 1980s, for example. Thailand has reported a 50 percent decrease in its poverty rate since 1960.

One of the channels of poverty is population growth. Population growth rates are substantially higher in low income populations. High infant mortality causes parents to compensate with large numbers of births. Children provide one of the few available means of old age security. Knowledge about birth control techniques is sparse and the availability of contraceptives is limited. Women frequently have low levels of education and in some cultures, large families are the only possible way for women to achieve status.

It will be virtually impossible to solve global environmental problems without simultaneously solving the problem of global poverty. And without the assistance of the industrialized world the strategies that developing countries will take to solve their poverty problems are likely to exacerbate the very environmental problems we have been talking about. Increased energy consumption to support industry will add greenhouse gases. Increased refrigeration will add more of the gases depleting the stratospheric ozone level. If all the countries of the world were to choose the path to development that we in the industrialized world have taken, the resulting levels of pollution would exceed the capacity of

the earth to absorb them. Similarly, biodiversity would fall in the face of new assaults on biologically rich areas as countries are forced to cash in their biological heritage simply to survive.

The principle of inertia applies to politics as fully as to physical bodies; a body moving in a particular direction will continue moving in that direction unless a significant outside force is introduced. A positive, helpful outside force must come from the industrialized world. Unfortunately many current policies in the industrialized nations are producing pressures that operate in exactly the opposite direction. Let me illustrate the point with two examples: trade policies and debt policies.

Trade policies have had a major role in distorting economic activity away from sustainable development in the Third World. The terms of trade for many Third World countries have deteriorated in the recent past. The terms of trade determine international purchasing power. When the terms of trade deteriorate, Third World exports purchase fewer imports. Some of the reasons for this deterioration are rather natural effects of markets rather than misguided policies. Included in this category are the import substitutions in the industrialized world (such as when optical fibers are substituted for copper in phone lines) and lower demand for Third World exports triggered by lower economic growth in the industrialized countries. But political factors are also important. When political forces in the developed countries conspire to eliminate or substantially reduce natural markets for the developing countries, these policies not only exacerbate the poverty in the developing nations, but they have a direct degrading effect on the environment.

The Multi-Fiber Arrangement, implemented in 1974, is a case in point. Its effect has been to severely reduce developing country exports of textiles and other products made from fibers. In developing countries fiber products are produced by labor-intensive techniques, causing the employment impact to be high. For local sustainable agriculture the opportunity to provide the fiber raw materials is another source of employment. By artificially reducing the markets for these products and the fibers from which these products are made, the agreement has forced some nations to substitute resource-intensive economic activities, such as timber exports, for more environmentally congenial fiber-based manufacturing in order to earn foreign exchange.

CAPITAL FLIGHT

Debt is another source of the deteriorating terms of trade. Many Third World countries have staggering levels of debt to service. In 1989 the Third World owed $1.2 trillion, nearly one half its collective GNP. Zambia's $6 billion debt represents over 300 percent of its GNP. In 1988 poor nations sent $43 billion more to the industrialized nations in interest and principal repayment than they received in new capital. Ironically capital is flowing out of the capital poor countries where it is desperately needed and into the capital rich countries. In periods of high real interest rates, servicing these debts puts a significant drain on foreign exchange earnings. Using these foreign exchange earnings to service the debt eliminates the possibility of using them to finance imports for sustainable activities to alleviate poverty. Furthermore, flooding the market with exports to earn foreign exchange reduces prices and contributes to the deteriorating terms of trade.

The large debts owed by many developing countries encourage these countries to overexploit their resource endowments to raise the necessary foreign exchange. Timber exports represent a case in point. As Gus Speth, president of the World Resources Institute, points out, "By an accident of history and geography, half of the Third World external debt and over two-thirds of global deforestation occur in the same fourteen developing countries."

Private banks hold most of the debt and they are not typically motivated by a desire to protect biodiversity. Nonetheless it is possible to find some common ground for negotiation of strategies to reduce the debt. Banks realize that complete repayment of the loans is probably not possible. Rather than write off the loans, an action which not only causes harm to the income statement, but creates adverse incentives for repayment of future loans, they are willing to consider alternative strategies.

One of the more innovative policies that explores common ground in international arrangements has become known as the debt-nature swap. It is innovative in two senses: (1) the uniqueness of the policy instrument and (2) the direct involvement of nongovernmental organizations in implementing the strategy. A debt-nature swap involves the purchase (at a discounted value in the secondary debt market) of a developing country debt usually by a nongovernmental environmental organization (NGO). The new holder of the debt, the NGO, offers to cancel the debt in return for an environmentally related action on the part of the debtor nation.

In July 1987, for example, an American environmental organization purchased $650,000 worth of Bolivia's foreign debt from a private bank at a discounted price of $100,000. It then swapped the face value of the debt with the government of Bolivia in return for an agreement to put together a public-private partnership. This partnership would develop a program that combines ecosystem conservation and regional development planning in 3.7 million acres of designated tropical forestland. The agreement also includes a $250,000 fund in local currency for establishing and administering a system for protecting the forest reserve.

The main advantage of such arrangements to the debtor nation is that it can pay off a significant foreign exchange obligation with domestic currency. Debt-nature swaps offer the realistic possibility to turn a major force for unsustainable economic activity (the debt crisis) into a force for resource conservation. It would clearly be naive, however, to believe that the debt-nature swap would serve as a sufficient vehicle for ending tropical deforestation. The magnitude of the debts and their importance in intensifying environmental degradation call for bolder measures to reduce the debt pressure and to enhance the status of environmental protection in developing countries. Foreign aid is one such vehicle.

AN ENVIRONMENTAL MARSHALL PLAN

A close look at the U.S. foreign aid situation is not comforting. The Bush Administration's proposed fiscal year 1990 foreign assistance budget came to $14 billion, but subtracting military aid and economic support to strategic countries (such as Israel) leaves only about $6 billion for development assistance. Most of this will be spent for purely political reasons having absolutely no connection to the need to alleviate poverty. Considering the political evolution of Eastern European countries, the number of claimants for these limited funds will increase.

It is difficult to escape the conclusion that increased financial transfers from the industrialized nations to the developing nations must be part of any package that affords adequate protection for biodiversity specifically and environmental protection generally. Furthermore, to be effective, these transfers should be targeted where they will do the most good, not where they will produce the greatest short-term political advantage (as they are now). Perhaps the time has come for an environmental version of the Marshall Plan, which was so important in facilitating Europe's recovery from World War II.

By being creative in the design of policy, the incentives of local and global communities can become compatible. In some cases being creative requires the use of conventional policy instruments in unconventional ways, but in others it requires the use of unconventional instruments in unconventional ways. Unconventional approaches are not pipe dreams. Most of them have been successfully employed in one form or another in local communities around the globe. The experience with these instruments in their current setting provides a model for their use on an international level. How well this model fits remains an open question, but it is better to sit down for a dinner with a full menu offering some novel, but interesting, choices rather than one offering only a limited selection of familiar, unappetizing fare.

THE FULL COST PRINCIPLE

One rather unconventional economic policy is now being used quite extensively in Europe and Japan, but in only a minor way in the United States. It starts from the premise that all production and consumption activities should bear their full cost, including the cost to the environment,

which has been so long neglected. This *full cost principle* is based upon the presumption that humanity has a right to a reasonably safe and healthy environment. Since this right has been held in common for the stratosphere and the international sections of the oceans, no administrative body has either the responsibility or the authority for protecting that right. As a result it has been involuntarily surrendered on a first-come, first-served basis without compensation.

The principle that some rights may necessarily be involuntarily transferred is recognized by the American legal system. Automobile accidents are a classic example; the right to safe passage is involuntarily surrendered at the moment of impact. But the legal system also recognizes that when involuntary transfers take place, compensation is to be awarded. Requiring compensation serves the twin purpose of attempting to restore victims to their pre-accident position, insofar as possible, and to provide incentives for all drivers to take the cost-justified level of precautions.

EMISSIONS TAXES?

One way of implementing the full cost principle, the means used in Europe and to a lesser extent in Japan, is an emissions tax. This involves charging a per unit fee on each unit of pollutant emitted into the environment. One of the most attractive features of this particular approach is that it can stimulate the development of new, environmentally benign technologies and it can stimulate the reduction of waste, not merely the control of the waste.

In a traditional command-and-control regulatory system based on emission or effluent standards, once the source has met the legal standard, further effort to reduce emissions is neither necessary nor in its economic interest. With an emissions tax, however, all uncontrolled emissions trigger an additional financial burden.

Adopting a new control technology that would permit additional emission reduction at reasonable cost would be an attractive strategy for the source facing emissions taxes, but not for a source currently meeting emission standards. By encouraging new markets for more environmentally benign technologies—an important component of the transition to sustainable development—emissions taxes could be expected to stimulate more research and development in both controlling and reducing emissions.

On a recent edition of the NBC "Evening News" an interesting piece lamented the fact that generating electricity with solar power was close to being economically competitive, but it still was not at the point where it could produce the lowest cost electricity. The report indicated that public support for the project was great, but that it produced electricity at about two cents per kilowatt hour more than more conventional fossil fuel plants. What the program didn't say, but should have, is that if those conventional plants were paying their full share of the cost, solar would be competitive right now! Wild idea, you say? New York State has just begun doing it on a more limited scale in order to promote rational utility planning.

Emissions taxes also produce revenue that could be used for coalition-building as a prelude to negotiating international environmental agreements while simultaneously assisting the Third World countries in their transition to new forms of development. The amount is potentially very large indeed. In the September 1989 issue of *Scientific American*, William Ruckelshaus estimated that a $1 per million BTUs tax on coal and a 60 cents per million BTUs tax on oil would raise $53 billion annually just in the United States.

What policy implications would flow from the acceptance of the full cost principle? Although all pollution including those gases responsible for global warming and ozone depletion impose an environmental cost, currently that cost is not being borne, or even recognized, by those who ultimately control the magnitude of the problem. Applying the full cost principle would send a strong signal to all users of the environment that the atmosphere is a scarce, precious resource and should be treated accordingly.

Products produced by manufacturing processes that are environmentally destructive would become relatively more expensive; those produced by environmentally benign production processes would become relatively cheaper. Consumer demand would switch from one to the other. Polluting activities that you and I engage in, such as driving our automobiles, would similarly become more expensive.

Implementing the full cost principle would end the implicit subsidy that all polluting activities have received since the beginning of time. When the level of economic activity was small, the corresponding subsidy was also small and therefore probably not worthy of political attention. Since the scale of economic activity has grown, however, the subsidy has become very large indeed; ignoring it leads to significant resource distortion.

For the global warming problem, one step in implementing this principle could take the form of a tax on all greenhouse gases emitted into the atmosphere. The "carbon tax," which is currently being widely discussed in Europe and the United States, could be one component of this package. Since carbon dioxide is only one of the greenhouse gases, however, taxes would necessarily be imposed on other gases as well. The appropriate level of this tax for each gas would depend upon its per unit contribution to the global warming problem; gases posing a larger per unit risk would bear higher tax rates.

Taxes on fossil fuels are not a radical concept. Gasoline taxes have routinely been levied for years. Though gasoline taxes are imposed on an input to combustion, rather than an emission rate, the administrative ease with which they can be implemented and the close relationship between the composition of the fuel and the composition of the emissions makes it a popular candidate for use as one component in a package of corrective measures to reduce global warming.

Unfortunately, close examination of the current system of gasoline taxes suggests they fall short of satisfying the full cost principle. Whereas the full cost principle requires that the tax rates reflect the damage caused by emissions, thereby fostering a reduction in emissions, current gasoline tax rates are commonly determined by the revenue needed to build more roads; added roadway capacity ultimately translates into more emissions, not fewer emissions. Because they are driven by the need to finance capacity expansion rather than to account for the environmental effects of combustion, gasoline taxes are currently not in conformance with the full cost principle.

Although applying the full cost principle for global warming also requires that the tax rates be uniformly applied around the world, that condition is a far cry from actual experience. According to the Energy Information Administration publication *International Energy Prices 1980—84*, in 1984 gasoline taxes (expressed in U.S. currency per gallon) ranged from 21 cents in the United States to over $1 in the majority of European countries. When the tax rates differ by a factor of five or more, the burden of reductions is not being efficiently borne. The plain truth is that as a nation we are not doing our fair share.

A common global fund could be established to receive and dispense the revenue created by these taxes. Controlled by representatives of the signatory nations, this fund could conceivably dispense funds for projects as diverse as reforestation or the promotion of solar-powered projects to provide income and subsistence to poor areas of the world. A fund financed by environmental taxes would help to reduce the twin causes of environmental problems: distorted market signals in the industrialized countries and poverty in the Third World.

One interesting precedent for this common fund aproach is the World Heritage Convention, which established a World Heritage Fund. This fund is used to protect environments of "outstanding universal value." Each signatory is required to contribute at least one percent of its contribution to the regular budget of UNESCO to the fund every two years. In practice this means that the fund is financed almost entirely by the industrial nations, but smaller nations can tap its resources. Some 90 nations have signed this agreement, suggesting that the fund arrangements have successfully exploited some common interests. Since subscribing to the agreement apparently confers benefits on the signatories, it is essentially self-enforcing. That is the good news. The bad news is the United States does not contribute to UNESCO.

Making explicit environmental costs that have been hidden is only one side of the coin; the other is eliminating inappropriate subsidies. Subsidies that are incompatible with the full cost principle should be eliminated. Implicit subsidies should be targeted as well as explicit subsidies. For example, when environmental resources are priced by the government (such as irrigation water in the American southwest) taxpayers should not pick up a significant proportion of the tab. That only leaves water significantly undervalued by those receiving the subsidies and encourages wasteful irrigation practices. Most beneficiaries of this policy are wealthy landowners, not poor farmers.

RESPECTING THE FUTURE

All resources should be used in a manner that respects the needs of future generations. For biological resources this implies that the harvest rates should be consistent with maintaining the population and not precipitating extinction; harvest rates and regeneration rates need to be synchronized. The use of finite resources, thereby denying their use to future generations, implies an obligation to maintain reasonable substitute options for succeeding generations. If we borrow from the future, we should remember to pay back the loan.

To protect biodiversity in Third World countries local communities should be entitled to property rights over flora and fauna within their border. For example, recognition and respect for local property rights could provide an additional means of resolving the diminishing supply of biologically rich tropical rain forests. One of the arguments for preserving biodiversity is that it offers a valuable gene pool for the development of future products such as medicines or food crops.

Typically, however, the nations that govern the forestland containing this biologically rich gene pool have not shared in the wealth created by the products derived from it. One solution to this problem is to establish the principle that the nations that contain these biologically rich resources within their borders would be entitled to a stipulated royalty on any and all products developed from the genes obtained from these preserves.

Currently, nations cutting down their tropical forests have little incentive to protect the gene pool harbored within those forests because they are unlikely to reap any of the rewards that will ultimately result. Exploitation of the gene pool and the economic rewards that result from it typically accrue only to those nations and to those companies that can afford the extensive research. By establishing the principle that stipulated royalty payments would accrue to the nation from which the original genes were extracted, local incentives would become more compatible with global incentives.

OUR THREE-PART ROLE

The search for solutions for environmental problems in the 21st century must recognize the pivotal role of poverty. Attempts to negotiate international agreements that ignore the legitimate interests of the poor are probably doomed to failure. The industrialized nations have a threefold role to play in exploring common interests. First, we must stop those policies that exacerbate Third World poverty. Second, we must revamp our incentives to encourage a transition to forms of development that are more environmentally benign by agreeing to pay the full cost of our activities. We need to lead by example. Third, we need to be more helpful to Third World nations as they seek their rightful place in the sun. This help will necessarily include increased financial flows from the capital rich countries to the capital poor countries.

To take these steps will require thinking and acting in somewhat unconventional ways. Whether the world community is equal to the task remains to be seen. Our leaders seem intent on suggesting that all problems are so minimal that they can be solved without sacrifice. Psychologists call this "denial." If you pretend the problems don't exist, it's easier than dealing with them. Hopefully someday a new breed of politician will arise that has the courage to lead us into the 21st century and the charisma to pull it off.